THE ROMAN ANTIQUITIES

OF

DIONYSIUS OF HALICARNASSUS

I

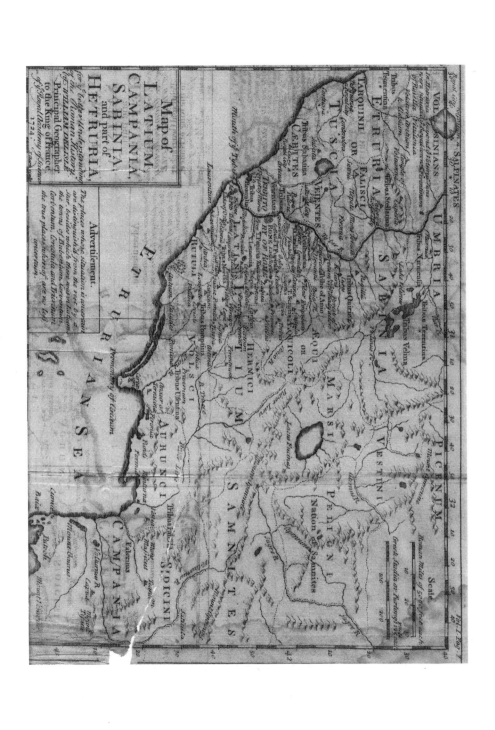

Map of
LATIUM,
CAMPANIA,
SABINIA,
and part of
HETRURIA.

for Cockburn's beginning
of the Roman History
&c WILLIAM DELISLE
Principal Geographer
to the King of France
& Royal Academy &c
1724.

Advertisement.

The places wherein situation is uncertain
are distinguished from the rest by a
star; besides which the accents show
the true place of the syllables &c
tortenium, Corgatula and Theatinum
the true places whereof are not here
uncertain.

THE ROMAN ANTIQUITIES

OF

DIONYSIUS OF HALICARNASSUS

I

Books I-VI. 54

Translated by Earnest Cary on the basis of Edward Spelman.

Edited by Giles Laurén

SOPHRON EDITOR

2017

ISBN 13: 978-0-9991401-2-3

ISBN 10:

Frontis. Environs of Rome.

Page xliv: Tarquinius Superbus by John Leech for A'Beckett's *Comic History of Rome*.

Back. Ancient Rome from Platner.

PUBLISHERS' STATEMENT

Sophron Editor strives to provide the best available texts at the lowest possible prices to encourage Classical Studies & Rhetoric. We pay no salaries, we have very little overhead, we rely on voluntary editors and we have no public relations, advertising, or marketing expenses. All of our editions are typeset, i.e. they are not scanned copies. Large and complex digital editions undertaken with limited means must result in a certain number of textual errors or inaccuracies. For the most part these are apparent, irritating, and do not affect the meaning of the text. As with all Sophron editions I will promptly correct all errors reported in the pages of these editions. Giles Laurén: enasophron@gmail.com.

Design by Sophron Editor

Contents

Foreword

The purpose of this edition of Dionysius of Halicarnassus is to make his complete *Roman Antiquities* available in English to the public in an inexpensive, two volume format.

This present text is taken from the the original Loeb edition using Earnest Cary's translation from Spelman. I have taken the raw English from Bill Thayer's excellent website, *Penelope*, and corrected it against the original. I have also retained some of Thayer' notes, marked 'Thayer note'. Cary's notes very usefully track parallel passages between Dionysius and Livy. The critical notes have not been retained, as unsuitable to a popular edition, and the curious scholar will have to refer to the origin Loeb edition(s).

Firstly a rhetorician, Dionysius wrote his history largely in the form of a sequence of speeches, all invented of course, but all the same interesting for their completeness and clarity. All possible reasons for and against any action are gracefully set forth with well ordered force. One feels that many of the topics of the speeches might have been set for students of rhetoric, as Cary believed. After all, to combine Roman history with rhetoric and Stoic ideals was the theme of the moment. His interest in words and their etymology is noteworthy.

Written in the Augustan era along with Virgil, Horace, Livy, Martial, they together invented a history for Rome. The Romans had conquered Greek armies, but not Greek minds. In the words of Horace:

> *Graecia capta ferum victorem cepit et artes intulit agresti Latio.*
> **Horace**. *Epistularum* II.1.156
>
> Greece, conquered Greece her conqueror subdued,
> And Rome grew polished, who till then was rude. **Conington**.

Who are these barbarians asked the Greeks? Although Greeks had occupied most of Italy for centuries, there is no mention of Rome in Herodotus, Thucydides, Diodorus or Polybius (who even mentions the Jews).

Dionysius, along with the authors cited above, all wrote with Stoic hindsight, attributing the Stoic virtues to (many mythical) early Romans. Together they wrote best ever exposition of the evolution of political systems. The speeches of Dionysius in particular make plain the various arguments of political factions. The influence of Augustan ideals on morals, law, history and Western civilisation endured so long as they were studied. Dionysius further served as a model for Josephus a century later when he created his history.

The historical sources available to the Augustan writers is an open question; certain annals are mentioned, but we have no notion of what they contained and it is remarkable that they were able to create histories much longer than Herodotus and Thucydides who wrote four centuries earlier.

We know that Varro[1] addressed early Roman history some fifty and more years earlier, and given the intervening wars and the destruction of his and other libraries, it may be that he was the principal source for the Augustans.

I would like to think that Dionysius is of interest to us today because of his knowledge of forensic rhetoric. His pupils were practical men living under an empire; political speeches were no longer needed and the future for young men was in the law courts. Dionysius instructed his pupils in the history of Roman institutions,

---

1   Marcus Terentius Varro (116-27) *De vita populi Romani. De gente populi Romani.* (lost) Studied with the Academic Antiochus of Ascalon at Athens & the first Roman philologist L. Aelius Stilo in Rome. Caesar appointed him to keep the future public library in 47.

elegantly gave them a glorious past and taught them to be effective in the law courts and successful in life.

Introduction

Life of Dionysius.

The few facts known about the life of Dionysius are virtually all given us by the author himself. At the close of the preface to the *Roman Antiquities* (chap. 8) he announces himself as Dionysius, the son of Alexander, and a native of Halicarnassus. He also informs us (chap. 7) that he had come to Italy at the time when Augustus Caesar put an end to the civil war in the middle of the 187th Olympiad (late in 30 B.C. or in 29), and that he had spent the following twenty-two years in acquainting himself with the language and the literature of the Romans, in gathering his materials, and in writing his History. The preface is dated (chap. 3) in the consulship of Nero and Piso (7 B.C.), and the first part, at least, of the work must have been published at that time. It is generally assumed that the entire History appeared then; but in Book VII. (70, 2) Dionysius refers to Book I. as having been already published. This leaves it an open question in how many instalments and at what intervals he issued the work. We do not know the exact date of his birth; but two casual statements in the History enable us to fix it within certain limits. He cites the disastrous campaign of Crassus against the Parthians as an event of his own lifetime (ii. 6, 4); and in describing the erection of the original Capitol he states that the new edifice, 'built in the days of our fathers,' stood on the same foundations as the old (iv. 61, 4). The first of these passages shows that he was born at least as early as 53, and perhaps as early as 54 or 55, since the reference may very well be to the whole Parthian expedition. The second allusion is more indefinite. The new Capitol, begun by Sulla shortly after the burning of the old structure in 83, was formally dedicated by Catulus in 69; nevertheless, as late as the beginning of 62 Caesar, in bringing charges of embezzlement against Catulus, claimed that many parts of the temple were still but half-finished and accordingly wished to have Pompey entrusted with the completion of the work.[1] We do not know how much justification there was for Caesar's action, though it is evident that it was

---

1   Dio Cassius, xxxvii. 44; *cf.* xliii. 14, 6.

primarily a political move; in any case, he was unsuccessful, and Catulus' name remained on the pediment of the temple. Whether Dionysius knew of Caesar's charges or attached any importance to them we can only conjecture. Egger,[2] taking these charges seriously, argued that Dionysius must have been born after 63; yet it is just as natural to believe that the historian dated the temple by the official dedication. The two passages, then, give as extreme limits for the date of Dionysius' birth 69 and 53, with some possibility of the narrower limits of 62 and 55. Modern scholars have generally assumed a date between 60 and 55, from the feeling that Dionysius must have been a fairly young man when he came to Rome and undertook to master a new language and literature. The only other reference in an ancient author to the time when Dionysius lived is even more indefinite than those just quoted. Strabo (*ca.* 63 B.C. *ca.* 21 A.D.), in speaking of Halicarnassus, names, as authors who claimed that city as their birthplace, Herodotus, Heracleitus the poet, and, 'in our time,' Dionysius the historian (xiv. 2, 16).

Halicarnassus had declined greatly in importance after the time of Maussolus, and finally suffered grievously at the hands of the pirates not far from the time when Dionysius was born. It was given a new lease of life by Quintus Cicero while he was serving as governor of Asia (61-58), if we may believe the enthusiastic tribute paid him by his brother.[3] Such was the city in which Dionysius apparently spent his youth and early manhood. Whether he composed any of his rhetorical treatises while still residing there is uncertain; but it is generally held that they were all written at Rome.

In Rome Dionysius was a teacher of rhetoric, probably giving private lessons; in one of his treatises addressed to a pupil he refers to 'our daily exercises.'[4] From these shorter works which took the form of letters addressed to friends, patrons or pupils, we learn the names of a number of

---

2   Max. Egger, Denys d' Halicarnasse, p. 3.
3   Cicero, ad *Quint, fratr.* i. 1, 8: *urbes complures dirutas ac paene desertas, in quibus unam Ioniae nobilissimam, alteram Cariae, Samum et Halicarnassum, per te esse recreatas.*
4   *On the Arrangement of Words,* chap. 20.

Introduction

his friends and associates; but unfortunately they are, with one or two exceptions, otherwise unknown to us. Aelius Tubero may have been the historian and jurist who was consul in 11 B.C., the same historian who is praised in the Antiquities (i. 80, 1). Melitius Rufus, a pupil, and his father, whom Dionysius calls a most valued friend, were evidently Romans. Cn. Pompeius Geminus may well have been a Greek, in spite of his name; Ammaeus also was probably a Greek, and so almost certainly were Demetrius and Zeno. Caecilius of Calacte, who is styled a dear friend, was a rhetorician and historian of whom a good deal is known. In the introduction to the *History* (chap. 7) Dionysius states that he gained some of his information orally from most learned men (Romans by implication) with whom he came in contact. It would be interesting indeed to know the names of some of these men and how intimately he associated with them; but, with the possible exception of Aelius Tubero, he nowhere names a contemporary Roman author, although he pays tribute to the many excellent works that were being produced in his day, – histories. speeches, and philosophical treatises, – by both Romans and Greeks.[5] From the circumstance that he gives particular credit to the ruling classes of Rome for the recent purification of literary taste, Roberts suggests that he may have been 'influenced more directly . . . by the Roman men of affairs with whom (or with whose sons) his vocation brought him into contact than by any Roman man of letters."[6] One avowed purpose in writing his History was to make a grateful return to Rome for the education and other advantages he had enjoyed there;[7] and this certainly suggests that he felt he had been made welcome in Rome.

We have no information regarding the date of his death. If he was the author of the summary of his History in five books which Photius (Cod. 84) attributes to him, he doubtless wrote this after the publication of the large work, and so must have lived for some little time at least after 7 B.C. There are several passages in his shorter works in which he promises to discuss this or that topic 'if I have the time,' or 'if it is possible,' or 'if

---

5   *On the Ancient Orators*, chap. 3.
6   W. Rhys Roberts, *Dionysius of Halicarnassus: The Three Literary Letters*, p. 35.
7   *Antiq.* i. 6, 5.

Heaven keeps us safe and sound.' These have sometimes been taken to indicate that he was already an old man or in poor health; but it is by no means necessary to put such a construction upon his words.

The Roman Antiquities.

The work which Dionysius undoubtedly regarded as his masterpiece and the practical embodiment of his theories regarding historical writing was the *Roman Antiquities*.[8] It treated the history of Rome from the earliest legendary times down to the beginning of the First Punic War, the point at which Polybius' history began. The work was in twenty books[9] of which the first ten are preserved, together with the greater part of the eleventh. Of the remaining books we have fragments amounting all told to a little more than the average length of one of the earlier books. Most of these fragments come from the great collection of historical extracts made at the direction of the emperor Constantine Porphyrogennetus in the tenth century.

In his preface Dionysius lays down two principles as fundamental for historians, first, that they should choose subjects noble and lofty and of great utility to their readers, and, second, that they should use the greatest care and discrimination in gathering their materials. He then proceeds to justify his own choice of subject and to describe the careful preparation he had made for his task. In two chapters, obviously imitated from Polybius' introduction, he gives a brief survey of the empires of the past, from the Assyrian to the Macedonian, with a glance at the Greek hegemonies, and points out how greatly Rome had surpassed them all, both in the extent of her dominion and in the length of time it had already endured. He then undertakes to answer the anticipated criticism of those who might censure him for choosing the humble beginnings of Rome as his particular theme

---

8   This is the traditional English rendering of the Greek title; if we were translating it to-day for the first time we should probably render it *Early History* (or *Ancient Lore*) *of Rome*.

9   Photius, Cod. 83. Stephanus of Byzantium cited numerous Italian place-names from the *Antiquities*. often giving the number of the book; the last book he names is the nineteenth.

Introduction

when there were so many glorious periods in her later history that would furnish excellent subjects. He declares that the Greeks for the most part were ignorant of Rome's early history, having been misled by baseless reports that attributed the founding of the city to some homeless wanderers, at once barbarians and slaves, and hence were inclined to rail at Fortune for unfairly bestowing the heritage of the Greeks upon the basest of barbarians. He promises to correct these erroneous impressions and to prove that Rome's founders were in reality Greeks, and Greeks from no mean tribes; he will also show that Rome from the very beginning produced countless instances of men as pious, just and brave as any other city ever did, and that it was due to these early leaders and to the customs and institutions handed down by them that their descendants advanced to so great power. Thus he hopes to reconcile his Greek readers to their subjection to Rome. He points out that there had been no accurate history of Rome written by Greeks, but only summary accounts, and even the Romans who had written histories of their country in Greek had passed lightly over events occurring before their own days. He feels, therefore, that in this earlier period of Rome's history he has found a noble theme virtually untouched as yet. By treating this period adequately he will confer immortal glory upon those worthy men of early Rome and encourage their descendants to emulate them in leading honourable and useful lives; at the same time he will have the opportunity of showing his goodwill toward all good men who delight in the contemplation of great and noble deeds, and also of making a grateful return to Rome for the cultural advantages and other blessings that he had enjoyed while residing there. He declares, however, that it is not for the sake of flattering the Romans that he has turned his attention to this subject, but out of regard for truth and justice, the proper objects of every history. He then describes his preparation for his task, – the twenty-two years he had spent in familiarizing himself with the language and literature of the Romans, the oral information he had received from the most learned men, and the approved Roman histories that he had read. Finally, he announces the period of Roman history to be covered in his work[10] and the topics to be

---

10 He does not explicitly state why he terminated his History with the beginning
     of the First Punic War, but the reasons are not far to seek. With this war

treated. He will relate the wars waged by Rome with other peoples and the seditions at home, her various forms of government, the best of her customs and the most important of her laws; in short, he will picture the whole life of the ancient city. As regards the form of his History, it will not be like the works of those who write of wars alone or treat solely of political constitutions, nor will it be monotonous and tiresome like the annalistic histories of Athens; but it will be a combination of every style, so as to appeal alike to statesmen and to philosophers as well as to those who desire mere undisturbed entertainment in their reading of history.

More than once in the course of his History (v. 56, xi. 1; cf. vii. 66) Dionysius interrupts his narrative to insist on the importance of acquainting the reader not only with the mere outcome of events, but also with the causes, remote as well as proximate, that led up to them, the circumstances in which the events occurred and the motives of the chief participants, — in fact, the whole background of the action. Such information, he says, is of the utmost importance to statesmen, in order that they may have precedents for the various situations that may confront them and may thus be able to persuade their fellow-citizens when they can adduce numerous examples from the past to show the advantage or the harm of a given course of action. Dionysius here shows an understanding of the true function of history, as he does also, in a measure, in his various protestations of devotion to the truth, though he nowhere sets up such a strict standard of absolute impartiality as did Polybius (i. 14, 4).

Unfortunately, in spite of these high ideals which Dionysius tried to keep before him, his *Antiquities* is an outstanding example of the mischievous results of that unnatural alliance between rhetoric and history which was the vogue after the time of Thucydides. The rhetoricians regarded a history as a work of art whose primary purpose was to give pleasure. Events in themselves seem to have been considered as of less

---

Rome emerged from the relative obscurity of her own peninsula and entered
upon her struggle for the supremacy of the Mediterranean. There were
already histories in Greek, notably that of Polybius, recounting her
achievements from this time onward; but for the period preceding the Punic
Wars Dionysius could feel that he was virtually a pioneer in his undertaking.

importance than the manner in which they were presented. Hence various liberties could be taken with the facts in order to produce a more telling effect; and as long as this was done not out of fear or favour, but simply from the desire to make the account more effective, the writer was not conscious of violating the truth. Dionysius doubtless thought that he was living up to his high ideals; but he was first and foremost a rhetorician and could see history only through a rhetorician's eyes. The desire to please is every-where in evidence; there is a constant straining after rhetorical and dramatic effects.

In conformity with the rhetorical tradition, he interlarded his narrative with speeches which he managed to insert on every possible occasion from the third book onward. One technical purpose which they were intended to serve – to give variety to the narrative —is clear from the very circumstance that there are scarcely any speeches at all in Books I. and II., which have a sufficiently diversified narrative to require no further efforts at variety, whereas from Book III. onward the speeches occupy very nearly one-third of the total text. Dionysius himself occasionally felt the need of some justification of his insertion of so many speeches and argued that, inasmuch as the crisis under consideration was settled by discussion, it was therefore important for the reader to know the arguments that were advanced on both sides (vii. 66; xi. 1). Yet he had no adequate conception of the talents required for carrying out this ambitious programme successfully. Possessing neither the historical sense nor psychological insight, nor even any special gift of imagination, he undertook to compose speeches for any and all occasions by the simple process of following certain stereotyped rhetorical rules. The main argument of many of his speeches he doubtless found already expressed in his sources, either in some detail or in the form of a brief résumé, while in other cases there was probably a mere form of statement that implied a speech at that point, numerous instances of each of these methods can be seen in Livy (who was not one of his sources) on the occasions where Dionysius inserts a speech. But it was little more than the main argument at best that he took over from his sources in most of the speeches of any length. The speeches were the part of a history in which the author was expected to give the freest reign to his rhetorical talents; and that Dionysius did not fail to make full use of this opportunity is evident from the many imitations of the classical Attic prose writers that are found in his speeches. One of his fundamental principles for the acquiring of a good style was the imitating of classical models, and in the speeches of the *Antiquities* we see how it was to be done. Not only do we find single phrases and sentences from Demosthenes, Thucydides and Xenophon paraphrased and amplified, but even the tenor of entire passages in those authors is imitated.[11] It is not at all surprising, therefore, that these speeches fail almost completely to perform their true function of revealing the character and the motives of the different speakers. Nor are they redeemed by any profound thoughts, unless in the imitated passages, or by any original sentiments; for the most part they are little more than a succession of cheap platitudes and rhetorical commonplaces. Indeed, we might almost believe at times that we were reading the declamations of Dionysius' own pupils.

It has generally been suspected that Dionysius invented a good many of his speeches outright, inserting them at points where there was no indication of any speech in his sources. One fairly clear instance of the sort is found in his account of Coriolanus (viii. 5-8). After giving much the same account as Livy does of the trick played on the Romans by Attius Tullus at Coriolanus' suggestion in order to provoke them into giving the Volscians a just cause for going to war, Dionysius then represents Coriolanus as summoned by the Volscian leaders to advise them how best to prosecute the war. Coriolanus,in a speech clearly modelled upon the one addressed to the Spartans by the exiled Alcibiades (Thuc. vi. 89 ff.), says much by way of self-justification, and finally offers a fresh plan for providing the Volscians with a just ground for war. There is no valid excuse for this second plan, the first one having already proved successful; Dionysius clearly wished to offer a parallel in his History to the famous episode in Thucydides. It is quite probable that several other speeches in this long account of Coriolanus also originated with Dionysius. Yet it must

11 His imitations of the authors named have been analysed by Flierle, *Ueber Nachahmungen des Demosthenes, Thucydides und Xenophon in den Reden der Röm. Archäologie des Dionysius von Halicarnass*, Leipzig:, 1890. The investigation should be continued to include Lysias and other orators.

be remembered that he drew largely on the late annalists, some of whose histories were very voluminous; and he may have found at least hints of speeches more frequently than has generally been supposed.

Quite in keeping with the tiresome speeches of the *Antiquities* are the long, circumstantial accounts of such events as Dionysius chose to emphasize in his narrative, and the cumulation of pathetic or gruesome details in tragic situations. His account of the combat between the Horatii and the Curiatii, followed by Horatius' slaying of his sister, occupies ten chapters (iii. 13-22) as against but three in Livy (i. 24-26); and there is even a greater disproportion in the length of their accounts of the events leading up to the combat (Dionys. iii. 2-12, Livy i. 22 f.) due in part to several long speeches in Dionysius. The outstanding instance of prolixity in the *Antiquities* is the account of Coriolanus. The events leading up to his exile (including 15 speeches) require 48 chapters (vii. 20-67), whereas Livy relates them in one-half of a single chapter (ii. 34, 7-12); the remaining events to the end of his life are told by Dionysius in 62 chapters (viii. 1-62), and by Livy in 6 (ii. 35-40). Almost everywhere in the extant portions of Dionysius his account is longer than that of Livy; but this relative fullness of detail was not maintained to the end of the History. To the struggle between the orders and to the Samnite wars he devoted less than four books (part of xiv. and xv.-xvii), where Livy has more than six (vi.-xi. and part of xii.). In other words, for events nearer his own day, for which the traditions should have been fuller and more reliable, he contented himself with a briefer narrative than for the earlier periods, which for most historians had been full of doubt and uncertainty, thereby exactly reversing the logical procedure of Livy. An exception is seen in his detailed account of the war with Pyrrhus, a war which aroused his special interest for more reasons than one. Nowhere is his fondness for minute detail more out of place than in his accounts of tragic events, such as the encounter of the triumphant Horatius with his sister, Tullia's behaviour when she forces the driver of her car to continue on his way over the dead body of her father, the grief of Lucretius when his daughter slays herself, Verginius' slaying of his own daughter, and Veturia's visit to the camp of her son Coriolanus. By his constant effort to make us realize the full pathos or horror of the scene he defeats his own purpose. The dignified restraint shown by Livy in relating these same events is far more impressive.

Dionysius perhaps felt that he was making a distinct contribution toward the solidarity of the Graeco-Roman world when he undertook to prove, as his principal thesis, the Greek origin of Rome's founders. Not only did he trace the Aborigines back through the Oenotrians to Arcadia, but he even showed that the ancestors of the Trojans had come originally from that same district of Greece; other Greek elements represented in the population of early Rome were the Pelasgians, naturally of Greek origin, Evander and his company from Arcadia, and some Peloponnesian soldiers in the following of Hercules, who had remained behind in Italy when that hero passed through the peninsula on his return from Spain to Argos. None of the various details of this theory was original with Dionysius. for he cites his authorities at every step; but he may have been the first to combine these separate strands of tradition into a single, comprehensive argument. The entire first book is devoted to the proving of this thesis; and the argument is further strengthened at the end of Book VII. by a detailed comparison of the ceremonies at the Ludi Romani with early Greek religious observances. As we saw from his introduction, he hoped by this demonstration to reconcile his fellow Greeks to Rome's supremacy; at the same time, he obviously understood the Romans of his day well enough to realize that, far from regarding Rome's glory as thereby diminished in any way, they would feel flattered by the thought of such a connexion with the heroic age of Greece. Incidentally, the proving of his thesis afforded him an excellent opportunity for dealing with the legendary period and thus giving greater variety to his work. But the acceptance of this theory was bound to give him an inverted view of the course of Roman history. Instead of recognizing the gradual evolution of the people and their institutions from very rude beginnings, he sees an advanced stage of civilization existing from the very first; and Rome's kings and later leaders are in such close contact with the Greek world that they borrow thence most of the new institutions that they establish from time to time. Thus he assumes that the *celeres*, the senate, the two consuls with joint powers, and the custom whereby the members of each *curia* dined together on holy days, were all based on Spartan models; that the division of the citizens into patricians and plebeians followed a similar division at Athens that Servius Tullius organized a Latin League on the analogy of the Amphictyonic League of Greece, and that even the dictatorship was suggested by the practice followed in various Greek cities of appointing an *aisymnetes* to deal with a particular emergency. Dionysius probably found most,if not all, of these institutions thus explained in his sources; in about half of the instances he qualifies his statement by the words 'in my opinion,' but this does not seem a sufficient criterion for deciding the authorship of these views.

Dionysius is so ready to praise Rome's ancient heroes and institutions on every occasion, with never a word of disapprobation, that his impartiality may well be questioned. On a number of occasions he praises the piety and other virtues of the early Romans, which secured for them the special favour of Heaven; once (xx. 6) he styles them the most holy and just of Greeks. A number of their laws and practices, especially some of those said to have been instituted by Romulus, are declared to be superior to those in vogue among the Greeks. Thus, Romulus' policy of colonizing captured cities and sometimes even granting them the franchise is contrasted with the ruthless practices of the leading Greek states and their narrow-minded policy of withholding the rights of citizenship from outsiders (ii. 16 f., xiv. 6); and his laws regarding marriage and the *patria potestas* are described as better than the corresponding Greek practices (ii. 24-27). Romulus is praised also for rejecting such of the myths as attributed any unseemly conduct to the gods and all grosser forms of religious worship (ii. 18 f.). Indeed, our historian even approves of the Roman censorship, the inquisitorial powers of which were not limited, as in Athens and Sparta, to the public behaviour of the citizens, but extended even inside the walls of private homes (xx. 13). But it is not the Greeks alone who are contrasted unfavourably with the old Romans; Dionysius is just as ready to point out to the Romans of his own day their failure to maintain the high standards set by their ancestors. He contrasts the spirit of mutual helpfulness and forbearance that characterized the relations of the plebeians and patricians in the early days with the era of bloodshed that began under Gaius Gracchus (ii. 11); similarly, he praises the simplicity of the first triumph (ii. 34), the excellent grounds on which Servius Tullius granted the franchise to manumitted slaves (iv. 24), the deference shown by the early consuls to the authority of the senate (v. 60), and the lawful and modest behaviour of the dictators down to the time of Sulla (v. 77), contrasting each of these practices and institutions with the evil forms they assumed in later days. In one instance (viii. 80) he leaves it to the reader to decide whether the traditional Roman practice or the practice of the Greeks which some had recently wished to introduce at Rome,was the better. The pointing of all these contrasts is part of the historian's function as moralist, the function which he had in mind when in his *Letter to Pompeius* (chap. 3) he said that the attitude of Herodotus toward the events he was describing was everywhere fair, showing pleasure in those that were good and grief at those that were bad. Dionysius doubtless endeavoured to be fair and sincere in his judgments; but he was. nevertheless, biased in favour of the Romans and in favour of the senatorial party, the Optimates of his own day. He even attempts to palliate one or two of the less savoury incidents associated with Rome's beginnings: he pictures Romulus as plunged into the depths of grief and despair at the death of Remus; and again, as addressing words of comfort and cheer to the captured Sabine maidens, assuring them that their seizure was in accordance with a good old Greek custom, and that it was the most distinguished way for women to be married! Livy makes no attempt to save the character of Romulus in the first instance, and in the second stops far short of Dionysius.

In the matter of religion, also, Dionysius makes no concealment of his attitude. He frequently refers to a divine providence. He speaks scornfully of the professors of atheistic philosophies, 'if philosophies they should be called,' who deny that the gods concern themselves with the affairs of mortals (ii. 68, 2; viii. 56, 1). He, for his part, is assured that the gods do sometimes intervene on behalf of the righteous (ii. 68 f.) and also to punish the wicked, as in the case of Pyrrhus (xx. 9 f.). The Romans, in particular, because of their piety and other virtues, had frequently been the recipients of divine favour, while the designs of their enemies were

Introduction

brought to naught(v. 54, 1; vi. 13; vii.12, 4; viii. 26, 3). The gods, he holds, manifest their will through portents, and the disregarding of these may be severely punished, as in the case of Crassus (ii. 6. 4). Hence he recorded from time to time a goodly number of portents which he regarded as particularly noteworthy. With respect to the myths, he looked upon many of them, in which the gods played shameful parts, as blasphemous (ii. 18, 3); and, though he recognized that some of the Greek myths had a certain value as allegorical interpretations of natural phenomena, or as consolations in misfortune or other similar ways, he nevertheless felt that for the ignorant mass of mankind they did more harm than good, and he was more inclined himself to accept the Roman religion (ii. 20). It is to be observed that in relating myths he nowhere implies his own belief in them, but generally introduces them with some qualifying phrase, such as 'it is said,' 'they say,' etc.

Dionysius doubtless made what he considered to be a thorough study of Roman political institutions; but his narrative constantly shows that he came far short of a real understanding of many of them. His failure to distinguish accurately between patricians and senators and between the *patrum auctoritas* and a *senatus consultum* is a source of no little confusion; but, worse still, he often uses the Attic term *προβούλευμα* (preliminary decree) both for *senatus consultum* and for *patrum auctoritas*. His frequent use of 'patricians' for 'senators' is easily explained when we compare Livy, who constantly uses the word *patres* for both patricians and senators. This ambiguous term was doubtless found by both historians in their sources; indeed, in a few instances Dionysius carelessly retained the word as 'fathers' (v. 33, 2; vi. 69, 2). In making his choice between the renderings 'patricians' and 'senators' he seems to have adopted the former wherever the *patres* seemed to be opposed as a class to the plebeians (*e.g.*, iv. 8, 2; viii. 82, 4; ix. 42, 3). The term *patrum auctoritas* was apparently no better understood by Livy than by Dionysius; even for the early period he several times represents the *auctoritas* as preceding the vote of the *comitia*, and after the Publilian law of 339, which required the *auctoritas* to be given before the people voted, he uses *patrum auctoritas* and *senatus consultum* indiscriminately. There is, in fact, every reason for believing that the term *patrum auctoritas* had become obsolete even in the time of the older annalists who were Livy's chief sources. But Dionysius, with sources before him that probably showed no greater misunderstanding of this term than does Livy, made matters much worse as the result of his assumption that the *patrum auctoritas*, and indeed any decree of the senate, was usually a preliminary decree to be ratified by the people. This view justified him in using the word προβούλευμα, the name given to the programme of business prepared by the Athenian *Boulê* for the consideration of the Ecclesia. It can hardly have been the desire to use the word προβούλευμα that led him to adopt its essential implications; for he often uses δόγμα or ψήφισμα in the same way for a decree of the senate that was to be ratified by the people. He must have had some reason in the first place for believing that the *patrum auctoritas* was a necessary preliminary to action by the people. We know that it was customary for the consuls, as a matter of practical convenience, to ask the senate's advice and secure its approval before bringing any important matter before the people, inasmuch as the action taken in the *comitia* would have to receive the *patrum auctoritas* later in order to be valid. If Dionysius was aware of this custom but not of its purpose, he might well reason that it was absurd for the senate to give its approval more than once to the same business, and hence, since he knew the *patrum auctoritas* was required for all votes of the people, he would naturally identify this term with the preliminary approval of the senate. It is true this view of the matter seems to be directly opposed to an important statement which he makes at the very outset. When defining the powers of the senate and of the people as established by Romulus, he states that the senate was to ratify the decisions of the people, but adds that in his own day the reverse principle was followed, the decrees of the senate then requiring the approval of the people (ii. 14, 3). The natural implication of his statement is that the change had come about in fairly late times, but he nowhere in the extant books has anything more definite to say on the subject. In a very few instances he speaks of the 'patricians' (doubtless to him identical with the senators) as ratifying a vote of the people afterwards, *e.g.*, in the case of the election of Numa (ii. 60, 3) and the appointment of the first tribunes (vi. 90, 2); but as early as the election of Ancus Marcius he represents the people as ratifying the choice of the senators (iii. 36, 1), and a little later speaks of this as the normal procedure (iv. 40, 2; 80, 2). In the last passage he is more explicit, declaring it to be the duty of the senate to consider in advance (*προβουλεύειν*) all matters relating to the general welfare, and the duty of the people to ratify their decision. It is fairly evident, then, that Dionysius' own theory was that a *προβούλευμα* of the senate had been necessary from the beginning. If his narrative occasionally violates this theory in practice, it is probably either because his sources were so explicit in particular instances that he felt he could not contradict them, or because he was negligent now and then and forgot to make his practice conform consistently to his theory. Another important matter in which he failed to make theory and practice coincide at all times will be mentioned a little later. It is not clear whether he believed the *plebiscita*, also, required a *προβούλευμα*; his language is at times ambiguous and his accounts of the procedure in the case of various *plebiscita* are inconsistent with one another. He held the mistaken view that all senators were patricians, even under the republic; for he believed that plebeians were made patricians before being admitted to the senate (ii. 47, 1; v. 13, 2). But it is not in constitutional matters only that he made serious errors; there is confusion also in his account of religious matters. Thus, he uses 'haruspex' for 'augur' in ii. 22, 3, and his account of the duties of the pontifices (ii. 73) contains many errors.[12]

A few words must be said about Dionysius' chronology. His date for the founding of Rome was 751 B.C., two years later than that adopted by Varro; and this difference between the two chronologies remains constant for the first 304 years of the city down to the time of the decemvirs (the period covered by Books I.-X.). At that point the gap widens: Dionysius represents the decemviral rule as continuing for a third year, while Varro assigned to it only two years. Accordingly, for the half- dozen years covered by Book XI. Dionysius' dates are three years later than those of Varro. The fragments of the last nine books do not give any dates; but three

---

12 On the subject of this paragraph see Edw. Schwartz in the *Real-Enc., s.v.* Dionysius, pp. 940 ff., and E. Bux, *Das Probuleuma bei Dionys.*

sporadic references in the earlier books to events of the third and first centuries B.C. show that for this late period his dates are the same as Varro's.[13] Dionysius devotes two chapters (i. 74 f.) to explaining how he arrived at the date 751 for the founding of the city, and for fuller information refers the reader to a separate work[14] that he had published to show how the Roman chronology was to be reduced to the Greek. There are other passages also which bear witness to the particular interest he felt in matters of chronology.[15] Notwithstanding all the attention he devoted to this side of his work, modern scholars have for the most part been very harsh in their judgments of him in this very regard, accusing him of carelessness generally in the matter of his dates and, in particular, of following one system of chronology for the period treated in his History and another for events nearer his own day. Our historian had to wait long for his vindication; but one of the most recent investigators in the field of Roman chronology, Oscar Leuze, has come ably to his defence and shown that at least the more important of these charges of inaccuracy rest upon misunderstanding of Dionysius' real meaning or of his usage.[16]

Like most of the later Greek historians, Dionysius uses the reckoning by Olympiads, usually adding the name of the Athenian archon. From the beginning of the republic he normally gives the Greek date only for the first year of each Olympiad, identifying the intervening years merely by the names of the Roman magistrates. As the Athenian official year began

13 8, 1 (265 B.C.); ii. 25, 7 (231 B.C.); i. 3, 4 (7 B.C.). See O. Leuze, *Die röm. Jahrzählung*, pp. 189-93, for a plausible explanation of the closing of the gap between the two chronologies before the end of the fourth century.

14 Χρόνοι, or Περὶ Χρόνων, cited by Clemens Alexandr., *Strom.* i. 102.

15 i. 63; ii. 59; iv. 6f.,30, 64; vi. 11; vii. 1.

16 *Die röm. Jahrzählung*, pp. 177-99. Of particular interest is his defence of Dionysius' date for the beginning of the First Punic War (pp. 184-87). Leuze argues that Dionysius is here following a usage of Polybius and Diodorus, who in a number of instances regard as the beginning of a war, not the formal declaration of war or the first armed clash, but the event that was the immediate cause of the conflict. In the case in question this was Rome's decision to aid the Mamertines, apparently at the end of the year 265. The *Antiquities* naturally included the events of the year 265 up to the sending of the Mamertine embassy to Rome.

Introduction

in mid-summer and the Olympiadic year of the historians either in mid-summer or early autumn, whereas the Roman consular year began, in later times, on January 1, though in earlier times at various seasons of the year, the Greek historians were confronted with an awkward problem in synchronizing Roman and Greek dates. The solution apparently followed by Dionysius, and probably by Polybius and Diodorus also, was to adopt the later Roman year of uniform length for all periods of Roman history, and to identify a given Roman year with the Olympiadic year in the course of which it began, rather than with that in which it ended (as is the modern practice). The dates given in the notes of the present edition follow this principle, only a single year being indicated as the modern equivalent of the Greek year, instead of parts of two years. Thus Olymp. 7, 1 is identified as 751 B.C. instead of 752/1. The only exceptions are a few dates of non-Roman events, where Dionysius was probably not concerned with the exact Roman equivalent.

Dionysius was in theory opposed to the annalistic method of writing history. In his *Letter to Pompeius* (chap. 3) he criticized Thucydides' chronological arrangement of events, by winters and summers, as seriously interrupting the continuity of the narrative, and praised Herodotus for adopting the topical order. Yet when he himself was to write a history of Rome he evidently found it impracticable to avoid following the annalistic method in vogue among the Romans. For the regal period, it is true, he arranges the events of each reign under the two headings of wars and peaceful achievements. But beginning with the establishment of the republic, he treats the events of each year by themselves, first naming the consuls or other chief magistrates. For the greater part of the period that he covers this method could cause no confusion, as the military campaigns were of short duration; and it had the further advantage of avoiding monotony, since the narrative was constantly alternating between wars abroad and dissensions at home.

As regards his sources, Dionysius states in his preface (chap. 7) that he had consulted the works of the approved Roman historians, – Cato, Fabius, Maximus (Servilianus?), Valerius Antias, Licinius Macer, Aelius (Tubero), Gellius, Calpurnius (Piso) and many others. —And that he had also derived information from conversations with the most learned men. And at the end of Book I. (chap. 89) he refers to his careful reading of many works by both Greek and Roman writers on the subject of the origin of the Romans. His claim certainly appears to be justified, so far at least as Book I. is concerned. In this one book he cites no fewer than thirty Greek authors, most of them historians or logographers, and seven Roman writers, – Cato, Tubero and Piso, of those named above, and Fabius Pictor, Lucius Alimentus, C. Sempronius (Tuditanus) and Varro. To the last-named he owns his indebtedness for his account of the old cities of the Aborigines (chaps. 14 f.); but he probably owes considerable more to him in this book in places where he has not named his source. After the birth of Romulus and Remus there was scarcely any further occasion for using Greek sources; and he usually mentioned the Roman historians only in cases where there were divergent traditions. He naturally considered it to be his task as a historian to reconcile the different traditions so far as possible and present a smooth, uninterrupted narrative and in the main he has succeeded very well in doing so.[17] But now and then he found such divergences among his sources that he could not ignore them. In such cases he presents the two or more versions and either expresses his own preference or, quite often, leaves the decision to the reader. At times he makes the decision with the greatest confidence, especially in matters of chronology. He is prompt to discover anachronisms, and rebukes rather sharply the historians who have carelessly perpetuated them; Licinius Macer and Cn. Gellius are thus censured on two occasions (vi. 11, 2; vii. 1, 4), also Fabius Pictor (iv. 6 f.; 30, 2 f.), while Calpurnius Piso Frugi is named in one instance (iv. 7, 5) as the only one to give the correct version. It is generally recognized that he followed the late annalists as his principal sources; their histories were generally very voluminous, and in them he could find the full, detailed accounts which he frequently gives. His political orientation is that of the annalists of Sulla's time, who were strong champions of the senate's supremacy. They wrote their annals as propaganda, deliberately falsifying their account of events from time to time in order to make it appear that the senate had held from the first, or

---

17 A number of contradictions that appear in the History are probably due to his using first one source and then another.

Introduction

at least from the beginning of the republic, the same dominant position in the State that it held in the second and first centuries before Christ. They did this by representing the senate as having been consulted in early times on various occasions where tradition made no mention of any action on its part.[18] Dionysius seems to have held the extreme view that even under the monarchy the senate had played a dominant part, the king's power being limited much as at Sparta (ii. 14, 1 f.; *cf.* vi. 66, 3). This was his theory; but in actual practice his narrative mentions very few specific occasions where the senate was consulted by the king, and we gain the impression that the power of the latter was virtually supreme. But from the moment of the establishing of the republic his account of events is in strict agreement with his theory. His failure to reconcile practice and theory earlier argues a lack of inventiveness either on his part or on that of his sources; it probably did not seem worth the trouble to work out the details. This view of the senate's original supremacy was the view taken also by Cicero in his *De Republica* but it was not the view of Livy, who followed earlier annalists and rightly held that the senate had only gradually gained its wide powers. It is just such differences in orientation as this that make it fairly certain that Dionysius was not using Livy as his source in the numerous passages where their accounts seem at first sight strikingly similar.[19] Besides the authors cited by Dionysius, he also mentions a number of inscriptions, both at Rome and elsewhere, and there are sporadic references to the annales maximi, the records of the censors, etc.; but he does not say that he had seen any of these himself, and it is probable that he found the references in the annalists.

The first historian to cite Dionysius was Plutarch, who modelled his style upon that of the *Antiquities*.[20] Schwartz held that Dionysius was Plutarch's sole source for his *Coriolanus*, but this view is opposed by Bux. The *Romulus* and *Numa* may each contain a little from the *Antiquities*, the *Camillus* is chiefly based on Livy.[21] Dionysius is twice quoted in the *Pyrrhus*,

18 A number of instances of this sort are discussed by Bux, *Das Probuleuma*, pp. 83-122.
19 See Schwartz, *Real-Enc.*, pp. 946-57, for an analysis of some of these passages.
20 Goetzler, *Einfluss des Dionys*, p. 194.
21 So Schwartz, *Real-Enc.*, pp. 943-45.

but not enough of his account is preserved to enable us to make any accurate comparison between the two.

Scripta Rhetorica.

The shorter works of Dionysius have generally gone under the name o f *Scripta Rhetorica*; but they contain more of literary criticism than of technical rhetoric. They are all in the form of letters addressed to some literary friend, patron or pupil. There is no internal evidence to show whether they were composed before or after the History was published; but it is generally assumed that Dionysius wrote them from time to time during the years that he was engaged upon his great work. Although no absolute dates can be assigned to these several treatises, the relative order in which they were composed can be determined in most cases by means of the frequent references in one to what the writer has already discussed or proposes to discuss in another. The order in which Roberts arranges them is as follows:

1. *First Letter to Ammaeus.*

2. *On the Arrangement of Words.*

3. *On the Ancient Orators.*

4. *On the Style of Demosthenes.*

5. *On Imitation*: Books I., II.

6. *Letter to Cn. Pompeius.*

7. *On Imitation*: Book III.

8. *On Dinarchus.*

9. *On Thucydides.*

10. *Second Letter to Ammaeus.*

Egger would transpose the second and third items, seeing a greater maturity of judgment in the treatise on the *Arrangement of Words*. As regards the *Dinarchus*, he says we can be sure only that it was later than the *Ancient Orators*.

The treatise on *Imitation* is known to us only from fragments. Only the first half of the study of the *Ancient Orators* is preserved, treating of Lysias, Isocrates and Isaeus; in the second part Demosthenes, Hyperides and Acschines were discussed. The treatise on the *Style of Demosthenes* is thought to be an enlarged edition of the discussion of Demosthenes in the earlier series. Other Works which have been lost were on the *Choice of Words*, on *Figures*, and on *Political Philosophy*, the latter a defence of the rhetoric of Isocrates and his school against its Epicurean detractors. The early editions attributed to Dionysius an *Ars Rhetorica*, but this is no longer held to be his work.

For a detailed account of the *Scripta Rhetorica* the reader is referred to Max. Egger, *Denys d'Halicarnasse*, pp. 20-246; a brief survey of these works may be found in W. Rhys Roberts, *Dionysius of Halicarnassus: The Three Literary Letters*, pp. 4-34. Roberts also gives (pp. 209-19) a bibliography of the *Scripta Rhetorica* down to the year 1900.

To his labours as literary critic Dionysius brought a wide and thorough acquaintance with the works of the Attic prose writers, a discriminating taste, and great industry and zeal. His chief merit as a critic lies in his purity of taste; he rejoiced in the recent triumph of Atticism over Asianism and did his best to strengthen that victory. His rhetorical works have much in common with those of Cicero, due to their both using many of the same sources. Like Cicero, Dionysius held Demosthenes in the greatest admiration; but this excessive admiration for one man seems to have made him unfair in his judgment of others: he tended to judge all the prose writers by the standards he set up for the orators. In other respects as well he is often narrow and superficial in his criticisms, and his manner is too dogmatic.

The first reference to Dionysius as a rhetorician in any extant author is in Quintilian, who merely names him three times in lists of rhetoricians. In the third century the circle of Libanius paid some attention to him.

From the fifth century onward he was regarded by the Byzantines as the supreme authority on rhetoric.

Manuscripts.

The manuscripts used by Jacoby for the first ten books of the *Antiquities* are as follows:

A. Chisianus 58, 10th cent.

B. Urbinas 105, l0th-11th cent.

C. Coislinianus 150, 16th cent.

D. Regius Parisinus 1654 and 1655, 16th cent.

E. Vaticanus 133, 15th cent.

F. Urbinas 106, 15th cent.

C and E also contain Book XI.; F contains only I.-V.

The MSS. used for Book XI. and those for the Fragments of XII.-XX. will be listed in Vol. VII.

A and B are by far the best of the MSS.; the others are all late, and some of them, especially C and D, contain numerous interpolations. The *editio princeps* was based on D. B was first used by Hudson, but he contented himself with giving its readings in his notes. The translators Bellanger and Spelman were prompt to adopt most of the good readings of B, and many were taken into the text by Reiske. Ritschl was the first to make a comparative study of A and B. As a result of his first investigation, based on insufficient evidence, he was inclined to rate A much higher than B; but later he showed a better appreciation of the good readings found only in B, and concluded that a sound text must rest upon a judicious use of both A and B,[22]— a conclusion in which Jacoby heartily concurred. Kiessling based his edition on B so far as possible.

---

22 His monographs on Dionysius were reprinted in his *Opuscula*, Vol. i., pp. 471-540.

The individual symbols of the late MSS. appear very infrequently in Jacoby's (and the present) critical apparatus, since these MSS. are rarely of any service in establishing the text. An occasional good reading found only in the margin of D (Dmg) may have been entered by R. Stephanus himself; in any event such readings are evidently based on conjecture rather than on the authority of any manuscript.

Editions

The important editions of the *Antiquities* follow: Robert Estienne (Stephanas), Paris. 1546. The *editio princeps* of the Greek text. Books I.-XI. Based on the very inferior Cod. Reg. Paris. 1654-55.

Friedrich Sylburg. Frankfort. 1586. Books I.-XI. and the *Excerpta de Legationibus*, translation (Gelenius' version revised) and notes. Sylburg made use, chiefly in his notes, of two MSS., a Romanus (not to be identified) and a Venetus (272). Reprinted in careless form at Leipzig in 1691.

John Hudson. Oxford, 1704. Books I.-XI. with the *Excerpta de Legationibus* and *Excerpta de Virtutibus et Vitiis*, a revision of Portus' Latin translation, and notes of various scholars. Hudson was the first to use the Urbinas (which he called Cod. Vaticanus), but cited its readings only in the notes.

J. J. Reiske, Leipzig, 1774-75. The text and translation of Hudson's edition with Reiske's own notes added. Too late to accomplish much in Vol. I., Reiske discovered that the printer was faithfully reproducing all the typographical errors of Hudson's edition; but from Book III. 21 onward he corrected the proof sheets and also for the first time inserted the good readings of B in the text. Dionysius is often cited by the pages of this edition.

Adolf Kiessling, Leipzig (Teubner), 1860-70. Based on B, so far as possible.

Carl Jacoby, Leipzig (Teubner), 1885-1905; Index, 1925.

Adolf Kiessling-Victor Prou, Paris (Didot), 1886. Greek text and Latin translation (Portus revised). An unfortunate edition. Kiessling, after getting the work fairly started, dropped it completely and Prou, who was called upon to complete the task, was far from possessing Kiessling's critical ability. Jacoby recognized the hand of Kiessling through the greater part of Books I.-III.; from that point on the edition has virtually no critical value.

Besides these complete editions of the *Antiquities*, selected chapters were edited by D. C. Grimm (*Archaeologiae Romanae quae ritus Romanos explicat Synopsis*), Leipzig, 1786; J. J. Ambrosch (i. 9-38; ii. 1-29; ii. 30-56; ii. 64-74) in four academic Festschriften, Breslau, 1840-46; Fr. Ritschl (i. 1-30), Bonn, 1846. Angelo Mai published at Milan, in 1816, some fragments from an epitome contained in a Milan MS., Cod. Ambrosianus Q 13 sup., and its copy, A 80 sup. These are now included (as the *Excerpta Ambrosiana*) among the Fragments of Books XII.-XX.

Translations.

The first Latin translation of the *Antiquities* (Books I.-XI.) was that of Lapus (or Lappus) Biragus, published at Treviso in 1480, three-quarters of a century before the first edition of the Greek text appeared. It possesses a special interest because it was based on two MSS., not as yet identified with any now extant, which were placed at the translator's disposal by Pope Paul II. Ritschl argued that one of these must have belonged to the better class of MSS. now represented by A and B, since the translation contains most of the additions to the text of the *editio princeps* that are found in one or both of the older MSS.[23] Lapus' translation was reprinted,

---

23   Opuscula, i. pp. 489, 493. Since some of the interpolations now found in C and D are included by Lapus, Ritschl concluded that he now and then consulted his later MS. for help (p. 530). Had Ritschl carried his investigation a little farther, he would have discovered that Lapus made diligent use of his older MS., closely related to B, only for Books I., II. and the first third of III., after which he practically ignored it. (The good readings which he has in common with B in the later books are in virtually every instance found also in C.) Down to iii. 23 he has most of the good readings of B, including a goodly number that appear in no other MS., but he avoids nearly all of B's errors; he

Introduction

'with corrections,' but also with a multitude of fresh typographical errors, at Paris in 1529, and again, as revised by Glareanus, at Basle in 1532. A fresh translation of Books I.-X. by Gelenius, based on the text of the *princeps*, appeared at Basle in 1549; for Book XI. he merely reprinted Lapus' translation. Sylburg (1586) revised the translation of Gelenius and added his own version of Book XL Aemilius Portus brought out a new translation (Lausanne, 1588); and this translation was adopted in the editions of Hudson and Reiske, and, with numerous corrections, in that of Kiessling-Prou.

An Italian translation by Francesco Venturi appeared at Venice in 1545, one year before the *editio princeps*. The translator names as his sources a Greek copy, very difficult to read, and a Latin translation [Lapus] full of errors. Apparently no serious use was made of the manuscript; it may well have proved to be generally inferior to Lapus' reading. In any case, Venturi's translation, with the exception of a few minor changes which were probably due to conjecture, presupposes the same Greek text as that of Lapus. Another Italian translation was published by M. Mastrofini, Rome, 1812-13.

A French version by G. F. le Jay (Paris, 1722) was loudly acclaimed by the admirers of the translator as representing perfection itself; but the two men who next translated the *Antiquities*, Bellanger and Spelman, showed that it was a servile translation of Portus' Latin version, errors and all. The following year Bellanger brought out, anonymously, his own translation, based on Hudson's text and the good readings of B contained in Hudson's notes. It is a smooth, fluent translation, but often rather free and at times little more than a paraphrase. It was reprinted later under Bellanger's own name.

---

also ignores the interpolations of C. From iii. 24 through Book XI. he nearly always agrees with C's readings, including a, number of the marginal interpolations; in a very few cases he supplies a few words missing in both B and C, so that one or the other of his MSS. must have been better than its present representative. Since he refers to the confused order of the text in both his MSS. at the end of Book XI., his older MS. cannot have been B; and the interpolated one cannot have been C, if C is correctly assigned to the sixteenth century.

Dionysius' Antiquities I

In German there have been translations by J. L. Benzler (1752; reprinted 1771-72) and by G. J. Schaller and A. H. Christian (Stuttgart, 1827-50). Benzler's version was quite free, that of Schaller (Books I.-IV.) accurate and scholarly; the part translated by Christian has not been seen by the present translator.

The only English version to appear hitherto is that of Edward Spelman, which was published with notes and dissertations at London in 1758. It is a good and, for the most part, fairly close translation of Hudson's text (Books I.-XI.) as improved by the good readings of the Urbinas and occasional conjectural emendations. See further below.

The Greek text here presented is based on the edition of Jacoby, but departs rather frequently from his text. All significant departures are indicated in the critical notes, but not, as a rule, minor details of orthography, elision and crasis, or corrections of obvious typographical errors that appear in his edition. Jacoby was fairly consistent in following out the principles which he had established with greater or less probability in two preliminary studies of Dionysian usage.[24] But in the case of some phrases and combinations of vowels for which he could not show that elision or crasis is normally to be expected, he vacillated in his attitude toward the MSS., sometimes following them in permitting hiatus and at other times emending; the present edition follows the MSS. (or some MS.) in all such cases. The MSS. are likewise followed in their spelling of the various forms of adjectives such as χαλκοῦς and χρυσοῦς. which appear in the contracted and the un-contracted forms with about equal frequency; Jacoby occasionally emended an un-contracted form. He adopted the late spellings ἐπαύσθην and ἠλάσθην wherever they have the authority of any MS,[25] and occasionally elsewhere; in the present text the Attic forms ἐπαύθην and ἠλάθην are everywhere restored.

---

24 (a) *Observationes criticae in Dionysii Hal. Antiquitates Romanas, in Acta Societatis Philol. Lipsiensis*, i. (1871), 287-344. (b) *Ueber die Sprache des Dionysios von Halikarnassos in der Röm. Archäologie*, Aarau, 1874.

25 In one instance C alone seems to show the σ; elsewhere the only MS. giving it is B (about half the time), but even in this MS. the σ has usually been deleted by a correcting hand.

Introduction

The present editor has permitted himself the liberty of spelling a few Latin proper names in the Greek text in the manner that many an editor would have liked to spell them, but as only a few of the earlier editors ventured to do in actual practice, and then only in the case of part of the names. It is hard to believe that Dionysius would have written such forms, for example, as Φαιστύλος for Φαυστύλος (compare his correct form Φαυστῖνος) Λωρεντόν (in Book I.) for Λαύρεντον (the form found in Book V.; cf. Λαυρεντῖνοι and Λαυρεντία), or Λαῦνα for Λαουϊνία in such a context as i. 59,3 (and if he wrote the correct form here, he must have used it elsewhere).

The critical apparatus lists only the more important variants and emendations; many simple emendations made by the early editors and adopted in subsequent editions are passed over in silence. No fresh collations of the MSS. have been available; but here and there an obvious error in Jacoby's report has been corrected or a suspicious entry queried.

The present translation is based on that of Spelman. His rendering of numerous passages, more especially in the speeches, is so spirited and so idiomatic, and often requires so few changes to make it seem thoroughly modern in tone, that it seemed desirable to use what was best of it in preparing this version for the Loeb Classical Library. If Spelman had been at his best more uniformly, a mild revision, to bring his translation into accord with the present Greek text, would have been all that was required. But the quality of his English is very uneven. He constructs a good many long, cumbersome sentences, in imitation of the Greek, shows an excessive fondness for the absolute use of the participle, and at times uses a vocabulary that seems more Latin than English. Where he thus departs from a good English style, and wherever his rendering is not sufficiently close to the Greek for the present purpose, changes have been freely made, some of them very drastic. No attempt has been made to preserve the antique flavour that characterizes Spelman's rendering, as a whole, inasmuch as the passages which he has rendered most successfully from other points of view are usually the most modern in diction. He did not translate the fragments; they appear here in English for the first time. The notes with which Spelman accompanied his version were scholarly and useful in their day, but have not the same interest now; accordingly, an entirely new set of notes has been prepared for this edition.

For the convenience of the reader parallel passages from Livy have been indicated in the notes, beginning with i. 64.

Bibliography

A BIBLIOGRAPHY of the *Roman Antiquities* covering the period from 1774 to 1876 was published by Jacoby in *Philologus*, xxxvi. (1877), pp. 129-31, 152-54. It was continued in the introductions to the several volumes of his edition, including the Index (1925). To the lists there given should be added:

Edw. Schwartz, in Pauly-Wissowa, *Real-Encydopadie, s.v.* Dionysius, cols. 934-61.

Max. Egger, *Denys d'Halicarnasse* (Paris, 1902) pp. 1-19, 247-98. An excellent study of Dionysius, more particularly as rhetorician.

H. Liers, *Die Theorie der Geschichtsschreibung des Dionys von Halikarnass*. Waldenburg, 1886.

Eiliv Skard, *Epigraphische Formeln bei Dionys von Halikarnass, in Symbolae Osloenses* xi. (1932). 55-60.

E. Gaida, *Die Schlachtschilderungen in den Antiquitates Romanae des Dionys von Halikarnass*, Breslau, 1934.

Introduction to Volume VII. (Vol. II)

MSS. OF BOOK XI

The manuscripts used by Kiessling and Jacoby for Book XI are as follows:

L = Laurentianus Plut. LXX 5 (15th cent.).

V=Vaticanus 133 (15th cent.).

M = Ambrosianus A 159 sup. (15th cent.).

C=Coislinianus 150 (16th cent.).

The best of these four MSS. is L, which appears to be a faithful copy of a badly damaged original: the scribe usually left gaps of appropriate length where he found the text illegible. Second best is V, which only occasionally shows interpolations; yet this V is the manuscript that was designated as E for the first ten books and regarded there as virtually negligible. Much inferior, however, even to V are M and C (the same C as for earlier books), which show many unskilful attempts to correct the text, especially by way of filling lacunae; see in particular chaps. 42 and 48-49.

All these MSS. derive from a poor archetype which, in addition to numerous shorter lacunae, had lost entire leaves at the end of Book XI, as well as earlier, and had some of the remaining leaves inserted out of place. See the note on chap. 44, 5 ; also vol. i. p. xli, n. 1, at end.

Excerpts from Books XII-XX. (Vol. II)

Approximately one-half of these excerpts come from the imposing collection made by order of the Emperor Constantine Porphyrogenitus, in the tenth century, from classical and later historians. The excerpts were classified under various heads, and a few of these sections have been preserved, some in but a single manuscript. The sections containing excerpts from Dionysius and the abbreviations used in citing them are as follows:

Ursin.— Περὶ πρεσβειῶν (*De legationibus*) , contained in several MSS.; see the list on p. x. First published by Ursinus, 1582; critical edition by C. de Boor, Berlin, 1903.

Vales.— Περὶ ἀρετῆς καὶ κακίας (*De virtutibus et vitiis*), preserved in the Codex Peirescianus (now Turonensis 980). Published by Valesius, 1634; critical edition by A. G. Roos, Berlin, 1910.

Esc.— Περὶ ἐπιβουλῶν (*De insidiis*), preserved in a single manuscript in the Escurial (Scorialensis Ω I 11). Edited by Feder, 1848 and 1849, and by

C. Müller in his *Frag. Hist. Graec.*, vol. ii., 1848. In numerous instances the same emendation was made independently, it would seem, by both these scholars; such corrections are indicated by the abbreviation Edd. Critical edition by C. de Boor, Berlin, 1905.

Ath.— Περὶ πολιορκιῶν. a few chapters from Book XX, contained in an early manuscript found on Mt. Athos, but now in Paris. Edited by C. Müller at the end of vol. ii. of his *Josephus*, Paris, 1847, and later by C. Wescher in his *Poliorcétique des Grecs*, Paris, 1868.

Another important source is:

Ambr.— A collection of miscellaneous excerpts, in chronological order, contained in a Milan manuscript (Ambrosianus Q 13 sup.), of the fifteenth century ; also in a second manuscript (A 80 sup.), which is a copy of the other and therefore rarely cited. This collection was carelessly edited by Angelo Mai in 1816. The numerous emendations of Struve mentioned in the critical notes were entered by that scholar in his copy of the Frankfort edition, now preserved in Munich.

Each new collection of excerpts, once discovered and published together with a Latin translation, has been included in the subsequent editions of the Antiquities.

The order in which the excerpts are here printed is that of Kiessling, followed by Jacoby, and is based on that of the Ambrosian collection. In a few cases the correctness of that order is open to serious question. Stephanus of Byzantium, by citing the particular books of the *Antiquities* in which he found the various places and peoples mentioned (see at end of Books XIII, XV-XIX), enables us to assign nearly all the excerpts to their proper books; but his references to Books XVII and XVIII are confused and leave it doubtful where the line of division came.

The present translation of the excerpts is the first to appear in English. Spelman did not translate the few that had been published in his day.

Sigla

BOOK XI

L = Laurentianus Plut. LXX 5.

V = Vaticanus 133.

M = Ambrosianus A 159 sup.

C = Coislinianus 150.

Ursin.

E = Scorialenses R III 14 and R III 21.

V = Vaticanus Graecus 1418.

R = Parisinus Graecus 2463.

B = Bruxellensis 11301-16.

M = Monacensis 267.

P = Palatinus Vaticanus Graecus 113.

O = All the MSS.

X = BMP.

Z = All the MSS. not otherwise cited.

Vales.

P = Peirescianus, now Turonensis.

Esc.

S = Scorialensis Ω I 11.

Edd. = Müller and Feder.

Ath.

A = Early MS. from Mt. Athos, now in Paris.

Ambr.

Q = Ambrosianus Q 13 sup.

A = Ambrosianus A 80 sup.

TARQUINIUS SUPERBUS MAKES HIMSELF KING.

Book I

1. Although it is much against my will to indulge in the explanatory statements usually given in the prefaces to histories, yet I am obliged to prefix to this work some remarks concerning myself. In doing this it is neither my intention to dwell too long on my own praise, which I know would be distasteful to the reader, nor have I the purpose of censuring other historians, as Anaximenes and Theopompus[1] did in the prefaces to their histories but I shall only show the reasons that induced me to undertake this work and give an accounting of the sources from which I gained the knowledge of the things that I am going to relate. For I am convinced that all who propose to leave such monuments of their minds to posterity as time shall not involve in one common ruin with their bodies, and particularly those who write histories, in which we have the right to assume that Truth, the source of both prudence and wisdom, is enshrined, ought, first of all, to make choice of noble and lofty subjects and such as will be of great utility to their readers, and then, with great care and pains, to provide themselves with the proper equipment for the treatment of their subject. For those who base historical works upon deeds inglorious or evil or unworthy of serious study, either because they crave to come to the knowledge of men and to get a name of some sort or other, or because they desire to display the wealth of their rhetoric, are neither admired by posterity for their fame nor praised for their eloquence; rather, they leave this opinion in the minds of all who take up their histories, that they themselves admired lives which were of a piece with the

---

1   Anaximenes of Lampsacus wrote a history of Greece (down to the battle of Mantinea) and a history of Philip of Macedon; also an epic on Alexander. Theopompus in his *Hellenica* continued the history of Thucydides from 411 down to the battle of Cnidus in 394; his *Philippica*, in 58 books, treated not only of Philip but of contemporary events elsewhere.

1

writings they published, since it is a just and a general opinion that a man's words are the images of his mind. Those, on the other hand, who, while making choice of the best subjects, are careless and indolent in compiling their narratives out of such reports as chance to come to their ears gain no praise by reason of that choice; for we do not deem it fitting that the histories of renowned cities and of men who have held supreme power should be written in an offhand or negligent manner. As I believe these considerations to be necessary and of the first importance to historians and as I have taken great care to observe them both, I have felt unwilling either to omit mention of them or to give it any other place than in the preface to my work.

2 That I have indeed made choice of a subject noble, lofty and useful to many will not, I think, require any lengthy argument, at least for those who are not utterly unacquainted with universal history. For if anyone turns his attention to the successive supremacies both of cities and of nations, as accounts of them have been handed down from times past, and then, surveying them severally and comparing them together, wishes to determine which of them obtained the widest dominion and both in peace and war performed the most brilliant achievements, he will find that the supremacy of the Romans has far surpassed all those that are recorded from earlier times, not only in the extent of its dominion and in the splendour of its achievements — which no account has as yet worthily celebrated — but also in the length of time during which it has endured down to our day. For the empire of the Assyrians, ancient as it was and running back to legendary times, held sway over only a small part of Asia. That of the Medes, after overthrowing the Assyrian empire and obtaining a still wider dominion, did not hold it long, but was overthrown in the fourth generation.[2] The Persians, who conquered the Medes, did, indeed, finally become masters of almost all Asia; but when they attacked the nations of Europe also, they did not reduce many of them to submission, and they continued in power not much above two hundred years.[3] The Macedonian dominion, which overthrew the might of the Persians, did, in the extent of its sway, exceed all its predecessors, yet even it did not flourish long, but after Alexander's death began to decline; for it was immediately partitioned among many commanders from the time of the Diadochi,[4] and although after their time it was able to go on to the second or third generation, yet it was weakened by its own dissensions and at the last destroyed by the Romans.[5] But even the Macedonian power did not subjugate every country and every sea; for it neither conquered Libya, with the exception of the small portion bordering on Egypt, nor subdued all Europe, but in the North advanced only as far as Thrace and in the West down to the Adriatic Sea.

3 Thus we see that the most famous of the earlier supremacies of which history has given us any account, after attaining to so great vigour and might, were overthrown. As for the Greek powers, it is not fitting to compare them to those just mentioned, since they gained neither magnitude of empire nor duration of eminence equal to theirs. For the Athenians ruled only the sea coast, during the space of sixty-eight years,[6] nor did their sway extend even over all that, but only to the part between the Euxine and the Pamphylian seas, when their naval supremacy was at its height. The

2   In 550 B.C., in the reign of Astyages, the fourth Median king according to Herodotus.

3   550-330 B.C.

4   *i.e.* "Successors," the term applied to the generals of Alexander who divided his empire among themselves after his death.

5   By the overthrow of Perseus in 168, or possibly by the defeat of Philip V in 197, followed by that of Antiochus in 190. Compare chap. 3 (end).

6   From *ca.* 472 to 404.

Lacedaemonians, when masters of the Peloponnesus and the rest of Greece, advanced their rule as far as Macedonia, but were checked by the Thebans before they had held it quite thirty years.[7] But Rome rules every country that is not inaccessible or uninhabited, and she is mistress of every sea, not only of that which lies inside the Pillars of Hercules but also of the Ocean, except that part of it which is not navigable;[8] she is the first and the only State recorded in all time that ever made the risings and the settings of the sun the boundaries of her dominion. Nor has her supremacy been of short duration, but more lasting than that of any other commonwealth or kingdom. For from the very beginning, immediately after her founding, she began to draw to herself the neighbouring nations, which were both numerous and warlike, and continually advanced, subjugating every rival. And it is now seven hundred and forty-five years from her foundation down to the consulship of Claudius Nero, consul for the second time, and of Calpurnius Piso, who were chosen in the one hundred and ninety-third Olympiad.[9] From the time that she mastered the whole of Italy she was emboldened to aspire to govern all mankind, and after driving from off the sea the Carthaginians, whose maritime strength was superior to that of all others, and subduing Macedonia, which until then was reputed to be the most powerful nation on land, she no longer had as rival any nation

---

7   This statement is puzzling, since the period actually extended from the surrender of Athens in 404 to the battle of Leuctra in 371. The text may be corrupt.

8   Dionysius may have had in mind Pytheas' report of a πεπηγυία Θάλασσα (a sea filled with floating ice?) in the far north. From Eratosthenes we learn also that that other early navigator, the Carthaginian Hanno, who sailed far south along the west coast of Africa, was finally forced by many difficulties (of what sort we are not told) to turn back. Thayer's Note: Hanno himself (*Periple*, § 18) says he uttered back for lack of supplies.

9   Nero and Piso were consuls in 7 B.C. This was the year 745 of the City according to Dionysius, who assigns its founding to the year 751. See chap. 74.

4

either barbarian or Greek; and it is now in my day already the seventh generation[10] that she has continued to hold sway over every region of the world, and there is no nation, as I may saw, that disputes her universal dominion or protests against being ruled by her. However, to prove my statement that I have neither made choice of the most trivial of subjects nor proposed to treat of mean and insignificant deeds, but am undertaking to write not only about the most illustrious city but also about brilliant achievements to whose like no man could point, I know not what more I need say.

4 But before I proceed, I desire to show in a few words that it is not without design and mature premeditation that I have turned to the early part of Rome's history, but that I have well-considered reasons to give for my choice, to forestall the censure of those who, fond of finding fault with everything and not as yet having heard of any of the matters which I am about to make known, may blame me because, in spite of the fact that this city, grown so famous in our days, had very humble and inglorious beginnings, unworthy of historical record, and that it was but a few generations ago, that is, since her overthrow of the Macedonian powers and her success in the Punic wars, that she arrived at distinction and glory, nevertheless, when I was at liberty to choose one of the famous periods in her history for my theme, I turned aside to one so barren of distinction as her antiquarian lore. For to this day almost all the Greeks are ignorant of the early history of Rome and the great majority of them have been imposed upon by sundry false opinions grounded upon stories which chance has brought to their ears and

---

10 This would normally mean six full generations plus part of another. If Dionysius was counting from the battle of Pydna (168), he must have reckoned a generation here at less than twenty-eight years (his usual estimate); but he may have felt that the Macedonian power was broken at Cynoscephalae (197). Or the seven generations may have been actually counted in some important family.

led to believe that, having come upon various vagabonds without house or home and barbarians, and even those not free men, as her founders, she in the course of time arrived at world domination, and this not through reverence for the gods and justice and every other virtue, but through some chance and the injustice of Fortune, which inconsiderately showers her greatest favours upon the most undeserving. And indeed the more malicious are wont to rail openly at Fortune for freely bestowing on the basest of barbarians the blessings of the Greeks. And yet why should I mention men at large, when even some historians have dared to express such views in the writing they have left, taking this method of humouring barbarian kings who detested Rome's supremacy, — princes to whom they were ever servilely devoted and with whom they associated as flatterers, — by presenting them with "histories" which were neither just nor true?[11]

5 In order, therefore, to remove these erroneous impressions, as have called them, from the minds of many and to substitute true ones in their room, I shall in this Book show who the founders of the city were, at what periods the various groups came together and through what turns of fortune they left their native countries. By this means I engage to prove that they were Greeks and came together from nations not the smallest nor least considerable. And beginning with the next Book I shall tell of the deeds they performed immediately after their founding of the city and of the customs and institutions by virtue of which their descendants advanced to so great dominion; and, so far as I am able, I shall omit nothing worthy of being recorded in history, to the end that I may instil in the minds of those who shall then be informed of the truth the fitting conception of this city, — unless they have already assumed an

---

11 Sylburg suggested that Hieronymus and Timaeus (see beginning of chap. 6) were among the writers Dionysius here had in mind and that Pyrrhus was one of the kings.

utterly violent and hostile attitude toward it, — and also that they may neither feel indignation at their present subjection, which is grounded on reason (for by an universal law of Nature, which time cannot destroy, it is ordained that superiors shall ever govern their inferiors), nor rail at Fortune for having wantonly bestowed upon an undeserving city a supremacy so great and already of so long continuance, particularly when they shall have learned from my history that Rome from the very beginning, immediately after its founding, produced infinite examples of virtue in men whose superiors, whether for piety or for justice or for life-long self-control or for warlike valour, no city, either Greek or barbarian, has ever produced. This, I say, is what I hope to accomplish, if my readers will but lay aside all resentment; for some such feeling is aroused by a promise of things which run counter to received opinion or excite wonder. And it is a fact that all those Romans who bestowed upon their country so great a dominion are unknown to the Greeks for want of a competent historian. For no accurate history of the Romans written in Greek language has hitherto appeared, but only very brief and summary epitomes.

6 The first historian, so far as I am aware, to touch upon the early period of the Romans was Hieronymus of Cardia, in his work on the Epigoni.[12] After him Timaeus of Sicily related the beginnings of their history in his general history and treated in a separate work the wars with Pyrrhus of Epirus.[13] Besides these, Antigonus, Polybius, Silenus[14] and innumerable other authors devoted

---

12 Hieronymus wrote a history of the **Diadochi** (the immediate successors of Alexander) and of their sons, sometimes called the **Epigoni** (*cf.* Diodorus 1. 3), covering the period down to the war of Pyrrhus in Italy.
13 Timaeus' great work was his history of Sicily down to the overthrow of Agathocles in 289. It included the histories of Italy and Carthage; hence Dionysius describes it as a "general history."
14 Antigonus, cited by Plutarch on early Roman history, is otherwise unknown. Polybius is too well known to require comment here. Silenus was one of the

themselves to the same themes, though in different ways, each of them recording some few things compiled without accurate investigation on his own part but from reports which chance had brought to his ears. Like to these in all respects are the histories of those Romans, also, who related in Greek the early achievements of the city; the oldest of these writers are Quintus Fabius[15] and Lucius Cincius,[16] who both flourished during the Punic wars. Each of these men related the events at which he himself had been present with great exactness, as being well acquainted with them, but touched only in a summary way upon the early events that followed the founding of the city. For these reasons, therefore, I have determined not to pass over a noble period of history which the older writers left untouched, a period, moreover, the accurate portrayal of which will lead to the following most excellent and just results: In the first place, the brave men who have fulfilled their destiny will gain immortal glory and be extolled by posterity, which things render human nature like upon the divine and prevent men's deeds from perishing together with their bodies. And again, both the present and future descendants of those godlike men will choose, not the pleasantest and easiest of lives, but rather the noblest and most ambitious, when they consider that all who are sprung from an illustrious origin ought to set a high value on themselves and indulge in no pursuit unworthy of their ancestors, And I, who have not turned aside to this work for the sake of flattery, but out of a regard for truth and justice, which ought to be the aim of every history, shall have an opportunity, in the first place, of expressing my attitude of goodwill toward all good men and toward all who take pleasure in the contemplation of great and noble deeds; and, in the

---

historians in the suite of Hannibal; his history of the Second Punic War was praised by Cicero and Nepos.

15　Q. Fabius Pictor.

16　L. Cincius Alimentus.

second place, of making the most grateful return that I may to the city and other blessings I have enjoyed during my residence in it.

7 Having thus given the reason for my choice of subject, I wish now to say something concerning the sources I used while preparing for my task. For it is possible that those who have already read Hieronymus, Timaeus, Polybius, or any of the other historians whom I just now mentioned as having slurred over their work, since they will not have found in those authors many things mentioned by me, will suspect me of inventing them and will demand to know how I came by the knowledge of these particulars. Lest anyone, therefore, should entertain such an opinion of me, it is best that I should state in advance what narratives and records I have used as sources. I arrived in Italy at the very time that Augustus Caesar put an end to the civil war, in the middle of the one hundred and eighty-seventh Olympiad.[17] and having from that time to this present day, a period of twenty-two years, lived at Rome, learned the language of the Romans and acquainted myself with their writings, I have devoted myself during all that time to matters bearing upon my subject. Some information I received orally from men of the greatest learning, with whom I associated; and the rest I gathered from histories written by the approved Roman authors — Porcius Cato, Fabius Maximus,[18] Valerius Antias, Licinius Macer, the Aelii, Gellii and Calpurnii,[19] and many others of note; with

17 Perhaps late in 30 B.C., if Dionysius wrote this preface *early* in the year 7 (chap. 3, 4); but the closing of the temple of Janus in January, 29, or Octavian's triumph in August may have marked for him the end of the war.

18 Probably Q. Fabius Maximus Servilianus (cos. 142); but we have very little evidence to go on. See Schanz-Hosius, *Röm. Literatturgesch.* i p. 174.

19 As Niebuhr pointed out (*Röm. Gesch.* ii note 11), these plurals are not to be taken literally, but in the sense of "men like Aelius," etc. We read of two Aelii, it is true, who were engaged in writing history — L. Aelius Tubero, a boyhood friend of Cicero, and his son, Quintus; but it is doubtful whether the father ever published his work, whereas the son's history is quoted several times. The only Gellius and the only Calpurnius known to have been

these works, which are like the Greek annalistic accounts, as a basis, I set about the writing of my history. So much, then, concerning myself. But it yet remains for me to say something also concerning the history itself — to what periods I limit it, what subjects I describe, and what form I give to the work.

8 I begin my history, then, with the most ancient legends, which the historians before me have omitted as a subject difficult to be cleared up with diligent study; and I bring the narrative down to the beginning of the First Punic War, which fell in the third year of the one hundred and twenty-eighth Olympiad.[20] I relate all the foreign wars that the city waged during that period and all the internal seditions with which she was agitated, showing from what causes they sprang and by what methods and by what arguments they were brought to an end. I give an account also of all the forms of government Rome used, both during the monarchy and after its overthrow, and show what was the character of each. I describe the best customs and the most remarkable laws; and, in short, I show the whole life of the ancient Romans. As to the form I give this work, it does not resemble that which the authors who make wars alone their subject have given to their histories, nor that which others who treat of the several forms of government by themselves have adopted, nor is it like the annalistic accounts which the authors of *Atthides* [21] have published (for these are monotonous and soon grow tedious to the reader), but it is a combination of every kind, forensic, speculative and narrative, to the intent that it may afford satisfaction both to those who occupy themselves with

---

historians were Cn. Gellius and L. Calpurnius Piso Frugi, sometimes styled Censorius (the ex-censor). Both lived in the time of the Gracchi and both wrote histories of Rome from the beginning down to their own day.

20 265 B.C., the date of the *casus belli.*

21 *Atthis* (an adjective meaning "Attic") was the name given to histories of Attica; there were many of these written in the fourth and third centuries. They made no pretension to literary style.

political debates and to those who are devoted to philosophical speculations,[22] as well as to any who may desire mere undisturbed entertainment in their reading of history Such things, therefore, will be the subjects of my history and such will be its form. I, the author, am Dionysius of Halicarnassus, the son of Alexander. And at this point I begin.

9 This city, mistress of the whole earth and sea, which the Romans now inhabit, is said to have had as its earliest occupants the barbarian Sicels, a native race. As to the condition of the place before their time, whether it was occupied by others or uninhabited, none can certainly say. But some time later the Aborigines gained possession of it, having taken it from the occupants after a long war. These people had previously lived on the mountains in unwalled villages and scattered groups; but when the Pelasgians,[23] with whom some other Greeks had united, assisted them in the war against their neighbours, they drove the Sicels out of this place, walled in many towns, and contrived to subjugate all the country that lies between the two rivers, the Liris and the Tiber. These rivers spring from the foot of the Apennine mountains, the range by which all Italy is divided into two parts throughout its length, and at points about eight hundred stades from one another discharge themselves into the Tyrrhenian Sea, the Tiber to the north, near the city of Ostia, and the Liris to the south, as it flows by Minturnae, both these cities being Roman colonies. And these people remained in this same place of abode, both never afterwards driven out by any others; but, although they continued to be one and the same people, their name was twice changed. Till the time of the Trojan war they preserved

---

22 A comparison of the introductory chapter of Book XI (§§ 1 and 4) makes it probable that the first group mentioned here were those who took an active part in public affairs, the second the political philosophers or theorists.

23 As will be seen a little later (chap. 17), Dionysius regarded the Pelasgians as a Greek nation.

their ancient name of Aborigines; but under Latinus, their king, who reigned at the time of that war, they began to be called Latins, and when Romulus founded the city named after himself sixteen generations after the taking of Troy, they took the name which they now bear. And in the course of time they contrived to raise themselves from the smallest nation to the greatest and from the most obscure to the most illustrious, not only by their humane reception of those who sought a home among them, but also by sharing the rights of citizenship with all who had been conquered by them in war after a brave resistance, by permitting all the slaves, too, who were manumitted among them to become citizens, and by disdaining no condition of men from whom the commonwealth might reap an advantage, but above everything else by their form of government, which they fashioned out of their many experiences, always extracting something useful from every occasion.

10 There are some who affirm that the Aborigines, from whom the Romans are originally descended, were natives of Italy, a stock which came into being spontaneously[24] (I call Italy all that peninsula which is bounded by the Ionian Gulf[25] and the Tyrrhenian Sea and, thirdly, by the Alps on the landward side); and these authors say that they were first called Aborigines because they were the founders of the families of their descendants, or, as we should call them, *genearchai* or *prôtogonoi*.[26] Others claim that certain vagabonds without house or home, coming together out of many places, met one another there by chance and took up their abode in the fastnesses, living by robbery and grazing their herds. And these

---

24 This clause is added, possibly by a scribe, as a definition of the well-known Greek word **autochthones**, here rendered "natives." The word means literally "sprung from the land itself," corresponding to the Latin *indigenae*. It was the proud boast of the Athenians that they were **autochthones**.

25 "The Ionian Gulf" or simply "the Ionian" is Dionysius' usual term for the Adriatic, or more particularly perhaps for the entrance to this sea.

26 "Founders of families" and "first-born" respectively.

writers change their name, also, to one more suitable to their condition, calling them Aberrigenes,[27] to show that they were wanderers; indeed, according to these, the race of the Aborigines would seem to be no different from those the ancients called Leleges; for this is the name they generally gave to the homeless and mixed peoples who had no fixed abode which they could call their country[28] Still others have a story to the effect that they were colonists sent out by those Ligurians who are neighbours of the Umbrians. For the Ligurians inhabit not only many parts of Italy but some parts of Gaul as well, but which of these lands is their native country is not known, since nothing certain is said of them further.

11 But the most learned of the Roman historians, among whom is Porcius Cato, who compiled with the greatest care the "origins"[29] of the Italian cities, Gaius Sempronius[30] and a great many others, say that they were Greeks, part of those who once dwelt in Achaia, and that they migrated many generations before the Trojan war. But they do not go on to indicate either the Greek tribe to which they belonged or the city from which they removed, or the date or the leader of the colony, or as the result of what turns of fortune they

---

27 From the Latin *aberrare* ("wander").

28 Strabo cites (vii. 7, 2) some verses of Hesiod in which the Leleges are described as λεκτοὺς ἐκ Γαίης λαούς, "peoples gathered out of earth," an etymological word-play which he thinks shows that Hesiod regarded them as having been from the beginning a collection of mixed peoples. This derivation of the name from the root λεγ ("gather") is the only one the ancients have handed down.

29 Cato's history seems to have consisted at first of one book, in which Rome's beginnings and the regal period were recounted, followed by two books devoted to the origin of the various Italian cities; hence the title *Origines*. Later he added four more books, in which an account was given of the Punic Wars and subsequent events.

30 Sempronius Tuditanus (cos. 129). Besides his *liber magistratuum* he seems to have written a historical work.

left their mother country; and although they are following a Greek legend, they have cited no Greek historian as their authority. It is uncertain, therefore, what the truth of the matter is. But if what they say is true, the Aborigines can be a colony of no other people but of those who are now called Arcadians; for these were the first of all the Greeks to cross the Ionian Gulf, under the leadership of Oenotrus, the son of Lycaon, and to settle in Italy. This Oenotrus was the fifth from Aezeius and Phoroneus, who were the first kings in the Peloponnesus. For Niobe was the daughter of Phoroneus, and Pelasgus was the son of Niobê and Zeus, it is said; Lycaon was the son of Aezeius and Deïanira was the daughter of Lycaon; Deïanira and Pelasgus were the parents of another Lycaon, whose son Oenotrus was born seventeen generations before the Trojan expedition. This, then, was the time when the Greeks sent the colony into Italy. Oenotrus left Greece because he was dissatisfied with his portion of his father's land; for, as Lycaon had twenty-two sons, it was necessary to divide Arcadia into as many shares. For this reason Oenotrus left the Peloponnesus, prepared a fleet, and crossed the Ionian Gulf with Peucetius, one of his brothers. They were accompanied by many of their own people — for this nation is said to have been very populous in early times — and by as many other Greeks as had less land than was sufficient for them. Peucetius landed his people above the Iapygian Promontory, which was the first part of Italy they made, and settled there; and from him the inhabitants of this region were called Peucetians. But Oenotrus with the greater part of the expedition came into the other sea that washes the western regions along the coast of Italy; it was then called the Ausonian Sea, from the Ausonians who dwelt beside it, but after the Tyrrhenians became masters at sea its name was changed to that which it now bears.

Book I

12 And finding there much land suitable for pasturage and much for tillage, but for the most part unoccupied, and even that which was inhabited not thickly populated, he cleared some of it of the barbarians and built small towns contiguous to one another on the mountains, which was the customary manner of habitation in use among the ancients. And all the land he occupied, which was very extensive, was called Oenotria, and all the people under his command Oenotrians, which was the third name they had borne. For in the reign of Aezeius they were called Aezeians, when Lycaon succeeded to the rule, Lycaonians, and after Oenotrus led them into Italy they were for a while called Oenotrians. What I say is supported by the testimony of Sophocles, the tragic poet, in his drama entitled *Triptolemus*; for he there represents Demeter as informing Triptolemus how large a tract of land he would have to travel over while sowing it with the seeds she had given him. For, after first referring to the eastern part of Italy, which reaches from the Iapygian Promontory to the Sicilian Strait, and then touching upon Sicily on the opposite side, she returns again to the western part of Italy and enumerates the most important nations that inhabit this coast, beginning with the settlement of the Oenotrians. But it is enough to quote merely the iambics in which he says:

> "And after this, — first, then, upon the right,
> Oenotria wide-outstretched and Tyrrhene Gulf,
> And next the Ligurian land shall welcome thee."[31]

And Antiochus of Syracuse,[32] a very early historian, in his account of the settlement of Italy, when enumerating the most ancient inhabitants in the order in which each of them held

---

31 Nauck, *Trag. Graec. Frag.*², p. 262, frg. 541.
32 Antiochus (latter half of fifth century) wrote a history of Sicily and a history of Italy. The former was used by Thucydides, and the latter is frequently cited by Strabo. The quotation here given is fragment. 3 in Müller, *Frag. Hist. Graec.* i. p. 181.

15

possession of any part of it, says that the first who are reported to have inhabited that country are the Oenotrians. His words are these: "Antiochus, the son of Xenophanes, wrote this account of Italy, which comprises all that is most credible and certain out of the ancient tales; this country, which is now called Italy, was formerly possessed by the Oenotrians." Then he relates in what manner they were governed and says that in the course of time Italus came to be their king, after whom they were named Italians; that this man was succeeded by Morges, after whom they were called Morgetes, and that Sicelus, being received as a guest by Morges and setting up a kingdom for himself, divided the nation. After which he adds these words: "Thus those who had been Oenotrians became Sicels, Morgetes and Italians."

13 Now let me also show the origin of the Oenotrian race, offering as my witness another of the early historians, Pherecydes of Athens,[33] who was a genealogist inferior to none. He thus expresses himself concerning the kings of Arcadia: "Of Pelasgus and Deïanira was born Lycaon; this man married Cyllenê, a Naiad nymph, after whom Mount Cyllenê is named." Then, having given an account of their children and of the places each of them inhabited, he mentions Oenotrus and Peucetius, in these words: "And Oenotrus, after whom are named the Oenotrians who live in Italy, and Peucetius, after whom are named the Peucetians who live on the Ionian Gulf." Such, then, are the accounts given by the ancient poets and writers of legends concerning the places of abode and the origin of the Oenotrians; and on their authority I assume that if the Aborigines were in reality a Greek nation, according to

---

33 Pherecydes (fifth century) was one of the more prominent of the early logographers and the first prose writer of Athens. His great work was a mythological history, beginning with a brief theogony but largely devoted to the genealogies of the great families of the heroic age. The following quotations appear as frg. 85 in Müller, F.H.G. i. p. 92.

the opinion of Cato, Sempronius and many others, they were descendants of these Oenotrians. For I find that the Pelasgians and Cretans and the other nations that lived in Italy came thither afterwards; nor can I discover that any other expedition more ancient than this came from Greece to the western parts of Europe. I am of the opinion that the Oenotrians, besides making themselves masters of many other regions in Italy, some of which they found unoccupied and others but thinly inhabited, also seized a portion of the country of the Umbrians, and that they were called Aborigines from their dwelling on the mountains[34] (for it is characteristic of the Arcadians to be fond of the mountains), in the same manner as at Athens some are called *Hyperakriori,*[35] and others *Paralioi.*[36] But if any are naturally slow in giving credit to accounts of ancient matters without due examination, let them be slow also in believing the Aborigines to be Ligurians, Umbrians, or any other barbarians, and let them suspend their judgment till they have heard what remains to be told and then determine which opinion out of all is the most probable.

14 Of the cities first inhabited by the Aborigines few remained in my day; the greatest part of them, having been laid waste both by wars and other calamities, are abandoned. These cities were in the Reatine territory, not far from the Apennine mountains, as Terentius Varro writes in his *Antiquities,*[37] the nearest being one day's journey

---

34 A hybrid etymology: *ab* + ὄρος (mountain).

35 People of the highlands.

36 People of the coast.

37 This monumental work of antiquarian lore is no longer extant. Varro was a native of Reate (49 Roman miles north-east of Rome), and may well have taken a particular interest in these old sites of the Aborigines. The latest discussion of this chapter is to be found in Nissen, *Italische Landeskunde*, ii. 1, pp471-6; Bunsen's article appeared in the Annali dell' Instituto di Corrispondenza Archeologica, vi. (1834), pp. 129 ff. See also *Smith's Dict. of Greek and Roman Geography, s.v.* Aborigines.

distant from Rome. I shall enumerate the most celebrated of them, following his account. Palatium, twenty-five stades distant from Reate (a city that was still inhabited by Romans down to my time),[38] near the Quintian Way.[39] Tribula, about sixty stades from Reate and standing upon a low hill. Suesbula, at the same distance from Tribula, near the Ceraunian Mountains. Suna, a famous city forty stades from Suesbula; in it there is a very ancient temple of Mars. Mefula, about thirty stades from Suna; its ruins and traces of its walls are pointed out. Orvinium, forty stades from Mefula, a city as famous and large as any in that region; for the foundations of its walls are still to be seen and some tombs of venerable antiquity, as well as the circuits of burying-places[40] extending over lofty mounds; and there is also an ancient temple of Minerva built on the summit.

At the distance of eighty stades from Reate, as one goes along the Curian Way[41] past Mount Coretus, stood Corsula, a town but recently destroyed. There is also pointed out an island, called Issa,

---

38 Bunsen emended the text so as to make the clause here included in parentheses refer to Palatium; he held that Reate was too well known to call for such an explanation.

39 The Via Quintia is not elsewhere mentioned, but seems to have been the more direct of two roads leading down the valley to the north-west of Reate. The names of the towns that immediately follow are probably corruptions of Trebula and Suessula. The Ceraunian Mountains are tentatively identified by Nissen with the Monte Rotondo of to-day.

40 The word **polyandrion** usually means a place where many are buried together; it is contrasted, as here, with individual tombs by Aelian, Var. Hist. xii. 21, and Pausanias ii.22, 9.

41 The Via Curia is thought to have been a second road leading north-west from Reate but running round the east and north sides of the chain of small lakes called by the collective name of Lacus Velinus or Palus Reatina. M'. Curius Dentatus in 272 drained the lowlands at the northern end of the valley, and he may well have constructed this road at that time. Mount Coretus is unknown. The Maruvium here named is not to be confused with the Marsian capital on the Fucine Lake. Cicero mentions the Septem Aquae in a letter to Atticus (iv. 15, 5).

surrounded by a lake; the Aborigines are said to have lived on this island without any artificial fortification, relying on the marshy waters of the lake instead of walls. Near Issa is Maruvium, situated on an arm of the same lake and distant forty stades from what they call the Septem Aquae.

Again, as one goes from Reate by the road towards the Listine district,[42] there is Batia,[43] thirty stades distant; then Tiora, called Matiene, at a distance of three hundred stades. In this city, they say, there was a very ancient oracle of Mars, the nature of which was similar to that of the oracle which legend says once existed at Dodona; only there a pigeon was said to prophesy, sitting on a sacred oak,[44] whereas among the Aborigines a heaven-sent bird,

---

42 This reading is due to Nissen, who believes that Listina (the district of Lista) was an earlier name for the district of Amiternum. In view of the story related at the end of the chapter Lista must have been fairly close to Amiternum, which was 33 miles east of Reate. The vulgate reading with Λατίνην, "the road to Latium" or possibly "to the Latin Way," has been taken to mean a road leading south-east from Reate towards the Fucine Lake, and Bunsen's emendation λίμνην was designed to make that direction still plainer. But the site, a few miles north-west of that lake, which various scholars have selected for Lista is more than 20 miles distant from Amiternum across a mountain pass; moreover, it lies in the country of the Aequians, which is not reported to have been occupied by the Sabines at any time. Nissen's view likewise places Lista distinctly outside the Reatine territory. But it is quite possible that the distance of 300 stades assigned to Tiora is seriously in error; we might then look for Tiora and Lista a little east of Interocreum, or somewhat more than half-way from Reate to Amiternum. Nissen unjustifiably assumes that in this entire section Dionysius is counting the stade as only one-tenth of a Roman mile, instead of one-eight of a mile, as he usually does.

43 Or Vatia.

44 At Dodona the god was said to dwell in the stem of an oak and to reveal his will from the branches of the tree, probably by the rustling of the leaves. In the time of Herodotus the oracles were interpreted by two or three aged women called πελειάδες or πέλειαι, both terms meaning "pigeons." According to some it was actually a pigeon that delivered the oracles.

ThayerNone of this gives you the faintest clue, gentle reader, where Tiora Matiene might be; and the reason for that is that the locality has not been

which they call *picus* and the Greeks *dryokolaptês*,[45] appearing on a pillar of wood, did the same. Twenty-four stades from the afore-mentioned city[46] stood Lista, the mother-city of the Aborigines, which at a still earlier time the Sabines had captured by a surprise attack, having set out against it from Amiternum by night. Those who survived the taking of the place, after being received by the Reatines, made many attempts to retake their former home, but being unable to do so, they consecrated the country to the gods, as if it were still their own, invoking curses against those who should enjoy the fruits of it.

15 Seventy stades from Reate stood Cutilia,[47] a famous city, beside a mountain. Not far from it there is a lake, four hundred feet in diameter, filled by ever-flowing natural springs and, it is said, bottomless. This lake, as having something divine about it, the inhabitants of the country look upon as sacred to Victory; and surrounding it with a palisade, so that no one may approach the water, they keep it inviolate; except that at certain times each year those whose sacred office it is go to the little island in the lake and perform the sacrifices required by custom. This island is about fifty feet in diameter and rises not more than a foot above the water; it is

---

identified: it's one of the countless thousands of lost places of Antiquity. If you read Italian, this excellent page (in turn part of Robert Tupone's site on the village of S. Anatolia, a frazione of Borgorose in Rieti province) goes into the matter in good detail.

45 Both the Greek and Latin words mean "woodpecker."

46 The context certainly suggests Tiora as the city referred to; but Holstenius understood Reate, and thus brought Lista between Cutilia and Reate, where the name Monte di Lesta is found to-day.

47 Also called Cutiliae. Its approximate size is determined by the remains of Aquae Cutiliae near by, a watering-place that was especially favoured by the Flavian emperors. It lay east of Reate, on the road last mentioned, if Nissen's identification of that road is correct. He suggests that the place is mentioned last, out of its natural order, in view of the important rôle the lake was to play later (see chap. 19).

not fixed, and floats about in any direction, according to as the wind gently wafts it from one place to another. An herb grows on the island like the flowering rush and also certain small shrubs, a phenomenon which to those who are unacquainted with the works of Nature seems unaccountable and a marvel second to none.[48]

16 The Aborigines are said to have settled first in these places after they had driven out the Umbrians. And making excursions from there, they warred not only upon the barbarians in general but particularly upon the Sicels, their neighbours, in order to dispossess them of their lands. First, a sacred band of young men went forth, consisting of a few who were sent out by their parents to seek a livelihood, according to a custom which I know many barbarians and Greeks have followed.[49] For whenever the population of any of their cities increased to such a degree that the produce of their lands no longer sufficed for them all, or the earth, injured by unseasonable changes of the weather, brought forth her fruits in less abundance than usual, or any other occurrence of like nature, either good or bad, introduced a necessity of lessening their numbers, they would dedicate to some god or other all the men born within a certain year, and providing them with arms, would send them out of their country. If, indeed, this was done by way of thanksgiving for populousness or for victory in war, they would first offer the usual sacrifices and then send forth their colonies under happy auspices; but if, having incurred the wrath of Heaven, they were seeking deliverance from the evils that beset them, they would perform much the same ceremony, but sorrowfully and begging forgiveness of the youths they were sending away. And those who departed,

---

48 The fullest account and explanation of this strange islet is given by Seneca (*Nat. Quaest.* iii. 25, 8). The lake is still to be seen, but the islet has disappeared.

49 The only recorded instance from the Greek world is that of the Chalcidians, who dedicated to Apollo one man in every ten and sent them to Delphi; these men later founded Rhegium (Strabo vi. 1, 6). Compare chap. 24 and note.

feeling that henceforth they would have no share in the land of their fathers but must acquire another, looked upon any land that received them in friendship or that they conquered in war as their country. And the god to whom they had been dedicated when they were sent out seemed generally to assist them and to prosper the colonies beyond all human expectation. In pursuance, therefore, of this custom some of the Aborigines also at that time, as their places were growing very populous (for they would not put any of their children to death, looking on this as one of the greatest of crimes), dedicated to some god or other the offspring of a certain year and when these children were grown to be men they sent them out of their country as colonists; and they, after leaving their own land, were continually plundering the Sicels. And as soon as they became masters of any places in the enemy's country the rest of the Aborigines, also, who needed lands now attacked each of them their neighbours with greater security and built various cities, some of which are inhabited to this day — Antemnae, Tellenae, Ficulea, which is near the Corniculan mountains, as they are called, and Tibur, where a quarter of the city is even to this day called the Sicel quarter;[50] and of all their neighbours they harassed the Sicels most. From these quarrels there arose a general war between the nations more important than any that had occurred previously in Italy, and it went on extending over a long period of time.

17 Afterwards some of the Pelasgians who inhabited Thessaly as it is now called, being obliged to leave their country, settled among the Aborigines and jointly with them made war upon the Sicels. It is possible that the Aborigines received them partly in the hope of gaining their assistance, but I believe it was chiefly on account of their kinship; for the Pelasgians, too, were a Greek nation originally

---

50 This would presumably be *vicus Siculus* or *regio Sicula* in Latin; no mention of the quarter is found elsewhere.

from the Peloponnesus. They were unfortunate in many ways but particularly in wandering much and in having no fixed abode. For they first lived in the neighbourhood of the Achaean Argos, as it is now called, being natives of the country, according to most accounts. They received their name originally from Pelasgus, their king. Pelasgus was the son of Zeus, it is said, and of Niobê the daughter of Phoroneus, who, as the legend goes, was the first mortal woman Zeus had knowledge of. In the sixth generation afterwards, leaving the Peloponnesus, they removed to the country which was then called Haemonia and now Thessaly. The leaders of the colony were Achaeus, Phthius and Pelasgus, the sons of Larisa and Poseidon. When they arrived in Haemonia they drove out the barbarian inhabitants and divided the country into three parts, calling them, after the names of their leaders, Phthiotis, Achaia and Pelasgiotis. After they had remained there five generations, during which they attained to the greatest prosperity while enjoying the produce of the most fertile plains in Thessaly, about the sixth generation they were driven out of it by the Curetes and Leleges, who are now called Aetolians and Locrians, and by many others who lived near Parnassus, their enemies being commanded by Deucalion, the son of Prometheus and Clymenê, the daughter of Oceanus.

18 And dispersing themselves in their flight, some went to Crete, others occupied some of the islands called the Cyclades, some settled in the region called Hestiaeotis near Olympus and Ossa, others crossed into Boeotia, Phocis and Euboea; and some, passing over into Asia, occupied many places on the coast along the Hellespont and many of the adjacent islands, particularly the one now called Lesbos, uniting with those who composed the first colony that was sent thither from Greece under Macar, the son of

Crinacus.[51] But the greater part of them, turning inland, took refuge among the inhabitants of Dodona, their kinsmen, against whom, as a sacred people, none would make war; and there they remained for a reasonable time. But when they perceived they were growing burdensome to their hosts, since the land could not support them all, they left it in obedience to an oracle that commanded them to sail to Italy, which was then called Saturnia. And having prepared a great many ships they set out to cross the Ionian Gulf, endeavouring to reach the nearest parts of Italy But as the wind was in the south and they were unacquainted with those regions, they were carried too far out to sea and landed at one of the mouths of the Po called the Spinetic mouth. In that very place they left their ships and such of their people as were least able to bear hardships, placing a guard over the ships, to the end that, if their affairs did not prosper, they might be sure of a retreat. Those who were left behind there surrounded their camp with a wall and brought in plenty of provisions in their ships; and when their affairs seemed to prosper satisfactorily, they built a city and called it by the same name as the mouth of the river.[52] These people attained to a greater degree of prosperity than any others who dwelt on the Ionian Gulf; for they had the mastery at sea for a long time, and out of their revenues from the sea they used to send tithes to the god at Delphi, which were among the most magnificent sent by any people. But later, when the barbarians in the neighbourhood made war upon them in great numbers, they deserted the city; and these barbarians in the course of time were driven out by the Romans. So perished that part of the Pelasgians that was left at Spina.

---

51 This is the form of the name given by Diodorus (v. 81) and others; the son's name usually appears as Macareus.
52 In reality it was, of course, the town Spina that gave its name to the *ostium Spineticum*.

Book I

19 Those, however, who had turned inland crossed the mountainous part of Italy and came to the territory of the Umbrians who were neighbours to the Aborigines. (The Umbrians inhabited a great many other part of Italy also and were an exceeding great and ancient people.) At first the Pelasgians made themselves masters of the lands where they first settled and took some of the small towns belonging to the Umbrians. But when a great army came together against them, they were terrified at the number of their enemies and betook themselves to the country of the Aborigines. And these, seeing fit to treat them as enemies, made haste to assemble out of the places nearest at hand, in order to drive them out of the country. But the Pelasgians luckily chanced to be encamped at that time near Cutilia, a city of the Aborigines hard by the sacred lake, and observing the little island circling round in it and learning from the captives they had taken in the fields the name of the inhabitants, they concluded that their oracle was now fulfilled. For this oracle, which had been delivered to them in Dodona and which Lucius Mallius,[53] no obscure man, says he himself saw engraved in ancient characters upon one of the tripods standing in the precinct of Zeus, was as follows:

> "Fare forth the Sicels' Saturnian land to seek,
> Aborigines' Cotylê,[54] too, where floats an isle;
> With these men mingling, to Phoebus send a tithe,
> And heads to Cronus' son, and send to the sire a man."[55]

---

53 Or Manlius. Nothing is known of the man beyond what may be inferred from the present passage.

54 A poetic variant of Cotylia, the Greek form of Cutilia.

55 Varro's version of this story is quoted by Macrobius (i. 7, 28 ff.). In the last verse of the oracle he has Ἀιδη for Κρονίδη. He says the oracle was at first taken to call for human heads as an offering to Dis and the sacrifice of men to Saturn. But several generations later Hercules taught the people a more humane interpretation: to Dis they should offer little images made in the likeness of men and Saturn should be honoured with lighted candles, since φῶτα meant "light" as well as "man."

20 When, therefore, the Aborigines advanced with a numerous army, the Pelasgians approached unarmed with olive branches in their hands, and telling them of their own fortunes, begged that they would receive them in a friendly manner to dwell with them, assuring them that they would not be troublesome, since Heaven itself was guiding them into this one particular country according to the oracle, which they explained to them. When the Aborigines heard this, they resolved to obey the oracle and to gain these Greeks as allies against their barbarian enemies, for they were hard pressed by their war with the Sicels. They accordingly made a treaty with the Pelasgians and assigned to them some of their own lands that lay near the sacred lake; the greater part of these were marshy and are still called Velia, in accordance with the ancient form of their language. For it was the custom of the ancient Greeks generally to place before those words that began with a vowel the syllable *ou*, written with one letter (this was like a gamma, formed by two oblique lines joined to one upright line), as ϝελένη, ϝάναξ, ϝοῖκος, ϝέαρ and many such words.[56] Afterwards, a considerable part of the Pelasgians, as the land was not sufficient to support them all, prevailed on the Aborigines to join them in an expedition against the Umbrians, and marching forth, they suddenly fell upon and captured Croton, a rich and large city of theirs. And using this place as a stronghold and fortress against the Umbrians, since it was sufficiently fortified as a place of defence in time of war and had fertile pastures lying round it, they made themselves masters also of a great many other places and with great zeal assisted the Aborigines in the war they were still engaged in against the Sicels, till they drove them out of their country. And the Pelasgians in

---

56 This letter, **vau**, later called digamma, has actually been found in numerous early inscriptions from various parts of Greece; its value was that of the Latin *v*, or English *w*. See Kühner-Blass, *Griech. Gram.* i. 1, §16 f. Dionysius assumes that Velia is an early form of ελεια ("marshy"). In his day the Latin *v* was usually represented in Greek by ου, sometimes by β.

common with the Aborigines settled many cities, some of which had been previously inhabited by the Sicels and others which they built themselves; among these are Caere, then called Agylla, and Pisae, Saturnia, Alsium and some others, of which they were in the course of time dispossessed by the Tyrrhenians.

21 But Falerii and Fescennium were even down to my day inhabited by Romans and preserved some small remains of the Pelasgian nation, though they had earlier belonged to the Sicels. In these cities there survived for a very long time many of the ancient customs formerly in use among the Greeks, such as the fashion of their arms of war, like Argolic bucklers and spears; and whenever they sent out an army beyond their borders, either to begin a war or to resist an invasion, certain holy men, unarmed, went ahead of the rest bearing the terms of peace;[57] similar, also, were the structure of their temples, the images of their gods, their purifications and sacrifices and many other things of that nature. But the most conspicuous monument which shows that those people who drove out the Sicels once lived at Argos in the temple of Juno at Falerii, built in the same fashion as the one at Argos; here, too, the manner of the sacrificial ceremonies was similar, holy women served the sacred precinct, and an unmarried girl, called the *canephorus* or "basket-bearer," performed the initial rites of the sacrifices, and there were choruses of virgins who praised the goddess in the songs of their country These people also possessed themselves of no inconsiderable part of the Campanian plains, as they are called, which afford not only very fertile pasturage but most pleasing prospects as well, having driven the Auronissi,[58] a barbarous nation, out of part of them. There they built various other cities and also Larisa, which they named after their mother-city in the

57 The *fetiales*; see ii, 72.
58 The name occurs nowhere else and is very probably a corruption of Aurunci.

Peloponnesus. Some of these cities were standing even to my day, having often changed their inhabitants. But Larisa has been long deserted and shows to the people of to-day no other sign of its ever having been inhabited but its name,[59] and even this is not generally known. It was not far from the place called Forum Popilii.[60] They also occupied a great many other places, both on the coast and in the interior, which they had taken from the Sicels.

22 The Sicels, being warred upon by both the Pelasgians and the Aborigines, found themselves incapable of making resistance any longer, and so, taking with them their wives and children and such of their possessions as were any other gold or silver, they abandoned all their country to these foes. Then, turning their course southward through the mountains, they proceeded through all the lower part of Italy, and being driven away from every place, they at last prepared rafts at the Strait and, watching for a downward current, passed over from Italy to the adjacent island. It was then occupied by the Sicanians, an Iberian nation, who, fleeing from the Ligurians, had but lately settled there and had caused the island, previously named Trinacria, from its triangular shape, to be called Sicania, after themselves. There were very few inhabitants in it for so large an island, and the greater part of it was as yet unoccupied. Accordingly, when the Sicels landed there they first settled in the western parts and afterwards in several others; and from these people the island began to be called Sicily. In this manner the Sicel nation left Italy, according to Hellanicus of Lesbos,[61] in the third

---

59 Larisa originally meant "citadel." Places with this name, of which there were several in Greece and Asia, seem to have been of Pelasgic origin.

60 This Forum Popilii was in the Falernian district at the northern end of the Campanian plain, a few miles south of Teanum.

61 Hellanicus (fifth century), the most prominent of the logographers, wrote histories of various Greek lands, including an *Atthis* for Attica and a *Phoronis* for Argos (*cf.* chap. 28, 3), as well as accounts of the Trojan expedition and the Persian invasion. He also compiled some chronological lists, such as *The*

generation before the Trojan war, and in the twenty-sixth year of the priesthood of Alcyonê at Argos.[62] But he says that two Italian expeditions passed over into Sicily, the first consisting of the Elymians, who had been driven out of their country by the Oenotrians, and the second, five years later, of the Ausonians, who fled from the Iapygians. As king of the latter group he names Sicelus, from whom both the people and the island got their name. But according to Philistus of Syracuse[63] the date of the crossing was the eightieth year before the Trojan war[64] and the people who passed over from Italy were neither Ausonians nor Elymians, but Ligurians, whose leader was Sicelus; this Sicelus, he says, was the son of Italus and in his reign the people were called Sicels, and he adds that these Ligurians had been driven out of their country by the Umbrians and Pelasgians. Antiochus of Syracuse[65] does not give the date of the crossing, but says the people who migrated were the Sicels, who had been forced to leave by the Oenotrians and Opicans, and that they chose Straton[66] as leader of the colony. But Thucydides writes[67] that the people who left Italy were the Sicels and those who drove them out the Opicans, and that the date was many years after the Trojan war. Such, then, are the reports given

---

Priestesses of Hera at Argos (*cf.* chap. 72, 2), with the apparent purpose of devising a scientific chronology. The present quotation appears as frg. 53 in Müller, *F.H.G.* i. p. 52.

62 Probably in the second quarter of the thirteenth century B.C.; but it is the certain that Hellanicus is here using the generation as a definite measure of time (usually reckoned as one-third of a century). Unfortunately the date of Alcyone's priesthood is not known.

63 Philistus (first half of fourth century) stood high in the counsels of the elder Dionysius, for a time, and particularly of the younger Dionysius. He was famous for his history of Sicily, which closely imitated the style of Thucydides. Müller, F.H.G. i. p. 185, frg. 2.

64 *ca.* 1263 B.C.

65 See p. 39, n. 2. Müller, *F. H. G.* i. p.181, frg. 1.

66 The name rests on conjecture. See critical note.

67 vi. 2.

by credible authorities concerning the Sicels who changed their abode from Italy to Sicily.

23 The Pelasgians, after conquering a large and fertile region, taking over many towns and building others, made great and rapid progress, becoming populous, rich and in every way prosperous. Nevertheless, they did not long enjoy their prosperity, but at the moment when they seemed to all the world to be in the most flourishing condition they were visited by divine wrath, and some of them were destroyed by calamities inflicted by the hand of Heaven, others by their barbarian neighbours; but the greatest part of them were again dispersed through Greece and the country of the barbarians (concerning whom, if I attempted to give a particular account, it would make a very long story), though some few of them remained in Italy through the care of the Aborigines. The first cause of the desolation of their cities seemed to be a drought which laid waste the land, when neither any fruit remained on the trees till it was ripe, but dropped while still green, nor did such of the seed corn as sent up shoots and flowered stand for the usual period till the ear was ripe, nor did sufficient grass grow for the cattle; and of the waters some were no longer fit to drink, others shrank during the summer, and others were totally dried up. And like misfortunes attended the offspring both of cattle and of women.[68] For they were either abortive or died at birth, some by their death destroying also those that bore them; and if any got safely past the danger of the delivery, they were either maimed or defective or, being injured by some other accident, were not fit to be reared. The rest of the people, also, particularly those in the prime of life, were afflicted with many unusual diseases and uncommon deaths. But when they asked the oracle what god or divinity they had offended to be thus

---

68 Similar calamities are mentioned, much more briefly, in Sophocles, *Oed. Rex* 25-27.

afflicted and by what means they might hope for relief, the god replied that, although they had obtained what they desired, they had neglected to pay what they had promised, and that the things of greatest value were still due from them. For the Pelasgians in a time of general scarcity in the land had vowed to offer[69] to Jupiter, Apollo and the Cabeiri tithes of all their future increase; but when their prayer had been answered, they set apart and offered to the gods the promised portion of all their fruits and cattle only, as if their vow had related to them alone. This is the account related by Myrsilus of Lesbos,[70] who uses almost the same words as I do now, except that he does not call the people Pelasgians, but Tyrrhenians, of which I shall give the reason a little later.[71]

24 When they heard the oracle which was brought to them, they were at a loss to guess the meaning of the message. While they were in this perplexity, one of the elders, conjecturing the sense of the saying, told them they had quite missed its meaning if they thought the gods complained of them without reason. Of material things they had indeed rendered to the gods all the first-fruits in the right and proper manner, but of human offspring, a thing of all others the most precious in the sight of the gods, the promised portion still remained due; if, however, the gods received their just share of this also, the oracle would be satisfied. There were, indeed, some who thought that he spoke aright, but others felt that there was treachery behind his words. And when some one proposed to ask the god whether it was acceptable to him to receive tithes of human beings, they sent their messengers a second time, and the god ordered them

---

69 The verbs καταθύσειν (here) and ἀπέθυσαν (just below) are rendered by the ambiguous word "offer"; for, though both are compounds of θύω ("sacrifice"), they sometimes mean merely "dedicate" or "devote."
70 Myrsilus (first half of third century) composed a history of Lesbos. This quotation is frg. 2 in Müller, *F. H. G.* iv. pp. 456 f.
71 In chaps. 25 and 29.

so to do.[72] Thereupon strife arose among them concerning the manner of choosing the tithes, and those who had the government of the cities first quarrelled among themselves and afterwards the rest of the people held their magistrates in suspicion. And there began to be disorderly emigrations, such as might well be expected from a people driven forth by a frenzy and madness inflicted by the hand of Heaven. Many households disappeared entirely when part of their members left; for the relations of those who departed were unwilling to be separated from their dearest friends and remain among their worst enemies. These, therefore, were the first to migrate from Italy and wander about Greece and many parts of the barbarian world; but after them others had the same experience, and this continued every year. For the rulers in these cities ceased not to select the first-fruits of the youth as soon as they arrived at manhood, both because they desired to render what was due to the gods and also because they feared uprisings on the part of lurking enemies. Many, also, under specious pretences were being driven away by their enemies through hatred; so that there were many

---

72 In a similar story related by Strabo v. 4, 12) the Sabines had vowed to dedicate all their increase of the year, and learning, as the result of a famine that later befell them, that they should have included their children, they dedicated these to Mars, and when the children had grown up, sent them out as colonists. Dionysius has already narrated (in chap. 16) a like procedure on the part of the Aborigines. This form of vow, when it involved the increase of a particular year, was called a *ver sacrum*, as we learn from Paulus Diaconus in his abridgement of Festus, p. 379. He states that it was a custom of the Italian peoples in times of dire peril to vow to sacrifice (*immolaturos*) all the living things that should be born to them during the following spring; but that, since it seemed to them cruel to slay innocent boys and girls, they reared these and then drove them forth, with their heads veiled, beyond the boundaries. It is not altogether clear in the case of the Pelasgians what the fate of the human tithes was, whether mere expulsion or actual sacrifice. In favour of the former view may be urged the fact of their respite until they had grown up; but the violent disturbances that accompanied the selection of the tithes would seem to point to a more cruel fate.

emigrations and the Pelasgian nation was scattered over most of the earth.

25 Not only were the Pelasgians superior to many in warfare, as the result of their training in the midst of dangers while they lived among warlike nations, but they also rose to the highest proficiency in seamanship, by reason of their living with the Tyrrhenians; and Necessity, which is quite sufficient to give daring to those in want of a livelihood, was their leader and director in every dangerous enterprise, so that wherever they went they conquered without difficulty. And the same people were called by the rest of the world both Tyrrhenians and Pelasgians, the former name being from the country out of which they had been driven and the latter in memory of their ancient origin. I mention this so that no one, when he hears poets or historians call the Pelasgians Tyrrhenians also, may wonder how the same people got both these names. Thus, with regard to them, Thucydides has a clear account[73] of the Thracian Actê and of the cities situated in it, which are inhabited by men who speak two languages. Concerning the Pelasgian nation these are his words: "There is also a Chalcidian element among them, but the largest element is Pelasgian, belonging to the Tyrrhenians who once inhabited Lemnos and Athens." And Sophocles makes the chorus in his drama *Inachus* speak the following anapaestic verses:

> "O fair-flowing Inachus, of ocean begot,
> That sire of all waters, thou rulest with might
> O'er the Argive fields and Hera's hills
> And Tyrrhene Pelasgians also."[74]

For the name of Tyrrhenia was then known throughout Greece, and all the western part of Italy was called by that name, the several nations of which it was composed having lost their distinctive

---

73 iv. 109.
74 Nauck, *T. G. F*², p. 189, frg. 248.

appellations. The same thing happened to many parts of Greece also, and particularly to that part of it which is now called the Peloponnesus; for it was after one of the nations that inhabited it, namely the Achaean, that the whole peninsula also, in which are comprised the Arcadian, the Ionian and many other nations, was called Achaia.

26 The time when the calamities of the Pelasgians began was about the second generation before the Trojan war; and they continued to occur even after that war, till the nation was reduced to very inconsiderable numbers. For, with the exception of Croton, the important city in Umbria,[75] and any others that they had founded in the land of the Aborigines, all the rest of the Pelasgian towns were destroyed. But Croton long preserved its ancient form, having only recently changed both its name and inhabitants; it is now a Roman colony, called Corthonia.[76] After the Pelasgians left the country their cities were seized by the various peoples which happened to live nearest them in each case, but chiefly by the Tyrrhenians, who made themselves masters of the greatest part and the best of them. As regards these Tyrrhenians, some declare them to be natives of Italy, but others call them foreigners. Those who make them a native race say that their name was given them from the forts, which they were the first of the inhabitants of this country to build; for covered buildings enclosed by walls are called by the Tyrrhenian as well as by the Greeks *tyrseis* or "towers."[77] So they will have it that they received their name from this circumstance in like manner as did

---

75 See chap. 20, 4.

76 *i.e.* Cortona. Compare the name Corythus used by Virgil (*Aen.* iii. 170).

77 The form **Tyrrhênoi** is the Attic development of **Tyrsênoi**, the form used by most of the Greeks.

the Mossynoeci[78] in Asia; for these also live in high wooden palisades resembling towers, which they call *mossynes*.

27 But those who relate a legendary tale about their having come from a foreign land say that Tyrrhenus, who was the leader of the colony, gave his name to the nation, and that he was a Lydian by birth, from the district formerly called Maeonia, and migrated in ancient times. They add that he was the fifth in descent from Zeus; for they say that the son of Zeus and Gê was Manes, the first king of that country, and his son by Callirrhoê, the daughter of Oceanus, was Cotys, who by Haliê, the daughter of earth-born Tyllus, had two sons, Asies and Atys, from the latter of whom by Callithea, the daughter of Choraeus, came Lydus and Tyrrhenus. Lydus, they continue, remaining there, inherited his father's kingdom, and from him the country was called Lydia; but Tyrrhenus, who was the leader of the colony, conquered a large portion of Italy and gave his name to those who had taken part in the expedition. Herodotus, however, says[79] that Tyrrhenus and his brother were the sons of Atys, the son of Manes, and that the migration of the Maeonians to Italy was not voluntary. For they say that in the reign of Atys there was a dearth in the country of the Maeonians and that the inhabitants, inspired by love of their native land, for a time contrived a great many methods to resist this calamity, one day permitting themselves but a moderate allowance of food and the next day fasting. But, as the mischief continued, they divided the people into two groups and cast lots to determine which should go out of the country and which should stay in it; of the sons of Atys

---

78 This people lived on the shore of the Euxine, a short distance west of Trapezus. Xenophon mentions them in the *Anabasis* (v. 4).

79 i. 94. But the quotation is inaccurate in two important details: Herodotus mentions only one son of Atys, Tyrrhenus, and says that Atys joined himself owing to the group destined to remain at home, but assigned his son to the other.

one was assigned to the one group the other to the other. And when the lot fell to that part of the people which was with Lydus to remain in the country, the other group departed after receiving their share of the common possessions; and landing in the western parts of Italy where the Umbrians dwelt, they remained there and built the cities that still existed even in his time.

28 I am aware that many other authors also have given this account of the Tyrrhenian race, some in the same terms, and others changing the character of the colony and the date. For some have said that Tyrrhenus was the son of Heracles by Omphalê, the Lydian, and that he, coming into Italy, dispossessed the Pelasgians of their cities, though not of all, but of those only that lay beyond the Tiber toward the north. Others declare that Tyrrhenus was the son of Telephus and that after the taking of Troy he came into Italy. But Xanthus of Lydia,[80] who was as well acquainted with ancient history as any man and who may be regarded as an authority second to none on the history of his own country, neither names Tyrrhenus in any part of his history as a ruler of the Lydians nor knows anything of the landing of a colony of Maeonians in Italy; nor does he make the least mention of Tyrrhenia as a Lydian colony, though he takes notice of several things of less importance. He says that Lydus and Torebus were the sons of Atys; that they, having divided the kingdom they had inherited from their father, both remained in Asia, and from them the nations over which they reigned received their names. His words are these: "From Lydus are sprung the Lydians, and from Torebus the Torebians. There is little difference in their language and even now each nation scoffs at many words used by the other,[81] even as do the Ionians and Dorians." Hellanicus of Lesbos says that the Tyrrhenians, who were

---

80 Xanthus, an older contemporary of Herodotus, was the first barbarian to write the history of his country in Greek. The passage here cited is garden as frg. 1 in Müller, *F. H. G.* i. p. 36.

previously called Pelasgians, received their present name after they
had settled in Italy. These are his words in the *Phoronis*:[82] "Phrastor
was the son of Pelasgus, their king, and Menippê, the daughter of
Peneus; his son was Amyntor, Amyntor's son was Teutamides, and
the latter's son was Nanas. In his reign the Pelasgians were driven
out of their country by the Greeks, and after leaving their ships on
the river Spines[83] in the Ionian Gulf, they took Croton, an inland
city; and proceeding from there, they colonized the country now
called Tyrrhenia." But the account Myrsilus gives is the reverse of
that given by Hellanicus. The Tyrrhenians, he says,[84] after they had
left their own country, were in the course of their wanderings called
Pelargoi or "Storks," from their resemblance to the birds of that
name, since they swarmed in flocks both into Greece and into the
barbarian lands; and they built the wall round the citadel of Athens
which is called the Pelargic wall.[85]

29 But in my opinion all who take the Tyrrhenians and the
Pelasgians to be one and the same nation are mistaken. It is no
wonder they were sometimes called by one another's names, since
the same thing has happened to certain other nations also, both
Greeks and barbarians, — for example, to the Trojans and
Phrygians, who lived near each other (indeed, many have thought

---

81 In other words, they simply spoke different dialects of a common language
and each nation jested at the "provincialisms" of the other. This explanation
obviates the numerous emendations that have been offered for the rare word
σιλλοῦσιν.

82 Müller, *F. H. G.* i. p. 45, frg. 1.

83 The Spinetic month of the Po. See chap. 18, 3.

84 Müller, *F. H. G.* iv. p. 457 frg. 3.

85 **Pelargikon** was the earlier form of the word, perhaps meaning "Stork's
Nest"; but its close resemblance to **Pelasgikon** gave rise in time to the belief
that the latter was the true form. The tradition that Pelasgians once dwelt in
Athens and built this wall on the acropolis does not appear to be much older
than the time of Herodotus. The next step was to show that even the form
Pelargikon had reference to the Pelasgians.

that those two nations were but one, differing in name only, not in fact). And the nations in Italy have been confused under a common name quite as often as any nations anywhere. For there was a time when the Latins, the Umbrians, the Ausonians and many others were all called Tyrrhenians by the Greeks, the remoteness of the countries inhabited by these nations making their exact distinctions obscure to those who lived at a distance. And many of the historians have taken Rome itself for a Tyrrhenian city. I am persuaded, therefore, that these nations changed their name along with their place of abode, but can not believe that they both had a common origin, for this reason, among many others, that their languages are different and preserve not the least resemblance to one another. "For neither the Crotoniats," says Herodotus,[86] "nor the Placians agree in language with any of their present neighbours, although they agree with each other; and it is clear that they preserve the fashion of speech which they brought with them into those regions." However, one may well marvel that, although the Crotoniats had a speech similar to that of the Placians, who lived near the Hellespont,[87] since both were originally Pelasgians, it was not at all similar to that of the Tyrrhenians, their nearest neighbours. For if kinship is to be regarded as the reason why two nations speak the same language, the contrary must, of course, be the reason for their speaking a different one, since surely it is not possible to believe that both these conditions arise from the same cause. For, although it might reasonably happen, on the one hand, that men of the same nation who have settled at a distance from one another would, as the result

---

86 Since Niebuhr first championed (*Röm. Gesch.* i. note 89, p. 39) the form of the name given by Dionysius as against Crestoniats (and Creston) found in Herodotus, the belief has steadily gained ground that the MSS. of Herodotus are in error. The latest editor of Herodotus, Legrand (1932), restores Κροτωνιῆται (and Κρότωνα) in the text.

87 Placia lay to the east of Cyzicus, at the foot of Mt. Olympus. It disappeared at an early date.

of associating with their neighbours, no longer preserve the same fashion of speech, yet it is not at all reasonable that men sprung from the same race and living in the same country should not in the least agree with one another in their language.

30 For this reason, therefore, I am persuaded that the Pelasgians are a different people from the Tyrrhenians. And I do not believe, either, that the Tyrrhenians were a colony of the Lydians; for they do not use the same language as the latter, nor can it be alleged that, though they no longer speak a similar tongue, they still retain some other indications of their mother country. For they neither worship the same gods as the Lydians nor make use of similar laws or institutions, but in these very respects they differ more from the Lydians than from the Pelasgians. Indeed, those probably come nearest to the truth who declare that the nation migrated from nowhere else, but was native to the country, since it is found to be a very ancient nation and to agree with no other either in its language or in its manner of living. And there is no reason why the Greeks should not have called them by this name, both from their living in towers and from the name of one of their rulers. The Romans, however, give them other names: from the country they once inhabited, named Etruria, they call them Etruscans, and from their knowledge of the ceremonies relating to divine worship, in which they excel others, they now call them, rather inaccurately, Tusci,[88] but formerly, with the same accuracy as the Greeks, they called them Thyoscoï.[89] Their own name for themselves, however, is the

---

88 The prevailing view to-day is that *Tusci* is for *Tursci*, *turs* being the same element that is seen in Τυρσηνός. *Etrusci* may be simply a lengthened form of *Tursci*, with *u* and *r* interchanged.

89 This statement is not borne out by information we have from any other source. It is merely an attempt to find a Greek etymology for *Tusci*. Θυοσκόοι were sacrificing priests.

same as that of one of their leaders, Rasenna. In another book[90] I shall show what cities the Tyrrhenians founded, what forms of government they established, how great power they acquired, what memorable achievements they performed, and what fortunes attended them. As for the Pelasgian nation, however, those who were not destroyed or dispersed among the various colonies (for a small number remained out of a great many) were left behind as fellow citizens of the Aborigines in these parts, where in the course of time their posterity, together with others, built the city of Rome. Such are the legends told about the Pelasgian race.

31 Soon after, another Greek expedition landed in this part of Italy, having migrated from Pallantium, a town of Arcadia, about the sixtieth year before the Trojan war,[91] as the Romans themselves say This colony had for its leader Evander, who is said to have been the son of Hermes and a local nymph of the Arcadians. The Greeks call her Themis and say that she was inspired, but the writers of the early history of Rome call her, in the native language, Carmenta. The nymph's name would be in Greek *Thespiōdos* or "prophetic singer"; for the Romans call songs *carmina*, and they agree that this woman, possessed by divine inspiration, foretold to the people in song the things that would come to pass. This expedition was not sent out by the common consent of the nation, but, a sedition having arisen among the people, the faction which was defeated left the country of their own accord. It chanced that the kingdom of the Aborigines had been inherited at that time by Faunus, a descendant of Mars, it is said, a man of prudence as well as energy, whom the Romans in their sacrifices and songs honour as one of the gods of their country. This man received the Arcadians, who were but few in

---

90 Nothing of the sort is found in the extant portions of the *Antiquities*. It is hardly probable that Dionysius intended to devote a separate work to the Etruscans.

91 *ca.* 1243 B.C.

number, with great friendship and gave them as much of his own land as they desired. And the Arcadians, as Themis by inspiration kept advising them, chose a hill, not far from the Tiber, which is now near the middle of the city of Rome, and by this hill built a small village sufficient for the complement of the two ships in which they had come from Greece. Yet this village was ordained by fate to excel in the course of time all other cities, whether Greek or barbarian, not only in its size, but also in the majesty of its empire and in every other form of prosperity, and to be celebrated above them all as long as mortality shall endure. They named the town Pallantium after their mother-city in Arcadia; now, however, the Romans call it Palatium, time having obscured the correct form, and this name has given occasion of the many to suggest absurd etymologies.

32 But some writers, among them Polybius of Megalopolis, related that the town was named after Pallas, a lad who died there; they say that he was the son of Hercules and Lavinia, the daughter of Evander, and that his maternal grandfather raised a tomb to him on the hill and called the place Pallantium, after the lad. But I have never seen any tomb of Pallas at Rome nor have I heard of any drink-offerings being made in his honour nor been able to discover anything else of that nature, although this family has not been left unremembered or without those honours with which divine beings are worshipped by men. For I have learned that public sacrifices are performed yearly by the Romans to Evander and to Carmenta in the same manner as to the other heroes and minor deities; and I have seen two altars that were erected, one to Carmenta under the Capitoline hill near the Porta Carmentalis, and the other to Evander by another hill, called the Aventine, not far from the Porta Trigemina; but I know of nothing of this kind that is done in honour of Pallas. As for the Arcadians, when they had joined in a single settlement at the foot of the hill, they proceeded to adorn their town with all the buildings to which they had been accustomed at home and to erect temples. And first they built a temple to the Lycaean Pan by the direction of Themis (for to the Arcadians Pan is the most ancient and the most honoured of all the gods), when they had found a suitable site for the purpose. This place the Romans call the Lupercal, but we should call it *Lykaion* or "Lycaeum." Now, it is true, since the district about the sacred precinct has been united with the city, it has become difficult to make out by conjecture the ancient nature of the place. Nevertheless, at first, we are told, there was a large cave under the hill overarched by a dense wood; deep springs issued from beneath the rocks, and the glen adjoining the cliffs was shaded by thick and lofty trees.[92] In this place they raised an altar to the god and performed their traditional sacrifice, which the Romans have continued to offer up to this day in the month of February, after the winter solstice,[93] without altering anything in the

---

92 The Lupercal was situated at the foot of the Palatine, probably at the southwest corner; it is further described in chap. 79, 8, and the Lupercalia in 80, 1. For a discussion of the various theories respecting the origin of the Lupercalia the reader is referred to Sir James Frazer's note on Ovid, *Fasti* ii. 267 (vol. ii pp. 327 ff. = pp. 389 ff. in his *L.C.L.* edition). When once the adjective Λυκαῖος (really "of Mt. Lycaeus," in Arcadia) was taken as the equivalent of *Lupercalis* and Lycaean Pan identified with the god worshipped at the Lupercalia, Λύκαιον and Λύκαια would naturally be equated with Lupercal and Lupercalia, in spite of the fact that these words as used in Greece meant the shrine and games of Zeus Lycaeus.

93 With the present passage should be compared three others in the *Antiquities* where Dionysius, for the benefit of his Greek public, indicates the season of the year in which a Roman date fell. Just below, in chap. 38, 3, he speaks of the Ides of May as being a little after the vernal equinox; in chap. 88.3, he places the Parilia (April 21) in the beginning of spring; and in ix. 25, 1, he says the new consuls assumed office near the summer solstice in the month of Sextilis (probably on the Calends of August). At first sight it might be thought that he was following an early Roman calendar that was a month or a little more in advance of the seasons. But the only calendar with which he can have had any personal acquaintance at Rome was the calendar as reformed

rites then performed. The manner of this sacrifice will be related later. Upon the summit of the hill they set apart the precinct of Victory and instituted sacrifices to her also, lasting throughout the year, which the Romans performed even in my time.

33 The Arcadians have a legend that this goddess was the daughter of Pallas, the son of Lycaon, and that she received those honours from mankind which she now enjoys at the desire of Athena, with whom she had been reared. For they say that Athena, as soon as she was born, was handed over to Pallas by Zeus and that she was reared by him till she grew up. They built also a temple to Ceres, to whom by the ministry of women they offered sacrifices without wine, according to the custom of the Greeks, none of which rites our time has changed. Moreover, they assigned a precinct to the Equestrian Neptune[94] and instituted the festival called by the Arcadians Hippocrateia and by the Romans Consualia,[95] during which it is customary among the latter for the horses and mules to rest from work and to have their heads crowned with flowers. They also consecrated many other precincts, altars and images of the gods and instituted purifications and sacrifices according to the customs of their own country, which continued to be performed down to my day in the same manner. Yet I should not be surprised if some of the ceremonies by reason of their great antiquity have been forgotten by their posterity and neglected; however, those that

---

by Julius Caesar, in effect since the year 46; and in three of the four passages he is describing a festival as it was still celebrated in his own day We are almost forced, then, to one of two conclusions, either that he was content to define the season very roughly, or else that he was using the term "solstice" loosely for the middle of winter or summer and "equinox" for a period midway between — a usage that it would be hard to parallel — and even delaying "spring" correspondingly Yet when it came to a Greek date as far back as the fall of Troy he could write with the greatest precision (chap. 63, 1).

94 Poseidon Hippios of the Greeks.
95 See note on ii. 31, 2.

are still practised are sufficient proofs that they are derived from the customs formerly in use among the Arcadians, of which I shall speak more at length elsewhere.[96] The Arcadians are said also to have been the first to introduce into Italy the use of Greek letters, which had lately appeared among them, and also music performed on such instruments as lyres, trigons[97] and flutes; for their predecessors had used no musical invention except shepherd's pipes. They are said also to have established laws, to have transformed men's mode of life from the prevailing bestiality to a state of civilization, and likewise to have introduced arts and professions and many other things conducive to the public good, and for these reasons to have been treated with great consideration by those who had received them. This was the next Greek nation after the Pelasgians to come into Italy and to take up a common residence with the Aborigines, establishing itself in the best part of Rome.

34 A few years after the Arcadians another Greek expedition came into Italy under the command of Hercules, who had just returned from the conquest of Spain and of all the region that extends to the setting of the sun. It was some of his followers who, begging Hercules to dismiss them from the expedition, remained in this region and built a town on a suitable hill, which they found at a distance of about three stades from Pallantium. This is now called the Capitoline hill, but by the men of that time the Saturnian hill, or, in Greek, the hill of Cronus. The greater part of those who stayed behind were Peloponnesians — people of Pheneus and Epeans of Elis, who no longer had any desire to return home, since their country had been laid waste in the war against Hercules.

---

96 Dionysius perhaps is thinking particularly of the passage in Book vii (72, 14-
    18), where he points out the close agreement even in details between a
    Roman and a Greek sacrifice. See also i. 80, 1 (the Lupercalia) and i. 34, 4;
    38, 2-3; 40, 3-5.
97 The trigon was a triangular harp.

There was also a small Trojan element mingled with these, consisting of prisoners taken from Ilium in the reign of Laomedon, at the time when Hercules conquered the city. And I am of the opinion that all the rest of the army, also, who were either wearied by their labours or irked by their wanderings, obtained their dismissal from the expedition and remained there. As for the name of the hill, some think it was an ancient name, as I have said, and that consequently the Epeans were especially pleased with the hill through memory of the hill of Cronus in Elis. This is in the territory of Pisa, near the river Alpheus, and the Eleans, regarding it as sacred to Cronus, assemble together at stated times to honour it with sacrifices and other marks of reverence. But Euxenus,[98] an ancient poet, and some others of the Italian mythographers think that the name was given to the place by the men from Pisa themselves, from its likeness to their hill of Cronus, that the Epeans together with Hercules erected the altar to Saturn which remains to this day at the foot of the hill near the ascent that leads from the Forum to the Capitol, and that it was they who instituted the sacrifice which the Romans still performed even in my time, observing the Greek ritual. But from the best conjectures I have been able to make, I find that even before the arrival of Hercules in Italy this place was sacred to Saturn and was called by the people of the country the Saturnian hill, and all the rest of the peninsula which is now called Italy was consecrated to this god, being called Saturnia[99] by the inhabitants, as may be found stated in some Sibylline prophecies and other oracles delivered by the gods. And in many parts of the country

---

98 No poet of this name is known, and Sylburg was perhaps right in proposing to read Ennius. Strictly speaking, Ennius was an Italian rather than a Roman, though it may be questioned whether Dionysius would have made the distinction. In the extant fragments of Ennius there is no reference to Hercules' visit, to say nothing of the Epeans.

99 Compare Virgil's use of *Saturnia tellus* (*Georg.* ii. 173, *Aen.* viii.329) and *Saturnia arva* (*Aen.* i. 569) for Italy.

there are temples dedicated to this god; certain cities bear the same name by which the whole peninsula was known at that time, and many places are called by the name of the god, particularly headlands and eminences.

35 But in the course of time the land came to be called Italy, after a ruler named Italus. This man, according to Antiochus of Syracuse,[100] was both a wise and good prince, and persuading some of his neighbours by arguments and subduing the rest by force, he made himself master of all the land which lies between the Napetine and Scylacian bays,[101] which was the first land, he says, to be called Italy, after Italus. And when he had possessed himself of this district and had many subjects, he immediately coveted the neighbouring peoples and brought many cities under his rule. He says further that Italus was an Oenotrian by birth. But Hellanicus of Lesbos[102] says that when Hercules was driving Geryon's cattle to Argos and was come to Italy, a calf escaped from the herd and in its flight wandered the whole length of the coast and then, swimming across the intervening strait of the sea, came into Sicily. Hercules, following the calf, inquired of the inhabitants wherever he came if anyone had seen it anywhere, and when the people of the island, who understood but little Greek and used their own speech when indicating the animal, called it *vitulus* (the name by which it is still known), he, in memory of the calf, called all the country it had wandered over Vitulia.[103] And it is no wonder that the name has been changed in the course of time to its present form, since many

---

100 For Antiochus see p. 39, n. 2 . This quotation is frg. 4 in Müller, *F. H. G.* i. pp. 181 f.

101 In other words, nearly all the "toe" of Italy south of the latitude of the Lacinian promontory.

102 For Hellanicus see p. 28, n. 6l. The quotation that follows is frg. 97 in Müller, *F H. G.* i. p. 58.

103 Hesychius cites the Greek word ἰταλός (originally Ϝιταλός) for "bull," and Timaeus, Varro and Festus state that Italia came from this root.

Greek names, too, have met with a similar fate. But whether, as Antiochus says, the country took this name from a ruler, which perhaps is more probable, or, as Hellanicus believes, from the bull, yet this at least is evident from both their accounts, that in Hercules' time, or a little earlier, it received this name. Before that it had been called Hesperia and Ausonia by the Greeks and Saturnia by the natives, as I have already stated.

36 There is another legend related by the inhabitants, to the effect that before the reign of Jupiter Saturn was lord in this land and that the celebrated manner of life[104] in his reign, abounding in the produce of every season, was enjoyed by none more than them. And, indeed, if anyone, setting aside the fabulous part of this account, will examine the merit of any country from which mankind received the greatest enjoyments immediately after their birth, whether they sprang from the earth, according to the ancient tradition, or came into being in some other manner, he will find none more beneficent to them than this. For, to compare one country with another of the same extent, Italy is, in my opinion, the best country, not only of Europe, but even of all the rest of the world. And yet I am not unaware that I shall not be believed by many when they reflect on Egypt, Libya, Babylonia and any other fertile countries there may be. But I, for my part, do not limit the wealth derived from the soil to one sort of produce, nor do I feel any eagerness to live where there are only rich arable lands and little or nothing else that is useful; but I account that country the best which is the most self-sufficient and generally stands least in need of imported commodities. And I am persuaded that Italy enjoys this universal fertility and diversity of advantages beyond any other land.

---

104 In Greek ὁ ἐπὶ Κρόνου βίος was proverbial for the Golden Age; compare the Latin *Saturnia regna*.

37 For Italy does not, while possessing a great deal of good arable land, lack trees, as does a grain-bearing country; nor, on the other hand, while suitable for growing all manner of trees, does it, when sown to grain, produce scanty crops, as does a timbered country; nor yet, while yielding both grain and trees in abundance, is it unsuitable for the grazing of cattle; nor can anyone say that, while it bears rich produce of crops and timber and herds, it is nevertheless disagreeable for men to live in. Nay, on the contrary, it abounds in practically everything that affords either pleasure or profit. To what grain-bearing country, indeed, watered, not with rivers, but with rains from heaven, do the plains of Campania yield, in which I have seen fields that produce even three crops in a year, summer's harvest following upon that of winter and autumn's upon that of summer? To what olive orchards are those of the Messapians, the Daunians, the Sabines and many others inferior? To what vineyards those of Tyrrhenia and the Alban and the Falernian districts, where the soil is wonderfully kind to vines and with the least labour produces the finest grapes in the greatest abundance? And besides the land that is cultivated one will find much that is left untilled as pasturage for sheep and goats, and still more extensive and more wonderful is the land suitable for grazing horses and cattle; for not only the marsh and meadow grass, which is very plentiful, but the dewy and well-watered grass of the glades, infinite in its abundance, furnish grazing for them in summer as well as in winter and keep them always in good condition. But most wonderful of all are the forests growing upon the rocky heights, in the glens and on the uncultivated hills, from which the inhabitants are abundantly supplied with fine timber suitable for the building of ships as well as for all other purposes. Nor are any of these materials hard to come at or at a distance from human need, but they are easy to handle and readily available, owing to the multitude of rivers that flow through the whole peninsula and make the transportation and exchange of everything the land produces inexpensive. Springs also of hot water have been discovered in many places, affording most pleasant baths and sovereign cures for chronic ailments. There are also mines of all sorts, plenty of wild beasts for hunting, and a great variety of sea fish, besides innumerable other things, some useful and others of a nature to excite wonder. But the finest thing of all is the climate, admirably tempered by the seasons, so that less than elsewhere is harm done by excessive cold or inordinate heat either to the growing fruits and grains or to the bodies of animals.

38 It is no wonder, therefore, that the ancients looked upon this country as sacred to Saturn, since they esteemed this god to be the giver and accomplisher of all happiness to mankind, — whether he ought to be called Cronus, as the Greeks deem fitting, or Saturn, as do the Romans, — and regarded him as embracing the whole universe, by whichever name he is called, and since they saw this country abounding in universal plenty and every charm mankind craves, and judged those places to be most agreeable both to divine and to human beings that are suited to them — for example, the mountains and woods to Pan, the meadows and verdant places to the nymphs, the shores and islands to the sea-gods, and all the other places to the god or genius to whom each is appropriate. It is said also that the ancients sacrificed human victims to Saturn, as was done at Carthage while that city stood and as is there is done to this day among the Gauls[105] and certain other western nations, and that Hercules, desiring to abolish the custom of this sacrifice, erected the altar upon the Saturnian hill and performed the initial rites of sacrifice with unblemished victims burning on a pure fire. And lest the people should feel any scruple at having neglected their traditional sacrifices, he taught them to appease the anger of the

---

105 Dionysius regularly uses the word Celts for Gauls; but it seems preferable to follow the English usage in the translation.

god by making effigies resembling the men they had been wont to bind hand and foot and throw into the stream of the Tiber, and dressing these in the same manner, to throw them into the river instead of the men, his purpose being that any superstitious dread remaining in the minds of all might be removed, since the semblance of the ancient rite would still be preserved. This the Romans continued to do every year even down to my day a little after the vernal equinox, in the month of May,[106] on what they call the Ides (the day they mean to be the middle of the month); on this day, after offering the preliminary sacrifices according to the laws, the *pontifices*, as the most important of the priests are called, and with them the virgins who guard the perpetual fire, the practors, and such of the other citizens as may lawfully be present at the rites, throw from the sacred bridge into the stream of the Tiber thirty effigies made in the likeness of men, which they call *Argei*.[107] But concerning the sacrifices and the other rites which the Roman people perform according to the manner both of the Greeks and of their own country I shall speak in another book.[108] At present, it seems requisite to give a more particular account of the arrival of Hercules in Italy and to omit nothing worthy of notice that he did there.

39 Of[109] the stories told concerning this god some are largely legend and some are nearer the truth. The legendary account of his

---

106 See p.42, n. 93.

107 According to Varro the number of these effigies, made of bulrushes, was twenty-seven, equal to the number of the chapels, also called *Argei*, situated in various parts of the city. The number thirty given by Dionysius would mean one for each *curia*; but this does not seem so probable. The sacred bridge was the *pons sublicius*. For a full discussion of the *Argei* see Sir James Frazer's note on Ovid, *Fasti* v .621 (vol. iv. pp. 74 ff., condensed in his *L.C.L.* edition, pp. 425 ff.).

108 In vii. 72, 14-18.

109 For chaps. 39-40 *cf.* Liv. i. 7, 4-14.

arrival is as follows: Hercules, being commanded by Eurystheus, among other labours, to drive Geryon's cattle from Erytheia[110] to Argos, performed the task, and having passed through many parts of Italy on his way home, came also to the neighbourhood of Pallantium in the country of the Aborigines; and there, finding much excellent grass for his cattle, he let them graze, and being overcome with weariness, lay down and gave himself over to sleep. Thereupon a robber of that region, named Cacus, chanced to come upon the cattle feeding with none to guard them and longed to possess them. But seeing Hercules lying there asleep, he imagined he could not drive them all away without being discovered and at the same time he perceived that the task was no easy one, either. So he secreted a few of them in the cave hard by, in which he lived, dragging each of them thither by the tail backwards. This might have destroyed all evidence of his theft, as the direction in which the oxen had gone would be at variance with their tracks. Hercules, then, arising from sleep soon afterwards, and having counted the cattle and found some were missing, was for some time at a loss to guess where they had gone, and supposing them to have strayed from their pasture, he sought them up and down the region; then, when he failed to find them, he came to the cave, and though he was deceived by the tracks, he felt, nevertheless, that he ought to search the place. But Cacus stood before the door, and when Hercules inquired after the cattle, denied that he had seen them, and when the other desired to search his cave, would not suffer him to do so, but called upon his neighbours for assistance, complaining of the violence offered to him by the stranger. And while Hercules was puzzled to know how he should act in the matter, he hit upon the expedient of driving the rest of the cattle to the cave. And thus, when those inside heard the lowing and perceived the smell of their

---

110 Erytheia ("Red" Island) was perhaps originally the fabulous land of the sunset glow. Later it was usually placed somewhere near the Pillars of Hercules.

companions outside, they bellowed to them in turn and thus their lowing betrayed the theft. Cacus, therefore, when his thievery was thus brought to light, put himself upon his defence and began to call out to his fellow herdsmen. But Hercules killed him by smiting him with his club and drove out the cattle; and when he saw that the place was well adapted to the harbouring of evil-doers, he demolished the cave, burying the robber under its ruins. Then, having purified himself in the river from the murder, he erected an altar near the place to Jupiter the Discoverer,[111] which is now in Rome near the Porta Trigemina, and sacrificed a calf to the god as a thank-offering for the finding of his cattle. This sacrifice the city of Rome continued to celebrate even down to my day, observing in it all the ceremonies of the Greeks just as he instituted them.

40 When the Aborigines and the Arcadians who lived at Pallantium learned of the death of Cacus and saw Hercules, they thought themselves very fortunate in being rid of the former, whom they detested for his robberies, and were struck with awe at the appearance of the latter, in whom they seemed to see something divine. The poorer among them, plucking branches of laurel which grew there in great plenty, crowned both him and themselves with it; and their kings also came to invite Hercules to be their guest. But when they heard from him his name, his lineage and his achievements, they recommended both their country and themselves to his friendship. And Evander, who had even before this heard Themis relate that it was ordained by fate that Hercules, the son of Jupiter and Alemena, changing his mortal nature, should become immortal by reason of his virtue, as soon as he learned who the stranger was, resolved to forestall all mankind by being the first to propitiate Hercules with divine honours, and he hastily erected an improvised altar and sacrificed upon it a calf that had not known

---

111 Jupiter Inventor.

the yoke, having first communicated the oracle to Hercules and asked him to perform the initial rites. And Hercules, admiring the hospitality of these men, entertained the common people with a feast, after sacrificing some of the cattle and setting apart the tithes of the rest of his booty; and to their kings he gave a large district belonging to the Ligurians and to some others of their neighbours, the rule of which they very much desired, after he had first expelled some lawless people from it. It is furthermore reported that he asked the inhabitants, since they were the first who had regarded him as a god, to perpetuate the honours they had paid him by offering up every year a calf that had not known the yoke and performing the sacrifice with Greek rites; and that he himself taught the sacrificial rites to two of the distinguished families, in order that their offerings might always be acceptable to him. Those who were then instructed in the Greek ceremony, they say, were the Potitii and the Pinarii, whose descendants continued for a long time to have the superintendence of these sacrifices, in the manner he had appointed, the Potitii presiding at the sacrifice and taking the first part of the burnt-offerings, while the Pinarii were excluded from tasting the inwards and held second rank in those ceremonies which had to be performed by both of them together. It is said that this disgrace was fixed upon them for having been late in arriving; for though they had been ordered to be present early in the morning, they did not come till the entrails had been eaten. To-day, however, the superintendence of the sacrifices no longer devolves on these families, but slaves purchased with the public money perform them. For what reasons this custom was changed and how the god manifested himself concerning the change in his ministers, I shall relate when I come to that part of the history[112] The altar on which Hercules offered up the tithes is called by the Romans the Greatest

---

112 In a portion of the work now lost.

Altar.[113] It stands near the place they call the Cattle Market[114] and no other is held in greater veneration by the inhabitants; for upon this altar oaths are taken and agreements made by those who wish to transact any business unalterably and the tithes of things are frequently offered there pursuant to vows. However, in its construction it is much inferior to its reputation. In many other places also in Italy precincts are dedicated to this god and altars erected to him, both in cities and along highways; and one could scarcely find any place in Italy in which the god is not honoured. Such, then, is the legendary account that has been handed down concerning him.

41 But the story which comes nearer to the truth and which has been adopted by many who have narrated his deeds in the form of history is as follows: Hercules, who was the greatest commander of his age, marched at the head of a large force through all the country that lies on this side of the Ocean, destroying any despotisms that were grievous and oppressive to their subjects, or commonwealths that outraged and injured the neighbouring states, or organized bands of men who lived in the manner of savages and lawlessly put strangers to death, and in their room establishing lawful monarchies, well-ordered governments and humane and sociable modes of life. Furthermore, he mingled barbarians with Greeks, and inhabitants of the inland with dwellers on the sea coast, groups which hitherto had been distrustful and unsocial in their dealings with each other; he also built cities in desert places, turned the course of rivers that overflowed the fields, cut roads through inaccessible mountains, and contrived other means by which every land and sea might lie open to the use of all mankind. And he came into Italy not alone nor yet bringing a herd of cattle (for neither does this country lies on the

---

113 *Ara maxima.*
114 *Forum boarium.*

road of those returning from Spain to Argos nor would he have been deemed worthy of so great an honour merely for passing through it), but at the head of a great army, after he had already conquered Spain, in order to subjugate and rule the people in this region; and he was obliged to tarry there a considerable time both because of the absence of his fleet, due to stormy weather that detained it, and because not all the nations of Italy willingly submitted to him. For, besides the other barbarians, the Ligurians, a numerous and warlike people seated in the passes of the Alps, endeavoured to prevent his entrance into Italy by force of arms, and in that place so great a battle was fought by the Greeks that all their missiles gave out in the course of the fighting. This war is mentioned by Aeschylus, among the ancient poets, in his *Prometheus Unbound*; for there Prometheus is represented as foretelling to Hercules in detail how everything else was to befall him on his expedition against Geryon and in particular recounting to him the difficult struggle he was to have in the war with the Ligurians. The verses are these:

> "And thou shalt come to Liguria's dauntless host,
> Where no fault shalt thou find, bold though thou art,
> With the fray: 'tis fated thy missiles all shall fail."[115]

42 After Hercules had defeated this people and gained the passes, some delivered up their cities to him of their own accord, particularly those who of Greek extraction or who had no considerable forces; but the greatest part of them were reduced by war and siege. Among those who were conquered in battle, they say, was Cacus, who is celebrated in the Roman legend, an exceedingly barbarous chieftain reigning over a savage people, who had set himself to oppose Hercules; he was established in the fastnesses and on that account was a pest to his neighbours. He, when he heard that Hercules lay encamped in the plain hard by, equipped his

---

115 Nauck, T.G.F.², p. 66, frg. 199.

followers like brigands and making a sudden raid while the army lay sleeping, he surrounded and drove off as much of their booty as he found unguarded. Afterwards, being besieged by the Greeks, he not only saw his forts taken by storm, but was himself slain amid his fastnesses. And when his forts had been demolished, those who had accompanied Hercules on the expedition (these were some Arcadians with Evander, and Faunus, king of the Aborigines) took over the districts round about, each group for itself. And it may be conjectured that those of the Greeks who remained there, that is, the Epeans and the Arcadians from Pheneus, as well as the Trojans, were left to guard the country. For among the various measures of Hercules that bespoke the true general none was more worthy of admiration than his practice of carrying along with him for a time on his expeditions the prisoners taken from the captured cities, and then, after they had cheerfully assisted him in his wars, settling them in the conquered regions and bestowing on them the riches he had gained from others. It was because of these deeds that Hercules gained the greatest name and renown in Italy, and not because of his passage through it, which was attended by nothing worthy of veneration.

43 Some say that he also left sons by two women in the region now inhabited by the Romans. One of these sons was Pallas, whom he had by the daughter of Evander, whose name, they say, was Lavinia; the other, Latinus, whose mother was a certain Hyperborean girl whom he brought with him as a hostage given to him by her father and preserved for some time untouched; but while he was on his voyage to Italy, he fell in love with her and got her with child. And when he was preparing to leave for Argos, he married her to Faunus, king of the Aborigines; for which reason Latinus is generally looked upon as the son of Faunus, not of Hercules. Pallas, they say, died before he arrived at puberty; but

Latinus, upon reaching man's estate, succeeded to the kingdom of the Aborigines, and when he was killed in the battle against the neighbouring Rutulians, without leaving any male issue, the kingdom devolved on Aeneas, the son of Anchises, his son-in-law. But these things happened at other times.

44 After Hercules had settled everything in Italy according to his desire and his naval force had arrived in safety from Spain, he sacrificed to the gods the tithes of his booty and built a small town named after himself[116] in the place where his fleet lay at anchor (it is now occupied by the Romans, and lying as it does between Neapolis and Pompeii, has at all times secure havens); and having gained fame and glory and received divine honours from all the inhabitants of Italy, he set sail for Sicily. Those who were left behind by him as a garrison to dwell in Italy and were settled around the Saturnian hill lived for some time under an independent government; but not long afterwards they adapted their manner of life, their laws and their religious ceremonies to those of the Aborigines, even as the Arcadians and, still earlier, the Pelasgians had done, and they shared in the same government with them, so that in time they came to be looked upon as of the same nation with them. But let this suffice concerning the expedition of Hercules and concerning the Peloponnesians who remained behind in Italy.

In the second generation after the departure of Hercules, and about the fifty-fifth year, according to the Romans' own account, the king of the Aborigines was Latinus, who passed for the son of Faunus, but was actually the son of Hercules; he was now in the thirty-fifth year of his reign.

45 At that time the Trojans who had fled with Aeneas from Troy after its capture landed at Laurentum, which is on the coast of the

---

116 Herculaneum.

Aborigines facing the Tyrrhenian sea, not far from the mouth of the Tiber. And having received from the Aborigines some land for their habitation and everything else they desired, they built a town on a hill not far from the sea and called it Lavinium. Soon after this they changed their ancient name and, together with the Aborigines, were called Latins, after the king of that country. And leaving Lavinium, they joined with the inhabitants of those parts in building a larger city, surrounded by a wall, which they called Alba; and setting out thence, they built many other cities, the cities of the so-called Prisci Latini, of which the greatest part were inhabited even to my day. Then, sixteen generations after the taking of Troy,[117] sending out a colony to Pallantium and Saturnia, where the Peloponnesians and the Arcadians had made their first settlement and where there were still left some remains of the ancient race, they settled these places and surrounded Pallantium with a wall, so that it then first received the form of a city. This settlement they called Rome, after Romulus, who was the leader of the colony and the seventeenth in descent from Aeneas. But also concerning the arrival of Aeneas in Italy, since some historians have been ignorant of it and others have related it in a different manner, I wish to give more than a cursory account, having compared the histories of those writers, both Greek and Roman, who are the best accredited. The stories concerning him are as follows:

46 When Troy had been taken by the Achaeans, either by the stratagem of the wooden horse, as Homer represents, or by the

---

117 See chap. 74, 2, and notes. We learn just below how the sixteen generations were reckoned: Romulus is declared to be seventeenth in descent from Aeneas. A comparison of the list of the Alban kings given in chaps. 70 f. shows that, strictly speaking, he was only sixteenth in descent, counting inclusively; but inasmuch as Ascanius' half-brother Silvius belonged in point of time to the following generation, he was evidently counted as third in the line of descent.

treachery of the Antenoridae,[118] or by some other means, the greatest part of the Trojans and of their allies then in the city were surprised and slain in their beds; for it seems that this calamity came upon them in the night, when they were not upon their guard. But Aeneas and his Trojan forces which he had brought from the cities of Dardanus and Ophrynium to the assistance of the people of Ilium, and as many others as had early notice of the calamity, while the Greeks were taking the lower town, fled together to the stronghold of Pergamus,[119] and occupied the citadel, which was fortified with its own wall; here were deposited the holy things of the Trojans inherited from their fathers and their great wealth in valuables, as was to be expected in a stronghold, and here also the flower of their army was stationed. Here they awaited and repulsed the enemy who were endeavouring to gain a foothold on the acropolis, and by making secret sallies they were able, through their familiarity with the narrow streets, to rescue the multitude which was seeking to escape at the taking of the city; and thus a larger number escaped than were taken prisoner. By hitting upon this plan Aeneas checked the immediate purpose of the enemy, which was to put all the citizens to the sword, and prevented them from taking the whole city by storm. But with respect to the future he reasoned very properly that it would be impossible to save a city the greater part of which was already in possession of the enemy, and he therefore decided to abandon the wall, bare of defenders, to the enemy and to save the inhabitants themselves as well as the holy objects inherited

---

118 The tradition that Antenor proved a traitor to his country is late, appearing first in Lycophron's *Alexandra* (verse 340), where the scholiast explains the cryptic words as meaning that Antenor raised a signal fire to the Greeks waiting at Tenedos and also released the Greek warriors from the wooden horse. Dictys relates (v. 8) that Antenor, with the aid of his wife Theano, handed over the Palladium to Odysseus and Diomed; and Dares (41) represents Antenor and Aeneas as opening the Scaean gate to the enemy.

119 Pergamus was the citadel of Troy (*Iliad* iv. 508; vi. 512).

from their fathers and all the valuables he could carry away Having thus resolved, he first sent out from the city the women and children together with the aged and all others whose condition required much time to make their escape, with orders to take the roads leading to Mount Ida, while the Achaeans, intent on capturing the citadel, were giving no thought to the pursuit of the multitude who were escaping from the city Of the army, he assigned one part to escort the inhabitants who were departing, in order that their flight might be as safe and free from hardships as the circumstances would permit; and they were ordered to take possession of the strongest parts of Mount Ida. With the rest of the troops, who were the most valiant, he remained upon the wall of the citadel and, by keeping the enemy occupied in assaulting it, he rendered less difficult the flight of those who had gone on ahead. But when Neoptolemus and his men gained a foothold on part of the acropolis and all the Achaeans rallied to their support, Aeneas abandoned the place; and opening the gates, he marched away with the rest of the fugitives in good order, carrying with him in the best chariots his father and the gods of his country, together with his wife and children and whatever else, either person or thing, was most precious.

47 In the meantime the Achaeans had taken the city by storm, and being intent on plunder, gave those who fled abundant opportunity of making their escape. Aeneas and his band overtook their people while still on the road, and being united now in one body, they seized the strongest parts of Mount Ida. Here they were joined not only by the inhabitants of Dardanus, who, upon seeing a great and unusual fire rising from Ilium, had in the night left their city undefended, — all except the men with Elymus and Aegestus, who had got ready some ships and had departed even earlier, — but also by the whole populace of Ophrynium and by those of the other Trojan cities who clung to their liberty; and in a very short time this force of the Trojans became a very large one. Accordingly, the fugitives who had escaped with Aeneas from the taking of the city and were tarrying on Mount Ida were in hopes of returning home soon, when the enemy should have sailed away; but the Achaeans, having reduced to slavery the people who were left in the city and in the places near by and having demolished the forts, were preparing to subdue those also who were in the mountains. When, however, the Trojans sent heralds to treat for peace and begged them not to reduce them to the necessity of making war, the Achaeans held an assembly and made peace with them upon the following terms: Aeneas and his people were to depart from the Troad with all the valuables they had saved in their flight within a certain fixed time, after first delivering up the forts to the Achaeans; and the Achaeans were to allow them a safe-conduct by land and sea throughout all their dominions when they departed in pursuance of these terms. Aeneas, having accepted these conditions, which he looked upon as the best possible in the circumstances, sent away Ascanius, his eldest son, with some of the allies, chiefly Phrygians, to the country of Dascylitis,[120] as it is called, in which lies the Ascanian lake, since he had been invited by the inhabitants to reign over them. But Ascanius did not tarry there for any great length of time; for when Scamandrius and the other descendants of Hector[121] who had been

---

120 This was the region about Dascylium on the Propontis, near the Mysian Olympus. The Ascanian lake actually lay some 50 miles to the east, being just west of Nicaea. Thayer's Note: Dascylium was rediscovered in the mid-20c, and some of the lapidary finds were wonderful.

121 Scamandrius was Hector's name for Astyanax (*Il.* vi. 402). According to the usual tradition, he was slain upon the capture of Troy. But the early logographers represented him as surviving and being carried off to Greece by Neoptolemus. And they usually spoke also of other sons of Hector (*cf.* Euripides, *Androm.* 224). There were various accounts of their return to the neighbourhood of Troy, or eventually to Troy itself, of which we have but a few brief fragments preserved. Two of these are found in Strabo (xiii. 1. 52f.; xiv. 5, 29).

permitted by Neoptolemus to return home from Greece, came to him, he went to Troy, in order to restore them to their ancestral kingdom. Regarding Ascanius, then, this is all that is told. As for Aeneas, after his fleet was ready, he embarked with the rest of his sons and his father, taking with him the images of the gods, and crossing the Hellespont, sailed to the nearest peninsula, which lies in front of Europe and is called Pallenê.[122] This country was occupied by a Thracian people called Crusaeans, who were allies of the Trojans and had assisted them during the war with greater zeal than any of the others.

48 This, then, is the most credible account concerning the flight of Aeneas and is the one which Hellanicus, among the ancient historians, adopts in his *Troica*.[123] There are different accounts given of the same events by some others, which I look upon as less probable than this. But let every reader judge as he thinks proper. Sophocles, the tragic poet, in his drama *Laocoön* represents Aeneas, just before the taking of the city, as removing his household to Mount Ida in obedience to the orders of his father Anchises, who recalled the injunctions of Aphroditê and from the omens that had lately happened in the case of Laocoön's family conjectured the approaching destruction of the city. His iambics, which are spoken by a messenger, are as follows:

---

122 This is certainly a strange way of describing Pallenê, the westernmost of the three Chalcidic peninsulas, but the description evidently goes back to Hellanicus (see chap. 48, 1) or even earlier; before the Peloponnesian war this region was often regarded as part of Thrace. Furthermore, Aeneia, the town the Trojans were said to have built during their stay there (chap. 49, 4), was not in Pallenê at all, but lay only a few miles south of Thessalonica, in the north-west corner of Chalcidicê. It would seem as if Pallenê were used loosely here for the whole eastern shore of the Thermaic gulf. This is not part of Thrace that Virgil had in mind as the first stopping-place of the Trojans (*Aen.* iii. 13-68); for the tomb of Polydorus was shown at Aenus, at the mouth of the Hebrus.

123 Müller, *F.H.G.* i. pp. 61 f, frg. 127. For Hellanicus see p. 28, n. 61.

"Now at the gates arrives the goddess' son,
Aeneas, his sire upon his shoulders borne
Aloft, while down that back by thunderbolt
Of Zeus once smit the linen mantle streams;[124]
Surrounding them the crowd of household slaves.
There follows a multitude beyond belief
Who long to join this Phrygian colony."[125]

But Menecrates of Xanthus[126] says that Aeneas betrayed the city to the Achaeans out of hatred for Alexander and that because of this service he was permitted by them to save his household. His account, which begins with the funeral of Achilles, runs on this wise: "The Achaeans were oppressed with grief and felt that the army had had its head lopped off. However, they celebrated his funeral feast and made war with all their might till Ilium was taken by the aid of Aeneas, who delivered it up to them. For Aeneas, being scorned by Alexander and excluded from his prerogatives, overthrew Priam; and having accomplished this, he became one of the Achaeans." Others say that he chanced to be tarrying at that time at the station where the Trojan ships lay; and others that he had been sent with a force into Phrygia by Priam upon some military expedition. Some give a more fabulous account of his

---

124 It is not certain whether καταστάζοντα is to be taken here literally ("dripping") or figuratively ("letting drop"); the construction of the sentence is without exact parallel, but there are analogies for interpreting it to mean simply "letting his robe stream, or fall, down his back." Plutarch (*De Virtute et Vitio*, 2) took the participle in a literal sense ("bedewing the robe down his back") and adds the explanation that the body of Anchises gave off a foul exudation. Whether he had any evidence before him, other than this passage of Sophocles, we can only conjecture. We are told that Anchises was struck, or grazed, by lightning because he foolishly boasted of his intimacy with Aphroditê. There were various stories concerning the permanent disability suffered by him in consequence, but the early tradition represented him as lamed.

125 Nauck, *T.G.F.*, p. 212, frg. 344.

126 Menecrates (fourth century?), a Lycian, wrote the history of his own country.

departure. But let the case stand according to each man's convictions.

49 What happened after his departure creates still greater difficulty for most historians. For some, after they have brought him as far as Thrace, say he died there; of this number are Cephalon of Gergis[127] and Hegesippus,[128] who wrote concerning Pallenê, both of them ancient and reputable men. Others make him leave Thrace and take him to Arcadia, and say that he lived in the Arcadian Orchomenus, in a place which, though situated inland, yet by reason of marshes and a river, is called Nesos or "Island";[129] and they add that the town called Capyae[130] was built by Aeneas and the Trojans and took its name from Capys the Troan. This is the account given by various other writers and by Ariaethus, the author of *Arcadica*.[131] And there are some who have the story that he came, indeed, to Arcadia and yet that his death did not occur there, but in Italy; this is stated by many others and especially by Agathyllus of Arcadia, the poet, who writes thus in an elegy:

> "Then to Arcadia came and in Nesos left his two daughters,
>> Fruit of his love for Anthemone fair and for lovely Codonê;
> Thence made haste to Hesperia's land and begat there male
>> offspring,
>> Romulus named."

---

127 A fictitious author under whose name Hegesianax of Alexandria in the Troad published some of his own works, especially his *Troica* (Athenaeus ix. 393d). Dionysius cites him again in chap. 72, 1.

128 Hegesippus of Mecyberna in Chalcidicê probably lived in the fourth or third century.

129 The city of Orchomenus, built on a hill between two plains, one of which was often a lake, and with a deep gorge on a third side, may perhaps answer this description. Or Nesos may have been in the northern plain (to-day a lake) near Caphyae.

130 More correctly Caphyae (Pausan. viii. 23, 2).

131 A history of Arcadia. We know nothing more about Ariaethus (Araethus?) and Agathyllus than is told here.

Book I

The arrival of Aeneas and the Trojans in Italy is attested by all the Romans and evidences of it are to be seen in the ceremonies observed by them both in their sacrifices and festivals, as well as in the Sibyl's utterances, in the Pythian oracles, and in many other things, which none ought to disdain as invented for the sake of embellishment. Among the Greeks, also, many distinct monuments remain to this day on the coasts where they landed and among the people with whom they tarried when detained by unfavourable weather. In mentioning these, though they are numerous, I shall be as brief as possible.[132] They first went to Thrace and landed on the

---

132 In the "digression," as Dionysius calls it (chap. 53, 4), which begins at this point, he gives a confident, straightforward account of the wanderings of Aeneas from Troy to Lavinium, without once naming a source or hinting at any variations in the legend. Kiessling (*De Dionysi Hal. Antiquitatum auctoribus Latinis*, p. 40) argued that he was here following Varro as his authority, as he does silently in various other places, and many scholars have accepted his conclusions; but unfortunately, for our knowledge of Varro's account, we have to depend on a few scattered quotations, found chiefly in Servius' commentary on the *Aeneid*. The route of Aeneas as traced by Virgil agrees so closely for the most part with that given by Dionysius as to suggest that both authors were drawing largely on the same source. The differences in their accounts can easily be explained when we bear in mind that one was a historian who prided himself on his chronological studies (chap. 74, 2) and the other a poet who gave free rein to his imagination. Thus, Dionysius was bound to reject the visit of Aeneas to Carthage if, as seems probable, he accepted Timaeus' date for the founding of that city (813; see chap. 74, 1). Chronological considerations may also account in part for Dionysius' silence concerning Cumae and Crete, though the Cumaean episode is evidently a late addition to the legend, perhaps due to Virgil himself; we shall see (chap. 55, 4) that Dionysius connected another Sibyl, living in the neighbourhood of Mt. Ida, with the destiny of the Trojan exiles, and this is doubtless the original form of the legend. One very important difference between the stories of Dionysius and Virgil is seen in the length of time assigned to the voyage from Troy to Lavinium; the historian allows just two years, the poet seven. For brief discussions of the growth of the Aeneas legend see Glover, *Vergil*, chap, iv; Nettleship, *Virgil*, pp. 47-50; Prescott, *Development of Virgil's Art*, pp. 153-168. A detailed comparison of the accounts of Dionysius and Virgil may be found in Wörner, *Die Sage von den Wanderungen des Aeneas bei Dionysios*

peninsula called Pallenê. It was inhabited, as I have said,[133] by barbarians called Crusaeans, who offered them a safe refuge. There they stayed the winter season and built a temple to Aphroditê on one of the promontories, and also a city called Aeneia, where they left all those who from fatigue were unable to continue the voyage and all who chose to remain there as in a country they were henceforth to look upon as their own. This city existed down to that period of the Macedonian rule which came into being under the successors of Alexander, but it was destroyed in the reign of Cassander, when Thessalonica was being founded; and the inhabitants of Aeneia with many others[134] removed to the newly-built city.

50 Setting sail from Pallenê, the Trojans came to Delos, of which Anius was king. Here there were many evidences of the presence of Aeneas and the Trojans as long as the island was inhabited and flourished. Then, coming to Cythera, another island, lying off the Peloponnesus, they built a temple there to Aphrodite. And while they were on their voyage from Cythera and not far from the Peloponnesus, one of Aeneas' companions, named Cinaethus, died and they buried him upon one of the promontories, which is now called Cinaethion after him. And having renewed their kinship with the Arcadians, concerning which I shall speak in a later chapter,[135] and having stayed a short time in those parts, they left some of their number there and came to Zacynthus. The Zacynthians, also, received them in a friendly manner on account of their kinship; for Dardanus, the son of Zeus and Electra, the daughter of Atlas, had,

---

und Vergilius, and also in his article on Aineias in Roscher's *Lexikon der griech. und rōm. Mythologie*, i. pp. 165-78.

133 Chap. 47, end.

134 But Aeneia is mentioned by Livy (xliv. 10, 7) as still in existence at a later time.

135 Chap. 61.

as they say, by Bateia two sons, Zacynthus and Erichthonius of whom the latter was the ancestor of Aeneas, and Zacynthus was the first settler of the island. In memory, therefore, of this kinship and by reason of the kindness of the inhabitants they stayed there some time, being also detained by unfavourable weather; and they offered to Aphroditê at the temple they had built to her a sacrifice which the entire population of Zacynthus performs to this day, and instituted games for young men, consisting among other events of a foot-race in which the one who comes first to the temple gains the prize. This is called the course of Aeneas and Aphroditê, and wooden statues of both are erected there. From there, after a voyage through the open sea, they landed at Leucas, which was still in the possession of the Acarnanians. Here again they built a temple to Aphroditê, which stands to-day on the little island between Dioryctus[136] and the city; it is called the temple of Aphroditê Aeneias.[137] And departing thence, they sailed to Actium and anchored off the promontory of the Ambracian Gulf; and from there they came to the city of Ambracia, which was then ruled by Ambrax, the son of Dexamenus, the son of Heracles. Monuments of their coming are left in both places: at Actium, the temple of Aphroditê Aeneias, and near to it that of the Great Gods, both of which existed even to my time; and in Ambracia, a temple of the same goddess and a hero-

---

136 Dioryctus (literally, a place "dug through") usually means the canal which made Leucas an island. But as Oberhummer has pointed out (*Akarnanien, . . . Leukas im Altertum*, p. 10, n. l) the only place for the little island here named would seem to have been in the canal; hence Dioryctus was evidently the name also of a place on the canal, probably on the Acarnanian side, at the end of the bridge mentioned by Strabo (x. 2, 8).

137 This cult-title of Aphroditê has been variously explained. See Farnell, *Cults of the Greek States*, ii. 638 ff., and Rossbach in Pauly-Wissowa, *Real-Enc., s.v.* Aineias, pp. l018 f. Malten, the latest to discuss the problem (*Archiv für Religionswissenschaft*, xxix (1931), pp. 33-59), regards this goddess as the mother of the race of the Aeneadae, and identifies her with the Mater Idaea, a variant form of the Great Mother; she is not to be confused with the Phoenician Astarte.

shrine of Aeneas near the little theatre. In this shrine there was a small archaic statue of wood, said to be of Aeneas, that was honoured with sacrifices by the priestesses they called *amphipoloi* or "handmaidens."

51 From Ambracia Anchises, sailing with the fleet along the coast, came to Buthrotum, a seaport of Epirus. But Aeneas with the most vigorous men of his army made a march of two days and came to Dodona, in order to consult the oracle; and there they found the Trojans who had come thither with Helenus. Then, after receiving responses concerning their colony and after dedicating to the god various Trojan offerings, including bronze mixing bowls, — some of which are still in existence and by their inscriptions, which are very ancient, show by whom they were given, — they rejoined the fleet after a march of about four days. The presence of the Trojans at Buthrotum is proved by a hill called Troy, where they encamped at that time. From Buthrotum they sailed along the coast and came to a place which was then called the Harbour of Anchises but now has a less significant name;[138] there also they built a temple to Aphroditê, and then crossed the Ionian Gulf, having for guides on the voyage Patron the Thyrian[139] and his men, who accompanied them of their own accord.[140] The greater part of these, after the army had arrived safely in Italy, returned home; but Patron with some of his friends, being prevailed on by Aeneas to join the colony stayed with the expedition. These, according to some, settled at

---

138 Onchesmus, opposite the northern point of Corcyra.

139 Θούριος generally means a man from Thurii in Italy. But Androtion is cited by Stephanus of Byzantium as using it for Θυριεύς, a man of Thyrium (or Thyreum) in Acarnania. Virgil (*Aen.* v. 298) names Patron, an Acarnanian, as one of the contestants in the funeral games in honour of Anchises.

140 Kiessling, rejecting this interpretation, supplied the word "Acarnanians" and retained the MS. reading συνεπισπώμενοι, the meaning then being: "having for guides . . . some Acarnanians who accompanied them of their own accord, bringing along with them Patron the Thyrian and his men."

Aluntium in Sicily. In memory of this service the Romans in the course of time bestowed Leucas and Anactorium, which they had taken from the Corinthians, upon the Acarnanians;[141] when the latter desired to restore the Oeniadae to their old home,[142] they gave them leave to do so, and also to enjoy the produce of the Echinades jointly with the Aetolians.[143] As for Aeneas and his companions, they did not all go ashore at the same place in Italy, but most of the ships came to anchor at the Promontory of Iapygia, which was then called the Salentine Promontory, and the others at a place named after Minerva,[144] where Aeneas himself chanced to set foot first in Italy This place is a promontory that offers a harbour in the summer, which from that time has been called the Harbour of Venus.[145] After this they sailed along the coast until they reached the strait, having Italy on the right hand, and left in these places also some traces of their arrival, among others a bronze *patera* in the temple of Juno, on which there is an ancient inscription showing the name of Aeneas as the one who dedicated it to the goddess.

52 When they were off Sicily, whether they had any design of landing there or were forced from their course by tempests, which

141 In 196 B.C. these two cities were apparently recognized by Rome as belonging to the Acarnanian League. The statement that the Romans had taken them from the Corinthians is utterly erroneous; the cities had been founded by the Corinthians, but had long been in the hands of the Acarnanians.

142 Or, "restore Oeniadae to its old status." Oeniadae was the name of both town and people. Our only other sources for this incident (Livy xxxviii. 11, 9; Polybius xxi. 32, 14) merely state that in the peace terms between Rome and the Aetolians in 189 it was provided that the city and territory of Oeniadae should belong to the Acarnanians.

143 We have no further information concerning this arrangement with regard to the Echinades. Oberhummer (*op. cit.*, p. 186, n. 4) suggests that these islands must have been divided up between the Aetolians and Acarnanians.

144 Castrum Minervae. The temple on this promontory was a well-known landmark.

145 Portus Veneris.

are common around this sea, they landed in that part of the island which is called Drepana. Here they found the Trojans who with Elymus and Aegestus had left Troy before them and who, being favoured by both fortune and the wind, and at the same time being not overburdened with baggage, had made a quick passage to Sicily and were settled near the river Crimisus in the country of the Sicanians. For the latter had bestowed the land upon them out of friendship because of their kinship to Aegestus, who had been born and reared in Sicily owing to the following circumstance. One of his ancestors, a distinguished man of Trojan birth, became at odds with Laomedon and the king seized him on some charge or other and put him to death, together with all his male children, lest he should suffer some mischief at their hands. But thinking it unseemly to put the man's daughters to death, as they were still maidens, and at the same time unsafe to permit them to live among the Trojans, he delivered them to some merchants, with orders to carry them as far away as possible. They were accompanied on the voyage by a youth of distinguished family, who was in love with one of them; and he married the girl when she arrived in Sicily. And during their stay among the Sicels they had a son, named Aegestus, who learned the manners and language of the inhabitants; but after the death of his parents, Priam being then king of Troy, he obtained leave to return home. And having assisted Priam in the war against the Achaeans, he then, when the city was about to be taken, sailed back again to Sicily, being accompanied in his flight by Elymus with the three ships which Achilles had had with him when he plunder the Trojan cities and had lost when they struck on some hidden rocks.[146] Aeneas, meeting with the men just named, showed them great

---

146 The incident here mentioned does not seem to be recorded by any other extant writer. The sacking of the Trojan cities was described in the lost *Cypria*.

kindness and built cities for them, Aegesta[147] and Elyma,[148] and even left some part of his army in these towns. It is my own surmise that he did this by deliberate choice, to the end that those who were worn out by hardships or otherwise irked by the sea might enjoy rest and a safe retreat. But some writers say that the loss of part of his fleet, which was set on fire by some of the women, who were dissatisfied with their wandering, obliged him to leave behind the people who belonged to the burned ships and for that reason could sail no longer with their companions.

53 There are many proofs of the coming of Aeneas and the Trojans to Sicily, but the most notable are the altar of Aphroditê Aeneias erected on the summit of Elymus and a temple erected to Aeneas in Aegesta; the former was built by Aeneas himself in his mother's honour, but the temple was an offering made by those of the expedition who remained behind to the memory of their deliverer. The Trojans with Elymus and Aegestus, then, remained in these parts and continued to be called Elymians; for Elymus was the first in dignity, as being of the royal family, and from him they all took their name. But Aeneas and his companions, leaving Sicily, crossed the Tyrrhenian sea and first came to anchor in Italy in the harbour of Palinurus, which is said to have got this name from one of the pilots of Aeneas who died there. After that they put in at an island which they called Leucosia, from a woman cousin of Aeneas

---

147 Called Segesta by the Romans.

148 Some of the early editors proposed to read Eryx for Elyma here and for Elymus in the next chapter, but later editors have retained the readings of the MSS. Neither Elyma nor Elymus is found anywhere else as the name of a city or mountain in Sicily, though Silius Italicus (*Pun.* xiv. 46 ff.) seems to state that both Acestes and Halymus (his names for the two Trojans) built cities named after themselves. There can be little doubt that Eryx, with the neighbouring mountain famous for its altar or temple of Aphroditê, was the place really meant; and it seems strange that Dionysius should have failed to make the identification, especially as he often gives both the earlier and later names of a place.

who died at that place. From there they came into a deep and excellent harbour of the Opicans, and when here also one of their number died, a prominent man named Misenus, they called the harbour after him. Then, putting in by chance at the island of Prochyta and at the promontory of Caieta, they named these places in the same manner, desiring that they should serve as memorials of women who died there, one of whom is said to have been a cousin of Aeneas and the other his nurse. At last they arrived at Laurentum in Italy, where, coming to the end of their wandering, they made an entrenched camp, and the place where they encamped has from that time been called Troy. It is distant from the sea about four stades.

It was necessary for me to relate these things and to make this digression, since some historians affirm that Aeneas did not even come into Italy with the Trojans, and some that it was another Aeneas, not the son of Anchises and Aphroditê, while yet others say that it was Ascanius, Aeneas' son, and others name still other persons. And there are those who claim that Aeneas, the son of Aphroditê, after he had settled his company in Italy, returned home, reigned over Troy, and dying, left his kingdom to Ascanius, his son, whose posterity possessed it for a long time. According to my conjecture these writers are deceived by mistaking the sense of Homer's verses. For in the *Iliad* he represents Poseidon as foretelling the future splendour of Aeneas and his posterity on this wise:

> "On great Aeneas shall devolve the reign,
> And sons succeeding sons the lasting line sustain."[149]

Thus, as they supposed that Homer knew these men reigned in Phrygia, they invented the return of Aeneas, as if it were not possible for them to reign over Trojans while living in Italy. But it was not impossible for Aeneas to reign over the Trojans he had

---

149 *Iliad* xx. 307 f. (Pope's translation).

taken with him, even though they were settled in another country. However, other reasons also might be given for this error.

54 But if it creates a difficulty for any that tombs of Aeneas are both said to exist, and are actually shown, in many places, whereas it is impossible for the same person to be buried in more than one place, let them consider that this difficulty arises in the case of many other men, too, particularly men who have had remarkable fortunes and led wandering lives; and let them know that, though only one place received their bodies, yet their monuments were erected among many peoples through the gratitude of those who had received some benefits from them, particularly if any of their race still survived or if any city had been built by them or if their residence among any people had been long and distinguished by great humanity — just such things, in fact, as we know are related of this hero. For he preserved Ilium from utter destruction at the time of its capture and sent away the Trojan allies safe to Bebrycia,[150] he left his son Ascanius as king in Phrygia, built a city named after himself in Pallenê, married off his daughters in Arcadia, left part of his army in Sicily, and during his residence in many other places had the reputation of conducting himself with great humanity; thus he gained the voluntary affection of those people and accordingly after he left this mortal life he was honoured with hero-shrines and monuments erected to him in many places. What reasons, pray, could anyone assign for his monuments in Italy if he never reigned in these parts or resided in them or if he was entirely unknown to the inhabitants? But this point shall be again discussed, according as my narrative shall from time to time require it to be made clear.

---

150 Bebrycia was an early name for the district about Lampsacus on the Hellespont. The incident here mentioned is otherwise unknown.

55 The failure of the Trojan fleet to sail any farther into Europe was due to the oracles which reached their fulfilment in those parts and to the divine power which revealed its will in many ways. For while their fleet lay at anchor off Laurentum and they had set up their tents near the shore, in the first place, when the men were oppressed with thirst and there was no water in the place (what I say I had from the inhabitants), springs of the sweetest water were seen rising out of the earth spontaneously, of which all the army drank and the place was flooded as the stream ran down to the sea from the springs. To-day however, the springs are no longer so full as to overflow, but there is just a little water collected in a hollow place, and the inhabitants say it is sacred to the Sun; and near it two altars are pointed out, one facing to the east, the other to the west, both of them Trojan structures, upon which, the story goes, Aeneas offered up his first sacrifice to the god as a thank-offering for the water. After that, while they were taking their repast upon the ground, many of them strewed parsley under their food to serve as a table; but others say that they thus used wheaten cakes, in order to keep their victuals clean. When all the victuals that were laid before them were consumed, first one of them ate of the parsley, or cakes, that were placed underneath, and then another. Thereupon one of Aeneas' sons, as the story goes, or some other of his messmates, happened to exclaim, "Look you, at last we have eaten even the table." As soon as they heard this, they all cried out with joy that the first part of the oracle was now fulfilled. For a certain oracle had been delivered to them, as some say, in Dodona,[151] but, according to others, in Erythrae, a place[152] on Mount Ida, where lived a Sibyl of

---

151 Varro, according to Servius' comment on the *Aeneid*, iii. 256, named Dodona as the place where Aeneas received the oracle about the "tables." Virgil (*Aen.* iii. 253-7), with a poet's licence, put the prophecy into the mouth of Celaeno, the harpy. *Cf.* p. 187, n. 1.

152 The text is uncertain here; see critical note. Most editors agree on Erythrae, though we do not hear elsewhere of any Erythrae near Ida; conjectures as to

that country, a prophetic nymph, who ordered them to sail westward till they came to a place where they should eat their tables; and that, when they found this had happened, they should follow a four-footed beast as their guide, and wherever the animal grew wearied, there they should build a city. Calling to mind, then, this prophecy, some at the command of Aeneas brought the images of the gods out of the ship to the place appointed by him, others prepared pedestals and altars for them, and the women with shouts and dancing accompanied the images. And Aeneas with his companions, when a sacrifice had been made ready, stood round the altar with the customary garlands on their heads.

56 While these were offering up their prayers, the sow which was the destined victim, being big with young and near her time, shook herself free as the priests were performing the initial rites, and fleeing from those who held her, ran back into the country. And Aeneas, understanding that this, then, was the four-footed beast the oracle intended as their guide, followed the sow with a few of his people at a small distance, fearing lest, disturbed by her pursuers, she might be frightened from the course fate had appointed for her. And the sow, after going about twenty-four stades from the sea, ran up a hill and there, spent with weariness, she lay down. But Aeneas, — for the oracles seemed now to be fulfilled, — observing that the place was not only in a poor part of the land, but also at a distance

---

the meaning of the following word vary from "near" to "oracle" and "cave." For the two words together Jacoby reads "red land." If Erythrae is the correct reading here, it would seem that Dionysius confused the Sibyl of Marpessus in the Troad with the famous Sibyl of Erythrae in Ionia. With this exception, the story here related may be assumed to be approximately the original form of the legend, which would naturally represent Aeneas as receiving the oracle from the local Sibyl before setting out on his voyage; later, when her fame became eclipsed by that of the Erythraean Sibyl, her role in the legend may have been transferred to the latter. For a recent discussion of the Sibyls see Buchholz in Roscher's *Lexikon der griech. und röm. Mythologie, s.v.* Sibylla.

from the sea, and that even the latter did not afford a safe anchorage, found himself in great perplexity whether they ought in obedience to the oracle to settle there, where they would lead a life of perpetual misery without enjoying any advantage, or ought to go farther in search of better land. While he was pondering thus and blaming the gods, on a sudden, they say, a voice came to him from the wood, — though the speaker was not to be see, — commanding him to stay there and build a city immediately, and not, by giving way to the difficulty occasioned by his present opinion, just because he would be establishing his abode in a barren country, to reject his future good fortune, that was indeed all but actually present. For it was fated that, beginning with this sorry and, at first, small habitation, he should in the course of time acquire a spacious and fertile country, and that his children and posterity should possess a vast empire which should be prolonged for many ages. For the present, therefore, this settlement should be a refuge for the Trojans, but, after as many years as the sow should bring forth young ones, another city, large and flourishing, should be built by his posterity. It is said that Aeneas, hearing this and looking upon the voice as something divine, did as the god commanded. But others say that while he was dismayed and had neglected himself in his grief, to such a degree that he neither came into the camp nor took any food, but spent that night just as he was, a great and wonderful vision of a dream appeared to him in the likeness of one of his country's gods and gave him the advice just before mentioned. Which of these accounts is the true one the gods only know.[153] The next day, it is said, the sow brought forth thirty young ones, and just that many

---

153 Virgil (*Aen*. viii. 42-48) represents the river-god Tiberinus as announcing the omen of the sow and her young to Aeneas and this omen is seen the very next day (vs. 81-85).

years later, in accordance with the oracle, another city was built by the Trojans, concerning which I shall speak in the proper place.[154]

57 Aeneas sacrificed the sow with her young to his household gods in the place where now stands the chapel, which the Lavinians looking as sacred and preserve inaccessible to all but themselves. Then, having ordered the Trojans to remove their camp to the hill, he placed the images of the gods in the best part of it and immediately addressed himself to the building of the town with the greatest zeal. And making descents into the country round about, he took from there such things as were of use to him in building and the loss of which was likely to be the most grievous to the owners, such as iron, timber and agricultural implements. But Latinus, the king of the country at that time, who was at war with a neighbouring people called the Rutulians and had fought some battles with ill success, received an account of what had passed in the most alarming form, to the effect that all his coast was being laid waste by a foreign army and that, if he did not immediately put a stop to their depredations, the war with his neighbours would seem to him a joy[155] in comparison. Latinus was struck with fear at this news, and immediately abandoning the war in which he was then engaged, he marched against the Trojans with a great army. But seeing them armed like Greeks, drawn up in good order and resolutely awaiting the conflict, he gave up the idea of hazarding an

154 Chap. 66.
155 Literally "gold." This expression seems to have become proverbial in comparisons between a lesser and a greater evil. See critical note. The critical note to the Greek text reads: χρυσὸς Cobet: ὀχυρὸς AB. Cobet, in his *Variae Lectiones*, pp. 235 f., points out several passages in Greek authors where χρυσὸς has been similarly corrupted (among them Dionysius ix. 25, 1, where only Ba reads χρυσός, the others χρηστός). The expression first appears in Euripides, *Troades* 431 ff.: δύστηνος, οὐκ οἶδ' οἷά νιν μένει παθεπῖν• ὡς χρυσὸς αὐτῷ ταμα καὶ Φρυγῶν κακὰ δόχει ποτ' εἶναι. "Wretch! — he knows not what sufferings wait for him, Such that my woes and Phrygia's yet shall seem As gold to them." (Way's translation in the L.C.L.).

immediate engagement, since he saw no probability now of defeating them at the first onset, as he had expected when he set out from home against them. And encamping on a hill, he thought he ought first to let his troops recover from their present fatigue, which from the length of the march and the eagerness of the pursuit was very great; and passing the night there, he was resolving to engage the enemy at break of day. But when he had reached this decision, a certain divinity of the place appeared to him in his sleep and bade him receive the Greeks into his land to dwell with his own subjects, adding that their coming was a great advantage to him and benefit to all the Aborigines alike. And the same night Aeneas' household gods appeared to him and admonished him to persuade Latinus to grant them of his own accord a settlement in the part of the country they desired and to treat the Greek forces rather as allies than as enemies. Thus the dream hindered both of them from beginning an engagement. And as soon as it was day and the armies were drawn up in order of battle, heralds came to each of the commanders from the other with the same request, that they should meet for a parley; and so it came to pass.

58 And first Latinus complained of the sudden war which they had made upon his subjects without any previous declaration and demanded that Aeneas tell him who he was and what he meant by plundering the country without any provocation, since he could not be ignorant that every one who is attacked in war defends himself against the aggressor; and he complained that when Aeneas might have obtained amicably and with the consent of the inhabitants whatever he could reasonably desire, he had chosen to take it by force, contrary to the universal sense of justice and with greater dishonour than credit to himself. After he had spoken thus Aeneas answered: "We are natives of Troy, not the least famous city among the Greeks; but since this has been captured and taken from us by the Achaeans after a ten-years' war, we have been wanderers, roving about for want both of a city and a country where we may henceforth live, and are come hither in obedience to the commands of the gods; and this land alone, as the oracles tell us, is left for us as the haven of our wandering. We are indeed taking from the country the things we need, with greater regard to our unfortunate situation than to propriety, — a course which until recently we by no means wished to pursue. But we will make compensation for them with many good services in return, offering you our bodies and our minds, well disciplined against dangers, to employ as you think proper in keeping your country free from the ravages of enemies and in heartily assisting you to conquer their lands. We humbly entreat you not to resent what we have done, realizing, as you must, that we did it, not out of wantonness, but constrained by necessity; and everything that is involuntary deserves forgiveness.[156] And you ought not to take any hostile resolution concerning us as we stretch forth our hands to you; but if you do so, we will first beg the gods and divinities who possess this land to forgive us even for what we do under the constraint of necessity and will then endeavour to defend ourselves against you who are the aggressors in the war; for this will not be the first nor the greatest war that we have experienced." When Latinus heard this he answered him: "Nay, but I cherish a kindly feeling towards the whole Greek race and am greatly grieved by the inevitable calamities of mankind. And I should be very solicitous for your safety if it were clear to me that you have come here in search of a habitation and that, contented with a suitable

---

156 In Thucydides iii. 40, 1, we find the expression ξύγγνωμόν δ' ἐστὶ τὸ ἀκούσιον. But Jacoby points out that the two passages are otherwise very different in their tenor, and hence concludes that Dionysius was not imitating the older historian. He believes, rather, that the source of both was a verse of some poet, probably ξύγγνωμόν ἐστ' . . . ἅπαν τἀκούσιον. The same sentiment, though not expressed in exactly the same words, is met with in Thuc. iv. 98.6, Plato, *Phaedrus* 233c, and Aristotle, *Eth. Nicom.*iii. 1, 1.

share of the land and enjoying in a spirit of friendship what shall be given you, you will not endeavour to deprive me of the sovereignty by force; and if the assurances you give me are real, I desire to give and receive pledges which will preserve our compact inviolate."

59 Aeneas having accepted this proposal, a treaty was made between the two nations and confirmed by oaths to this effect: the Aborigines were to grant to the Trojans as much land as they desired, that is, the space of about forty stades in every direction from the hill; the Trojans, on their part, were to assist the Aborigines in the war they were then engaged in and also to join them with their forces upon every other occasion when summoned; and, mutually, both nations were to aid each other to the utmost of their power, both with their arms and with their counsel. After they had concluded this treaty and had given pledges by handing over children as hostages, they marched with joint forces against the cities of the Rutulians; and having soon subdued all opposition there, they came to the town of the Trojans, which was still but half-finished, and all working with a common zeal, they fortified the town with a wall. This town Aeneas called Lavinium, after the daughter of Latinus, according to the Romans' own account; for her name, they say, was Lavinia. But according to some of the Greek mythographers he named it after the daughter of Anius, the king of the Delians, who was also called Lavinia; for as she was the first to die of illness at the time of the building of the city and was buried in the place where she died, the city was made her memorial. She is said to have embarked with the Trojans after having been given by her father to Aeneas at his desire as a prophetess and a wise woman. While Lavinium was building, the following omens are said to have appeared to the Trojans. When a fire broke out spontaneously in the forest, a wolf, they say, brought some dry wood in his mouth and threw it upon the fire, and an eagle, flying thither, fanned the flame with the motion of his wings. But working in opposition to these, a fox, after wetting his tail in the river, endeavoured to beat out the flames; and now those that were kindling it would prevail, and now the fox that was trying to put it out. But at last the two former got the upper hand, and the other went away, unable to do anything further. Aeneas, on observing this, said that the colony would become illustrious and an object of wonder and would gain the greatest renown, but that as it increased it would be envied by its neighbours and prove grievous to them; nevertheless, it would overcome its adversaries, the good fortune that it had received from Heaven being more powerful than the envy of men that would oppose it. These very clear indications are said to have been given of what was to happen to the city; of which there are monuments now standing in the forum of the Lavinians, in the form of bronze images of the animals, which have been preserved for a very long time.

60 After the Trojans' city was built all were extremely desirous of enjoying the mutual benefit of their new alliance. And their kings setting the example, united the excellence of the two races, the native and the foreign, by ties of marriage, Latinus giving his daughter Lavinia to Aeneas. Thereupon the rest also conceived the same desire as their kings; and combining in a very brief time their customs, laws and religious ceremonies, forming ties through intermarriages and becoming mingled together in the wars they jointly waged, and all calling themselves by the common name of Latins, after the king of the Aborigines, they adhered so firmly to their pact that no lapse of time has yet severed them from one another.

The nations, therefore, which came together and shared in a common life and from which the Roman people derived their origin before the city they now inhabit was built, are these: first, the

Aborigines, who drove the Sicels out of these parts and were originally Greeks from the Peloponnesus, the same who with Oenotrus removed from the country now called Arcadia, according to my opinion; then, the Pelasgians, who came from Haemonia, as it was then called, but now Thessaly; third, those who came into Italy with Evander from the city of Pallantium; after them the Epeans and Pheneats, who were part of the Peloponnesian army commanded by Hercules, with whom a Trojan element also was commingled; and, last of all, the Trojans who had escaped with Aeneas from Ilium, Dardanus and the other Trojan cities.

61 That the Trojans, too, were a nation as truly Greek as any and formerly came from the Peloponnesus has long been asserted by some authors and shall be briefly related by me also. The account concerning them is as follows. Atlas was the first king of the country now called Arcadia, and he lived near the mountain called Thaumasius.[157] He had seven daughters, who are said to be numbered now among the constellations under the name of the Pleiades; Zeus married one of these, Electra, and had by her two sons, Iasus and Dardanus.[158] Iasus remained unmarried, but Dardanus married Chrysê, the daughter of Pallas, by whom he had two sons, Idaeus and Deimas; and these, succeeding Atlas in the kingdom, reigned for some time in Arcadia. Afterwards, a great deluge occurring throughout Arcadia, the plains were overflowed and for a long time could not be tilled; and the inhabitants, living upon the mountains and eking out a sorry livelihood, decided that the land remaining would not be sufficient for the support of them all, and so divided themselves into two groups, one of which

---

157 This mountain is mentioned by Pausanias (viii. 36, 2) and by Stephanus of Byzantium. Cauconius, suggested by Jacoby, appears to be purely a conjectural name.

158 One of very many conflicting ancient tales about the Pleiades; for a comprehensive survey see Allen's Star Names, s.v. Taurus.

remained in Arcadia, after making Deimas, the son of Dardanus, their king, while the other left the Peloponnesus on board a large fleet. And sailing along the coast of Europe, they came to a gulf called Melas and chanced to land on a certain island of Thrace, as to which I am unable to say whether it was previously inhabited or not. They called the island Samothrace, a name compounded of the name of a man and the name of a place. For it belongs to Thrace and its first settler was Samon, the son of Hermes and a nymph of Cyllenê, named Rhenê. Here they remained but a short time, since the life proved to be no easy one for them, forced to contend, as they were, with both a poor soil and a boisterous sea; but leaving some few of their people in the island, the greater part of them removed once more and went to Asia under Dardanus as leader of their colony (for Iasus had died in the island, being struck with a thunderbolt for desiring to have intercourse with Demeter), and disembarking in the strait now called the Hellespont, they settled in the region which was afterwards called Phrygia. Idaeus, the son of Dardanus, with part of the company occupied the mountains which are now called after him the Idaean mountains, and there built a temple to the Mother of the Gods and instituted mysteries and ceremonies which are observed to this day throughout all Phrygia. And Dardanus built a city named after himself in the region now called the Troad; the land was given to him by Teucer, the king, after whom the country was anciently called Teucris. Many authors, and particularly Phanodemus, who wrote about the ancient lore of Attica,[159] say that Teucer had come into Asia from Attica, where he had been chief of the deme called Xypetê, and of this tale they offer many proofs. They add that, having possessed himself of a large and fertile country with but a small native population, he was glad to see Dardanus and the Greeks who came with him, both because he hoped for their assistance in his wars against the

159 His work was an *Atthis* (*cf.* p. 27, n. 1). Müller, *Frag. Hist. Graec.* i. 367, 8).

barbarians and because he desired that the land should not remain unoccupied.

62 But the subject requires that I relate also how Aeneas was descended: this, too, I shall do briefly. Dardanus, after the death of Chrysê, the daughter of Pallas, by whom he had his first sons, married Bateia, the daughter of Teucer, and by her had Erichthonius, who is said to have been the most fortunate of all men, since he inherited both the kingdom of his father and that of his maternal grandfather. Of Erichthonius and Callirrhoê, the daughter of Scamander,[160] was born Tros, from whom the nation has received its name; of Tros and Acallaris, the daughter of Eumedes, Assaracus; of Assaracus and Clytodora, the daughter of Laomedon, Capys; of Capys and a Naiad nymph, Hieromnemê, Anchises; of Anchises and Aphroditê, Aeneas. Thus I have shown that the Trojan race, too, was originally Greek.

63 Concerning the time when Lavinium was built there are various reports, but to me the most probable seems to be that which places it in the second year after the departure of the Trojans from Troy[161] For Ilium was taken at the end of the spring, seventeen days before the summer solstice, and the eighth from the end of the month Thargelion,[162] according to the calendar of the Athenians; and there still remained twenty days after the solstice to complete

---

160 The river-god of the Scamander River, one of the rivers on the plain of Troy: it thus makes perfect sense that Tros should be considered a descendant of Scamander.

161 This would be 1181 B.C. according to Dionysius, since Eratosthenes, whose chronology he follows (chap. 74, 2), placed the fall of Troy in 1183.

162 The Athenians divided their months into three periods of ten days each (nine in the last period in the shorter months), in the first two of which they counted the days forwards, as we do, while in the third they reckoned backwards from the end of the month. The eighth from the end of the month, reckoning inclusively, would be the 23rd (or 22nd). Their year seems to have begun with the new moon immediately following the summer solstice.

that year. During the thirty-seven days that followed the taking of the city I imagine the Achaeans were employed in regulating the affairs of the city, in receiving embassies from those who had withdrawn themselves, and in concluding a treaty with them. In the following year, which was the first after the taking of the city, the Trojans set sail about the autumnal equinox, crossed the Hellespont, and landing in Thrace, passed the winter season there, during which they received the fugitives who kept flocking to them and made the necessary preparations for their voyage. And leaving Thrace in the beginning of spring, they sailed as far as Sicily; when they had landed there that year came to an end, and they passed the second winter in assisting the Elymians to found their cities in Sicily But as soon as conditions were favourable for navigation they set sail from the island, and crossing the Tyrrhenian sea, arrived at last at Laurentum on the coast of the Aborigines in the middle of the summer. And having received the ground from them, they founded Lavinium, thus bringing to an end the second year from the taking of Troy With regard to these matters, then, I have thus shown my opinion.

64 But[163] when Aeneas had sufficiently adorned the city with temples and other public buildings, of which the greatest part remained even to my day, the next year, which was the third after his departure from Troy, he reigned over the Trojans only. But in the fourth year, Latinus having died, he succeeded to his kingdom also, not only in consideration of his relationship to him by marriage, Lavinia being the heiress after the death of Latinus, but also because of his being commander in the war against the neighbouring tribes. For the Rutulians had again revolted from Latinus, choosing for

---

163 *Cf.* Livy 1, 2. From this point onward parallel passages in Livy will be thus indicated by a note attached to the initial word of a chapter or series of chapters in Dionysius.

their leader one of the deserters, named Tyrrhenus,[164] who was a nephew of Amata,[165] the wife of Latinus. This man, blaming Latinus in the matter of Lavinia's marriage, because he had ignored his kinsmen and allied his family with outsiders, and being goaded on by Amata and encouraged by others, had gone over to the Rutulians with the forces he commanded. War arose out of these complaints and in a sharp battle that ensued Latinus, Tyrrhenus and many others were slain; nevertheless, Aeneas and his people gained the victory. Thereupon Aeneas succeeded to the kingdom of his father-in-law; but when he had reigned three years after the death of Latinus, in the fourth he lost his life in battle. For the Rutulians marched out in full force from their cities against him, and with them Mezentius, king of the Tyrrhenians, who thought his own country in danger; for he was troubled at seeing the Greek power already making rapid headway. A severe battle took place not far from Lavinium and many were slain on both sides, but when night came on the armies separated; and when the body of Aeneas was nowhere to be seen, some concluded that it had been translated to the gods and others that it had perished in the river beside which the battle was fought. And the Latins built a hero-shrine to him with this inscription: "To the father and god of this place,[166] who presides

---

164 It is perhaps wiser to follow the MSS. in the spelling of this name than to emend to Turnus. Granted that Τύρνος might easily have been changed to Τυρρηνός by a scribe, yet it is just as conceivable that Greek writers, seeing in Turnus nothing but a modified form of Tyrrhenus, may have preferred to use the normal form; we have already met with a Tyrrhenus as the eponymous founder of the Tyrrhenian race (chaps. 27 f.). Yet for Turnus Herdonius (iv. 45.47 f.) Dionysius evidently used the spelling Τύρνος (corrupted to Τύρδος in the MSS.).

165 In the case of this name we may emend to Amata with little hesitation, since the form Amita ("paternal aunt") is not appropriate as a proper name and is unlike any Greek name.

166 Dionysius evidently uses χθόνιος here to translate the Latin term *indiges*. Livy (1. 2, 6) does not specifically cite the inscription, but says *Iovem Indigitem appellant*.

over the waters of the river Numicius." But there are some who say the shrine was erected by Aeneas in honour of Anchises, who died in the year before this war. It is a small mound, round which have been set out in regular rows trees that are well worth seeing.

65 Aeneas having departed this life about the seventh year after the taking of Troy, Euryleon, who in the flight had been renamed Ascanius, succeeded to the rule over the Latins. At this time the Trojans were undergoing a siege; the forces of the enemy were increasing daily, and the Latins were unable to assist those who were shut up in Lavinium. Ascanius and his men, therefore, first invited the enemy to a friendly and reasonable accommodation, but when no heed was paid to them, they were forced to allow their enemies to put an end to the war upon their own terms. When, however, the king of the Tyrrhenians, among other intolerable conditions that he imposed upon them, as upon a people already become his slaves, commanded them to bring to the Tyrrhenians every year all the wine the country of the Latins produced, they looked upon this as a thing beyond all endurance, and following the advice of Ascanius, voted that the fruit of the vine should be sacred to Jupiter. Then, exhorting one another to prove their zeal and valour and praying the gods to assist them in their dangerous enterprise, they fixed upon a moonless night and sallied out of the city. And they immediately attacked that part of the enemy's rampart which lay nearest to the city and which, being designed as an advanced post to cover the rest of their forces, had been constructed in a strong position and was defended by the choicest youth of the Tyrrhenians, under the command of Lausus, the son of Mezentius; and their attack being unforeseen, they easily made themselves masters of the stronghold. While they were employed in taking this post, those of the enemy who were encamped on the plains, seeing an unusual light and hearing the cries of the men who were perishing, left the level country and were fleeing to the mountains. During this time there was great confusion and tumult, as was but natural with an army moving at night; for they expected the enemy would every moment fall upon them while they were withdrawing in disorder and with ranks broken. The Latins, after they had taken the fort by storm and learned that the rest of the army was in disorder, pressed after them, killing and pursuing. And not only did none of the enemy attempt to turn and resist, but it was not even possible for them to know in what evil plight they were, and in their confusion and helplessness some were falling over precipices and perishing, while others were becoming entangled in blind ravines and were being taken prisoner; but most of them, failing to recognize their comrades in the dark, treated them as enemies, and the greatest part of their loss was due to their slaying of one another. Mezentius with a few of his men seized a hill, but when he learned of the fate of his son and of the numbers he had lost and discovered the nature of the place in which he had shut himself up, realizing that he was lacking in everything needful, he sent heralds to Lavinium to treat for peace. And since Ascanius advised the Latins to husband their good fortune, Mezentius obtained permission to retire under a truce with the forces he had left; and from that time, laying aside all his enmity with the Latins, he was their constant friend.

66 In the thirtieth year[167] after the founding of Lavinium Ascanius, the son of Aeneas, in pursuance of the oracle given to his father, built another city and transferred both the inhabitants of Lavinium and the other Latins who were desirous of a better habitation to this newly-built city, which he called Alba. Alba means in the Greek tongue *Leukê* or "White"; but for the sake of clearness it is distinguished from another city of the same name by the

---

167 *Cf.* Livy i. 3, 3-4. According to Dionysius' reckoning (see p. 84, n. 161), Alba was founded in 1151 B.C.

addition of an epithet descriptive of its shape, and its name is now, as it were, a compound, made up of the two terms, Alba Longa, that is *Leukê Makra* or "Long White (town)." This city is now uninhabited, since in the time of Tullus Hostilius, king of the Romans, Alba seemed to be contending with her colony for the sovereignty and hence was destroyed; but Rome, though she razed her mother-city to the ground, nevertheless welcomed its citizens into her midst. But these events belong to a later time. To return to its founding, Alba was built near a mountain and a lake, occupying the space between the two, which served the city in place of walls and rendered it difficult to be taken. For the mountain is extremely strong and high and the lake is deep and large; and its waters are received by the plain when the sluices are opened, the inhabitants having it in their power to husband the supply as much as they wish. Lying below the city are plains marvellous to behold and rich in producing wines and fruits of all sorts in no degree inferior to the rest of Italy, and particularly what they call the Alban wine, which is sweet and excellent and, with the exception of the Falernian, certainly superior to all others.

67 While the city was building, a most remarkable prodigy said to have occurred. A temple with an inner sanctuary had been built for the images of the gods which Aeneas had brought with him from the Troad and set up in Lavinium, and the statues had been removed from Lavinium to this sanctuary; but during the following night, although the doors were most carefully closed and the walls of the enclosure and the roof of the temple suffered no injury, the statues changed their position and were found upon their old pedestals. And after being brought back again from Lavinium with supplications and propitiatory sacrifices they returned in like manner to the same place. Upon this the people were for someone time in doubt what they should do, being unwilling either to live apart from their ancestral gods or to return again to their deserted habitation. But at last they hit upon an expedient which promised to meet satisfactorily both these difficulties. This was to let the images remain where they were and to conduct men back from Alba to Lavinium to live there and take care of them. Those who were sent to Lavinium to have charge of their rites were six hundred in number; they removed thither with their entire households, and Aegestus was appointed their chief. As for these gods, the Romans call them Penates. Some who translate the name into the Greek language render it *Patrooi*, others *Genethlioi*, some *Ktêsioi*, others *Mychioi*, and still others *Herkeioi*.[168] Each of these seems to be giving them their name from some one of their attributes, and it is probable that they are all expressing more or less the same idea. Concerning their figure and appearance, Timaeus, the historian, makes the statement that the holy objects preserved in the sanctuary at Lavinium are iron and bronze *caducei* or "heralds' wands," and a Trojan earthenware vessel; this, he says, he himself learned from the inhabitants.[169] For my part, I believe that in the case of those things which it is not lawful for all to see I ought neither to hear about them from those who do see them nor to describe them; and I am indignant with every one else, too, who presumes to inquire into or to know more than what is permitted by law.

68 But the things which I myself know by having seen them and concerning which no scruple forbids me to write are as follows. They show you in Rome a temple[170] built not far from the Forum in

---

168 These Greek terms, all adjectives in form, mean the gods, respectively, (a) of the race, (b) of the family, (c) of house and property, (d) of the inner house, (e) of the front court.

169 Müller, *Frag. Hist. Graec.* i. 197, 20. For Timaeus see p. 7, n. 13.

170 The *aedes deum Penatium in Velia* (Livy xiv. 16, 5; *Mon. Ancyr.* iv. 7; Varro, *de Ling. Lat.* v. 54). The statues really represented the Dioscuri, but had long been identified with the Penates. Servius (on *Aen.* iii. 12), citing Varro, says that on the base of the statues was the inscription *MAGNIS DIIS*; but there

the short street that leads to the Carinae; it is a small shrine, and is darkened by the height of the adjacent buildings.[171] The place is called in the native speech Velia. In this temple there are images of the Trojan gods which it is lawful for all to see, with an inscription showing them to be the Penates. They are two seated youths holding spears, and are pieces of ancient workmanship. We have seen many other statues also of these gods in ancient temples and in all of them are represented two youths in military garb. These it is permitted to see, and it is also permitted to hear and to write about them what Callistratus,[172] the author of the history of Samothrace, relates, and also Satyrus, who collected the ancient legends, and many others, too, among whom the poet Arctinus is the earliest we know of. At any rate, the following is the account they give. Chrysê, the daughter of Pallas, when she was married to Dardanus, brought for her dowry the gifts of Athena, that is, the Palladia and the sacred symbols of the Great Gods, in whose mysteries she had been instructed. When the Arcadians, fleeing from the deluge,[173] left the Peloponnesus and established their abode in the Thracian island.[174] Dardanus built there a temple to these gods, whose particular names he kept secret from all any others, and performed the mysteries in their honour which are observed to this day by the Samothracians.

<hr>

was probably more to the inscription, including *PENATIBVS*.

171 The innocent-looking phrase "darkened by the height of the adjacent buildings" is an expansion of ὑπεροχῇ σκοτεινός, literally "in high shade"; exactly how the phrase is translated — it's as ambiguous in Greek as it is in English — has a bearing on the topography of Rome and the identification of some of its ancient monuments: see P. B. Whitehead, The Church of SS. Cosma e Damiano in Rome (AJA 31:1-18).

172 Müller, *Frag. Hist. Graec.* iv. 335 f., 10. Domitius Callistratus seems to have been a Roman freedman. Satyrus is unknown, but was probably not the same as the biographer of that name. Arctinus was regarded in later times as the author of two of the poems in Epic Cycle, the *Aethiopis* and the *Iliou Persis*; but classical writers cited the poems anonymously.

173 See chap. 61, 2.

174 Samothrace.

Then, when he was conducting the greater part of the people into Asia, he left the sacred rites and mysteries of the gods with those who remained in the island, but packed up and carried with him the Palladia and the images of the gods. And upon consulting the oracle concerning the place where he should settle, among other things that he learned he received this answer relating to the custody of the holy objects:

"In the town thou buildest worship undying found
To gods ancestral; guard them, sacrifice,
Adore with choirs. For whilst these holy things
In thy land remain, Zeus' daughter's gifts of old
Bestowed upon thy souse, secure from harm
Thy city shall abide forevermore."

69 Dardanus, accordingly, left the statues in the city which he founded and named after himself, but when Ilium was settled later, they were removed thither by his descendants; and the people of Ilium built a temple and a sanctuary for them upon the citadel and preserved them with all possible care, looking upon them as sent from Heaven and as pledges of the city's safety. And while the lower town was being captured, Aeneas, possessing himself of the citadel, took out of the sanctuary the images of the Great Gods and the Palladium which still remained (for Odysseus and Diomed, they say, when they came into Ilium by night, had stolen the other away), and carrying them with him out of the city, brought them into Italy. Arctinus, however, says that only one Palladium was given by Zeus to Dardanus and that this remained in Ilium, hidden in the sanctuary, till the city was being taken; but that from this a copy was made, differing in no respect from the original, and exposed to public view, on purpose to deceive those who might be planning to steal it, and that the Achaeans, having formed such a plan, took the copy away. I say therefore, upon the authority of the men above-mentioned, that the holy objects brought into Italy by Aeneas were the images of the Great Gods, to whom the Samothracians, of all the Greeks, pay the greatest worship, and the Palladium, famous in legend, which they say is kept by the holy virgins in the temple of Vesta, where the perpetual fire is also preserved; but concerning these matters I shall speak hereafter.[175] And there may also be other objects besides these which are kept secret from us who are not initiated. But let this suffice concerning the holy objects of the Trojans.

70 Upon[176] the death of the Ascanius in the thirty-eighth year of his reign, Silvius, his brother, succeeded to the rule. He was born of Lavinia, the daughter of Latinus, after the death of Aeneas, and they say that he was brought up on the mountains by the herdsmen. For when Ascanius took over the rule, Lavinia, becoming alarmed lest her relationship as step-mother might draw upon her some severity from him, and being then with child, entrusted herself to a certain Tyrrhenus,[177] who had charge of the royal herds of swine and whom she knew to have been on very intimate terms with Latinus. He, carrying her into the lonely woods as if she were an ordinary woman, and taking care that she was not seen by anyone who knew her, supported her in a house he built in the forest, which was known to but few. And when the child was born, he took it up and reared it, naming it, from the wood, Silvius, or, as one might say in Greek, *Hylaios*. But in the course of time, finding that the Latins made great search for the woman and that the people accused Ascanius of having put her to death, he acquainted them with the whole matter and brought the woman and her son out of the forest. From this experience Silvius got his name, as I have related, and so

---

175 ii. 66.

176 For chaps. 70-71 *cf.* Livy i. 3, 6-10.

177 The name appears as Tyrrheus or Tyrrhus in Virgil (*Aen.* vii. 485), the only other author who mentions such an individual. Tyrrh(e)us, like Turnus, is apparently a modified form of Tyrrhenus; *cf.* p. 86, n. 164.

did all his posterity. And he became king after the death of his brother, though not without a contest with one of the sons of Ascanius, — Iulus, the eldest, — who claimed the succession to his father's rule; the issue was decided by vote of the people, who were influenced chiefly by this consideration, among others, that Silvius' mother was heiress to the kingdom. Upon Iulus was conferred, instead of the sovereignty, a certain sacred authority and honour preferable to the royal dignity both for security and ease of life, and this prerogative[178] was enjoyed even to my day by his posterity, who were called Julii after him. This house became the greatest and at the same time the most illustrious of any we know of, and produced the most distinguished commanders, whose virtues were so many proofs of their nobility. But concerning them I shall say what is requisite in another place.[179]

71 Silvius, after holding the sovereignty twenty-nine years, was succeeded by Aeneas, his son, who reigned thirty-one years. After him, Latinus reigned fifty-one, then Alba, thirty-nine; after Alba, Capetus reigned twenty-six, then Capys twenty-eight, and after Capys, Capetus held the rule for thirteen years. Then Tiberinus reigned for a period of eight years. This king, it is said, was slain in a battle that was fought near a river, and being carried away by the stream, gave his name to the river, which had previously been called the Albula. Tiberinus' successor, Agrippa, reigned forty-one years. After Agrippa, Allodius, a tyrannical creature and odious to the gods, reigned nineteen years. Contemptuous of the divine powers, he had contrived imitations of lightning and sounds resembling thunder-claps, with which he proposed to terrify people as if he were a god. But rain and lightning descended upon his house, and the lake beside which it stood rose to an unusual height, so that he

178 The reference is probably to the office of *pontifex maximus*, held by both
    Julius Caesar and Augustus.
179 This promise is not fulfilled in the extant portions of the history.

was overwhelmed and destroyed with his whole household. And even now when the lake is clear in a certain part, which happens whenever the flow of water subsides and the depths are undisturbed,[180] the ruins of porticoes and other traces of a dwelling appear. Aventinus, after whom was named one of the seven hills that are joined to make the city of Rome, succeeded him in the sovereignty and reigned thirty-seven years, and after him Proca twenty-three years. Then Amulius, having unjustly possessed himself of the kingdom which belonged to Numitor, his elder brother, reigned forty-two years, But when Amulius had been slain by Romulus and Remus, the sons of the holy maiden, as shall presently be related, Numitor, the maternal grandfather of the youths, after his brother's death resumed the sovereignty which by law belonged to him. In the next year of Numitor's reign, which was the four hundred and thirty-second after the taking of Troy, the Albans sent out a colony, under the leadership of Romulus and Remus, and founded Rome, in the beginning of the first year of the seventh Olympiad, when Daïcles of Messenê was victor in the foot race, and at Athens Charops was in the first year of his ten-year term as archon.[181]

72 But as there is great dispute concerning both the time of the building of the city and the founders of it, I have thought it incumbent on me also not to give merely a cursory account of these things, as if they were universally agreed on. For Cephalon of

---

180 Kirby F. Smith has pointed out (*Am. Journ. Philol.* xvi., 1895, p. 205) that the Alban Lake is fed entirely from the bottom by gushing springs, so that νᾶμα here has its ordinary meaning of "spring" or "running water," and σταθερός is used with particular appropriateness of the depths of this lake.

181 751 B.C. According to the common tradition the archonship, which was at first held for life, was in 752 limited to a ten-year term, and finally, *ca.* 683, to a single year. See Grote, *History of Greece,* Part ii., chap, x (beginning); von Schoeffer in Pauly-Wissowa, *Real-Encyclopädie, s.v.* Archontes, cols. 569 f.

Gergis,[182] a very ancient writer, says that the city was built in the second generation after the Trojan war by those who had escaped from Troy with Aeneas, and he names as the founder of it Romus,[183] who was the leader of the colony and one of Aeneas' sons; he adds that Aeneas had four sons, Ascanius, Euryleon, Romulus and Remus. And Demagoras,[184] Agathyllus and many others agree with him as regards both the time and the leader of the colony. But the author of the history of the priestesses at Argos[185] and of what happened in the days of each of them says that Aeneas came into Italy from the land of the Molossians with Odysseus[186] and became the founder of the city, which he named after Romê, one of the Trojan women. He says that this woman, growing weary with wandering, stirred up the other Trojan women and together with them set fire to the ships. And Damastes of Sigeum[187] and some others agree with him. But Aristotle, the philosopher, relates[188] that some of the Achaeans, while they were doubling Cape Malea on their return from Troy, were overtaken by a violent storm, and being for some time driven out of their course by the winds, wandered

182 See p. 64, n. 127.

183 Ρῶμος was the name invented by the Greeks for the founder of Rome before they had heard of any Romulus or Remus; later they used it as the equivalent of Remus. It seems best to translate it as Romus (or Romos), except where we are clearly dealing with the Roman legend of the twin brothers. See recent discussions of the growth of the legend by Carter in Roscher's *Lexikon der griech. u. röm. Mythologie*, *s.v.* Romulus, cols. 167-83; Rosenberg in Pauly-Wissowa, *Real-Enc.*, *s.v.* Romulus, cols. 1074-92; De Sanctis, *Storia dei Romani*, i. pp. 206-17.

184 Demagoras of Samos apparently wrote a work on Trojan or Samothracian antiquities. Agathyllus has already been cited in chap. 49, 2.

185 The author of this work was Hellanicus (see p. 28, n. 61). The present quotation is frag. 53 (end) in Müller, *Frag. Hist. Graec.* i. 52.

186 A variant reading is "after Odysseus." See critical note.

187 Damastes (*ca.* 400) wrote the genealogies of the Greek leaders before Troy; also a description of the earth and its peoples, to accompany his map of the world.

188 Probably in his *Instituta Barbarica.* Müller, *Frag. Hist. Graec.* ii. 178, 242.

over many parts of the sea, till at last they came to this place in the land of the Opicans which is called Latinium,[189] lying on the Tyrrhenian sea. And being pleased with the sight of land, they hauled up their ships, stayed there the winter season, and were preparing to sail at the beginning of spring; but when their ships were set on fire in the night and they were unable to sail away, they were compelled against their will to fix their abode in the place where they had landed. This fate, he says, was brought upon them by the captive women they were carrying with them from Troy, who burned the ships, fearing that the Achaeans in returning home would carry them into slavery. Callias,[190] who wrote of the deeds of Agathocles, says that Romê, one of the Trojan women who came into Italy with the other Trojans, married Latinus, the king of the Aborigines, by whom she had three son, Romus, Romulus and Telegonus, . . . and having built a city, gave it the name of their mother. Xenagoras, the historian,[191] writes that Odysseus and Circê had three sons, Romus, Anteias and Ardeias, who built three cities and called them after their own names.[192] Dionysius of Chalcis[193] names Romus as the founder of the city, but says that according to some this man was the son of Ascanius, and according to others the son of Emathion. There are others who declare that Rome was built by Romus, the son of Italus and Leucaria, the daughter of Latinus.

---

189 Probably originally an adjective (like the later Λατίνη), "the Latin land." Some have wished to read Latium or Lavinium.

190 Callias wrote the history of Agathocles in 22 books. His account was so biased in favour of that tyrant that he was accused of having been heavily bribed by him.

191 Xenagoras (date uncertain) wrote a historical work called Χρόνοι and a book about islands. Müller, *Frag. Hist. Graec.* iv. 527, 6.

192 Rome, Antium and Ardea.

193 Dionysius of Chalcis (fourth century?) wrote several books of Κτίσεις or "Foundings of Cities." Müller, *Frag. Hist. Graec.* iv. 395, 11.

73 I could cite many other Greek historians who assign different founders to the city, but, not to appear prolix, I shall come to the Roman historians. The Romans, to be sure, have not so much as one single historian or chronicler who is ancient; however, each of their historians has taken something out of ancient accounts that are preserved on sacred tablets.[194] Some of these say that Romulus and Remus, the founders of Rome, were the sons of Aeneas, others say that they were the sons of a daughter of Aeneas, without going on to determine who was their father; that they were delivered as hostages by Aeneas to Latinus, the king of the Aborigines, when the treaty was made between the inhabitants and the new-comers, and that Latinus, after giving them a kindly welcome, not only did them many good offices, but, upon dying without male issue, left them his successors to some part of his kingdom. Others say that after the death of Aeneas Ascanius, having succeeded to the entire sovereignty of the Latins, divided both the country and the forces of the Latins into three parts, two of which he gave to his brothers, Romulus and Remus. He himself, they say, built Alba and some other towns; Remus built cities which he named Capua, after Capys, his great-grandfather, Anchisa, after his grandfather Anchises, Aeneia (which was afterwards called Janiculum), after his father, and Rome, after himself.[195] This last city was for some time deserted, but upon the arrival of another colony, which the Albans sent out under the leadership of Romulus and Remus, it received again its ancient name. So that, according to this account, there were two settlements of Rome, one a little after the Trojan war, and the other fifteen generations after the first.[196] And if anyone desires to look into the remoter past, even a third Rome will be found, more ancient than

194 This probably refers to the *annales maximi*, the brief record of magistrates, prodigies and important public events of each year kept by the *pontifex maximus*. *Cf.* iv. 30, 3.

195 Anchisa and Aeneia are otherwise unknown. See critical note.

196 See chap. 45, 3.

these, one that was founded before Aeneas and the Trojans came into Italy. This is related by no ordinary or modern historian, but by Antiochus of Syracuse, whom I have mentioned before.[197] He says that when Morges reigned in Italy (which at that time comprehended all the seacoast from Tarentum to Posidonia),[198] a man came to him who had been banished from Rome. His words are these: "When Italus was growing old, Morges reigned. In his reign there came a man who had been banished from Rome; his name was Sicelus." According to the Syracusan historian, therefore, an ancient Rome is found even earlier than the Trojan war. However, as he has left it doubtful whether it was situated in the same region where the present city stands or whether some other place happened to be called by this name, I, too, can form no conjecture. But as regards the ancient settlements of Rome, I think that what has already been said is sufficient.

74 As to the last settlement or founding of the city, or whatever we ought to call it, Timaeus of Sicily,[199] following what principle I do not know, places it at the same time as the founding of Carthage, that is, in the thirty-eighth year before the first Olympiad;[200] Lucius Cincius, a member of the senate, places it about the fourth year of the twelfth Olympiad,[201] and Quintus Fabius in the first year of the eighth Olympiad.[202] Porcius Cato does not give the time according to Greek reckoning, but being as careful as any writer in gathering the data of ancient history, he places its founding four hundred and thirty-two years after the Trojan war; and this time, being compared

---

197 Chap. 12, 3; 22, 5; 35, 1. The present quotation is found in Müller, *Frag. Hist. Graec.* i. 182, 7.
198 Later Paestum.
199 See p. 7, n. 61.
200 813 B.C.
201 728 B.C.
202 747 B.C.

with the *Chronicles* of Eratosthenes,[203] corresponds to the first year of the seventh Olympiad.[204] That the canons of Eratosthenes are sound I have shown in another treatise,[205] where I have also shown how the Roman chronology is to be synchronized with that of the Greeks. For I did not think it sufficient, like Polybius of Megalopolis,[206] to say merely that I believe Rome was built in the second year of the seventh Olympiad,[207] nor to let my belief rest without further examination upon the single tablet preserved by the high priests, the only one of its kind, but I determined to set forth the reasons that had appealed to me, so that all might examine them who so desired. In that treatise, therefore, the detailed exposition is given; but in the course of the present work also the most essential of the conclusions there reached will be mentioned. The matter stands thus: It is generally agreed that the invasion of the Gauls,[208] during which the city of Rome was taken, happened during the archonship of Pyrgion at Athens, in the first year of the ninety-eighth Olympiad.[209] Now if the time before the taking of the city is reckoned back to Lucius Junius Brutus and Lucius Tarquinius Collatinus, the first consuls at Rome after the overthrow of the kings, it comprehends one hundred and twenty years. This is proved in many other ways, but particularly by the records of the censors, which the son receives in succession from the father and takes great

---

203 Eratosthenes was perhaps the most versatile scholar of antiquity. Eminent not only as an astronomer, mathematician and geographer, he also won distinction as an historian, philosopher and grammarian. His *Chronographiae* was an annalistic history, both political and literary, in which especial attention was devoted to the accurate determination of the chronology. The work began with the fall of Troy, which he placed in 1183 B.C.

204 751 B.C.

205 This work, now lost, is cited by Clement of Alexandria (*Strom.* i. 102) as Χρόνοι.

206 Probably in a lost portion of his Book VI.

207 750 B.C.

208 Literally "Celts." See p. 49, n. 105.

209 387 B.C.

care to transmit to posterity, like family rites; and there are many illustrious men of censorian families who preserve these records. In them I find that in the second year before the taking of the city there was a census of the Roman people, to which, as to the rest of them, there is affixed the date, as follows: "In the consulship of Lucius Valerius Potitus and Titus Manlius Capitolinus, in the one hundred and nineteenth year after the expulsion of the kings." So that the Gallic invasion, which we find to have occurred in the second year after the census, happened when the hundred and twenty years were completed. If, now, this interval of time is found to consist of thirty Olympiads, it must be allowed that the first consuls to be chosen entered upon their magistracy in the first year of the sixty-eighth Olympiad, the same year that Isagoras was archon at Athens.[210]

75 And, again, if from the expulsion of the kings the time is reckoned back to Romulus, the first ruler of the city, it amounts to two hundred and forty-four years. This is known from the order in which the kings succeeded one another and the number of years each of them ruled. For Romulus, the founder of Rome, reigned thirty-seven years, it is said, and after his death the city was a year without a king. Then Numa Pompilius, who was chosen by the people, reigned forty-three years; after Numa, Tullus Hostilius thirty-two; and his successor, Ancus Marcius, twenty-four; after Marcius, Lucius Tarquinius, called Priscus, thirty-eight; Servius Tullius, who succeeded him, forty-four. And the slayer of Servius, Lucius Tarquinius, the tyrannical prince who, from his contempt of justice, was called Superbus, extended his reign to the twenty-fifth year. As the reigns, therefore, of the kings amount to two hundred and forty-four years or sixty-one Olympiads, it follows necessarily that Romulus, the first ruler of the city, began his reign in the first

210 507 B.C.

year of the seventh Olympiad, when Charops at Athens was in the first year of his ten-year term as archon.[211] For the count of the years requires this; and that each king reigned the number of years is shown in that treatise of mine to which I have referred.

This, therefore, is the account given by those who lived before me and adopted by me concerning the time of the settlement of the city which now rules supreme. As to its founders, who they were and by what turns of fortune they were induced to lead out the colony, and any other details told concerning its settlement, all this has been related by many, and the greatest part of it in a different manner by some; and I, also, shall relate the most probable of these stories. They are as follows:

76 When[212] Amulius succeeded to the kingdom of the Albans, after forcibly excluding his elder brother Numitor from the dignity that was his by inheritance, he not only showed great contempt for justice in everything else that he did, but he finally plotted to deprive Numitor's family of issue, both from fear of suffer punishment for his usurpation and also because of his desire never to be dispossessed of the sovereignty. Having long resolved upon this course, he first observed the neighbourhood where Aegestus, Numitor's son, who was just coming to man's estate, was wont to follow the chase, and having placed an ambush in the most hidden part of it, he caused him to be slain when he had come out to hunt; and after the deed was committed he contrived to have it reported that the youth had been killed by robbers. Nevertheless, the rumour thus concocted could not prevail over the truth which he was trying to keep concealed, but many, though it was unsafe to do so, ventured to tell what had been done. Numitor was aware of the crime, but his judgment being superior to his grief, he affected

211 751 B.C.
212 *Cf.* Livy i. 3, 11.

ignorance, resolving to defer his resentment to a less dangerous time. And Amulius, supposing that the truth about the youth had been kept secret, set a second plan on foot, as follows: he appointed Numitor's daughter, Ilia, — or, as some state, Rhea, surnamed Silvia, — who was then ripe for marriage, to be a priestess of Vesta, lest, if she first entered a husband's house, she might bring forth avengers for her family. These holy maidens who were entrusted with the custody of the perpetual fire and with the carrying out of any other rites that it was customary for virgins to perform in behalf of the commonwealth were required to remain undefiled by marriage for a period of not less than five[213] years. Amulius was carrying out his plan under specious pretences, as if he were conferring honour and dignity on his brother's family; for he was not the author of this law, which was a general one, nor, again, was his brother the first person of consideration whom he had obliged to yield obedience to it, but it was both customary and honourable among the Albans for maidens of the highest birth to be appointed to the service of Vesta. But Numitor, perceiving that these measures of his brother proceeded from no good intention, dissembled his resentment, lest he should incur the ill-will of the people, and stifled his complaints upon this occasion also.

77 The[214] fourth year after this, Ilia, upon going to a grove consecrated to Mars to fetch pure water for use in the sacrifices, was ravished by somebody or other in the sacred precinct. Some say that the author of the deed was one of the maiden's suitors, who was carried away by his passion for the girl;[215] others say that it was

---

213 Thirty years was the period required at Rome from the time of Numa; *cf.* ii. 67, 2. Some early editors wished to emend the present passage to agree with the later practice.

214 *Cf.* Livy i. 4, 1-3.

215 The last clause (literally, "loving the girl") may well be a gloss to explain the preceding words "one of the maiden's suitors." See critical note.

Amulius himself, and that, since his purpose was to destroy her quite as much as to satisfy his passion, he had arrayed himself in such armour as would render him most terrible to behold and that he also kept his features disguised as effectively as possible. But most writers relate a fabulous story to the effect that it was a spectre of the divinity to whom the place was consecrated; and they add that the adventure was attended by many supernatural signs, including a sudden disappearance of the sun and a darkness that spread over the sky, and that the appearance of the spectre was far more marvellous than that of a man both in stature and in beauty. And they say that the ravisher, to comfort the maiden (by which it became clear that it was a god), commanded her not to grieve at all at what had happened, since she had been united in marriage to the divinity of the place and as a result of her violation should bear two sons who would far excel all men in valour and warlike achievements. And having said this, he was wrapped in a cloud and, being lifted from the earth, was borne upwards through the air. This is not a proper place to consider what opinion we ought to entertain of such tales, whether we should scorn them as instances of human frailty attributed to the gods, — since god is incapable of any action that is unworthy of his incorruptible and blessed nature, — or whether we should admit even these stories, upon the supposition that all the substance of the universe is mixed, and that between the race of gods and that of men some third order of being exists which is that of the daemons, who, uniting sometimes with human beings and sometimes with the gods, beget, it is said, the fabled race of heroes. This, I say, is not a proper place to consider these things, and, moreover, what the philosophers have said concerning them is sufficient. But, be that as it may, the maid after her violation feigned illness (for this her mother advised out of regard both for her own safety and for the sacred services of the gods) and no longer attended the sacrifices, but her duties were performed by the other virgins who were joined with her in the same ministry.

78 But Amulius, moved either by his own knowledge of what had happened or by a natural suspicion of the truth, began to inquire into her long absence from the sacrifices, in order to discover the real reason. To this end he kept sending in to her some physicians in whom he had the greatest confidence; and then, since the women alleged that her ailment was one that must be kept secret from others, he left his wife to watch her. She, having by a woman's marking of the signs discovered what was a secret to the others, informed him of it, and he, lest the girl should be delivered in secret, for she was now near her time, caused her to be guarded by armed men. And summoning his brother to the council, he not only announced the deflowering of the girl, of which the rest knew naught, but even accused her parents of being her accomplices; and he ordered Numitor not to hide the guilty man, but to expose him. Numitor said he was amazed at what he heard, and protesting his innocence of everything that was alleged, desired time to test the truth of it. Having with difficulty obtained this delay, and being informed by his wife of the affair as his daughter had related it in the beginning, he acquainted the council with the rape committed by the god and also related what the god had said concerning the twins, and asked that his story should be believed only if the fruit of her travail should prove to be such as the god had foretold; for the time of her delivery was near at hand, so that it would not be long, if he were playing the rogue, before the fact would come to light. Moreover, he offered to put at their disposal for examination the women who were watching his daughter, and he was ready to submit to any and every test. As he spoke thus the majority of the councillors were persuaded, but Amulius declared that his demands were altogether insincere, and was bent on destroying the girl by every means. While this was taking place, those who had been appointed to keep guard over Ilia at the time of her delivery came to announce that she had given birth to male twins. And at once Numitor began to urge at length the same arguments, showing the deed to be the work of the god and demanding that they take no unlawful action against his daughter, who was innocent of her condition. On the other hand, Amulius thought that even in connexion with her delivery there had been some human trickery and that the women had provided another child, either unknown to the guards or with their connivance, and he said much more to the same purport. When the councillors found that the king's decision was inspired by implacable anger, they, too, voted, as he demanded, that the law should be carried out which provided that a Vestal who suffered herself to be defiled should be scourged with rods and put to death and her offspring thrown into the current of the river. To-day, however, the sacred law ordains that such offenders shall be buried alive.

79 Up[216] to this point the greater part of the historians give the same account or differ but slightly, some in the direction of what is legendary, others of what is more probable; but they disagree in what follows. Some say that the girl was put to death immediately; others that she remained in a secret prison under a guard, which caused the people to believe that she had been put to death secretly. The latter authors say that Amulius was moved to do this when his daughter begged him to grant her the life of her cousin; for, having been brought up together and being of the same age, they loved each other like sisters. Amulius, accordingly, to please her, — for she was his only daughter, — saved Ilia from death, but kept her confined in a secret prison; and she was at length set at liberty after the death of Amulius. Thus do the accounts of the ancient authors

---

216 *Cf.* Livy i. 4, 3-9.

vary concerning Ilia, and yet both opinions carry with them an appearance of truth; for this reason I, also, have mentioned them both, but each of my readers will decide for himself which to believe.

But concerning the babes born of Ilia, Quintus Fabius, called Pictor, whom Lucius Cincius, Porcius Cato, Calpurnius Piso and most of the other historians have followed, writes thus: By the order of Amulius some of his servants took the babes in an ark and carried them to the river, distant about a hundred and twenty stades from the city, with the intention of throwing them into it. But when they drew near and perceived that the Tiber, swollen by continual rains, had left its natural bed and overflowed the plains, they came down from the top of the Palatine hill[217] to that part of the water that lay nearest (for they could no longer advance any farther) and set down the ark upon the flood where it washed the foot of the hill. The ark floated for some time, and then, as the waters retired by degrees from their extreme limits, it struck against a stone and, overturning, threw out the babes, who lay whimpering and wallowing in the mud. Upon this, a she-wolf that had just whelped appeared and, her udder being distended with milk, gave them her paps to suck and with her tongue licked off the mud with which they were besmeared. In the meantime the herdsmen happened to be driving their flocks forth to pasture (for the place was now become passable) and one of them, seeing the wolf thus fondling the babes, was for some time struck dumb with astonishment and disbelief of what he saw. Then going away and getting together as many as he could of his fellows who kept their herds near at hand (for they would not believe what he said), he led them to see the sight themselves. When these also drew near and saw the wolf

---

217 From this point the word Παλλάντιον will be rendered "Palatine hill" instead of "Pallantium," only the context shows clearly that the village itself is meant.

caring for the babes as if they had been her young and the babes clinging to her as to their mother, they thought they were beholding a supernatural sight and advanced in a body, shouting to terrify the creature. The wolf, however, far from being provoked at the approach of the men, but as if she had been tame, withdrew gently from the babes and went away, paying little heed to the rabble of shepherds. Now there was not far off a holy place, arched over by a dense wood, and a hollow rock from which springs issued; the wood was said to be consecrated to Pan, and there was an altar there to that god.[218] To this place, then, the wolf came and hid herself. The grove, to be sure, no longer remains, but the cave from which the spring flows is still pointed out, built up[219] against the side of the Palatine hill on the road which leads to the Circus, and near it is a sacred precinct in which there is a statue commemorating the incident; it represents a she-wolf suckling two infants, the figures being in bronze and of ancient workmanship.[220] This spot is said to have been a holy place of the Arcadians who formerly settled there with Evander.

As soon as the beast was gone the herdsmen took up the babes, and believing that the god desired their preservation, were eager to bring them up. There was among them the keeper of the royal herds of swine, whose name was Faustulus, an upright man, who

---

218 Compare the description of the Lupercal already given in chap. 32.
219 The cave became a shrine and received some sort of architectural adornment, which must have included at least a dignified entrance. The Lupercal is named in the *Monumentum Ancyranum* (4, 2) in a list of public buildings repaired by Augustus.
220 The statue here mentioned is doubtless the one erected by Cn. and Q. Ogulnius near the *Ficus Ruminalis* in 295 B.C (Livy x. 23). Another similar group stood on the summit of the Capitol, and was struck by lightning in 65 B.C. The wolf of this second group is almost certainly the famous one still preserved in the Palazzo dei Conservatori, since the animal's hind legs show the effects of lightning; the wolf is dated about 600 B.C., but the infants are a modern restoration.

had been in town upon some necessary business at the time when the deflowering of Ilia and her delivery were made public. And afterwards, when the babes were being carried to the river, he had by some providential chance taken the same road to the Palatine hill and gone along with those who were carrying them. This man, without giving the least intimation to the others that he knew anything of the affair, asked that the babes might be delivered to him, and having received them by general consent, he carried them home to his wife. And finding that she had just given birth to a child and was grieving because it was still-born, he comforted her and gave her these children to substitute in its place, informing her of every circumstance of their fortune from the beginning. And as they grew older he gave to one the name of Romulus and to the other that of Remus. When they came to be men, they showed themselves both in dignity of aspect and elevation of mind not like swineherds and neatherds, but such as we might expect those to be who are born of royal race and are looked upon as the offspring of the gods; and as such they are still celebrated by the Romans in the hymns of their country, But their life was that of herdsmen, and they lived by their own labour, generally upon the mountains in huts which they built, roofs and all,[221] out of sticks and reeds. One of these, called the hut of Romulus,[222] remained even to my day on the flank of the

---

221 This meaning (on the analogy of such words as αὔτανδρος, αὐτόκλαδος, αὐτόρριζος, seems to be the one required here. The only meaning given in the lexicons, "self-covered" or "roofed by nature," would imply huts depending for their roofs on natural shelters, such as overhanging rocks or overarching trees, — in other words, huts technically roofless. But the thatched roof of the "hut of Romulus" was to the Romans one of its most striking features; see next note, καλάμων, here rendered "reeds," in accordance with its usual meaning, is also used sometimes for "straw," which may be what Dionysius intended.

222 The present passage gives us our most detailed account of the *casa Romuli.* Plutarch (Rom. 20) adds the detail that it stood near the *scalae Caci,* a landmark on the south-west corner of the Palatine hill. There was also

Palatine hill which faces towards the Circus, and it is preserved holy by those who have charge of these matters; they add nothing to it to render it more stately, but if any part of it is injured, either by storms or by the lapse of time, they repair the damage and restore the hut as nearly as possible to its former condition.

When Romulus and Remus were about eighteen years of age, they had some dispute about the pasture with Numitor's herdsmen, whose herds were quartered on the Aventine hill, which is over against the Palatine. They frequently accused one another either of grazing the meadow-land that did not belong to them or of monopolizing that which belonged to both in common, or of whatever the matter chanced to be. From this wrangling they had recourse sometimes to blows and then to arms. Finally Numitor's men, having received many wounds at the hands of the youths and lost some of their number and being at last driven by force from the places in dispute, devised a stratagem against them. They placed an ambuscade in the hidden part of the ravine and having concerted the time of the attack with those who lay in wait for the youths, the rest in a body attacked the others' folds by night. No wit happened that Romulus, together with the chief men of the village, had gone at the time to a place called Caenina to offer sacrifices for the community according to the custom of the country; but Remus, being informed of the foe's attack, hastily armed himself and with a few of the villagers who had already got together went out to oppose them. And they, instead of awaiting him, retired, in order to draw him to the place where they intended to face about and attack

---

another *casa Romuli* on the Capitoline, probably a replica of the first. Vitruvius (ii. 1, 5), after mentioning the primitive custom of constructing roofs out of reeds, brushwood or straw, cites the hut of Romulus on the Capitoline as a good example of the ancient practice. *Cf.* Virgil (*Aen.* viii. 654), *Romuleoque recens horrebat regia culmo*; and Ovid's similar description of the original temple of Vesta (*Fasti* vi. 261 f.).

him to advantage. Remus, being unaware of their stratagem, pursued them for a long distance, till he passed the place where the rest lay in ambush; thereupon these men rose up and at the same time the others who had been fleeing faced about. And having surrounded Remus and his men, they overwhelmed them with a shower of stones and took them prisoners; for they had received orders from their masters to bring the youths to them alive. Thus Remus was captured and led away.

80 But[223] Aelius Tubero,[224] a shrewd man and careful in collecting his historical data, writes that Numitor's people, knowing beforehand that the youths were going to celebrate in honour of Pan the Lupercalia,[225] the Arcadian festival as instituted by Evander, set an ambush for that moment in the celebration when the youths living near the Palatine were, after offering sacrifice, to proceed from the Lupercal and run round the village naked, their loins girt with the skins of the victims just sacrificed. This ceremony signified a sort of traditional purification of the villagers, and is still performed even to this day. On this occasion, then, the herdsmen lay in wait in the narrow part of the road for the youths who were taking part in the ceremony, and when the first band with Remus came abreast of them, that with Romulus and the rest being behind (for they were divided into three bands and ran at a distance from one another), without waiting for the others they set up a shout and all rushed upon the first group, and, surrounding them, some threw darts at them, others stones, and others whatever they could lay their hands on. And the youths, startled by the unexpected attack and at a loss how to act, fighting unarmed as they were against armed men, were

223 *Cf.* Livy i. 5, 1-3.
224 See p. 9, n. 19.
225 For a detailed discussion of the Lupercalia the reader is referred to Sir James Frazer's note on Ovid's *Fasti* ii. 267 (Vol. ii. pp. 327 ff.; condensed in his L.C.L. edition, pp. 389 ff.).

easily overpowered. Remus, therefore, having fallen into the hands of the enemy in this manner or in the way Fabius relates, was being led away, bound, to Alba. When Romulus heard of his brother's fate, he thought he ought to follow immediately with the stoutest of the herdsmen in the hope of overtaking Remus while he was still on the road, but he was dissuaded by Faustulus. For seeing that his haste was too frenzied, this man, who was looked upon as the father of the youths and who had hitherto kept everything a secret from them, lest they should venture upon some hazardous enterprise before they were in their prime, now at last, compelled by necessity, took Romulus aside and told him everything. When the youth heard every circumstance of their fortune from the beginning, he was touched both with compassion for his mother and with solicitude for Numitor. And after taking much counsel with Faustulus, he decided to give up his plan for an immediate attack, but to get ready a larger force, in order to free his whole family from the lawlessness of Amulius, and he resolved to risk the direst peril for the sake of the greatest rewards, but to act in concert with his grandfather in whatever the other should see fit to do.

81 This[226] plan having been decided upon as the best, Romulus called together all the inhabitants of the village and after asking them to hasten into Alba immediately, but not all by the same gates nor in a body, lest the suspicions of the citizens should be aroused, and then to stay in the market-place and be ready to do whatever should be ordered, he himself set out first for the city. In the meantime those who had carried off Remus brought him before the king and complained of all the outrageous treatment they had received from the youths, producing their wounded, and threatening, if they found no redress, to desert their herds. And Amulius, desiring to please both the countrymen, who had come in

---

226 For chaps. 81-83 *cf.* Livy i. 5, 4-6, 2.

great numbers, and Numitor (for he happened to be present and share the exasperation of his retainers), and longing to see peace throughout the country, and at the same time suspecting the boldness of the youth, so fearless was in his answers, gave judgment against him; but he left his punishment to Numitor, saying that the one who had done an injury could be punished by none so justly as by the one who had suffered it. While Numitor's herdsmen were leading Remus away with his hands bound behind him and mocking him, Numitor followed and not only admired his grace of body, so much was there that was kingly in his bearing, but also observed his nobility of spirit, which he preserved even in distress, not turning to lamentations and entreaties, as all do under such afflictions, but with a becoming silence going away to his fate. As soon as they were arrived at his house he ordered all the rest to withdraw, and Remus being left alone, he asked him who he was and of what parents; for he did not believe such a man could be meanly born. Remus answered that he knew this much only from the account he had received from the man who brought him up, that he with his twin brother had been exposed in a wood as soon as they were born and had then been taken up by the herdsmen and reared by them. Upon which Numitor, after a short pause, either because he suspected something of the truth or because Heaven was bringing the matter to light, said to him: "I need not inform you, Remus, that you are in my power to be punished in whatever way I may see fit, and that those who brought you here, having suffered many grievous wrongs at your hands, would give much to have you put to death. All this you know. But if I should free you from death and every other punishment, would you show your gratitude and serve me when I desire your assistance in an affair that will conduce to the advantage of us both?" The youth, having in answer said everything which the hope of life prompts those who are in despair of it to say and promise to those on whom their fate depends,

Numitor ordered him to be unbound. And commanding everybody to leave the place, he acquainted him with his own misfortunes — how Amulius, though his brother, had deprived him of his kingdom and bereft him of his children, having secretly slain his son while he was hunting and keeping his daughter bound in prison, and in all other respects continued to treat him as a master would treat his slave.

82 Having spoken thus and accompanied his words with many lamentations, he entreated Remus to avenge the wrongs of his house. And when the youth gladly embraced the proposal and begged him to set him at the task immediately, Numitor commended his eagerness and said: "I myself will determine the proper time for the enterprise; but do you meanwhile send a message privately to your brother, informing him that you are safe and asking him to come here in all haste." Thereupon a man who seemed likely to serve their purpose was found and sent; and he, meeting Romulus not far from the city, delivered his message. Romulus was greatly rejoiced at this and went in haste to Numitor; and having embraced them both, he first spoke words of greeting and then related how he and his brother had been exposed and brought up and all the other circumstances he had learned from Faustulus. The others, who wished his story might be true and needed few proofs in order to believe it, heard what he said with pleasure. And as soon as they knew one another they proceeded to consult together and consider the proper method and occasion for making their attack. While they were thus employed, Faustulus was brought before Amulius. For, fearing lest the information given by Romulus might not be credited by Numitor, in an affair of so great moment, without manifest proofs, he soon afterwards followed him to town, taking the ark with him as evidence of the exposing of the babes. But as he was entering the gates in great confusion, taking all

114

possible pains to conceal what he carried, one of the guards observed him (for there was fear of an incursion of the enemy and the gates were being guarded by those who were most fully trusted by the king) and laid hold of him; and insisting upon knowing what the concealed object was, he forcibly threw back his garment. As soon as he saw the ark and found the man embarrassed, he demanded to know the cause of his confusion and what he meant by not carrying openly an article that required no secrecy. In the meantime more of the guards flocked to them and one of them recognized the ark, having himself carried the children in it to the river; and he so informed those who were present. Upon this they seized Faustulus, and carrying him to the king himself, acquainted him with all that had passed. Amulius, having terrified the man by the threat of torture if he did not willingly tell the truth, first asked him if the children were alive; and learning that they were, he desired to know in what manner they had been preserved. And when the other had given him a full account of everything as it had happened, the king said: "Well then, since you have spoken the truth about these matters, say where they may now be found; for it is not right that they who are my relations should any longer live ingloriously among herdsmen, particularly since it is due to the providence of the gods that they have been preserved."

83 But Faustulus, suspecting from the king's unaccountable mildness that his intentions were not in harmony with his professions, answer him in this manner: "The youths are upon the mountains tending their herds, which is their way of life, and I was sent by them to their mother to give her an account of their fortunes; but, hearing that she was in your custody, I was intending to ask your daughter to have me brought to her. And was bringing the ark with me that I might support my words with a manifest proof. Now, therefore, since you have decided to have the youths brought here, not only am I glad, but I ask you to send such persons with me as you wish. I will point out to them the youths and they shall acquaint them with your commands." This he said in the desire to discover some means of delaying the death of the youths and at the same time in the hope of making his own escape from the hands of those who were conducting him, as soon as he should arrive upon the mountains. And Amulius speedily sent the most trustworthy of his guards with secret orders to seize and bring before him the persons whom the swineherd should point out to them. Having done this, he at once determined to summon his brother and keep him under mild guard[227] till he had ordered the present business to his satisfaction, and he sent for him as if for some other purpose; but the messenger who was sent, yielding both to his good-will toward the man in danger and to compassion for his fate, informed Numitor of the design of Amulius. And Numitor, having revealed to the youths the danger that threatened them and exhorted them to show themselves brave men, came to the palace with a considerable band of his retainers and friends and loyal servants. These were joined by the countrymen who had entered the city earlier and now came from the market-place with swords concealed under their clothes, a sturdy company. And having by a concerted attack forced the entrance, which was defended by only a few heavy-armed troops, they easily slew Amulius and afterwards made themselves masters of the citadel. Such is the account given by Fabius.

84 But others, who hold that nothing bordering on the fabulous has any place in historical writing, declare that the exposing of the babes by the servants in a manner not in accordance with their instructions is improbable, and they ridicule the tameness of the

227 Literally "under guard without chains," probably a translation of the Latin *libera custodia*. In later times persons of rank were often thus kept under surveillance in their own houses or in the house of a magistrate.

she-wolf that suckled the children as a story full of melodramatic absurdity In place of this they give the following account of the matter: Numitor, upon learning that Ilia was with child, procured other new-born infants and when she had given birth to her babes, he substituted the former in place of the latter. Then he gave the supposititious children to those who were guarding her at the time of her delivery to be carried away, having either secured the loyalty of the guards by money or contrived this exchange by the help of women; and when Amulius had received them, he made away with them by some means or other. As for the babes that were born of Ilia, their grandfather, who was above all things solicitous for their preservation, handed them over to Faustulus. This Faustulus, they say, was of Arcadian extraction, being descended from those Arcadians who came over with Evander; he lived near the Palatine hill and had the care of Amulius' possessions, and he was prevailed on by his brother, named Faustinus, who had the oversight of Numitor's herds that fed near the Aventine hill, to do Numitor the favour of bringing up the children. They say, moreover, that the one who nursed and suckled them was not a she-wolf, but, as may well be supposed, a woman, the wife of Faustulus, named Laurentia, who, having formerly prostituted her beauty, had received from the people living round the Palatine hill the nickname of Lupa.[228] This is an ancient Greek[229] term applied to women who prostitute themselves for gain; but they are now called by a more respectable name, *hetaerae* or "companions." But some who were ignorant of this invented the myth of the she-wolf, this animal being called in the Latin tongue *lupa*. The story continues that after the children

228 *Cf.* Livy i. 4, 7. *lupa* is found in various Latin authors in the sense of "prostitute," and *lupanar* meant "brothel."

229 It would seem as if "Greek" must be an error here for "Latin." Not even the Greek equivalent of *lupa* (λύκαινα) is found used in this sense. Hesychius' gloss, λύπτα (for λύππα?): ἑταίρα, πόρνη, may well have been taken from some Roman history.

were weaned they were sent by those who were rearing them to Gabii, a town not far from the Palatine hill, to be instructed in Greek learning; and there they were brought up by some personal friends of Faustulus, being taught letters, music, and the use of Greek arms until they grew to manhood. After their return to their supposed parents the quarrel arose between them and Numitor's herdsmen concerning their common pastures; thereupon they beat Numitor's men so that these drove away their cattle, doing this by Numitor's direction, to the intent that it might serve as a basis for his complaints and at the same time as an excuse for the crowd of herdsmen to come to town. When this had been brought about, Numitor raised a clamour against Amulius, declaring that he was treated outrageously, being plundered by the herdsmen of Amulius, and demanding that Amulius, if he was not responsible for any of this, should deliver up to him the herdsman and his sons for trial; and Amulius, wishing to clear himself of the charge, ordered not only those who were complained of, but all the rest who were accused of having been present at the conflict, to come and stand trial before Numitor. Then, when great numbers came to town together with the accused, ostensibly to attend the trial, the grandfather of the youths acquainted them with all the circumstances of their fortune, and telling them that now, if ever, was the time to avenge themselves, he straightway made his attack upon Amulius with the crowd of herdsmen. These, then, are the accounts that are given of the birth and rearing of the founders of Rome.

85 I[230] am now going to relate the events that happened at the very time of its founding; for this part of my account still remains. When Numitor, upon the death of Amulius, had resumed his rule and had spent a little time in restoring the city from its late disorder

---

230 For chaps. 85-88 *cf.* Livy i. 6, 3-7, 3.

to its former orderly state, he presently thought of providing an independent rule for the youths by founding another city. At the same time, the inhabitants being much increased in number, he thought it good policy to get rid of some part of them, particularly of those who had once been his enemies, lest he might have cause to suspect any of his subjects. And having communicated this plan to the youths and gained their approval, he gave them, as a district to rule, the region where they had been brought up in their infancy, and, for subjects, not only that part of the people which he suspected of a design to begin rebellion anew, but also any who were willing to migrate voluntarily. Among these, as is likely to happen when a city sends out a colony, there were great numbers of the common people, but there were also a sufficient number of the prominent men of the best class, and of the Trojan element all those who were esteemed the noblest in birth, some of whose posterity remained even to my day, consisting of about fifty families. The youths were supplied with money, arms and corn, with slaves and beasts of burden and everything else that was of use in the building of a city. After they had led their people out of Alba and intermingled with them the local population that still remained in Pallantium and Saturnia, they divided the whole multitude into two parts. This they did in the hope of arousing a spirit of emulation, so that through their rivalry with each other their tasks might be the sooner finished; however, it produced the greatest of evils, discord. For each group, exalting its own leader, extolled him as the proper person to command them all; and the youths themselves, being now no longer one in mind or feeling it necessary to entertain brotherly sentiments toward each, since each expected to command the other, scorned equality and craved superiority. For some time their ambitions were concealed, but later they burst forth on the occasion which I shall now describe. They did not both favour the same site for the building of the city; for Romulus proposed to settle the

Palatine hill, among other reasons, because of the good fortune of the place where they had been preserved and brought up, whereas Remus favoured the place that is now named after him Remoria.[231] And indeed this place is very suitable for a city, being a hill not far from the Tiber and about thirty stades from Rome. From this rivalry their unsociable love of rule immediately began to disclose itself; for on the one who now yielded the victor would inevitably impose his will on all occasions alike.

86 Meanwhile, some time having elapsed and their discord in no degree abating, the two agreed to refer the matter to their grandfather and for that purpose went to Alba. He advised them to leave it to the decision of the gods which of them should give his name to the colony and be its leader. And having appointed for them a day, he ordered them to place themselves early in the morning at a distance from one another, in such stations as each of them should think proper, and after first offering to the gods the customary sacrifices, to watch for auspicious birds; and he ordered that he to whom the more favourable birds first appeared should rule the colony. The youths, approving of this, went away and according to their agreement appeared on the day appointed for the test. Romulus chose for his station the Palatine hill, where he proposed settling the colony, and Remus the Aventine hill adjoining it, or, according to others, Remoria; and a guard attended them both, to prevent their reporting things otherwise than as they appeared. When they had taken their respective stations, Romulus, after a short pause, from eagerness and jealousy of his brother, — though possibly Heaven was thus directing him, — even before he saw any omen at all, sent messengers to his brother desiring him to come immediately, as if he had been the first to see some auspicious

---

231 This hill cannot be identified. The name was also given (according to Paulus in his epitome of Festus, p. 276) to a site on the summit of the Aventine where Remus was said to have taken the auspices (chap. 86).

birds. But while the persons he sent were proceeding with no great haste, feeling ashamed of the fraud, six vultures appeared to Remus, flying from the right; and he, seeing the birds, rejoiced greatly. And not long afterwards the men sent by Romulus took him thence and brought him to the Palatine hill. When they were together, Remus asked Romulus what birds he had been the first to see, and Romulus knew not what to answer. But thereupon twelve auspicious vultures were seen flying; and upon seeing these he took courage, and pointing them out to Remus, said: "Why do you demand to know what happened a long time ago? For surely you see these birds yourself." But Remus was indignant and complained bitterly because he had been deceived by him; and he refused to yield to him his right to the colony.

87 Thereupon greater strife arose between them than before, as each, while secretly striving for the advantage, was ostensibly willing to accept equality, for the following reason. Their grandfather, as I have stated, had ordered that he to whom the more favourable birds first appeared should rule the colony; but, as the same kind of birds had been seen by both, one had the advantage of seeing them first and the other that of seeing the greater number. The rest of the people also espoused their quarrel, and arming themselves without orders from their leaders, began war; and a sharp battle ensued in which many were slain on both sides. In the course of this battle, as some say, Faustulus, who had brought up the youths, wishing to put an end to the strife of the brothers and being unable to do so, threw himself unarmed into the midst of the combatants, seeking the speediest death, which fell out accordingly. Some say also that the stone lion which stood in the principal part of the Forum near the rostra was placed over the body of Faustulus, who was buried by those who found him in the place where he fell. Remus having been slain in this action, Romulus, who had gained a most melancholy victory through the death of his brother and the mutual slaughter of citizens, buried Remus at Remoria, since when alive he had clung to it as the site for the new city. As for himself, in his grief and repentance for what had happened, he became dejected and lost all desire for life. But when Laurentia, who had received the babes when newly born and brought them up and loved them no less than a mother, entreated and comforted him, he listened to her and rose up, and gathering together the Latins who had not been slain in the battle (they were now little more than three thousand out of a very great multitude at first, when he led out the colony), he built a city on the Palatine hill.

The account I have given seems to me the most probable of the stories about the death of Remus. However, if any has been handed down that differs from this, let that also be related. Some, indeed, say that Remus yielded the leadership to Romulus, though not without resentment and anger at the fraud, but that after the wall was built, wishing to demonstrate the weakness of the fortification, he cried, "Well, as for this wall, one of your enemies could as easily cross it as I do," and immediately leaped over it. Thereupon Celer, one of the men standing on the wall, who was overseer of the work, said, "Well, as for this enemy, one of us could easily punish him," and striking him on the head with a matlock, he killed him then and there. Such is said to have been the outcome of the quarrel between the brothers.

88 When no obstacle now remained to the building of the city, Romulus appointed a day on which he planned to begin the work, after first propitiating the gods. And having prepared everything that would be required for the sacrifices and for the entertainment of the people, when the appointed time came, he himself first offered sacrifice to the gods and ordered all the rest to do the same according to their abilities. He then in the first place took the omens, which were favourable. After that, having commanded fires to be lighted before the tents, he caused the people to come out and leap over the flames in order to expiate their guilt. When he thought everything had been done which he conceived to be acceptable to the gods, he called all the people to the appointed place and described a quadrangular figure about the hill, tracing with a plough drawn by a bull and a cow yoked together a continuous furrow designed to receive the foundation of the wall; and from that time this custom has continued among the Romans of ploughing a furrow round the site where they plan to build a city. After he had done this and sacrificed the bull and the cow and also performed the initial rites over many other victims, he set the people to work. This day the Romans celebrate every year even down to my time as one of their greatest festivals and call it the Parilia.[232] On this day, which comes in the beginning of spring, the husbandmen and herdsmen offer up a sacrifice of thanksgiving for the increase of their cattle. But whether they had celebrated this day in even earlier times as a day of rejoicing and for that reason looked upon it as the most suitable for the founding of the city, or whether, because it marked the beginning of the building of the city, they consecrated it and thought they should honour on it the gods who are propitious to shepherds, I cannot say for certain.

89 Such, then, are the facts concerning the origin of the Romans which I have been able to discover after reading very diligently many works written by both Greek and Roman authors. Hence, from now on let the reader forever renounce the views of those who make Rome a retreat of barbarians, fugitive and vagabonds, and let

---

232 The Parilia, or more properly Palilia, was an ancient festival celebrated by the shepherds and herdsmen on the 21st of April in honour of the divinity Pales. See the detailed description of its observance in Ovid, *Fasti* iv. 721 ff., with Sir James Frazer's note on that passage (vol. iii pp. 336-42; condensed in his L.C.L. edition, pp. 411-13).

him confidently affirm it to be a Greek city, — which will be easy
when he shows that it is at once the most hospitable and friendly of
all cities, and when he bears in mind that the Aborigines were
Oenotrians, and these in turn Arcadians, and remembers those who
joined with them in their settlement, the Pelasgians who were
Argives by descent and came into Italy from Thessaly; and recalls,
moreover, the arrival of Evander and the Arcadians, who settled
round the Palatine hill, after the Aborigines had granted the place to
them; and also the Peloponnesians, who, coming along with
Hercules, settled upon the Saturnian hill; and, last of all, those who
left the Troad and were intermixed with the earlier settlers. For one
will find no nation that is more ancient or more Greek than these.
But the admixtures of the barbarians with the Romans, by which
the city forgot many of its ancient institutions, happened at a later
time. And it may well seem a cause of wonder to many who reflect
on the natural course of events that Rome did not become entirely
barbarized after receiving the Opicans, the Marsians, the Samnites,
the Tyrrhenians, the Bruttians and many thousands of Umbrians,
Ligurians, Iberians and Gauls, besides innumerable other nations,
some of whom came from Italy itself and some from other regions
and differed from one another both in their language and habits; for
their very ways of life, diverse as they were and thrown into turmoil
by such dissonance, might have been expected to cause many
innovations in the ancient order of the city. For many others by
living among barbarians have in a short time forgotten all their
Greek heritage, so that they neither speak the Greek language nor
observe the customs of the Greeks nor acknowledge the same gods
nor have the same equitable laws (by which most of all the spirit of
the Greeks differs from that of the barbarians) nor agree with them
in anything else whatever that relates to the ordinary intercourse of
life. Those Achaeans who are settled near the Euxine sea are a
sufficient proof of my contention; for, though originally Eleans, of a

nation the most Greek of any, they are now the most savage of all barbarians.[233]

90 The language spoken by the Romans is neither utterly barbarous nor absolutely Greek, but a mixture, as it were, of both, the greater part of which is Aeolic;[234] and the only disadvantage they have experienced from their intermingling with these various nations is that they do not pronounce all their sounds properly. But all other indications of a Greek origin they preserve beyond any other colonists. For it is not merely recently, since they have enjoyed the full tide of good fortune to instruct them in the amenities of life, that they have begun to live humanely; nor is it merely since they first aimed at the conquest of countries lying beyond the sea, after overthrowing the Carthaginian and Macedonian empires, but rather from the time when they first joined in founding the city, that they have lived like Greeks; and they do not attempt anything more illustrious in the pursuit of virtue now than formerly. I have innumerable things to say upon this subject and can adduce many arguments and present the testimony of credible authors; but I reserve all this for the account I purpose to write of their government.[235] I shall now resume the thread of my narrative, after

233 These Asiatic Achaeans were a barbarian people of the Caucasus, whose name was made to coincide with that of the Greek Achaeans; hence the belief arose that they were an offshoot of the latter. Strabo connected them either with the Boeotian Orchomenus (ix. 2, 42) or with Phthiotis (xi. 2,12); other writers do not go into the same detail. The name "Eleans" in the text must be regarded as very uncertain; see the critical note.

234 Dionysius is probably thinking particularly of the letter digamma (*cf.* p. 26, n. 56) which Quintilian (i. 4, 8; i. 7, 26) calls the Aeolic letter, and the preservation in Aeolic, as well as Doric, of the original ā, as in φάμα (Lat. *fāma*), a, as in μάτηρ (Lat. *māter*), as contrasted with the Ionic φήμη, μήτηρ. Quintilian, too, regards the Aeolic dialect as being closest to Latin (i. 6, 31).

235 See especially vii. 70 ff., where Dionysius reminds the reader of the promise made here. As contrasted with Book I, which deals with the origin of the Romans, all the rest of the work could be thought of as an account of their government.

prefacing to the following Book a recapitulation of what is contained in this.

Book II

1 The city of Rome is situated in the western part of Italy near the river Tiber, which empties into the Tyrrhenian sea about midway along the coast; from the sea the city is distant one hundred and twenty stades. Its first known occupants were certain barbarians, natives of the country, called Sicels, who also occupied many other parts of Italy and of whom not a few distinct memorials are left even to our times; among other things there are even some names of places said to be Sicel names, which show that this people formerly dwelt in the land. They were driven out by the Aborigines, who occupied the place in their turn; these were descendants of the Oenotrians who inhabited the seacoast from Tarentum to Posidonia. They were a band of holy youths consecrated to the gods according to their local custom and sent out by their parents, it is said, to inhabit the country which Heaven should give them. The Oenotrians were an Arcadian tribe who had of their own accord left the country then called Lycaonia and now Arcadia, in search of a better land, under the leadership of Oenotrus, the son of Lycaon, from whom the nation received its name. While the Aborigines occupied this region the first who joined with them in their settlement were the Pelasgians, a wandering people who came from the country then called Haemonia and now Thessaly where they had lived for some time. After the Pelasgians came the Arcadians from the city of Pallantium, who had chosen as leader of their colony Evander, the son of Hermes and the nymph Themis. These built a town beside one of the seven hills that stands near the middle of Rome, calling the place Pallantium, from their mother-city in Arcadia. Not long afterwards, when Hercules came into Italy on his return home with his army from Erytheia, a certain part of his force, consisting of Greeks, remained behind and settled near

Pallantium, beside another of the hills that are now inclosed within the city. This was then called by the inhabitants Saturnian hill, but is now called the Capitoline hill by the Romans. The greater part of these men were Epeans who had abandoned their city in Elis after their country had been laid waste by Hercules.

2 In the sixteenth generation after the Trojan war the Albans united both these places into one settlement, surrounding them with a wall and a ditch. For until then there were only folds for cattle and sheep and quarters of the other herdsmen, as the land round about yielded plenty of grass, not only for winter but also for summer pasture, by reason of the rivers that refresh and water it. The Albans were a mixed nation composed of Pelasgians, of Arcadians, of the Epeans who came from Elis, and, last of all, of the Trojans who came into Italy with Aeneas, the son of Anchises and Aphroditê, after the taking of Troy. It is probable that a barbarian element also from among the neighbouring peoples or a remnant of the ancient inhabitants of the place was mixed with the Greek. But all these people, having lost their tribal designations, came to be called by one common name, Latins, after Latinus, who had been king of this country. The walled city, then, was built by these tribes in the four hundred and thirty-second year after the taking of Troy, and in the seventh Olympiad.[1] The leaders of the colony were twin brothers of the royal family, Romulus being the name of one and Remus of the other. On the mother's side they were descended from Aeneas and were Dardanidae; it is hard to say with certainty who their father was, but the Romans believe them to have been the sons of Mars. However, they did not both continue to be leaders of the colony, since they quarrelled over the command; but after one of them had been slain in the battle that ensued, Romulus, who survived, became the founder of the city and called it after his own name. The great

---

[1] 751 B.C.

numbers of which the colony had originally consisted when sent out with him were now reduced to a few, the survivors amounting to three thousand foot and three hundred horse.

3 When, therefore, the ditch was finished, the rampart completed and the necessary work on the houses done, and the situation required that they should consider also what form of government they were going to have, Romulus called an assembly of the people by the advice of his grandfather, who had instructed him what to say, and told them that the city, considering that it was newly built, was sufficiently adorned both with public and private buildings; but he asked them all to bear in mind that these were not the most valuable things in cities. For neither in foreign wars, he said, are deep ditches and high ramparts sufficient to give the inhabitants an undisturbed assurance of their safety, but guarantee one thing only, namely, that they shall suffer no harm through being surprised by an incursion of the enemy; nor, again, when civil commotions afflict the State, do private houses and dwellings afford anyone a safe retreat. For these have been contrived by men for the enjoyment of leisure and tranquillity in their lives, and with them neither those of their neighbours who plot against them are prevented from doing mischief nor do those who are plotted against feel any confidence that they are free from danger; and no city that has gained splendour from these adornments only has ever yet become prosperous and great for a long period, nor, again, has any city from a want of magnificence either in public or in private buildings ever been hindered from becoming great and prosperous. But it is other things that preserve cities and make them great from small beginnings: in foreign wars, strength in arms, which is acquired by courage and exercise; and in civil commotions, unanimity among the citizens, and this, he showed, could be most effectually achieved for the commonwealth by the prudent and just life of each citizen.

Those who practise warlike exercises and at the same time are masters of their passions are the greatest ornaments to their country, and these are the men who provide both the commonwealth with impregnable walls and themselves in their private lives with safe refuges; but men of bravery, justice and the other virtues are the result of the form of government when this has been established wisely, and, on the other hand, men who are cowardly, rapacious and the slaves of base passions are the product of evil institutions. He added that he was informed by men who were older and had wide acquaintance with history that of many large colonies planted in fruitful regions some had been immediately destroyed by falling into seditions, and others, after holding out for a short time, had been forced to become subject to their neighbours and to exchange their more fruitful country for a worse fortune, becoming slaves instead of free men; while others, few in numbers and settling in places that were by no means desirable, had continued, in the first place, to be free themselves, and, in the second place, to command others; and neither the successes of the smaller colonies nor the misfortunes of those that were large were due to any other cause than their form of government. If, therefore, there had been but one mode of life among all mankind which made cities prosperous, the choosing of it would not have been difficult for them; but, as it was, he understood there were many types of government among both the Greeks and barbarians, and out of all of them he heard three especially commended by those who had lived under them, and of these systems none was perfect, but each had some fatal defects inherent in it, so that the choice among them was difficult. He therefore asked them to deliberate at leisure and say whether they would be governed by one man or by a few, or whether they would establish laws and entrust the protection of the public interests to the whole body of the people. "And whichever form of government you establish," he said, "I am ready to comply with your desire, for I neither consider myself unworthy to command nor refuse to obey. So far as honours are concerned, I am satisfied with those you have conferred on me, first, by appointing me leader of the colony, and, again, by giving my name to the city. For of these neither a foreign war nor civil dissension nor time, that destroyer of all that is excellent, nor any other stroke of hostile fortune can deprive me; but both in life and in death these honours will be mine to enjoy for all time to come."

4 Such was the speech that Romulus, following the instructions of his grandfather, as I have said, made to the people. And they, having consulted together by themselves, returned this answer: "We have no need of a new form of government and we are not going to change the one which our ancestors approved of as the best and handed down to us. In this we show both a deference for the judgment of our elders, whose superior wisdom we recognize in establishing it, and our own satisfaction with our present condition. For we could not reasonably complain of this form of government, which has afforded us under our kings the greatest of human blessings — liberty and the rule over others. Concerning the form of government, then, this is our decision; and to this honour we conceive none has so good a title as you yourself by reason both of your royal birth and of your merit, but above all because we have had you as the leader of our colony and recognize in you great ability and great wisdom, which we have seen displayed quite as much in your actions as in your words." Romulus, hearing this, said it was a great satisfaction to him to be judged worthy of the kingly office by his fellow men, but that he would not accept the honour until Heaven, too, had given its sanction by favourable omens.

5 And when the people approved, he appointed a day on which he proposed to consult the auspices concerning the sovereignty; and when the time was come, he rose at break of day and went forth from his tent. Then, taking his stand under the open sky in a clear space and first offering the customary sacrifice, he prayed to King Jupiter and to the other gods whom he had chosen for the patrons of the colony, that, if it was their pleasure he should be king of the city, some favourable signs might appear in the sky. After this prayer a flash of lightning darted across the sky from the left to the right. Now the Romans look upon the lightning that passes from the left to the right as a favourable omen, having been thus instructed either by the Tyrrhenians or by their own ancestors. Their reason is, in my opinion, that the best seat and station for those who take the auspices is that which looks toward the east, from whence both the sun and the moon rise as well as the planets and fixed stars; and the revolution of the firmament, by which all things contained in it are sometimes above the earth and sometimes beneath it, begins its circular motion thence. Now to those who look toward the east the parts[2] facing toward the north are on the left and those extending toward the south are on the right, and the former are by nature more honourable than the latter. For in the northern parts the pole of the axis upon which the firmament turns is elevated, and of the five zones which girdle the sphere the one called the arctic zone is always visible on this side; whereas in the southern parts the other zone, called the antarctic, is depressed and invisible on that side. So it is reasonable to assume that those signs in the heavens and in mid-air are the best which appear on the best side; and since the parts that are turned toward the east have preëminence over the western parts, and, of the eastern parts themselves, the northern are higher than the southern, the former would seem to be the best. But some relate that the ancestors of the Romans from very early times, even before they had learned it from the Tyrrhenians, looked upon the lightning that came from the left as a favourable omen. For they say that when Ascanius, the son of Aeneas, was warred upon and

2   "Parts" in this chapter means regions of the sky.

besieged by the Tyrrhenians led by their king Mezentius, and was upon the point of making a final sally out of the town, his situation being now desperate, he prayed with lamentations to Jupiter and to the rest of the gods to encourage this sally with favourable omens, and thereupon out of a clear sky there appeared a flash of lightning coming from the left; and as this battle had the happiest outcome, this sign continued to be regarded as favourable by his posterity.

6 When Romulus, therefore, upon the occasion mentioned had received the sanction of Heaven also, he called the people together in assembly; and having given them an account of these omens, he was chosen king by them and established it as a custom, to be observed by all his successors, that none of them should accept the office of king or any other magistracy until Heaven, too, had given its sanction. And this custom relating to the auspices long continued to be observed by the Romans, not only while the city was ruled by kings, but also, after the overthrow of the monarchy, in the elections of their consuls, praetors and other legal magistrates; but it has fallen into disuse in our days except as a certain semblance of it remains merely for form's sake. For those who are about to assume the magistracies pass the night out of doors, and rising at break of day, offer certain prayers under the open sky; whereupon some of the augurs present, who are paid by the State, declare that a flash of lightning coming from the left has given them a sign, although there really has not been any. And the others, taking their omen from this report, depart in order to take over their magistracies, some of them assuming this alone to be sufficient, that no omens have appeared opposing or forbidding their intended action, others acting even in opposition to the will of the god; indeed, there are times when they resort to violence and rather seize than receive the magistracies. Because of such men many armies of the Romans have been utterly destroyed on land, many fleets have been lost with all their people at sea, and other great and dreadful reverses have befallen the commonwealth, some in foreign wars and others in civil dissensions. But the most remarkable and the greatest instance happened in my time when Licinius Crassus, a man inferior to no commander of his age, led his army against the Parthian nation contrary to the will of Heaven and in contempt of the innumerable omens that opposed his expedition. But to tell about the contempt of the divine power that prevails among some people in these days would be a long story.

7 Romulus, who was thus chosen king by both men and gods, is allowed to have been a man of great military ability and personal bravery and of the greatest sagacity in instituting the best kind of government. I shall relate such of his political and military achievements as may be thought worthy of mention in a history; and first I shall speak of the form of government that he instituted, which I regard as the most self-sufficient of all political systems both for peace and for war. This was the plan of it: He divided all the people into three groups, and set over each as leader its most distinguished man. Then he subdivided each of these three groups into ten others, and appointed as many of the bravest men to be the leaders of these also. The larger divisions he called tribes and the smaller *curiae*, as they are still termed even in our day. These names may be translated into Greek as follows: a tribe by *phylê* and *trittys*, and a *curia* by *phratra* and *lochos*;[3] the commanders of the tribes,

3   Dionysius is here thinking of these divisions of the people both as political and military units. The ordinary Greek equivalent of "tribe" is **phylê**, but etymologically **trittys** is probably the same word as *tribus*, both originally meaning a "third"; in actual practice, however, **trittys** was used of the third of a tribe. **Phratra** or **phratria**, "brotherhood" or "clan," was also the third of a tribe, and the **phratries** in their organization and rites offer a number of parallels to the *curiae* (cf. chap. 23). **Lochos** is a military term, "company," of indefinite size. The **phylarchoi** were the commanders of the cavalry contingents furnished by each tribe, and the **lochagoi** were infantry captains. The **trittyarchoi** and **phratriarchoi** were simply the heads of their respective political divisions.

whom the Romans call tribunes, by *phylarchoi* and *trittyarchoi*, and the commanders of the *curiae*, whom they call *curiones*, by *phratriarchoi* and *lochagoi*. These *curiae* were again divided by him into ten parts, each commanded by its own leader, who was called *decurio* in the native language. The people being thus divided and assigned to tribes and *curiae*, he divided the land into thirty equal portions and assigned one of them to each *curia*, having first set apart as much of it as was sufficient for the support of the temples and shrines and also reserved some part of the land for the use of the public. This was one division made by Romulus, both of the men and of the land, which involved the greatest equality for all alike.

8 But there was another division again of the men only, which assigned kindly services and honours in accordance with merit, of which I am now going to give an account. He distinguished those who were eminent for their birth, approved for their virtue and wealthy for those times, provided they already had children, from the obscure, the lowly and the poor. Those of the lower rank he called "plebeians" (the Greek would call them *démotikoi* or "men of the people"), and those of the higher rank "fathers," either because they had children or from their distinguished birth or for all these reasons. One may suspect that he found his model in the system of government which at that time still prevailed at Athens. For the Athenians had divided their population into two parts, the *eupatridai* or "well-born," as they called those who were of the noble families and powerful by reason of their wealth, to whom the government of the city was committed, and the *agroikoi* or "husbandmen," consisting of the rest of the citizens, who had no voice in public affairs, though in the course of time these, also, were admitted to

---

4   Both the Latin *plebeius* and the Greek **dêmotikos** are adjectives, "belonging to the *plebs* or **dêmos**."

5   Called also **geômoroi** or **geôrgoi**.

the offices.[6] Those who give the most probable account of the Roman government say it was for the reasons I have given that those men were called "fathers" and their posterity "patricians";[7] but others, considering the matter in the light of their own envy and desirous of casting reproach on the city for the ignoble birth of its founders, say they were not called patricians for the reasons just cited, but because these men only could point out their fathers,[8] — as if all the rest were fugitives and unable to name free men as their fathers. As proof of this they cite the fact that, whenever the kings thought proper to assemble the patricians, the heralds called them both by their own names and by the names of their fathers, whereas public servants summoned the plebeians *en masse* to the assemblies by the sound of ox horns. But in reality neither the calling of the patricians by the heralds is any proof of their nobility nor is the sound of the horn any mark of the obscurity of the plebeians; but the former was an indication of honour and the latter of expedition, since it was not possible in a short time to call every one of the multitude by name.

9 After Romulus had distinguished those of superior rank from their inferiors, he next established laws by which the duties of each were prescribed. The patricians were to be priests, magistrates and judges, and were to assist him in the management of public affairs, devoting themselves to the business of the city. The plebeians were excused from these duties, as being unacquainted with them and because of their small means wanting leisure to attend to them, but were to apply themselves to agriculture, the breeding of cattle and

---

6   Dionysius ignores the **dêmiourgoi** (artisans), the third class of the three into which Theseus, according to tradition, divided the population.

7   This is the explanation given by Livy (i. 8, 7).

8   *Cf.* Livy x. 8, 10 (part of a speech): *patricios . . . qui patrem ciere possent, id est nihil ultra quam ingenuos.* This derivation of *patricius* from *pater* and *cieo* is a good example of Roman etymologising at its worst.

the exercise of gainful trades. This was to prevent them from engaging in seditions, as happens in other cities when either the magistrates mistreat the lowly, or the common people and the needy envy those in authority He placed the plebeians as a trust in the hands of the patricians, by allowing every plebeian to choose for his patron any patrician whom he himself wished. In this he improved upon an ancient Greek custom that was in use among the Thessalians for a long time and among the Athenians in the beginning. For the former treated their clients with haughtiness, imposing on them duties unbecoming to free men; and whenever they disobeyed any of their commands, they beat them and misused them in all other respects as if had been slaves they had purchased. The Athenians called their clients *thêtes* or "hirelings," because they served for hire, and the Thessalians called theirs *penestai* or "toilers," by the very name reproaching them with their condition. But Romulus not only recommended the relationship by a handsome designation, calling this protection of the poor and lowly a "patronage," but he also assigned friendly offices to both parties, thus making the connexion between them a bond of kindness befitting fellow citizens.

10 The regulations which he then instituted concerning patronage and which long continued in use among the Romans were as follows: It was the duty of the patricians to explain to their clients the laws, of which they were ignorant; to take the same care of them when absent as present, doing everything for them that fathers do for their sons with regard both to money and to the contracts that related to money; to bring suit on behalf of their clients when they were wronged in connexion with contracts, and to defend them against any who brought charges against them; and, to put the matter briefly, to secure for them both in private and in public affairs all that tranquillity of which they particularly stood in need. It was the duty of the clients to assist their patrons in providing dowries for their daughters upon their marriage if the fathers had not sufficient means; to pay their ransom to the enemy if any of them or of their children were taken prisoner; to discharge out of their own purses their patrons' losses in private suits and the pecuniary fines which they were condemned to pay to the State, making these contributions to them not as loans but as thank-offerings; and to share with their patrons the costs incurred in their magistracies and dignities[9] and other public expenditures, in the same manner as if they were their relations. For both patrons and clients alike it was impious and unlawful to accuse each other in law-suits or to bear witness or to give their votes against each other or to be found in the number of each other's enemies; and whoever was convicted of doing any of these things was guilty of treason by virtue of the law sanctioned by Romulus, and might lawfully be put to death by any man who so wished as a victim devoted to the Jupiter of the infernal regions.[10] For it was customary among the Romans, whenever they wished to put people to death without incurring any penalty, to devote their persons to some god or other, and particularly to the gods of the lower world; and this was the course what Romulus then adopted. Accordingly, the connexions between the clients and patrons continued for many generations, differing in no wise from the ties of blood-relationship and being handed down to their children's children. And it was a matter of great praise to men of illustrious families to have as many clients as possible and not only to preserve the succession of hereditary patronages but also by their own merit to acquire others. And it is incredible how great the contest of goodwill was between the

---

9   The word γερηφορία should mean literally the "bearing, or enjoyment, of privileges," hence a "position of honour" or a "dignity." Presumably the reference is to priesthoods.

10   *i.e.* Dis or Pluto.

patrons and clients, as each side strove not to be outdone by the other in kindness, the clients feeling that they should render all possible services to their patrons and the patrons wishing by all means not to occasion any trouble to their clients and accepting no gifts of money. So superior was their manner of life to all pleasure; for they measured their happiness by virtue, not by fortune.

11 It was not only in the city itself that the plebeians were under the protection of the patricians, but every colony of Rome and every city that had joined in alliance and friendship with her and also every city conquered in war had such protectors and patrons among the Romans as they wished. And the senate has often referred the controversies of these cities and nations to their Roman patrons and regarded their decisions binding. And indeed, so secure was the Romans' harmony, which owed its birth to the regulations of Romulus, that they never in the course of six hundred and thirty years[11] proceeded to bloodshed and mutual slaughter, though many great controversies arose between the populace and their magistrates concerning public policy, as is apt to happen in all cities, whether large or small; but by persuading and informing one another, by yielding in some things and gaining other things from their opponents, who yielded in turn, they settled their disputes in a manner befitting fellow citizens. But from the time that Gaius Gracchus, while holding the tribunician power, destroyed the harmony of the government they have been perpetually slaying and banishing one another from the city and refraining from no irreparable acts in order to gain the upper hand. However, for the narration of these events another occasion will be more suitable.

---

11 Dionysius ignores the bloodshed in connexion with the slaying of Tiberius Gracchus in 133 and the execution of many Gracchans that followed. The overthrow of Gaius Gracchus occurred at the very beginning of the year 121, which was the year 631 of the City according to Dionysius' reckoning.

12 As[12] soon as Romulus had regulated these matters he determined to appoint senators to assist him in administering the public business, and to this end he chose a hundred men from among the patricians, selecting them in the following manner. He himself appointed one, the best out of their whole number, to whom he thought fit to entrust the government of the city[13] whenever he himself should lead the army beyond the borders. He next ordered each of the tribes to choose three men who were then at the age of greatest prudence and were distinguished by their birth. After these nine were chosen he ordered each *curia* likewise to name three patricians who were the most worthy. Then adding to the first nine, who had been named by the tribes, the ninety who were chosen by the *curiae*, and appointing as their head the man he himself had first selected, he completed the number of a hundred senators. The name of this council may be expressed in Greek by *gerousia* or "council of elders," and it is called by the Romans to this day;[14] but whether it received its name from the advanced age of the men who were appointed to it or from their merit, I cannot say for certain. For the ancients used to call the older men and those of greatest merit *gerontes* or "elders." The members of the senate were called Conscript[15] Fathers, and they retained that name down to my time. This council, also, was a Greek institution. At any rate, the Greek kings, both those who inherited the realms of their ancestors and those who were elected by the people themselves to be their rulers, had a council composed of the best men, as both Homer and the most ancient of the poets testify; and the authority of the ancient kings was not arbitrary and absolute as it is in our days.

---

12 *Cf.* Livy i. 8, 7.
13 The reference is to the *praefectus urbi.*
14 *i.e. senatus.*
15 Literally, "enrolled." For the usual explanation of *Patres Conscripti* see Livy ii. 1, 11.

13 After[16] Romulus had also instituted the senatorial body, consisting of the hundred men, he perceived, we may suppose, that he would also require a body of young men whose services he could use both for the guarding of his person and for urgent business, and accordingly he chose three hundred men, the most robust of body and from the most illustrious families, whom the *curiae* named in the same manner that they had named the senators, each *curia* choosing ten young men; and these he kept always about his person. They were all called by one common name, *celeres*; according to most writers this was because of the "celerity" required in the services they were to perform (for those who are ready and quick at their tasks the Romans call *celeres*), but Valerius Antias says that they were thus named after their commander. For among them, also, the most distinguished man was their commander; under him were three centurions, and under these in turn were others who held the inferior commands. In the city these *celeres* constantly attended Romulus, armed with spears, and executed his orders; and on campaigns they charged before him and defended his person. And as a rule it was they who gave a favourable issue to the contest, as they were the first to engage in battle and the last of all to desist. They fought on horseback where there was level ground favourable for cavalry manoeuvres, and on foot where it was rough and inconvenient for horses. This custom Romulus borrowed, I believe, from the Lacedaemonians, having learned that among them, also, three hundred of the noblest youths attended the kings as their guards and also as their defenders in war, fighting both on horseback and on foot.

14 Having made these regulations, he distinguished the honours and powers which he wished each class to have. For the king he had reserved these prerogatives: in the first place, the supremacy in

---

16 *Cf.* Livy i.15, 8.

religious ceremonies and sacrifices and the conduct of everything relating to the worship of the gods; secondly, the guardianship of the laws and customs of the country and the general oversight of justice in all cases, whether founded on the law of nature or the civil law; he was also the judge in person the greatest crimes, leaving the lesser to the senators, but seeing to it that no error was made in their decisions; he was to summon the senate and call together the popular assembly, to deliver his opinion first and carry out the decision of the majority. These prerogatives he granted to the king and, in addition, the absolute command in war. To the senate he assigned honour and authority as follows: to deliberate and give their votes concerning everything the king should refer to them, the decision of the majority to prevail. This also Romulus took over from the constitution of the Lacedaemonians; for their kings, too, did not have arbitrary power to do everything they wished, but the *gerousia* exercised complete control of public affairs. To the populace he granted these three privileges: to choose magistrates, to ratify laws, and to decide concerning war whenever the king left the decision to them; yet even in these matters their authority was not unrestricted, since the concurrence of the senate was necessary to give effect to their decisions. The people did not give their votes all at the same time, but were summoned to meet by *curiae,* and whatever was resolved upon by the majority of the *curiae* was reported to the senate. But in our day this practice is reversed, since the senate does not deliberate upon the resolutions passed by the people, but the people have full power over the decrees of the senate; and which of the two customs is better I leave it open to others to determine. By this division of authority not only were the civil affairs administered in a prudent and orderly manner, but the business of war also was carried on with dispatch and strict obedience. For whenever the king thought proper to lead out his army there was then no necessity for tribunes to be chosen by tribes, or centurions by centuries, or commanders of the horse appointed, nor was it necessary for the army to be numbered or to be divided into centuries or for every man to be assigned to his appropriate post. But the king gave his orders to the tribunes and these to the centurions and they in turn to the decurions, each of whom led out those who were under his command; and whether the whole army or part of it was called, at a single summons they presented themselves ready with arms in hand at the designated post.

15 By these institutions Romulus sufficiently regulated and suitably disposed the city both for peace and for war: and he made it large and populous by the following means. In the first place, he obliged the inhabitants to bring up all their male children and the first-born of the females, and forbade them to destroy any children under three years of age unless they were maimed or monstrous from their very birth. These he did not forbid their parents to expose, provided they first showed them to their five nearest neighbours and these also approved. Against those who disobeyed this law he fixed various penalties, including the confiscation of half their property. Secondly, finding that many of the cities in Italy were very badly governed, both by tyrannies and by oligarchies, he undertook to welcome and attract to himself the fugitives from these cities, who were very numerous, paying no regard either to their calamities or to their fortunes, provided only they were free men. His purpose was to increase the power of the Romans and to lessen that of their neighbours; but he invented a specious pretext for his course, making it appear that he was showing honour to a god. For he consecrated the place between the Capitol and the citadel which is now called in the language of the Romans "the space between the two groves,"[17] — a term that was really descriptive at that time of the actual conditions, as the place was shaded by thick woods on

---

17 *inter duos lucos*; *cf.* Livy i. 8, 5-6.

both sides where it joined the hills, — and made it an asylum for suppliants. And built a temple there, — but to what god or divinity he dedicated it I cannot say for certain, — he engaged, under the colour of religion, to protect those who fled to it from suffering any harm at the hands of their enemies; and if they chose to remain with him, he promised them citizenship and a share of the land he should take from the enemy. And people came flocking thither from all parts, fleeing from their calamities at home; nor had they afterwards any thought of removing to any other place, but were held there by daily instances of his sociability and kindness.

16 There was yet a third policy of Romulus, which the Greeks ought to have practised above all others, it being, in my opinion, the best of all political measures, as it laid the most solid foundation for the liberty of the Romans and was no slight factor in raising them to their position of supremacy. It was this: not to slay all the men of military age or to enslave the rest of the population of the cities captured in war or to allow their land to go back to pasturage for sheep, but rather to send settlers thither to possess some part of the country by lot and to make the conquered cities Roman colonies, and even to grant citizenship to some of them. By these and other like measures he made the colony great from a small beginning, as the actual results showed; for the number of those who joined with him in founding Rome did not amount to more than three thousand foot nor quite to three hundred horse, whereas he left behind him when he disappeared from among men forty-six thousand foot and about a thousand horse. Romulus having instituted these measures, not alone the kings who ruled the city after him but also the annual magistrates after them pursued the same policy, with occasional additions, so successfully that the Roman people became inferior in numbers to none of the nations that were accounted the most populous.

Book II

17 When I compare the customs of the Greeks with these, I can find no reason to extol either those of the Lacedaemonians or of the Thebans or of the Athenians, who pride themselves most on their wisdom; all of whom, jealous of their noble birth and granting citizenship to none or to very few (I say nothing of the fact that some even expelled foreigners), not only received no advantage from this haughty attitude, but actually suffered the greatest harm because of it. Thus, the Spartans after their defeat at Leuctra,[18] where they lost seventeen hundred men, were no longer able to restore their city to its former position after that calamity, but shamefully abandoned their supremacy And the Thebans and Athenians through the single disaster at Chaeronea[19] were deprived by the Macedonians not only of the leadership of Greece but at the same time of the liberty they had inherited from their ancestors. But Rome, while engaged in great wars both in Spain and Italy and employed in recovering Sicily and Sardinia, which had revolted, at a time when the situation in Macedonia and Greece had become hostile to her and Carthage was again contending for the supremacy, and when all but a small portion of Italy was not only in open rebellion but was also drawing upon her the Hannibalic war, as it was called, — though surrounded, I say, by so many dangers at one and the same time, Rome was so far from being overcome by these misfortunes that she derived from them a strength even greater than she had had before, being enabled to meet every danger, thanks to the number of her soldiers, and not, as some imagine, to the favour of Fortune; since for all of Fortune's assistance the city might have been utterly submerged by the single disaster at Cannae, where of six thousand horse only three hundred and seventy survived, and of eighty thousand foot enrolled in the army of the commonwealth little more than three thousand escaped.

18 371 B.C.
19 338 B.C.

18 It is not only these institutions of Romulus that I admire, but also those which I am going to relate. He understood that the good government of cities was due to certain causes which all statesmen prate of but few succeed in making effective: first, the favour of the gods, the enjoyment of which gives success to men's every enterprise; next, moderation and justice, as a result of which the citizens, being less disposed to injure one another, are more harmonious, and make honour, rather than the most shameful pleasures, the measure of their happiness; and, lastly, bravery in war, which renders the other virtues also useful to their possessors. And he thought that none of these advantages is the effect of chance, but recognized that good laws and the emulation of worthy pursuits render a State pious, temperate, devoted to justice, and brave in war. He took great care, therefore, to encourage these, beginning with the worship of the gods and genii. He established temples, sacred precincts and altars, arranged for the setting up of statues, determined the representations and symbols of the gods, and declared their powers, the beneficent gifts which they have made to mankind, the particular festivals that should be celebrated in honour of each god or genius, the sacrifices with which they delight to be honoured by men, as well as the holidays, festal assemblies, days of rest, and everything alike of that nature, in all of which he followed the best customs in use among the Greeks. But he rejected all the traditional myths concerning the gods that contain blasphemies or calumnies against them, looking upon these as wicked, useless and indecent, and unworthy, not only of the gods, but even of good men; and he accustomed people both to think and to speak the best of the gods and to attribute to them no conduct unworthy of their blessed nature.

19 Indeed, there is no tradition among the Romans either of Caelus being castrated by his own sons or of Saturn destroying his own offspring to secure himself from their attempts or of Jupiter dethroning Saturn and confining his own father in the dungeon of Tartarus, or, indeed, of wars, wounds, or bonds of the gods, or of their servitude among men. And no festival is observed among them as a day of mourning or by the wearing of black garments and the beating of breasts and the lamentations of women because of the disappearance of deities, such as the Greeks perform in commemorating the rape of Persephonê and the adventures of Dionysus and all the other things of like nature. And one will see among them, even though their manners are now corrupted, no ecstatic transports, no Corybantic frenzies, no begging under the colour of religion, no bacchanals[20] or secret mysteries, no all-night vigils of men and women together in the temples, nor any other mummery of this kind; but alike in all their words and actions with respect to the gods a reverence is shown such as is seen among neither Greeks nor barbarians. And, — the thing which I myself have marvelled at most, — notwithstanding the influx into Rome of innumerable nations which are under every necessity of worshipping their ancestral gods according to the customs of their respective countries, yet the city has never officially adopted any of those foreign practices, as has been the experience of many cities in the past; but, even though she has, in pursuance of oracles, introduced certain rites from abroad, she celebrates them in accordance with her own traditions, after banishing all fabulous

---

20 The Bacchic rites, introduced into Rome shortly after the close of the Second Punic War, were soon being celebrated with such licentious excesses and were accompanied by the plotting of so many crimes that the most drastic action was taken by the senate and consuls in 186 to punish the guilty and prevent all further celebration of the rites. An abstract of the decree passed by the senate (the *Senatus Consultum de Bacchanalibus*), contained in an official letter of the consuls to some local magistrates in southern Italy, is still preserved on a bronze tablet and is one of our earliest Latin documents. It appears in the *Corpus Inscript. Lat.* i. 196 and x.104, also in F. D. Allen's *Remnants of Early Latin*, pp. 28-31.

clap-trap. The rites of the Idaean goddess[21] are a case in point; for the praetors perform sacrifices and celebrated games in her honour every year according to the Roman customs, but the priest and priestess of the goddess are Phrygians, and it is they who carry her image in procession through the city, begging alms in her name according to their custom, and wearing figures upon their breasts[22] and striking their timbrels while their followers play tunes upon their flutes in honour of the Mother of the Gods. But by a law and decree of the senate no native Roman walks in procession through the city arrayed in a parti-coloured robe, begging alms or escorted by flute-players, or worships the god with the Phrygian ceremonies. So cautious are they about admitting any foreign religious customs and so great is their aversion to all pompous display that is wanting in decorum.

20 Let no one imagine, however, that I am not sensible that some of the Greek myths are useful to mankind, part of them explaining, as they do, the works of Nature by allegories, others being designed as a consolation for human misfortunes, some freeing the mind of its agitations and terrors and clearing away unsound opinions, and others invented for some other useful purpose. But, though I am as well acquainted as anyone with these matters, nevertheless my attitude toward the myths is one of caution, and I am more inclined to accept the theology of the Romans, when I consider that the advantages from the Greek myths are slight and cannot be of profit

---

21 The official title of Cybelê in Rome was *Mater Deum Magna Idaea*, commonly shortened to *Mater Magna* or *Mater Idaea*. The sacred black stone, which was her symbol, was brought from Pessinus in Asia Minor in 204 B.C., in response to a Sibylline oracle which declared that only thus could Hannibal be driven out of Italy. The games established in her honour were the Megalesia.

22 Polybius twice (xxi. 6, 7; 37, 5) refers to the "figures and pectorals" of the Galli, the priests of Cybelê; but we have no further information regarding them.

to many, but only to those who have examined the end for which they are designed; and this philosophic attitude is shared by few. The great multitude, unacquainted with philosophy, are prone to take these stories about the gods in the worse sense and to fall into one of two errors: they either despise the gods as buffeted by many misfortunes, or else refrain from none of the most shameful and lawless deeds when they see them attributed to the gods.

21 But let the consideration of these matters be left to those who have set aside the theoretical part of philosophy exclusively for their contemplation. To return to the government established by Romulus, I have thought the following things also worthy the notice of history. In the first place, he appointed a great number of persons to carry on the worship of the gods. At any rate, no one could name any other newly-founded city in which so many priests and ministers of the gods were appointed from the beginning. For, apart from those who held family priesthoods, sixty were appointed in his reign to perform by tribes and *curiae* the public sacrifices on behalf of the commonwealth; I am merely repeating what Terentius Varro, the most learned man of his age, his written in his *Antiquities*. In the next place, whereas others generally choose in a careless and inconsiderate manner those who are to preside over religious matters, some thinking fit to make public sale of this honour and others disposing of it by lot, he would not allow the priesthoods to be either purchased for money or assigned by lot, but made a law that each *curia* should choose two men over fifty years of age, of distinguished birth and exceptional merit, of competent fortune, and without any bodily defects; and he ordered that these should enjoy their honours, not for any fixed period, but for life, freed from military service by their age and from civil burdens by the law.

22 And because some rites were to be performed by women, others by children whose fathers and mothers were living,[23] to the end that these also might be administered in the best manner, he ordered that the wives of the priests should be associated with their husbands in the priesthood; and that in the case of any rites which men were forbidden by the law of the country to celebrate, their wives should perform them and their children should assist as their duties required; and that the priests who had no children should choose out of the other families of each *curia* the most beautiful boy and girl, the boy to assist in the rites till the age of manhood, and the girl so long as she remained unmarried. These arrangements also he borrowed, in my opinion, from the practices of the Greeks. For all the duties that are performed in the Greek ceremonies by the maidens whom they call *kanêphoroi* and *arrhéphoroi*[24] are performed by those whom the Romans call *tutulatae*,[25] who wear on their heads the same kind of crowns with which the statues of the Ephesian Artemis are adorned among the Greeks. And all the functions which among the Tyrrhenians and still earlier among the Pelasgians were performed by those they called *cadmili*[26] in the rites of the Curetes

---

23　*Patrimi matrimique*. This requirement, very familiar in Roman ritual, would not appear to have been so common among the Greeks. Allusions to such a παῖς ἀμφιθαλής are extremely rare, and then only in connexion with festivals or, in one instance, a wedding.

24　The "basket-bearers" and the "bearers of the symbols (?)" of Athena Polias. But there is great dispute as regards both the spelling and the meaning of the second word.

25　*Tutulatae* is due to Kiessling's conjecture. The feminine form does not occur elsewhere, but the masculine *tutulati* is attested by a gloss in Festus (pp. 354 f.). The word was descriptive of those who wore their hair plaited up in the shape of a cone (*tutulus*). This was an ancient style of arranging the hair, and was prescribed in the case of the *flaminica Dialis*.

26　*Cadmili* is another form resting on conjecture. Elsewhere the word occurs only once in the singular, as a proper name. Cadmilus (sometimes written Casmilus) was one of the Cabeiri worshipped in Samothrace and was identified with Hermes. The name was probably of Oriental origin.

and in those of the Great Gods, were performed in the same manner by those attendants of the priests who are now called by the Romans *camilli*.[27] Furthermore, Romulus ordered one soothsayer out of each tribe to be present at the sacrifices. This soothsayer we call *hieroskopos* or "inspector of the vitals," and the Romans, preserving something of the ancient name, *aruspex*.[28] He also made a law that all the priests and ministers of the gods should be chosen by the *curiae* and that their election should be confirmed by those who interpret the will of the gods by the art of divination.

23 After he had made these regulations concerning the ministers of the gods, he again, as I have stated,[29] assigned the sacrifices in an appropriate manner to the various *curiae*, appointing for each of them gods and genii whom they were always to worship, and determined the expenditures for the sacrifices, which were to be paid to them out of the public treasury. The members of each *curia* performed their appointed sacrifices together with their own priests, and on holy days they feasted together at their common table. For a banqueting-hall had been built for each *curia*, and in it there was consecrated, just as in the Greek *prytanea*, a common table for all the members of the *curia*. These banqueting-halls had the same name as the *curiae* themselves, and are called so to our day. This institution, it seems to me, Romulus took over from the practice of the Lacedaemonians in the case of their *phiditia*,[30] which were then the vogue. It would seem that Lycurgus, who had learned the institution

---

27 The *camilli* were free-born youths who assisted in the sacrifices of the *flamen Dialis*; in time, however, the term came to be applied to those assisting in other religious rites. The word was probably introduced from Etruria. Varro connected it with Casmilus (or Cadmilus), but most scholars to-day reject this derivation.

28 *Aruspex* or, more properly, *haruspex*, meant "inspector of the entrails"; but the element *haru-* is not, as Dionysius supposed, a corruption of *hiero-*.

29 Chap. 21, 2-3.

30 The Spartan name for συσσίτια, the public messes.

from the Cretans, introduced it at Sparta to the great advantage of his country; for he thereby in time of peace directed the citizens' lives toward frugality and temperance in their daily repasts, and in time of war inspired every man with a sense of shame and concern not to forsake his comrade with whom he had offered libations and sacrifices and shared in common rites. And not alone for his wisdom in these matters does Romulus deserve praise, but also for the frugality of the sacrifices that he appointed for the honouring of the gods, the greatest part of which, if not all, remained to my day, being still performed in the ancient manner. At any rate, I myself have seen in the sacred edifices repasts set before the gods upon ancient wooden tables, in baskets and small earthen plates, consisting of barley bread, cakes and spelt, with the first-offerings of some fruits, and other things of like nature, simple, cheap, and devoid of all vulgar display. I have seen also the libation wines that had been mixed, not in silver and gold vessels, but in little earthen cups and jugs, and I have greatly admired these men for adhering to the customs of their ancestors and not degenerating from their ancient rites into a boastful magnificence. There are, it is true, other institutions, worthy to be both remembered and related, which were established by Numa Pompilius, who ruled the city after Romulus, a man of consummate wisdom and of rare sagacity in interpreting the will of the gods, and of them I shall speak later; and yet others were added by Tullus Hostilius, the second[31] king after Romulus, and by all the kings who followed him. But the seeds of them were sown and the foundations laid by Romulus, who established the principal rites of their religion.

24 Romulus also seems to have been the author of that good discipline in other matters by the observance of which the Romans have kept their commonwealth flourishing for many generations; for

---

31 Literally the "third," counting inclusively.

he established many good and useful laws, the greater part of them unwritten, but some committed to writing. There is no need for me to mention most of them, but I will give a short account of those which I have admired most of all and which I have regarded as suitable to illustrate the character of the rest of this man's legislation, showing how austere it was, how averse to vice, and how closely it resembled the life of the heroic age. However, I will first observe that all who have established constitutions, barbarian as well as Greek, seem to me to have recognized correctly the general principle that every State, since it consists of many families, is most likely to enjoy tranquillity[32] when the lives of the individual citizens are untroubled, and to have a very tempestuous time when the private affairs of the citizens are in a bad way, and that every prudent statesman, whether he be a lawgiver or a king, ought to introduce such laws as will make the citizens just and temperate in their lives. Yet by what practices and by what laws this result may be accomplished they do not all seem to me to have understood equally well, but some of them seem to have gone widely and almost completely astray in the principal and fundamental parts of their legislation. For example, in the matter of marriage and commerce with women, from which the lawgiver ought to begin (even as Nature has begun thence to form our lives), some, taking their example from the beasts, have allowed men to have intercourse with women freely and promiscuously, thinking thus to free their lives from the frenzies of love, of save them from murderous jealousy, and to deliver them from many other evils which come upon both private houses and whole States through women. Others have banished this wanton and bestial intercourse from their States by joining a man to one woman; and yet for the preservation of the marriage ties and the chastity of women they have never attempted

---

32 Literally, "to sail right," that is, on an even keel. Here, as often in Greek
    writers, the State is likened to a ship.

to make even the slightest regulation whatsoever, but have given up the idea as something impracticable. Others have neither permitted sexual intercourse without marriage, like some barbarians, nor neglected the guarding of their women, like the Lacedaemonians, but have established many laws to keep them within bounds. And some have even appointed a magistrate to look after the good conduct of women; this provision, however, for their guarding was found insufficient and too weak to accomplish its purpose, being incapable of bringing the woman of un-virtuous nature to the necessity of a modest behaviour.

25 But Romulus, without giving either to the husband an action against his wife for adultery or for leaving his home without cause, or to the wife an action against her husband on the ground of ill-usage[33] or for leaving her without reason, and without making any laws for the returning or recovery of the dowry, or regulating anything of this nature, by a single law which effectually provides for all these things, as the results themselves have shown, led the women to behave themselves with modesty and great decorum. The law was to this effect, that a woman joined to her husband by a holy marriage should share in all his possessions and sacred rites. The ancient Romans designated holy and lawful marriages by the term *"farreate,"*[34] from the sharing of *far*, which we call *zea*;[35] for this was the ancient and, for a long time, the ordinary food of all the Romans, and their country produces an abundance of excellent spelt. And as we Greeks regard barley as the most ancient grain, and for that reason begin our sacrifices with barley-corns which we call

---

33 The term can also mean the mismanagement of her property.

34 *Farracius* or *farraceus* is an adjective, "of spelt." It is not used by any extant writer in connexion with marriages; but we do find the participles *farreatus* and *confarreatus* thus used, and especially the noun *confarreatio*. See note 37, p. 155.

35 Both words mean "spelt," a coarse variety of wheat. Farina?

oulai, so the Romans, in the belief that spelt is both the most valuable and the most ancient of grains, in all burnt offerings begin the sacrifice with that.[36] For this custom still remains, not having deteriorated into first-offerings of greater expense. The participation of the wives with their husbands in this holiest and first food and their union with them founded on the sharing of all their fortunes took its name[37] from this sharing of the spelt and forged the compelling bond of an indissoluble union, and there was nothing that could annul these marriages. This law obliged both the married women, as having no other refuge, to conform themselves entirely to the temper of their husbands, and the husbands to rule their wives as necessary and inseparable possessions. Accordingly, if a wife was virtuous and in all things obedient to her husband, she was mistress of the house to the same degree as her husband was master of it, and after the death of her husband she was heir to his property in the same manner as a daughter was to that of her father; that is, if he died without children and intestate, she was mistress of all that he left, and if he had children, she shared equally with them. But if she did any wrong, the injured party was her judge and determined the degree of her punishment. Other offences, however, were judged by her relations together with her husband; among them was adultery, or where it was found she had drunk wine — a thing which the Greeks would look upon as the least of all faults. For Romulus permitted them to punish both these acts with death, as being the gravest offences women could be guilty of, since he looked upon adultery as the source of reckless folly, and drunkenness as the source of adultery. And both these offences continued for a long time to be punished by the Romans with merciless severity. The wisdom of this law concerning wives is attested by the length of time it was in force; for it is agreed that during the space of five

36 The *mola salsa.*
37 *Confarreatio.*

hundred and twenty years no marriage was ever dissolved at Rome. But it is said that in the one hundred and thirty-seventh Olympiad, in the consulship of Marcus Pomponius and Gaius Papirius,[38] Spurius Carvilius, a man of distinction, was the first to divorce his wife,[39] and that he was obliged by the censors to swear that he had married for the purpose of having children (his wife, it seems, was barren); yet because of his action, though it was based on necessity, he was ever afterwards hated by the people.

26 These, then, are the excellent laws which Romulus enacted concerning women, by which he rendered them more observant of propriety in relation to their husbands. But those he established with respect to reverence and dutifulness of children toward their parents, to the end that they should honour and obey them in all things, both in their words and actions, were still more august and of greater dignity and vastly superior to our laws. For those who established the Greek constitutions set a very short time for sons to be under the rule of their fathers, some till the expiration of the third year after they reached manhood, others as long as they continued unmarried, and some till their names were entered in the public registers, as I have learned from the laws of Solon, Pittacus and Charondas, men celebrated for their great wisdom. The punishments, also, which they ordered for disobedience in children toward their parents were not grievous: for they permitted fathers to

---

38 231 B.C.

39 Gellius (iv. 3), Valerius Maximus (ii. 1, 4) and Plutarch (*Thes. et Rom.* 6) give this same tradition regarding Carvilius, but differ widely as to his date. Gellius is in virtual agreement with Dionysius, but Valerius gives 604 B.C. and Plutarch 524. Moreover, Valerius states elsewhere (ii. 9, 2) that L. Annius repudiated his wife in 307/6, a date confirmed by Livy (ix. 43, 25). It seems most probable that Dionysius and Gellius are wrong in their date. Scholars who accept this late date admit an earlier voluntary dissolution of marriage or assume that the ancient authors were thinking of different forms of marriage or of different grounds for divorce.

turn their sons out of doors and to disinherit them, but nothing further. But mild punishments are not sufficient to restrain the folly of youth and its stubborn ways or to give self-control to those who have been heedless of all that is honourable; and accordingly among the Greeks many unseemly deeds are committed by children against their parents. But the lawgiver of the Romans gave virtually full power to the father over his son, even during his whole life, whether he thought proper to imprison him, to scourge him, to put him in chains and keep him at work in the fields, or to put him to death, and this even though the son were already engaged in public affairs, though he were numbered among the highest magistrates, and though he were celebrated for his zeal for the commonwealth. Indeed, in virtue of this law men of distinction, while delivering speeches from the rostra hostile to the senate and pleasing to the people, have been dragged down from thence and carried away by their fathers to undergo such punishment as these thought fit; and while they were being led away through the Forum, none present, neither consul, tribune, nor the very populace, which was flattered by them and thought all power inferior to its own, could rescue them. I forbear to mention how many brave men, urged by their valour and zeal to proof some noble deed that their fathers had not ordered, have been put to death by those very fathers, as is related of Manlius Torquatus[40] and many others. But concerning them I shall speak in the proper place.

27 And not even at this point did the Roman lawgiver stop in giving the father power over the son, but he even allowed him to sell

40 The son of the Manlius Torquatus who was consul in 340 B.C. Just before the battle with the Latins at the foot of Mt. Vesuvius the consuls issued strict orders that no Roman should engage in single combat with a Latin on pain of death; but this youth could not resist the taunts of a Tusculan foe, and accepted his challenge. When he returned triumphantly with the spoils of his enemy, his father ordered his death. The portion of the *Antiquities* in which this incident was related is no longer extant.

his son, without concerning himself whether this permission might be regarded as cruel and harsher than was compatible with a natural affection. And, — a thing which anyone who has been educated in the lax manners of the Greeks may wonder at above all things and look upon as harsh and tyrannical, — he even gave leave to the father to make a profit by selling his son as often as three times, thereby giving greater power to the father over his son than to the master over his slaves. For a slave who has once been sold and has later obtained his liberty is his own master ever after, but a son who had once been sold by his father, if he became free, came again under his father's power, and if he was a second time sold and a second time freed, he was still, as at first, his father's slave; but after the third sale he was freed from his father. This law, whether written or unwritten, — I cannot say positively which, — the kings observed in the beginning, looking upon it as the best of all laws; and after the overthrow of the monarchy, when the Romans first decided to expose in the Forum for the consideration of the whole body of citizens all their ancestral customs and laws, together with those introduced from abroad, to the end that the rights of the people might not be changed as often as the powers of the magistrates, the decemvirs, who were authorized by the people to collect and transcribe the laws, recorded it among the rest, and it now stands on the fourth of the Twelve Tables, as they are called, which they then set up in the Forum. And that the decemvirs, who were appointed after three hundred years to transcribe these laws, did not first introduce this law among the Romans, but that, finding it long before in use, they dared not repeal it, I infer from many other considerations and particularly from the laws of Numa Pompilius, the successor of Romulus, among which there is recorded the following: "If a father gives his son leave to marry a woman who by the laws is to be the sharer of his sacred rites and possessions, he shall no longer have the power of selling his son." Now he would never have written this unless the father had by all former laws been allowed to sell his sons, But enough has been said concerning these matters, and I desire also to give a summary account of the other measures by which Romulus regulated the lives of the private citizens.

28 Observing that the means by which the whole body of citizens, the greater part of whom are hard to guide, can be induced to lead a life of moderation, to prefer justice to gain, to cultivate perseverance in hardships, and to look upon nothing as more valuable than virtue, is not oral instruction, but the habitual practice of such employments as lead to each virtue, and knowing that the great mass of men come to practise them through necessity rather than choice, and hence, if there is nothing to restrain them, return to their natural disposition, he appointed slaves and foreigners to exercise those trades that are sedentary and mechanical and promote shameful passions, looking upon them as the destroyers and corruptors both of the bodies and souls of all who practise them; and such trades were for a very long time held in disgrace by the Romans and were carried on by none of the native-born citizens. The only employments he left to free men were two, agriculture and warfare; for he observed that men so employed become masters of their appetite, are less entangled in illicit love affairs, and follow that kind of covetousness only which leads them, not to injure one another, but to enrich themselves at the expense of the enemy. But, as he regarded each of these occupations, when separate from the other, as incomplete and conducive to fault-finding, instead of appointing one part of the men to till the land and the other to lay waste the enemy's country, according to the practice of the Lacedaemonians,[41] he ordered the same persons to

---

41 The Spartan masters were the warrior class and the Helots were primarily tillers of the soil. Nevertheless, each Spartan soldier was accompanied to war by several Helots, who fought as light-armed troops.

exercise the employments both of husbandmen and soldiers. In time
of peace he accustomed them to remain at their tasks in the country,
except when it was necessary for them to come to market, upon
which occasions they were to meet in the city in order to traffic, and
to that end he appointed every ninth[42] day for the markets; and
when war came he taught them to perform the duties of soldiers
and not to yield to others either in the hardships or advantages that
war brought. For he divided equally among them the lands, slaves
and money that he took from the enemy, and thus caused them to
take part cheerfully in his campaigns.

29 In the case of wrongs committed by the citizens against one
another he did not permit the trials to be delayed, but caused them
to be held promptly, sometimes deciding the suits himself and
sometimes referring them to others; and he proportioned the
punishment to the magnitude of the crime. Observing, also, that
nothing restrains men from all evil actions so effectually as fear, he
contrived many things to inspire it, such as the place where he sat in
judgment in the most conspicuous part of the Forum, the very
formidable appearance of the soldiers who attended him, three
hundred in number, and the rods and axes borne by twelve men, [43]
who scourged in the Forum those whose offences deserved it and
beheaded others in public who were guilty of the greatest crimes.
Such then, was the general character of the government established
by Romulus; the details I have mentioned are sufficient to enable
one to form a judgment of the rest.

30 The[44] other deeds reported of this man, both in his wars and
at home, which may be thought deserving of mention in a history

---

42 "Every ninth day," reckoning inclusively, means every eighth day by modern
reckoning. The name of these market-days was *nundinae*, from *novem* and
dies.

43 The lictors; *cf.* Livy i. 8, 2-3.

44 For chaps. 30-31 *cf.* Livy i, 9.

are as follows. Inasmuch as many nations that were both numerous and brave in war dwelt round about Rome and none of them was friendly to the Romans, he desired to conciliate them by intermarriages, which, in the opinion of the ancients, was the surest method of cementing friendships; but considering that the cities in question would not of their own accord unite with the Romans, who were just getting settled together in one city, and who neither were powerful by reason of their wealth nor had performed any brilliant exploit, but that they would yield to force if no insolence accompanied such compulsion, he determined, with the approval of Numitor, his grandfather, to bring about the desired intermarriages by a wholesale seizure of virgins. After he had taken this resolution, he first made a vow to the god[45] who presides over secret counsels to celebrate sacrifices and festivals every year if his enterprise should succeed. Then, having laid his plan before the senate and gaining their approval, he announced that he would hold a festival and general assemblage in honour of Neptune, and he sent word round about to the nearest cities, inviting all who wished to do so to be present at the assemblage and to take part in the contests; for he was going to hold contests of all sorts, both between horses and between men. And when many strangers came with their wives and children to the festival, he first offered the sacrifices to Neptune and held the contests: then, on the last day, on which he was to dismiss the assemblage, he ordered the young men, when he himself should raise the signal, to seize all the virgins who had come to the spectacle, each group taking those they should first encounter, to keep them that night without violating their chastity and bring them to him the next day. So the young men divided themselves into several groups, and as soon as they saw the signal raised, fell to seizing the virgins; and straightway the strangers were in an uproar and fled, suspecting some greater mischief. The next day, when the

45 Consus. See p. 162 and note 47 (end).

virgins were brought before Romulus, he comforted them in their despair with the assurance that they had been seized, not out of wantonness, but for the purpose of marriage; for he pointed out that this was an ancient Greek custom[46] and that of all methods of contracting marriages for women it was the most illustrious, and he asked them to cherish those whom Fortune had given them for their husbands. Then counting them and finding their number to be six hundred and eighty-three, he chose an equal number of unmarried men to whom he united them according to the customs of each woman's country, basing the marriages on a communion of fire and water, in the same manner as marriages are performed even down to our times.

31 Some state that these things happened in the first year of Romulus' reign, but Gnaeus Gellius says it was in the fourth, which is more probable. For it is not likely that the head of a newly-built city would undertake such an enterprise before establishing its government. As regards the reason for the seizing of the virgins, some ascribe it to a scarcity of women, others to the seeking of pretext for war; but those who give the most plausible account — and with them I agree — attribute it to the design of contracting an alliance with the neighbouring cities, founded on affinity. And the Romans even to my day continued to celebrate the festival then instituted by Romulus, calling it the Consualia,[47] in the course of

46 It is to be regretted that Dionysius did not see fit to cite some specific instances of this practice from the Greek world. But probably he merely inferred such an early custom from some of the marriage rites of a later day, such as the procedure of the Spartan bridegrooms described by Plutarch (*Lycurg.* 15).

47 The Consualia was in origin a harvest festival held in honour of Consus, an ancient Italic god of agriculture. His altar was kept covered with earth except at these festivals (*cf.* Plutarch, *Rom.* 14, 3), perhaps to commemorate an ancient practice of storing the garnered grain underground or else to symbolize the secret processes of nature in the production of crops. At the Consualia horses and mules were given a holiday and crowned with flowers,

which a subterranean altar, erected near the Circus Maximus, is uncovered by the removal of the soil round about it and honoured with sacrifices and burnt-offerings of first-fruits and a course is run both by horses yoked to chariots and by single horses. The god to whom these honours are paid is called Consus by the Romans, being the same, according to some who render the name into our tongue, as Poseidon Seisichthon or the "Earth-shaker"; and they say that this god was honoured with a subterranean altar because he holds the earth.[48] I know also from hearsay another tradition, to the effect that the festival is indeed celebrated in honour of Neptune and the horse-races are held in his honour, but that the subterranean altar was erected later to a certain divinity whose name may not be uttered, who presides over and is the guardian of hidden counsels; for a secret altar has never been erected to Neptune, they say, in any part of the world by either Greeks or barbarians. But it is hard to say what the truth of the matter is.

32 When,[49] now, the report of the seizure of the virgins and of their marriage was spread among the neighbouring cities, some of these were incensed at the proceeding itself, though others, considering the motive from which it sprang and the outcome to which it led, bore it with moderation; but, at any rate, in the course of time it occasioned several wars, of which the rest were of small consequence, but that against the Sabines was a great and difficult one. All these wars ended happily, as the oracles had foretold to Romulus before he undertook the task, indicating as they did that

---

as we have already seen (i. 33, 2). Because of the races held on his festival the god came to be identified with Poseidon Hippios. The name Consus is evidently derived from the verb *condere* ("to store up"); but the Romans connected it with *consilium* and thought of him as a god of counsels and secret plans.

48 Or "upholds the earth." Compare his Greek epithet Γαιήοχος ("Earth-upholding").

49 For chaps. 32-36 *cf.* Livy i.10; 11, 1-5.

the difficulties and dangers would be great but that their outcome would be prosperous. The first cities that made war upon him were Caenina, Antemnae and Crustumerium. They put forward as a pretext the seizure of the virgins and their failure to receive satisfaction on their account; but the truth was that they were displeased at the founding of Rome and at its great and rapid increase and felt that they ought not to permit this city to grow up as a common menace to all its neighbours. For the time being, then, these cities were sending ambassadors to the Sabines, asking them to take command of the war, since they possessed the greatest military strength and were most powerful by reason of their wealth and were laying claim to the rule over their neighbours and inasmuch as they had suffered from the Romans' insolence quite as much as any of the rest; for the greater part of the virgins who had been seized belonged to them.

33 But when they found they were accomplishing nothing, since the embassies from Romulus opposed them and courted the Sabine people both by their words and by their actions, they were vexed at the waste of time — for the Sabines were forever affecting delays and putting off to distant dates the deliberation concerning the war — and resolved to make war upon the Romans by themselves alone, believing that their own strength, if the three cities joined forces, was sufficient to conquer one inconsiderable city. This was their plan: but they did not all assemble together promptly enough in one camp, since the Caeninenses, who seemed to be most eager in promoting the war, rashly set out ahead of the others. When these men, then, had taken the field and were wasting the country that bordered on their own, Romulus led out his army, and unexpectedly falling upon the enemy while they were as yet off their guard, he made himself master of their camp, which was but just completed. Then following close upon the heels of those who fled into the city, where the inhabitants had not as yet learned of the defeat of their forces, and finding the walls unguarded and the gates unbarred, he took the town by storm; and when the king of the Caeninenses met him with a strong body of men, he fought with him, and slaying him with his own hands, stripped him of his arms.

34 The town being taken in this manner, he ordered the prisoners to deliver up their arms, and taking such of their children for hostages as he thought fit, he marched against the Antemnates. And having conquered their army also, in the same manner as the other, by falling upon them unexpectedly while they were still dispersed in foraging, and having accorded the same treatment to the prisoners, he led his army home, carrying with him the spoils of those who had been slain in battle and the choicest part of the booty as an offering to the gods; and he offered many sacrifices besides. Romulus himself came last in the procession, clad in a purple robe and wearing a crown of laurel upon his head, and, that he might maintain the royal dignity, he rode in a chariot drawn by four horses.[50] The rest of the army, both foot and horse, followed, ranged in their several divisions, praising the gods in songs of their country and extolling their general in improvised verses. They were met by the citizens with their wives and children, who, ranging themselves on each side of the road, congratulated them upon their victory and expressed their welcome in every other way When the army entered the city, they found mixing bowls filled to the brim with wine and tables loaded down with all sorts of viands, which were placed before the most distinguished houses in order that all who pleased might take their fill. Such was the victorious procession, marked by the carrying of trophies and concluding with a sacrifice, which the Romans call a triumph, as it was first instituted by Romulus. But in

50 Plutarch (*Romulus* 16) corrects Dionysius on this point, claiming that the first Tarquin, or, according to some, Publicola, was the first to use a chariot in the triumphal procession.

our day the triumph had become a very costly and ostentatious pageant, being attended with a theatrical pomp that is designed rather as a display of wealth than as approbation of valour, and it has departed in every respect from its ancient simplicity. After the procession and the sacrifice Romulus built a small temple on the summit of the Capitoline hill to Jupiter whom the Romans call Feretrius; indeed, the ancient traces of it still remain, of which the longest sides are less than fifteen feet. In this temple he consecrated the spoils of the king of the Caeninenses, whom he had slain with his own hand. As for Jupiter Feretrius, to whom Romulus dedicated these arms, one will not err from the truth whether one wishes to call him *Tropaiouchos*, or *Skylophoros*, as some will have it, or, since he excels all things and comprehends universal nature and motion, *Hyperpheretês*.[51]

35 After the king had offered to the gods the sacrifices of thanksgiving and the first-fruits of victory, before entering upon any other business, he assembled the senate to deliberate with them in what manner the conquered cities should be treated, and he himself first delivered the opinion he thought the best. When all the senators who were present had approved of the counsels of their chief as both safe and brilliant and had praised all the other advantages that were likely to accrue from them to the commonwealth, not only for the moment but for all future time, he gave command for the assembling of all the women belonging to the race of the Antemnates and of the Caeninenses who had been seized with the rest. And when they had assembled, lamenting, throwing themselves at his feet and bewailing the calamities of their native cities, he commanded them to cease their lamentations and be silent, then

---

51   These three Greek words mean, respectively, "Bearer (or Receiver) of Trophies," "Bearer of Spoils," and "Supreme." Dionysius obviously derived *Feretrius* from *ferre* ("to bear"); but modern scholars agree with Propertius (iv. 10, 46) in connecting it with *ferire* ("to strike").

spoke to them as follows: "Your fathers and brothers and your entire cities deserve to suffer every severity for having preferred to our friendship a war that was neither necessary nor honourable. We, however, have resolved for many reasons to treat them with moderation; for we not only fear the vengeance of the gods, which ever threatens the arrogant, and dread the ill-will of men, but we are also persuaded that mercy contributes not a little to alleviate the common ills of mankind, and we realize that we ourselves may one day stand in need of that of others. And we believe that to you, whose behaviour towards your husbands has thus far been blameless, this will be no small honour and favour. We suffer this offence of theirs, therefore, to go unpunished and take from your fellow citizens neither their liberty nor their possessions nor any other advantages they enjoy; and both to those who desire to remain there and to those who wish to change their abode we grant full liberty to make their choice, not only without danger but without fear of repenting. But, to prevent their ever repeating their fault or the finding of any occasion to induce their cities to break off their alliance with us, the best means, we consider, and that which will at the same time conduce to the reputation and security of both, is for us to make those cities colonies of Rome and to send a sufficient number of our own people from here to inhabit them jointly with your fellow citizens. Depart, therefore, with good courage; and redouble your love and regard for your husbands, to whom your parents and brothers owe their preservation and your countries their liberty." The women, hearing this, were greatly pleased, and shedding many tears of joy, left the Forum; but Romulus sent a colony of three hundred men into each city, to whom these cities gave a third part of their lands to be divided among them by lot. And those of the Caeninenses and Antemnates who desired to remove to Rome they brought thither together with their wives and children, permitting them to retain their allotments of land and to take with them all their possessions; and the king immediately enrolled them, numbering not less than three thousand, in the tribes and the *curiae*, so that the Romans had then for the first time six thousand foot in all upon the register. Thus Caenina and Antemnae, no inconsiderable cities, whose inhabitants were of Greek origin (for the Aborigines had taken the cities from the Sicels and occupied them, these Aborigines being, as I said before, part of those Oenotrians who had come out of Arcadia),[52] after this war became Roman colonies.

36 Romulus, having attended to these matters, led out his army against the Crustumerians, who were better prepared than the armies of the other cities had been. And after he had reduced them both in a pitched battle and in an assault upon their city, although they had shown great bravery in the struggle, he did not think fit to punish them any further, but made this city also a Roman colony like the two former. Crustumerium was a colony of the Albans sent out many years before the founding of Rome. The fame of the general's valour in war and of his clemency to the conquered being spread through many cities, many brave men joined him, bringing with them considerable bodies of troops, who migrated with their whole families. From one of these leaders, who came from Tyrrhenia and whose name was Caelius, one of the hills, on which he settled, is to this day called the Caelian. Whole cities also submitted to him, beginning with Medullia, and became Roman colonies. But the Sabines, seeing these things, were displeased and blamed one another for not having crushed the power of the Romans while it was in its infancy, instead of which they were now to contend with it when it was greatly increased. They determined, therefore, to make amends for their former mistake by sending out an army of respectable size. And soon afterwards, assembling a

---

52 i. 13.

general council in the greatest and most famous city in the nation, called Cures, they voted for the war and appointed Titus, surnamed Tatius, the king of that city, to be their general. After the Sabines had come to this decision, the assembly broke up and all returned home to their several cities, where they busied themselves with their preparations for the war, planning to advance on Rome with a great army the following year.

37 In the meantime Romulus also was making the best preparations he could in his turn, realizing that he was to defend himself against a warlike people. With this in view, he raised the wall of the Palatine hill by building higher ramparts upon it as a further security to the inhabitants, and fortified the adjacent hills — the Aventine and the one now called the Capitoline — with ditches and strong palisades, and upon these hills he ordered the husbandmen with their flocks to pass the nights, securing each of them by a sufficient garrison; and likewise any other place that promised to afford them security he fortified with ditches and palisades and kept under guard. In the meantime there came to him a man of action and reputation for military achievements, named Lucumo, lately become his friend, who brought with him from the city of Solonium[53] a considerable body of Tyrrhenian mercenaries. There came to him also from the Albans, sent by his grandfather, a goodly number of soldiers with their attendants, and with them artificers for making engines of war; these men were adequately supplied with provisions, arms, and all necessary equipment. When everything was ready for the war on both sides, the Sabines, who planned to take the field at the beginning of spring, resolved first to send an embassy to the enemy

---

53 Solonium was an ancient city about twelve miles from Rome, near the Ostian Way. It disappeared at an early date, but its name survived in the *Solonius ager*. The statement of Dionysius is confirmed by Propertius iv. 1. 31, where the latest editions, following the Neapolitan MS., read *hinc Tities Ramnesque viri Luceresque Soloni* (instead of *coloni*).

both to ask for the return of the women and to demand satisfaction for their seizure, just so that they might seem to have undertaken the war from necessity when they failed to get justice, and they were sending the heralds for this purpose. Romulus, however, asked that the women, since they themselves were not unwilling to live with their husbands, should be permitted to remain with them; but he offered to grant the Sabines anything else they desired, provided they asked it as from friends and did not begin war. Thereupon the others, agreeing to none of his proposals, led out their army, which consisted of twenty-five thousand foot and almost a thousand horse. And the Roman army was not much smaller than that of the Sabines, the foot amounting to twenty thousand and the horse to eight hundred; it was encamped before the city in two divisions, one of them, under Romulus himself, being posted on the Esquiline hill, and the other, commanded by Lucumo, the Tyrrhenian, on the Quirinal, which did not as yet have that name.

38 Tatius,[54] the king of the Sabines, being informed of their preparations, broke camp in the night and led his army through the country, without doing any damage to the property in the fields, and before sunrise encamped on the plain that lies between the Quirinal and Capitoline hills. But observing all the posts to be securely guarded by the enemy and no strong position left for his army, he fell into great perplexity, not knowing what use to make of the enforced delay. While he was thus at his wit's end, he met with an unexpected piece of good fortune, the strongest of the fortresses being delivered up to him in the following circumstances. It seems that, while the Sabines were passing by the foot of the Capitoline to view the place and see whether any part of the hill could be taken within by surprise of or by force, they were observed from above by a maiden whose name was Tarpeia, the daughter of a distinguished

---

54 For chaps. 38-44 *cf.* Liv i. 11, 6-12, 10.

man who had been entrusted with the guarding of the place. This maiden, as both Fabius and Cincius relate, conceived a desire for the bracelets which the men wore on their left arms and for their rings; for at that time the Sabines wore ornaments of gold and were no less luxurious in their habits than the Tyrrhenians.[55] But according to the account given by Lucius Piso, the ex-censor, she was inspired by the desire of performing a noble deed, namely, to deprive the enemy of their defensive arms and thus deliver them up to her fellow citizens. Which of these accounts is the truer may be conjectured by what happened afterwards. This girl, therefore, sending out one of her maids by a little gate which was not known to be open, desired the king of the Sabines to come and confer with her in private, as if she had an affair of necessity and importance to communicate to him. Tatius, in the hope of having the place betrayed to him, accepted the proposal and came to the place appointed; and the maiden, approaching within speaking distance, informed him that her father had gone out of the fortress during the night on some business, but that she had the keys of the gates, and if they came in the night, she would deliver up the place to them upon condition that they gave her as a reward for her treachery the things which all the Sabines wore on their left arms. And when Tatius consented to this, she received his sworn pledge for the faithful performance of the agreement and gave him hers. Then having appointed, as the place to which the Sabines were to repair, the strongest part of the fortress, and the most unguarded hour of the night as the time for the enterprise, she returned without being observed by those inside.

39 So far all the Roman historians agree, but not in what follows. For Piso, the ex-censor, whom I mentioned before, says that a

---

55 It need hardly be pointed out how inconsistent this description of the Sabines is with the traditional view of their character as given below at the end of chapter 49.

messenger was sent out of the place by Tarpeia in the night to inform Romulus of the agreement she had made with the Sabines, in consequence of which she proposed, by taking advantage of the ambiguity of the expression in that agreement, to demand their defensive arms, and asking him at the same time to send a reinforcement to the fortress that night, so that the enemy together with their commander, being deprived of their arms, might be taken prisoners; but the messenger, he says, deserted to the Sabine commander and acquainted him with the designs of Tarpeia. Nevertheless, Fabius and Cincius say that no such thing occurred, but they insist that girl kept her treacherous compact. In what follows, however, all are once more in agreement. For they say that upon the arrival of the king of the Sabines with the flower of his army, Tarpeia, keeping her promise, opened to the enemy the gate agreed upon, and rousing the garrison, urged them to save themselves speedily by other exits unknown to the enemy, as if the Sabines were already masters of the place; that after the flight of the garrison the Sabines, finding the gates open, possessed themselves of the stronghold, now stripped of its guards, and that Tarpeia, alleging that she had kept her part of the agreement, insisted upon receiving the reward of her treachery according to the oaths.

40 Here again Piso says that, when the Sabines were ready to give the girl the gold they wore on their left arms, Tarpeia demanded of them their shields and not their ornaments. But Tatius resented the imposition and at the same time thought of an expedient by which he might not violate the agreement. Accordingly, he decided to give her the arms as the girl demanded, but to contrive that she should make no use of them; and immediately poising his shield, he hurled it at her with all his might, and ordered the rest to do the same; and thus Tarpeia, being pelted from all sides, fell under the number and force of the blows and died, overwhelmed by the shields. But Fabius attributes this fraud in the performance of the agreement to the Sabines; for they, being obliged by the agreement to give her the gold as she demanded, were angered at the magnitude of the reward and hurled their shields at her as if they had engaged themselves by their oaths to give her these. But what followed gives the greater appearance of truth to the statement of Piso. For she was honoured with a monument in the place where she fell and lies buried on the most sacred hill of the city and the Romans every year perform libations to her (I relate what Piso writes); whereas, if she had died in betraying her country to the enemy, it is not to be supposed that she would have received any of these honours, either from those whom she had betrayed or from those who had slain her, but, if there had been any remains of her body, they would in the course of time have been dug up and cast out of the city, in order to warn and deter others from committing the like crimes. But let everyone judge of the matters as he pleases.

41 As for Tatius and the Sabines, having become masters of a strong fortress and having without any trouble taken the greatest part of the Romans' baggage, they carried on the war thereafter in safety. And as the armies lay encamped at a short distance from each other and many occasions offered, there were many essays and skirmishes, which were not attended with any great advantages or losses to either side, and there were also two very severe pitched battles, in which all the forces were opposed to each other and there was great slaughter on both sides. For, as the time dragged along, they both came to the same resolution, namely, to decide the issue by a general engagement. Whereupon leaders of both armies, who were masters of the art of war, as well as common soldiers, trained in many engagements, advanced into the plain that lay between the two camps and performed memorable feats both in attacking and receiving the enemy as well as in rallying and renewing the fight on equal terms. Those who from the ramparts were spectators of this doubtful battle, which, often varying, favoured each side in turn, when their own men had the advantage, inspired them with fresh courage by their exhortations and songs of victory, and when they were hard pressed and pursued, prevented them by their prayers and lamentations from proving utter cowards; and thanks to these shouts of encouragement and entreaty the combatants were compelled to endure the perils of the struggle even beyond their strength. And so, after they had thus carried on the contest all that day without a decision, darkness now coming on, they both gladly retired to their own camps.

42 But on the following days they buried their dead, took care of the wounded and reinforced their armies; then, resolving to engaged in another battle, they met again in the same plain as before and fought till night. In this battle, when the Romans had the advantage on both wings (the right was commanded by Romulus himself and the left by Lucumo, the Tyrrhenian) but in the centre the battle remained as yet undecided, one man prevented the utter defeat of the Sabines and rallied their wavering forces to renew the struggle with the victors. This man, whose name was Mettius Curtius, was of great physical strength and courageous in action, but he was famous especially for his contempt of all fear and danger. He had been appointed to command those fighting in the centre of the line and was victorious over those who opposed him; but wishing to restore the battle in the wings also, where the Sabine troops were by now in difficulties and being forced back, he encouraged those about him, and pursuing such of the enemy's forces as were fleeing and scattered, he drove them back to the gates of the city. This obliged Romulus to leave the victory but half completed and to return and make a drive against the victorious troops of the enemy. Upon the departure of Romulus with his forces those of the Sabines who had been in trouble were once more upon equal terms with their opponents, and the whole danger was now centred round Curtius and his victorious troops. For some time the Sabines received the onset of the Romans and fought brilliantly, but when large numbers joined in attacking them, they gave way and began to seek safety in their camp, Curtius amply securing their retreat, so that they were not driven back in disorder, but retired without precipitation. For he himself stood his ground fighting and awaited Romulus as he approached; and there ensued a great and glorious engagement between the leaders themselves as they fell upon each other. But at last Curtius, having received many wounds and lost much blood, retired by degrees till he came to a deep lake in his rear which its difficult for him to make his way round, his enemies being massed on all sides of it, and impossible to pass through by reason of the quantity of mud on the marshy shore surrounding it and the depth of water that stood in the middle. When he came to the lake, he threw himself into the water, armed as he was, and Romulus, supposing that he would immediately perish in the lake, — moreover, it was not possible to pursue him through so much mud and water, — turned upon the rest of the Sabines. But Curtius with great difficulty got safely out of the lake after a time without losing his arms and was led away to the camp. This place is now filled up, but it is called from this incident the Lacus Curtius, being about in the middle of the Roman Forum.[56]

43 Romulus, while pursuing the others, had drawn near the Capitoline and had great hopes of capturing the stronghold, but being weakened by many other wounds and stunned by a severe blow from a stone which was hurled from the heights and hit him on the temple, he was taken up half dead by those about him and

---

56 *Cf.* Livy i. 13, 5.

carried inside the walls. When the Romans no longer saw their leader, they were seized with fear and the right wing turned to flight; but the troops that were posted on the left with Lucumo stood their ground for some time, encouraged by their leader, a man most famous for his warlike prowess and who had performed many exploits during the course of this war. But when he in his turn was pierced through the side with a javelin and fell through weakness, they also gave way; and thereupon the whole Roman army was in flight, and the Sabines, taking courage, pursued them up to the city. But as they were already drawing near the gates they were repulsed, when the youths whom the king had appointed to guard the walls sallied out against them with their forces fresh; and when Romulus, too, who by this time was in some degree recovered of his wound, came out to their assistance with all possible speed, the fortune of the battle quickly turned and veered strongly to the other side. For those who were fleeing recovered themselves from their late fear on the unexpected appearance of their leader, and reforming their lines, no longer hesitated to come to blows with the enemy; while the latter, who but now had been driving the fugitives into the city and thought there was nothing that could prevent them from taking the city itself by storm, when they saw this sudden and unexpected change, took thought for their own safety But they found it no easy matter to retreat to their camp, pursued as they were down from a height and through a hollow way, and in this rout they sustained heavy losses. And so, after they had thus fought that day without a decision and both had met with unexpected turns of fortune, the sun now being near his setting, they parted.

44 But during the following days the Sabines were taking counsel whether they should lead their forces back home, after doing all possible damage to the enemy's country, or should send for another army from home and still hold out obstinately until they should put an end to the war in the most honourable manner. They considered that it would be a bad thing for them to return home with the shame of having effected nothing or to stay there when none of their attempts succeeded according to their expectations. And to treat with the enemy concerning an accommodation, which they looked upon as the only honourable means of putting an end to the war, they conceived to be no more fitting for them than for the Romans. On the other side, the Romans were not less, but even more, perplexed than the Sabines what course to take in the present juncture. For they could not resolve either to restore the women or to retain them, believing that the former course involved an acknowledgment of defeat and that it would be necessary to submit to whatever else might be imposed upon them, and that the alternative course would necessitate their witnessing many terrible sights as their country was being laid waste and the flower of their youth destroyed; and, if they should treat with the Sabines for peace, they despaired of obtaining any moderate terms, not only for many other reasons, but chiefly because the proud and headstrong treat an enemy who resorts to courting them, not with moderation, but with severity.

45 While[57] both sides were consuming the time in these considerations, neither daring to renew the fight nor treating for peace, the wives of the Romans who were of the Sabine race and the cause of the war, assembling in one place apart from their husbands and consulting together, determined to make the first overtures themselves to both armies concerning an accommodation. The one who proposed this measure to the rest of the women was named Hersilia, a woman of no obscure birth among the Sabines. Some say that, though already married, she was seized with the others as supposedly a virgin; but those who give the most probable

---

57 For chaps. 45-47 *cf.* Livy i. 13.

account say that she remained with her daughter of her own free will, for according to them her only daughter was among those who had been seized. After the women had taken this resolution they came to the senate, and having obtained an audience, they made long pleas, begging to be permitted to go out to their relations and declaring that they had many excellent grounds for hoping to bring the two nations together and establish friendship between them. When the senators who were present in council with the king heard this, they were exceedingly pleased and looked upon it, in view of their present difficulties, as the only solution. Thereupon a decree of the senate was passed to the effect that those Sabine women who had children should, upon leaving them with their husbands, have permission to go as ambassadors to their countrymen, and that those who had several children should take along as many of them as they wished and endeavour to reconcile the two nations. After this the women went out dressed in mourning, some of them also carrying their infant children. When they arrived in the camp of the Sabines, lamenting and falling at the feet of those they met, they aroused great compassion in all who saw them and none could refrain from tears. And when the councillors had been called together to receive them and the king had command them to state their reasons for coming, Hersilia, who had proposed the plan and was at the head of the embassy, delivered a long and pathetic plea, begging them to grant peace to those who were interceding for their husbands and on whose account, she pointed out, the war had been undertaken. As to the terms, however, on which peace should be made, she said the leaders, coming together by themselves, might settle them with a view to the advantage of both parties.

46 After she had spoken thus, all the women with their children threw themselves at the feet of the king and remained prostrate till those who were present raised them from the ground and promised to do everything that was reasonable and in their power. Then, having ordered them to withdraw from the council and having consulted together, they decided to make peace. And first a truce was agreed upon between the two nations; then the kings met together and a treaty of friendship was concluded. The terms agreed upon by the two, which they confirmed by their oaths, were as follows: that Romulus and Tatius should be kings of the Romans with equal authority and should enjoy equal honours; that the city, preserving its name, should from its founder be called Rome; that each individual citizen should as before be called a Roman, but that the people collectively should be comprehended under one general appellation and from the city of Tatius[58] be called Quirites, and that all the Sabines who wished might live in Rome, joining in common rites with the Romans and being assigned to tribes and *curiae*. After they had sworn to this treaty and, to confirm their oaths, had erected altars near the middle of the Sacred Way, as it is called, they mingled together. And all the commanders returned home with their forces except Tatius, the king, and three persons of the most illustrious families, who remained at Rome and received those honours which their posterity after them enjoyed; these were Volusus[59] Valerius and Tallus, surnamed Tyrannius, with Mettius Curtius, the man who swam cross the lake with his arms, and with them there remained also their companions, relations and clients, no fewer in number than the former inhabitants.

47 Everything being thus settled, the kings thought proper, since the city had received a great increase of people, to double the number of the patricians by adding to the most distinguished

---

58 Cures; see chap. 36, 3; 48. Dionysius is giving the ordinary Roman derivation of Quirites. The word may, however, come directly from the Sabine *quiris* (chap. 48, end) and mean the "spear men."

59 The name should probably be Volesus, as spelled by Livy (i. 58, 6; ii.18, 6) and other Roman writers.

families others from among the new settlers equal in number to the old, and they called these "new patricians." Of these a hundred persons, chosen by the *curiae*, were enrolled with the original senators. Concerning these matters almost all the writers of Roman history agree. But some few differ regarding the number of the newly-enrolled senators, for they say it was not a hundred, but fifty, that were added to the senate. Concerning the honours, also, which the kings conferred on the women in return for having reconciled them, not all the Roman historians agree; for some write that, besides many other signal marks of honour which they bestowed upon them, they gave their names to the *curiae*, which were thirty, as I have said, that being the number of the women who went upon the embassy But Terentius Varro does not agree with them in this particular, for he says that Romulus gave the names to the *curiae* earlier than this, when he first divided the people, some of these names being taken from men who were their leaders and others from districts; and he says that the number of the women who went upon the embassy was not thirty, but five hundred and twenty-seven, and he thinks it very improbable that the kings would have deprived so many women of this honour to bestow it upon only a few of them. But as regards these matters, it has not seemed to me fitting either to omit all mention of them or to say more than is sufficient.

48 Concerning the city of Cures from which Tatius and his followers came (for the course of my narrative requires that I should speak of them also, and say who they were and whence), we have received the following account. In the territory of Reate, when the Aborigines were in possession of it, a certain maiden of that country, who was of the highest birth, went into the temple of Enyalius to dance. The Sabines and the Romans, who have learned it from them, give to Enyalius the name of Quirinus, without being able to affirm for certain whether he is Mars or some other god who enjoys the same honours as Mars. For some think that both these names are used of one and the same god who presides over martial combats; others, that the names are applied to two different gods of war. Be that as it may, this maiden, while she was dancing in the temple, was on a sudden seized with divine inspiration, and quitting the dance, ran into the inner sanctuary of the god; after which, being with child by this divinity, as everybody believed, she brought forth a son named Modius, with the surname Fabidius, who, being arrived at manhood, had not a human but a divine form and was renowned above all others for his warlike deeds. And conceiving a desire to found a city on his own account, he gathered together a great number of people of the neighbourhood and in a very short time built the city called Cures: he gave it this name, as some say, from the divinity whose son he was reputed to be, or, as others state, from a spear, since the Sabines call spears *cures*.[60] This is the account given by Terentius Varro.

49 But Zenodotus of Troezen, a . . . historian,[61] relates that the Umbrians, a native race, first dwelt in the Reatine territory, as it is called, and that, being driven from there by the Pelasgians, they came into the country which they now inhabit, and changing their name with their place of habitation, from Umbrians were called Sabines. But Porcius Cato says that the Sabine race received its name from Sabus, the son of Sancus, a divinity of that country, and that this Sancus was by some called Jupiter Fidius. He says also that their first place of abode was a certain village called Testruna, situated near the city of Amiternum; that from there the Sabines made an incursion at that time into the Reatine territory, which was inhabited by the Aborigines together with the Pelasgians,[62] and took

---

60 Or **quires**. The Greek spelling can represent either form.
61 The Greek text suggests the loss of an adjective or phrase qualifying "historian." See critical note.
62 The word "Pelasgians" is due to Reiske. See critical note and i. 19 f.

their most famous city, Cutiliae, by force of arms and occupied it; and that, sending colonies out of the Reatine territory, they built many cities, in which they lived without fortifying them, among others the city called Cures. He further states that the country they occupied was distant from the Adriatic about two hundred and eighty stades and from the Tyrrhenian Sea two hundred and forty, and that its length was a little less than a thousand stades. There is also another account given of the Sabines in the native histories, to the effect that a colony of Lacedaemonians settled among them at the time when Lycurgus, being guardian to his nephew Eunomus, gave his laws to Sparta. For the story goes that some of the Spartans, disliking the severity of his laws and separating from the rest, quitted the city entirely, and after being borne through a vast stretch of sea, made a vow to the gods to settle in the first land they should reach; for a longing came upon them for any land whatsoever. At last they made that part of Italy which lies near the Pomentine plains[63] and they called the place where they first landed Foronia, in memory of their being *borne*[64] through the sea, and built a temple owing to the goddess Foronia, to whom they had addressed their vows; this goddess, by the alteration of one letter, they now call Feronia. And some of them, setting out from thence, settled among the Sabines. It is for this reason, they say, that many of the habits of the Sabines are Spartan, particularly their fondness for war and their frugality and a severity in all the actions of their lives. But this is enough about the Sabine race.

---

63 The *Pomptinus ager* of Livy (ii. 34; iv. 25). The marginal lands stretching round the Pontine marshes.

64 One wonders why the author of this fanciful etymology did not connect Feronia directly with the verb φέρεσθαι ("to be borne along"), instead of assuming an earlier spelling Foronia, not otherwise attested, and deriving that form from the abstract noun φόρησις. The name has not as yet been satisfactorily explained.

50 Romulus and Tatius immediately enlarged the city by adding to it two other hills, the Quirinal, as it is called, and the Caelian; and separating their habitations, each of them had his particular place of residence. Romulus occupied the Palatine and Caelian hills, the latter being next to the Palatine, and Tatius the Capitoline hill, which he had seized in the beginning, and the Quirinal. And cutting down the wood that grew on the plain at the foot of the Capitoline and filling up the greatest part of the lake, which, since it lay in a hollow, was kept well supplied by the waters that came down from the hills, they converted the plain into a forum, which the Romans continue to use even now; there they held their assemblies, transacting their business in the temple of Vulcan, which stands a little above the Forum. They built temples also and consecrated altars to those gods to whom they had addressed their vows during their battles: Romulus to Jupiter Stator,[65] near the Porta Mugonia, as it is called, which leads to the Palatine hill from the Sacred Way, because this god had heard his vows and had caused his army to stop in its flight and to renew the battle; and Tatius to the Sun and Moon, to Saturn and to Rhea, and, besides these, to Vesta, Vulcan, Diana, Enyalius, and to other gods whose names are difficult to be expressed in the Greek language; and in every *curia* he dedicated tables to Juno called Quiritis,[66] which remain even to this day. For five years, then, the kings reigned together in perfect harmony, during which time they engaged in one joint undertaking, the expedition against the Camerini; for these people, who kept sending out bands of robbers and doing great injury to the country of the Romans, would not agree to have the case submitted to judicial investigation, though often summoned by the Romans to do so.

---

65 "The "Stayer" of their flight.
66 The name also appears as Quiris, Curis and Cur(r)itis. It was variously derived from *currus* ("car"), from the Sabine *curis* ("spear") and from Cures, the city.

After conquering the Camerini in a pitched battle (for they came to blows with them) and later besieging and taking their town by storm, they disarmed the inhabitants and deprived them of a third part of their land, which they divided among their own people.[67] And when the Camerini proceeded to harass the new settlers, they marched out against them, and having put them to flight, divided all their possessions among their own people, but permitted as many of the inhabitants as wished to so to live at Rome. These amounted to about four thousand, whom they distributed among the *curiae*, and they made their city a Roman colony. Cameria was a colony of the Albans planted long before the founding of Rome, and anciently one of the most celebrated habitations of the Aborigines.

51 But[68] in the sixth year, the government of the city devolved once more upon Romulus alone, Tatius having lost his life as the result of a plot which the principal men of Lavinium formed against him. The occasion for the plot was this. Some friends of Tatius had led out a band of robbers into the territory of the Lavinians, where they seized a great many of their effects and drove away their herds of cattle, killing or wounding those who came to the rescue. Upon the arrival of an embassy from the injured to demand satisfaction, Romulus decided that those who had done the injury should be delivered up for punishment to those they had wronged. Tatius, however, espousing the cause of his friends, would not consent that any persons should be taken into custody by their enemies before trial, and particularly Roman citizens by outsiders, but ordered those who complained that they had been injured to come to Rome and proceed against the others according to law. The ambassadors, accordingly, having failed to obtain any satisfaction, went away full of resentment; and some of the Sabines, incensed at their action,

---

67 More than an entire line is supplied here, following Kiessling's suggestion. See critical note.

68 For chaps. 51-52 *cf.* Livy i.14, 1-3.

followed them and set upon them while they were asleep in their tents, which they had pitched near the road when evening overtook them, and not only robbed them of their money, but cut the throats of all they found still in their beds; those, however, who perceived the plot promptly and were able to make their escape got back to their city. After this ambassadors came both from Lavinium and from many cities, complaining of this lawless deed and threatening war if they should not obtain justice.

52 This violence committed against the ambassadors appeared to Romulus, as indeed it was, a terrible crime and one calling for speedy expiation, since it had been in violation of a sacred law; and finding that Tatius was making light of it, he himself, without further delay, caused those who had been guilty of the outrage to be seized and delivered up in chains to the ambassadors to be led away. But Tatius not only was angered at the indignity which he complained he had received from his colleague in the delivering up of the men, but was also moved with compassion for those who were being led away (for one of the guilty persons was actually a relation of his); and immediately, taking his soldiers with him, he went in haste to their assistance, and overtaking the ambassadors on the road, he took the prisoners from them. But not long afterwards, as some say, when he had gone with Romulus to Lavinium in order to perform a sacrifice which it was necessary for the kings to offer to the ancestral gods for the prosperity of the city, the friends and relations of the ambassadors who had been murdered, having conspired against him, slew him at the altar with the knives and spits used in cutting up and roasting the oxen. But Licinius[69] writes that he did not go with Romulus nor, indeed, on account of any sacrifices, but that he went alone, with the intention of persuading those who had received the injuries to forgive the authors of them,

---

69 Licinius Macer.

and that when weight people became angry because the men were not delivered up to them in accordance with the decision both of Romulus and of the Roman senate, and the relations of the slain men rushed upon him in great numbers, he was no longer able to escape summary justice and was stoned to death by them. Such was the end to which Tatius came, after he had warred against Romulus for three years and had been his colleague for five. His body was brought to Rome, where it was given honourable burial; and the city offers public libations to him every year.

53 But[70] Romulus, now established for the second time as sole ruler, expiated the crime committed against the ambassadors by forbidding those who had perpetrated the outrage the use of fire and water; for upon the death of Tatius they had all fled from the city. After that, he brought to trial the Lavinians who had conspired against Tatius and who had been delivered up by their own city, and when they seemed to plead, with considerable justice, that they had but avenged violence with violence, he freed them of the charge. After he had attended to these matters, he led out his army against the city of Fidenae, which was situated forty stades from Rome and was at that time both large and populous. For on an occasion when the Romans were oppressed by famine and provisions which the people of Crustumerium had sent to them were being brought down the river in boats, the Fidenates crowded aboard the boats in great numbers, seized the provisions and killed some of the men who defended them, and when called upon to make satisfaction, they refused to do so. Romulus, incensed at this, made an incursion into their territory with a considerable force, and having possessed himself of a great quantity of booty, was preparing to lead his army home; but when the Fidenates came out against him, he gave them battle. After a severe struggle, in which many fell on both sides, the

---

70 *Cf.* Livy, i. 14, 4-11.

enemy were defeated and put to flight, and Romulus, following close upon their heels, rushed inside the walls along with the fugitives. When the city had been taken at the first assault, he punished a few of the citizens, and left a guard of three hundred men there; and taking from the inhabitants a part of their territory, which he divided among his own people, he made this city also a Roman colony. It had been founded by the Albans at the same time with Nomentum and Crustumerium, three brothers having been the leaders of the colony, of whom the eldest built Fidenae.

54 After this war Romulus undertook another against the Camerini, who had attacked the Roman colonists in their midst while the city of Rome was suffering from a pestilence; it was this situation in particular that encouraged the Camerini, and believing that the Roman nation would be totally destroyed by the calamity, they killed some of the colonists and expelled the rest. In revenge for this Romulus, after he had a second time made himself master of the city, put to death the authors of the revolt and permitted his soldiers to plunder the city; and he also took away half the land besides that which had been previously granted to the Roman settlers. And having left a garrison in the city sufficient to quell any future uprising of the inhabitants, he departed with his forces. As the result of this expedition he celebrated a second triumph, and out of the spoils he dedicated a chariot and four in bronze to Vulcan, and near it he set up his own statue with an inscription in Greek characters setting forth his deeds. The[71] third war Romulus engaged in was against the most powerful city of the Tyrrhenian race at that time, called Veii, distant from Rome about a hundred stades; it is situated on a high and craggy rock and is as large as Athens. The Veientes made the taking of Fidenae the pretext for this war, and sending ambassadors, they bade the Romans withdraw

---

71 For chap. 54, 3-55, 6 *cf.* Livy, i.15, 1-5.

their garrison from that city and restore to its original possessors the territory they had taken from them and were now occupying. And when their demand was not heeded, they took the field with a great army and established their camp in a conspicuous place near Fidenae. Romulus, however, having received advance information of their march, had set out with the flower of his army and lay ready at Fidenae to receive them. When all their preparations were made for the struggle, both armies advanced into the plain and came to grips, and they continued fighting with great ardour for a long time, till the coming on of night parted them, after they had proved themselves evenly matched in the struggle. This was the course of the first battle.

55 But in a second battle, which was fought not long afterwards, the Romans were victorious as the result of the strategy of their general, who had occupied in the night a certain height not far distant from the enemy's camp and placed there in ambush the choicest both of the horse and foot that had come to him from Rome since the last action. The two armies met in the plain and fought in the same manner as before; but when Romulus raised the signal to the troops that lay in ambush on the height, these, raising the battle cry, rushed upon the Veientes from the rear, and being themselves fresh while the enemy were fatigued, they put them to flight with no great difficulty. Some few of them were slain in battle, but the great part, throwing themselves into the Tiber, which flows by Fidenae, with the intention of swimming across the river, were drowned; for, being wounded and spent with labour, they were unable to swim across, while others, who did not know how to swim and had not looked ahead, having lost all presence of mind in face of the danger, perished in the eddies of the river. If, now, the Veientes had realized that their first plans had been ill-advised and had remained quiet after this, they would have met with no greater misfortune; but, as it was, hoping to repair their former losses and believing that if they attacked with a larger force they would easily conquer in the war, they set out a second time against the Romans with a large army, consisting both of the levy from the city itself and of others of the same race[72] who in virtue of their league came to their assistance. Upon this, another severe battle was fought near Fidenae, in which the Romans were victorious, after killing many of the Veientes and taking more of them prisoners. Even their camp was taken, which was full of money, arms and slaves, and likewise their boats, which were laden with great store of provisions; and in these the multitude of prisoners were carried down the river to Rome. This was the third triumph that Romulus celebrated, and it was much more magnificent than either of the former. And when, not long afterwards, ambassadors arrived from the Veientes to seek an end to the war and to ask pardon for their offences, Romulus imposed the following penalties upon them: to deliver up to the Romans the country adjacent to the Tiber, called the Seven Districts,[73] and to abandon the salt-works near the mouth of the river, and also to bring fifty hostages as a pledge that they would attempt no uprising in the future. When the Veientes submitted to all these demands, he made a treaty with them for one hundred years and engraved terms of it on pillars. He then dismissed without ransom all the prisoners who desired to return home; but those who preferred to remain in Rome — and these were far more numerous than the others — he made citizens, distributing them among the *curiae* and assigning to them allotments of land on this side of the Tiber.

56 These[74] are the memorable wars which Romulus waged. His failure to subdue any more of the neighbouring nations seems to

---

72 *i.e.* Etruscans.
73 Septem Pagi.
74 *Cf.* Livy, i. 16, 1-4.

have been due to his sudden death, which happened while he was still in the vigour of his age for warlike achievements. There are many different stories concerning it. Those who give a rather fabulous account of his life say that while he was haranguing his men in the camp, sudden darkness rushed down out of a clear sky and a violent storm burst, after which he was nowhere to be seen; and these writers believe that he was caught up into heaven by his father, Mars. But those who write the more plausible accounts say that he was killed by his own people; and the reason they allege for his murder is that he released without the common consent, contrary to custom, the hostages he had taken from the Veientes, and that he no longer comported himself in the same manner toward the original citizens and toward those who were enrolled later, but showed greater honour to the former and slighted the latter, and also because of his great cruelty in the punishment of delinquents (for instance, he had ordered a group of Romans who were accused of brigandage against the neighbouring peoples to be hurled down the precipice[75] after he had sat alone in judgment upon them, although they were neither of mean birth nor few in number), but chiefly because he now seemed to be harsh and arbitrary and to be exercising his power more like a tyrant than a king. For these reasons, they say, the patricians formed a conspiracy against him and resolved to slay him; and having carried out the deed in the senate-house, they divided his body into several pieces, that it might not be seen, and then came out, each one hiding his part of the body under his robes, and afterwards burying it in secret. Others say that while haranguing the people he was slain by the new citizens of Rome, and that they undertook the murder at the time when the rain and the darkness occurred, the assembly of the people being then dispersed and their chief left without his guard. And for this reason, they say, the day on which this event happened got its name

---

75 The Tarpeian rock.

from the flight of the people and is called *Populifugia*[76] down to our times. Be that as it may, the incidents that occurred by the direction of Heaven in connexion with this man's conception and death would seem to give no small authority to the view of those who make gods of mortal men and place the souls of illustrious persons in heaven. For they say that at the time when his mother was violated, whether by some man or by a god, there was a total eclipse of the sun and a general darkness as in the night covered the earth, and that at his death the same thing happened. Such, then, is reported to have been the death of Romulus, who built Rome and was chosen by her citizens as their first king. He left no issue, and after reigning thirty-seven years, died in the fifty-fifth year of his age; for he was very young when he obtained the rule, being no more than eighteen years old, as is agreed by all who have written his history.

57 The[77] following year there was no king of the Romans elected, but a certain magistracy, called by them an interregnum, had the oversight of public affairs, being created in much the following manner: The patricians who had been enrolled in the senate under Romulus, being, as I have said,[78] two hundred in number, were divided into *decuriae*;[79] then, when lots had been cast, the first ten persons upon whom the lot fell were invested by the rest with the absolute rule of the State. They did not, however, all reign together, but successively, each for five days, during which time they

---

76 Or *Poplifugia*. The same explanation of the origin of the festival is given by Plutarch (*Rom.* 29), who also records the more common version that the original "flight of the people" occurred shortly after the departure of the Gauls, at a time when several Latin tribes suddenly appeared before the city. According to a third view, found in Macrobius (iii. 2, 14), Etruscans were the invaders.

77 For chaps. 57-58 *cf.* Livy i. 17; 18, 1 and 5.

78 Chap. 47, 1.

79 Groups of ten.

had both the rods and the other insignia of the royal power. The first, after his power had expired, handed over the government to the second, and he to the third, and so on to the last. After the first ten had reigned their appointed time of fifty days, ten others received the rule from them, and from those in turn others. But presently the people decided to abolish the rule of the *decuriae*, being irked by all the changes of power, since the men did not all have either the same purposes or the same natural abilities. Thereupon the senators, calling the people together in assembly by tribes and *curiae*, permitted them to consider the form of government and determine whether they wished to entrust the public interests to a king or to annual magistrates. The people, however, did not take the choice upon themselves, but referred the decision to the senators, intimating that they would be satisfied with whichever form of government the others should approve. The senators all favoured establishing a monarchical form of government, but strife arose over the question from which group the future king should be chosen. For some thought that the one who was to govern the commonwealth ought to be chosen from among the original senators, and others that he should be chosen from among those who had been admitted afterwards and whom they called new senators.

58 The contest being drawn out to a great length, they at last reached an agreement on the basis that one of two courses should be followed — either the older senators should choose the king, who must not, however, be one of themselves, but might be anyone else whom they should regard as most suitable, or the new senators should do the same. The older senators accepted the right of choosing, and after a long consultation among themselves decided that, since by their agreement they themselves were excluded from the sovereignty, they would not confer it on any of the newly-appointed senators, either, but would find some man from outside who would espouse neither party, and declare him king, as the most effectual means of putting an end to party strife. After they had come to this resolution, they chose a man of the Sabine race, the son of Pompilius Pompon, a person of distinction, whose name was Numa. He was in that stage of life, being near forty, in which prudence is the most conspicuous, and of an aspect full of royal dignity; and he enjoyed the greatest renown for wisdom, not only among the citizens of Cures,[80] but among all the neighbouring peoples as well. After reaching this decision the senators assembled the people, and that one of their number who was then the *interrex*, coming forward, told them that the senators had unanimously resolved to establish a monarchical form of government and that he, having been empowered to decide who should succeed to the rule, chose Numa Pompilius as king of the State. After this he appointed ambassadors from among the patricians and sent them to conduct Numa to Rome that he might assume the royal power. This happened in the third year of the sixteenth Olympiad,[81] at which Pythagoras, a Lacedaemonian, won the foot-race.

59 Up[82] to this point, then, I have nothing to allege in contradiction to those who have published the history of this man but in regard to what follows I am at a loss what to say. For many have written that Numa was a disciple of Pythagoras and that when he was chosen king by the Romans he was studying philosophy at Croton. But the date of Pythagoras contradicts this account, since he was not merely a few years younger than Numa, but actually lived four whole generations later, as we learn from universal

---

80 Cures is here taken as a leading city of the Sabines; see the editor's note at ii, 46, which gathers further passages of Dionysius and much additional information.

81 713 B.C.

82 *Cf.* Livy i. 18, 2-4.

history; for Numa succeeded to the sovereignty of the Romans in the middle of the sixteenth Olympiad, whereas Pythagoras resided in Italy after the fiftieth Olympiad.[83] But I can advance yet a stronger argument to prove that the chronology is incompatible with the reports handed down about Numa, and that is, that at the time when he was called to the sovereignty by the Romans the city of Croton did not yet exist; for it was not until four whole years after Numa had begun to rule the Romans that Myscelus founded this city, in the third year of the seventeenth Olympiad.[84] Accordingly, it was impossible for Numa either to have studied philosophy with Pythagoras the Samian, who flourished four generations after him, or to have resided in Croton, a city not as yet in existence when the Romans called him to the sovereignty. But if I may express my own opinion, those who have written his history seem to have taken these two admitted facts, namely, the residence of Pythagoras in Italy and the wisdom of Numa (for he has been allowed by everybody to have been a wise man), and combining them, to have made Numa a disciple of Pythagoras, without going on to inquire whether they both flourished at the same period — unless, indeed, one is going to assume that there was another Pythagoras who taught philosophy before the Samian, and that with him Numa associated. But I do not know how this could be proved, since it is not supported, so far as I know, by the testimony of any author of note, either Greek or Roman. But I have said enough on this subject.

60 When the ambassadors came to Numa to invite him to the sovereignty, he for some time refused it and long persisted in his resolution not to accept the royal power. But when his brothers kept urging him insistently and at last his father argued that the offer of so great an honour ought not to be rejected, he consented to

---

83 580/79 B.C.
84 709 B.C.

become king. As soon as the Romans were informed of this by the ambassadors, they conceived a great yearning for the man before they saw him, esteeming it a sufficient proof of his wisdom that, while the others had valued sovereignty beyond measure, looking upon it as the source of happiness, he alone despised it as a paltry thing and unworthy of serious attention. And when he approached the city, they met him upon the road and with great applause, salutations and other honours conducted him into the city. After that, an assembly of the people was held, in which the tribes by *curiae* gave their votes in his favour; and when the resolution of the people had been confirmed by the patricians, and, last of all, the augurs had reported that the heavenly signs were auspicious, he assumed the office. The Romans say that he undertook no military campaign, but that, being a pious and just man, he passed the whole period of his reign in peace and caused the State to be most excellently governed.[85] They relate also many marvellous stories about him, attributing his human wisdom to the suggestions of the gods. For they fabulously affirm that a certain nymph, Egeria, used to visit him and instruct him on each occasion in the art of reigning, though others say that it was not a nymph, but one of the Muses. And this, they claim, became clear to every one; for, when people were incredulous at first, as may well be supposed, and regarded the story concerning the goddess as an invention, he, in order to give the unbelievers a manifest proof of his converse with this divinity, did as follows, pursuant to her instructions. He invited to the house where he lived a great many of the Romans, all men of worth, and having shown them his apartments, very meanly provided with furniture and particularly lacking in everything that was necessary to entertain a numerous company, he ordered them to depart for the time being, but invited them to dinner in the evening. And when they came at the appointed hour, he showed them rich couches and

85 For §§ 4-7 *cf.* Livy i. 19, 1-5.

tables laden with a multitude of beautiful cups, and when they were at table, he set before them a banquet consisting of all sorts of viands, such a banquet, indeed, as it would not have been easy for any man in those days to have prepared in a long time. The Romans were astonished at everything they saw, and from that time they entertained a firm belief that some goddess held converse with him.

61 But those who banish everything that is fabulous from history say that the report concerning Egeria was invented by Numa, to the end that, when once the people were possessed with a fear of the gods, they might more readily pay regard to him and willingly receive the laws he should enact, as coming from the gods. They say that in this he followed the example of the Greeks, emulating the wisdom both of Minos the Cretan and of Lycurgus the Lacedaemonian. For the former of these claimed to hold converse with Zeus, and going frequently to the Dictaean mountain, in which the Cretan legends say that the new-born Zeus was brought up by the Curetes, he used to descend into the holy cave; and having composed his laws there, he would produce them, affirming that he had received them from Zeus. And Lycurgus, paying visits to Delphi, said he was forming his code of laws under the instruction of Apollo. But, as I am sensible that to give a particular account of the legendary histories, and especially of those relating to gods, would require a long discussion, I shall omit doing so, and shall relate instead the benefits which the Romans seem to me to have received from this man's rule, according to the information I have derived from their own histories. But first I will show in what confusion the affairs of the State were before he came to the throne.

62 After the death of Romulus the senate, being now in full control of the government and having held the supreme power for one year, as I have related,[86] began to be at odds with itself and to

---

86 Chap. 57.

split into factions over questions of pre-eminence and equality. For the Alban element, who together with Romulus had planted the colony, claimed the right, not only of delivering their opinions first and enjoying the greatest honours, but also of being courted by the newcomers. Those, on the other hand, who had been admitted afterwards into the number of the patricians from among the new settlers thought that they ought not to be excluded from any honours or to stand in an inferior position to the others. This was felt particularly by those who were of the Sabine race and who, in virtue the treaty made by Romulus with Tatius, supposed they had been granted citizenship by the original inhabitants on equal terms, and that they had shown the same favour to the former in their turn. The senate being thus at odds, the clients also were divided into two parties and each joined their respective factions. There were, too, among the plebeians not a few, lately admitted into the number of the citizens, who, having never assisted Romulus in any of his wars, had been neglected by him and had received neither a share of land nor any booty. These, having no home, but being poor and vagabonds, were by necessity enemies to their superiors and quite ripe for revolution. So Numa, having found the affairs of the State in such a raging sea of confusion, first relieved the poor among the plebeians by distributing to them some small part of the land which Romulus had possessed and of the public land; and afterwards he allayed the strife of the patricians, not by depriving them of anything the founders of the city had gained, but by bestowing some other honours on the new settlers. And having attuned the whole body of the people, like a musical instrument, to the sole consideration of the public good and enlarged the circuit of the city by the addition of the Quirinal hill (for till that time it was still without a wall), he then addressed himself to the other measures of government, labouring to inculcate these two things by the possession of which he conceived the State would become prosperous and great: first, piety, by informing his subjects that the gods are the givers and guardians of every blessing to mortal men, and, second, justice, through which, he showed them, the blessings also which the gods bestow bring honest enjoyment to their possessors.

63 As regards the laws and institutions by which he made great progress in both these directions, I do not think it fitting that I should enter into all the details, not only because I fear the length of such a discussion but also because I do not regard the recording of them as necessary to a history intended for Greeks; but I shall give a summary account of the principal measures, which are sufficient to reveal the man's whole purpose, beginning with his regulations concerning the worship of the gods. I should state, however, that all those rites which he found established by Romulus, either in custom or in law, he left untouched, looking upon them all as established in the best possible manner. But whatever he thought had been overlooked by his predecessor, he added, consecrating many precincts to those gods who had hitherto received no honours, erecting many altars and temples, instituting festivals in honour of each, and appointing priests to have charge of their sanctuaries and rites, and enacting laws concerning purifications, ceremonies, expiations and many other observances and honours in greater number than are to be found in any other city, either Greek or barbarian, even in those that have prided themselves the most at one time or another upon their piety. He also ordered that Romulus himself, as one who had shown a greatness beyond mortal nature, should be honoured, under the name of Quirinus, by the erection of a temple and by sacrifices throughout the year. For[87] while the Romans were yet in doubt whether divine providence or human treachery had been the cause of his disappearance, a certain man,

---

87   *Cf.* Livy i. 16, 5-8.

named Julius, descended from Ascanius, who was a husbandman and of such a blameless life that he would never have told an untruth for his private advantage, arrived in the Forum and said that, as he was coming in from the country, he saw Romulus departing from the city fully armed and that, as he drew near to him, he heard him say these words: "Julius, announce to the Romans from me, that the genius to whom I was allotted at my birth is conducting me to the gods, now that I have finished my mortal life, and that I am Quirinus." Numa, having reduced his whole system of religious laws to writing, divided them into eight parts, that being the number of the different classes of religious ceremonies.

64 The first division of religious rites he assigned to the thirty *curiones*, who, as I have stated,[88] perform the public sacrifices for the *curiae*. The second, to those called by the Greeks *stephanêphoroi*[89] or "wearers of the crown" and by the Romans *flamines*;[90] they are given this name from their wearing caps and fillets, called † *flama*,[91] which they continue to wear even to this day. The third, to the commanders of the *celeres*, who, as I have stated,[92] were appointed to be the body-guards of the kings and fought both as cavalry and

---

88 Chap. 23, 1-2.
89 **Stephanêphoros** was a title given in various Greek states to magistrates entitled to wear a crown as a symbol of their office: here the word is used as the best Greek equivalent for "wearers of the fillet."
90 *Cf.* Livy i. 20, 2.
91 An error for *fila*? Dionysius is here giving the usual Roman etymology of *flamen*, which is preserved to us by Varro (*de Ling. Lat.* v. 84) and by Festus (p. 87). Both authorities state that these priests got their name from the *filum*, the fillet of wool which they wore round about the top of their caps. It is hard to believe that our author could have confused *filum* with *flammeum*, the bridal veil; see the critical note. The true etymology of *flamen* is disputed; but there is much to be said in favour of deriving it are *flare* ("to blow"), since one of the first duties of a priest would be to blow up the fire for the sacrifices.
92 Chap. 13.

infantry; for these also performed certain specified religious rites. The fourth, to those who interpret the signs sent by the gods and determine what they portend both to private persons and to the public; these, from one branch of the speculations belonging to their art, the Romans call augurs, and we should call them *oiônopoloi* or "soothsayers by means of birds"; they are skilled in all sorts of divination in use among the Romans, whether founded on signs appearing in the heavens, in mid-air or on the earth. The fifth he assigned to the virgins who are the guardians of the sacred fire and who are called Vestals by the Romans, after the goddess whom they serve, he himself having been the first to build a temple at Rome to Vesta and to appoint virgins to be her priestesses.[93] But concerning them it is necessary to make a few statements that are most essential, since the subject requires it; for there are problems that have been thought worthy of investigation by many Roman historians in connexion with this topic and those authors who have not diligently examined into the causes of these matters have published rather worthless accounts.

65 At any rate, as regards the building of the temple of Vesta, some ascribe it to Romulus, looking upon it as an inconceivable thing that, when a city was being founded by a man skilled in divination, a public hearth[94] should not have been erected first of all, particularly since the founder had been brought up at Alba, where the temple of this goddess had been established from ancient times, and since his mother had been her priestess. And recognizing two classes of religious ceremonies — the one public and common to all the citizens, and the other private and confined to particular families — they declare that on both these grounds Romulus was under every obligation to worship this goddess. For they say that

93 *Cf.* Livy i. 20, 3.
94 The word ἑστία means, as a common noun, "hearth," and, as a proper noun, Hestia, the hearth-goddess, corresponding to the Roman Vesta.

nothing is more necessary for men than a public hearth, and that nothing more nearly concerned Romulus, in view of his descent, since his ancestors had brought the sacred rites of this goddess from Ilium and his mother had been her priestess. Those, then, who for these reasons ascribe the building of the temple to Romulus rather than to Numa seem to be right, in so far as the general principle is concerned, that when a city was being founded, it was necessary for a hearth to be established first of all, particularly by a man who was not unskilled in matters of religion; but of the details relating to the building of the present temple and to the virgins who are in the service of the goddess they seem to have been ignorant. For, in the first place, it was not Romulus who consecrated to the goddess this place where the sacred fire is preserved (a strong proof of this is that it is outside of what they call Roma Quadrata,[95] which he surrounded with a wall, whereas all men place the shrine of the public hearth in the best part of a city and nobody outside of the walls); and, in the second place, he did not appoint the service of the goddess to be performed by virgins, being mindful, I believe, of the experience that had befallen his mother, who while she was serving the goddess lost her virginity; for he doubtless felt that the remembrance of his domestic misfortunes would make it impossible for him to punish according to the traditional laws any of the priestesses he should find to have been violated. For this reason, therefore, he did not build a common temple of Vesta nor did he appoint virgins to be her priestesses; but having erected a hearth in each of the thirty *curiae* on which the members sacrificed, he appointed the chiefs of the *curiae* to be the priests of those hearths, therein imitating the customs of the Greeks that are still observed in the most ancient cities. At any rate, what are called *prytanea* among

---

95 A later name for the old Palatine city, which, according to the theory of the augurs, was quadrangular.

them are temples of Hestia, and are served by the chief magistrates of the cities.[96]

66 Numa, upon taking over the rule, did not disturb the individual hearths of the *curiae*, but erected one common to them all in the space between the Capitoline hill and the Palatine (for these hills had already been united by a single wall into one city, and the Forum, in which the temple is built, lies between them), and he enacted, in accordance with the ancestral custom of the Latins, that the guarding of the holy things should be committed to virgins. There is some doubt, however, what it is that is kept in this temple and for what reason the care of it has been assigned to virgins, some affirming that nothing is preserved there but the fire, which is visible to everybody. And they very reasonably argue that the custody of the fire was committed to virgins, rather than to men, because fire is incorrupt and a virgin is undefiled, and the most chaste of mortal things must be agreeable to the purest of those that are divine. And they regard the fire as consecrated to Vesta because that goddess, being the earth[97] and occupying the central place in the universe, kindles the celestial fires from herself. But there are some who say that besides the fire there are some holy things in the temple of the goddess that may not be revealed to the public, of which only the pontiffs and the virgins have knowledge. As a strong confirmation of this story they cite what happened at the burning of the temple during the First Punic War between the Romans and the

---

96 Apparently each capital city among the Greeks had a prytaneum, containing the common hearth of the State, where the sacred fire was kept burning. This building would serve naturally as the headquarters of the chief magistrates (though in Athens the archons removed at an early date to the Thesmotheteum and the prytaneis took their meals in the Tholos); and here were entertained foreign ambassadors and also citizens who had deserved well of the State.

97 Vesta is similarly identified with the earth by Ovid, *Fasti* vi. 267. See Sir James Frazer's instructive note on that passage (vol. iv. pp. 201 f.).

Carthaginians over Sicily. For when the temple caught fire and the virgins fled from the flames, one of the pontiffs, Lucius Caecilius, called Metellus, a man of consular rank, the same who exhibited a hundred and thirty-eight elephants in the memorable triumph which he celebrated for his defeat of the Carthaginians in Sicily,[98] neglecting his own safety for the sake of the public good, ventured to force his way into the burning structure, and, snatching up the holy things which the virgins had abandoned, saved them from the fire; for which he received the honours from the State, as the inscription upon his statue on the Capitol testifies. Taking this incident, then, as an admitted fact, they add some conjectures of their own. Thus, some affirm that the objects preserved here are a part of those holy things which were once in Samothrace; that Dardanus removed them out of that island into the city which he himself had built, and that Aeneas, when he fled from the Troad, brought them along with the other holy things into Italy. But others declare that it is the Palladium that fell from Heaven, the same that was in the possession of the people of Ilium; for they hold that Aeneas, being well acquainted with it, brought it into Italy, whereas the Achaeans stole away the copy, — an incident about which many stories have been related both by poets and by historians. For my part, I find from very many evidences that there are indeed some holy things, unknown to the public, kept by the virgins, and not the fire alone; but what they are I do not think should be inquired into too curiously, either by me of by anyone else who wishes to observe the reverence due to the gods.

67 The virgins who serve the goddess were originally four and were chosen by the kings according to the principles established by Numa, but afterwards, from the multiplicity of the sacred rites they perform, their number was increased to six, and has so remained

---

98 At Panormus, in 250. The temple of Vesta was burned in 241.

down to our time. They live in the temple of the goddess, into which none who wish are hindered from entering in the daytime, whereas it is not lawful for any man to remain there at night. They were required to remain undefiled by marriage for the space of thirty years, devoting themselves to offering sacrifices and performing the other rites ordained by law. During the first ten years their duty was to learn their functions, in the second ten to perform them, and during the remaining ten to teach others. After the expiration of the term of thirty years nothing hindered those who so desired from marrying, upon laying aside their fillets and the other insignia of their priesthood. And some, though very few, have done this; but they came to ends that were not at all happy or enviable. In consequence, the rest, looking upon their misfortunes as ominous, remain virgins in the temple of the goddess till their death, and then once more another is chosen by the pontiffs to supply the vacancy. Many high honours have been granted them by the commonwealth, as a result of which they feel no desire either for marriage or for children; and severe penalties have been established for their misdeeds. It is the pontiffs who by law both inquire into and punish these offences; to Vestals who are guilty of lesser misdemeanours they scourge with rods, but those who have suffered defilement they deliver up to the most shameful and the most miserable death. While they are yet alive they are carried upon a bier with all the formality of a funeral, their friends and relations attending them with lamentations, and after being brought as far as the Colline Gate, they are placed in an underground cell prepared within the walls, clad in their funeral attire; but they are not given a monument or funeral rites or any other customary solemnities. There are many indications, it seems, when a priestess is not performing her holy functions with purity, but the principal one is the extinction of the fire, which the Romans dread above all misfortunes, looking upon it, from whatever cause it proceeds, as an omen that portends the destruction of the city; and they bring fire again into the temple with many supplicatory rites, concerning which I shall speak on the proper occasion.[99]

68 However, it is also well worth relating in what manner the goddess has manifested herself in favour of those virgins who have been falsely accused. For these things, however incredible they may be, have been believed by the Romans and their historians have related much about them. To be sure, the professors of the atheistic philosophies, — if, indeed, their theories deserve the name of philosophy, — who ridicule all the manifestations of the gods which have taken place among either the Greeks or barbarians, will also laugh these reports to scorn and attribute them to human imposture, on the ground that none of the gods concern themselves in anything relating to mankind. Those, however, who do not absolve the gods from the care of human affairs, but, after looking deeply into history, hold that they are favourable to the good and hostile to the wicked, will not regard even these manifestations as incredible. It is said, then, that once, when the fire had been extinguished through some negligence on the part of Aemilia, who had the care of it at the time and had entrusted it to another virgin, one of those who had been newly chosen and were then learning their duties, the whole city was in great commotion and an inquiry was made by the pontiffs whether there might not have been some defilement of the priestess to account for the extinction of the fire. Thereupon, they say, Aemilia, who was innocent, but distracted at what had happened, stretched out her hands toward the altar and in the presence of the priests and the rest of the virgins cried: "O Vesta, guardian of the Romans' city, if, during the space of nearly thirty years, I have performed the sacred offices to thee in a holy and proper manner, keeping a pure mind and a chaste body, do

---

99 This promise is not fulfilled in the extant portions of the history.

thou manifest thyself in my defence and assist me and do not suffer thy priestess to die the most miserable of all deaths; but if I have been guilty of any impious deed, let my punishment expiate the guilt of the city" Having said this, she tore off the band of the linen garment she had on and threw it upon the altar, they say, following her prayer; and from the ashes, which had been long cold and retained no spark, a great flame flared up through the linen, so that the city no longer required either expiations or a new fire.

69 But what I am going to relate is still more wonderful and more like a myth. They say that somebody unjustly accused one of the holy virgins, whose name was Tuccia, and although he was unable to point to the extinction of the fire as evidence, he advanced false arguments based on plausible proofs and depositions; and that the virgin, being ordered to make her defence, said only this, that she would clear herself from the accusation by her deeds. Having said this and called upon the goddess to be her guide, she led the way to the Tiber, with the consent of the pontiffs and escorted by the whole population of the city; and when she came to the river, she was so hardy as to undertake the task which, according to the proverb, is among the most impossible of achievement: she drew up water from the river in a sieve, and carrying it as far as the Forum, poured it out at the feet of the pontiffs. After which, they say, her accuser, though great search was made for him, could never be found either alive or dead. But, though I have yet many other things to say concerning the manifestations of this goddess, I regard what has already been said as sufficient.

70 The sixth division of his religious institutions was devoted to those the Romans call *Salii*, whom Numa himself appointed out of the patricians, choosing twelve young men of the most graceful appearance.[100] These are the *Salii* whose holy things are deposited

---

100 *Cf.* Livy i. 20, 4.

on the Palatine hill and who are themselves called the (*Salii*) *Palatini*; for the (*Salii*) Agonales, [101] by some called the *Salii Collini*, the repository of whose holy things is on the Quirinal hill,[102] were appointed after Numa's time by King Hostilius, in pursuance of a vow he had made in the war against the Sabines. All these *Salii* are a kind of dancers and singers of hymns in praise of the gods of war. Their festival falls about the time of the Panathenaea,[103] in the month which they call March, and is celebrated at the public expense for many days, during which they proceed through the city with their dances to the Forum and to the Capitol and to many other places both private and public. They wear embroidered tunics girt about with wide girdles of bronze, and over these are fastened, with brooches, robes striped with scarlet and bordered with purple, which they call *trabeae*; this garment is peculiar to the Romans and a mark of the greatest honour. On their heads they wear *apices*, as they are called, that is, high caps contracted into the shape of a cone, which the Greeks call *kyrbasiai*. They have each of them a sword hanging at their girdle and in their right hand they hold a spear or a staff or something else of the sort, and on their left arm a Thracian buckler, which resembles a lozenge-shaped shield with its sides drawn in,[104] such as those are said to carry who among the Greeks perform the sacred rites of the Curetes. And, in my opinion

---

101 Usually called **Agonenses**.

102 "Colline hill," the absurd reading of the MSS. and editors, cannot be from the hand of Dionysius.

103 "Panathenaea" does not here mean the well-known Athenian festival (which took place in August), but the Quinquatria, the Roman festival in honour of Minerva (March 19-23). The principal celebration of the *Salii* began on the first of March and continued until at least the 24th; Polybius (xxi. 10, 12) gives the total period as thirty days.

104 "Lozenge-shaped" here doubtless means oval. What have been identified as these sacred *ancilia* are seen depicted on a few ancient coins and gems. They are of the shape often called "figure of eight." This was not the shape of the Thracian buckler, which is described as crescent-shaped.

at least, the *Salii*, if the word be translated into Greek, are Curetes, whom, because they are *kouroi* or "young men," we call by that name from their age, whereas the Romans call them *Salii* from their lively motions. For to leap and skip is by them called *salire*; and for the same reason they call all other dancers *saltatores*, deriving their name from the *Salii*, because their dancing also is attended by much leaping and capering. Whether I have been well advised or not in giving them this appellation, anyone who pleases may gather from their actions. For they execute their movements in arms, keeping time to a flute, sometimes all together, sometimes by turns, and while dancing sing certain traditional hymns. But this dance and exercise performed by armed men and the noise they make by striking their bucklers with their daggers, if we may base any conjectures on the ancient accounts, was originated by the Curetes. I need not mention the legend[105] which is related concerning them, since almost everybody is acquainted with it.

71 Among the vast number of bucklers which both the *Salii* themselves bear and some of their servants carry suspended from rods, they say there is one that fell from heaven and was found in the palace of Numa, though no one had brought it thither and no buckler of that shape had ever before been known among the Italians; and that for both these reasons the Romans concluded that this buckler had been sent by the gods. They add that Numa, desiring that it should be honoured by being carried through the city on holy days by the most distinguished young men and that annual sacrifices should be offered to it, but at the same time being fearful both of the plot of his enemies and of its disappearance by theft, caused many other bucklers to be made resembling the one

---

105 The legend that made them the protectors of the infant Zeus in the island of
   Crete; see chap. 61, 2. They were said to have clashed their spears against
   their shields in order to drown the cries of the infant Zeus, lest his
   whereabouts should be discovered.

which fell from heaven, Mamurius, an artificer, having undertake the work; so that, as a result of the perfect resemblance of the man-made imitations, the shape of the buckler sent by the gods was rendered inconspicuous and difficult to be distinguished by those who might plot to possess themselves of it. This dancing after the manner of the Curetes was a native institution among the Romans and was held in great honour by them, as I gather from many other indications and especially from what takes place in their processions both in the Circus and in the theatres. For in all of them young men clad in handsome tunics, with helmets, swords and bucklers, march in file. These are the leaders of the procession and are called by the Romans, from a game of which the Lydians seem to have been the inventors, *ludiones*;[106] they show merely a certain resemblance, in my opinion, to the *Salii*, since they do not, like the *Salii*, do any of the things characteristic of the Curetes, either in their hymns or dancing. And it was necessary that the *Salii* should be free men and native Romans and that both their fathers and mothers should be living; whereas the others are of any condition whatsoever. But why should I say more about them?

72 The seventh division of his sacred institutions was devoted to the college of the *fetiales*;[107] these may be called in Greek *eirênodikai* or "arbiters of peace." They are chosen men, from the best families, and exercise their holy office for life; King Numa was also the first who instituted this holy magistracy among the Romans. But whether he took his example from those called the Aequicoli,[108] according to the opinion of some, or from the city of Ardea, as

---

106 From the well-known chapter (vii. 2) in which Livy describes the beginnings of drama at Rome we learn that these *ludiones* or "players" were at first mere dancers and only later pantomimists.

107 *Cf.* Livy i. 24 and 32. Livy does not mention the *fetiales* until the reign of Numa's successor, Tullus Hostilius.

108 Another name for the Aequi; but in time the word seems to have been interpreted as meaning: "lovers of justice" (from *aequum* and *colere*).

Gellius writes, I cannot say. It is sufficient for me to state that before Numa's reign the college of the *fetiales* did not exist among the Romans. It was instituted by Numa when he was upon the point of making war on the people of Fidenae, who had raided and ravaged his territories, in order to see whether they would come to an accommodation with him without war; and that is what they actually did, being constrained by necessity. But since the college of the *fetiales* is not in use among the Greeks, I think it incumbent on me to relate how many and how great affairs fall under its jurisdiction, to the end that those who are unacquainted with the piety practised by the Romans of those times may not be surprised to find that all their wars had the most successful outcome; for it will appear that the origins and motives of them all were most holy, and for this reason especially the gods were propitious to them in the dangers that attended them. The multitude of duties, to be sure, that fall within the province of these *fetiales* makes it no easy matter to enumerate them all; but to indicate them by a summary outline, they are as follows: It is their duty to take care that the Romans do not enter upon an unjust war against any city in alliance with them, and if others begin the violation of treaties against them, to go as ambassadors and first make formal demand for justice, and then, if the others refuse to comply with their demands, to sanction war. In like manner, if any people in alliance with the Romans complain of having been injured by them and demand justice, these men are to determine whether they have suffered anything in violation of their alliance; and if they find their complaints well grounded, they are to seize the accused and deliver them up to the injured parties. They are also to take cognizance of the crimes committed against ambassadors, to take care that treaties are religiously observed, to make peace, and if they find that peace has been made otherwise than is prescribed by the holy laws, to set it aside; and to inquire into and expiate the transgressions of the generals in so far as they relate to oaths and treaties, concerning which I shall speak in the proper places. As to the functions they performed in the quality of heralds when they went to any city thought to have injured the Romans (for these things also are worthy of our knowledge, since they were carried out with great regard to both religion and justice), I have received the following account: One of these *fetiales*, chosen by his colleagues, wearing his sacred robes and insignia to distinguish him from all others, proceeded towards the city whose inhabitants had done the injury; and, stopping at the border, he called upon Jupiter and the rest of the gods to witness that he was come to demand justice on behalf of the Roman State. Thereupon he took an oath that he was going to a city that had done an injury; and having uttered the most dreadful imprecation against himself and Rome, if what he averred was not true, he the entered their borders. Afterwards, he called to witness the first person he met, whether it was one of the countrymen or one of the townspeople, and having repeated the same imprecations, he advanced towards the city. And before he entered it he called to witness in the same manner the gate-keeper or the first person he met at the gates, after which he proceeded to the forum; and taking his stand there, he discussed with the magistrates the reasons for his coming, adding everywhere the same oaths and imprecations. If, then, they were disposed to offer satisfaction by delivering up the guilty, he departed as a friend taking leave of friends, carrying the prisoners with him. Or, if they desired time to deliberate, he allowed them ten days, after which he returned and waited till they had made this request three times. But after the expiration of the thirty days, if the city still persisted in refusing to grant him justice, he called both the celestial and infernal gods to witness and went away, saying no more than this, that the Roman State would deliberate at its leisure concerning these people. Afterwards he, together with the other *fetiales*, appeared before the senate and declared that they had done everything that was ordained by the holy laws, and that, if the senators wished to vote for war, there would be no obstacle on the part of the gods. But if any of these things was omitted, neither the senate nor the people had the power to vote for war. Such, then, is the account we have received concerning the *fetiales*.

73 The last branch of the ordinances of Numa related to the sacred offices allotted to those who held the higher priesthoods and the greatest power among the Romans.[109] These, from one of the duties they perform, namely, the repairing of the wooden bridge,[110] are in their own language called *pontifices*; but they have jurisdiction over the most weighty matters. For they the judges in all religious causes wherein private citizens, magistrates or the ministers of the gods are concerned; they make laws for the observance of any religious rites, not established by written law or custom, which may seem to them worthy of receiving the sanction of law and custom; they inquire into the conduct of all magistrates to whom the performance of any sacrifice or other religious duty is committed, and also into that of all the priests; they take care that their servants and ministers whom they employ in religious rites commit no error in the matter of the sacred laws; to the laymen who are unacquainted with such matters they are the expounders and interpreters of everything relating to the worship of the gods and genii; and if they find that any disobey their orders, they inflict punishment upon them with due regard to every offence; moreover, they are not liable to any prosecution or punishment, nor are they accountable to the senate or to the people, at least concerning religious matters. Hence, if anyone wishes to call them *hierodidaskaloi, hieronomoi, hierophylakes*, or, as I think proper,

---

109 *Cf.* Livy i. 20, 5-7.

110 According to Dionysius himself (iii. 45) the *pons sublicius* was built by Ancus Marcius; but it will be noted that he does not say explicitly that these priests bore the name *pontifices* from the first.

hierophantai,[111] he will not be in error. When one of them dies, another is appointed in his place, being chosen, not by the people, but by the *pontifices* themselves, who select the person they think best qualified among their fellow citizens; and the one thus approved of receives the priesthood, provided the omens are favourable to him. These — not to speak of others less important — are the greatest and the most notable regulations made by Numa concerning religious worship and divided by him according to the different classes of sacred rites; and through these it came about that the city increased in piety.

74 His regulations, moreover, that tended to inspire frugality and moderation in the life of the individual citizen and to create a passion for justice, which preserves the harmony of the State, were exceedingly numerous, some of them being comprehended in written laws, and others not written down but embodied in custom and long usage. To treat of all these would be a difficult task; but mention of the two of them which have been most frequently cited will suffice to give evidence of the rest. First, to the end that people should be content with what they had and should not covet what belonged to others, there was the law that appointed boundaries to every man's possessions. For, having ordered every one to draw a line around his own land and to place stones on the bounds, he consecrated these stones to Jupiter Terminalis and ordained that all should assemble at the place every year on a fixed day and offer sacrifices to them; and he made the festival in honour of these gods of boundaries among the most dignified of all. This festival the Romans call Terminalia, from the boundaries, and the boundaries themselves, by the change of one letter as compared with our

---

111 These words mean respectively "teachers of religion," "supervisors of religion," "guardians of religion" and "interpreters of religion." The last is the term regularly employed by Dionysius when he translates the word *pontifices*.

language, they call *termines*.[112] He also enacted that, if any person demolished or displaced these boundary stones he should be looked upon as devoted to the god, to the end that anyone who wished might kill him as a sacrilegious person with impunity and without incurring any stain of guilt. He established this law with reference not only to private possessions but also to those belonging to the public; for he marked these also with boundary stones, to the end that the gods of boundaries might distinguish the lands of the Romans from those of their neighbours, and the public lands from such as belonged to private persons. Memorials of this custom are observed by the Romans down to our times, purely as a religious form. For they look upon these boundary stones as gods and sacrifice to them yearly, offering up no kind of animal (for it is not lawful to stain these stones with blood), but cakes made of cereals and other first-fruits of the earth. But they ought still to observe the motive, as well, which led Numa to regard these boundary stones as gods and content themselves with their own possessions without appropriating those of others either by violence or by fraud; whereas now there are some who, in disregard of what is best and of the example of their ancestors, instead of distinguishing that which is theirs from that which belongs to others, set as bounds to their possessions, not the law, but their greed to possess everything, — which is disgraceful behaviour. But we leave the considerations of these matters to others.

---

112 When Dionysius says that the Latin and Greek words differ by only one letter he is almost certainly referring to the stem (*termin-*: τερμον-) or to the nominative singular (*termen*: τέρμων); he would naturally disregard the case-endings, since he regularly inflects Latin words as if they were Greek. The form τέρμινας, *i.e. terminēs*, can hardly be from the hand of Dionysius, who must have known that most nouns terminating in -*men* were neuter (compare his κάρμινα, *carmina*, in i. 31). The true form here should evidently be either τέρμινα or τερμίνους *i.e. termina* or *termini* (to cite them in the nominative).

Book II

75 By such laws Numa brought the State to frugality and moderation. And in order to encourage the observance of justice in the matter of contracts, he hit upon a device which was unknown to all who have established the most celebrated constitutions. For, observing that contracts made in public and before witnesses are, out of respect for the persons present, generally observed and that few are guilty of any violation of them, but that those which are made without witnesses — and these are much more numerous than the others — rest on no other security than the faith of those who make them, he thought it incumbent on him to make this faith the chief object of his care and to render it worthy of divine worship. For he felt that Justice, Themis, Nemesis, and those the Greeks call Erinyes, with other concepts of the kind, had been sufficiently revered and worshipped as gods by the men of former times, but that Faith, than which there is nothing greater nor more sacred among men, was not yet worshipped either by states in their public capacity or by private persons. As the result of these reflexions he, first of all men, erected a temple to the Public Faith and instituted sacrifices in her honour at the public expense in the same manner as to the rest of the gods.[113] And in truth the result was bound to be that this attitude of good faith and constancy on the part of the State toward all men would in the course of time render the behaviour of the individual citizens similar. In any case, so revered and inviolable a thing was good faith in their estimation, that the greatest oath a man could take was by his own faith, and this had greater weight than all the testimony taken together. And if there was any dispute between one man and another concerning a contract entered into without witnesses, the faith of either of the parties was sufficient to decide the controversy and prevent it from going any farther. And the magistrates and courts of justice based their decisions in most causes on the oaths of the parties attesting by

113 *Cf.* Livy i. 21, 1 and 4.

their faith. Such regulations, devised by Numa at that time to encourage moderation and enforce justice, rendered the Roman State more orderly than the best regulated household.

76 But the measures which I am now going to relate made it both careful to provide itself with necessaries and industrious in acquiring the advantages that flow from labour. For this man, considering that a State which was to love justice and to continue in the practice of moderation ought to abound in all things necessary to the support of life, divided the whole country into what are called *pagi* or "districts," and over each of these districts he appointed an official whose duty it was to inspect and visit the lands lying in his own jurisdiction. These men, going their rounds frequently, made a record of the lands that were well and ill cultivated and laid it before the king, who repaid the diligence of the careful husbandmen with commendations and favours, and by reprimanding and fining the slothful encouraged them to cultivate their lands with greater attention. Accordingly, the people, being freed from wars and exempt from any attendance on the affairs of the State, and at the same time being disgraced and punished for idleness and sloth, all became husbandmen and looked upon the riches which the earth yields and which of all others are the most just as more enjoyable than the precarious influence of a military life. And by the same means Numa came to be beloved of his subjects, the example of his neighbours, and the theme of posterity. It was owing to these measures that neither civil dissension broke the harmony of the State nor foreign war interrupted the observance of his most excellent and admirable institutions. For their neighbours were so far from looking upon the peaceful tranquillity of the Romans as an opportunity for attacking them, that, if at any time they were at war with one another, they chose the Romans for mediators and wished to settle their enmities under the arbitration of Numa. This man, therefore, I should take no shame in placing among the foremost of those who have been celebrated for their felicity in life. For he was of royal birth and of royal appearance; and he pursued an education which was not the kind of useless training that deals only with words,[114] but a discipline that taught him to practise piety and every other virtue. When he was young he was thought worthy to assume the sovereignty over the Romans, who had invited him to that dignity upon the reputation of his virtue; and he continued to command the obedience of his subjects during his whole life. He lived to a very advanced age without any impairment of his faculties and without suffering any blow at Fortune's hands; and he died the easiest of all deaths, being withered by age, the genius who had been allotted to him from his birth having continued the same favour to him till he disappeared from among men. He lived more than eighty years and reigned forty-three, leaving behind him, according to most historians, four sons and one daughter, whose posterity remain to this day; but according to Gnaeus Gellius he left only one daughter, who was the mother of Ancus Marcius, the second[115] king of the Romans after him. His death was greatly lamented by the state, which gave him a most splendid funeral. He lies buried upon the Janiculum, on the other side of the river Tiber. Such is the account we have received concerning Numa Pompilius.

---

114 A thrust at the sophists or rhetoricians.
115 Literally, "the third," counting inclusively.

Book III

1 After[1] the death of Numa Pompilius the senate, being once more in full control of the commonwealth, resolved to abide by the same form of government, and as the people did not adopt any contrary opinion, they appointed some of the older senators to govern as *interreges* for a definite number of days.[2] These men, pursuant to the unanimous desire of the people, chose as king Tullus Hostilius, whose descent was as follows. From Medullia, a city which had been built by the Albans and made a Roman colony by Romulus after he had taken it by capitulation, a man of distinguished birth and great fortune, named Hostilius, had removed to Rome and married a woman of the Sabine race, the daughter of Hersilius, the same woman who had advised her country-women to go as envoys to their fathers on behalf of their husbands at the time when the Sabines were making war against the Romans, and was regarded as the person chiefly responsible for the alliance then concluded by the leaders of the two nations.[3] This man, after taking part with Romulus in many wars and performing mighty deeds in the battles with the Sabines, died, leaving an only son, a young child at the time, and was buried by the kings in the principal part of the Forum and honoured with a monument and an inscription testifying to his valour. His only son, having come to manhood and married a woman of distinction, had by her Tullus Hostilius, a man of action, the same who was now chosen king by a vote passed by the citizens concerning him according to the laws; and the decision of the people was confirmed by favourable omens from Heaven. The year in which he assumed the sovereignty was the second of the twenty-

---

1 *Cf.* Livy i. 22, 1 f.
2 *Cf.* ii, 57.
3 *Cf.* ii, 45 f.

seventh Olympiad,[4] the one in which Eurybates, an Athenian, won the prize in the foot-race, Leostratus being archon at Athens. Tullus, immediately upon his accession, gained the hearts of all the labouring class and of the needy among the populace by performing an act of the most splendid kind. It was this: The kings before him had possessed much fertile land, especially reserved for them, from the revenues of which they not only offered sacrifices to the gods, but also had abundant provision for their private needs. This land Romulus had acquired in war by dispossessing the former owners, and when he died childless, Numa Pompilius, his successor, had enjoyed its use; it was no longer the property of the state, but the inherited possession of the successive kings. Tullus now permitted this land to be divided equally among such of the Romans as had no allotment, declaring that his own patrimony was sufficient both for the sacrifices and for his personal expenditures. By this act of humanity he relieved the poor among the citizens by freeing them from the necessity of labouring as serfs on the estates of others. And, to the end that none might lack a habitation either, he included within the city wall the hill called the Caelian, where those Romans who were unprovided with dwellings were allotted a sufficient amount of ground and built houses; and he himself had his residence in this quarter. These, then, are the memorable actions reported of this king so far as regards his civil administration.

2 Many[5] military exploits are related of him, but the greatest are those which I shall now narrate, beginning with the war against the Albans. The man responsible for the quarrel between the two cities and the severing of their bond of kinship was an Alban named Cluilius,[6] who had been honoured with the chief magistracy; this

---

4   670 B.C. For the chronology see Intro. pp. xxvi ff.
5   For chaps. 2 f. *cf.* Livy i. 22, 3-7.
6   The traditional spelling of this name is followed in the translation, though it is uncertain whether Dionysius thought of it as Cluilius or Cloelius. See critical

man, vexed at the prosperity of the Romans and unable to contain his envy, and being by nature headstrong and somewhat inclined to madness, resolved to involve the cities in war with each other. But not seeing how he could persuade the Albans to permit him to lead an army against the Romans without just and urgent reasons, he contrived a plan of the following sort: he permitted the poorest and boldest of the Albans to pillage the fields of the Romans, promising them immunity, and so caused many to overrun the neighbouring territory in a series of plundering raids, as they would now be pursuing without danger gains from which they would never desist even under the constraint of fear. In doing this he was following a very natural line of reasoning, as the event bore witness. For he assumed that the Romans would not submit to being plundered but would rush to arms, and he would thus have an opportunity of accusing them to his people as the aggressors in the war; and he also believed that the majority of the Albans, envying the prosperity of their colony, would gladly listen to these false accusations and would begin war against the Romans. And that is just what happened. For when the worst elements of each city fell to robbing and plundering each other and at last a Roman army made an incursion into the territory of the Albans and killed or took prisoner many of the bandits, Cluilius assembled the people and inveighed against the Romans at great length, showed them many who were wounded, produced the relations of those who had been seized or slain, and at the same time added other circumstances of his own invention; whereupon it was voted on his motion to send an embassy first of all to demand satisfaction for what had happened, and then, if the Romans refused it, to begin war against them.

3 Upon the arrival of the ambassadors at Rome, Tullus, suspecting that they had come to demand satisfaction, resolved to

note.

220

anticipate them in doing this, since he wished to turn upon the Albans the blame for breaking the compact between them and their colony. For there existed a treaty between the two cities which had been made in the reign of Romulus, wherein, among other articles, it was stipulated that neither of them should begin a war, but if either complained of any injury whatsoever, that city would demand satisfaction from the city which had done the injury, and failing to obtain it, should then make war as a matter of necessity, the treaty being looked upon as already broken. Tullus, therefore, taking care that the Romans should not be the first called upon to give satisfaction and, by refusing it, become guilty in the eyes of the Albans, ordered the most distinguished of his friends to entertain the ambassadors of the Albans with every courtesy and to detain them inside their homes while he himself, pretending to be occupied with some necessary business, put off their audience. The following night he sent to Alba some Romans of distinction, duly instructed as to the course they should pursue, together with the *fetiales*,[7] to demand satisfaction from the Albans for the injuries the Romans had received. These, having performed their journey before sunrise, found Cluilius in the market-place at the time when the early morning crowd was gathered there. And having set forth the injuries which the Romans had received at the hands of the Albans, they demanded that he should act in conformity with the compact between the cities. But Cluilius, alleging that the Albans had been first in sending envoys to Rome to demand satisfaction and had not even been vouchsafed an answer, ordered the Romans to depart, on the ground that they had violated the terms of the treaty, and declared war against them. The chief of the embassy, however, as he was departing, demanded from Cluilius an answer to just this one question, namely, whether he admitted that those were violating the treaty who, being the first called upon to give satisfaction, had

7   *Cf.* ii. 72.

refused to comply with any part of their obligation. And when Cluilius said he did, he exclaimed: "Well, then, I call the gods, whom we made witnesses of our treaty, to witness that the Romans, having been the first to be refused satisfaction, will be undertaking a just war against the violators of that treaty, and that it is you Albans who have avoided giving satisfaction, as the events themselves show. For you, being the first called upon for satisfaction, have refused it and you have been the first to declare war against us. Look, therefore, for vengeance to come upon you ere long with the sword." Tullus, having learned of all this from the ambassadors upon their return to Rome, then ordered the Albans to be brought before him and to state the reasons for their coming; and when they had delivered the message entrusted to them by Cluilius and were threatening war in case they did not obtain satisfaction, he replied: "I have anticipated you in doing this, and having obtained nothing that the treaty directs, I declare against the Albans the war that is both necessary and just."

4 After[8] these pretences they both prepared themselves for war not only arming their own forces but also calling to their assistance those of their subjects. And when they had everything ready the two armies drew near to each other and encamped at the distance of forty stades from Rome, the Albans at the Cluilian Ditches,[9] as they are called (for they still preserve the name of the man who constructed them) and the Romans a little farther inside,[10] having chosen the most convenient place for their camp. When the two armies saw each other's forces neither inferior in numbers nor poorly armed nor to be despised in respect of their other preparations, they lost their impetuous ardour for the combat,

---

8   For chaps. 4-12 *cf.* Livy i. 23.

9   *Fossae Cluiliae*. Livy also places this landmark at the same distance (five miles) from Rome; nothing more is known about it.

10 *i.e.*, nearer to Rome.

which they had felt at first because of their expectation of defeating the enemy by their very onset, and they took thought rather of defending themselves by building their ramparts to a greater height than of being the first to attack. At the same time the most intelligent among them began to reflect, feeling that they were not being governed by the best counsels, and there was a spirit of faultfinding against those in authority. And as the time dragged on in vain (for they were not injuring one another to any notable extent by sudden dashes of the light-armed troops or by skirmishes of the horse), the man who was looked upon as responsible for the war, Cluilius, being irked at lying idle, resolved to march out with his army and challenge the enemy to battle, and if they declined it, to attack their entrenchments. And having made his preparations for an engagement and all the plans necessary for an attack upon the enemy's ramparts, in case that should prove necessary, when night came on he went to sleep in the general's tent, attended by his usual guard; but about daybreak he was found dead, no signs appearing on his body either of wounds, strangling, poison, or any other violent death.

5 This unfortunate event appearing extraordinary to everybody, as one would naturally expect, and the cause of it being enquired into — for no preceding illness could be alleged — those who ascribed all human fortunes to divine providence said that this death had been due to the anger of the gods, because he had kindled an unjust and unnecessary war between the mother-city and her colony. But others, who looked upon war as a profitable business and thought they had been deprived of great gains, attributed the event to human treachery and envy, accusing some of his fellow citizens of the opposing faction of having made away with him by secret and untraceable poisons that they had discovered. Still others alleged that, being overcome with grief and despair, he had taken his own life, since all his plans were becoming difficult and impracticable and none of the things that he had looked forward to in the beginning when he first took hold of affairs was succeeding according to his desire. But those who were not influenced by either friendship or enmity for the general and based their judgment of what had happened on the soundest grounds were of the opinion that neither the anger of the gods nor the envy of the opposing faction nor despair of his plans had put an end to his life, but rather Nature's stern law and fate, when once he had finished the destined course which is marked out for everyone that is born. Such, then, was the end that Cluilius met, before he had performed any noble deed. In his place Mettius Fufetius was chosen general by those in the camp and invested with absolute power;[11] he was a man without either ability to conduct a war or constancy to preserve a peace, one who, though he had been at first as zealous as any of the Albans in creating strife between the two cities and for that reason had been honoured with the command after the death of Cluilius, yet after he had obtained it and perceived the many difficulties and embarrassments with which the business was attended, no longer adhered to the same plans, but resolved to delay and put off matters, since he observed that not all the Albans now had the same ardour for war and also that the victims, whenever he offered sacrifice concerning battle, were unfavourable. And at last he even determined to invite the enemy to an accommodation, taking the initiative himself in sending heralds, after he had been informed of a danger from the outside which threatened both the Albans and Romans, a danger which, if they did not terminate their war with each other by a treaty, was unavoidable and bound to destroy both armies. The danger was this:

---

11 Livy styles him *dictator* (i. 23, 4; 27, 1) but calls Cluilius *rex* (i. 23,4).

Book III

6 The Veientes and Fidenates, who inhabited large and populous cities, had in the reign of Romulus engaged in a war with the Romans for command and sovereignty, and after losing many armies in the course of the war and being punished by the loss of part of their territory, they had been forced to become subjects of the conquerors; concerning which I have given a precise account in the preceding Book.[12] But having enjoyed an uninterrupted peace during the reign of Numa Pompilius, they had greatly increased in population, wealth and every other form of prosperity. Elated, therefore, by these advantages, they again aspired to freedom, assumed a bolder spirit and prepared to yield obedience to the Romans no longer. For a time, indeed, their intention of revolting remained undiscovered, but during the Alban war it became manifest. For when they learned that the Romans had marched out with all their forces to engaged the Albans, they thought that they had now got the most favourable opportunity for their attack, and through their most influential men they entered into a secret conspiracy. It was arranged that all who were capable of bearing arms should assemble in Fidenae, going secretly, a few at a time, so as to escape as far as possible the notice of those against whom the plot was aimed, and should remain there awaiting the moment when the armies of the Romans and Albans should quit their camps and march out to battle, the actual time to be indicated to them by means of signals given by some scouts posted on the mountains; and as soon as the signals were raised they were all to take arms and advance in haste against the combatants (the road leading from Fidenae to the camps was not a long one, but only a march of two or three hours at most), and appearing on the battlefield at the time when presumably the conflict would be over, they were to regard neither side as friends, but whether the Romans or the Albans had won, were to slay the victors. This was the plan of action on which

12 ii. 53-55.

the chiefs of those cities had determined. If, therefore, the Albans, in their contempt for the Romans, had rushed more boldly into an engagement and had resolved to stake everything upon the issue of a single battle, nothing could have hindered the treachery contrived against them from remaining secret and both their armies from being destroyed. But as it was, their delay in beginning war, contrary to all expectations, and the length of time they employed in making their preparations were bringing their foes' plans to nought. For some of the conspirators, either seeking to compass their private advantage or envying their leaders and those who had been the authors of the undertaking or fearing that others might lay information — a thing which has often happened in conspiracies where there are many accomplices and the execution is long delayed — or being compelled by the will of Heaven, which could not consent that a wicked design should meet with success, informed their enemies of the treachery.

7 Fufetius, upon learning of this, grew still more desirous of making an accommodation, feeling that they now had no choice left of any other course. The king of the Romans also had received information of this conspiracy from his friends in Fidenae, so that he, too, made no delay but hearkened to the overtures made by Fufetius. When the two met in the space between the camps, each being attended by his council consisting of persons of competent judgment, they first embraced, according to their former custom, and exchanged the greetings usual among friends and relations, and then proceeded to discuss an accommodation. And first the Alban leader began as follows:

"It seems to me necessary to begin my speech by setting forth the reasons why I have determined to take the initiative in proposing a termination of the war, though neither defeated by you Romans in battle nor hindered from supplying my army with provisions nor reduced to any other necessity, to the end that you may not imagine that a recognition of the weakness of my own force or a belief that yours is difficult to overcome makes me seek a plausible excuse for ending the war. For, should you entertain such an opinion of us, you would be intolerably severe, and, as if you were already victorious in the war, you could not bring yourself to do anything reasonable. In order, therefore, that you may not impute to me false reasons for my purpose to end the war, listen to the true reasons. My country having appointed me general with absolute power, as soon as I took over the command I considered what were the causes which had disturbed the peace of our cities. And finding them trivial and petty and of too little consequence to dissolve so great a friendship and kinship, I concluded that neither we Albans nor you Romans had been governed by the best counsels. And I was further convinced of this and led to condemn the great madness that we both have shown, when once I had taken hold of affairs and began to sound out each man's private opinion. For I found that the Albans neither in their private meetings nor in their public assemblies were all of one mind regarding the war; and the signs from Heaven, whenever I consulted the victims concerning battle, presenting, as they did, far greater difficulties than those based on human reasoning, caused me great dismay and anxiety. In view, therefore, of these considerations, I restrained my eagerness for armed conflicts and devised delays and postponements of the war, in the belief that you Romans would make the first overtures towards peace. And indeed you should have done this, Tullus, since you are our colony, and not have waited till your mother-city set the example. For the founders of cities have a right to receive as great respect from their colonies as parents from their children. But while we have been delaying and watching each other, to see which side should first make friendly overtures, another motive, more compelling than any arguments drawn from human reason, has arisen to draw us together. And since I learned of this while it was yet a secret to you, I felt that I ought no longer to aim at appearances in concluding peace. For dreadful designs are being formed against us, Tullus, and a deadly plot has been woven against both of us, a plot which was bound to overwhelm and destroy us easily and without effort, bursting upon us like a conflagration or a flood. The authors of these wicked designs are the chiefs of the Fidenates and Veientes, who have conspired together. Hear now the nature of their plot and how the knowledge of their secret design came to me."

8 With these words he gave to one of those present the letters which a certain man had brought to him from his friends at Fidenae, and desired him to read them out; and at the same time he produced the man who had brought the letters. After they were read and the man had informed them of everything he had learned by word of mouth from the persons who had despatched the letters, all present were seized with great astonishment, as one would naturally expect upon their hearing of so great and so unexpected a danger. Then Fufetius, after a short pause, continued:

"You have now heard, Romans, the reasons why I have thus far been postponing armed conflicts with you and have now thought fit to make the first overtures concerning peace. After this it is for you to consider whether, in order to avenge the seizure of some miserable oxen and sheep, you ought to continue to carry on an implacable war against your founders and fathers, in the course of which, whether conquered or conquerors, you are sure to be destroyed, or, laying aside your enmity toward your kinsmen, to march with us against our common foes, who have plotted not only to revolt from you but also to attack you — although they have neither suffered any harm nor had any reason to fear that they should suffer any — and, what is more, have not attacked us openly, according to the universally recognized laws of war, but under cover of darkness, so that their treachery could least be suspected and guarded against. But I need say no more to convince you that we ought to lay aside our enmity and march with all speed against these impious men (for it would be madness to think otherwise), since you are already resolved and will pursue that resolution. But in what manner the terms of reconciliation may prove honourable and advantageous to both cities (for probably you have long been eager to hear this) I shall now endeavour to explain. For my part, I hold that that mutual reconciliation is the best and the most becoming to kinsmen and friends, in which there is no rancour nor remembrance of past injuries, but a general and sincere remission of everything that has been done or suffered on both sides; less honourable than this form of reconciliation is one by which, indeed, the mass of the people are absolved of blame, but those who have injured one another are compelled to undergo such a trial as reason and law direct. Of these two methods of reconciliation, now, it is my opinion that we ought to choose the one which is the more honourable and magnanimous, and we ought to pass a decree of general amnesty. However, if you, Tullus, do not wish a reconciliation of this kind, but prefer that the accusers and the accused should mutually give and receive satisfaction, the Albans are also ready to do this, after first settling our mutual hatreds. And if, besides this, you have any other method to suggest which is either more honourable or more just, you cannot lay it before us too soon, and for doing so I shall be greatly obliged to you."

9 After Fufetius had thus spoken, the king of the Romans answered him and said:

"We also, Fufetius, felt that it would be a grave calamity for us if we were forced to decide this war between kinsmen by blood and slaughter, and whenever we performed the sacrifices preparatory to war we were forbidden by them to begin an engagement. As regards the secret conspiracy entered into by the Fidenates and Veientes against us both, we have learned of it, a little ahead of you, through our friends in their midst, and we are not unprepared against their plot, but have taken measures not only to suffer no mischief ourselves but also to punish those foes in such a manner as their treachery deserves. Nor were we less disposed than you to put an end to the war without a battle rather than by the sword; yet we did not consider it fitting that we should be the first to send ambassadors to propose an accommodation, since we had not been the first to begin the war, but had merely defended ourselves against those who had begun it. But once you are ready to lay down your arms, we will gladly receive your proposal, and will not scrutinize too closely the terms of the reconciliation, but will accept those that are the best and the most magnanimous, forgiving every injury and offence we have received from the city of Alba — if, indeed, those deserve to be called public offences of the city for which your general Cluilius was responsible, and has paid no mean penalty to the gods for the wrongs he did us both. Let every occasion, therefore, for complaint, whether private or public, be removed and let no memory of past injuries any longer remain — even as you also, Fufetius, think fitting. Yet it is not enough for us to consider merely how we may compose our present enmity toward one another, but we must further take measures to prevent our ever going to war again; for the purpose of our present meeting is not to obtain a postponement but rather an end of our evils. What settlement of the war, therefore, will be enduring and what contribution must each of us make toward the situation, in order that we may be friends both now and for all time? This, Fufetius, you have omitted to tell us; but I shall endeavour to go on and supply this omission also. If, on the one hand, the Albans would cease to envy the Romans the advantages they possess, advantages which were acquired not without great perils and many hardships (in any case you have suffered no injury at our hands, great or slight, but you hate us for this reason alone, that we seem to be better off than you); and if, on the other hand, the Romans would cease to suspect the Albans of always plotting against them and would cease to be on their guard against them as against enemies (for no one can be a firm friend to one who distrusts him). How, then, shall each of these results be brought about? Not by inserting them in the treaty, nor by our both swearing to them over the sacrificial victims — for these are small and weak assurances — but by looking upon each other's fortunes as common to us both. For there is only one cure, Fufetius, for the bitterness which men feel over the advantages of others, and that is for the envious no longer to regard the advantages of the envied as other than their own. In order to accomplish this, I think the Romans ought to place equally at the disposal of the Albans all the advantages they either now or shall hereafter possess; and that the Albans ought cheerfully the accept this offer and all of you, if possible, or at least the most and the best of you, become residents of Rome. Was it not, indeed, a fine thing for the Sabines and Tyrrhenians to leave their own cities and transfer their habitation to Rome? And for you, who are our nearest kinsmen, will it not accordingly be a fine thing if this same step is taken? If, however, you refuse to inhabit the same city with us, which is already large and will be larger, but are going to cling to your ancestral hearths, do this at least: appoint a single council to consider what shall be of advantage to each city, and give the supremacy to that one of the two cities which is the more powerful and is in a position to render the greater services to the weaker. This is what I recommend, and if these proposals are carried out I believe that we shall then be lasting friends; whereas, so long as we inhabit two cities of equal eminence, as at present, there never will be harmony between us."

10 Fufetius, hearing this, desired time for taking counsel; and withdrawing from the assembly along with the Albans who were present, he consulted with them whether they should accept the proposals. Then, having taken the opinions of all, he returned to the assembly and spoke as follows: "We do not think it best, Tullus, to abandon our country or to desert the sanctuaries of our fathers, the hearths of our ancestors, and the place which our forbears have possessed for nearly five hundred years, particularly when we are not compelled to such a course either by war or by any other calamity inflicted by the hand of Heaven. But we are not opposed to establishing a single council and letting one of the two cities rule over the other. Let this article, then, also be inserted in the treaty, if agreeable, and let every excuse for war be removed."

These conditions having been agreed upon, they fell to disputing which of the two cities should be given the supremacy and many words were spoken by both of them upon this subject, each contending that his own city should rule over the other. The claims advanced by the Alban leader were as follows:

"As for us, Tullus, we deserve to rule over even all the rest of Italy, inasmuch as we represent a Greek nation and the greatest nation of all that inhabit this country. But to the sovereignty of the Latin nation, even if no other, we think ourselves entitled, not without reason, but in accordance with the universal law which Nature bestowed upon all men, that ancestors should rule their posterity. And above all our other colonies, against whom we have thus far no reason to complain, we think we ought to rule your city, having sent our colony thither not so long ago that the stock sprung from us is already extinct, exhausted by the lapse of time, but only the third generation before the present. If, indeed, Nature, inverting human rights, shall ever command the young to rule over the old and posterity over their progenitors, then we shall submit to seeing the mother-city ruled by its colony, but not before. This, then, is one argument we offer in support of our claim, in virtue of which we will never willingly yield the command to you. Another argument — and do not take this as said by way of censure or reproach of you Romans, but only from necessity — is the fact that the Alban race has to this day continued the same that it was under the founders of the city, and one cannot point to any race of mankind, except the Greeks and Latins, to whom we have granted citizenship; whereas you have corrupted the purity of your body politic by admitting Tyrrhenians, Sabines, and some others who were homeless, vagabonds and barbarians, and that in great numbers too, so that the true-born element among you that went out from our midst is become small, or rather a tiny fraction, in comparison with those who have been brought in and are of alien race. And if we should yield the command to you, the base-born will rule over the true-born, barbarians over Greeks, and immigrants over the native-born. For you cannot even say this much for yourself, that you have not permitted this immigrant mob to gain any control of public affairs but that you native-born citizens are yourselves the rulers and councillors of the commonwealth. Why, even for your kings you choose outsiders, and the greatest part of your senate consists of these newcomers; and to none of these conditions can you assert that you submit willingly. For what man of superior rank willingly allows himself to be ruled by an inferior? It would be great folly and baseness, therefore, on our part to accept willingly those evils which you must own you submit to through necessity. My last argument is this: The city of Alba has so far made no alteration in any part of its constitution, though it is already the eighteenth generation that it has been inhabited, but continues to observe in due form all its customs and traditions; whereas your city is still without order and discipline, due to its being newly founded and a conglomeration of many races, and it will require long ages and manifold turns of

233

fortune in order to be regulated and freed from those troubles and dissensions with which it is now agitated. But all will agree that order ought to rule over confusion, experience over inexperience, and health over sickness; and you do wrong in demanding the reverse."

11 After Fufetius had thus spoken, Tullus answered and said:

"The right which is derived from Nature and the virtue of one's ancestors, Fufetius and ye men of Alba, is common to us both; for we both boast the same ancestors, so that on this score neither of use ought to have any advantage or suffer any disadvantage. But as to your claim that by a kind of necessary law of Nature mother-cities should invariably rule over their colonies, it is neither true nor just. Indeed, there are many races of mankind among which the mother-cities do not rule over their colonies but are subject to them. The greatest and the most conspicuous instance of this is the Spartan state, which claims the right not only to rule over the other Greeks but even over the Doric nation, of which she is a colony. But why should I mention the others? For you who colonized our city are yourself a colony of the Lavinians. If, therefore, it is a law of Nature that the mother-city should rule over its colony, would not the Lavinians be the first to issue their just orders to both of us? To your first claim, then, and the one which carries with it the most specious appearance, this is a sufficient answer. But since you also undertook to compare the ways of life of the two cities, Fufetius, asserting that the nobility of the Albans has always remained the same while ours has been 'corrupted' by the various admixtures of foreigners, and demanded that the base-born should not rule over the well-born nor newcomers over the native-born, know, then, that in making this claim, too, you are greatly mistaken. For we are so far from being ashamed of having made the privileges of our city free to all who desired them that we even take the greatest pride in this course; moreover, we are not the originators of this admirable practice, but took the example from the city of Athens, which enjoys the greatest reputation among the Greeks, due in no small measure, if indeed not chiefly, to this very policy. And this principle, which has been to us the source of many advantages, affords us no ground either for complaint or regret, as if we had committed some error. Our chief magistracies and membership in the senate are held and the other honours among us are enjoyed, not by men possessed of great fortunes, nor by those who can show a long line of ancestors all natives of the country, but by such as are worthy of these honours; for we look upon the nobility of men as consisting in nothing else than in virtue. The rest of the populace are the body of the commonwealth, contributing strength and power to the decisions of the best men. It is owing to this humane policy that our city, from a small and contemptible beginning, is become large and formidable to its neighbours, and it is this policy which you condemn, Fufetius, that has laid for the Romans the foundation of that supremacy which none of the other Latins disputes with us. For the power of states consists in the force of arms, and this in turn depends upon a multitude of citizens; whereas, for small states that are sparsely populated and for that reason weak it is not possible to rule others, nay, even to rule themselves. On the whole, I am of the opinion that a man should only then disparage the government of other states and extol his own when he can show that his own, by following the principles he lays down, is grown flourishing and great, and that the states he censures, by not adopting them, are in an unhappy plight. But this is not our situation. On the contrary, your city, beginning with greater brilliance and enjoying greater resources than ours, has shrunk to lesser importance, while we, from small beginnings at first, have in a short time made Rome greater than all the neighbouring cities by following the very policies you condemned. And as for our factional strife — since this also,

Fufetius, met with your censure — it tends, not to destroy and diminish the commonwealth, but to preserve and enhance it. For there is emulation between our youths and our older men and between the newcomers and those who invited them in, to see which of us shall do more for the common welfare. In short, those who are going to rule others ought to be endowed with these two qualities, strength in war and prudence in counsel, both of which are present in our case. And that this is no empty boast, experience, more powerful than any argument, bears us witness. It is certain in any case that the city could not have attained to such greatness and power in the third generation after its founding, had not both valour and prudence abounded in it. Sufficient proof of its strength is afforded by the behaviour of many cities of the Latin race which owe their founding to you, but which, nevertheless, scorning your city, have come over us, choosing rather to be ruled by the Romans than by the Albans, because they look upon us as capable of doing both good to our friends and harm to our enemies, and upon you as capable of neither. I had many other arguments, and valid ones, Fufetius, to advance against the claims which you have presented; but as I see that argument is futile and that the result will be the same whether I say much or little to you, who, though our adversaries, are at the same time the arbiters of justice, I will make an end of speaking. However, since I conceive that there is but one way of deciding our differences which is the best and has been made use of by many, both barbarians and Greeks, when hatred has arisen between them either over the supremacy or over some territory in dispute, I shall propose this and then conclude, Let each of us fight the battle with some part of our forces and limit the fortune of war to a very small number of combatants; and let us give to that city whose champions shall overcome their adversaries the supremacy over the other. For such contests as cannot be determined by arguments are decided by arms."

236

12 These were the reasons urged by the two generals to support the pretensions of their respective cities to the supremacy; and the outcome of the discussion was the adoption of the plan Tullus proposed. For both the Albans and Romans who were present at the conference, in their desire to put a speedy end to the war, resolved to decide the controversy by arms. This also being agreed to, the question arose concerning the number of the combatants, since the two generals were not of the same mind. For Tullus desired that the fate of the war might be decided by the smallest possible number of combatants, the most distinguished man among the Albans fighting the bravest of the Romans in single combat, and he cheerfully offered himself to fight for his own country, inviting the Alban leader to emulate him. He pointed out that for those who have assumed the command of armies combats for sovereignty and power are glorious, not only when they conquer brave men, but also when they are conquered by the brave; and he enumerated all the generals and kings who had risked their lives for their country, regarding it as a reproach to them to have a greater share of the honours than others but a smaller share of the dangers. The Alban, however, while approving of the proposal to commit the fate of the cities to a few champions, would not agree to decide it by single combat. He owned that when commanders of the armies were seeking to establish their own power a combat between them for the supremacy was noble and necessary, but when states themselves were contending for the first place he thought the risk of single combat not only hazardous but even dishonourable, whether they met with good or ill fortune. And he proposed that three chosen men from each city should fight in the presence of all the Albans and Romans, declaring that this was the most suitable number for deciding any matter in controversy, as containing in itself a beginning, a middle and an end. This proposal meeting with the approval of both Romans and Albans, the conference broke up and each side returned to its own camp.

13 After[13] this the generals assembled their respective armies and gave them an account both of what they had said to each other and of the terms upon which they had agreed to put an end to the war. And both armies having with great approbation ratified the agreement entered into by their generals, there arose a wonderful emulation among the officers and soldiers alike, since a great many were eager to carry off the prize of valour in the combat and expressed their emulation not only by their words but also by their actions, so that their leaders found great difficulty in selecting the most suitable champions. For if anyone was renowned for his illustrious ancestry or remarkable for his strength of body, famous for some brave deed in action, or distinguished by some other good fortune or bold achievement, he insisted upon being chosen first among the three champions. This emulation, which was running to great lengths in both armies, was checked by the Alban general, who called to mind that some divine providence, long since foreseeing this conflict between the two cities, had arranged that their future champions should be sprung of no obscure families and should be brave in arms, most comely in appearance, and distinguished from the generality of mankind by their birth, which should be unusual and wonderful because of its extraordinary nature. It seems that Sicinius, an Alban, had at one and the same time married his twin daughters to Horatius, a Roman, and to Curiatius,[14] an Alban; and the two wives came with child at the same time and each was brought to bed, at her first lying-in, of three male children. The parents, looking upon the event as a happy omen both to their cities and families, brought up all these children

---

13 For chaps. 13-20 *cf.* Livy i. 24 f.
14 On the spelling Curiatius see the critical note.

till they arrived at manhood. And Heaven, as I said in the beginning, gave them beauty and strength and nobility of mind, so that they were not inferior to any of those most highly endowed by Nature. It was to these men that Fufetius resolved to commit the combat for supremacy; and having invited the Roman king to a conference, he addressed him as follows:

14 "Tullus, some god who keeps watch over both our cities would seem, just as upon many other occasions, so especially in what relates to this combat to have made his goodwill manifest. For that the champions who are to fight on behalf of all their people should be found inferior to none in birth, brave in arms, most comely in appearance, and that they should furthermore have been born of one father and mother, and, most wonderful of all, that they should have come into the world on the same day, the Horatii with you and the Curiatii with us, all this, I say, has every appearance of a remarkable instance of divine favour. Why therefore, do we not accept this great providence of the god and each of us invite the triplets on his side to engage in the combat for the supremacy? For not only all the other advantages which we could desire in the best-qualified champions are to be found in these men, but, as they are brothers, they will be more unwilling than any others among either the Romans or the Albans to forsake their companions when in distress; and furthermore, the emulation of the other youths, which cannot easily be appeased in any other way, will be promptly settled. For I surmise that among you also, as well as among the Albans, there is a kind of strife among many of those who lay claim to bravery; but if we inform them that some providential fortune has anticipated all human efforts and has itself furnished us with champions qualified to engage upon equal terms in the cause of the cities, we shall easily persuade them to desist. For they will then look upon themselves as inferior to the triplets, not in point of bravery, but only in respect of a special boon of Nature and of the favour of a Chance that is equally inclined toward both sides."[15]

15 After Fufetius had thus spoken and his proposal had bee received with general approbation (for the most important both of the Romans and Albans were with the two leaders), Tullus, after a short pause, spoke as follows:

"In other respects, Fufetius, you seem to me to have reasoned well; for it must be some wonderful fortune that has produced in both our cities in our generation a similarity of birth never known before. But of one consideration you seem to be unaware — a matter which will cause great reluctance in the youths if we ask them to fight with one another. For the mother of our Horatii is sister to the mother of the Alban Curiatii, and the young men have been brought up in the arms of both the women and cherish and love one another no less than their own brothers. Consider, therefore, whether, as they are cousins and have been brought up together, it would not be impious in us to put arms in their hands and invite them to mutual slaughter. For the pollution of kindred blood, if they are compelled to stain their hands with one another's blood, will deservedly fall upon us who compel them."

To this Fufetius answered: "Neither have I failed, Tullus, to note the kinship of the youths, nor did I purpose to compel them to fight with their cousins unless they themselves were inclined to undertake the combat. But as soon as this plan came into my mind I sent for the Alban Curiatii and sounded them in private to learn whether they were willing to engage in the combat; and it was only after they had accepted the proposal with incredible and wonderful alacrity that I decided to disclose my plan and bring it forward for

---

15 Literally, "equally inclined toward the adversary." Nature and Chance have specially favoured these six men above all their fellows, but as between the Alban triplets and the Roman triplets the scales are evenly balanced.

consideration. And I advise you to take the same course yourself — to send for the triplets on your side and sound out their disposition. And if they, too, agree of their own accord to risk their lives for their country, accept the favour; but if they hesitate, bring no compulsion to bear upon them. I predict, however, the same result with them as with our own youths — that is, if they are such men as we have been informed, like the few most highly endowed by Nature, and are brave in arms; for the reputation of their valour has reached us also."

16 Tullus, accordingly, approved of this advice and made a truce for ten days, in order to have time to deliberate and give his answer after learning the disposition of the Horatii; and thereupon he returned to the city. During the following days he consulted with the most important men, and when the greater part of them favoured accepting the proposals of Fufetius, he sent for the three brothers and said to them:

"Horatii, Fufetius the Alb an informed me at a conference the last time we met at the camp that by divine providence three brave champions were at hand for each city, the noblest and most suitable of any we could hope to find — the Curiatii among the Albans and you among the Romans. He added that upon learning of this he had himself first inquired whether your cousins were willing to give their lives to their country, and that, finding them very eager to undertake the combat on behalf of all their people, he could now bring forward this proposal with confidence; and he asked me also to sound you out, to learn whether you would be willing to risk your lives for your country by engaging with the Curiatii, or whether you choose to yield this honour to others. I, in view of your valour and your gallantry in action, which are not concealed from public notice, assumed[16] that you of all other would embrace this danger for the

---

16 This verb is missing from the Greek text; see critical note.

sake of winning the prize of valour; but fearing lest your kinship with the three Alban brothers might prove an obstacle to your zeal, I requested time for deliberation and made a truce for ten days. And when I came here I assembled the senate and laid the matter before them for their consideration. It was the opinion of the majority that if you of you own free will accepted the combat, which is a noble one an worthy of you and which I myself was eager to wage alone on behalf of all our people, they should praise your resolution an accept the favour from you; but if, to avoid the pollution of kindred blood — for surely it would be no admission of cowardice on your part — you felt that those who are not related to them ought to be called upon to undertake the combat, they should bring no compulsion to bear upon you. This, then, being the vote of the senate, which will neither be offended with you if you show reluctance to undertake the task nor feel itself under any slight obligation to you if you rate your country more highly than your kinship, deliberate carefully and well."

17 The youths upon hearing these words withdrew to one side, and after a short conference together returned to give their answer; and the eldest[17] on behalf of them all spoke as follows: "If we were free and sole masters of our own decisions, Tullus, and you had given us the opportunity to deliberate concerning the combat with our cousins, we should without further delay have given your our thoughts upon it. But since our father is still living, without whose advice we do not think it proper to say or do the least thing, we ask you to wait a short time for our answer till we have talked with him." Tullus having commended their filial devotion and told them to do as they proposed, they went home to their father. And acquainting

---

17 The first-born of the triplets is spoken of as the eldest, just as in the biblical story of Esau and Jacob we read, "and the elder shall serve the younger" (Gen. 25:23). And just below (chap. 18, end), the triplets take their places "according to age."

him with the proposals of Fufetius and with what Tullus had said to them and, last of all, with their own answer, they desired his advice. And he answered and said: "But indeed this is dutiful conduct on your part, my sons, when you live for your father and do nothing without my advice. But it is time for you to show that you yourselves now have discretion in such matters at least. Assume, therefore, that my life is now over, and let me know what you yourselves would have chosen to do if you had deliberated without your father upon your own affairs." And the eldest answered him thus: "Father, we would have accepted this combat for the supremacy and would have been ready to suffer whatever should be the will of Heaven; for we had rather be dead than to live unworthy both of you and of our ancestors. As for the bond of kinship with our cousins, we shall not be the first to break it, but since it has already been broken by fate, we shall acquiesce therein. For if the Curiatii esteem kinship less than honour, the Horatii also will not value the ties of blood more highly than valour." Their father, upon learning their disposition, rejoiced exceedingly, and lifting his hands to Heaven, said he rendered thanks to the gods for having given him noble sons. Then, throwing his arms about each in turn and giving the tenderest of embraces and kisses, he said: "You have my opinion also, my brave sons. Go, then, to Tullus and give him the answer that is both dutiful and honourable." The youths went away pleased with the exhortation of their father, and going to the king, they accepted the combat; and he, after assembling the senate and sounding the praises of the youths, sent ambassadors to the Alban to inform him that the Romans accepted his proposal and would offer the Horatii to fight for the sovereignty.

18 As my subject requires not only that a full account of the way the battle was fought should be given, but also that the subsequent tragic events, which resemble the sudden reversals of fortune seen upon the stage, should be related in no perfunctory manner, I shall endeavour, as far as I am able, to give an accurate account of every incident. When the time came, then, for giving effect to the terms of the agreement, the Roman forces marched out in full strength, and afterwards the youths, when they had offered up their prayers to the gods of their fathers; they advanced accompanied by the king while the entire throng that filed the city acclaimed them and strewed flowers upon their heads. By this time the Albans' army also had marched out. And when the armies had encamped near one another, leaving as an interval between their camps the boundary that separated the Roman territory from that of the Albans, each side occupying the site of its previous camp, they first offered sacrifice and swore over the burnt offerings that they would acquiesce in whatever fate the event of the combat between the cousins should allot to each city and that they would keep inviolate their agreement, neither they nor their posterity making use of any deceit. Then, after performing the rites which religion required, both the Romans and Albans laid aside their arms an came out in front of their camps to be spectators of the combat leaving an interval of three or four stades for the champions. And presently appeared the Alban general conducting the Curiatii and the Roman king escorting the Horatii, all of them armed in the most splendid fashion and withal dressed like men about to die. When they came near to one another they gave their swords to their armour-bearers, and running to one another, embraced weeping and calling each other by the tenderest names, so that al the spectators were moved to tears and accused both themselves and their leaders of great heartlessness, in that, when it was possible to decide the battle by other champions, they had limited the combat on behalf of the cities to men of kindred blood and compelled the pollution of fratricide. The youths, after their embraces were over, received their swords from their armour-bearers, and the bystanders having retired, they took their places according to age and began the combat.

19 For a time[18] quiet and silence prevailed in both armies, and then there was shouting by both sides together and alternate exhortations to the combatants; and there were vows and lamentations and continual expressions of every other emotion experienced in battle, some of them caused by what was either being enacted or witnessed by each side, and others by their apprehensions of the outcome; and the things they imagined outnumbered those which actually were happening. For it was impossible to see very clearly, owing to the great distance, and the partiality of each side for their own champions interpreted everything that passed to match their desire; then, too, the frequent advances and retreats of the combatants and their many sudden countercharges rendered any accurate judgment out of the question; and this situation lasted a considerable time. For the champions on both sides not only were alike in strength of body but were well matched also in nobility of spirit, and they had their entire bodies protected by the choicest armour, leaving no part exposed which if wounded would bring on swift death. So that many, both of the Romans and of the Albans, from their eager rivalry and from their partiality for their own champions, were unconsciously putting themselves in the position of the combatants and desired rather to be actors in the drama that was being enacted than spectators. At last the eldest of the Albans, closing with his adversary and giving and receiving blow after blow, happened somehow to run his sword through the Roman's groin. The latter was already stupefied from his other wounds, and now receiving this

---

18 The following description of the varied feelings that swayed the spectators of the combat is obviously inspired by the dramatic account in Thucydides (vii. 71) of the naval battle in the harbour of Syracuse, notwithstanding the total difference in details.

final blow, a mortal one, he fell down dead, his limbs no longer supporting him. When the spectators of the combat saw this they all cried out together, the Albans as already victorious, the Romans as vanquished; for they concluded that their two champions would be easily dispatched by the three Albans. In the meantime, the Roman who had fought by the side of the fallen champion, seeing the Alban rejoicing in his success, quickly rushed upon him, and after inflicting many wounds and receiving many himself, happened to plunge his sword into his neck and killed him. After Fortune had thus in a short time made a great alteration both in the state of the combatants and in the feelings of the spectators, and the Romans had now recovered from their former dejection while the Albans had had their joy snatched away, another shift of Fortune, by giving a check to the success of the Romans, sunk their hopes and raised the confidence of their enemies. For when the Alban fell, his brother who stood next to him closed with the Roman who had struck him down; and each, as it chanced, gave the other a dangerous wound at the same time, the Alban plunging his sword down through the Roman's back into his bowels, and the Roman throwing himself under the shield of his adversary and slashing one of his thighs.

20 The one who had received the mortal wound died instantly, and the other, who had been wounded in the thigh, was scarcely able to stand, but limped and frequently leaned upon his shield. Nevertheless, he still made a show of resistance and with his surviving brother advanced against the Roman, who stood his ground; and they surrounded him, one coming up to him from in front and the other from behind. The Roman, fearing that, being thus surrounded by them and obliged to fight with two adversaries attacking him from two sides, he might easily be overcome — he was still uninjured — hit upon the plan of separating his enemies and fighting each one singly He thought he could most easily separate them by feigning flight; for then he would not be pursued by both the Albans, but only by one of them, since he saw that the other no longer had control of his limbs. With this thought in mind he fled as fast as he could; and it was his good fortune not to be disappointed in his expectation. For the Alban who was not mortally wounded followed at his heels, while the other, being unable to keep going was falling altogether too far behind. Then indeed the Albans encouraged their men and the Romans reproached their champion with cowardice, the former singing songs of triumph and crowning themselves with garlands as if the contest were already won, and the others lamenting as if Fortune would never raise them up again. But the Roman, having carefully waited for his opportunity, turned quickly and, before the Alban could put himself on his guard, struck him a blow on the arm with his sword and clove his elbow in twain, and when his hand fell to the ground together with his sword, he struck one more blow, a mortal one, and dispatched the Alban; then, rushing from him to the last of his adversaries, who was half dead and fainting, he slew him also. And taking the spoils from the bodies of his cousins, he hastened to the city, wishing to give his father the first news of his victory.

21 But[19] it was ordained after all that even he, as he was but a mortal, should not be fortunate in everything, but should feel some stroke of the envious god[20] who, having from an insignificant man made him great in a brief moment of time and raised him to wonderful and unexpected distinction, plunged him the same day into the unhappy state of being his sister's murderer. For when he arrived near the gates he saw a multitude of people of all conditions pouring out from the city and among them his sister running to meet him. At the first sight of her he was distressed that a virgin ripe

---

19 For chaps. 21 f. *cf.* Livy i. 26.
20 Fortune.

for marriage should have deserted her household tasks at her mother's side and joined a crowd of strangers. And though he indulged in many absurd reflections, he was at last inclining to those which were honourable and generous, feeling that in her yearning to be the first to embrace her surviving brother and in her desire to receive an account from him of the gallant behaviour of her dead brothers she had disregarded decorum in a moment of feminine weakness. However, it was not, after all, her yearning for her brothers that had led her to venture forth in this unusual manner, but it was because she was overpowered by love for one of her cousins to whom her father had promised her in marriage, a passion which she had till then kept secret; and when she had overheard a man who came from the camp relating the details of the combat, she could no longer contain herself, but leaving the house, rushed to the city gates like a maenad, without paying any heed to her nurse who called her and ran to bring her back. But when she got outside the city and saw her brother exulting and wearing the garlands of victory with which the king had crowned him, and his friends carrying the spoils of the slain, among which was an embroidered robe which she herself with the assistance of her mother had woven and sent as a present to her betrothed against their nuptial day (for it is the custom of the Latins to array themselves in embroidered robes when they go to fetch their brides), when, therefore, she saw this robe stained with blood, she rent her garment, and beating her breast with both hands, fell to lamenting and calling upon her cousin by name, so that great astonishment came upon all who were present there. After she had bewailed the death of her betrothed she stared with fixed gaze at her brother and said: "Most abominable wretch, so you rejoice in having slain your cousins and deprived your most unhappy sister of wedlock! Miserable fellow! Why, you are not even touched with pity for your slain kinsmen, whom you were wont to call your brothers, but instead, as if you had performed some noble deed, you are beside yourself with joy and wear garlands in honour of such calamities. Of what wild beast, then, have you the heart?" And he, answering her, said: "The heart of a citizen who loves his country and punishes those who wish her ill, whether they happen to be foreigners or his own people. And among such I count even you; for though you know that the greatest of blessings and of woes have happened to us at one and the same time — I mean the victory of your country, which I, your brother, am bringing home with me, and the death of your brothers — you neither rejoice in the public happiness of your country, wicked wretch, nor grieve at the private calamities of your own family, but, overlooking your own brothers, you lament the fate of your betrothed, and this, too, not after taking yourself off somewhere alone under cover of darkness, curse you! but before the eyes of the whole world; and you reproach me for my valour and my crowns of victory, you pretender to virginity, you hater of your brothers and disgrace to your ancestors! Since, therefore, you mourn, not for your brothers, but for your cousins, and since, though your body is with the living, your soul is with him who is dead, go to him on whom you call and cease to dishonour either your father or your brothers."

After these words, being unable in his hatred of baseness to observe moderation, but yielding to the anger which swayed him, he ran his sword through her side; and having slain his sister, he went to his father. But so averse to baseness and so stern were the manners and thoughts of the Romans of that day and, to compare them with the actions and lives of those of our age, so cruel and harsh and so little removed from the savagery of wild beasts, that the father, upon being informed of this terrible calamity, far from resenting it, looked upon it as a glorious and becoming action. In fact, he would neither permit his daughter's body to be brought into the house nor allow her to be buried in the tomb of her ancestors or given any funeral or burial robe or other customary rites; but as she lay there where she had been cast, in the place where she was slain, the passers-by, bringing stones and earth, buried her like any corpse which had none to give it proper burial. Besides these instances of the father's severity there were still others that I shall mention. Thus, as if in gratitude for some glorious and fortunate achievements, he offered that very day to the gods of his ancestors the sacrifices he had vowed, and entertained his relations at a splendid[21] banquet, just as upon the greatest festivals, making less account of his private calamities than of the public advantages of his country. This not only Horatius but many other prominent Romans after him are said to have done; I refer to their offering sacrifice and wearing crowns and celebrating triumphs immediately after the death of their sons when through them the commonwealth had met with good fortune. Of these I shall make mention in the proper places.[22]

22 After the combat between the triplets, the Romans who were then in the camp buried the slain brothers in a splendid manner in the places where they had fallen, and having offered to the gods the customary sacrifices for victory, were passing their time in rejoicings. On the other side, the Albans were grieving over what had happened and blaming their leader for bad generalship; and the greatest part of them spent that night without food and without any other care for their bodies. The next day the king of the Romans called them to an assembly and consoled them with many assurances that he would lay no command upon them that was either dishonourable, grievous or unbecoming to kinsmen, but that with impartial judgment he would take thought for what was best and most advantageous for both cities; and having continued

---

21 Another adjective may have been lost after "splendid." See critical note.
22 No such places are found in the extant books of the *Antiquities*.

Fufetius, their ruler, in the same office and made no other change in the government, he led his army home.

After he had celebrated the triumph which the senate had decreed for him and had entered upon the administration of civil affairs, some citizens of importance came to him bringing Horatius for trial, on the ground that because of his slaying of his sister he was not free of the guilt of shedding a kinsman's blood; and being given a hearing, they argued at length, citing the laws which forbade the slaying of anyone without a trial, and recounting instances of the anger of all[23] the gods against the cities which neglected to punish those who were polluted. But the father spoke in defence of the youth and blamed his daughter, declaring that the act was a punishment, not a murder, and claiming that he himself was the proper judge of the calamities of his own family, since he was the father of both. And a great deal having been said on both sides, the king was in great perplexity what decision to pronounce in the cause. For he did not think it seemly either to acquit any person of murder who confessed he had put his sister to death before a trial — and that, too, for an act which the laws did not concede to be a capital offence — lest by so doing he should transfer the curse and pollution from the criminal to his own household, or to punish as a murderer any person who had chosen to risk his life for his country and had brought her so great power, especially as he was acquitted of blame by his father, to whom before all others both nature and the law gave the right of taking vengeance in the case of his daughter. Not knowing, therefore, how to deal with the situation, he at last decided it was best to leave the decision to the people. And the Roman people, becoming upon this occasion judges for the first

---

23 The word "all" is disturbing here. There is much to be said for Schwartz's emendation ἀπαντῶντα ("meeting," "befalling"), the meaning then being "instances of the anger of the gods visited upon the cities."

time in a cause of a capital nature, sided with the opinion of the father and acquitted Horatius of the murder.

Nevertheless, the king did not believe that the judgment thus passed upon Horatius by men was a sufficient atonement to satisfy those who desired to observe due reverence toward the gods; but sending for the pontiffs, he ordered them to appease the gods and other divinities and to purify Horatius with those lustrations with which it was customary for involuntary homicides to be expiated. The pontiffs erected two altars, one to Juno, to whom the care of sisters is allotted, and the other to a certain god or lesser divinity of the country called in their language Janus, to whom was now added the name Curiatius, derived from that of the cousins who had been slain by Horatius;[24] and after they had offered certain sacrifices upon these altars, they finally, among other expiations, led Horatius under the yoke. It is customary among the Romans, when enemies deliver up their arms and submit to their power, to fix two pieces of wood upright in the ground and fasten a third to the top of them transversely, then to lead the captives under this structure, and after they have passed through, to grant them their liberty and leave to return home. This they call a yoke; and it was the last of the customary expiatory ceremonies used upon this occasion by those who purified Horatius. The place in the city where they performed this expiation is regarded by all the Romans as sacred; it is in the street that leads down from the Carinae as one goes towards Cuprius Street.[25] Here the altars then erected still remain, and over them extends a beam which is fixed in each of the opposite walls;

---

24 *Cf.* Schol. Bob. to Cic. *pro Milone*, 7: *constitutis duabus aris Iano Curiatio et Iunoni Sororiae, superque eas iniecto tigillo, Horatius sub iugum traductus est.*

25 The *vicus Cuprius* (often written *Cyprius* because a false etymology) was a street running north and south across the Carinae, the west end of the western spur of the Esquiline. The *tigillum* was evidently higher up on this spur in the part called the Mons Oppius.

the beam lies over the heads of those who go[26] out of this street and is called in the Roman tongue "the Sister's Beam." This place, then, is still preserved in the city as a monument to this man's misfortune and honoured by the Romans with sacrifices every year. Another memorial of the bravery he displayed in the combat is the small corner pillar standing at the entrance to one of the two porticos[27] in the Forum, upon which were placed the spoils of the three Alban brothers. The arms, it is true, have disappeared because of the lapse of time, but the pillar still preserves its name and is called *pila Horatia* or "the Horatian Pillar."[28] The Romans also have a law, enacted in consequence of this episode and observed even to this day, which confers immortal honour and glory upon these men; it provides that the parents of triplets shall receive from the public treasury the cost of rearing them until they are grown. With this, the incidents relating to the family of the Horatii, which showed some remarkable and unexpected reversals of fortune, came to an end.

23 The[29] king of the Romans, after letting a year pass, during which he made the necessary preparations for war, resolved to lead out his army against the city of the Fidenates. The grounds he alleged for the war were that this people, being called upon to justify themselves in the matter of the plot that they had formed against the Romans and Albans, had paid no heed, but immediately taking up arms, shutting their gates, and bringing in the allied forces of the Veientes, had openly revolted, and that when ambassadors arrived from Rome to inquire the reason for their revolt, they had answered that they no longer had anything in common with the Romans since

---

26 *Sororium tigillum.*
27 The Basilica Julia and the Basilica Aemilia.
28 The Latin term was ambiguous, *pila* meaning either "pillar" or "javelins." With the disappearance of the arms it was natural enough to interpret it in the first sense; but Livy (i. 26,10) takes it in the second.
29 For chaps. 23-30 *cf.* Livy 1. 27.

the death of Romulus, their king, to whom they had sworn their oaths of friendship. Seizing on these grounds for war, Tullus was not only arming his own forces, but also sending for those of his allies. The most numerous as well as the best auxiliary troops were brought to him from Alba by Mettius Fufetius, and they were equipped with such splendid arms as to excel all the other allied forces. Tullus, therefore, believing that Mettius had been actuated by zeal and by the best motives in deciding to take part in the war, commended him and communicated to him all his plans. But this man, who was accused by his fellow citizens of having mismanaged the recent war and was furthermore charged with treason, in view of the fact that he continued in the supreme command of the city for the third year by order of Tullus, disdaining now to hold any longer a command that was subject to another's command or to be subordinated rather than himself to lead, devised an abominable plot. He sent ambassadors here and there secretly to the enemies of the Romans while they were as yet wavering in their resolution to revolt and encouraged them not to hesitate, promising that he himself would join them in attacking the Romans during the battle; and these activities and plans he kept secret from everybody. Tullus, as soon as he had got ready his own army as well as that of his allies, marched against the enemy and after crossing the river Anio encamped near Fidenae. And finding a considerable army both of the Fidenates and of their allies drawn up before the city, he lay quiet that day; but on the next he sent for Fufetius, the Alban, and the closest of his other friends and took counsel with them concerning the best method of conducting the war. And when all were in favour of engaging promptly and not wasting time, he assigned them their several posts and commands, and having fixed the next day for the battle, he dismissed the council.

Book III

In the meantime Fufetius, the Alban — for his treachery was still a secret to many even of his own friends — calling together the most prominent centurions and tribunes among the Albans, addressed them as follows:

"Tribunes and centurions, I am going to disclose to you important and unexpected things which I have hitherto been concealing; and I beg of you to keep them secret if you do not wish to ruin me, and to assist me in carrying them out if you think their realization will be advantageous. The present occasion does not permit of many words, as the time is short; so I shall mention only the most essential matters. I, from the time we were subordinated to the Romans up to this day, have led a life full of shame and grief, though honoured by the king with the supreme command, which I am now holding for the third year and may, if I should so desire, hold as long as I live. But regarding it as the greatest of all evils to be the only fortunate man in a time of public misfortune, and taking it to heart that, contrary to all the rights mankind look upon as sacred, we have been deprived by the Romans of our supremacy, I took thought how we might recover it without experiencing any great disaster. And although I considered many plans of every sort, the only way I could discover that promised success, and at the same time the easiest and the least dangerous one, was in case a war should be started against them by the neighbouring states. For I assumed that when confronted by such a war they would have need of allies and particularly of us. As to the next step, I assumed that it would not require much argument to convince you that it is more glorious as well as more fitting to fight for our liberty than for the supremacy of the Romans.

"With these thoughts in mind I secretly stirred up a war against the Romans on the part of their subjects, encouraging the Veientes and Fidenates to take up arms by a promise of my assistance in the war. And thus far I have escaped the Romans' notice as I contrived these things and kept in my own hands the opportune moment for the attack. Just consider now the many advantages we shall derive from this course. First, by not having openly planned a revolt, in which there would have been a double danger — either of being hurried or unprepared and of putting everything to the hazard while trusting to our own strength only, or, while we were making preparations and gathering assistance, of being forestalled by an enemy already prepared — we shall now experience neither of these difficulties but shall enjoy the advantage of both. In the next place, we shall not be attempting to destroy the great and formidable power and good fortune of our adversaries by force, but rather by those means by which every thing that is overbearing and not easy to be subdued by force is taken, namely, by guile and deceit; and we shall be neither the first nor the only people who have resorted to these means, Besides, as our own force is not strong enough to be arrayed against the whole power of the Romans and their allies, we have also added the forces of the Fidenates and the Veientes, whose great numbers you see before you; and I have taken the following precautions that these auxiliaries who have been added to our numbers may with all confidence be depended on to adhere to our alliance. For it will not be in our territory that the Fidenates will be fighting, but while they are defending their own country they will at the same time be protecting ours. Then, too, we shall have this advantage, which men look upon as the most gratifying of all and which has fallen to the lot of but few in times past, namely, that, while receiving a benefit from our allies, we shall ourselves be thought to be conferring one upon them. And if this enterprise turns out according to our wish, as is reasonable to expect, the Fidenates and the Veientes, in delivering us from a grievous subjection, will feel grateful to us, as if it were they themselves who had received this favour at our hands.

Book III

"These are the preparations which I have made after much thought and which I regard as sufficient to inspire you with the courage and zeal to revolt. Now hear from me the manner in which I have planned to carry out the undertaking. Tullus has assigned me my post under the hill and has given me the command of one of the wings. When we are about to engage the enemy, I will break ranks and begin to lead up the hill; and you will then follow me with your companies in their proper order. When I have gained the top of the hill and am securely posted, hear in what manner I shall handle the situation after that. If I find my plans turning out according to my wish, that is, if I see that the enemy has become emboldened through confidence in our assistance, and the Romans disheartened and terrified, in the belief that they have been betrayed by us, and contemplating, as they likely will, flight rather than fight, I will fall upon them and cover the field with the bodies of the slain, since I shall be rushing down hill from higher ground and shall be attacking with a courageous and orderly force men who are frightened and dispersed. For a terrible thing in warfare is the sudden impression, even though ill-grounded, of the treachery of allies or of an attack by fresh enemies, and we know that many great armies in the past have been utterly destroyed by no other kind of terror so much as by an impression for which there was no ground. But in our case it will be no vain report, no unseen terror, but a deed more dreadful than anything ever seen or experienced. If, however, I find that the contrary of my calculations is in fact coming to pass (for mention must be made also of those things which are wont to happen contrary to human expectations, since our lives bring us many improbable experiences as well), I too shall then endeavour to do the contrary of what I have just proposed. For I shall lead you against the enemy in conjunction with the Romans and shall share with them the victory, pretending that I occupied the heights with the intention of surrounding the foes drawn up against me; and my

257

claim will seem credible, since I shall have made my actions agree with my explanation. Thus, without sharing in the dangers of either side, we shall have a part in the good fortune of both.

"I, then, have determined upon these measures, and with the assistance of the gods I shall carry them out, as being the most advantageous, not only to the Albans, but also to the rest of the Latins. It is your part, in the first place, to observe secrecy, and next, to maintain good order, to obey promptly the orders you shall receive, to fight zealously yourselves and to infuse the same zeal into those who are under your command, remembering that we are not contending for liberty upon the same terms as other people, who have been accustomed to obey others and who have received that form of government from their ancestors. For we are freemen descended from freemen, and to us our ancestors have handed down the tradition of holding sway over our neighbours as a mode of life preserved by them for someone five hundred years; of which let us not deprive our posterity. And let none of you entertain the fear that by showing a will to do this he will be breaking a compact and violating the oaths by which it was confirmed; on the contrary, let him consider that he will be restoring to its original force the compact which the Romans have violated, a compact far from unimportant, but one which human nature has established and the universal law of both Greeks and barbarians confirms, namely, that fathers shall rule over and give just commands to their children, and mother-cities to their colonies. This compact, which is forever inseparable from human nature, is not being violated by us, who demand that it shall always remain in force, and none of the gods or lesser divinities will be wroth with us, as guilty of an impious action, if we resent being slaves to our own posterity; but it is being violated by those who have broken it from the beginning and have attempted by an impious act to set up the law of man above that of Heaven.

And it is reasonable to expect that the anger of the gods will be directed against them rather than against us, and that the indignation of men will fall upon them rather than upon us. If, therefore, you all believe that these plans will be the most advantageous, let us pursue them, calling the gods and other divinities to our assistance. But if any one of you is minded to the contrary and either believes that we ought never to recover the ancient dignity of our city, or, while awaiting a more favourable opportunity, favours deferring our undertaking for the present, let him not hesitate to propose his thoughts to the assembly. For we shall follow whatever plan meets with your unanimous approval."

24 Those who were present having approved of this advice and promised to carry out all his orders, he bound each of them by an oath and then dismissed the assembly The next day the armies both of the Fidenates and of their allies marched out of their camp at sunrise and drew up in order of battle; and on the other side the Romans came out against them and took their positions. Tullus himself and the Romans formed the left wing, which was opposite to the Veientes (for these occupied the enemy's right), while Mettius Fufetius and the Albans drew up on the right wing of the Roman army, over against the Fidenates, beside the flank of the hill. When the armies drew near one another and before they came within range of each other's missiles, the Albans, separating themselves from the rest of the army, began to lead their companies up the hill in good order. The Fidenates, learning of this and feeling confident that the Albans' promises to betray the Romans were coming true before their eyes, now fell to attacking the Romans with greater boldness, and the right wing of the Romans, left unprotected by their allies, was being broken and was suffering severely; but the left, where Tullus himself fought among the flower of the cavalry, carried on the struggle vigorously. In the meantime a horseman rode up to those who were fighting under the king and said: "Our right wing is suffering, Tullus. For the Albans have deserted their posts and are hastening up to the heights, and the Fidenates, opposite to whom they were stationed, extend beyond our wing that is now left unprotected, and are going to surround us." The Romans, upon hearing this and seeing the haste with which the Albans were rushing up the hill, were seized with such fear of being surrounded by the enemy that it did not occur to them either to fight or to stand their ground, Thereupon Tullus, they say, not at all disturbed in mind by so great and so unexpected a misfortune, made use of a stratagem by which he not only saved the Roman army, which was threatened with manifest ruin, but also shattered and brought to nought all the plans of the enemy. For, as soon as he had heard the messenger, he raised his voice, so as to be heard even by the enemy, and cried: "Romans, we are victorious over the enemy. For the Albans have occupied for us this hill hard by, as you see, by my orders, so as to get behind the enemy and fall upon them. Consider, therefore, that we have our greatest foes where we want them, some of us attacking them in front and others in the rear, in a position where, being unable either to advance or to retire, hemmed in as they are on the flanks by the river and by the hill, they will make handsome atonement to us. Forward, then, and show your utter contempt of them."

25 These words he repeated as he rode past all the ranks. And immediately the Fidenates became afraid of counter-treachery suspecting that the Alban had deceived them by a stratagem, since they did not see either that he had changed his battle order so as to face the other way or that he was promptly charging the Romans, according to his promise; but the Romans, on their side, were emboldened by the words of Tullus and filled with confidence, and giving a great shout, they rushed in a body against the enemy. Upon this, the Fidenates gave way and fled toward their city in disorder. The Roman king hurled his cavalry against them while they were in this fear and confusion, and pursued them for some distance; but when he learned that they were dispersed and separated from one another and neither likely to take thought for getting together again nor in fact able to do so, he gave over the pursuit and marched against those of the enemy whose ranks were still unbroken and standing their ground. And now there took place a brilliant engagement of the infantry and a still more brilliant one on the part of the cavalry. For the Veientes, who were posted at this point, did not give way in terror at the charge of the Roman horse, but maintained the fight for a considerable time. Then, learning that their left wing was beaten and that the whole army of the Fidenates and of their other allies was in headlong flight, and fearing to be surrounded by the troops that had returned from the pursuit, they also broke their ranks and fled, endeavouring to save themselves by crossing the river. Accordingly, those among them who were strongest, least disabled by their wounds, and had some ability to swim, got across the river, without their arms, while all who lacked any of these advantages perished in the eddies; for the stream of the Tiber near Fidenae is rapid and has many windings. Tullus ordered a detachment of the horse to cut down those of the enemy who were pressing toward the river, while he himself led the rest of the army to the camp of the Veientes and captured it by storm. This was the situation of the Romans after they had been unexpectedly preserved from destruction.

26 When the Alban observed that Tullus had already won a brilliant victory, he also marched down from the heights with his own troops and pursued those of the Fidenates who were fleeing, in order that he might be seen by all the Romans performing some part of the duty of an ally; and he destroyed many of the enemy who had become dispersed in the left. Tullus, though he understood his purpose and understood his double treachery, thought he ought to utter no reproaches for the present till he should have the man in his power, but addressing himself to many of those who were present, he pretended to applaud the Alban's withdrawal to the heights, as if it had been prompted by the best motive; and sending a party of horse to him, he requested him to give the final proof of his zeal by hunting down and slaying the many Fidenates who had been unable to get inside the walls and were dispersed about the country. And Fufetius, imagining that he had succeeded in one of his two hopes and that Tullus was unacquainted with his treachery, rejoiced, and riding over the plains for a considerable time, he cut down all whom he found; but when the sun was now set, he returned from the pursuit with his horsemen to the Roman camp and passed the following night in making merry with his friends.

Tullus remained in the camp of the Veientes till the first watch and questioned the most prominent of the prisoners concerning the leaders of the revolt; and when he learned that Mettius Fufetius, the Alban, was also one of the conspirators and considered that his actions agreed with the information of the prisoners, he mounted his horse, and taking with him the most faithful of his friends, rode off to Rome. Then, sending to the houses of the senators, he assembled them before midnight and informed them of the treachery of the Alban, producing the prisoners as witnesses, and informed them of the stratagem by which he himself had outwitted both their enemies and the Fidenates.[30] And he asked them, now that the war was ended in the most successful manner, to consider the problems that remained — how the traitors ought to be punished and the city of Alba rendered more circumspect for the

---

30 Probably we should either supply "secret" before "enemies" (so Reiske) or substitute Albans for Fidenates (Spelman).

future. That the authors of these wicked designs should be punished seemed to all both just and necessary, but how this was to be most easily and safely accomplished was a problem that caused them great perplexity. For they thought it obviously impossible to put to death a great number of brave Albans in a secret and clandestine manner, whereas, if they should attempt openly to apprehend and punish the guilty, they assumed that the Albans would not permit it but would rush to arms; and they were unwilling to carry on war at the same time with the Fidenates and Tyrrhenians and with the Albans, who had come to them as allies. While they were in this perplexity, Tullus delivered the final opinion, which met with the approval of all; but of this I shall speak presently.

27 The distance between Fidenae and Rome being forty stades, Tullus rode full speed to the camp, and sending for Marcus Horatius, the survivor of the triplets, before it was quite day, he commanded him to take the flower of the cavalry and infantry, and proceeding to Alba, to enter the city as a friend, and then, as soon as he had secured the submission of the inhabitants, to raze the city to the foundations without sparing a single building, whether private or public, except the temples; but as for the citizens, he was neither to kill nor injure any of them, but to permit them to retain their possessions. After sending him on his way he assembled the tribunes and centurions, and having acquainted them with the resolutions of the senate, he placed them as a guard about his person. Soon after, the Alban came, pretending to express his joy over their common victory and to congratulate Tullus upon it. The latter, still concealing his intention, commended him and declared he was deserving of great rewards; at the same time he asked him to write down the names of such of the other Albans also as had performed any notable exploit in the battle and to bring the list to him, in order that they also might get their share of the fruits of victory. Mettius, accordingly, greatly pleased at this, entered upon a tablet and gave to him a list of his most intimate friends who had been the accomplices in his secret designs. Then the Roman king ordered all the troops to come to an assembly after first laying aside their arms. And when they assembled he ordered the Alban general together with his tribunes and centurions to stand directly beside the tribunal; next to these the rest of the Albans were to take their place in the assembly, drawn up in their ranks, and behind the Albans the remainder of the allied forces, while outside of them all he stationed Romans, including the most resolute, with swords concealed under their garments. When he thought he had his foes where he wanted them, he rose up and spoke as follows:

28 "Romans and you others, both friends and allies, those who dared openly to make war against us, the Fidenates and their allies, have been punished by us with the aid of the gods, and either will cease for the future to trouble us or will receive an even severer chastisement than that they have just experienced. It is now time, since our first enterprise has succeeded to our wish, to punish those other enemies also who bear the name of friends and were taken into this war to assist us in harrying our common foes, but have broken faith with us, and entering into secret treaties with those enemies, have attempted to destroy us all. For these are much worse than open enemies and deserve a severer punishment, since it is both easy to guard against the latter when one is treacherously attacked and possible to repulse them when they are at grips as enemies, but when friends act the part of enemies it is neither easy to guard against them nor possible for those who are taken by surprise to repulse them. And such are the allies sent us by the city of Alba with treacherous intent, although they have received no injury from us but many considerable benefits. For, as we are their colony, we have not wrested away any part of their dominion but have acquired our own strength and power from our own wars; and by making our city a bulwark against the greatest and most warlike nations we have effectually secured them from a war with the Tyrrhenians and Sabines. In the prosperity, therefore, of our city they above all others should have rejoiced, and have grieved at its adversity no less than at their own. But they, it appears, continued not only to begrudge us the advantages we had but also to begrudge themselves the good fortune they enjoyed because of us, and at last, unable any longer to contain their festering hatred, they declared war against us. But finding us well prepared for the struggle and themselves, therefore, in no condition to do any harm, they invited us to a reconciliation and friendship and asked that our strife over the supremacy should be decided by three men from each city. These proposals also we accepted, and after winning in the combat became masters of their city. Well, then, what did we do after that? Though it was in our power to take hostages from them, to leave a garrison in their city, to destroy some of the principal authors of the war between the two cities and to banish others, to change the form of their government according to our own interest, to punish them with the forfeiture of a part of their lands and effects, and — the thing that was easiest of all — to disarm them, by which means we should have strengthened our rule, we did not see fit to do any of these things, but, consulting our filial obligations to our mother-city rather than the security of our power and considering the good opinion of all the world as more important than our own private advantage, we allowed them to enjoy all that was theirs and permitted Mettius Fufetius, as being supposedly the best of the Albans — since they themselves had honoured him with the chief magistracy — to administer their affairs up to the present time.

"For which favours hear now what gratitude they showed, at a time when we needed the goodwill of our friends and allies more than ever. They made a secret compact with our common enemies by which they engaged to fall upon us in conjunction with them in the course of the battle; and when the two armies approached each other they deserted the post to which they had been assigned and made off for the hills near by at a run, eager to occupy the strong positions ahead of anyone else. And if their attempt had succeeded according to their wish, nothing could have prevented us, surrounded at once by our enemies and by our friends, from being all destroyed, and the fruit of the many battles we had fought for the sovereignty of our city from being lost in a single day. But since their plan has miscarried, owing, in the first place, to the goodwill of the gods (for I at any rate ascribe all worthy achievements to them), and, second, to the stratagem I made use of, which contributed not a little to inspire the enemy with fear and you with confidence (for the statement I made during the battle, that the Albans were taking possession of the heights by my orders with a view of surrounding the enemy, was all a fiction and a stratagem contrived by myself), since, I say, things have turned out to our advantage, we should not be the men we ought to be if we did not take revenge on these traitors. For, apart from the other ties which, by reason of their kinship to us, they ought to have preserved inviolate, they recently made a treaty with us confirmed by oaths, and then, without either fearing the gods whom they had made witnesses of the treaty or showing any regard for justice itself and the condemnation of men, or considering the greatness of the danger if their treachery should not succeed according to their wish, endeavoured to destroy us, who are both their colony and their benefactors, in the most miserable fashion, thus arraying themselves, though our founders, on the side of our most deadly foes and our greatest enemies."

29 While he was thus speaking the Albans had recourse to lamentations and entreaties of every kind, the common people declaring that they had no knowledge of the intrigues of Mettius, and their commanders alleging that they had not learned of his secret plans till they were in the midst of the battle itself, when it was not in their power either to prevent his orders or to refuse obedience to them; and some even ascribed their action to the necessity imposed against their will by their affinity or kinship to the man. But the king, having commanded them to be silent, addressed them thus:

"I, too, Albans, am not unaware of any of these things that you urge in your defence, but am of the opinion that the generality of you had no knowledge of this treachery, since secrets are not apt to be kept even for a moment when many share in the knowledge of them; and I also believe that only a small number of the tribunes and centurions were accomplices in the conspiracy formed against us, but that the greater part of them were deceived and forced into a position where they were compelled to act against their will. Nevertheless, even if nothing of all this were true, but if all the Albans, as well you who are here present as those who are left in your city, had felt a desire to hurt us, and if you had not now for the first time, but long since, taken this resolution, yet on account of their kinship to you the Romans would feel under every necessity to bear even this injustice at your hands. But against the possibility of your forming some wicked plot against us hereafter, as the result either of compulsion or deception on the part of the leaders of your state, there is but one precaution and provision, and that is for us all to become citizens of the same city and to regard one only as our fatherland, in whose prosperity and adversity everyone will have that share which Fortune allots to him. For so long as each of our two peoples decides what is advantageous and disadvantageous on the basis of a different judgment, as is now the case, the friendship between us will not be enduring, particularly when those who are the first to plot against the others are either to gain an advantage if they succeed, or, if they fail, are to be secured by their kinship from any serious retribution, while those against whom the attempt is made, if they are subdued, are to suffer the extreme penalties, and if they escape, are not, like enemies, to remember their wrongs — as has happened in the present instance.

"Know, then, that the Romans last night came to the following resolutions, I myself having assembled the senate and proposed the decree: it is ordered that your city be demolished and that no buildings, either public or private, be left standing except the temples; that all the inhabitants, while continuing in the possession of the allotments of land they now enjoy and being deprived of none of their slaves, cattle and other effects, reside henceforth at Rome; that such of your lands as belong to the public be divided among those of the Albans who have none, except the sacred possessions from which the sacrifices to the gods were provided; that I take charge of the construction of the houses in which you newcomers are to establish your homes, determining in what parts of the city they shall be, and assist the poorest among you in the expense of building; that the mass of your population be incorporated with our plebeians and be distributed among the tribes and *curiae*, but that the following families be admitted to the senate, hold magistracies and be numbered with the patricians, to wit, the Julii, the Servilii, the Curiatii, the Quintilii, the Cloelii, the Geganii, and the Metilii;[31] and that Mettius and his accomplices in the treachery suffer such punishments as we shall ordain when we come to sit in judgment upon each of the accused. For we shall deprive none of them either of a trial or of the privilege of making a defence."

---

31 *Cf.* Livy i. 30, 2.

Book III

30 At these words of Tullus the poorer sort of the Albans were very well satisfied to become residents of Rome and to have lands allotted to them, and they received with loud acclaim the terms granted them. But those among them who were distinguished for their dignities and fortunes were grieved at the thought of having to leave the city of their birth and to abandon the hearths of their ancestors and pass the rest of their lives in a foreign country; nevertheless, being reduced to the last extremity, they could think of nothing to say. Tullus, seeing the disposition of the multitude, ordered Mettius to make his defence, if he wished to say anything in answer to the charges. But he, unable to justify himself against the accusers and witnesses, said that the Alban senate had secretly given him these orders when he led his army forth to war, and he asked the Albans, for whom he had endeavoured to recover the supremacy, to come to his aid and to permit neither their city to be razed nor the most illustrious of the citizens to be haled to punishment. Upon this, a tumult arose in the assembly and, some of them rushing to arms, those who surrounded the multitude, upon a given signal, held up their swords. And when all were terrified, Tullus rose up again and said: "It is no longer in your power, Albans, to act seditiously or even to make any false move. For if you dare attempt any disturbance, you shall all be slain by these troops (pointing to those who held their swords in their hands). Accept, then, the terms offered to you and become henceforth Romans. For you must do one of two things, either live at Rome or have no other country. For early this morning Marcus Horatius set forth, sent by me, to raze your city to the foundations and to remove all the inhabitants to Rome. Knowing, then, that these orders are as good as executed already, cease to court destruction and do as you are bidden. As for Mettius Fufetius, who has not only laid snares for us in secret but even now has not hesitated to call the turbulent and seditious to arms, I shall punish him in such manner as his wicked and deceitful heart deserves."

At these words, that part of the assembly which was in an irritated mood, cowered in fear, restrained by inevitable necessity. Fufetius alone still showed his resentment and cried out, appealing to the treaty which he himself was convicted of having violated, and even in his distress abated nothing of his boldness; but the lictors seized him at the command of King Tullus, and tearing off his clothes, scourged his body with many stripes. After he had been sufficiently punished in this manner, they brought up two teams of horses and with long traces fastened his arms to one of them and his feet to the other; then, as the drivers urged their teams apart, the wretch was mangled upon the ground and, being dragged by the two teams in opposite directions, was soon torn apart. This was the miserable and shameful end of Mettius Fufetius. For the trial of his friends and the accomplices of his treachery the king set up courts and put to death such of the accused as were found guilty, pursuant to the law respecting deserters and traitors.

31 In[32] the meantime Marcus Horatius, who had been sent on with the picked troops to destroy Alba, having quickly made the march and finding the gates open and the walls unguarded, easily made himself master of the city. Then, assembling the people, he informed them of everything which had happened during the battle and read to them the decree of the Roman senate. And though the inhabitants had recourse to supplications and begged for time in which to send an embassy, he proceeded without any delay to raze the houses and walls and every other building, both public and private; but he conducted the inhabitants to Rome with great care, permitting them to take their animals and their goods with them. And Tullus, upon arriving from the camp, distributed them among

---

32 *Cf.* Livy i. 29.

the Roman tribes and *curiae*, assisted them in building houses in such parts of the city as they themselves preferred, allotted a sufficient portion of the public lands to those of the labouring class, and by other acts of humanity relieved the needs of the multitude. Thus the city of Alba, which had been built by Ascanius, the son whom Aeneas, Anchises' son, had by Creusa, the daughter of Priam, after having stood for four hundred and eighty-seven years from its founding, during which time it had greatly increased in population, wealth and every form of prosperity, and after having colonized the thirty cities of the Latins and during all this time held the leadership of that nation, was destroyed by the last colony it had planted, and remains uninhabited to this day.

King Tullus, after letting the following winter pass, led out his army once more against the Fidenates at the beginning of spring. These had publicly received no assistance whatever from any of the cities in alliance with them, but some mercenaries had resorted to them from many places, and relying upon these, they were emboldened to come out from their city; then, after arraying themselves for battle and slaying many in the struggle that ensued and losing even more of their own men, they were again shut up inside the town. And when Tullus had surrounded the city with palisades and ditches and reduced those within to the last extremity, they were obliged to surrender themselves to the king upon his own terms. Having in this manner become master of the city, Tullus put to death the authors of the revolt, but released all the rest, leaving them in the enjoyment of all their possessions in the same manner as before and restoring to them their previous form of government. He then disbanded his army, and returning to Rome, rendered to the gods the trophy-bearing procession and sacrifices of thanksgiving, this being the second triumph he celebrated.

32 After[33] this war another arose against the Romans on the part of the Sabine nation, the beginning and occasion of which was this. There is a sanctuary, honoured in common by the Sabines and the Latins, that is held in the greatest reverence and is dedicated to a goddess named Feronia; some of those who translate the name into Greek call her *Anthophoros* or "Flower Bearer," others *Philostephanos* or "Lover of Garlands," and still others *Persephonê*. To this sanctuary people used to resort from the neighbouring cities on the appointed days of festival, many of them performing vows and offering sacrifice to the goddess and many with the purpose of trafficking during the festive gathering as merchants, artisans and husbandmen; and here were held fairs more celebrated than in any other places in Italy At this festival some Romans of considerable importance happened to be present on a certain occasion and were seized by some of the Sabines, who imprisoned them and robbed them of their money. And when an embassy was sent concerning them, the Sabines refused to give any satisfaction, but retained both the persons and the money of the men whom they had seized, and in their turn accused the Romans of having received the fugitives of the Sabines by establishing a sacred asylum (of which I gave an account in the preceding Book).[34] As a result of these accusations the two nations became involved in war, and when both had taken the field with large forces a pitched battle occurred between them; and both sides continued to fight with equal fortunes until night parted them, leaving the victory in doubt. During the following days both of them, upon learning the number of the slain and wounded, were unwilling to hazard another battle but left their camps and retired.

---

33 For chaps. 32 f. *cf.* Livy i. 30, 4-10.
34 ii. 15.

Book III

They let that year pass without further action, and then, having increased their forces, they again marched out against one another and near the city of Eretum, distant one hundred and sixty stades from Rome, engaged in a battle in which many fell on both sides. And when that battle also continued doubtful for a long time, Tullus, lifting his hands to heaven, made a vow to the gods that if he conquered the Sabines that day he would institute public festivals in honour of Saturn and Ops (the Romans celebrate them every year after they have gathered in all the fruits of the earth)[35] and would double the number of the Salii, as they are called. These are youths of noble families who at appointed times dance, fully armed, to the sound of the flute and sing certain traditional hymns, as I have explained in the preceding Book.[36] After this vow the Romans were filled with a kind of confidence and, like fresh troops falling on those that are exhausted, they at last broke the enemy's line in the late afternoon and forced the first ranks to begin flight. Then, pursuing them as they fled to their camp, they cut down many more round the trenches, and even then did not turn back, but having stayed there the following night and cleared the ramparts of their defenders, they made themselves masters of the camp. After this action they ravaged as much of the territory of the Sabines as they wished, but when no one any longer came out against them to protect the country, they returned home. Because of this victory the king triumphed a third time; and not long afterwards, when the Sabines sent ambassadors, he put an end to the war, having first received from them the captives that they had taken in their foraging expeditions, together with the deserters, and levied the penalty which the Roman senate, estimating the damage at a certain sum of money, had imposed upon them for the cattle, the beasts of

---

35 The Saturnalia and Opalia, in mid-December.
36 ii. 70.

burden and the other effects that they had taken from the husbandmen.

33 Although the Sabines had ended the war upon these conditions an had set up pillars in their temples on which the terms of the treaty were inscribed, nevertheless, as soon as the Romans were engaged in a war not likely to be soon terminated against the cities of the Latins, who had all united against them, for reasons which I shall presently[37] mention, they welcomed the situation and forgot those oaths and the treaty as much a if they never had been made. And thinking that they now had a favourable opportunity to recover from the Romans many times as much money as they had paid them, they went out, at first in small numbers and secretly, and plundered the neighbouring country; but afterward many met together and in an open manner, and since their first attempt had turned out as they wished and no assistance had come to the defence of the husbandmen, they despised their enemies and proposed to march even on Rome itself, for which purpose they were gathering an army out of every city. They also made overtures to the cities of the Latins with regard to an alliance, but were not able to conclude a treaty of friendship and alliance with that nation. For Tullus, being informed of their intention, made a truce with the Latins and determined to march against the Sabines; and to this end he armed all the forces of the Romans, which since he had annexed the Alban state, were double the number they had been before, and sent to his other allies for all the troops they could furnish. The Sabines, too, had already assembled their army, and when the two forces drew near one another they encamped near a place called the Knaves' Wood,[38] leaving a small interval between them. The next day they engaged and the fight continued doubtful for a long time;

---

37 In chap. 34.
38 *Silva malitiosa* (Livy i. 30, 9), probably a hide-out of brigands.

but at length, in the late afternoon, the Sabines gave way, unable to stand before the Roman horse, and many of them were slain in the flight. The Romans stripped the spoils from the dead, plundered their camp and ravaged the best part of the country, after which they returned home. This was the outcome of the war that occurred between the Romans and the Sabines in the reign of Tullus.

34 The cities of the Latins now became at odds with the Romans for the first time, being unwilling after the razing of the Albans' city to yield the leadership to the Romans who had destroyed it. It seems that when fifteen years had passed after the destruction of Alba the Roman king, sending embassies to the thirty cities which had been at once colonies and subjects of Alba, summoned them to obey the orders of the Romans inasmuch as the Romans had succeeded to the Alban's supremacy over the Latin race as well as to everything else that the Albans had possessed. He pointed out that there were two methods of acquisition by which men became masters of what had belonged to others, one the result of compulsion, the other of choice, and that the Romans had by both these methods acquired the supremacy over the cities which the Albans had held. For when the Albans had become enemies of the Romans, the latter had conquered them by arms, and after the others had lost their own city the Romans had given them a share in theirs, so that it was but reasonable that the Albans both perforce and voluntarily should yield to the Romans the sovereignty they had exercised over their subjects. The Latin cities gave no answer separately to the ambassadors, but in a general assembly of the whole nation held at Ferentinum[39] they passed a vote not to yield the sovereignty to the

---

39 Dionysius frequently gives this name to the place of assembly of the Latins, as if there had been a town there. Livy usually says *ad lucum Ferentinae* ("at the grove of Ferentina") but also speaks of the *aqua Ferentina* ("spring of Ferentina"). This place should not be confused with the Ferentinum situated on the Via Latina in the land of the Hernicans.

Romans, and immediately chose two generals, Ancus Publicius of the city of Cora and Spusius Vecilius of Lavinium, and invested them with absolute power with regard to both peace and war. These were the causes of the war between the Romans and their kinsmen, a war that lasted for five years and was carried on more or less like a civil war and after the ancient fashion. For, as they never engaged in pitched battles with all their forces ranged against all those of the foe, no great disaster occurred nor any wholesale slaughter, and none of their cities went through the experience of being razed or enslaved or suffer any other irreparable calamity as the result of being captured in war; but making incursions into one another's country when the corn was ripe, they foraged it, and them returning home with their armies, exchanged prisoners. However, one city of the Latin nation called Medullia, which earlier had become a colony of the Romans in the reign of Romulus, as I stated in the preceding Book,[40] and had revolted again to their countrymen, was brought to terms after a siege by the Roman king and persuaded not to revolt for the future; but no other of the calamities which wars bring in their train was felt by either side at that time. Accordingly, as the Romans were eager for peace, a treaty was readily concluded that left no rancour.[41]

35 These[42] were the achievements performed during his reign by King Tullus Hostilius, a man worthy of exceptional praise for his boldness in war and his prudence in the face of danger, but, above both these qualifications, because, though he was not precipitate in entering upon war, when he was once engaged in it he steadily pursued it until he had the upper hand in every way over his adversaries. After he had reigned thirty-two years he lost his life when his house caught fire, and with him his wife and children and

40 ii. 36, 2.
41 *Cf.* Livy i. 32, 3.
42 *Cf.* Livy i. 31, 5-8.

all his household perished in the flames. Some say that his house was set on fire by a thunderbolt, Heaven having become angered at his neglect of some sacred rites (for they say that in his reign some ancestral sacrifices were omitted and that he introduced others that were foreign to the Romans), but the majority state that the disaster was due to human treachery and ascribe it to Marcius, who ruled the state after him. For they say that this man, who was the son of Numa Pompilius' daughter, was indignant at being in a private station himself, though of royal descent, and seeing that Tullus had children growing up, he suspected very strongly that upon the death of Tullus the kingdom would fall to them. With these thoughts in mind, they say, he had long since formed a plot against the king, and had many of the Romans aiding him to gain the sovereignty; and being a friend of Tullus and one of his closest confidants, he was watching for a suitable opportunity to appear for making his attack. Accordingly, when Tullus proposed to perform a certain sacrifice at home which he wished only his near relations to know about and that day chanced to be very stormy, with rain and sleet and darkness, so that those who were upon guard before the house had left their station, Marcius, looking upon this as a favourable opportunity, entered the house together with his friends, who had swords under their garments, and having killed the king and his children and all the rest whom he encountered, he set fire to the house in several places, and after doing this spread the report that the fire had been due to a thunderbolt. But for my part I do not accept this story, regarding it as neither true nor plausible, but I subscribe rather to the former account, believing that Tullus met with this end by the judgment of Heaven. For, in the first place, it is improbable that the undertaking in which so many were concerned could have been kept secret, and, besides, the author of it could not be certain that after the death of Hostilius the Romans would choose him as king of the state; furthermore, even if men were loyal to him and steadfast, yet it was unlikely that the gods would act with an ignorance resembling that of men. For after the tribes had given their votes, it would be necessary that the gods, by auspicious omens, should sanction the awarding of the kingdom to him; and which of the gods or other divinities was going to permit a man who was impure and stained with the unjust murder of so many persons to approach the altars, begin the sacrifices, and perform the other religious ceremonies? I, then, for these reasons do not attribute the catastrophe to the treachery of men, but to the will of Heaven; however, let everyone judge as he pleases.

36 After[43] the death of Tullus Hostilius, the *interreges* appointed by the senate according to ancestral usage chose Marcius, surnamed Ancus, king of the state; and when the people had confirmed the decision of the senate and the signs from Heaven were favourable, Marcius, after fulfilling all the customary requirements, entered upon the government in the second year of the thirty-fifth Olympiad[44] (the one in which Sphaerus, a Lacedaemonian, gained the prize),[45] at the time when Damasias held the annual archonship at Athens. This king, finding that many of the religious ceremonies instituted by Numa Pompilius, his maternal grandfather, were being neglected, and seeing the greatest part of the Romans devoted to the pursuit of war and gain and no longer cultivating the land as aforetime, assembled the people and exhorted them to worship the gods once more as they had done in Numa's reign. He pointed out to them that it was owing to their neglect of the gods that not only many pestilences had fallen upon the city, by which no small part of the population had been destroyed, but also that King Hostilius, who had not shown the proper regard for the gods, had suffered for a long time from a complication of bodily ailments and at last, no

43 *Cf.* Livy i. 32, 1 f.
44 638 B.C.
45 In the short-distance foot-race. See critical note.

longer sound even in his understanding but weakened in mind as well as in body, had come to a pitiable end, both he and his family. He then commended the system of government established by Numa for the Romans as excellent and wise and one which supplied every citizen with daily plenty from the most lawful employments; and he advised them to restore this system once more by applying themselves to agriculture and cattle-breeding and to those occupations that were free from all injustice, and to scorn rapine and violence and the profits accruing from war. By these and similar appeals he inspired in all a great desire both for peaceful tranquillity and for sober industry. After this, he called together the pontiffs, and receiving from them the commentaries on religious rites which Pompilius had composed, he caused them to be transcribed on tablets and exposed in the Forum for everyone to examine. These have since been destroyed by time, for, brazen pillars being not yet in use at that time, the laws and the ordinances concerning religious rites were engraved on oaken boards; but after the expulsion of the kings they were again copied off for the use of the public by Gaius Papirius, a pontiff, who had the superintendence of all religious matters. After Marcius had re-established the religious rites which had fallen into abeyance and turned the idle people to their proper employments, he commended the careful husbandmen and reprimanded those who managed their lands ill as citizens not to be depended on.

37 While[46] instituting these administrative measures he hoped above all else to pass his whole life free from war and troubles, like his grandfather, but he found his purpose crossed by fortune and, contrary to his inclinations, was forced to become a warrior and to live no part of his life free from danger and turbulence. For at the very time that he entered upon the government and was establishing

46 For chaps. 37-39, 2 *cf.* Livy i. 32-33, 5.

his tranquil regime the Latins, despising him and looking upon him as incapable of conducting wars through want of courage, sent bands of robbers from each of their cities into the parts of the Roman territory that lay next to them, in consequence of which many of the Romans were suffering injury. And when ambassadors came from the king and summoned them to make satisfaction to the Romans according to the treaty, they alleged that they neither had any knowledge of the robberies complained of, asserting that these had been committed without the general consent of the nation, nor had become accountable to the Romans for anything they did. For they had not made the treaty with them, they say, but with Tullus, and by the death of Tullus their treaty of peace had been terminated. Marcius, therefore, compelled by these reasons and the answers[47] of the Latins, led out an army against them, and laying siege to the city of Politorium, he took it by capitulation before any aid reached the besieged from the other Latins. However, he did not treat the inhabitants with any severity, but, allowing them to retain their possessions, transferred the whole population to Rome and distributed them among the tribes.

38 The next year, since the Latins had sent settlers to Politorium, which was then uninhabited, and were cultivating the lands of the Politorini, Marcius marched against them with his army. And when the Latins came outside the walls and drew up in order of battle, he defeated them and took the town a second time; and having burnt the houses and razed the walls, so the enemy might not again use it as a base of operations nor cultivate the land, he led his army home. The next year the Latins marched against the city of Medullia, in which there were Roman colonists, and besieging it, attacked the walls on all sides and took it by storm. At the same time Marcius

---

47 The text is uncertain here. Possibly we should read with Grasberger "haughty answers," an expression used several times by Dionysius, in place of "reasons and answers."

took Tellenae, a prominent city of the Latins, after he had overcome the inhabitants in a pitched battle and had reduced the place by an assault upon the walls; after which he transferred the prisoners to Rome without taking any of their possessions from them, and set apart for them a place in the city in which to build houses. And when Medullia had been for three years subject to the Latins, he recovered it in the fourth year, after defeating the inhabitants in many great battles. A little later he captured Ficana, a city which he had already taken two years before by capitulation, afterwards transferring all the inhabitants to Rome but doing no other harm to the city — a course in which he seemed to have acted with greater clemency than prudence. For the Latins sent colonists thither and occupying the land of the Ficancnses, they enjoyed its produce themselves; so that Marcius was obliged to lead his army a second time against this city and, after making himself master of it with great difficulty, to burn the houses and raze the walls.

39 After this the Latins and Romans fought two pitched battles with large armies In the first, after they had been engaged a considerable time without any seeming advantage on either side, they parted, each returning to their own camp. But in the later contest the Romans gained the victory and pursued the Latins to their camp. After these actions there was no other pitched battle fought between them, but continual incursions were made by both into the neighbouring territory and there were also skirmishes between the horse and light-armed foot who patrolled the country; in these the victors were generally the Romans, who had their forces in the field posted secretly in advantageous strongholds, under the command of Tarquinius the Tyrrhenian. About the same time the Fidenates also revolted from the Romans. They did not, indeed, openly declare war, but ravaged their country by making raids in small numbers and secretly. Against these Marcius led out an army of light troops, and before the Fidenates had made the necessary preparations for war he encamped near their city. At first they pretended not to know what injuries they had committed to draw the Roman army against them, and when the king informed them that he had come to punish them for their plundering and ravaging of his territory, they excused themselves by alleging that their city was not responsible for these injuries, and asked for time in which to make an investigation and to search out the guilty; and they consumed many days in doing nothing that should have been done, but rather in sending to their allies secretly for assistance and busying themselves with the preparing of arms.

40 Marcius, having learned of their purpose, proceeded to dig mines leading under the walls of the city from his own camp; and when the work was finally completed, he broke camp and led his army against the city, taking along many siege-engines and scaling-ladders and the other equipment he had prepared for an assault, and approaching a different point from that where the walls were undermined. Then, the Fidenates had rushed in great numbers to those parts of the city that were being stormed, and were stoutly repulsing the assaults, the Romans who had been detailed for the purpose opened the mouths of the mines and found themselves within the walls; and destroying all who came to meet them, they threw open the gates to the besiegers. When many of the Fidenates had been slain in the taking of the town, Marcius ordered the rest to deliver up their arms, and made proclamation that all should repair to a certain place in the city. Thereupon he caused a few of them who had been the authors of the revolt to be scourged and put to death, and having given leave to his soldiers to plunder all their houses and left a sufficient garrison there, he marched with his army against the Sabines. For these also had failed to abide by the terms of the peace which they had made with King Tullus, and making incursions into the territory of the Romans, were again laying waste the neighbouring country. When Marcius, therefore, learned from spies and deserters the proper time to put his plan into execution, while the Sabines were dispersed and plundering the fields, he marched in person with the infantry to the enemy's camp, which was weakly guarded, and took the ramparts at the first onset; and he ordered Tarquinius to hasten with the cavalry against those who were dispersed in foraging. The Sabines, learning that the Roman cavalry was coming against them, left their plunder and the other booty they were carrying and driving off, and fled to their camp; and when they perceived that this too was in the possession of the infantry, they were at a loss which way to turn and endeavoured to reach the woods and mountains. But being pursued by the light-armed foot and the horse, the greater part of them were destroyed, though some few escaped. And after this misfortune, sending ambassadors once more to Rome, they obtained such a peace as they desired. For the war which was still going on between the Romans and the Latin cities rendered both a truce and a peace with their other foes necessary.

41 About[48] the fourth year after this war Marcius, the Roman king, leading his own army of citizens and sending for as many auxiliaries as he could obtain from his allies, marched against the Veientes and laid waste a large part of their country. These had been the aggressors the year before by making an incursion into the Roman territory, where they seized much property and slew many of the inhabitants. And when the Veientes came out against him with a large army and encamped beyond the river Tiber, near Fidenae, Marcius set out with his army as rapidly as possible; and being superior in cavalry, he first cut them off from the roads leading into the country, and then, forcing them to come to a

48 *Cf.* Livy i. 33, 9.

pitched battle, defeated them and captured their camp. Having succeeded in this war also according to his desire, he returned to Rome and conducted in honour of the gods the procession in celebration of his victory and the customary triumph. The second year after this, the Veientes having again broken the truce they had made with Marcius and demanding to get back the salt-works which they had surrendered by treaty in the reign of Romulus,[49] he fought a second battle with them, one more important than the first, near the salt works; and having easily won it, he continued from that time forth in undisputed possession of the salt-works. The prize for valour in this battle also was won by Tarquinius, the commander of the horse; and Marcius, looking upon him as the bravest man in the whole army, kept honouring him in various ways, among other things making him both a patrician and a senator. Marcius also engaged in a war with the Volscians, since bands of robbers from this nation too were setting out to plunder the fields of the Romans. And marching against them with a large army, he captured much booty; then, laying siege to one of their cities called Velitrae, he surrounded it with a ditch and palisades and, being master of the open country, prepared to assault the walls. But when the elders came out with the emblems of suppliants and not only promised to make good the damage they had done, in such manner as the king should determine, but also agreed to deliver up the guilty to be punished, he made a truce with them, and, after accepting the satisfaction they freely offered, he concluded a treaty of peace and friendship.

42 Again, some others of the Sabine nation who had not yet felt the Roman power, the inhabitants of . . .,[50] a great and prosperous city, without having any grounds of complaint against the Romans

---

49 See ii. 55, 5.
50 The name of the city has been lost from the MSS. Compare the similar case of Politorium in chap. 37, 4.

but being driven to envy of their prosperity, which was increasing disproportionately, and being a very warlike people, began at first with brigandage and the raiding of their fields in small bodies, but afterwards, lured by the hope of booty, made war upon them openly and ravaged much of the neighbouring territory, inflicting severe damage. But they were not permitted either to carry off their booty or themselves to retire unscathed, for the Roman king, hastening to the rescue, pitched his camp near theirs and forced them to come to an engagement. A great battle, therefore, was fought and many fell on both sides, but the Romans won by reason of their skill and their endurance of toil, virtues to which they had been long accustomed, and they proved far superior to the Sabines; and pursuing them closely as they fled, dispersed and in disorder, toward their camp, they wrought great slaughter. Then, having also captured their camp, which was full of all sorts of valuables, and recovered the captives the Sabines had taken in their raids, they returned home. These in brief are the military exploits of this king that have been remembered and recorded by the Romans. I shall now mention the achievements of his civil administration.

43 In[51] the first place, he made no small addition to the city by enclosing the hill called the Aventine within its walls. This is a hill of moderate height and about eighteen stades in circumference, which was then covered with trees of every kind, particularly with many beautiful laurels, so that one place on the hill is called Lauretum or "Laurel Grove" by the Romans; but the whole is now covered with buildings, including, among many others, the temple of Diana. The Aventine is separated from another of the hills that are included within the city of Rome, called the Palatine Hill (round which was built the first city to be established), by a deep and narrow ravine, but in after times the whole hollow between the two hills was filled

---

51 *Cf.* Livy i. 33, 2.

up. Marcius, observing that this hill would serve as a stronghold against the city for any army that approached, encompassed it with a wall and ditch and settled here the populations that he had transferred from Tellenae and Politorium and the other cities he had taken. This is one peace-time achievement recorded of this king that was at once splendid and practical; thereby the city was not only enlarged by the addition of another city but also rendered less vulnerable to the attack of a strong enemy force.

44 Another peace-time achievement was of even greater consequence than the one just mentioned, as it made the city richer in all the conveniences of life and encouraged it to embark upon nobler undertakings. The river Tiber, descending from the Apennine mountains and flowing close by Rome, discharges itself upon harbourless and exposed shores made by the Tyrrhenian Sea; but this river was of small and negligible advantage to Rome because of having at its mouth no trading post where the commodities brought in by sea and down the river from the country above could be received and exchanged with the merchants. But as it is navigable quite up to its source for river boats of considerable size and as far as Rome itself for sea-going ships of great burden, he resolved to build a seaport at its outlet, making use of the river's mouth itself for a harbour. For the Tiber broadens greatly where it unites with the sea and forms great bays equal to those of the best seaports; and, most wonderful of all, its mouth is not blocked by sandbanks piled up by the sea, as happens in the case of many even of the large rivers, nor does it by wandering this way and that through fens and marshes spend itself before its stream unites with the sea, but it is everywhere navigable and discharges itself through its one genuine mouth, repelling the surge that comes from the main, notwithstanding the frequency and violence of the west wind on that coast. Accordingly, oared ships however large and merchantmen up to three thousand bushels[52] burden enter at the mouth of the river and are rowed and towed up to Rome, while those of a larger size ride at anchor off the mouth, where they are unloaded and loaded again by river boats. Upon the elbow of land that lies between the river and the sea the king built a city and surrounded it with a wall, naming it from its situation Ostia,[53] or, as we should call it, *thyra* or "portal"; and by this means he made Rome not only an inland city but also a seaport, and gave it a taste of the good things from beyond the sea.

45 He[54] also built a wall round the high hill called the Janiculum, situated on the other side of the river Tiber, and stationed there an adequate garrison for the security of those who navigated the river; for the Tyrrhenians, being masters of all the country on the other side of the river, had been plundering the merchants. He also is said to have built the wooden bridge over the Tiber, which was required to be constructed without brass or iron, being held together by its beams alone. This bridge they preserve to the present day, looking upon it as sacred; and if any part of it gives out the pontiffs attend to it, offering certain traditional sacrifices while it is being repaired.[55] These are the memorable achievements of this king during his reign, and he handed Rome on to his successors in much better condition than he himself had received it. After reigning twenty-four years he died, leaving two sons, one still a child in years and the elder just growing a beard.[56]

---

52 Literally "three thousand [measures]."

53 *Cf.* Livy i. 33, 9.

54 *Cf.* Livy i. 33, 6.

55 The *pons sublicius* ("pile-bridge") leading to the Janiculum was for centuries the only bridge at Rome. Dionysius has already, in discussing the *pontifices* (ii. 73, 1), stated that they were so named from one of their important duties, the repairing of the wooden bridge. Thus he follows Varro (*L.L.* v. 83) in deriving *pontifex* from *pons* and *facere*.

56 *Cf.* Livy i. 35, 1.

46 After the death of Ancus Marcius the senate, being empowered by the people to establish whatever form of government they thought fit, again resolved to abide by the same form and appointed *interreges*.[57] These, having assembled the people for the election, chosen Lucius Tarquinius as king; and the omens from Heaven having confirmed the decision of the people, Tarquinius took over the sovereignty about the second year of the forty-first Olympiad[58] (the one in which Cleondas, a Theban, gained the prize),[59] Heniochides being archon at Athens. I shall now relate, following the account I have found in the Roman annals, from what sort of ancestors this Tarquinius was sprung, from what country he came, the reasons for his removing to Rome, and by what course of conduct he came to be king.[60] There was a certain Corinthian, Demaratus by name, of the family of the Bacchiadae, who, having chosen to engage in commerce, sailed to Italy in a ship of his own with his own cargo; and having sold the cargo in the Tyrrhenian cities, which were at the time the most flourishing in all Italy, and gained great profit thereby, he no longer desired to put into any other ports, but continued to ply the same sea, carrying a Greek cargo to the Tyrrhenians and a Tyrrhenian cargo to Greece, by which means he became possessed of great wealth. But when Corinth fell a prey to sedition and the tyranny of Cypselus was rising in revolt against the Bacchiadae,[61] Demaratus thought it was not safe for him to live under a tyranny with his great riches, particularly as he was of the oligarchic family; and accordingly,

57 *Cf.* ii. 57, iii. 1.
58 614 B.C.
59 In the short-distance foot-race. See the critical note on chap. 36.
60 For chaps. 46, 2-48, 4 *cf.* Livy i. 34.
61 The Bacchiadae were the ruling family at Corinth in early times. The kings after Bacchis (*ca.* 926-891 B.C.) were all chosen from among his descendants, and after the abolition of the monarchy, the family ruled as an oligarchy. Cypselus (father of the famous Periander), who overthrew their rule *ca.* 657, soon became so popular a ruler that he dispensed with a bodyguard.

getting together all of his substance that he could, he sailed away from Corinth. And having from his continual intercourse with the Tyrrhenians many good friends among them, particularly at Tarquinii, which was a large and flourishing city at that time, he built a house there and married a woman of illustrious birth. By her he had two sons, to whom he gave Tyrrhenian names, calling one Arruns and the other Lucumo; and having instructed them in both the Greek and Tyrrhenian learning, he married them, when they were grown, to two women of the most distinguished families.

47 Not long afterward the elder of his sons died without acknowledged issue, and a few days later Demaratus himself died of grief, leaving his surviving son Lucumo heir to his entire fortune. Lucumo, having thus inherited the great wealth of his father, had aspired to public life and a part in the administration of the commonwealth and to be one of its foremost citizens. But being repulsed on every side by the native-born citizens and excluded, not only from the first, but even from the middle rank, he resented his disfranchisement. And hearing that the Romans gladly received all strangers and made them citizens, he resolved to get together all his riches and remove thither, taking with him his wife and such of his friends and household as wished to go along; and those who were eager to depart with him were many. When they were come to the hill called Janiculum, from which Rome is first discerned by those who come from Tyrrhenia, an eagle, descending on a sudden, snatched his cap from his head and flew up again with it, and rising in a circular flight, hid himself in the depths of the circumambient air, then of a sudden replaced the cap on his head, fitting it on as it had been before.[62] This prodigy appearing wonderful and

---

62 Livy's account of this episode (i. 34, 8) is as follows: *ibi ei carpento sedenti cum uxore aquila suspensis demissa leniter alis pilleum aufert, superque carpentum cum magno clangore volitans, rursus velut ministerio divinitus missa capiti apte reponit; inde sublimis abiit.* At first sight this appears the

extraordinary to them all, the wife of Lucumo, Tanaquil by name, who had a good understanding through her ancestors, of the Tyrrhenians' augural science, took him aside from the others and, embracing him, filled him with great hopes of rising from his private station to the royal power. She advised him, however, to consider by what means he might render himself worthy to receive the sovereignty by the free choice of the Romans.

48 Lucumo was overjoyed at this omen, and as he was now approaching the gates he besought the gods that the prediction might be fulfilled and that his arrival might be attended with good fortune; then he entered the city. After this, gaining an audience with King Marcius, he first informed him who he was and then told him that, being desirous of settling at Rome, he had brought with him all his paternal fortune, which, as it exceeded the limits suitable for a private citizen, he said he proposed to place at the disposal of the king and of the Roman state for the general good. And having met with a favourable reception from the king, who assigned him and his Tyrrhenian followers to one of the tribes and to one of the *curiae*, he built a house upon a site in the city which was allotted to him as sufficient for the purpose, and received a portion of land. After he had settled these matters and had become one of the citizens, he was informed that every Roman had a common name and, after the common name, another, derived from his family and ancestors, and wishing to be like them in this respect also, he took the name of Lucius instead of Lucumo as his common name, and that of Tarquinius as his family name, from the

more straightforward account, and Schnelle (see critical note) proposed to rearrange the clauses of Dionysius' account to conform to it. But Dionysius was probably following a different tradition, according to which the eagle was represented as temporarily disappearing in order to descend then direct from Heaven as it were, with Tarquinius' cap. Palaeographically Schnelle's proposal is very improbable.

city in which he had been born and brought up. In a very short time he gained the friendship of the king by presenting him with those things which he saw he needed most and by supplying him with all the money he required to carry on his wars. On campaigns he fought most bravely of all, whether of the infantry or of the cavalry, and wherever there was need of good judgment he was counted among the shrewdest counsellors. Yet the favour of the king did not deprive him of the goodwill of the rest of the Romans; for he not only won to himself many of the patricians by his kindly services but also gained the affections of the populace by his cordial greetings, his agreeable conversation, his dispensing of money and his friendliness in other ways.

49 This was the character of Tarquinius and for these reasons he became during the lifetime of Marcius the most illustrious of all the Romans, and after that king's death was adjudged by all as worthy of the kingship. When he had succeeded to the sovereignty he first made war upon the people of Apiolae, as it was called, a city of no small note among the Latins.[63] For the Apiolani and all the rest of the Latins, looking upon the treaty of peace as having been terminated after the death of Ancus Marcius, were laying waste the Roman territory by plundering and pillaging. Tarquinius, desiring to take revenge upon them for these injuries, set out with a large force and ravaged the most fruitful part of their country; then, when important reinforcements came to the Apiolani from their Latin neighbours, he fought two battles with them and, having gained the victory in both, proceeded to besiege the city, causing his troops to assault the walls in relays; and the besieged, being but few contending against many and not having a moment's respite, were at last subdued. The city being taken by storm, the greater part of the Apiolani were slain fighting, but a few after delivering up their

---

63 *Cf.* Livy i. 35, 7.

arms were sold together with the rest of the booty; their wives and children were carried away into slavery by the Romans and the city was plundered and burned. After the king had done this and had razed the walls to the foundations, he returned home with his army. Soon afterwards[64] he undertook another expedition against the city of the Crustumerians. This was a colony of the Latins and in the reign of Romulus had submitted to the Romans; but after Tarquinius succeeded to the sovereignty it began again to incline on the side of the Latins. However, it was not necessary to reduce this place by a siege and great effort; for the Crustumerians, having become aware both of the magnitude of the force that was coming against them and of their own weakness, since no aid came to them from the rest of the Latins, opened their gates; and the oldest and most honoured of the citizens, coming out, delivered up the city to Tarquinius, asking only that he treat them with clemency and moderation. This fell out according to his wish, and entering the city, he put none of the Crustumerians to death and punished only a very few, who had been the authors of the revolt, with perpetual banishment, while permitting all the rest to retain their possessions and to enjoy Roman citizenship as before; but, in order to prevent any uprising for the future, he left Roman colonists in their midst.

50 The Nomentans also, having formed the same plans, met with the same fate. For they kept sending bands of robbers to pillage the fields of the Romans and openly became their enemies, relying upon the assistance of the Latins. But when Tarquinius set out against them and the aid from the Latins was too late in arriving, they were unable to resist so great a force by themselves, and coming out of the town with the tokens of suppliants, they surrendered. The inhabitants of the city called Collatia undertook to try the fortune of battle with the Roman forces and for that purpose came out of

---

64 For chaps. 49, 4-54.3 *cf.* Livy i. 38, 1-4.

their city; but being worsted in every engagement and having many of their men wounded, they were again forced to take refuge inside their walls, and they kept sending to the various Latin cities asking for assistance. But as these were too slow about relieving them and the enemy was attacking their walls in many places, they were at length obliged to deliver up their town. They did not, however, meet with the same lenient treatment as had the Nomentans and Crustumerians, for the king disarmed them and fined them in a sum of money; and leaving a sufficient garrison in the city, he appointed his own nephew, Tarquinius Arruns, to rule over them with absolute power for life. This man, who had been born after the death both of his father Arruns and of his grandfather Demaratus, had inherited from neither the part of their respective fortunes which otherwise would have fallen to his share and for this reason he was surnamed Egerius or "the Indigent"; for that is the name the Romans give to poor men and beggars. But from the time when he took charge of this city both he himself and all his descendants were given the surname of Collatinus.

After the surrender of Collatia the king marched against the place called Corniculum; this also was a city of the Latin race. And having ravaged their territory in great security, since none offered to defend it, he encamped close by[65] the city itself and invited the inhabitants to enter into a league of friendship. But since they were unwilling to come to terms, but relied on the strength of their walls and expected allies to come from many directions, he invested the city on all sides and assaulted the walls. The Corniculans resisted long and bravely, inflicting numerous losses upon the besiegers, but becoming worn out with continual labour and no longer being unanimous (for some wished to deliver up the town and others to

---

65 Adopting Kiessling's emendation (see critical note) in place of the reading of the MSS., which means "marched toward the city itself."

hold out to the last) and their distress being greatly increased by this very dissension, the town was taken by storm. The bravest part of the people were slain fighting during the capture of the town, while the craven, who owed their preservation to their cowardice, were sold for slaves together with their wives and children; and the city was plundered by the conquerors and burned. The Latins, resenting this proceeding, voted to lead a joint army against the Romans; and having raised a numerous force, they made an irruption into the most fruitful part of their country, carrying off thence many captives and possessing themselves of much booty. King Tarquinius marched out against them with his light troops who were ready for action, but too late to overtake them, he invaded their country and treated it in similar fashion. Many other such reverses and successes happened alternately to each side in the expeditions they made against one another's borders; and they fought one pitched battle with all their forces near the city of Fidenae, in which many fell on both sides though the Romans gained the victory and forced the Latins to abandon their camp by night and retire to their own cities.

51 After this engagement Tarquinius led his army in good order to their cities, making offers of friendship; and the Latins, since they had no national army assembled and no confidence in their own preparations, accepted his proposals. And some of them proceeded to surrender their cities, observing that in the case of the cities which were taken by storm the inhabitants were made slaves and the cities razed, while those which surrendered by capitulation were treated with no other severity than to be obliged to yield obedience to the conquerors. First, then, Ficulea, a city of note, submitted to him upon fair terms, then Cameria; and their example was followed by some small towns and strong fortresses. But the rest of the Latins, becoming alarmed at this and fearing that he would subjugate the whole nation, met together in their assembly at Ferentinum and voted, not only to lead out their own forces from every city, but also to call the strongest of the neighbouring peoples to their aid; and to that end they sent ambassadors to the Tyrrhenians and Sabines to ask for assistance. The Sabines promised that as soon as they should hear that the Latins had invaded the territory of the Romans they too would take up arms and ravage that part of their territory which lay next to them; and the Tyrrhenians engaged to send to their assistance whatever forces they themselves should not need,[66] though not all were of the same mind, but only five cities, namely, Clusium, Arretium, Volaterrae, Rusellae, and, in addition to these, Vetulonia.

52 The Latins, elated by these hopes, got ready a large army of their own forces and having added to it the troops from the Tyrrhenians, invaded the Roman territory; and at the same time the cities of the Sabine nation which had promised to take part with them in the war proceeded to lay waste the country that bordered their own. Thereupon the Roman king, who in the meantime had also got ready a large and excellent army, marched in haste against the enemy. But thinking it unsafe to attack the Sabines and the Latins at the same time and to divide his forces into two bodies, he determined to lead his whole army against the Latins, and encamped near them. At first both sides were reluctant to hazard an engagement with all their forces, being alarmed at each other's preparations; but the light-armed troops, coming down from their entrenchments, engaged in constant skirmishes with one another, generally without any advantage on either side. After a time, however, these skirmishes produced a spirit of rivalry in both armies and each side supported its own men, at first in small numbers, but at last they were all forced to come out of their camps. The troops which now engaged, being used to fighting and being nearly equal

66 Or, reading ἧς ἄν δεηθῶσιν (see critical note), "whatever forces they [the Latins] should need."

in numbers, both foot and horse, animated by the same warlike ardour, and believing that they were running the supreme risk, fought on both sides with noteworthy bravery; and they separated, without a decision, when night overtook them. But the different feelings of the two sides after the action made it clear which of them had fought better than their opponents. For on the next day the Latins stirred no more out of their camp, while the Roman king, leading out his troops into the plain, was ready to fight another engagement and for a long time kept his lines in battle formation. But when the enemy did not come out against him, he took the spoils from their dead, and carrying off his own dead, led his army with great exultation back to his own camp.

53 The Latins having received fresh aid from the Tyrrhenians during the days that followed, a second battle was fought, much greater than the former, in which King Tarquinius gained a most signal victory, the credit for which was allowed by all to belong to him personally. For when the Roman line was already in distress and its close formation was being broken on the left wing, Tarquinius, as soon as he learned of this reverse to his forces (for he happened then to be fighting on the right wing), wheeling the best troops of horse about and taking along the flower of the foot, led them behind his own army and passing by the left wing, advanced even beyond the solid ranks of his line of battle. Then, wheeling his troops to the right and all clapping spurs to their horses, he charged the Tyrrhenians in flank (for these were fighting on the enemy's right wing and had put to flight those who stood opposite to them), and by thus appearing to them unexpectedly he caused them great alarm and confusion. In the meantime the Roman foot also, having recovered themselves from their earlier fear, advanced against the enemy; and thereupon there followed a great slaughter of the Tyrrhenians and the utter rout of their right wing. Tarquinius, having ordered the commanders of the infantry to follow in good order and slowly, led the cavalry himself at full speed to the enemy's camp; and arriving there ahead of those who were endeavouring to save themselves from the rout, he captured the entrenchments at the very first onset. For the troops which had been left there, being neither aware as yet of the misfortune that had befallen their own men nor able, by reason of the suddenness of the attack, to recognize the cavalry that approached, permitted them to enter. After the camp of the Latins had been taken, those of the enemy who were retiring thither from the rout of their army, as to a safe retreat, were slain by the cavalry, who had possessed themselves of it, while others, endeavouring to escape from the camp into the plain, were met by the serried ranks to Roman infantry and cut down; but the greater part of them, being crowded by one another and trodden under foot, perished on the palisades or in the trenches in the most miserable and ignoble manner. Consequently, those who were left alive, finding no means of saving themselves, were obliged to surrender to the conquerors. Tarquinius, having taken possession of many prisoners and much booty, sold the former and granted the plunder of the camp to the soldiers.

54 After this success he led his army against the cities of the Latins, in order to reduce by battle those who would not voluntarily surrender to him; but he did not find it necessary to lay siege to any of them. For all had recourse to supplications and prayers, and sending ambassadors to him from the whole nation, they asked him to put an end to the war upon such conditions as he himself wished, and delivered up their cities to him. The king, becoming master of their cities upon these terms, treated them all with the greatest clemency and moderation; for he neither put any of the Latins to death nor forced any into exile, nor laid a fine upon any of them, but allowed them to enjoy their lands and to retain their traditional forms of government. He did, however, order them to deliver up the deserters and captives to the Romans without ransom, to restore to their masters the slaves they had captured in their incursions, to repay the money they had taken from the husbandmen, and to make good every other damage or loss they had occasioned in their raids. Upon their performing these commands they were to be friends and allies of the Romans, doing everything that they should command. This was the outcome of the war between the Romans and the Latins; and King Tarquinius celebrated the customary triumph for his victory in this war.

55 The[67] following year he led his army against the Sabines, who had long since been aware of his purpose and preparations against them. They were unwilling, however, to let the war to be brought into their own country, but having got ready an adequate force in their turn, they were advancing to meet him. And upon the confines of their territory they engaged in a battle which lasted till night, neither army being victorious, but both suffering very severely. At all events, during the following days neither the Sabine general nor the Roman king led his forces out of their entrenchments, but both broke camp and returned home without doing any injury to the other's territory. The intention of both was the same, namely, to lead out a new and larger force against the other's country at the beginning of spring. After they had made all their preparations, the Sabines first took the field, strengthened with a sufficient body of Tyrrhenian auxiliaries, and encamped near Fidenae, at the confluence of the Anio and the Tiber rivers. They pitched two camps opposite and adjoining each other, the united stream of both rivers running between them, over which was built a wooden bridge resting on boats and rafts, thus affording quick communication between them and making them one camp. Tarquinius, being

---

67   For chaps. 55-57.1 *cf.* Livy i. 36, 1 f., 37.

informed of their irruption, marched out in his turn with the Roman army and pitched his camp a little above theirs, near the river Anio, upon a strongly situated hill. But though both armies had all the zeal imaginable for the war, no pitched battle, either great or small, occurred between them; for Tarquinius by a timely stratagem ruined all the plans of the Sabines and gained possession of both their camps. His stratagem was this:

56 He got together boats and rafts on the one side of the two rivers near which he himself lay encamped and filled them with dry sticks and brushwood, also with pitch and sulphur, and then waiting for a favourable wind, about the time of the morning watch he ordered the firewood to be set on fire and the boats and rafts turned adrift to drop downstream. These covered the intervening distance in a very short time, and being driven against the bridge, set fire to it in many places. The Sabines, seeing a vast flame flare up on a sudden, ran to lend their assistance and tried all means possible to extinguish the fire. While they were thus employed Tarquinius arrived about dawn, leading the Roman army in order of battle, and attacked one of the camps; and since the greater part of the guards had left their posts to run to the fire, though some few turned and resisted, he gained possession of it without any trouble. While these things were going on another part of the Roman army came up and took the other camp of the Sabines also, which lay on the other side of the river. This detachment, having been sent on ahead by Tarquinius about the first watch, had crossed in boats and rafts the river formed by the uniting of the two streams, at a place where their passage was not likely to be discovered by the Sabines, and had got near to the other camp at the same time that they saw the bridge on fire; for this was their signal for the attack. Of those who were found in the camps some were slain by the Romans while fighting, but any others threw themselves into the confluence of the rivers, and being unable to get through the whirlpools, were swallowed up; and not a few of them perished in the flames while they were endeavouring to save the bridge. Tarquinius, having taken both camps, gave leave to the soldiers to divide among themselves the booty that was found in them; but the prisoners, who were very numerous, not only of the Sabines themselves but also of the Tyrrhenians, he carried to Rome, where he kept them under strict guard.

57 The Sabines, subdued by this calamity, grew sensible of their own weakness, and sending ambassadors, concluded a truce from the war for six years. But the Tyrrhenians, angered not only because they had been often defeated by the Romans, but also because Tarquinius had refused to restore to them the prisoners he held when they sent an embassy to demand them, but retained them as hostages, passed a vote that all the Tyrrhenian cities should carry on the war jointly against the Romans and that any city refusing to take part in the expedition should be excluded from their league. After passing this vote they led out their forces and, crossing the Tiber, encamped near Fidenae. And having gained possession of that city by treachery, there being a sedition among the inhabitants, and having taken a great many prisoners and carried off much booty from the Roman territory, they returned home, leaving a sufficient garrison in Fidenae; for they thought this city would be an excellent base from which to carry on the war against the Romans. But King Tarquinius, having for the ensuing year armed all the Romans and taken as many troops as he could get from his allies, led them out against the enemy at the beginning of spring, before the Tyrrhenians could be assembled from all their cities and march against him as they had done before. Then, having divided his whole army into two parts, he put himself at the head of the Roman troops and led them against the cities of the Tyrrhenians, while he gave the command of the allies, consisting chiefly of the Latins, to Egerius, his kinsman, and ordered him to march against the enemy in Fidenae. This force of allies, through contempt of the enemy, placed their camp in an unsafe position near Fidenae and barely missed being totally destroyed; for the garrison in the town, having secretly sent for fresh aid from the Tyrrhenians and watched for a suitable occasion, sallied forth from the town and captured the enemy's camp at the first onset, as it was carelessly guarded, and slew many of those who had gone out for forage. But the army of Romans, commanded by Tarquinius, laid waste and ravaged the country of the Veientes and carried off much booty, and when numerous reinforcements assembled from all the Tyrrhenian cities to aid the Veientes, the Romans engaged them in battle and gained an incontestable victory. After this they marched through the enemy's country, plundering it with impunity; and having taken many prisoners and much booty — for it was prosperous country — they returned home when the summer was now ending.

58 The Veientes, therefore, having suffered greatly from that battle, stirred no more out of their city but suffered their country to be laid waste before their eyes. King Tarquinius made three incursions into their territory and for a period of three years deprived them of the produce of their land; but when he had laid waste the greater part of their country and was unable to do any further damage to it, he led his army against the city of the Caeretani, which earlier had been called Agylla while it was inhabited by the Pelasgians but after falling under the power of the Tyrrhenians had been renamed Caere,[68] and was as flourishing and populous as any city in Tyrrhenia. From this city a large army

---

68 Dionysius made his Latin names conform as far as possible to recognized Greek types. Not fancying such a nominative as Καῖρε, he constructed a form Καίρητα (Caerēta) from the stem of the Latin word. Other Greek writers used Καίρη, Καιρέα and even Καῖρε.

marched out to defend the country; but after destroying many of the enemy and losing still more of their own men they fled back into the city. The Romans, being masters of their country, which afforded them plenty of everything, continued there many days, and when it was time to depart they carried away all the booty they could and returned home. Tarquinius, now that his expedition against the Veientes had succeeded according to his desire, led out his army against the enemies in Fidenae, wishing to drive out the garrison that was there and at the same time being anxious to punish those who had handed over the walls to the Tyrrhenians. Accordingly, not only a pitched battle took place between the Romans and those who sallied out of the city, but also sharp fighting in the attacks that were made upon the walls. At any rate, the city was taken by storm, and the garrison, together with the rest of the Tyrrhenian prisoners, were kept in chains under a guard. As for those of the Fidenates who appeared to have been the authors of the revolt, some were scourged and beheaded in public and others were condemned to perpetual banishment; and their possessions were distributed by lot among those Romans who were left both as colonists and as a garrison for the city.

59 The last battle between the Romans and Tyrrhenians was fought near the city of Eretum in the territory of the Sabines. For the Tyrrhenians had been prevailed on by the influential men there to march through that country on their expedition against the Romans, on the assurance that the Sabines would join them in the campaign; for the six-years' truce, looking to peace, which the Sabines had made with Tarquinius, had already expired, and many of them longed to retrieve their former defeats, now that a sufficient body of youths had grown up in the meantime in their cities. But their attempt did not succeed according to their desire, the Roman army appearing too soon, nor was it possible for aid to be sent publicly to the Tyrrhenians from any of the Sabine cities; but a few went to their assistance of their own accord, attracted by the liberal pay. This battle, the greatest of any that had yet taken place between the two nations, gave a wonderful increase to the power of the Romans, who were gained a most glorious victory, for which both the senate and people decreed a triumph to King Tarquinius. But it broke the spirits of the Tyrrhenians, who, after sending out all the forces from every city to the struggle, received back in safety only a few out of all that great number. For some of them were cut down while fighting in the battle, and others, having in the route found themselves in rough country from which they could not extricate themselves, surrendered to the conquerors. The leading men of their cities, therefore, having met with so great a calamity, acted as became prudent men. For when King Tarquinius led another army against them, they met in a general assembly and voted to treat with him about ending the war; and they sent to him the oldest and most honoured men from each city, giving them full powers to settle the terms of peace.

60 The king, after he had heard the many arguments they advanced to move him to clemency and moderation and had been reminded of his kinship to their nation, said he desired to learn from them just this one thing, whether they still contended for equal rights and were come to make peace upon certain conditions, or acknowledged themselves to be vanquished and were ready to deliver up their cities to him. Upon their replying that they were not only delivering up their cities to him but should also be satisfied with a peace upon any fair terms they could get, he was greatly pleased at this and said: "Hear now upon what fair terms I will put an end to the war and what favours I am granting you. I am not eager either to put any of the Tyrrhenians to death or to banish any from their country or to punish any with the loss of their possessions. I impose no garrisons or tributes upon any of your cities, but permit each of them to enjoy its own laws and its ancient form of government. But in granting you this I think I ought to obtain one thing from you in return for all that I am giving, and that is the sovereignty over your cities — something that I shall possess even against your will as long as I am more powerful in arms, though I prefer to obtain it with your consent rather than without it. Inform your cities of this, and I promise to grant you an armistice till you return.

61 The ambassadors, having received this answer, departed, and after a few days returned, not merely with words alone, but bringing the insignia of sovereignty with which they used to decorate their own kings. These were a crown of gold, an ivory throne, a sceptre with an eagle perched on its head, a purple tunic decorated with gold, and an embroidered purple robe like those the kings of Lydia and Persia used to wear, except that it was not rectangular in shape like theirs, but semicircular.[69] This kind of robe is called *toga* by the Romans and *tēbenna*[70] by the Greeks; but I do not know where the Greeks learned the name, for it does not seem to me to be a Greek word. And according to some historians they also brought to Tarquinius the twelve axes, taking one from each city. For it seems to have been a Tyrrhenian custom for each king of the several cities to be preceded by a lictor bearing an axe together with the bundle of rods, and whenever the twelve cities undertook any joint military expedition, for the twelve axes to be handed over to the one man who was invested with absolute power. However, not all the authorities agree with those who express this opinion, but some

---

69 Dionysius is here describing the insignia of a Roman triumphator (*cf.* chap. 62, 2 and v. 47, 3). The tunic is the *tunica palmata* and the robe the toga *picta*.

70 The word τήβεννα (of uncertain origin) is found only in late Greek writers. Dionysius has already used it to represent the Latin *trabea* (ii. 70, 2), and Polybius used it for the *paludamentum* (x. 4, 8).

maintain that even before the reign of Tarquinius twelve axes were carried before the kings of Rome and that Romulus instituted this custom as soon as he received the sovereignty. But there is nothing to prevent our believing that the Tyrrhenians were the authors of this practice, that Romulus adopted its use from them, and that the twelve axes also were brought to Tarquinius together with the other royal ornaments, just as the Romans even to-day give sceptres and diadems to kings in confirmation of their power; since, even without receiving those ornaments from the Romans, these kings make use of them.

62 Tarquinius, however, did not avail himself of these honours as soon as he received them, according to most of the Roman historians, but left it to the senate and people to decide whether he should accept them or not; and when they unanimously approved, he then accepted them and from that time till he died always wore a crown of gold and an embroidered purple robe and sat on a throne of ivory holding an ivory sceptre in his hand, and the twelve lictors, bearing the axes and rods, attended him when he sat in judgment and preceded him when he went abroad. All these ornaments were retained by the kings who succeeded him, and, after the expulsion of the kings, by the annual consuls — all except the crown and the embroidered robe; these alone were taken from them, being looked upon as vulgar and invidious. Yet whenever they return victorious from a war and are honoured with a triumph by the senate, they then not only wear gold[71] but are also clad in embroidered purple robes. This, then, was the outcome of the war between Tarquinius and the Tyrrhenians after it had lasted nine years.

63 Since there now remained as a rival to the Romans for the supremacy only the Sabine race, which not only possessed warlike

---

71 The crown actually worn was of laurel, but a public slave held the golden crown of Jupiter above the victor's head.

men but also inhabited a large and fertile country lying not far from Rome, Tarquinius was extremely desirous of subduing these also and declared war against them. He complained that their cities had refused to deliver up those who had promised the Tyrrhenians that if they entered their country with an army they would make their cities friendly to them and hostile to the Romans. The Sabines not only cheerfully accepted the war, being unwilling to be deprived of the most influential of their citizens, but also, before the Roman army could come against them, they themselves invaded the others' territory. As soon as King Tarquinius heard that the Sabines had crossed the river Anio and that all the country round their camp was being laid waste, he took with him such of the Roman youth as were most lightly equipped, and led them with all possible speed against those of the enemy who were dispersed in foraging. Then, having slain many of them and taken away all the booty which they were driving off, he pitched his camp near theirs; and after remaining quiet there for a few days till not only the remainder of his army from Rome had reached him but the auxiliary forces also from his allies had assembled, he descended into the plain ready to give battle.

64 When the Sabines saw the Romans eagerly advancing to the combat, they also led out their forces, which were not inferior to the enemy either in numbers or in courage, and engaging, they fought with all possible bravery, so long as they had to contend only with those who were arrayed opposite them. Then, learning that another hostile army was advancing in their rear in orderly battle formation, they deserted their standards and turned to flight. The troops that appeared behind the Sabines were chosen men of the Romans, both horse and foot, whom Tarquinius had placed in ambush in suitable positions during the night. The unexpected appearance of these troops struck such terror into the Sabines that they displayed no further deed of bravery, but, feeling that they had been outmanoeuvred by the enemy and overwhelmed by an irresistible calamity, they endeavoured to save themselves, some in one direction and some in another; and it was in this route that the greatest slaughter occurred among them, while they were being pursued by the Roman horse and surrounded on all sides. Consequently, those of their number who escaped to the nearest cities were very few and the greater part of those who were not slain in the battle fell into the hands of the Romans. Indeed, not even the forces that were left in the camp had the courage to repulse the assault of the enemy or to hazard an engagement, but, terrified by their unexpected misfortune, surrendered both themselves and their entrenchments without striking a blow. The Sabine cities, feeling that they had been outmanoeuvred and deprived of the victory by their foes, not by valour but by deceit, were preparing to send out again a more numerous army and a more experienced commander. But Tarquinius, being informed of their intention, hastily collected his army, and before the enemy's forces were all assembled, forestalled them by crossing the river Anio. Upon learning of this the Sabine general marched out with his newly raised army as speedily as possible and encamped near the Romans upon a high and steep hill; however, he judged it inadvisable to engage in battle till he was joined by the rest of the Sabine forces, but by continually sending some of the cavalry against the enemy's foragers and placing ambuscades in the woods and glades he barred the Romans from the roads leading into his country

65 While the Sabine general was conducting the war in this manner many skirmishes took place between small parties both of the light-armed foot and the horse, but no general action between all the forces. The time being thus protracted, Tarquinius was angered at the delay and resolved to lead his army against the enemy's camp; and he attacked it repeatedly. Then, finding that it could not easily be taken by forcible means, because of its strength, he determined to reduce those within by famine; and by building forts upon all the roads that led to the camp and hindering them from going out to get wood for themselves and forage for their horses and from procuring many other necessities from the country, he reduced them to so great a shortage of everything that they were obliged to take advantage of a stormy night of rain and wind and flee from their camp in a shameful manner, leaving behind them their beasts of burden, their tents, their wounded, and all their warlike stores. The next day the Romans, learning of their departure, took possession of their camp without opposition and after seizing the tents, the beasts of burden, and the personal effects, returned to Rome with the prisoners. This war continued to be waged for five years in succession, and in its course both sides continually plundered one another's country and engaged in many battles, some of lesser and some of greater importance, the advantage occasionally resting with the Sabines but usually with the Romans; in the last battle, however, the war came to a definite end. The Sabines, it seems, did not as before go forth to war in successive bands, but all who were any other an age to bear arms went out together; and all the Romans, with the forces of the Latins, the Tyrrhenians and the rest of their allies, were advancing to meet the enemy. The Sabine general, dividing his forces, formed two camps, while the Roman king made three divisions of his troops and pitched three camps not far apart. He commanded the Roman contingent himself and made his nephew Arruns leader of the Tyrrhenian auxiliaries, while over the Latins and the other allies he placed a man who was valiant in warfare and of most competent judgment, but a foreigner without a country. This man's first name was Servius and his family name Tullius; it was he whom the Romans, after the death of Lucius Tarquinius without male issue, permitted to rule the state, since they admired him for his abilities in both peace and war. But I shall give an account of this man's birth, education and fortunes and of the divine manifestation made with regard to him when I come to that part of my narrative.[72]

66 On this occasion, then, when both armies had made the necessary preparations for the struggle, they engaged; the Romans were posted on the left wing, the Tyrrhenians on the right, and the Latins in the centre of the line. After a hard battle that lasted the whole day the Romans were far superior; and having slain many of the enemy, who had acquitted themselves as brave men, and having taken many more of them prisoners in the rout, they possessed themselves of both Sabine camps, where they seized a rich store of booty. And now being masters of all the open country without fear of opposition, they laid it waste with fire and sword and every kind of injury; but as the summer drew to an end, they broke camp and returned home. And King Tarquinius in honour of this victory triumphed for the third time during his own reign. The following year, when he was preparing to lead his army once more against the cities of the Sabines and had determined to reduce them by siege, there was not one of those cities that any longer took any brave or vigorous resolution, but all unanimously determined, before incurring the risk of slavery for themselves and the razing of their cities, to put an end to the war. And the most important men among the Sabines came from every city to King Tarquinius, who had already taken the field with all his forces, to deliver up their walled cities to him and to beg him to make reasonable terms. Tarquinius gladly accepted this submission of the nation, unattended as it was by any hazards, and made a treaty of peace and friendship with them upon the same conditions upon which he had earlier received

---

72 See iv. 1 ff.

the submission of the Tyrrhenians; and he restored their captives to them without ransom.

67 These are the military achievements of Tarquinius which are recorded; those that relate to peace and to the civil administration (for these too I do not wish to pass over without mention) are as follows: As soon as he had assumed the sovereignty, being anxious to gain the affections of the common people, after the example of his predecessors, he won them over by such services as these: He chose a hundred persons out of the whole body of the plebeians who were acknowledged by all to be possessed of some warlike prowess or political sagacity, and having made them patricians, he enrolled them among the senators; and then for the first time the Romans had three hundred senators, instead of two hundred,[73] as previously Next, he added to the four holy virgins who had the custody of the perpetual fire two others; for the sacrifices performed on behalf of the state at which these priestesses of Vesta were required to be present being now increased, the four were not thought sufficient. The example of Tarquinius was followed by the rest of the kings and to this day six priestesses of Vesta are appointed. He seems also to have first devised the punishments which are inflicted by the pontiffs on those Vestals who do not preserve their chastity, being moved to do so either by his own judgment or, as some believe, in obedience to a dream; and these punishments, according to the interpreters of religious rites, were found after his death among the Sibylline oracles. For in his reign a priestess named Pinaria, the daughter of Publius, was discovered to be approaching the sacrifices in a state of unchastity The manner of punishing the Vestals who have been debauched has been described by me in the preceding Book.[74] Tarquinius also adorned the Forum, where justice is

---

73 *Cf.* ii. 47, 1 f. and Livy i. 35, 6.
74 ii. 67.

administered, the assemblies of the people held, and other civil matters transacted, by surrounding it with shops and porticos.[75] And he was the first to build the walls of the city, which previously had been of temporary and careless construction, with huge[76] stones regularly squared.[77] He also began the digging of the sewers, through which all the water that collects from the streets is conveyed into the Tiber — a wonderful work exceeding all description.[78] Indeed, in my opinion the three most magnificent works of Rome, in which the greatness of her empire is best seen, are the aqueducts, the paved roads and the construction of the sewers. I say this with respect not only to the usefulness of the work (concerning which I shall speak in the proper place), but also to the magnitude of the cost, of which one may judge by a single circumstance, if one takes as his authority Gaius Acilius,[79] who says that once, when the sewers had been neglected and were no longer passable for the water, the censors let out the cleaning and repairing of them at a thousand talents.

68 Tarquinius[80] also built the Circus Maximus,[81] which lies between the Aventine and Palatine Hills, and was the first to erect covered seats round it on scaffolding (for till then the spectators had stood), the wooden stands being supported by beams. And dividing the places among the thirty *curiae*, he assigned to each *curia* a particular section, so that every spectator was seated in his proper place. This work also was destined to become in time one of the most beautiful and most admirable structures in Rome.[82] For the Circus is three stades and a half in length and four plethra in

---

75 *Cf.* Livy i. 35, 10.
76 Literally, "large enough to load a wagon."
77 *Cf.* Livy i. 38, 6.
78 *Cf.* Livy, *ibid.*
79 A senator of the second century B.C. who wrote a history of Rome in Greek.
80 *Cf.* Livy i. 35, 8 f.
81 Literally, "the largest of the hippodromes."

breadth.[83] Round about it on the two longer sides and one of the shorter sides a canal has been dug, ten feet in depth and width, to receive water.[84] Behind the canal are erected porticos three stories high, of which the lowest story has stone seats, gradually rising, as in the theatres, one above the other, and the two upper stories wooden seats. The two longer porticos are united into one and joined together by means of the shorter one, which is crescent-shaped, so that all three form a single portico like an amphitheatre,[85] eight stades in circuit and capable of holding 150,000 persons. The other of the shorter sides is left uncovered and contains vaulted starting-places for the horses, which are all opened by means of a single rope.[86] On the outside of the Circus there is another portico of one story which has shops in it and habitations over them. In this portico there are entrances and ascents for the spectators at every shop, so that the countless thousands of people may enter and depart without inconvenience.

---

82 From this point Dionysius describes the Circus as it existed in his own day; in later times its size and splendour were still further increased.

83 A stade was 600 Greek feet, a plethron 100 feet.

84 The original purpose of the canal was to protect the spectators from any wild beasts that might get out of control in the arena. Under Nero it was filled in.

85 It is obvious from his use of the adjective ἀμφιθέατρος here and in the similar passage, iv. 44, 1, that Dionysius did not think of this word as necessarily implying a circular or elliptical structure, as it soon came to do, but that he used it in the original sense of "having seats on all sides." The U-shaped figure which he describes — two long parallel sides connected by a shorter, semicircular end — was essentially that of the Greek hippodromes to be seen at Olympia and elsewhere. But the circus was narrower than the hippodrome, and the arrangement of the starting-places (*carceres*) was different.

86 The ὕσπληξ was the rope drawn across the bounds of a Greek racecourse and let down as a starting signal. In the Circus the barriers at each entrance consisted of folding gates, which were all thrown open at the same moment by slaves, two at each barrier; possibly this was done with the aid of a rope or ropes. Spelman took the phrase figuratively in the sense of "at one signal."

69 This king also undertook to construct the temple to Jupiter, Juno and Minerva, in fulfilment of the vow he had made to these gods in his last battle against the Sabines.[87] Having, therefore, surrounded the hill on which he proposed to build the temple with high retaining walls in many places, since it required much preparation (for it was neither easy of access nor level, but steep, and terminated in a sharp peak), he filled in the space between the retaining walls and the summit with great quantities of earth and, by levelling it, made the place most suitable for receiving temples. But he was prevented by death from laying the foundations of the temple; for he lived but four years after the end of the war. Many years later, however, Tarquinius, the second[88] king after him, the one who was driven from the throne, laid the founds of this structure and built the greater part of it. Yet even he did not complete the work, but it was finished under the annual magistrates who were consuls in the third year after his expulsion.

It is fitting to relate also the incidents that preceded the building of it as they have been handed down by all the compilers of Roman history.[89] When Tarquinius was preparing to build the temple he called the augurs together and ordered them first to consult the auspices concerning the site itself, in order to learn what place in the city was the most suitable to be consecrated and the most acceptable to the gods themselves; and upon their indicating the hill that commands the Forum, which was then called the Tarpeian, but now the Capitoline Hill, he ordered them to consult the auspices once more and declare in what part of the hill the foundations must be laid. But this was not at all easy; for there were upon the hill many altars both of the gods and of the lesser divinities not far apart from

---

87 *Cf.* Livy i. 38, 7; 55, 1.
88 Literally, "the third," counting inclusively.
89 Livy (i. 55, 2-4) refers the incident that follows to the reign of the second Tarquin.

313

one another, which would have to be moved to some other place and the whole area given up to the sanctuary that was to be built to the gods. The augurs thought proper to consult the auspices concerning each one of the altars that were erected there, and if the gods were willing to withdraw, then to move them elsewhere. The rest of the gods and lesser divinities, then, gave them leave to move their altars elsewhere, but Terminus and Juventas,[90] although the augurs besought them with great earnestness and importunity, could not be prevailed on and refused to leave their places. Accordingly, their altars were included within the circuit of the temples,[91] and one of them now stands in the vestibule of Minerva's shrine and the other in the shrine itself near the statue[92] of the goddess. From this circumstance the augurs concluded that no occasion would ever cause the removal of the boundaries of the Romans' city or impair its vigour; and both have proved true down to my day, which is already the twenty-fourth generation.[93]

70 The most celebrated of the augurs, the one who changed the position of the altars and marked out the area for temple of Jupiter

---

90 Livy (*l.c.*) names Terminus only.

91 Inasmuch as the temple of Jupiter Capitolinus actually consisted of three shrines under one roof (see iv. 61, 4), Dionysius could speak of it either in the singular or plural. He has already used the plural once before, near the beginning of the chapter.

92 The Greek word indicates that it was a seated statue.

93 Ambrosch, believing, with some of the early editors, that Dionysius often used γενεά for a definite period of 27 years, proposed to read "twenty-first" here; see critical note. But the interval involved (extending from 576 B.C., at the very latest, to 7 B.C.) was a little more than twenty-one full generations of 27 years each; so that he needed to read "twenty-second," or else assume 28 years to the generation. Dodwell was almost certainly right in declaring that Dionysius did not use γενεά for any definite number of years. He showed that for the earliest times and down through the regal period at Rome he regularly counted as a generation the reign of each successive king; and he argued that for the republican period he counted his generations by the records of some important family, probably that of Julius Caesar.

and in other things foretold the will of the gods to the people by his prophetic art, had for his common and first name Nevius,[94] and for his family name Attius; and he is conceded to have been the most favoured by the gods of all the experts in his profession and to have gained the greatest reputation by it, having displayed some extraordinary and incredible instances of his augural skill. Of these I shall give one, which I have selected because it has seemed the most wonderful to me; but first I shall relate from what chance he got his start and by what opportunities vouchsafed to him by the gods he attained to such distinction as to make all the other augurs of his day appear negligible in comparison. His father was a poor man who cultivated a cheap plot of ground, and Nevius, as a boy, assisted him in such tasks as his years could bear; among his other employments he used to drive the swine out to pasture and tend them. One day he fell asleep, and upon waking missed some of the swine. At first he wept, dreading the blows his father would give him; then, going to the chapel of some heroes[95] that had been built on the farm, he besought them to assist him in finding his swine, promising that if they did so he would offer up to them the largest cluster of grapes on the farm. And having found the swine shortly afterwards, he wished to perform his vow to the heroes, but found himself in great perplexity, being unable to discover the largest cluster of grapes. In his anxiety over the matter he prayed to the gods to reveal to him by omens what he sought. Then by a divine inspiration he divided the vineyard into two parts, taking one on his right hand and the other on his left, after which he observed the omens that showed over each; and when there appeared in one of them such birds as he desired, he again divided that into two parts and distinguished in the same manner the birds that came to it.

---

94 It seems best to retain the spelling of this name given by the MSS., since there is doubt as to the form which Dionysius would have used. See critical note.

95 The *lares compitales*.

Having continued this method of dividing the places and coming up to the last vine that was pointed out by the birds, he found an incredibly huge cluster. As he was carrying it to the chapel of the heroes he was observed by his father; and when the latter marvelled at the size of the cluster and inquired where he had got it, the boy informed him of the whole matter from the beginning. His father concluded, as was indeed the case, that there were some innate rudiments of the art of divination in the boy, and taking him to the city, he put him in the hands of elementary teachers; then, after he had acquired sufficient general learning, he placed him under the most celebrated master among the Tyrrhenians to learn the augural art. Thus Nevius, who possessed an innate skill of divination and had now added to it the knowledge acquired from the Tyrrhenians, naturally far surpassed, as I said, all the other augurs. And the augurs in the city, even though he was not of their college, used to invite him to their public consultations because of the success of his predictions, and they foretold nothing without his approval.

71 This Nevius,[96] when Tarquinius once desired to create three new tribes out of the knights he had previously enrolled, and to give his own name and the names of his personal friends to these additional tribes, alone violently opposed it and would not allow any of the institutions of Romulus to be altered. The king, resenting this opposition and being angry with Nevius, endeavoured to bring his science to nought and show him up as a charlatan who did not speak a word of truth. With this purpose in mind he summoned Nevius before the tribunal when a large crowd was present in the Forum; and having first informed those about him in what manner he expected to show the augur to be a false prophet, he received Nevius upon his arrival with friendly greetings and said: "Now is the time, Nevius, for you to display the accuracy of your prophetic

---

96 *Cf.* Livy i. 36, 2-7.

science. For I have in mind to undertake a great project, and I wish
to know whether it is possible. Go, therefore, take the auspices and
return speedily. I will sit here and wait for you." The augur did as he
was ordered, and returning soon after, said he had obtained
favourable omens and declared the undertaking to be possible. But
Tarquinius laughed at his words, and taking out a razor and a
whetstone from his bosom, said to him: "Now you are convicted,
Nevius, of imposing on us and openly lying about the will of the
gods, since you have dared to affirm that even impossible things are
possible. I wanted to know from the auspices whether if I strike the
whetstone with this razor I shall be able to cut it in halves." At this,
laughter arose from all who stood round the tribunal; but Nevius,
nothing daunted by their raillery and clamour, said: "Strike the
whetstone confidently, as you propose, Tarquinius. For it will be cut
asunder, or I am ready to submit to any punishment." The king,
surprised at the confidence of the augur, struck the razor against the
whetstone, and the edge of the steel, making its way quite through
the stone, not only cut the whetstone asunder but also cut off a part
of the hand that held it. All the others who beheld this wonderful
and incredible feat cried out in their astonishment; and Tarquinius,
ashamed of having made this trial of the man's skill and desiring to
atone for his unseemly reproaches, resolved to win back the goodwill
of Nevius himself, seeing in him one favoured above all men by the
gods. Among many other instances of kindness by which he won
him over, he caused a bronze statue of him to be made and set up in
the Forum to perpetuate his memory with posterity. This statue still
remained down to my time, standing in front of the senate-house
near the sacred fig-tree; it was shorter than a man of average stature
and the head was covered with the mantle. At a small distance from
the statue both the whetstone and the razor are said to be buried in

the earth under a certain altar. The place is called a well[97] by the Romans. Such then, is the account given of this augur.

72 King Tarquinius,[98] being now obliged to desist from warlike activities by reason of old age (for he was eighty years old), lost his life by the treachery of the sons of Ancus Marcius. They had endeavoured even before this to dethrone him, indeed had frequently made the attempt, in the hope that when he had been removed the royal power would devolve upon them; for they looked upon it as theirs by inheritance from their father and supposed that it would very readily be granted to them by the citizens. When they failed in their expectation, they formed against him a plot from which there would be no escape; but Heaven did not allow it to go unpunished. I shall now relate the nature of their plot, beginning with their first attempt. Nevius, that skilful augur who, as I said, once opposed the king when he wished to increase the number of the tribes, had, at the very time when he was enjoying the greatest repute for his art and exceeded all the Romans in power, suddenly disappeared, either through the envy of some rival in his own profession or through the plotting of enemies or some other mischance, and none of his relations could either guess his fate or find his body. And while the people were grieving over and resenting the calamity and entertaining many suspicions against many persons, the sons of Marcius, observing this impulse on the part of the multitude, endeavoured to put the blame for the pollution upon King Tarquinius, though they had no proof or evidence to offer in support of their accusation, but relied upon these two specious arguments: first, that the king, having resolved to make many unlawful innovations in the constitution, wished to get rid of the

---

97 *Puteal* was the Roman name for this place. Strictly speaking, *puteal* was the curbing round the well, *puteus* the well itself. A *puteal* was constructed about a spot that had been struck by lightning.

98 For chaps. 72 f. *cf.* Livy i. 40-41, 1.

man who was sure to oppose him again as he had done on the former occasions, and second, that, when a dreadful calamity had occurred, he had caused no search to be made for the perpetrators, but had neglected the matter — a thing, they said, which no innocent man would have done. And having gathered about them strong bands of partisans, both patricians and plebeians, upon whom they had lavished their fortunes, they made many accusations against Tarquinius and exhorted the people not to permit a polluted person to lay hands on the sacrifices and defile the royal dignity, especially one who was not a Roman, but some newcomer and a man without a country. By delivering such harangues in the Forum these men, who were bold and not lacking in eloquence, inflamed the minds of many of the plebeians, and these, when Tarquinius came into the Forum to offer his defence, endeavoured to drive him out as an impure person. However, they were not strong enough to prevail over the truth or to persuade the people to depose him from power. And after both Tarquinius himself had made a powerful defence and refuted the calumny against him, and his son-in-law Tullius, to whom he had given one of his two daughters in marriage and who had the greatest influence with the people, had stirred the Romans to compassion, the accusers were looked upon as slanderers and wicked men, and they left the Forum in great disgrace.

73 Having failed in this attempt and having, with the aid of their friends, found reconciliation with Tarquinius, who bore their folly with moderation because of the favours he had received from their father, and looked upon their repentance as sufficient to correct their rashness, they continued for three years in this pretence of friendship; but as soon as they thought they had a favourable opportunity, they contrived the following treacherous plot against him: They dressed up two youths, the boldest of their accomplices, and arming them with billhooks, sent them to the king's house at midday, after instructing them what they were to say and do and showing them in what manner they were to make their attack. These youths, upon approaching the palace, fell to abusing each other, as if they had received some injury, and even proceeded to blows, while both with a loud voice implored the king's assistance; and many of their accomplices, ostensibly rustics, were present, taking part with one or the other of them in his grievance and giving testimony in his favour. When the king ordered them to be brought before him and commanded them to inform him of the subject of their quarrel, they pretended their dispute was about some goats, and both of them bawling at the same time and gesticulating passionately, after the manner of rustics, without saying anything to the purpose, they provoked much laughter on the part of all. And when they thought that the derision which they were exciting offered the proper moment for putting their design into execution, they wounded the king on the head with their billhooks, after which they endeavoured to escape out of doors. But when an outcry was raised at this calamity and assistance came from many sides. they were ubable to escape and were seized by those who had pursued them; and later, after being put to the torture and forced to name the authors of the conspiracy, they at length met with the punishment they deserved.[99]

---

99 See the critical note.

Book IV

1 King Tarquinius,[1] accordingly, who had conferred not a few important benefits upon the Romans, died in the manner I have mentioned, after holding the sovereignty for thirty-eight years, leaving two grandsons who were infants and two daughters already married. His son-in-law Tullius succeeded him in the sovereignty in the fourth year of the fiftieth Olympiad[2] (the one in which Epitelides, a Lacedaemonian, won the short-distance footrace), Archestratides being archon at Athens. It is now the proper time to mention those particulars relating to Tullius which we at first omitted,[3] namely, who his parents were and what deeds he performed while he was yet a private citizen, before his accession to the sovereignty. Concerning his family, then, the account with which I can best agree is this: There lived at Corniculum, a city of the Latin nation, a man of the royal family named Tullius, who was married to Ocrisia, a woman far excelling all the other women in Corniculum in beauty and modesty. When this city was taken by the Romans, Tullius himself was slain while fighting, and Ocrisia, then with child, was selected from the spoils and taken by King Tarquinius, who gave her to his wife. She, having been informed of everything that related to this woman, freed her soon afterwards and continued to treat her with kindness and honour above all other women. While Ocrisia was yet a slave she bore a son, to whom, when he had left the nursery, she gave the name of Tullius, from his father, as his proper and family name, and also that of Servius as his common and first name, from her own condition, since she had

---

1 For chaps. 1 f. *cf.* Livy i. 39.
2 576 B.C.
3 See iii. 65, 6.

been a slave when she had given birth to him. Servius, if translated into the Greek tongue, would be *doulios* or "servile."

2 There is also current in the local records another story relating to his birth which raises the circumstances attending to the realm of the fabulous, and we have found it in many Roman histories. This account — if it be pleasing to the gods and the lesser divinities that it be related — is somewhat as follows: They say that from the hearth in the palace, on which the Romans offer various other sacrifices and also consecrate the first portion of their meals, there rose up above the fire a man's privy member, and that Ocrisia was the first to see it as she was carrying the customary cakes to the fire, and immediately informed the king and queen of it. Tarquinius, they add, upon hearing this and left beholding the prodigy, was astonished; but Tanaquil, who was not only wise in other matters but also inferior to none of the Tyrrhenians in her knowledge of divination, told him it was ordained by fate that from the royal hearth should issue a scion superior to the race of mortals, to be born of the woman who should conceive by that phantom. And the other soothsayers affirming the same thing, the king thought it fitting that Ocrisia, to whom the prodigy had first appeared, should have intercourse with it. Thereupon this woman, having adorned herself as brides are usually adorned, was shut up alone in the room in which the prodigy had been seen. And one of the gods or lesser divinities, whether Vulcan, as some think, or the tutelary deity of the house,[4] having had intercourse with her and afterwards disappearing, she conceived and was delivered of Tullius at the proper time. This fabulous account, although it seems not altogether credible, is rendered less incredible by reason of another manifestation of the gods relating to Tullius which was wonderful and extraordinary For when he had fallen asleep one day while

---

4   The *lar familiaris*.

sitting in the portico of the palace about noon, a fire shone forth from his head. This was seen by his mother and by the king's wife, as they were walking through the portico, as well as by all who happened to be present with them at the time. The flame continued to illumine his whole head till his mother ran to him and wakened him; and with the ending of his sleep the flame was dispersed and vanished. Such are the accounts that are given of his birth.

3 The memorable actions he performed before becoming king, in consideration of which Tarquinius admired him and the Roman people honoured him next to the king, are these: When, scarcely more than a boy as yet, he was serving in the cavalry in the first campaign that Tarquinius undertook against the Tyrrhenians, he was thought to have fought so splendidly that he straightway became famous and received the prize of valour ahead of all others. Afterwards, when another expedition was undertaken against the same nation and a sharp battle was fought near the city of Eretum, he showed himself the bravest of all and was again crowned by the king as first in valour. And when he was about twenty years old he was appointed to command the auxiliary forces sent by the Latins, and assisted King Tarquinius in obtaining the sovereignty over the Tyrrhenians. In the first war that arose against the Sabines, being general of the horse, he put to flight that of the enemy, pursuing them as far as the city of Antemnae, and again received the prize of valour because of this battle. He also took part in many other engagements against the same nation, sometimes commanding the horse and sometimes the foot, in all of which he showed himself a man of the greatest courage and was always the first to be crowned ahead of the others. And when that nation came to surrender themselves and deliver up their cities to the Romans, he was regarded by Tarquinius as the chief cause of his gaining this dominion also, and was crowned by him with the victor's crown.

Moreover, he not only had the shrewdest understanding of public affairs, but was inferior to none in his ability to express his plans; and he possessed in an eminent degree the power of accommodating himself to every circumstance of fortune and to every kind of person. Because of these accomplishments the Romans thought proper to transfer him by their votes from the plebeian to the patrician order, an honour they had previously conferred on Tarquinius, and, still earlier, on Numa Pompilius. The king also made him his son-in-law, giving him one of his two daughters in marriage, and whatever business his infirmities or his age rendered him incapable of performing by himself, he ordered Tullius to transact, not only entrusting to him the private interests of his own family, but also asking him to manage the public business of the commonwealth. In all these employments he was found faithful and just, and the people felt that it made no difference whether it was Tarquinius or Tullius who looked after the public affairs, so effectually had he won them to himself by the services he had rendered to them.

4 This man,[5] therefore, being endowed with a nature adequately equipped for command and also supplied by Fortune with many great opportunities for attaining it, believed, when Tarquinius died by the treachery of the sons of Ancus Marcius, who desired to recover their father's kingdom, as I have related in the preceding book,[6] that he was called to the kingship by the very course of events and so, being a man of action, he did not let the opportunity slip from his grasp. The person who helped him to seize possession of the supreme power and the author of all his good fortune was the wife of the deceased king, who aided him both because he was her son-in-law and also because she knew from many oracles that it was

5   For chaps. 4 f. *cf.* Livy i. 41.
6   iii. 72 f.

ordained by fate that this man should be king of the Romans. It chanced that her son, a youth, had died shortly before and that two infant sons were left by him. She, therefore, reflecting on the desolation of her house and being under the greatest apprehension lest, if the sons of Marcius possessed themselves of the sovereignty, they should destroy these infants and extirpate all the royal family, first commanded that the gates of the palace should be shut and guards stationed there with orders to allow no one to pass either in or out. Then, ordering all the rest to leave the room in which they had laid Tarquinius when he was at the point of death, she detained Ocrisia, Tullius and her daughter who was married to Tullius, and after ordering the children to be brought by their nurses, she spoke to them as follows:

"Our king Tarquinius, in whose home you received your nurture and training, Tullius, and who honoured you above all his friends and relations, has finished his destined course, the victim of an impious crime, without having either made any disposition by will of his private interests or left injunctions concerning the public business of the commonwealth, and without having had it in his power even to embrace any of us and utter his last farewells. And these unhappy children here are left destitute and orphaned and in imminent danger of their lives. For if the power falls into the hands of the Marcii, the murderers of their grandfather, they will be put to death by them in the most piteous manner. Even the lives of you men, to whom Tarquinius gave his daughters in preference to them, will not be safe, should his murderers obtain the sovereignty, any more than the lives of the rest of his friends and relations or of us miserable women; but they will endeavour to destroy us all both openly and secretly. Bearing all this in mind, then, we must not permit the wicked murderers of Tarquinius and the enemies of us all to obtain so great power, but must oppose and prevent them, now by craft and deceit, since these means are necessary at present, but when our first attempt has succeeded, then coming to grips with them openly with all our might and with arms, if those too shall be necessary. But they will not be necessary if we are willing to take the proper measures now. And what are these measures? Let us, in the first place, conceal the king's death and cause a report to be spread among the people that he has received no mortal wound, and let the physicians state that in a few days they will show him safe and sound. Then I will appear in public and will announce to the people, as if Tarquinius had so enjoined, that he has committed to one of his two sons-in-law (naming you, Tullius) the care and guardianship both of his private interests and of the public business till he is recovered of his wounds; and the Romans, far from being displeased, will be glad to see the state administered by you, who often have administered it already in the past. Then, when we have averted the present danger — for the power of our enemies will be at an end the moment the king is reported to be alive — do you assume the rods and the military power and summon before the people those who formed the plot to assassinate Tarquinius, beginning with the sons of Marcius, and cause them to stand trial. After you have punished all these, with death, if they submit to be tried, or with perpetual banishment and the confiscation of their estates, if they let their case go by default, which I think they will be more apt to do, then at last set about establishing your government. Win the affections of the people by kindly affability, take great care that no injustice be committed, and gain the favour of the poorer citizens by sundry benefactions and gifts. Afterwards, when we see a proper time, let us announce that Tarquinius is dead and hold a public funeral for him. And as for you, Tullius, if you, who have been brought up and educated by us, have partaken of every advantage that sons receive from their mother and father, and are married to our daughter, shall in addition actually become king of the Romans, it is but just, since I helped to win this also for you, that you should show all the kindness of a father to these little children, and when they come to manhood and are capable of handling public affairs, that you should appoint the elder to be leader of the Romans."

5 With these words she thrust each of the children in turn into the arms of both her son-in-law and her daughter and roused great compassion in them both; then, when it was the proper time, she went out of the room and ordered the servants to get everything ready for dressing the king's wounds and to call the physicians. And letting that night pass, the next day, when the people flocked in great numbers to the palace, she appeared at the windows that gave upon the narrow street before the gates and first informed them who the persons were who had plotted the murder of the king, and produced in chains those whom they had sent to commit the deed. Then, finding that many lamented the calamity and were angry at the authors of it, she at last told them that these men had gained naught from their wicked designs, since they had not been able to kill Tarquinius. This statement being received with universal joy, she then commended Tullus to them as the person appointed by the king to be the guardian of all his interests, both private and public, till he himself recovered. The people, therefore, went away greatly rejoicing, in the belief that the king had suffered no fatal injury, and continued for a long time in that opinion. Afterwards Tullius, attended by a strong body of men and taking along the king's lictors, went to the Forum and caused proclamation to be made for the March to appear and stand trial; and upon their failure to obey, he pronounced sentence of perpetual banishment against them, and having confiscated their property, he was now in secure possession of the sovereignty of Tarquinius.

6 I[7] shall interrupt the narration of what follows that I may give the reasons which have induced me to disagree with Fabius and the rest of the historians who affirm that the children left by Tarquinius were his sons, to the end that none who have read those histories may suspect that I am inventing when I call them his grandsons rather than his sons. For it is sheer heedlessness and indolence that has led these historians to publish that account of them without first examining any of the impossibilities and absurdities that are fatal to it. Each of these absurdities I will endeavour to point out in a few words. Tarquinius packed up and removed from Tyrrhenia with all his household at an age the most capable of reflection; for it is reported that he already aspired to take part in public life, to hold magistracies and to handle public affairs, and that he removed from there because he was not allowed to share in any position of honour in the state. Anyone else, then, might have assumed that he was at least in his thirtieth year when he left Tyrrhenia, since it is from this age onwards, as rule, that the laws call to the magistracies and to the administration of public affairs those who desire such a career; but I will suppose him five whole years younger than this and put him in his twenty-fifth year when he removed. Moreover, all the Roman historians agree that he brought with him a Tyrrhenian wife, whom he had married while his father was yet alive. He came to Rome in the first year of the reign of Ancus Marcius, as Gellius[8] writes, but according to Licinius,[1] in the eighth year. Grant, then, that he came in the year Licinius states and not before; for he could not have come after that time, since in the ninth year of the reign of Ancus he was sent by the king to command the cavalry in the war against the Latins, as both these historians state. Now, if he was not more than twenty-five years old when he came to Rome, and, having been received into the friendship of Ancus, who was then king, in the

---

7   For chaps. 6 f. *cf.* Livy i. 46, 4.
8   For these annalists see i. 7, 3 and note.

eighth year of his reign (for Ancus reigned twenty-four years), and if he himself reigned thirty-eight, as all agree, he must have been fourscore years old when he died; for this is the sum obtained by adding up the years. If his wife was five years younger, as may well be supposed, she was presumably in her seventy-fifth year when Tarquinius died. Accordingly, if she conceived her second and last son when she was in her fiftieth year (for at a more advanced age a woman no longer conceives, but this is itself the limit of her child-bearing, as those authors write who have looked into these things), this son could not have been less than twenty-five years old when his father died, and Lucius, the elder, not less than twenty-seven; hence the sons whom Tarquinius left by this wife could not have been infants. But surely, if her sons had been grown men when their father died, it cannot be imagined either that their mother would have been so miserable a creature or so infatuated as to deprive her own children of the sovereignty their father had left them and bestow it upon an outsider and the son of a slave-woman, or, again, that her sons themselves, when thus deprived of their father's sovereignty, would have borne the injustice in so abject and supine a manner, and that at an age when they were at the very height of their powers both of speech and of action. For Tullius neither had the advantage of them in birth, being the son of a slave-woman, nor excelled them much in the dignity of age, being only three years older than one of them; so that they would not willingly have yielded the kingship to him.

7 This view involves some other absurdities, too, of which all the Roman historians have been ignorant, with the exception of one whom I shall name presently. For it has been agreed that Tullius, having succeeded to the kingdom after the death of Tarquinius, held it for forty-four years; so that, if the eldest of the Tarquinii was twenty-seven years old when he was deprived of the sovereignty, he must have been above seventy when he killed Tullius. But he was then in the prime of life, according to the tradition handed down by the historians, and they state that he himself lifted up Tullius, and carrying him out of the senate-house, hurled him down the steps. His expulsion from the kingship happened in the twenty-fifth year after this, and in that same year he is represented as making war against the people of Ardea and performing all the duties himself; but it is not reasonable to suppose that a man ninety-six years old should be taking part in wars. And after his expulsion he still makes war against the Romans for no less than fourteen years, being present himself, they say, at all the engagements — which is contrary to all common sense. Thus, according to them, he must have lived above one hundred and ten years; but this length of life is not produced by our climes.[9] Some of the Roman historians, being sensible of these absurdities, have endeavoured to solve them by means of other absurdities, alleging that not Tanaquil but one Gegania, of whom no other account has come down to us, was the mother of the children. But here again, the marriage of Tarquinius is unseasonable, he being then very near fourscore years old, and the begetting of children by men of that age is incredible;[10] nor was he a childless man, who would wish by all means for children, for he

---

9   There were tales current in the Graeco-Roman world of the remarkable longevity enjoyed by the inhabitants of various remote regions. Thus, according to Herodotus, some of the Ethiopians lived to the age of 120 and over; and Strabo mentions reports that some tribes of India lived 130 years and that the Seres lived more than 200, while the Hyperboreans were credited with 1000 years. Of the half-dozen Greeks recorded as having passed the century mark, Gorgias led with from 105 to 109 years. The Romans of the historical period, so far as records tell, all fell short of a century.

Thayer's Note: Strabo either ridicules these tales or repeats them with an audible sniff, to judge from the company he puts them in; the references in the Geography are: xv. i. 34, 37, and 57.

10   No such feat is recorded of any Greek or Roman. But Masinissa, the loyal ally of Scipio Africanus, is said to have had a son when he had passed his 86th year (Livy, *Periocha* to Book L).

330

had two daughters and these already married. In the light, therefore, of these various impossibilities and absurdities, I state that the children were not the sons, but the grandsons, of Tarquinius, agreeing therein with Lucius Piso Frugi[11] (for he in his *Annals* is the only historian who has given this account); unless, indeed, the children were the king's grandsons by birth and his sons by adoption and this circumstance misled all the other Roman historians. Now that these explanations have been made by way of preface, it is time to resume my narrative where it was broken off.

8 When Tullius, after receiving the guardianship of the kingdom and expelling the faction of the Marcii, thought he was now in secure possession of the sovereignty, he honoured King Tarquinius, as if he had but recently died of his wounds, with a very costly funeral, an imposing monument, and the other usual honours. And from that time, as guardian of the royal children, he took under his protection and care both their private fortunes and the public interests of the commonwealth. The patricians, however, were not pleased with these proceedings, but felt indignation and resentment, being unwilling that Tullius should build up a kind of royal power for himself without either a decree of the senate or the other formalities prescribed by law. And the most powerful of them met together frequently and discussed with one another means of putting an end to his illegal rule; and they resolved that in the first time Tullius should assemble them in the senate-house they would compel him to lay aside the rods and the other symbols of royalty, and that after this was done they would appoint the magistrates called *interreges*[12] and through them choose a man to rule the state in accordance with the laws. While they were making these plans, Tullius, becoming aware of their purpose, applied himself to

11 For this annalist see the note on i. 7, 3.
12 *Cf.* ii. 57.

flattering and courting the poorer citizens, and hopes of retaining the sovereignty through them; and having called an assembly of the people, he brought the children forward to the tribunal and delivered a speech somewhat as follows:

9 "I find myself under great obligation, citizens, to take care of these infant children. For Tarquinius, their grandfather, received me when I was fatherless and without a country, and brought me up, holding me in no respect inferior to his own children. He also gave me one of his two daughters in marriage, and during the whole course of his life continued to honour and love me, as you also know, with the same affection as if I had been his own son. And after that treacherous attack was made upon him he entrusted me with the guardianship of these children in case he should suffer the fate of all mortals. Who, therefore, will think me pious towards the gods or just towards men if I abandon and betray the orphans to whom I owe so great a debt of gratitude? But, to the best of my ability, I shall neither betray the trust reposed in me nor yet abandon the children in their forlorn condition. You too ought in justice to remember the benefits their grandfather conferred upon the commonwealth in reducing to your obedience so many cities of the Latins, your rivals for the sovereignty, in making all the Tyrrhenians, the most powerful of your neighbours, your subjects, and in forcing the Sabine nation to submit to you — all of which he effected at the cost of many great dangers. As long, therefore, as he himself was living, it became you to give him thanks for the benefits you had received from him; and now that he is dead, it becomes you to make a grateful return to his posterity, and not to bury the remembrance of their deeds together with the persons of your benefactors. Consider, therefore, that you have all jointly been left guardians of these little children, and confirm to them the sovereignty which their grandfather left them. For they would not receive so great an advantage from my guardianship, which is that of one man only, as from the joint assistance of you all. I have been compelled to say these things because I have perceived that some persons are conspiring against them and desire to hand the sovereignty over the others. I ask you, Romans, also to call to mind the struggles I have undergone in the interest of your supremacy — struggles neither inconsiderable nor few, which I need not relate to you who are familiar with them — and to repay to these little children the gratitude you owe me in return. For it has not been with a view to securing a sovereignty of my own — of which, if that had been my aim, I was as worthy as anyone — but in order to aid the family of Tarquinius, that I have chosen to direct public affairs. And I entreat you as a suppliant not to abandon these orphans, who are now, indeed, only in danger of losing the sovereignty, but, if this first attempt of their enemies succeeds, will also be expelled from the city. But on this subject I need say no more to you, since you both know what is required and will perform your duty.

"Hear from me now the benefits I myself have arranged to confer upon you and the reasons that induced me to summon this assembly. Those among you who already have debts which through poverty they are unable to discharge, I am eager to help, since they are citizens and have undergone many hardships in the service of their country; hence, in order that these men who have securely established the common liberty may not be deprived of their own, I am giving them from my own means enough to pay their debts. And those who shall hereafter borrow I will not permit to be haled to prison on account of their debts, but will make a law that no one shall lend money on the security of the persons of free men; for I hold that it is enough for the lenders to possess the property of those who contracted the debts. And in order to lighten for the future the burden also of the war taxes you pay to the public treasury, by

which the poor are oppressed and obliged to borrow, I will order all
the citizens to give in a valuation of their property and everyone to
pay his share of the taxes according to that valuation, as I learn is
done in the greatest and best governed cities;[13] for I regard it as both
just and advantageous to the public that those who possess much
should pay much in taxes and those who have little should pay little.
I also believe that the public lands, which you have obtained by your
arms and now enjoy, should not, as at present, be held by those who
are the most shameless, whether they got them by favour or
acquired them by purchase, but by those among you who have no
allotment of land, to the end that you, being free men, may not be
serfs to others or cultivate others' lands instead of your own;[14] for a
noble spirit cannot dwell in the breasts of men who are in want of
the necessaries of daily life. But, above all these things, I have
determined to make the government fair and impartial and justice
the same for all and towards all. For some have reached that degree
of presumption that they take upon themselves to maltreat the
common people and do not look upon the poor among you as being
even free men. To the end, therefore, that the more powerful may
both receive justice from and do justice to their inferior impartially, I
will establish such laws as shall prevent violence and preserve justice,
and I myself will never cease to take thought for the equality of all
the citizens."

10 While he was thus speaking there was much praise from the
assembly, some commending him for his loyalty and justice to his
benefactors, others for his humanity and generosity to the poor, and
still others for his moderation and democratic spirit towards those of
humbler station; but all loved and admired him for being a lawful
and just ruler. The assembly having been dismissed, during the

---

13   Dionysius was doubtless thinking particularly of Solon's division of the
     Athenians into four classes for purposes of taxation.
14   *Cf.* Livy i. 46, 1.

following days he ordered lists to be made of all the debtors who were unable to keep their pledges, with the amount each owed and the names of the creditors; and when this list had been delivered to him, he commanded tables to be placed in the Forum and in the presence of all the citizens counted out to the lenders the amount of the debts. Having finished with this, he published a royal edict commanding that all those who were enjoying the use of the public lands and holding them for their own should quit possession within a certain specified time, and that those citizens who had no allotments of land should give in their names to him. He also drew up laws, in some cases renewing old laws that had been introduced by Romulus and Numa Pompilius and had fallen into abeyance, and establishing others himself. While he was pursuing these measures, the patricians were growing indignant as they saw the power of the senate being overthrown, and they proceeded to a plan of action which was no longer the same as before, but the opposite. For whereas at first they had determined to deprive him of his illegal power, to appoint *interreges*, and through them to choose one who should hold the office legally, they now thought they ought to acquiesce in the existing state of affairs and not to interfere at all. For it occurred to them that, if the senate attempted to place a man of its own choosing at the head of affairs, the people, when they came to give their votes, would oppose him; whereas, if they should leave the choice of the king to the people, all the *curiae* would elect Tullius and the result would be that he would seem to hold the office legally. They thought it better, therefore, to permit him to continue in the possession of the sovereignty by stealth and by deceiving the citizens rather than after persuading them and receiving it openly. But none of their calculations availed them aught, so artfully did Tullius outmanoeuvre them and get possession of the royal power against their will. For having long before caused a report to be spread through the city that the patricians were plotting against him, he came into the Forum meanly dressed and with a dejected countenance, accompanied by his mother Ocrisia, Tanaquil, the wife of Tarquinius, and all the royal family. And when great crowds flocked together at so unexpected a sight, he called an assembly, and ascending the tribunal, addressed them much as follows:

11 "It is no longer the children of Tarquinius alone whom I see in danger of suffering some injury at the hands of their enemies, but I am already coming to fear for my own life, lest I receive a bitter requital for my justice. For the patricians are plotting against me and I have received information that some of them are conspiring to kill me, not because they can charge me with any crime, great or trivial, but because they resent the benefits I have conferred and am prepared to confer upon the people and feel that they are being treated unjustly. The money-lenders, for their part, feel aggrieved because I did not permit the poor among you to be haled to prison by them because of their debts and to be deprived of their liberty. And those who misappropriate and hold what belongs to the state, finding themselves obliged to give up the land which you acquired with your blood, are as angry as if they were being deprived of their inheritances instead of merely restoring what belongs to others. Those, again, who have been exempt from war taxes resent being compelled to give in a valuation of their property and to pay taxes i n proportion to those valuations. But the general complaint of them all is that they will have to accustom themselves to live according to written laws and impartially dispense justice to you and receive it from you, instead of abusing the poor, as they now do, as if they were so many purchased slaves. And making common cause of these complaints, they have taken counsel and sworn to recall the exiles and to restore the kingdom to Marcius' sons, against whom you passed a vote forbidding them the use of fire and water for having assassinated Tarquinius, your king, a worthy man and a lover of his country, and, after they had committed such an act of pollution, for having failed to appear for their trial and thus condemned themselves to exile. And if I had not received early information of these designs, they would, with the assistance of a foreign force, have brought back the exiles into the city in the dead of night. You all know, of course, what would have been the consequence of this, even without my mentioning it — that the Marcii, with the support of the patricians, after getting control of affairs without any trouble, would first have seized me, as the guardian of the royal family and as the person who had pronounced sentence against them, and after that would have destroyed these children and all the other kinsmen and friends of Tarquinius; and, as they have much of the savage and the tyrant in their nature, they would have treated our wives, mothers and daughters and all the female sex like slaves. If, therefore, it is *your* pleasure also, citizens, to recall the assassins and make them kings, to banish the sons of your benefactors and to deprive them of the kingdom their grandfather left them, we shall submit to our fate. But we all, together with our wives and children, make supplication to you by all the gods and lesser divinities who watch over the lives of men that, in return for the many benefits Tarquinius, the grandfather of these children, never ceased to confer upon you, and in return for the many services I myself, as far as I have been able, have done you, you will grant us this single boon — to declare your own sentiments. For if you have come to believe that any others are more worthy than we of this honour, the children, with all the other relations of Tarquinius, shall withdraw, leaving the city to you. As for me, I shall take a more generous resolution in my own case For I have already lived long enough both for virtue and for glory, and if I am disappointed of your goodwill, which I have preferred to every other good thing, I could never bring myself to live in disgrace among any other people. Take the rods, then, and give them to the patricians, if you wish; I shall not trouble you with my presence."

12 While he was speaking these words and seemed about to leave the tribunal, they all raised a tremendous clamour, and mingling tears with their entreaties, besought him to remain and to retain control of affairs, fearing no one. Thereupon some of his partisans, who had stationed themselves in different parts of the Forum, following his instructions, cried out, "Make him king," and demanded that the *curiae* should be called together and a vote taken; and after these had set the example, the whole populace was promptly of the same opinion. Tullius, seeing this, no longer let the occasion slip, but told them that he felt very grateful to them for remembering his services; and after promising to confer even more benefits if they should make him king, he appointed a day for the election, at which he ordered everybody to be present including those from the country. When the people had assembled he called the *curiae* and took the vote of each *curia* separately. And upon being judged worthy of the kingship by all the *curiae*, he then accepted it from the populace, telling the senate to go hang; for he did not ask that body to ratify the decision of the people, as it was accustomed to do.[15] After coming to the sovereignty in this manner, he introduced many reforms in the civil administration and also carried on a great and memorable war against the Tyrrhenians. But I shall first give an account of his administrative reforms.

13 Immediately upon receiving the sovereignty he divided the public lands among those of the Romans who served others for hire. Next he caused both the laws relating to private contracts an those

15 *Cf.* Livy i. 41, 6 f.; 46, 1. In the first passage he states that *Tullius primus iniussu populi voluntate patrum regnavit*; and in the second he said that when the young Tarquinius hinted that he was ruling without the sanction of the people, he proceeded to conciliate the plebeians and then, putting the question to a vote of the people, was declared king by them.

concerning torts to be ratified by the *curiae*; these laws were about fifty in number, of which I need not make any mention a present. He also added two hills to the city, those called the Viminal and the Esquiline,[16] each of which has the size of a fairly large city. These he divided among such of the Romans as had no homes of their own, so that they might build houses there; and he himself fixed his habitation there, in the best part of the Esquiline Hill.[17] This king was the last who enlarged the circuit of the city, by adding these two hills to the other five, after he had first consulted the auspices, as the law directed, and performed the other religious rites. Farther than this the building of the city has not yet progressed, since the gods, they say, have not permitted it; but all the inhabited places round it, which are many and large, are unprotected and without walls, and very easy to be taken by any enemies who may come. If anyone wishes to estimate the size of Rome by looking at these suburbs he will necessarily be misled for want of a definite clue by which to determine up to what point it is still the city and where it ceases to be the city; so closely is the city connected with the country, giving the beholder the impression of a city stretching out indefinitely. But if one should wish to measure Rome by the wall, which, though hard to be discovered by reason of the buildings that surround it in many places, yet preserves in several parts of it some traces of its ancient structure, and to compare it with the circuit of the city of Athens, the circuit of Rome would not seem to him very much larger than the other. But for an account of the extent and beauty of the city of Rome, as it existed in my day, another occasion will be more suitable.[18]

---

16 Livy (i. 44, 3) states that Tullius added the Viminal and the Quirinal, and enlarged the Esquiline. Strabo (v. 3, 7) agrees with Dionysius. The Quirinal had already been added by Numa according to Dionysius (ii. 62, 5).

17 Livy (*l.c.*) says that he established his residence on the Esquiline *ut loco dignitas fieret*.

18 No such passage is to be found in the extant portions of the *Antiquities*.

14 After Tullius had surrounded the seven hills with one wall, he divided the city into four regions,[19] which he named after the hills, calling the first the Palatine, the second the Suburan,[20] the third the Colline,[21] and the fourth the Esquiline region; and by this means he made the city contain four tribes, whereas it previously had consisted of but three.[22] And he ordered that the citizens inhabiting each of the four regions should, like persons living in villages, neither take up another abode nor be enrolled elsewhere; and the levies of troops, the collection of taxes for military purposes, and the other services which every citizen was bound to offer to the commonwealth, he no longer based upon the three national tribes, as aforetime, but upon the four local tribes established by himself. And over each region he appointed commanders, like heads of tribes or villages, whom he ordered to know what house each man lived in. After this he commanded that there should be erected in every street[23] by the inhabitants of the neighbourhood chapels to heroes whose statues stood in front of the houses,[24] and he made a law that sacrifices should be performed to them every year, each family contributing a honey-cake. He directed also that the persons attending and assisting those who performed the sacrifices at these shrines[25] on behalf of the neighbourhood should not be free men,

---

19 *Cf.* Livy i. 43, 13.
20 This was named from the Subura, which was not a hill, but a valley entering the Forum from the northeast.
21 This name was derived from Collis, a common term for the Quirinal.
22 The Ramnes, Tities and Luceres.
23 The word στενωπός usually means a narrow passage or lane, but in this chapter it is used for the Roman *compitum* (compare 13 lines below), and this we know was a cross-road.
24 This seems to be the literal meaning of προνώπιος, but evidently the word is used here to express *compitalis*, the heroes being the *lares compitales*. These *lares* doubtless reminded Dionysius of the Greek herms, and his descriptive adjective is more appropriate to the latter.
25 Literally, "in the places before the houses." Of the emendations proposed (see the critical note), that of Casaubon means "to the (heroes) in front of the

but slaves, the ministry of servants being looked upon as pleasing to the heroes. This festival the Romans still continued to celebrate even in my day in the most solemn and sumptuous manner a few days after the Saturnalia, calling it the Compitalia, after the streets; for *compiti*,[26] is their name for streets.[27] And they still observe the ancient custom in connexion with those sacrifices, propitiating the heroes by the ministry of their servants, and during these days removing every badge of their servitude, in order that the slaves, being softened by this instance of humanity, which has something great and solemn about it, may make themselves more agreeable to their masters and be less sensible of the severity of their condition.

15 Tullius[28] also divided the country[29] as a whole into twenty-six parts, according to Fabius, who calls these divisions tribes also and, adding the four city tribes to them, says that there were thirty tribes in all under Tullius. But according to Vennonius[30] he divided the country into thirty-one parts, so that with the four city tribes the number was rounded out to the thirty-five tribes that exist down to our day. However, Cato, who is more worthy of credence than either of these authors, does not specify the number of the parts

---

houses," that of Bücheler "at the crossroads."

26 The usual plural was *compita*, but the form *compiti* is occasionally found.

27 See note 21 on p. 340.

28 The first section of this chapter is badly confused in the MSS. and two entire lines are missing from all but two of the extant MSS. Unfortunately we have no confirmation of the statements attributed by Dionysius to Fabius Pictor, Vennonius and Cato. The relation of the country districts to the city tribes is a moot question and it is not at all certain that the districts here mentioned are identical with the **pagi**, as Dionysius assumed. The number of tribes at this early period concerning have been as large even as thirty. Indeed, Dionysius himself in describing the trial of Coriolanus (vii. 64, 6) states that there were twenty-one tribes then; and Livy (vi. 5) records the same number for 387 B.C.

29 *i.e.*, the country as distinguished from the city.

30 An annalist of whom almost nothing is known. He seems to have lived in the second century B.C.

into which the country was divided. After Tullius, therefore, had divided the country into a certain number of parts, whatever that number was, he built places of refuge upon such lofty eminences as could afford ample security for the husbandmen, and called them by a Greek name, *pagi* or "hills."[31] Thither all the inhabitants fled from the fields whenever a raid was made by enemies, and generally passed the night there. These places also had their governors, whose duty it was to know not only the names of all the husbandmen who belonged to the same district but also the lands which afforded them their livelihood. And whenever there was occasion to summon the countrymen to take arms or to collect the taxes that were assessed against each of them, these governors assembled the men together and collected the money. And in order that the number of these husbandmen might not be hard to ascertain, but might be easy to compute and be known at once, he ordered them to erect altars to the gods who presided over and were guardians of the district, and directed them to assemble every year and honour these gods with public sacrifices. This occasion also he made one of the most solemn festivals, calling it the Paganalia; and he drew up laws concerning these sacrifices, which the Romans still observe. Towards the expense of this sacrifice and of this assemblage he ordered all those of the same district to contribute each of them a certain piece of money, the men paying one kind, the women another and the children a third kind. When these pieces of money were counted by those who presided over the sacrifices, the number of people, distinguished by their sex and age, became known. And wishing also, as Lucius Piso writes in the first book of his *Annals*, to know the number of the inhabitants of the city, and of all who were born and

31 Dionysius was misled by the Greek word πάγος (a rocky hill) to apply the Latin term primarily to the natural stronghold rather than to the district it served. While both words are doubtless from the same root **pag-**, "fix," the meanings developed along different lines; *pagus* seems to have meant a "fixed" or marked area.

died and arrived at the age of manhood, he prescribed the piece of money which their relations were to pay for each — into the treasury of Ilithyia (called by the Romans Juno Lucina) for those who were born, into that of the Venus of the Grove (called by them Libitina)[32] for those who died, and into the treasury of Juventas for those who were arriving at manhood. By means of these pieces of money he would know every year both the number of all the inhabitants and which of them were of military age. After he had made these regulations, he ordered all the Romans to register their names and give in a monetary valuation of their property, at the same time taking the oath required by law that they had given in a true valuation in good faith; they were also to set down the names of their fathers, with their own age and the names of their wives and children, and every man was to declare in what tribe of the city or in what district of the country he lived. If any failed to give in their valuation, the penalty he established was that their property should be forfeited and they themselves whipped and sold for slaves. This law continued in force among the Romans for a long time.

16 After all had given in their valuations, Tullius took the registers and determining both the number of the citizens and the size of their estates, introduced the wisest of all measures, and one which has been the source of the greatest advantages to the Romans, as the results have shown.[33] The measure was this: He selected from the whole number of the citizens one part, consisting of those whose property was rated the highest and amounted to no

---

32 Libitina was a goddess of corpses, but in the course of time, perhaps through a confusion of Libitina with Libentina (an epithet of Venus), she came to be identified with Venus. Not only was the register of deaths kept in her temple, but everything necessary for a funeral might be bought or hired there.

33 On the Servian constitution and census described in chaps. 16-22 *cf.* Livy i. 42, 4-43, 11.

less than one hundred minae.[34] Of these he formed eighty centuries, whom he ordered to be armed with Argolic bucklers, with spears, brazen helmets, corslets, greaves and swords. Dividing these centuries into two groups, he made forty centuries of younger men, whom he appointed to take the field in time of war, and forty of older men, whose duty it was, when the youth went forth to war, to remain in the city and guard everything inside the walls. This was the first class; in wars it occupied a position in the forefront of the whole army. Next, from those who were left he took another part whose rating was under ten thousand drachmae but not less than seventy-five minae. Of these he formed twenty centuries and ordered them to wear the same armour as those of the first class, except that he took from them the corslets, and instead of the bucklers gave them shields.[35] Here also he distinguished between those who were over forty-five years old and those who were of military age, constituting ten centuries of the younger men, whose duty it was to serve their country in the field, and ten of the older, to whom he committed the defence of the walls. This was the second class; in engagements they were drawn up behind those fighting in the front ranks. The third class he constituted out of those who were left, taking such as had a rating of less than seven thousand five hundred drachmae but not less than fifty minae. The armour of these he diminished not only by taking away the corslets, as from the second class, but also the greaves. He formed likewise twenty

---

34 In giving Greek equivalents for the Roman sums involved in the census Dionysius amused himself by stating the amounts alternately in minae and in drachmae (1 mina = 100 drachmae). Assuming equivalence between the drachma and the Roman denarius, he gave to the latter its earlier value of 10 asses. Thus his figures when given in drachmae are just one-tenth as large as Livy's figures expressed in asses. The sums named by the two historians agree except in the case of the fifth class, where Dionysius gives 1,250 drachmae as against Livy's 11,000 asses.

35 The Greek word here used means a large, oblong shield, Livy's *scutum*. The Argolic buckler or **clipeus**, on the other hand, was a round shield.

centuries of these, dividing them, like the former, according to their age and assigning ten centuries to the younger men and ten to the older. In battles the post and station of these centuries was in the third line from the front.

17 Again taking from the remainder those whose property amounted to less than five thousand drachmae but was as much as twenty-five minae, he formed a fourth class. This he also divided into twenty centuries, ten of which he composed of such as were in the vigour of their age, and the other ten of those who were just past it, in the same manner as with the former classes. He ordered the arms of these to be shields, swords and spears, and their post in engagements to be in the last line. The fifth class, consisting of those whose property was between twenty-five minae and twelve minae and a half, he divided into thirty centuries. These were also distinguished according to their age, fifteen of the centuries being composed of the older men and fifteen of the younger. These he armed with javelins and slings, and placed outside the line of battle. He ordered four unarmed centuries to follow those that were armed, two of them consisting of armourers and carpenters and of those whose business it was to prepare everything that might be of use in time of war, and the other two of trumpeters and horn-blowers and such as sounded the various calls with any other instruments. The artisans were attached to the second class and divided according to their age, one of their centuries following the older centuries, and the other the younger centuries; the trumpeters and horn-blowers were added to the fourth class, and one of their centuries also consisted of the older men and the other of the younger.[36] Out of all the centuries the bravest men were chosen as

---

36 Livy on the contrary, says that the artisans were attached to the first class and the musicians to the fifth.

centurions, and each of these commanders took care that his century should yield a ready obedience to orders.

18 This was the arrangement he made of the entire infantry, consisting of both the heavy-armed and light-armed troops. As for the cavalry, he chose them out of such as had the highest rating and were of distinguished birth, forming eighteen centuries of them, and added them to the first eighty centuries of the heavy-armed infantry; these centuries of cavalry were also commanded by persons of the greatest distinction. The rest of the citizens, who had a rating of less than twelve minae and a half but were more numerous than those already mentioned, he put into a single century and exempted them from service in the army and from every sort of tax. Thus there were six divisions which the Romans call *classes*, by a slight change of the Greek word *klêseis*[37] (for the verb which we Greeks pronounce in the imperative mood *kalei*, the Romans call *cala*,[38] and the classes they anciently called *caleses*), and the centuries included in these divisions amounted to one hundred and ninety-three. The first class contained ninety-eight centuries, counting the cavalry; the second, twenty-two, counting the artificers; the third, twenty; the fourth, again, contained twenty-two, counting the trumpeters and horn-blowers; the fifth, thirty; and the last of all, one century, consisting of the poor citizens.

19 In pursuance of this arrangement he levied troops according to the division of the centuries, and imposed taxes[39] in proportion to the valuation of their possessions. For instance, whenever he had

---

37 κλῆσις means a "calling" or "summoning."

38 This root is seen in *Calendae* (Kalendae), in *comitia calata*, and in *intercalare*. The statement about an early form *calesis* (better *calasis*) is probably pure conjecture.

39 The Greek word εἰσφορά, translated "tax" in these chapters, means a special tax, particularly one levied for war purposes; it is here equivalent to the Roman *tributum*.

occasion to raise ten thousand men, or, if it should so happen, twenty thousand, he would divide that number among the hundred and ninety-three centuries and then order each century to furnish the number of men that fell to its share. As to the expenditures that would be needed for the provisioning of soldiers while on duty and for the various warlike supplies, he would first calculate how much money would be sufficient, and having in like manner divided that sum among the hundred and ninety-three centuries, he would order every man to pay his share towards it in proportion to his rating. Thus it happened that those who had the largest possessions, being fewer in number but distributed into more centuries, were obliged to serve oftener and without any intermission, and to pay greater taxes than the rest; that those who had small and moderate possessions, being more numerous but distributed into fewer centuries, serve seldom and in rotation and paid small taxes, and that those whose possessions were not sufficient to maintain them were exempt from all burdens. Tullius made none of these regulations without reason, but from the conviction that all men look upon their possessions as the prizes at stake in war and that it is for the sake of retaining these that they all endure its hardships; he thought it right, therefore, that those who had greater prizes at stake should suffer greater hardships, both with their persons and with their possessions, that those who had less at stake should be less burdened in respect to both, and that those who had no loss to fear should endure no hardships, but be exempt from taxes by reason of their poverty and from military service because they paid no tax. For at that time the Romans received no pay as soldiers from the public treasury but served at their own expense. Accordingly, he did not think it right either that those should pay taxes who were so far from having wherewithal to pay them that they were in want of the necessities of daily life, or that such as contributed nothing to the public taxes should, like mercenary troops, be maintained in the field at the expense of others.

20 Having by this means laid upon the rich the whole burden of both the dangers and expenses and observing that they were discontented, he contrived by another method to relieve their uneasiness and mitigate their resentment by granting to them an advantage which would make them complete masters of the commonwealth, while he excluded the poor from any part in the government; and he effected this without the plebeians noticing it. This advantage that he gave to the rich related to the assemblies, where the matters of greatest moment were ratified by the people. I have already said before[40] that by the ancient laws the people had control over the three most important and vital matters: they elected the magistrates, both civil and military; they sanctioned and repealed laws; and they declared war and made peace. In discussing and deciding these matters they voted by *curiae*, and citizens of the smallest means had an equal vote with those of the greatest; but as the rich were few in number, as may well be supposed, and the poor much more numerous, the latter carried everything by a majority of votes. Tullius, observing this, transferred this preponderance of votes from the poor to the rich. For whenever he thought proper to have magistrates elected, a law considered, or war to be declared, he assembled the people by centuries instead of by *curiae*. And the first centuries that he called to express their opinion[41] were those with the highest rating, consisting of the eighteen centuries of cavalry and the eighty centuries of infantry. As these centuries amounted to three more than all the rest together, if they agreed they prevailed

---

40 ii. 14, 3.

41 If taken literally, this expression is erroneous. The popular assemblies were not deliberative bodies; they could merely vote "aye" or "no" to a specific proposal. But probably Dionysius meant no more by his expression than "give their vote."

over the others and the matter was decided. But in case these were not all of the same mind, then he called the twenty-two centuries of the second class; and if the votes were still divided, he called the centuries of the third class, and, in the fourth place, those of the fourth class; and this he continued to do till ninety-seven centuries concurred in the same opinion. And if after the calling of the fifth class this had not yet happened but the opinions of the hundred and ninety-two centuries were equally divided, he then called the last century, consisting of the mass of the citizens who were poor and for that reason exempt from all military service and taxes; and whichever side this century joined, that side carried the day. But this seldom happened and was next to impossible. Generally the question was determined by calling the first class, and it rarely went as far as the fourth; so that the fifth and the last were superfluous.

21 In establishing this political system, which gave so great an advantage to the rich, Tullius outwitted the people, as I said, without their noticing it and excluded the poor from any part in public affairs. For they all thought that they had an equal share in the government because every man was asked his opinion, each in his own century; but they were deceived in this, that the whole century, whether it consisted of a small or a very large number of citizens, had but one vote; and also in that the centuries which voted first, consisting of men of the highest rating, though they were more in number than all the rest, yet contained fewer citizens; but, above all, in that the poor, who were very numerous, had but one vote and were the last called. When this had been brought about, the rich, though paying out large sums and exposed without intermission to the dangers of war, were less inclined to feel aggrieved now that they had obtained control of the most important matters and had taken the whole power out of the hands of those who were not performing the same services; and the poor, who had but the slightest share in the government, finding themselves exempt both from taxes and from military service, prudently and quietly submitted to this diminution of their power; and the commonwealth itself had the advantage of seeing the same persons who were to deliberate concerning its interests allotted the greatest share of the dangers and ready to do whatever required to be done. This form of government was maintained by the Romans for many generations, but is altered in our times and changed to a more democratic form, some urgent needs having forced the change, which was effected, not by abolishing the centuries, but by no longer observing the strict ancient manner of calling them[42] — a fact which I myself have noted, having often been present at the elections of their magistrates. But this is not the proper occasion to discuss these matters.

22 Thereupon[43] Tullius, having completed the business of the census, commanded all the citizens to assemble in arms in the largest field before the city;[44] and having drawn up the horse in their respective squadrons and the foot in their massed ranks, and placed the light-armed troops each in their own centuries, he performed an

---

42 No ancient writer gives us an explicit account of this reform of the *comitia centuriata*; but from scattered allusions it is known that each of the five classes later contained 80 companies (one of *seniores* and one of *iuniores* from each of the 35 tribes). To these 350 centuries must be added the centuries of knights (probably 18, as before, though 35 and even 70 have been suggested), and perhaps also those of the artisans and musicians (4 as before?) and the one century of *proletarii*. The knights no longer voted first, but one century out of the first class (or possibly out of all five classes) was chosen by lot to give its vote first; then followed the knights and the several classes in a fixed order. This reform may have been introduced at the time when the last two tribes were created, in 241 B.C. Livy's statement (i. 43, 12) is tantalizingly brief.

43 *Cf.* Livy i. 44, 1 f.

44 The Campus Martius.

expiatory sacrifice for them with a bull, a ram and a boar.[45] These victims he ordered to be led three times round the army and then sacrificed them to Mars, to whom that field is consecrated. The Romans are to this day purified by this same expiatory sacrifice, after the completion of each census, by those who are invested with the most sacred magistracy,[46] and they call the purification a *lustrum*.[47]

The number of all the Romans who then gave in a valuation of their possessions was, as appears by the censors' records, 84,700.[48] This king also took no small care to enlarge the body of citizens, hitting upon a method that had been overlooked by all the kings before him. For they, by receiving foreigners and bestowing upon them equal rights of citizenship without rejecting any, whatever their birth or condition, had indeed rendered the city populous; but Tullius permitted even manumitted slaves to enjoy these same rights, unless they chose to return to their own countries. For he ordered these also to report the value of their property at the same time as all the other free men, and he distributed them among the four city tribes, in which the body of freedmen, however numerous, continued to be ranked even to my day; and he permitted them to share in all the privileges which were open to the rest of the plebeians.

---

45 The sacrifice referred to is of course the well-known *suovetaurilia*. It seems incredible that Dionysius could have overlooked the obvious meaning of this compound word and substituted a goat for the boar, as our MSS. do. Roscher pointed out that the later Greeks sometimes performed a triple sacrifice of a bull, a ram and a goat, and he suggested that the knowledge of such a sacrifice may have misled a scribe who was less familiar with Roman customs.
46 The censorship.
47 From this original meaning the word *lustrum* came to be applied also to the entire period from one census to the next, and finally could be used of any five-year period.
48 Livy (*l.c.*) reports 80,000, Eutropius (i. 7) 83,000.

23 The patricians being displeased and indignant at this, he called an assembly of the people and told them that he wondered at those who were displeased at his course, first, for thinking that free men differed from slaves by their very nature rather than by their condition, and, second, for not determining by men's habits and character, rather than by the accidents of their fortune, those who were worthy of honours, particularly when they saw how unstable a thing good fortune is and how subject to sudden change, and how difficult it is for anyone, even of the most fortunate, to say how long it will remain with him. He asked them also to consider how many states, both barbarian and Greek, had passed from slavery to freedom and how many from freedom to slavery. He called it great folly on their part if, after they had granted liberty to such of their slaves as deserved it, they envied them the rights of citizens; and he advised them, if they thought them bad men, not to make them free, and if good men, not to ignore them because they were foreigners. He declared that they were doing an absurd and stupid thing, if, while permitting all strangers to share the rights of citizenship without distinguishing their condition or inquiring closely whether any of them had been manumitted or not, they regarded such as had been slaves among themselves as unworthy of this favour. And he said that, though they thought themselves wiser than other people, they did not even see what lay at their very feet and was to be observed every day and what was clear to the most ordinary men, namely, that not only the masters would take great care not to manumit any of their slaves rashly, for fear of granting the greatest of human blessings indiscriminately, but the slaves too would be more zealous to observe their masters faithfully when they knew that if they were thought worthy of liberty they should presently become citizens of a great and flourishing state and receive both these blessings from their masters. He concluded by speaking of the advantage that would result from this policy, reminding those who understood such matters, and informing the ignorant, that to a state which aimed at supremacy and thought itself worthy of great things nothing was so essential as a large population, in order that it might be equal to carrying on all its wars with its own armed forces and might not exhaust itself as well as its wealth in hiring mercenary troops; and for this reason, he said, the former kings had granted citizenship to all foreigners. But if they enacted this law also, great numbers of youths would be reared from those who were manumitted and the state would never lack for armed forces of its own, but would always have sufficient troops, even if it should be forced to make war against all the world. And besides this advantage to the public, the richest men would privately receive many benefits if they permitted the freedmen to share in the government, since in the assemblies and in the voting and in their other acts as citizens they would receive their reward in the very situations in which they most needed it, and furthermore would be leaving the children of these freedmen as so many clients to their posterity. These arguments of Tullius induced the patricians to permit this custom to be introduced into the commonwealth, and to this day it continues to be observed by the Romans as one of their sacred and unalterable usages.

24 Now that I have come to this part of my narrative, I think it necessary to give an account of the customs which at that time prevailed among the Romans with regard to slaves, in order that no one may accuse either the king who first undertook to make citizens of those who had been slaves, or the Romans who accepted the law, of recklessly abandoning their noble traditions. The Romans acquired their slaves by the most just means; for they either purchased them from the state at an auction[49] as part of the spoils,

---

49   Literally "sold under the spear." Dionysius here uses a Latinism (*sub hasta vendere*).

or the general permitted the soldiers to keep the prisoners they had taken together with the rest of the booty, or else they bought them of those who had obtained possession of them by these same means. So that neither Tullius, who established this custom, nor those who received and maintained thought they were doing anything dishonourable or detrimental to the public interest, if those who had lost both their country and their liberty in war and had proved loyal to those who had enslaved them, or to those who had purchased them from these, had both those blessings restored to them by their masters. Most of these slaves obtained their liberty as a free gift because of meritorious conduct, and this was the best kind of discharge from their masters; but a few paid a ransom raised by lawful and honest labour.

This, however, is not the case in our day, but things have come to such a state of confusion and the noble traditions of the Roman commonwealth have become so debased and sullied, that some who have made a fortune by robbery, housebreaking, prostitution and every other base means, purchase their freedom with the money so acquired and straightway are Romans. Others, who have been confidants and accomplices of their masters in poisonings, receive from them this favour as their reward. Some are freed in order that, when they have received the monthly allowance of corn given by the public or some other largesse distributed by the men in power to the poor among the citizens, they may bring it to those who granted them their freedom. And others owe their freedom to the levity of their masters and to their vain thirst for popularity. I, at any rate, know of some who have allowed all their slaves to be freed after their death, in order that they might be called good men when they were dead and that many people might follow their biers wearing

354

their liberty-caps;[50] indeed, some of those taking part in these processions, as one might have heard from those who knew, have been malefactors just out of jail, who had committed crimes deserving of a thousand deaths. Most people, nevertheless, as they look upon these stains[51] that can scarce be washed away from the city, are grieved and condemn the custom, looking upon it as unseemly that a dominant city which aspires to rule the whole world should make such men citizens.

One might justly condemn many other customs also which were wisely devised by the ancients but are shamefully abused by the men of to-day. Yet, for my part, I do not believe that this law ought to be abolished, lest as a result some greater evil should break out to the detriment of the public; but I do say that it ought to be amended, as far as possible, and that great reproaches and disgraces hard to be wiped out should not be permitted entrance into the body politic. And I could wish that the censors, preferably, or, if that may not be, then the consuls, would take upon themselves the care of this matter, since it requires the control of some it magistracy, and that they would make inquiries about the persons who are freed each year — who they are and for what reason they have been freed and how — just as they inquire into the lives of the knights and senators; after which they should enrol in the tribes such of them as they find worthy to be citizens and allow them to remain in the city, but should expel from the city the foul and corrupt herd under the specious pretence of sending them out as a colony These are the things, then, which as the subject required it, I thought it both

---

50 The *pilleus* was a brimless (or almost brimless) cap, generally of felt. In the form worn by all Romans at the Saturnalia and by newly emancipated slaves it was nearly cylindrical.

51 There is probably an intentional pun in the Greek between σπίλους ("stains") and πίλους" ("caps") just above. A few lines later the historian substitutes another word (ῥύπους) for σπίλους.

necessary and just to say to those who censure the customs of the Romans.

25 Tullius showed himself a friend to the people, not only in these measures by which he seemed to lessen the authority of the senate and the power of the patricians, but also in those by which he diminished the royal power, of half of which he deprived himself. For whereas the kings before him had thought proper to have all causes brought before them and had determined all suits both private and public as they themselves thought fit, he, making a distinction between public and private suits, took cognizance himself of all crimes which affected the public, but in private cases appointed private persons to be judges, prescribing for them as norms and standards the laws which he himself had established.

When[52] he had arranged affairs in the city in the best manner, he conceived a desire to perpetuate his memory with posterity by some illustrious enterprise. And upon turning his attention to the monuments both of ancient kings and statesmen by which they had gained reputation and glory he did not envy either that Assyrian woman[53] for having built the walls of Babylon, or the kings of Egypt for having raised the pyramids at Memphis, or any other prince for whatever monument he might have erected as a display of his riches and of the multitude of workmen at his command. On the contrary, he regarded all these things as trivial and ephemeral and unworthy of serious attention, mere beguilements for the eyes, but no real aids to the conduct of life or to the administration of public affairs, since they led to nothing more than a reputation for great felicity on the part of those who built them. But the things that he regarded as worthy of praise and emulation were the works of the mind, the advantages from which are enjoyed by the greatest number of

---

52 For chaps. 25, 3-26, 5 *Cf.* Livy i. 45, 1-3.
53 Semiramis.

people and for the greatest length of time. And of all the achievements of this nature he admired most the plan of Amphictyon, the son of Hellen,[54] who, seeing the Greek nation weak and easy to be destroyed by the barbarians who surrounded them, brought them together in a general council and assemblage of the whole nation, named after him the Amphictyonic council; and then, apart from the particular laws by which each city was governed, established others common to all, which they call the Amphictyonic laws, in consequence of which they lived in mutual friendship, and fulfilling the obligations of kinship by their actions rather than by their professions, continued troublesome and formidable neighbours to the barbarians. His example was followed by the Ionians who, leaving Europe, settled in the maritime parts of Caria, and also by the Dorians, who built their cities in the same region and erected temples at the common expense — the Ionians building the temple of Diana at Ephesus and the Dorians that of Apollo at Triopium — where they assembled with their wives and children at the appointed times, joined together in sacrificing and celebrating the festival, engaged in various contests, equestrian, gymnastic and musical, and made joint offerings to the gods. After they had witnessed the spectacles, celebrated the festival, and received the other evidences of goodwill from one another, if any difference had arisen between one city and another, arbiters sat in judgment and decided the controversy; and they also consulted together concerning the means both of carrying on the war against

---

54 The Greek words can mean either "the son of Hellen" or "the Greek"; but the latter does not seem to be a very natural way of describing him. Other writers regularly regarded Amphictyon as the son of Deucalion and Pyrrha, and thus the brother of Hellen. Spelman proposed to add the word ἀδελφοῦ ("brother") to the Greek text here. The ancients did not all accept this aetiological myth as the true explanation of the Amphictyons and the Amphictyonic League. Several of the later authors rightly recognized in ἀμφικτύονες a mere variant of ἀμφικτίονες ("those dwelling round about," "neighbours"), the equivalent of Homer's περικτίονες.

the barbarians and of maintaining their mutual concord. These and the like examples inspired Tullius also with a desire of bringing together and uniting all the cities belonging to the Latin race, so that they might not, as the result of engaging in strife at home and in wars with one another, be deprived of their liberty by the neighbouring barbarians.

26 After he had taken this resolution he called together the most important men of every city, stating that he was summoning them to take counsel with him about matters of great consequence and of mutual concern. When they had assembled, he caused the Roman senate and these men who came from the cities to meet together, and made a long speech exhorting them to concord, pointing out what a fine thing it is when a number of states agree together and what a disgraceful sight when kinsmen are at variance, and declaring that concord is a source of strength to weak states, while mutual slaughter reduces and weakens even the strongest. After this he went on to show them that the Latins ought to have the command over their neighbours and, being Greeks, ought to give laws to barbarians, and that the Romans ought to have the leadership of all the Latins, not only because they excelled in the size of their city and the greatness of their achievements, but also because they, more than the others, had enjoyed the favour of divine providence and in consequence had attained to so great eminence. Having said this, he advised them to build a temple of refuge at Rome at their joint expense, to which the cities should repair every year and offer up sacrifices both individually and in common, and also celebrate festivals at such times as they should appoint; and if any difference should arise between these cities, they should terminate it over the sacrifices, submitting their complaints to the rest of the cities for decision. By enlarging upon these and the many other advantages they would reap from the appointment of a general council, he prevailed on all who were present at the session to give their consent. And later, with the money contributed by all the cities, he built the temple of Diana, which stands upon the Aventine, the largest of all the hills in Rome; and he drew up laws relating to the mutual rights of the cities and prescribed the manner in which everything else that concerned the festival and the general assembly should be performed. And to the end that no lapse of time should obliterate these laws, he erected a bronze pillar upon which he engraved both the decrees of the council and the names of the cities which had taken part in it. This pillar still existed down to my time in the temple of Diana, with the inscription in the characters that were anciently used in Greece.[55] This alone would serve as no slight proof that the founders of Rome were not barbarians; for if they had been, they would not have used Greek characters. These are the most important and most conspicuous administrative measures that are recorded of this king, besides many others of less note and certainty. His military operations were directed against one nation only, that of the Tyrrhenians; of these I shall now give an account.

27 After[56] the death of Tarquinius those cities which had yielded the sovereignty to him refused to observe the terms of their treaties any longer, disdaining to submit to Tullius, since he was a man of lowly birth, and anticipating great advantages for themselves from the discord that had arisen between the patricians and their ruler. The people called the Veientes were the leaders of this revolt; and when Tullus sent ambassadors they replied that they had no treaty with him either concerning their yielding the sovereignty or concerning friendship and an alliance. These having set the example, the people of Caere and Tarquinii followed it, and at last

---

55 The Romans got their alphabet from the Greeks (Chalcidians) who settled at Cumae and Neapolis.

56 *Cf.* Livy i. 42, 2 f.

all Tyrrhenia was in arms. This war lasted for twenty years without intermission, during which time both sides made many irruptions into one another's territories with great armies and fought one pitched battle after another. But Tullius, after being successful in all the battles in which he engaged, both against the several cities and against the whole nation, and after being honoured with three most splendid triumphs, at last forced those who refused to be ruled to accept the yoke[57] against their will. In the twentieth year, therefore, the twelve cities, having become exhausted by the war both in men and in money, again met together and decided to yield the sovereignty to the Romans upon the same terms as previously. And so the men chosen as envoys from each city arrived with the tokens of suppliants, and entrusting their cities to Tullius, begged of him not to adopt any extreme measures against them. Tullius told them that because of their folly and their impiety towards the gods whom they had made sponsors of their treaties, only to violate their agreements afterwards, they deserved many severe punishments; but that, since they acknowledged their fault and were come with the fillets of suppliants and with entreaties to deprecate the resentment they had merited, they should fail of none of the clemency and moderation of the Romans at this time. Having said this, he put an end to the war against them, and in the case of most of the cities, without imposing any conditions or harbouring any resentment for past injuries, he permitted them to retain the same government as before and also to enjoy their own possessions as long as they should abide by the treaties made with them by Tarquinius. But in the case of the three cities of Caere, Tarquinii and Veii, which had not only begun the revolt but had also induced the rest to make war upon the Romans, he punished them by seizing a part of their lands, which

---

57 Literally "bridle" or "bit," a different metaphor but with essentially the same meaning.

he portioned out among those who had lately been added to the body of Roman citizens.

Besides these achievements in both peace and war, he built two temples to Fortune, who seemed to have favoured him all his life, one in the market called the Cattle Market, the other on the banks of the Tiber to the Fortune which he named Fortuna Virilis,[58] as she is called by the Romans even to this day. And being now advanced in years and not far from a natural death, he was treacherously slain by Tarquinius, his son-in-law, and by his own daughter. I shall also relate the manner in which this treacherous deed was carried out; but first I must go back and mention a few things that preceded it.

28 Tullius[59] had two daughters by his wife Tarquinia, who King Tarquinius had given to him in marriage. When these maidens were of marriageable age, he gave them to the nephew of their mother, who were also the grandsons of Tarquinius joining the elder daughter to the elder nephew and the younger to the younger, since he thought they would thus live most harmoniously with their husbands. But it happened that each of his sons-in-law was joined by an adverse fate in the matter of dissimilarity of character. For the wife of Lucius, the elder of the two brothers, who was of a bold, arrogant and tyrannical nature was a good woman, modest and fond of her father; on the other hand, the wife of Arruns, the younger brother, a man of great mildness and prudence, was a wicked woman who hated her father and was capable of any rash action. Thus it chanced that each of the husbands tried to follow his own bent, but was drawn in the opposite direction by his wife. For when the wicked husband desired to drive his father-in-law from the throne and was devising every means to accomplish this, his wife by

---

58 Dionysius is probably in error here; Varro (*L.L.* vi. 17) states that this temple on the banks of the Tiber was dedicated to *Fors Fortuna*.

59 For chaps. 28-40 *cf.* Livy i. 42, 1 f.; 46-48.

her prayers and tears endeavoured to prevail on him to desist. And when the good husband thought himself obliged to abstain from all attempts against the life of his father-in-law and to wait till he should end his days by the course of nature, and tried to prevent his brother from doing what was wrong, his wicked wife, by her remonstrances and reproaches and by reviling him with a want of spirit, sought to draw him in the opposite direction. But when nothing was accomplished by either the entreaties of the virtuous wife as she urged upon her unjust husband the best course, or by the exhortations of the wicked wife when she strove to incite to impious deeds the husband who was not by nature evil, but each husband followed his natural bent and thought his wife troublesome because her wishes differed from his own, nothing remained but for the first wife to lament and submit to her fate and for her audacious sister to rage and endeavour to rid herself of her husband. At last this wicked woman, grown desperate and believing her sister's husband to be most suitable to her own character, sent for him, as if she wanted to talk with him concerning a matter of urgent importance.

29 And when he came, after first ordering those who were in the room to withdraw, that she might talk with him in private, she said: "May I, Tarquinius, speak freely and without risk all my thoughts concerning our common interests? And will you keep to yourself what you shall hear? Or is it better for me to remain silent and not to communicate plans that require secrecy?" And when Tarquinius bade her say what she wished, and gave her assurances, by such oaths as she herself proposed, that he would keep everything to himself, Tullia, laying aside all shame from that moment, said to him: "How long, Tarquinius, do you intend to permit yourself to be deprived of the kingship? Are you descended from mean and obscure ancestors, that you refuse to entertain high thoughts of yourself? But everyone knows that your early ancestors, who were

Greeks and descended from Hercules, exercised the sovereign power in the flourishing city of Corinth for many generations, as I am informed, and that your grandfather, Tarquinius, after removing from Tyrrhenia, was able by his merits to become king of this state; and not only his possessions, but his kingdom as well, ought to descend to you who are the elder of his grandsons. Or have you been given a body incapable of performing the duties of a king because of some weakness and deformity? But surely you are endowed both with strength equal to those most highly favoured by Nature and with a presence worthy of your royal birth. Or is it neither of these, but your youth, as yet weak and far from being capable of forming sound judgments, that holds you back and causes you to decline the government of the state — you who want not many years from being fifty? Yet at about this age a man's judgment is naturally at its best.[60] Well, then, is it the high birth of the man who is now in control of affairs and his popularity with the best citizens — which makes him difficult to attack — that forces you to submit? But in both these respects too he happens to be unfortunate, as not even he himself is unaware. Moreover, boldness and willingness to undergo danger are inherent in your character, qualities most necessary to one who is going to reign. You have sufficient wealth also, numerous friends, and many other important qualifications for public life. Why, then, do you still hesitate and wait for an occasion to be provided by chance, an occasion that will come bringing to you the kingship without your having made any effort to obtain it? And that, I presume, will be after the death of Tullius! As if Fate waited on men's delays or Nature dispensed death to each man according to his age, and the outcome of all human affairs were not, on the contrary, obscure and difficult to be

60 *Cf.* Solon 27 Edmonds (*L.C.L.*), i. 13: ἑπτὰ δὲ νοῦν καὶ γλῶσσαν ἐν ἑβδομάσιν μέγ' ἄριστος ὀκτώ τ'. — "in seven sevens and in eight he is at his best in mind and tongue."

foreseen! But I will declare frankly, even though you may call me bold for it, what seems to me to be the reason why you reach out for no coveted honour or glory. You have a wife whose disposition is in no respect like your own and who by her allurements and enchantments has softened you; and by her you will insensibly be transformed from a man into a nonentity. Just so have I a husband who is timorous and has nothing of a man in him, who makes me humble though I am worthy of great things, and though I am fair of body, yet because of him I have withered away. But if it had been possible for you to take me as your wife and for me to get you as my husband, we had not lived so long in a private station. Why, therefore, do we not ourselves correct this error of fate by exchanging our marital ties, you removing your wife from life and I making this disposition of my husband? And when we have put them out of the way and are joined together, we will then consider in security what remains to be done, having rid ourselves of what now causes our distress. For though one may hesitate to commit all the other crimes, yet for the sake of a throne one cannot be blamed for daring anything."[61]

30 Such were Tullia's words, and Tarquinius, gladly agreeing to the course she proposed, immediately exchanged pledges with her, and then, after celebrating the rites preliminary to their unholy nuptials, he departed. Not long after this the elder daughter of Tullius and the year Tarquinius died the same kind of death.

Here again, I find myself obliged to make mention of Fabius and to show him guilty of negligence in his investigation of the chronology of events. For when he comes to the death of Arruns he

---

61 *Cf.* Euripides, *Phoen.* 524 f.: εἴπερ γὰρ ἀδικεῖν χρή, τυραννίδος πέρι κάλλιστον ἀδικεῖν, τἆλλα δ' εὐσεβεῖν χρεών — "If wrong e'er be right, for a throne's sake, Were wrong most right: — be god in all else feared." — Way in *L.C.L.* These lines, according to Cicero (*de Off.* iii. 21), were often quoted by Caesar.

commits not only one error, as I said before,[62] in stating that he was the son of Tarquinius, but also another in saying that after his death he was buried by his mother Tanaquil, who could not possibly have been alive at that time. For it was shown in the beginning that when Tarquinius died Tanaquil was seventy-five years of age; and if to the seventy-five years forty more are added (for we find in the annals that Arruns died in the fortieth year of the reign of Tullius), Tanaquil must have been one hundred and fifteen years old. So little evidence of a laborious inquiry after truth do we find in that author's history.

After this deed of theirs Tarquinius married Tullia without any further delay, though the marriage had neither the sanction of her father nor the approval of her mother, but he took her of her own gift. As soon as these impious and bloodthirsty natures were commingled they began plotting to drive Tullius from the throne if he would not willingly resign his power. They got together band of their adherents, appealed to such of the patricians as were ill-disposed towards the king and his popular institutions, and bribed the poorest among the plebeians who had no regard for justice and all this they did without any secrecy. Tullius, seeing what was afoot, was not only disturbed because of his fears for his own safety, if he should be caught unprepared and come to some harm, but was especially grieved at the thought that he should be forced to take up arms against his own daughter and his son-in-law and to punish them as enemies. Accordingly, he repeatedly invited Tarquinius and his friends to confer with him, and sought, with by reproaches, now by admonitions, and again by arguments, to prevent him from doing him any wrong. When Tarquinius gave no heed to what he said but declared he would plead his cause before the senate, Tullius called

---

62 In chap. 6.

the senators together and said to them: "Senators,[63] it has become clear to me that Tarquinius is gathering bands of conspirators against me and is anxious to drive me from power. I desire to learn from him, therefore, in the presence of you all, what wrong he has personally received from me or what injury he has seen the commonwealth suffer at my hands, that he should be forming these plots against me. Answer me, then, Tarquinius, concealing nothing, and say what you have to accuse me of, since you have asked that these men should hear you."

31 Tarquinius answered him: "My arriving, Tullius, is brief and founded on justice, and for that reason I have chosen to lay it before these men. Tarquinius, my grandfather, obtained the sovereignty of the Romans after fighting many hard battles in its defence. He being dead, I am his successor according to the laws common to all men, both Greeks and barbarians, and it is my right, just as it is of any others who succeed to the estates of their grandfathers, to inherit not only his property but his kingship as well. You have, it is true, delivered up to me the property that he left, but you are depriving me of the kingship and have retained possession of it for so long a time now, though you obtained it wrongfully. For neither did any *interreges* appoint you king nor did the senate pass a vote in your favour, nor did you obtain this power by a legal election of the people, as my grandfather and all the kings before him obtained it; but by bribing and corrupting in every way possible the crowd of vagabonds and paupers, who had been disfranchised for convictions or for debts and had no concern for the public interests, and by not admitting even then that you were seeking the power for yourself, but by pretending that you were going to guard it for us who were orphans and infants, you came into control of affairs and kept

---

63 Dionysius usually makes no attempt to render literally the Latin mode of address — *patres* or *patres conscripti*.

promising in the hearing of all that when we came to manhood you would hand over the sovereignty to me as the elder brother. You ought, therefore, if you desired to do right, when you handed over to me the estate of my grandfather, to have delivered up his kingship also together with his property, following the example of all the upright guardians who, having taken upon themselves the care of royal children bereft of their parents, have rightly and justly restored to them the kingdoms of their fathers and ancestors when they came to be men. But if you thought I had not yet attained a proper degree of prudence and that by reason of my youth I was still unequal to the government of so great a state, yet when I attained to my full vigour of body and mind at the age of thirty, you ought, at the same time that you gave me your daughter in marriage, to have put also the affairs of the state into my hands; for it was at that very age that you yourselves first undertook both the guardianship of our family and the oversight of the kingship.

32 "If you had done this you would, in the first place, have gained the reputation of a loyal and just man, and again, you would have reigned with me and shared in every honour; and you would have been called my benefactor, my father, my preserver, and all the other laudatory names that men bestow in recognition of noble actions, instead of depriving me for all these forty-four years of what was mine, though I was neither maimed in body nor stupid in mind. And after that have you the assurance to ask me what ill-treatment provokes me to look upon you as my enemy and for what reason I accuse you? Nay, do *you,* answer *me* rather, Tullius, and declare why you think me unworthy to inherit the honours of my grandfather and what specious reason you allege for depriving me of them. Is it because you do not regard me as the legitimate offspring of his blood, but as some supposititious and illegitimate child? If so, why did you act as guardian to one who was a stranger to his blood, and why did you deliver up his estate to me as soon as I reached manhood? Or is it that you still look upon me as an orphan child and incapable of handling the business of the state — me who am not far from fifty years old? Lay aside now the dissimulation of your shameless questions and cease at last to play the rogue. However, if you have any just reason to allege against what I have said, I am ready to leave the decision to these men as judges, than whom you can name none better in the city. But if you attempt to run away from this tribunal and fly for refuge, as is ever your habit, to the rabble you mislead by your cajolery, I will not permit it. For I am prepared, not only to speak in defence of my rights, but also, if this should fail to convince you, to act with force."

33 When he had done speaking, Tullius took the floor and said: "Anything, it seems, senators, that is unexpected is to be expected by a mortal man, and nothing should be regarded as incredible, since Tarquinius here is set upon deposing *me* from my office, though I received him when he was an infant and, when his enemies were forming designs against his life, preserved him and brought him up, and when he came to be a man, saw fit to take him for a son-in-law and in the event of my death was intending to leave him heir to all that I possessed. But now that everything has happened to me contrary to my expectation and I myself am accused of wrongdoing, I shall lament my misfortune later on, but at present I will plead my just cause against him. I took upon myself, Tarquinius, the guardianship of your brother and yourself when you were left infants, not of my own will, but compelled by the circumstances, since those who aspired to the kingship had openly assassinated your grandfather and were said to be plotting secretly against you and the rest of his kin; and all your friends acknowledged that if those men once got the power into their hands they would not leave even a seed of the race of Tarquinius. And there was no one else to care for you and guard you but a woman, the mother of your father, and she, by reason of her great age, herself stood in need of others to care for her; but you children were left in my charge alone, to be guarded in your destitute condition — though you now call me a stranger and in no degree related to you. Nevertheless, when I had been put in command of such a situation, I not only punished the assassins of your grandfather and reared you boys to manhood, but, as I had no male issue, I proposed to make you the owners of what I possessed. You have now, Tarquinius, the account of my guardianship, and you will not venture to say that a word of it is false.

34 "But concerning the kingship, since this is the point of your accusation, learn not only by what means I obtained it, but also for what reasons I am not resigning it either to you or to anyone else. When I took upon myself the oversight of the commonwealth, finding that there were certain plots forming against me, I desired to surrender the conduct of affairs to the people; and having called them all together in assembly, I offered to resign the power to them, exchanging this envied sovereignty, the source of more pains than pleasures, for a quiet life free from danger. But the Romans would not permit me to follow this preference, nor did they see fit to make anyone else master of the state, but retained me and by their votes gave me the kingship — a thing which belonged to them, Tarquinius, rather than to you or your brother — in the same manner as they had entrusted the government to your grandfather, who was a foreigner and in no way related to the king who preceded him; and yet King Ancus Marcius had left sons in their prime of life, not grandchildren and infants, as you and your brother were left by Tarquinius. But if it were a general law that the heirs to the estate and possessions of deceased kings should also be heirs to their kingly office, Tarquinius, your grandfather would not have succeeded to the sovereignty upon the death of Ancus, but rather the elder of the king's sons. But the Roman people did not call to power the heir of the father, but rather the person who was worthy to rule. For they held that, while property belongs to those who acquired it, the kingly office belongs to those who conferred it, and that the former, when anything happens to its owners, ought to descend to the natural heirs or the testamentary heirs, but that the latter, when the persons who received it die, should return to those who gave it. Unless, indeed, you have some claim to offer to the effect that your grandfather received the kingship upon certain express conditions, whereby he was not to be deprived of it himself and could also leave it to you, his grandsons, and that it was not in the power of the people to take it from you and confer it upon me. If you have any such claim to allege, why do you not produce the contract? But you cannot do so. And if I did not obtain the office in the most justifiable manner, as you say, since I was neither chosen by the *interreges* nor entrusted with the government by the senate and the other legal requirements were not observed, then surely it is these men here that I am wronging and not you, and I deserve to be deprived of power by them, not by you. But I am not wronging either these men nor anyone else. The length of my reign, which has now lasted forty years,[64] bears me witness that power was both then justly given to me and is now justly vested in me; for during this time none of the Romans ever thought I reigned unjustly, nor did either the people or the senate ever endeavour to drive me from power.

35 "But — to pass over all these matters and to come to grip with your charges — if I had been depriving you of a deposit that had been left in my hands by your grandfather in trust for you and,

---

64 Kiessling proposed to read "forty-four years," which is not improbable in view of the use of the exact number by Tarquinius above (chap. 32, 1).

contrary to all the established rules of justice recognized by mankind, had been retaining the kingship which was yours, you ought to have gone to those who granted the power to me and to have vented your indignation and reproaches, both against me, for continuing to hold what did not belong to me, and against them, for having conferred on me what belonged to others; for you would easily have convinced them if you had been able to urge any just claim. If, however, you had no confidence in this argument and yet thought that I had no right to rule the state and that you were a more suitable person to be entrusted with its oversight, you ought to have done as follows — to have made an investigation of my mistakes and enumerated your own services and then to have challenged me to a trial for the determination of our respective merits. Neither of these things did you do; but, after all this time, as if recovered from a long fit of drunkenness, you now come to accuse me, and even now not where you should have come. For it is not here that you should present these charges — do not take any offence at this statement of mine, senators, for it is not with a view of taking the decision away from you that I say this, but from the desire to expose this man's calumnies — but you ought to have told me beforehand to call an assembly of the people and there to have accused me. However, since you have avoided doing so, I will do it for you, and having called the people together, I will appoint them judges of any crimes of which you may accuse me, and will again leave it to them to decide which of us two is the more suitable to hold the sovereignty; and whatever they shall unanimously decide I ought to do, I will do. As for you, this is a sufficient answer, since it is all the same whether one urges many or few just claims against unreasonable adversaries; for mere words naturally cannot bring any argument which will persuade them to be honest.

36 "But I have been surprised, senators, that any of *you* wish to remove me from power and have conspired with this man against me. I should like to learn from them what injury provokes them to attack me and at what action of mine they are offended. Is it because they know that great numbers during my reign have been put to death without a trial, banished from their country, deprived of their possessions, or have met with any other misfortune which they have not merited? Or, though they can accuse most of none of these tyrannical misdeeds, are they acquainted with any outrages I have been guilty of toward married women, or insults to their maiden daughters, or any other wanton attempt upon a person of free condition? If I have been guilty of any such crime I should deserve to be deprived at the same time both of the kingship and of my life. Well then, am I haughty, am I burdensome by my severity, and can no one bear the arrogance of my administration? And yet which of my predecessors constantly used his power with such moderation and kindliness, treating all the citizens as an indulgent father treats his own children? What, I did not even desire to retain all the power which you, following the traditions of your fathers, gave to me, but after establishing laws, which you all confirmed, relating to the most essential matters, I then granted to you the privilege of giving and receiving justice in accordance with these laws; and to these rules of justice which I prescribed for others I showed myself the first to yield obedience, like any private citizen. Nor did I make myself the judge of all sorts of crimes, but causes of a private nature I restored to your jurisdiction — a thing which none of the former kings ever did. But it appears that it is no wrongdoing on my part that has drawn upon me the ill-will of certain persons, but it is rather the benefits I have conferred on the plebeians that grieve you unjustly — concerning which I have often given you my reasons. But there is no need for such explanations now. If you believe that Tarquinius here by taking over the government will administer affairs better than I, I shall not envy the commonwealth a better ruler; and after I have surrendered the sovereignty to the people, from whom I received it, and have become a private citizen, I shall endeavour to make it plain to all that I not only know how to rule well, but can also obey with equanimity."

37 After this speech, which covered the conspirators with shame, Tullius dismissed the meeting and then, summoning the heralds he ordered them to go through all the streets and call the people together to an assembly. And when the whole populace of the city had flocked to the Forum, he came forward to the tribunal and made a long and moving harangue, enumerating all military achievements he had performed, both during the lifetime of Tarquinius and after his death, and recounting in addition one by one all his administrative measures from which the commonwealth appeared to have reaped many great advantages. And when everything he said met with great applause and all the people earnestly desired to know for what reasons he mentioned these things, at last he said that Tarquinius accused him of retaining the kingship unjustly, since it belonged to himself; for Tarquinius claimed that his grandfather at his death had left him the sovereignty together with his property, and that the people did not have it in their power to bestow on another what was not their own to give. This raising a general clamour and indignation among the people, he ordered them to be silent and asked them to feel no displeasure or resentment at his words, but in case Tarquinius had any just claim to advance in support of his pretensions, to summon him and if, after learning what he had to say, they should find that he was being wronged and was the more suitable man to rule, to entrust him with the leadership of the commonwealth. As for himself, he said, he now resigned the sovereignty and restored it to those to whom it belonged and from whom he had received it. After he had said this and was on the point of descending from the tribunal, there was a general outcry and many begged of him with groans not to surrender the sovereignty to anyone; and some of them even called out to stone Tarquinius. He, however, fearing summary punishment, since the crowds were already making a rush against him, fled, and his companions with him, while the entire populace with joy, applause, and many acclamations conducted Tullius as far as his house and saw him safely established there.

38 When Tarquinius failed in this attempt also, he was dismayed that from the senate, upon which he had chiefly relied, no assistance had come to him, and remaining at home for some time, he conversed only with his friends. Afterwards, when his wife advised him no longer to play the weakling or hesitate, but to have done with words and proceed to deeds, after he should first have obtained a reconciliation with Tullius by the intercession of friends — to the end that the king, trusting him as having become his friend, might be the less upon his guard against him — believing that her advice was most excellent, he began to pretend to repent of his past behaviour and through friends besought Tullius with many entreaties to forgive him. And he very easily persuaded the man, who was not only by his nature inclined to reconciliation but was also averse to waging an implacable contest with his daughter and his son-in-law; then, as soon as he saw a favourable opportunity, when the people were dispersed about the country for the gathering of the harvest, he appeared in public with his friends, all having swords under their garments, and giving the axes to some of his servants, he himself assumed the royal apparel and all the other insignia of royalty Then, going to the Forum, he took his stand before the senate-house and ordered the herald to summon the senators thither; indeed, many of the patricians who were privy to his design and were urging him on were by prearrangement ready in the Forum. And so the senators assembled. In the meantime someone went and informed Tullius, who was at home, that Tarquinius had appeared in public in royal apparel and was calling a meeting of the senate. And he, astonished at the other's rashness, set out from his house with more haste than prudence, attended by but a few. And going into the senate-house and seeing Tarquinius seated on the throne with all the other insignia of royalty, he exclaim: "Who, most wicked of men, gave you authority to assume this attire?" To which the other replied: "Your boldness and impudence, Tullius; for, though you were not even a free man, but a slave and the son of a slave mother, whom my grandfather got from among the captives, you nevertheless have dared to proclaim yourself king of the Romans." When Tullius heard this, he was so exasperated at the reproach that, heedless of his own safety, he rushed at him with the intent of forcing him to quit the throne. Tarquinius was pleased to see this, and leaping from his seat, seized and bore off the old man, who cried out and called upon his servants to assist him. When he got outside the senate-house, being a man of great vigour and in his prime, he raised him aloft and hurled him down the steps that lead from the senate-house to the comitium. The old man got up from his fall with great difficulty, and seeing the whole neighbourhood crowded with the followers of Tarquinius and noting a great dearth of his own friends, he set out for home lamenting, only a few persons supporting and escorting him, and as he went he dripped much blood and his entire body was in a wretched plight from his fall.

39 What happened next, terrible to hear yet astonishing and incredible to have been done — the deeds of his impious daughter — have been handed down to us. She, having been informed that her father had gone to the senate-house, and being in haste to know what would be the outcome of the affair, entered her carriage and rode to the Forum; and there, hearing what had passed and seeing Tarquinius standing upon the steps before the senate-house, she was the first person to salute him as king, which she did in a loud voice, and prayed to the gods that his seizing of the sovereignty might redound to the advantage of the Roman state. And after all the rest who had assisted him in gaining the sovereignty had also saluted him as king, she took him aside and said to him: "The first steps, Tarquinius, you have taken in the manner that was fitting; but it is impossible for you to hold the kingship securely so long as Tullius survives. For by his harangues he will again stir up the populace against you if he remains alive but the least part of this day; and you know how attached the whole body of the plebeians is to him. But come, even before he gets home, send some men and put him out of the way." Having said this, she again entered her carriage and departed. Tarquinius upon this occasion also approved of the advice of his most impious wife, and sent some of his servants against Tullius armed with swords; and they, swiftly covering the interval, overtook Tullius when he was already near his house and slew him. While his body lay freshly slain and quivering where it had been flung, his daughter arrived; and, the street through which her carriage was obliged to pass being very narrow, the mules became fractious at the sight of the body, and the groom who was leading them, moved by the piteous spectacle, stopped short and looked at his mistress. Upon her asking what possessed him not to lead the team on, he said: "Do you not see your father lying dead, Tullia, and that there is no other way but over his body?" This angered her to such a degree that she snatched up the stool from under her feet and hurled it at the groom, saying "Will you not lead on, accursed wretch, even over the body" Thereupon the groom, with lamentations caused more by the shocking deed than by the blow, led the mules forcibly over the body. This street, which before was called Orbian[65] Street, is, from this horrid and detestable incident, called by the Romans in their own language Impious Street, that is, *vicus Sceleratus*.

40 Such[66] was the death which fell to the lot of Tullius after he had reigned forty-four years. The Romans say that this man was the first who altered ancestral customs and laws by receiving the sovereignty, not from the senate and the people jointly, like all the former kings, but from the people alone, the poorer sort of whom he had won over by bribery and many other ways of courting popular favour; and this is true. For before this time, upon the death of a king it was the custom for the people to grant to the senate authority to establish such a form of government as they should think fit; and the senate created *interreges*, who appointed the best man king, whether he was a native Roman or a foreigner. And if the senate approved of the one so chosen and the people by their votes confirmed the choice, and if the auguries also gave their sanction to it, he assumed the sovereignty; but if any one of these formalities was lacking, they named a second, and then a third, if it so happened that the second was likewise not found unobjectionable by both men and gods. Tullius, on the contrary, at first assumed the guise of royal guardian, as I said before,[67] after which he gained the affections of the people by certain ingratiating acts and was appointed king by them alone. But as he proved to be a man of mildness and moderation, by his subsequent actions he put an end to the complaints caused by his not having observed the laws in all respects, and gave occasion for many to believe that, if he had not been made away with too soon, he would have changed the form of

---

65 Or Urbian (ὄρβιος may represent either form). The *clivus Orbius* (or *Urbius*) led up to the Carinae to the top of the Mons Oppius, a spur of the Esquiline. It was on the Esquiline that Tullius had his residence (chap. 13, 2).
66 *Cf.* Livy i. 48, 8 f.
67 See chap. 5, 2; 8, 1.

government to a democracy. And they say it was for this reason chiefly that some of the patricians joined in the conspiracy against him; that, being unable by any other means to overthrow his power, they took Tarquinius as an ally in their undertaking and aided him in gaining the sovereignty, it being their wish not only to weaken the power of the plebeians, which had received no small addition from the political measures of Tullius, but also to recover their own former dignity.

The death of Tullius having occasioned a great tumult and lamentation throughout the whole city, Tarquinius was afraid lest if the body should be carried through the Forum, according to the custom of the Romans, adorned with the royal robes and the other marks of honour usual in royal funerals, some attack might be made against him by the populace before he had firmly established his authority; and accordingly he would not permit any of the usual ceremonies to be performed in his honour. But the wife of Tullius, who was daughter to Tarquinius, the former king, with a few of her friends carried the body out of the city at night as if it had been that of some ordinary person; and after uttering many lamentations over the fate both of herself and of her husband and heaping countless imprecations upon her son-in-law and her daughter, she buried the body in the ground. Then, returning home from the sepulchre, she lived but one day after the burial, dying the following night. The manner of her death was not generally known. Some said that in her grief she lost all desire to live and died by her own hand; others, that she was put to death by her son-in-law and her daughter because of her compassion and affection for her husband. For the reasons mentioned, then, the body of Tullius could not be given a royal funeral and a stately monument; but his achievements have won lasting remembrance for all time. And it was made clear by another prodigy that this man was dear to the gods; in consequence of which that fabulous and incredible opinion I have already mentioned[68] concerning his birth also came to be regarded by many as true. For in the temple of Fortune which he himself had built there stood a gilded wooden statue of Tullius,[69] and when a conflagration occurred and everything else was destroyed, this statue alone remained uninjured by the flames. And even to this day, although the temple itself and all the objects in it, which were restored to their formed condition after the fire, are obviously the products of modern art, the statue, as aforetime, is of ancient workmanship; for it still remains an object of veneration by the Romans. Concerning Tullus these are all the facts that have been handed down to us.

41 He[70] was succeeded in the sovereignty over the Romans by Lucius Tarquinius, who obtained it, not in accordance with the laws, but by arms, in the fourth year of the sixty-first Olympiad[71] (the one in which Agatharchus of Corcyra won the foot-race), Thericles being archon at Athens. This man, despising not only the populace, but the patricians as well, by whom he had been brought to power, confounded and abolished the customs, the laws, and the whole native form of government, by which the former kings had ordered the commonwealth, and transformed his rule into an avowed tyranny. And first he placed about his person a guard of very daring men, both natives and foreigners, armed with swords and spears, who camped round the palace at night and attended him in the

---

68 In chap. 2.

69 As this statue was muffled up in a couple of robes, there was considerable difference of opinion as to whom it represented. Ovid (*Fasti* vi. 570 ff.) took it to be Tullius himself, but Pliny (*N. H.* viii. 194, 197) believed it was the goddess Fortune, while Livy (x. 23, 3) apparently regarded it as Chastity (Pudicitia). The temple, which stood in the Forum Boarium, has already been mentioned (chap. 27, 7); it was destroyed in the great fire of 213 B.C.

70 For chaps. 41 f. *cf.* Livy i. 49, 1-7.

71 532 B.C.

daytime wherever he went, effectually securing him from the attempts of conspirators. Secondly, he did not appear in public often or at stated times, but only rarely and unexpectedly; and he transacted the public business at home, for the most part, and in the presence of none but his most intimate friends, and only occasionally in the Forum. To none who sought an audience would he grant it unless he himself had sent for them; and even to those who did gain access to him he was not gracious or mild, but, as is the way with tyrants, harsh and irascible, and his aspect was terrifying rather than genial. His decisions in controversies relating to contracts he rendered, not with regard to justice and law, but according to his own moods. For these reasons the Romans gave him the surname of Superbus, which in our language means "the haughty"; and his grandfather they called Priscus, or, as we should say, "the elder," since both his names[72] were the same as those of the younger man.

42 When he thought he was now in secure possession of the sovereignty, he suborned the basest of his friends to bring charges against many of the prominent men and place them on trial for their lives. He began with such as were hostile to him and resented his driving of Tullius from power; and next he accused all those whom he thought to be aggrieved by the change and those who had great riches. When the accusers brought these men to trial, charging them with various fictitious crimes but chiefly with conspiring against the king, it was by Tarquinius himself, sitting as judge, that the charges were heard. Some of the accused he condemned to death and others to banishment, and seizing the property of both the slain and the exiled, he assigned some small part to the accusers but retained the largest part for himself. The result was therefore bound to be that many influential men, knowing the motives

---

72 Both had the praenomen Lucius.

underlying the plots against them, voluntarily, before they could be convicted of the charges brought against them, left the city to the tyrant, and the number of these was much greater than of the others. There were some who were even seized in their homes or in the country and secretly murdered by him, men of note, and not even their bodies were seen again. After he had destroyed the best part of the senate by death or by exile for life, he constituted another senate himself by working his own followers into the honours of the men who had disappeared;[73] nevertheless, not even these men were permitted by him to do or say anything but what he himself commanded. Consequently, when the senators who were left of those who had been enrolled in the senate under Tullius and who had hitherto been at odds with the plebeians and had expected the change in the form of government to turn out to their advantage (for Tarquinius had held out such promises to them with a view of deluding and tricking them) now found that they had no longer any share in the government, but that they too, as well as the plebeians, had been deprived of their freedom of speech, although they lamented their fate and suspected that things would be still more terrible in the future than they were at the moment, yet, having no power to prevent what was going on, they were forced to acquiesce in the existing state of affairs.

43 The plebeians, seeing this, looked upon them as justly punished and in their simplicity rejoiced at their discomfiture, imagining that the tyranny would be burdensome to the senators alone and would involve no danger to themselves. Nevertheless, to them also came even more hardships not long afterwards. For the laws drawn up by Tullius, by which they all received justice alike from each other and by which they were secured from being injured

---

73 Livy (i. 49, 6), on the contrary, states that Tarquinius determined to appoint no new members to the senate, in order that its small numbers might cause it to be scorned.

by the patricians, as before, in their contracts with them, were all abolished by Tarquinius, who did not leave even the tables on which the laws were written, but ordered these also to be removed from the Forum and destroyed. After this he abolished the taxes based on the census and revived the original form of taxation; and whenever he required money, the poorest citizen contributed the same amount as the richest. This measure ruined a large part of the plebeians, since every man was obliged to pay ten drachmae as his individual share of the very first tax. He also forbade the holding in future of any of the assemblies to which hitherto the inhabitants of the villages, the members of the *curiae*, or the residents of a neighbourhood, both in the city and in the country, had resorted in order to perform religious ceremonies and sacrifices in common,[74] lest large numbers of people, meeting together, should form secret conspiracies to overthrow his power. He had spies scattered about in many places who secretly inquired into everything that was said and done, while remaining undiscovered by most persons; and by insinuating themselves into the conversation of their neighbours and sometimes by reviling the tyrant themselves they sounded every man's sentiments. Afterwards they informed the tyrant of all who were dissatisfied with the existing state of affairs; and the punishments of those who were found guilty were severe and relentless.

44 Nor[75] was he satisfied merely with these illegal vexations o the plebeians, but, after selecting from among them such as were loyal to himself and fit for war, he compelled the rest to labour on the public works in the city; for he believed that monarchs are exposed to the greatest danger when the worst and the most needy of the citizens live in idleness, and at the same time he was eager to complete during his own reign the works his grandfather had left

---

74 See chap. 14, 3; 15, 3.
75 *Cf.* Livy i. 56, 1 f.; 57, 2.

half finished, namely, to extend to the river the drainage canals[76] which the other had begun to dig and also to surround the Circus,[77] which had been carried up no higher than the foundations, with covered porticos. At these undertakings all the poor laboured, receiving from him but a moderate allowance of grain. Some of them were employed in quarrying stone, others in hewing timber, some in driving the wagons that transported these materials, and others in carrying the burdens themselves upon their shoulders, still others in digging the subterranean drains and constructing the arches over them and in erecting the porticos and serving the various artisans who were thus employed; and smiths, carpenters and masons were taken from their private undertakings and kept at work in the service of the public. Thus the people, being worn out by these works, had no rest; so that the patricians, seeing their hardships and servitude, rejoiced in their turn and forgot their own miseries. Yet neither of them attempted to put a stop to these proceedings.

45 Tarquinius,[78] considering that those rulers who have not go their power legally but have obtained it by arms require a bod guard, not of natives only, but also of foreigners,[79] earnestly endeavoured to gain the friendship of the most illustrious and most powerful man of the whole Latin nation, by giving his daughter to him in marriage. This man was Octavius Mamilius, who traced his lineage back to Telegonus, the son of Ulysses and Circe; he lived in the city of Tusculum and was looked upon as a man of singular sagacity in political matters and a competent military commander. When Tarquinius had gained the friendship of this man and through him had won over the chief men at the head of affairs in

---

76 The underground sewers; cf. iii. 67, 5.
77 Literally, "the amphitheatrical race-course."
78 For chaps. 45-48 cf. Livy i. 49, 8-52, 5.
79 Cf. Aristotle, *Politics* 1285a, 28.

each city, he resolved then at last to try his strength in warfare in the open and to lead an expedition against the Sabines, who refused to obey his orders and looked upon themselves as released from the terms of their treaty upon the death of Tullius, with whom they had made it. After he had taken this resolution he sent messengers to invite to the council at Ferentinum[80] those who were accustomed to meet together there on behalf of the Latin nation, and appointed a day, intimating that he wished to consult with them concerning some important matters of mutual interest. The Latins, accordingly, appeared, but Tarquinius, who had summoned them, did not come at the time appointed. They waited for a long time and the majority of them regarded his behaviour as an insult. Among them was a certain man, named Turnus Herdonius, who lived in the city of Corilla and was powerful by reason of both of his riches and of his friends, valiant in war and not without ability in political debate; he was not only at variance with Mamilius, owing to their rivalry for power in the state, but also, on account of Mamilius, an enemy to Tarquinius, because the king had seen fit to take the other for his son-in-law in preference to himself. This man now inveighed at length against Tarquinius, enumerating all the other actions of the man which seemed to show evidence of arrogance and presumption, and laying particular stress upon his not appearing at the assembly which he himself had summoned, when all the rest were present. But Mamilius attempted to excuse Tarquinius, attributing his delay to some unavoidable cause, and asked that the assembly might be adjourned to the next day; and the presiding officers of the Latins were prevailed on to do so.

46 The next day Tarquinius appeared and, the assembly having been called together, he first excused his delay in a few words and at once entered upon a discussion of the supremacy, which he insisted

---

80 See the note on iii. 34, 3.

belonged to him by right, since Tarquinius, his grandfather, had held it, having acquired it by war; and he offered in evidence the treaties made by the various cities with Tarquinius. After saying a great deal in favour of his claim and concerning the treaties, and promising to confer great advantages on the cities in case they should continue in their friendship, he at last endeavoured to persuade them to join him in an expedition against the Sabines. When he had ceased speaking, Turnus, the man who had censured him for his failure to appear in time, came forward and sought to dissuade the council from yielding to him the supremacy, both on the ground that it did not belong to him by right and also because it would not be in the interest of the Latins to yield it to him; and he dwelt long upon both these points. He said that the treaties they had made with the grandfather of Tarquinius, when they granted to him the supremacy, had been terminated after his death, no clause having been added to those treaties providing that the same grant should descend to his posterity; and he showed that the man who claimed the right to inherit the grants made to his grandfather was of all men the most lawless and most wicked, and he recounted the things he had done in order to possess himself of the sovereignty over the Romans. After enumerating many terrible charges against him, he ended by informing them that Tarquinius did not hold even the kingship over the Romans in accordance with the laws by taking it with their consent, like the former kings, but had prevailed by arms and violence; and that, having established a tyranny, he was putting some of the citizens to death, banishing others, despoiling others of their estates, and taking from all of them their liberty both of speech and of action. He declared it would be an act of great folly and madness to hope for anything good and beneficent from a wicked and impious nature and to imagine that a man who had not spared such as were nearest to him both in blood and friendship would spare those who were strangers to him; and he advised them, as long as they had not yet accepted the yoke of slavery, to fight to the end against accepting it, judging from the misfortunes of others what it would be their own fate to suffer.

47 After Turnus had thus inveighed against Tarquinius and most of those present had been greatly moved by his words, Tarquinius asked that the following day might be set for his defence. His request was granted, and when the assembly had been dismissed, he summoned his most intimate friends and consulted with them how he ought to handle the situation. These began to suggest to him the arguments he should use in his defence and to run over the means by which he should endeavour to win back the favour of the majority; but Tarquinius himself declared that the situation did not call for any such measures, and gave it as his own opinion that he ought not to attempt to refute the accusations, but rather to destroy the accuser himself. When all had praised this opinion, he arranged with them the details of the attack and then set about carrying out a plot that was least likely to be foreseen by any man and guarded against. Seeking out the most evil among the servants of Turnus who conducted his pack animals with the baggage and bribing them with money, he persuaded them to take from him a large number of swords at nightfall and put them away in the baggage-chests[81] where they would not be in sight. The next day, when the assembly had convened, Tarquinius came forward and said that his defence against the accusations was a brief one, and he proposed that his accuser himself should be the judge of all the charges. "For, councillors," he said, "Turnus here, as a judge, himself acquitted me of everything of which he now accuses me, when he desired my

---

81 The word used in the text, σκευοφόροις, ordinarily means either "pack-animals" or "porters," neither of which meanings suits the context. Warmington suggests "baggage-chests," cf. οἰνοφόρον "wine-jar"; Capps would read σκευοφορίοις in the sense of "strongboxes." But possibly the compound means simply the baggage itself (so Polybius, vi. 40, 3).

daughter in marriage. But since he was thought unworthy of the marriage, as was but natural (for who in his senses would have refused Mamilius, the man of highest birth and greatest merit among the Latins, and consented to take for his son-in-law this man who cannot trace his family back even five generations?), in resentment for this slight he has now come to accuse me. Whereas, if he knew me to be such a man as he now charges, he ought not to have desired me then for a father-in-law; and if he thought me a good man when he asked me for my daughter in marriage, he ought not now to traduce me as a wicked man. So much concerning myself. As for you, councillors, who are running the greatest of dangers, it is not for you to consider now whether I am a good or a bad man (for this you may inquire into afterwards) but to provide both for your own safety and for the liberty of your respective cities. For a plot is being formed by this fine demagogue against you who are the chief men of your cities and are at the head of affairs; and he is prepared, after he has put the most prominent of you to death, to attempt to seize the sovereignty over the Latins, and has come here for that purpose. I do not say this from conjecture but from my certain knowledge, having last night received information of it from one of the accomplices in the conspiracy. And I will give you an incontestible proof of what I say, if you will go to his lodging, by showing you the arms that are concealed there."

48 After he had thus spoken they all cried out, and fearing for the men's safety, demanded that he prove the matter and not impose upon them. And Turnus, since he was unaware of the treachery, cheerfully offered to submit to the investigation and invited the presiding officers to search his lodging, saying that one of two things ought to come of it — either that he himself should be put to death, if he were found to have provided more arms than were necessary for his journey, or that the person who had accused him falsely should be punished. This offer was accepted; and those who went to his lodging found the swords which had been hidden in the baggage-chests by the servants. After this they would not permit Turnus to say anything more in his defence, but cast him into a pit and promptly dispatched him by burying him alive. As for Tarquinius, they praised him in the assembly as the common benefactor of all their cities for having saved the lives of their chief citizens, and they appointed him leader of their nation upon the same terms as they had appointed Tarquinius, his grandfather, and, after him, Tullius; and having engraved the treaty on pillars and confirmed it by oaths, they dismissed the assembly

49 After Tarquinius had obtained the supremacy over the Latins he sent ambassadors to the cities of the Hernicans and to those of the Volscians to invite them also to enter into a treaty of friendship and alliance with him. The Hernicans unanimously voted in favour of the alliance, but of the Volscians only two cities, Ecetra and Antium, accepted the invitation. And as a means of providing that the treaties made with those cities might endure forever Tarquinius resolved to designate a temple for the joint use of the Romans, the Latins, the Hernicans and such of the Volscians as had entered into the alliance, in order that, coming together each year at the appointed place, they might celebrate a general festival, feast together and share in common sacrifices. This proposal being cheerfully accepted by all of them, he appointed for their place of assembly a high mountain situated almost at the centre of these nations and commanding the city of the Albans; and he made a law that upon this mountain an annual festival should be celebrated, during which they should all abstain from acts of hostility against any of the others and should perform common sacrifices to Jupiter Latiaris, as he is called, and feast together, and he appointed the share each city was to contribute towards these sacrifices and the portion each of them was to receive. The cities that shared in this festival and sacrifice were forty-seven. These festivals and sacrifices the Romans celebrate to this day, calling them the "Latin Festivals";[82] and some of the cities that take part in them bring lambs, some cheeses, others a certain measure of milk, and others something of like nature.[83] And one bull is sacrificed in common by all of them, each city receiving its appointed share of the meat. The sacrifices they offer are on behalf of all and the Romans have the superintendence of them.

50 When[84] he had strengthened his power by these alliances also, he resolved to lead an army against the Sabines, choosing such of the Romans as he least suspected of being apt to assert their liberty if they became possessed of arms, and adding to them the auxiliary forces that had come from his allies, which were much more numerous than those of the Romans. And having laid waste the enemy's country and defeated in battle those who came to close quarters with him, he led his forces against the people called the Pometini, who lived in the city of Suessa[85] and had the reputation of both more prosperous than any of their neighbours and, because of their great good fortune, of being troublesome and oppressive to them all. He accused them of certain acts of brigandage and robbery and of giving haughty answers when asked for satisfaction therefor. But they were expecting war and were ready and in arms.

---

82 *Feriae Latinae.*

83 The MSS. add "a kind of honey-cake." This looks like a scribe's comment on some word that has been lost; or the word "honey-cake(s)" itself may have stood in the original text. Reiske proposed to read: "and others something of like nature, such as nuts and honey-cakes." Sintenis suggested: "and others an *itrion* (a cake made of sesame and honey), and others something of like nature," omitting the words "a kind of honey-cake."

84 *Cf.* Livy i. 53, 1-3.

85 This ancient Volscian city was often called Suessa Pometia. Its name survived in the adjectival forms Pomptinus and Pontinus.

Tarquinius engaged them in battle upon the frontiers, and after killing many of them and putting the rest to flight, he shut them up within their walls; and when they no longer ventured out of the city, he encamped near by, and surrounding it with a ditch and palisades, made continuous assaults upon the walls. The inhabitants defended themselves and withstood the hardships of the siege for a considerable time; but when their provisions began to fail and their strength was spent, since they neither received any assistance nor even obtained any respite, but the same men had to toil both night and day, they were taken by storm. Tarquinius, being now master of the city, put to death all he found in arms and permitted the soldiers to carry off the women and children and such others as allowed themselves to be made prisoners, together with a multitude of slaves not easy to be numbered; and he also gave them leave to carry away all the plunder of the city that they found both inside the walls and in the country. As to the silver and gold that was found there, he ordered it all to be brought to one place, and having reserved a tenth part of it to build a temple, he distributed the rest among the soldiers. The quantity of silver and gold taken upon this occasion was so considerable that every one of the soldiers received for his share five minae of silver, and the tenth part reserved for the gods amounted to no less than four hundred talents.[86]

51 While he was still tarrying at Suessa a messenger brought the news that the flower of the Sabine youth had set out and made an irruption into the territory of the Romans in two large armies and were laying waste the country, one of them being encamped near Eretum and the other near Fidenae, and that unless a strong force

---

86 Livy i. 55, 8 f.; *cf.* 53, 3) favours Fabius Pictor's estimate of 40 talents as the amount realized from the sale of the booty and devoted to the construction of the temple of Jupiter Capitolinus, as against Piso's statement that the amount was 40,000 pounds of silver. The 400 talents of Dionysius are probably meant to be the equivalent of Piso's figure.

should oppose them everything there would be lost. When Tarquinius heard this he left a small part of his army at Suessa, ordering them to guard the spoils and the baggage, and leading the rest of his forces in light marching order against that body of the Sabines which was encamped near Eretum, he pitched camp upon an eminence within a short distance of the enemy. And the generals of the Sabines having resolved to send for the army that was at Fidenae and to give battle at daybreak, Tarquinius learned of their intention (for the bearer of the letter from these generals to the others had been captured) and availed himself of this fortunate incident by employing the following stratagem: He divided his army into two bodies and sent one of them in the night without the enemy's knowledge to occupy the road that led from Fidenae; and drawing up the other division as soon as it was fully day, he marched out of his camp as if to give battle. The Sabines, seeing the small number of the enemy and believing that their other army from Fidenae would come up at any moment, boldly marched out against them. These armies, therefore, engaged and the battle was for a long time doubtful; then the troops which had been sent out in advance by Tarquinius during the night turned back in their march and prepared to attack the Sabines in the rear. The Sabines, upon seeing them and recognizing them by their arms and their standards, were upset in their calculations, and throwing away their arms, sought to save themselves by flight. But escape was impossible for most of them, surrounded as they were by enemies, and the Roman horse, pressing upon them from all sides, hemmed them in; so that only a few were prompt enough to escape disaster, but the greater part were either cut down by the enemy or surrendered. Nor was there any resistance made even by those who were left in the camp, but this was taken at the first onset; and there, besides the Sabines' own effects, all the possessions that had been stolen from the Romans, together with many captives, were recovered still uninjured and were restored to those who had lost them.

52 After Tarquinius had succeeded in his first attempt he marched with his forces against the rest of the Sabines who were encamped near Fidenae and were not yet aware of the destruction of their companions. It happened that these also had set out from their camp and were already on the march when, coming near to the Roman army, they saw the heads of their commanders fixed upon pikes (for the Romans held them forward in order to strike the enemy with terror), and learning thus that their other army had been destroyed, they no longer performed any deed of bravery, but turning to supplications and entreaties, they surrendered. The Sabines, having had both their armies snatched away in so shameful and disgraceful a manner, were reduced to slender hopes, and fearing that their cities would be taken by assault, they sent ambassadors to treat for peace, offering to surrender, become subjects of Tarquinius, and pay tribute for the future. He accordingly made peace with them and received the submission of their cities upon the same terms,[87] and then returned to Suessa. Thence he marched with the forces he had left there, the spoils he had taken, and the rest of his baggage, to Rome, bringing back his army loaded with riches. After that he also made many incursions into the country of the Volscians, sometimes with his whole army and sometimes with part of it, and captured much booty. But when now most of his undertakings were succeeding according to his wish, a war broke out on the part of his neighbours which proved not only of long duration (for it lasted seven years without

---

87 This may possibly mean "upon the very terms they offered"; but it is more probable that some words have been lost from the text. Sylburg (see critical note) proposed: "on the same terms on which his grandfather (had done so)"; *cf.* iii. 66, 3. Schnelle proposed: "on the same terms that they had made with Tullius"; *cf.* iv. 45, 2.

intermission) but also important because of the severe and unexpected misfortunes with which it was attended. I will relate briefly from what causes it sprang and how it ended, since it was brought to a conclusion by a clever ruse and a novel stratagem.

53 There[88] was a city of the Latins, which had been founded by the Albans, distant one hundred stades from Rome and standing upon the road that leads to Praeneste. The name of this city was Gabii. To-day not all parts of it are still inhabited, but only those that lie next the highway and are given up to inns; but at that time it was as large and populous as any city. One may judge both of its extent and importance by observing the ruins of the buildings in many places and the circuit of the wall, most parts of which are still standing. To this city had flocked some of the Pometini who had escaped from Suessa when Tarquinius took their town and many of the banished Romans. These, by begging and imploring the Gabini to avenge the injuries they had received and by promising great rewards if they should be restored to their own possessions, and also by showing the overthrow of the tyrant to be not only possible but easy, since the people in Rome too would aid them, prevailed upon them, with the encouragement of the Volscians (for these also had sent ambassadors to them and desired their alliance) to make war upon Tarquinius. After this both the Gabini and the Romans made incursions into and laid waste one another's territories with large armies and, as was to be expected, engaged in battles, now with small numbers on each side and now with all their forces. In these actions the Gabini often put the Romans to flight and pursuing them up to their walls,[89] slew many and ravaged their country with impunity; and often the Romans drove the Gabini back and shutting

88 For chaps.53-58 *cf.* Livy i. 53, 4-54, 10.
89 Kiessling (see critical note) would place the phrase "up to their walls" after "ravaged their country with impunity" Cobet after "the Romans drove the Gabini back."

them up within their city, carried off their slaves together with much booty.

54 As these things happened continually, both of them were obliged to fortify the strongholds in their territories and to garrison them so that they might serve as places of refuge for the husbandmen; and sallying out from these strongholds in a body they would fall upon and destroy bands of robbers and any small groups they might discover that had been detached from a large army and, as would naturally be expected in forages, were observing no order, through contempt of the enemy And the both were obliged in their fear of the sudden assaults of the other to raise the walls and dig ditches around those parts of their cities that were vulnerable and could easily be taken by means o scaling-ladders. Tarquinius was particularly active in taking these precautions and employed a large number of workmen in strengthening those parts of the city walls that looked toward Gabii by widening the ditch, raising the walls, and placing the towers at shorter intervals; for on this side the city seemed to be the weakest, the rest of the circuit being tolerably secure and difficult of approach. But, as is apt to happen to all cities in the course of long wars, when the country is laid waste by the continual incursions of the enemy and no longer produces its fruits, both were bound to experience a dearth of all provisions and to feel terrible discouragement regarding the future; but the want of necessaries was felt more keenly by the Romans than by the Gabini and the poorest among them, who suffered most, thought a treaty ought to be made with the enemy and an end put to the war upon any terms they might grant.

55 While Tarquinius was dismayed at the situation and neither willing to end the war upon dishonourable terms nor able to hold out any longer, but was contriving all sorts of schemes and devising ruses of every kind, the eldest[90] of his sons, Sextus by name, privately communicated to him his own plan; and when Tarquinius, who thought the enterprise bold and full of danger, yet not impossible after all, had given him leave to act as he thought fit, he pretended to be at odds with his father about putting an end to the war. Then, after being scourged with rods in the Forum by his father's order and receiving other indignities, so that the affair became noised abroad, he first sent some of his most intimate friends as deserters to inform the Gabini secretly that he had resolved to betake himself to them and make war against his father, provided he should receive pledges that they would protect him as well as the rest of the Roman fugitives and not deliver him up to his father in the hope of settling their private enmities to their own advantage. When the Gabini listened to this proposal gladly and agreed not to do him any wrong, he went over to them as a deserter, taking with him many of his friends and clients, and also, in order to increase their belief in the genuineness of his revolt from his father, carrying along a great deal of silver and gold. And many flocked to him afterwards from Rome, pretending to flee from the tyranny of Tarquinius, so that he now had a strong body of men about him. The Gabini looked upon the large numbers who came over to them as a great accession of strength and made no doubt of reducing Rome in a short time. Their delusion was further increased by the actions of this rebellious son, who continually made incursions into his father's territory and captured much booty; for his father, knowing beforehand what parts he would visit, took care that there should be plenty of plunder there and that the places should be unguarded, and he kept sending men to be destroyed by his son, selecting from among the citizens those whom he held in suspicion. In consequence of all this the Gabini, believing the man to be their

---

90   Livy (i. 53, 5) calls Sextus the youngest son.

loyal friend and an excellent general — and many of them had also been bribed by him — promoted him to the supreme command.

56 After Sextus had obtained so great power by deception and trickery, he sent one of his servants to his father, without the knowledge of the Gabini, both to inform him of the power he had gained and to inquire what he should now do. Tarquinius, who did not wish even the servant to learn the instructions that he sent his son, led the messenger into the garden that lay beside the palace. It happened that in this garden there were poppies growing, already full of heads and ready to be gathered; and walking among these, he kept striking and knocking off the heads of all the tallest poppies with his staff. Having done this, he sent the messenger away without giving any answer to his repeated inquiries. Herein, it seems to me, he imitated the thought of Thrasybulus the Milesian. For Thrasybulus returned no verbal answer to Periander, the tyrant of Corinth, by the messenger Periander once sent him to inquire how he might most securely establish his power; but, ordering the messenger to follow him into a field of wheat and breaking off the ears that stood above the rest, he threw them upon the ground, thereby intimating that Periander ought to lop off and destroy the most illustrious of the citizens. When, therefore, Tarquinius did a like thing on this occasion, Sextus understood his father's meaning and knew that he was ordering him to put to death the most eminent of the Gabini. He accordingly called an assembly of the people, and after saying a great deal about himself he told them that, having fled to them with his friends upon the assurance they had given him, he was in danger of being seized by certain persons and delivered up to his father and that he was ready to resign his power and desired to quit their city before any mischief befell him; and while saying this he wept and lamented his fate as those do who are in very truth in terror of their lives.

Book IV

57 When the people became incensed at this and were eagerly demanding to know who the men were who were intending to betray them, he named Antistius Petro, who not only had been the author of many excellent measures in time of peace but had also often commanded their armies and had thus become the most distinguished of all the citizens. And when this man endeavoured to clear himself and, from the consciousness of his innocence, offered to submit to any examination whatever, Sextus said he wished to send some others to search Petro's house, but that he himself would stay with him in the assembly till the persons sent should return. It seems that he had bribed some of the servants of Petro to take the letters prepared for Petro's destruction and sealed with the seal of Tarquinius and to hide them in their master's house. And when the men sent to make the search (for Petro made no objection but gave permission for his house to be searched), having discovered the letters in the place where they had been hidden, appeared in the assembly with many sealed letters, among them the one addressed to Antistius, Sextus declared he recognized his father's seal, and breaking open the letter, he gave it to the secretary and ordered him to read it. The purport of the letter was that Antistius should, if possible, deliver up his son to him alive, but if he could not do this, that he should cut off his head and send it. In return for this Tarquinius said that, besides the rewards he had already promised, he would grant Roman citizenship both to him and those who had assisted him in the business, and would admit them all into the number of the patricians, and furthermore bestow on them houses, allotments of land and many other fine gifts. Thereupon the Gabini became so incensed against Antistius, who was thunderstruck at this unexpected calamity and unable in his grief to utter a word, that they stoned him to death and appointed Sextus to inquire into and punish the crimes of his accomplices. Sextus committed the guarding of the gates to his own followers, lest any of the accused should escape him; and sending to the houses of the most prominent of the Gabini, he put many good men to death.

58 While these things were going on and all the city was in an uproar, as was natural in consequence of so great a calamity, Tarquinius, having been informed by letter of all that was passing, marched thither with his army, approached the city about the middle of the night, and then, when the gates had been opened by those appointed for the purpose, entered with his forces and made himself master of the city without any trouble. When this disaster became known, all the citizens bewailed the fate awaiting them; for they expected slaughter, enslavement and all the horrors that usually befall those captured by tyrants, and, as the best that could happen to them, had already condemned themselves to slavery, the loss of their property and like calamities. However, Tarquinius did none of the things that they were expecting and dreading even though he was harsh of temper and inexorable in punishing his enemies. For he neither put any of the Gabini to death, nor banished any from the city, nor punished any of them with disfranchisement or the loss of their property; but calling an assembly of the people and changing to the part of a king from that of a tyrant, he told them that he not only restored their own city to them and allowed them to keep the property they possessed, but in addition granted to all of them the rights of Roman citizens. It was not, however, out of goodwill to the Gabini that he adopted this course, but in order to establish more securely his mastery over the Romans. For he believed that the strongest safeguard both for himself and for his family would be the loyalty of those who, contrary to their expectation, had been preserved and had recovered all their possessions. And, in order that they might no longer have any fear regarding the future or any doubt of the permanence of his concessions, he ordered the terms upon which they were to be friends to be set down in writing, and then ratified the treaty immediately in the assembly and took an oath over the victims to observe it. There is a memorial of this treaty at Rome in the temple of Jupiter Fidius,[91] whom the Romans call Sancus; it is a wooden shield covered with the hide of the ox that was sacrificed at the time they confirmed the treaty by their oaths, and upon it are inscribed in ancient characters the terms of the treaty. After Tarquinius had thus settled matters and appointed his son Sextus king of the Gabini, he led his army home. Such was the outcome of the war with the Gabini.

59 After[92] this achievement Tarquinius gave the people a respite from military expeditions and wars, and being desirous of performing the vows made by his grandfather, devoted himself to the building of the sanctuaries. For the elder Tarquinius, while h was engaged in an action during his last war with the Sabines, had made a vow to build temples to Jupiter, Juno and Minerva if he should gain the victory; and he had finished off the peak on which he proposed to erect the temples to these gods by means of retaining walls and high banks of earth, as I mentioned in the preceding Book;[93] but he did not live long enough to complete the building of the temples. Tarquinius, therefore, proposing to erect this structure with the tenth part of the spoils taken at Suessa, set all the artisans at the work. It was at this time, they say, that a wonderful prodigy appeared under ground; for when they were digging the foundations and the excavation had been carried down to a great depth, there was found the head of a man newly slain with the face like that of a living man and the blood which flowed from the severed head warm and fresh. Tarquinius, seeing this prodigy, ordered the workmen to leave off digging, and assembling the native soothsayers, inquired of

---

91 The full Roman title was *Semo Sancus Dius Fidius*. For Sancus see ii. 49, 2.
92 For chaps. 59-61 *cf.* Livy i. 55.
93 iii. 69, 1.

them what the prodigy meant. And when they could give no explanation but conceded to the Tyrrhenians the mastery of this science, he inquired of them who was the ablest soothsayer among the Tyrrhenians, and when he had found out, sent the most distinguished of the citizens to him as ambassadors.

60 When these men came to the house of the soothsayer they met by chance a youth who was just coming out, and informing him that they were ambassadors sent from Rome who wanted to speak with the soothsayer, they asked him to announce them to him. The youth replied: "The man you wish to speak with is my father. He is busy at present, but in a short time you may be admitted to him. And while you are waiting for him, acquaint me with the reason of your coming. For if, through inexperience, you are in danger of committing an error in phrasing your question when you have been informed by me you will be able to avoid any mistake; for the correct form of question is not the least important part of the art of divination." The ambassadors resolved to follow his advice and related the prodigy to him. And when the youth had heard it, after a short pause he said: "Hear me, Romans. My father will interpret this prodigy to you and will tell you no untruth, since it is not right for a soothsayer to speak falsely; but, in order that you may be guilty of no error or falsehood in what you say or in the answers you give to his questions (for it is of importance to you to know these things beforehand), be instructed by me. After you have related the prodigy to him he will tell you that he does not fully understand what you say and will circumscribe with his staff some piece of ground or other; then he will say to you: 'This is the Tarpeian Hill, and this is part of it that faces the east, this the part that faces the west, this point is north and the opposite is south.' These parts he will point out to you with his staff and then ask you in which of these parts the head was found. What answer, therefore, do I advise you to make?

400

Do not admit that the prodigy was found in any of these places he shall inquire about when he points them out with his staff, but say that it appeared among you at Rome on the Tarpeian Hill. If you stick to these answers and do not allow yourselves to be misled by him, he, well knowing that fate cannot be changed, will interpret to you without concealment what the prodigy means."

61 Having received these instructions, the ambassadors, as soon as the old man was at leisure and a servant came out to fetch them, went in and related the prodigy to the soothsayer. He, craftily endeavouring to mislead them, drew circular lines upon the ground and then other straight lines, and asked them with reference to each place in turn whether the head had been found there; but the ambassadors, not at all disturbed in mind, stuck to the one answer suggested to them by the soothsayer's son, always naming Rome and the Tarpeian Hill, and asked the interpreter not to appropriate the omen to himself,[94] but to answer in the most sincere and just manner. The soothsayer, accordingly, finding it impossible for him either to impose upon the men or to appropriate the omen, said to them: "Romans, tell your fellow citizens it is ordained by fate that the place in which you found the head shall be the head of all Italy." Since that time the place is called the Capitoline Hill from the head that was found there; for the Romans call heads *capita*. Tarquinius, having heard these things from the ambassadors, set the artisans to work and built the greater part of the temple, though he was not able to complete the whole work, being driven from power too soon; but the Roman people brought it to completion in the third consulship. It stood upon a high base and was eight hundred feet in circuit, each side measuring close to two hundred feet; indeed, one would find the excess of the length over the width to be but slight, in

---

94 *i.e.*, not to make it apply to the actual spot on Etruscan soil to which he was pointing.

fact not a full fifteen feet. For the temple that was built in the time of our fathers after the burning of this one[95] was erected upon the same foundations, and differed from the ancient structure in nothing but the costliness of the materials, having three rows of columns on the front, facing the south, and a single row on each side. The temple consists of three parallel shrines, separated by party walls; the middle shrine is dedicated to Jupiter, while on one side stands that of Juno and on the other that of Minerva, all three being under one pediment and one roof.

62 It is said that during the reign of Tarquinius another very wonderful piece of good luck also came to the Roman state, conferred upon it by the favour of some god or other divinity; and this good fortune was not of short duration, but throughout the whole existence of the country it has often saved it from great calamities. A certain woman who was not a native of the country came to the tyrant wishing to sell him nine books filled with Sibylline oracles; but when Tarquinius refused to purchase the books at the price she asked, she went away and burned three of them. And not long afterwards, bringing the remaining six books, she offered to sell them for the same price. But when they thought her a fool and mocked at her for asking the same price for the smaller number of books that she had been unable to get for even the larger number, she again went away and burned half of those that were left; then, bringing the remaining books, she asked the same amount of money for these. Tarquinius, wondering at the woman's purpose, sent for the augurs and acquainting them with the matter, asked them what he should do. These, knowing by certain signs that he had rejected a god-sent blessing, and declaring it to be a great misfortune that he had not purchased all the books, directed him to

---

95 The old temple was burned in 83 B.C. Concerning the erection of the new edifice see Introd., p. viii.

pay the woman all the money she asked and to get the oracles that were left. The woman, after delivering the books and bidding him take great care of them, disappeared from among men. Tarquinius chose two men of distinction from among the citizens and appointing two public slaves to assist them, entrusted to them the guarding of the books; and when one of these men, named Marcus Atilius, seemed to have been faithless to his trust[96] and was informed upon by one of the public slaves, he ordered him to be sewed up in a leather bag and thrown into the sea as a parricide.[97] Since the expulsion of the kings, the commonwealth, taking upon itself the guarding of these oracles, entrusts the care of them to persons of the greatest distinction, who hold this office for life, being exempt from military service and from all civil employments, and it assigns public slaves to assist them, in whose absence the others are not permitted to inspect the oracles. In short, there is no possession of the Romans, sacred or profane, which they guard so carefully as they do the Sibylline oracles. They consult them, by order of the senate, when the state is in the grip of party strife or some great misfortune has happened to them in war, or some important prodigies and apparitions have been seen which are difficult of interpretation, as has often happened. These oracles till the time of

---

96 Or, adopting Bücheler's emendation (see critical note), "to have been guilty of [giving out] information" or "guilty in the matter of an inquiry." Atilius, according to Zonaras (vii. 11), was accused of accepting a bribe to permit the copying of some of the oracles.

97 The etymology of *par(r)icidium* is much disputed, but from very early times the word seems to have meant the murder of a near relative, especially the murder of a parent, which perhaps gave rise to the normal form *parricidium*, as if for *patricidium*. The word also came to be used, as here, of treason — the "murder of the fatherland." Those found guilty of this crime were punished by being sewed up in a leather bag together with a dog, a cock, a viper and an ape and then cast into the sea. See J. Strachan-Davidson, *Problems of the Roman Criminal Law*, vol. i., pp. 21-24.

the Marsian War, as it was called,[98] were kept underground in the temple of Jupiter Capitolinus in a stone chest under the guard of ten men.[99] But when the temple was burned after the close of the one hundred and seventy-third Olympiad,[100] either purposely, as some think, or by accident, these oracles together with all the offerings consecrated to the god were destroyed by the fire. Those which are now extant have been scraped together from many places, some from the cities of Italy, others from Erythrae in Asia (whither three envoys were sent by vote of the senate to copy them), and others were brought from other cities, transcribed by private persons. Some of these are found to be interpolations among the genuine Sibylline oracles, being recognized as such by means of the so-called acrostics.[101] In all this I am following the account given by Terentius Varro in his work on religion.[102]

63 Besides these achievements of Tarquinius both in peace and in war, he founded two colonies.[103] One of them, called Signia, was not planned, but was due to chance, the soldiers having established their winter quarters in the place and built their camp in such a manner as not to differ in any respect from a city. But it was with deliberate purpose that he settled Circeii, because the place was advantageously situated in relation both to the Pomptine plain, which is the largest of all the plains in the Latin country, and to the sea that is contiguous to it. For it is a fairly high rock in the nature of

---

98 The "Social War," 91-88 B.C.

99 These ten men had replaced the original two; after Sulla there were fifteen (the *quindecimviri sacris faciundis*).

100 83 B.C.; *cf.* ch. 61, 4.

101 The oracles were written in Greek hexameters. Those regarded as genuine were composed as acrostics, the initial letters of the successive verses spelling out the words of the first verse (or first verses, probably, if the oracle was a long one). See Cicero, *de Div.* ii. 54, 111 f.; also H. Diels, *Sibyllinische Blätter*.

102 This was the second part of his *Antiquities*.

103 *Cf.* Livy i. 56, 3.

a peninsula, situated on the Tyrrhenian Sea; and tradition has it that Circe, the daughter of the Sun, lived there. He assigned both these colonies to two of his sons as their founders, giving Circeii to Arruns and Signia to Titus; and being now no longer in any fear concerning his power, he was both driven from power and exiled because of the outrageous deed of Sextus, his eldest son, who ruined a married woman. Of this calamity that was to overtake his house, Heaven had forewarned him by numerous omens,[104] and particularly by this final one: Two eagles, coming in the spring to the garden near the palace, made their aerie on the top of a tall palm tree. While these eagles had their young as yet unfledged, a flock of vultures, flying to the aerie, destroyed it and killed the young birds; and when the eagles returned from their feeding, the vultures, tearing them[105] and striking them with the flat of their wings, drove them from the palm tree. Tarquinius, seeing these omens, took all possible precautions to avert his destiny but proved unable to conquer fate; for when the patricians set themselves against him and the people were of the same mind, he was driven from power. Who the authors of this insurrection were and by what means they came into control of affairs, I shall endeavour to relate briefly.

64 Tarquinius[106] was then laying siege to Ardea, alleging as his reason that it was receiving the Roman fugitives and assisting them in their endeavours to return home. The truth was, however, that he had designs against this city on account of its wealth, since it was the most flourishing of all the cities in Italy. But as the Ardeates bravely defended themselves and the siege was proving a lengthy one, both the Romans who were in the camp, being fatigued by the length of the war, and those at Rome, who had become exhausted by the war taxes, were ready to revolt if any occasion offered for

---

104 For one of these see Livy, i. 56, 4.
105 Perhaps we should follow Reiske in supplying "with their beaks."
106 For chaps. 64-67 cf. Livy i. 57 f.

making a beginning. At this time Sextus, the eldest son of Tarquinius, being sent by his father to a city called Collatia to perform certain military services, lodged at the house of his kinsman, Lucius Tarquinius, surnamed Collatinus. This man is said by Fabius to have been the son of Egerius, who, as I have shown earlier,[107] was the nephew of Tarquinius the first Roman king of that name, and having been appointed governor of Collatia, was not only himself called Collatinus from his living there, but also left the same surname to his posterity. But, for my part, I am persuaded that he too was a grandson of Egerius,[108] inasmuch as he was of the same age as the sons of Tarquinius, as Fabius and the other historians have recorded; for the chronology confirms me in this opinion. Now it happened that Collatinus was then at the camp, but his wife, who was a Roman woman, the daughter of Lucretius, a man of distinction, entertained him, as a kinsman of her husband, with great cordiality and friendliness. This matron, who excelled all the Roman women in beauty as well as in virtue, Sextus tried to seduce; he had already long entertained this desire, whenever he visited his kinsman, and he thought he now had a favourable opportunity. Going, therefore, to bed after supper, he waited a great part of the night, and then, when he thought all were asleep, he got up and came to the room where he knew Lucretia slept, and without being discovered by her slaves, who lay asleep at the door, he went into the room sword in hand.

65 When he paused at the woman's bedside and she, hearing the noise, awakened and asked who it was, he told her his name and bade her be silent and remain in the room, threatening to kill her if she attempted either to escape or to cry out. Having terrified the woman in this manner, he offered her two alternatives, bidding her

107 iii. 50, 3.
108 That is, as Tarquinius likewise was a grandson of the elder Tarquinius.

choose whichever she herself preferred — death with dishonour or life with happiness. "For," he said, "if you will consent to gratify me, I will make you my wife, and with me you shall reign, for the present, over the city my father has given me, and, after his death, over the Romans, the Latins, the Tyrrhenians, and all the other nations he rules; for I know that I shall succeed to my father's kingdom, as is right, since I am his eldest son. But why need I inform you of the many advantages which attend royalty, all of which you shall share with me, since you are well acquainted with them? If, however, you endeavour to resist from a desire to preserve your virtue, I will kill you and then slay one of your slaves, and having laid both your bodies together, will state that I had caught you misbehaving with the slave and punished you to avenge the dishonour of my kinsman; so that your death will be attended with shame and reproach and your body will be deprived both of burial and every other customary rite." And as he kept urgently repeating his threats and entreaties and swearing that he was speaking the truth as to each alternative, Lucretia, fearing the ignominy of the death he threatened, was forced to yield and to allow him to accomplish his desire.

66 When it was day, Sextus, having gratified his wicked and baneful passion, returned to the camp. But Lucretia, overwhelmed with shame at what had happened, got into her carriage in all haste, dressed in black raiment under which she had a dagger concealed, and set out for Rome, without saying a word to any person who saluted her when they met or making answer to those who wished to know what had befallen her, but continued thoughtful and downcast, with her eyes full of tears. When she came to her father's house, where some of his relations happened to be present, she threw herself at his feet and embracing his knees, wept for some time without uttering a word. And when he raised her up and asked her what had befallen her, she said: "I come to you as a suppliant, father, having endured terrible and intolerable outrage, and I beg you to avenge me and not to overlook your daughter's having suffered worse things than death." When her father as well as all the others was struck with wonder at hearing this and he asked her to tell who had outraged her and in what manner, she said: "You will hear of my misfortunes very soon, father; but first grant me this favour I ask of you. Send for as many of your friends and kinsmen as you can, so that they may hear the report from me, the victim of terrible wrongs, rather than from others. And when you have learned to what shameful and dire straits I was reduced, consult with them in what manner you will avenge both me and yourself. But do not let the time between be long."

67 When, in response to his hasty and urgent summons, the most prominent men had come to his house as she desired, she began at the beginning and told them all that had happened. Then after embracing her father and addressing many entreaties both to him and to all present and praying to the gods and other divinities to grant her a speedy departure from life, she drew the dagger she was keeping concealed under her robes, and plunging it into he breast, with a single stroke pierced her heart. Upon this the women beat their breasts and filled the house with their shrieks and lamentations, but her father, enfolding her body in his arms, embraced it, and calling her by name again and again, ministered to her, as though she might recover from her wound, until in his arms, gasping and breathing out her life, she expired. This dreadful scene struck the Romans who were present with so much horror and compassion that they all cried out with one voice that they would rather die a thousand deaths in defence of their liberty than suffer such outrages to be committed by the tyrants. There was among them a certain man, named Publius Valerius, a descendant of one of those Sabines who came to Rome with Tatius, and a man of action and prudence. This man was sent by them to the camp both to acquaint the husband of Lucretia with what had happened and with his aid to bring about a revolt of the army from the tyrants. He was no sooner outside the gates than he chanced to meet Collatinus, who was coming to the city from the camp and knew nothing of the misfortunes that had befallen his household. And with him came Lucius Junius, surnamed Brutus, which, translated into the Greek language, would be *êlithios* or "dullard." Concerning this man, since the Romans say that he was the prime mover in the expulsion of the tyrants, I must say a few words before continuing my account, to explain who he was and of what descent and for what reason he got his surname, which did not at all describe him.

68 The[109] father of Brutus was Marcus Junius, a descendant of one of the colonists in the company of Aeneas, and a man who for his merits was ranked among the most illustrious of the Romans; his mother was Tarquinia, a daughter of the first King Tarquinius. He himself enjoyed the best upbringing and education that his country afforded and he had a nature not averse to any noble accomplishment. Tarquinius, after he had caused Tullius to be slain, put Junius' father also to death secretly, together with many other worthy men, not for any crime, but because he was in possession of the inheritance of an ancient family enriched by the good fortune of his ancestors, the spoils of which Tarquinius coveted; and together with the father he slew the elder son, who showed indications of a noble spirit unlikely to permit the death of his father to go unavenged. Thereupon Brutus, being still a youth and entirely destitute of all assistance from his family, undertook to follow the most prudent of all courses, which was to feign a stupidity that was not his; and he continued from that time to maintain this pretence

109 For chaps. 68 f. *cf.* Livy i. 56, 5-12.

of folly from which he acquired his surname, till he thought the proper time had come to throw it off. This saved him from suffering any harm at the hands of the tyrant at a time when many good men were perishing.

69 For Tarquinius, despising in him this stupidity, which was only apparent and not real, took all his inheritance from him, an allowing him a small maintenance for his daily support, kept him under his own authority, as an orphan who still stood in need of guardians, and permitted him to live with his own sons, not by way of honouring him as a kinsman, which was the pretence he made to his friends, but in order that Brutus, by saying many stupid things and by acting the part of a real fool, might amuse the lads. And when he sent two of his sons, Arruns and Titus, to consult the Delphic oracle concerning the plague[110] (for some uncommon malady had in his reign descended upon both maids and boys, and many died of it, but it fell with the greatest severity and without hope of cure upon women with child, destroying the mothers in travail together with their infants), desiring to learn from the god both the cause of this distemper and the remedy for it, he sent Brutus along with the lads, at their request, so that they might have somebody to laugh at and abuse. When the youths had come to the oracle and had received answers concerning the matter upon which they were sent, they made their offerings to the god and laughed much at Brutus for offering a wooden staff to Apollo; in reality he had secretly hollowed the whole length of it like a tube and inserted a rod of gold. After this they inquired of the god which of them was destined to succeed to the sovereignty of Rome; and the god answered, "the one who should first kiss his mother." The youths, therefore, not knowing the meaning of the oracle, agreed together to kiss their mother at the

---

110 Livy states (i. 56, 4 f.) that the oracle was consulted concerning an omen that had appeared in the palace.

same time, desiring to possess the kingship jointly; but Brutus, understanding what the god meant, as soon as he landed in Italy, stooped to the earth and kissed it, looking upon that as the common mother of all mankind. Such, then, were the earlier events in the life of this man.

70 On[111] the occasion in question, when Brutus had heard Valerius relate all that had befallen Lucretia and describe her violent death, he lifted up his hands to Heaven and said: "O Jupiter and all ye gods who keep watch over the lives of men, has that time now come in expectation of which I have both keeping up this pretence in my manner of life? Has fate ordained that the Romans shall by me and through me be delivered from this intolerable tyranny?" Having said this, he went in all haste to the house together with Collatinus and Valerius. When they came in Collatinus, seeing Lucretia lying in the midst and her father embracing her, uttered a loud cry and, throwing his arms about his wife's body, kept kissing her and calling her name and talking to her as if she had been alive; for he was out of his mind by reason of his calamity While he and her father were pouring forth their lamentations in turn and the whole house was filled with wailing and mourning, Brutus, looking at them, said: "You will have countless opportunities, Lucretius, Collatinus, and all of you who are kinsmen of this woman, to bewail her fate; but now let us consider how to avenge her, for that is what the present moment calls for." His advice seemed good; and sitting down by themselves and ordering the slaves and attendants to withdraw, they consulted together what they ought to do. And first Brutus began to speak about himself, telling them that what was generally believed to be his stupidity was not real, but only assumed, and informing them of the reasons which had induced him to submit to this pretence; whereupon they regarded him as the wisest

111 For chaps. 70 f. *cf.* Livy i. 59, 1 f., 7.

of all men. Next he endeavoured to persuade them all to be of one mind in expelling both Tarquinius and his sons from Rome; and he used many alluring arguments to this end. When he found they were all of the same mind, he told them that what was needed was neither words nor promises, but deeds, if any of the needful things were to be accomplished; and he declared that he himself would take the lead in such deeds. Having said this, he took the dagger with which Lucretia had slain herself, and going to the body (for it still lay in view, a most piteous spectacle), he swore by Mars and all the other gods that he would do everything in his power to overthrow the dominion of the Tarquinii and that he would neither be reconciled to the tyrants himself nor tolerate any who should be reconciled to them, but would look upon every man who thought otherwise as an enemy and till his death would pursue with unrelenting hatred both the tyranny and its abettors; and if he should violate his oath, he prayed that he and his children might meet with the same end as Lucretia.

71 Having said this, he called upon all the rest also to take the same oath; and they, no longer hesitating, rose up, and receiving the dagger from one another, swore. After they had taken the oath they at once considered in what manner they should go about their undertaking. And Brutus advised them as follows: "First, let us keep the gates under guard, so that Tarquinius may have no intelligence of what is being said and done in the city against the tyranny till everything on our side is in readiness. After that, let us carry the body of this woman, stained as it is with blood, into the Forum, and exposing it to the public view, call an assembly of the people. When they are assembled and we see the Forum crowded, let Lucretius and Collatinus come forward and bewail their misfortunes, after first relating everything that has happened. Next, let each of the others come forward, inveigh against the tyranny, and summon the citizens to liberty. It will be what all Romans have devoutly wished if they see us, the patricians, making the first move on behalf of liberty. For they have suffered many dreadful wrongs at the hands of the tyrant and need but slight encouragement. And when we find the people ager to overthrow the monarchy, let us give them an opportunity to vote that Tarquinius shall no longer rule over the Romans, and let us send their decree to this effect to the soldiers in the camp in all haste. For when those who have arms in their hands hear that the whole city is alienated from the tyrant they will become zealous for the liberty of their country and will no longer, as hitherto, be restrained by bribes or able to bear the insolent acts of the sons and flatterers of Tarquinius." After he had spoken thus, Valerius took up the discussion and said: "In other respccts you seem to me to reason well, Junius; but concerning the assembly of the people, I wish to know further who is to summon it according to law and propose the vote to the *curiae*. For this is the business of a magistrate and none of us holds a magistracy." To this Brutus answered: "*I* will, Valerius; for I am commander of the *celeres* and I have the power by law of calling an assembly of the people when I please.[112] The tyrant gave me this most important magistracy in the belief that I was a fool and either would not be aware of the power attaching to it or, if I did recognize it, would not use it. And I myself will deliver the first speech against the tyrant."

72 Upon hearing this they all applauded him for beginning with an honourable and lawful principle, and they asked him to tell the rest of his plans. And he continued: "Since you have resolved to follow this course, let us further consider what magistracy shall govern the commonwealth after the expulsion of the kings, and by what man it shall be created, and, even before that, what form of government we shall establish as we get rid of the tyrant. For it is

---

112 *Cf.* ii. 13 and Livy i. 59, 7.

better to have considered everything before attempting so important an undertaking and to have left nothing unexamined or unconsidered. Let each one of you, accordingly, declare his opinion concerning these matters." After this many speeches were made by many different men. Some were o f the opinion that they ought to establish a monarchical government again, and they recounted the great benefits the state had received from all the former kings. Others believed that they ought no longer to entrust the government to a single ruler, and they enumerated the tyrannical excesses which many other kings and Tarquinius, last of all, had committed against their own people; but they thought they ought to make the senate supreme in all matters, according to the practice of many Greek cities. And still others liked neither of these forms of government, but advised them to establish a democracy like at Athens; they pointed to the insolence and avarice of the few and to the seditions usually stirred up by the lower classes against their superiors, and they declared that for a free commonwealth the equality of the citizens was of all forms of government the safest and the most becoming.

73 The choice appearing to all of them difficult and hard to decide upon by reason of the evils attendant upon each form of government, Brutus took up the discussion as the final speaker and said: "It is my opinion, Lucretius, Collatinus, and all of you here present, good men yourselves and descended from good men, that we ought not in the present situation to establish any new form of government. For the time to which we are limited by the circumstances is short, so that it is not easy to reform the constitution of the state, and the very attempt to change it, even though we should happen to be guided by the very best counsels, is precarious and not without danger. And besides, it will be possible later, when we are rid of the tyranny, to deliberate with greater freedom and at leisure and thus choose a better form of government in place of a poorer one — if, indeed, there is any constitution better than the one which Romulus, Pompilius and all the succeeding kings instituted and handed down to us, by means of which our commonwealth has continued to be great and prosperous and to rule over many subjects. But as for the evils which generally attend monarchies and because of which they degenerate into a tyrannical cruelty and are abhorred by all mankind, I advise you to correct these now and at the same time to take precautions that they shall never again occur hereafter. And what are these evils? In the first place, since most people look at the names of things and, influenced by them, either admit some that are hurtful or shrink from others that are useful, of which monarchy happens to be one, I advise you to change the name of the government and no longer to call those who shall have the supreme power either kings or monarchs, but to give them a more modest and humane title. In the next place, I advise you not to make one man's judgment the supreme authority over all, but to entrust the royal power to two men, as I am informed the Lacedaemonians have been doing now for many generations, in consequence of which form of government they are said to be the best governed and the most prosperous people among the Greeks. For the rulers will be less arrogant and vexatious when the power is divided between two and each has the same authority; moreover, mutual respect, the ability of each to prevent the other from living as suits his pleasure, and a rivalry between them for the attainment of a reputation for virtue would be most likely to result from such equality of power and honour.

74 "And inasmuch as the insignia which have been granted to the kings are numerous, I believe that if any of these are grievous and invidious in the eyes of the multitude we ought to modify some of them and abolish others — I mean these sceptres and golden crowns, the purple and gold-embroidered robes — unless it be upon certain festal occasions and in triumphal processions, when the rulers will assume them in honour of the gods; for they will offend no one if they are seldom used. But I think we ought to leave to the men the ivory chair, in which they will sit in judgment, and also the white robe bordered with purple, together with the twelve axes to be carried before them when they appear in public. There is one thing more which in my opinion will be of greater advantage than all that I have mentioned and the most effectual means of preventing those who shall receive this magistracy from committing many errors, and that is, not to permit the same persons to hold office for life (for a magistracy unlimited in time and not obliged to give any account of its actions is grievous to all and productive of tyranny), but to limit the power of the magistracy to a year, as the Athenians do. For this principle, by which the same person both rules and is ruled in turn and surrenders his authority before his mind has been corrupted, restrains arrogant dispositions and does not permit men's natures to grow intoxicated with power. If we establish these regulations we should be able to enjoy all the benefits that flow from monarchy and at the same time to be rid of the evils that attend it. But to the end that the name, too, of the kingly power, which is traditional with us and made its way into our commonwealth with favourable auguries that manifested the approbation of the gods, may be preserved for form's sake, let there always be appointed a king of sacred rites,[113] who shall enjoy the honour for life exempt from all military and civil duties and, like the "king" at Athens,[114] exercising this single function, the superintendence of the sacrifices, and no other.

---

113 The *rex sacrorum*, sometimes styled *rex sacrificulus*.

114 This, the reading of Reiske (see critical note), seems necessary to give an intelligible meaning to the explanatory clause. The second of the nine archons at Athens was called βασιλεύς, but his term of office was limited to a single year.

75 "In what manner each of these measures shall be effected I will now tell you. I will summon the assembly, as I said, since this power is accorded me by law, and will propose this resolution: That Tarquinius be banished with his wife and children, and that they and their posterity as well be forever debarred both from the city and from the Roman territory. After the citizens have passed this vote I will explain to them the form of government we propose to establish; next, I will choose an *interrex* to appoint the magistrates who are to take over the administration of public affairs, and I will then resign the command of the *celeres*. Let the *interrex* appointed by me call together the centuriate assembly, and having nominated the persons who are to hold the annual magistracy, let him permit the citizens to vote upon them; and if the majority of the centuries are in favour of ratifying his choice of men and the auguries concerning them are favourable, let these men assume the axes and the other insignia of royalty and see to it that our country shall enjoy its liberty and that the Tarquinii shall nevermore return. For they will endeavour, be assured, by persuasion, violence, fraud and every other means to get back into power unless we are upon our guard against them.

"These are the most important and essential measures that I have to propose to you at present and to advise you to adopt. As for the details, which are many and not easy to examine with precision at the present time (for we are brought to an acute crisis), I think we ought to leave them to the men themselves who are to take over the magistracy. But I do say that these magistrates ought to consult with the senate in everything, as the kings formerly did, and to do nothing without your advice, and that they ought to lay before the people the decrees of the senate, according to the practice of our ancestors, depriving them of none of the privileges which they possessed in earlier times. For thus their magistracy will be most secure and most excellent."

76 After Junius Brutus had delivered this opinion they all approved it, and straightway consulting about the persons who were to take over the magistracies, they decided that Spurius Lucretius, the father of the woman who had killed herself, should be appointed *interrex*, and that Lucius Junius Brutus and Lucius Tarquinius Collatinus should be nominated by him to exercise the power of the kings. And they ordered that these magistrates should be called in their language *consules*; this, translated into the Greek language, may signify *symbouloi* ("counsellors") or *probouloi* ("pre-counsellors"), for the Romans call our *symboulai* ("counsels") *consilia*. But in the course of time they came to be called by the Greeks *hypatoi* ("supreme") from the greatness of their power, because they command all the citizens and have the highest rank; for the ancients called that which was outstanding and superlative *hypaton*.

Having discussed and settled these matters, they besought the gods to assist them in the pursuit of their holy and just aims, and then went to the Forum.[115] They were followed by their slaves, who carried upon a bier spread with black cloth the body of Lucretia, unprepared for burial and stained with blood; and directing them to place it in a high and conspicuous position before the senate-house, they called an assembly of the people. When a crowd had gathered, not only of those who were in the Forum at the time but also of those who came from all parts of the city (for the heralds had gone through all the streets to summon the people thither), Brutus ascended the tribunal from which it was the custom for those who assembled the people to address them, and having placed the patricians near them, spoke as follows:

---

115 *Cf.* Livy (i. 59, 3-7), who describes scenes in the Forum at Collatia as well as in the Roman Forum.

Book IV

77 "Citizens,[116] as I am going to speak to you upon urgent matters of general interest, I desire first to say a few words about myself. For by some, perhaps, or more accurately, as I know, by many of you, I shall be thought to be disordered in my intellect when I, a man of unsound mind, attempt to speak upon matters of the greatest importance — a man who, as being not mentally sound, has need of guardians. Know, then, that the general opinion you all entertained of me as of a fool was false and contrived by me and by me alone. That which compelled me to live, not as my nature demanded or as beseemed me, but as was agreeable to Tarquinius and seemed likely to be to my own advantage, was the fear I felt for my life. For my father was put to death by Tarquinius upon his accession to the sovereignty, in order that he might possess himself of his property, which was very considerable, and my elder brother, who would have avenged his father's death if he had not been put out of the way, was secretly murdered by the tyrant; nor was it clear that he would spare me, either, now left destitute of my nearest relations, if I had not pretended a folly that was not genuine. This fiction, finding credit with the tyrant, saved me from the same treatment that they had experienced and has preserved me to this day; but since the time has come at last which I have prayed for and looked forward to, I am now laying it aside for the first time, after maintaining it for twenty-five years. So much concerning myself.

78 "The state of public affairs, because of which I have called you together, is this: Inasmuch as Tarquinius neither obtained the sovereignty in accordance with our ancestral customs and laws, nor, since he obtained it — in whatever manner he got it — has he been exercising it in an honourable or kingly manner, but has surpassed in insolence and lawlessness all the tyrants the world ever saw, we patricians met together and resolved to deprive him of his power, a

---

116 For chaps. 77-84 *cf.* Livy i. 59, 8-11.

419

thing we ought to have done long ago, but are doing now when a favourable opportunity has offered. And we have called you together, plebeians, in order to declare our own decision and then ask for your assistance in achieving liberty for our country, a blessing which we night have hitherto been able to enjoy since Tarquinius obtained the sovereignty, nor shall hereafter be able to enjoy if we show weakness now. Had I as much time as I could wish, or were I about to speak to men unacquainted with the facts, I should have enumerated all the lawless deeds of the tyrant for which he deserves to die, not once, but many times, at the hands of all. But since the time permitted me by the circumstances is short, and in this brief time there is little that needs to be said but much to be done, and since I am speaking to those who are acquainted with the facts, I shall remind you merely of those of his deeds that are the most heinous and the most conspicuous and do not admit of any excuse.

79 "This is that Tarquinius, citizens, who, before he took over the sovereignty, destroyed his own brother Arruns by poison because he would not consent to become wicked, in which abominable crime he was assisted by his brother's wife, the sister of his own wife, whom this enemy of the gods had even long before debauched. This is the man who on the same days and with the same poisons killed his wedded wife, a virtuous woman who had also been the mother of children by him, and did not even deign to clear himself of the blame for both of these poisonings and make it appear that they were not his work, by assuming a mourning garb and some slight pretence of grief; nay, close upon the heels of his committing those monstrous deeds and before the funeral-pyre which had received those miserable bodies had died away, he gave a banquet to his friends, celebrated his nuptials, and led the murderess of her husband as a bride to the bed of her sister, thus fulfilling the abominable contract he had made with her and being the first and the only man who ever introduced into the city of Rome such impious and execrable crimes unknown to any nation in the world, either Greek or barbarian. And how infamous and dreadful, plebeians, were the crimes he committed against both his parents-in-law when they were already in the sunset of their lives! Servius Tullius, the most excellent of your kings and your greatest benefactor, he openly murdered and would not permit his body to be honoured with either the funeral or the burial that were customary; and Tarquinia, the wife of Tullius, whom, as she was the sister of his father and had always shown great kindness to him, it was fitting that he should honour as a mother, he destroyed, unhappy woman, by the noose, without allowing her time to mourn her husband under the sod and to perform the customary sacrifices for him. Thus he treated those by whom he had been preserved, by whom he had been reared, and whom after their death he was to have succeeded if he had waited but a short time till death came to them in the course of nature.

80 "But why do I censure these crimes committed against his relations and his kin by marriage when, apart from them, I have so many other unlawful acts of which to accuse him, which he has committed against his country and against us all — if, indeed, they ought to be called merely unlawful acts and not rather the subversion and extinction of all that is sanctioned by our laws and customs? Take, for instance, the sovereignty — to begin with that. How did he obtain it? Did he follow the example of the former kings? Far from it! The others were all advanced to the sovereignty by you according to our ancestral customs and laws, first, by a decree of the senate, which body has been given the right to deliberate first concerning all public affairs; next, by the appointment of *interreges*, whom the senate entrusts with the selection of the most suitable man from among those who are worthy of the sovereignty; after that, by a vote of the people in the comitia, by which vote the law requires that all matters of the greatest moment shall be ratified; and, last of all, by the approbation of the auguries, sacrificial victims and other signs, without which human diligence and foresight would be of no avail. Well, then, which of these things does any one of you know to have been done when Tarquinius was obtaining the sovereignty? What preliminary decree of the senate was there? What decision on the part of the *interreges*? What vote of the people? What favourable auguries? I do not ask whether all these formalities were observed, though it was necessary, if all was to be well, that nothing founded either in custom or in law should have been omitted; but if it can be shown that any one of them was observed, I am content not to quibble about those that were omitted. How, then, did he come to the sovereignty? By arms, by violence, and by the conspiracies of wicked men, according to the custom of tyrants, in spite of your disapproval and indignation. Well, but after he had obtained the sovereignty — in whatever manner he got it — did he use it in a fashion becoming a king, in imitation of his predecessors, whose words and actions were invariably such that they handed down the city to their successors more prosperous and greater than they themselves had received it? What man in his senses could say so, when he sees to what a pitiable and wretched state we all have been brought by him?

81 "I shall say nothing of the calamities we who are patricians have suffered, of which no one even of our enemies could hear without tears, since we are left but few out of many, have been brought low from having been exalted, and have come to poverty and dire want after being stripped of many enviable possessions. Of all those illustrious men, those great and able leaders because of whom our city was once distinguished, some have been put to death and others banished. But what is your condition, plebeians? Has not Tarquinius taken away your laws? Has he not abolished your assemblages for the performance of religious rites and sacrifices? Has he not put an end to your electing of magistrates, to your voting, and to your meeting in assembly to discuss public affairs? Does he not force you, like slaves purchased with money, to endure shameful hardships in quarrying stone, hewing timber, carrying burdens, and wasting your strength in deep pits and caverns, without allowing you the least respite from your miseries? What, then, will be the limit of our calamities? And when shall we recover the liberty our fathers enjoyed? When Tarquinius dies? To be sure! And how shall we be in a better condition then? Why should it not be a worse? For we shall have three Tarquinii sprung from the one, all far more abominable than their sire. For when one who from a private station has become a tyrant and has begun late to be wicked, is an expert in all tyrannical mischief, what kind of men may we expect those to be who are sprung from him, whose parentage has been depraved, whose nurture has been depraved, and who never had an opportunity of seeing or hearing of anything done with the moderation befitting free citizens? In order, therefore, that you may not merely guess at their accursed natures, but may know with certainty what kind of whelps the tyranny of Tarquinius is secretly rearing up for your destruction, behold the deed of one of them, the eldest of the three.

82 "This woman is the daughter of Spurius Lucretius, whom the tyrant, when he went to the war, appointed prefect of the city,[117] and the wife of Tarquinius Collatinus, a kinsman of the tyrant who has undergone many hardships for their sake. Yet this woman, who desired to preserve her virtue and loved her husband as becomes a good wife, could not, when Sextus was entertained last night at her

---

117 *Cf.* Livy i. 59, 12.

house as a kinsman and Collatinus was absent at the time in camp, escape the unbridled insolence of tyranny, but like a captive constrained by necessity, had to submit to indignities that it is not right any woman of free condition should suffer. Resenting this treatment and looking upon the outrage as intolerable, she related to her father and the rest of her kinsmen the straits to which she had been reduced, and after earnestly entreating and adjuring them to avenge the wrongs she had suffered, she drew out the dagger she had concealed under the folds of her dress and before her father's very eyes, plebeians, plunged the steel into her vitals. O admirable woman and worthy of great praise for your noble resolution! You are gone, you are dead, being unable to bear the tyrant's insolence and despising all the pleasures of life in order to avoid suffering any such indignity again. After this example, Lucretia, when you, who were given a woman's nature, have shown the resolution of a brave man, shall we, who were born men, show ourselves inferior to women in courage? To you, because you had been deprived by force of your spotless chastity by submission to a tyrant during one night, death appeared sweeter and more blessed than life; and shall not the same feelings sway us, whom Tarquinius, by a tyranny, not of one day only, but of twenty-five years, has deprived of all the pleasures of life in depriving us of our liberty? Life is intolerable to us, plebeians, while we wallow amid such wretchedness — to us who are the descendants of those men who thought themselves worthy to give laws to others and exposed themselves to many dangers for the sake of power and fame. Nay, but we must all choose one of two things — life with liberty or death with glory. An opportunity has come such as we have been praying for. Tarquinius is absent from the city, the patricians are the leaders of the enterprise, and naught will be lacking to us if we enter upon the undertaking with zeal — neither men, money, arms, generals, nor any other equipment of warfare, for the city is full of all these; and it would be disgraceful if we, who aspire to rule the Volscians, the Sabines and countless other peoples, should ourselves submit to be slaves of others, and should undertake many wars to gratify the ambition of Tarquinius but not one to recover our own liberty.

83 "What resources, therefore, what assistance shall we have for our undertaking? For this remains to be discussed. First there are the hopes we place in the gods, whose rites, temples and altars Tarquinius pollutes with hands stained with blood and defiled with every kind of crime against his own people every time he begins the sacrifices and libations. Next, there are the hopes that we place in ourselves, who are neither few in number nor unskilled in war. Besides these advantages there are the forces of our allies, who, so long as they are not called upon by us, will not presume to busy themselves with our affairs, but if they see us acting the part of brave men, will gladly assist us in the war; for tyranny is odious to all who desire to be free. But if any of you are afraid that the citizens who are in the camp with Tarquinius will assist him and make war upon us, their fears are groundless. For the tyranny is grievous to them also and the desire of liberty is implanted by Nature in the minds of all men, and every excuse for a change is sufficient for those who are compelled to bear hardships; and if you by your votes order them to come to the aid of their country, neither fear nor favour, nor any of the other motives that compel or persuade men to commit injustice, will keep them with the tyrants. But if by reason of an evil nature or a bad upbringing the love of tyranny is, after all, rooted in some of them — though surely there are not many such — we will bring strong compulsion to bear upon these men too, so that they will become good citizens instead of bad. For we have, as hostages for them in the city, their children, wives and parents, who are dearer to every man than his own life. By promising to restore these to them if they will desert the tyrants, and by passing a vote of amnesty for the mistakes they have made, we shall easily prevail upon them to join us. Advance to the struggle, therefore, plebeians, with confidence and with good hopes for the future; for this war which you are about to undertake is the most glorious of all the wars you have ever waged. Ye gods of our ancestors, kindly guardians of this land, and ye other divinities, to whom the care of our fathers was allotted, and thou City, dearest to the gods of all cities, the city in which we received our birth and nurture, we shall defend you with our counsels, our words, our hands and our lives, and we are ready to suffer everything that Heaven and Fate shall bring. And I predict that our glorious endeavours will be crowned with success. May all here present, emboldened by the same confidence and united in the same sentiments, both preserve us and be preserved by us!"

84 While Brutus was thus addressing the people everything he said was received by them with continual acclamations signifying both their approval and their encouragement. Most of them even wept with pleasure at hearing these wonderful and unexpected words, and various emotions, in no wise resembling one another, affected the mind of each of his hearers. For pain was mingled with pleasure, the former arising from the terrible experiences that were past and the latter from the blessings that were anticipated; and anger went hand in hand with fear, the former encouraging them to despise their own safety in order to injure the objects of their hatred, while the latter, occasioned by the thought of the difficulty of overthrowing the tyranny, inspired them with reluctance toward the enterprise. But when he had done speaking, they all cried out, as from a single mouth, to lead them to arms. Then Brutus, pleased at this, said: "On this condition, that you first hear the resolution of the senate and confirm it. For we have resolved that the Tarquinii and all their posterity shall be banished both from the city of Rome and from all the territory ruled by the Romans; that no one shall be permitted to say or do anything about their restoration; and that if anyone shall be found to be working contrary to these decisions he shall be put to death. If it is your pleasure that this resolution be confirmed, divide yourselves into your *curiae* and give your votes; and let the enjoyment of this right be the beginning of your liberty." This was done; and all the *curiae* having given their votes for the banishment of the tyrants, Brutus again came forward and said: "Now that our first measures have been confirmed in the manner required, hear also what we have further resolved concerning the form of our government. It was our decision, upon considering what magistracy should be in control of affairs, not to establish the kingship again, but to appoint two annual magistrates to hold the royal power, these men to be whomever you yourselves shall choose in the *comitia*, voting by centuries. If, therefore, this also is your pleasure, give your votes to that effect." The people approved of this resolution likewise, not a single vote being given against it. After that, Brutus, coming forward, appointed Spurius Lucretius as *interrex* to preside over the *comitia* for the election of magistrates, according to ancestral custom. And he, dismissing the assembly, ordered all the people to go promptly in arms to the field[118] where it was their custom to elect their magistrates. When they were come thither, he chose two men to perform the functions which had belonged to the kings — Brutus and Collatinus; and the people, being called by centuries, confirmed their appointment.[119] Such were the measures taken in the city at that time.

85 As[120] soon as King Tarquinius heard by the first messengers who had found means to escape from the city before the gates were shut that Brutus was holding the assembled people enthralled,

118 The Campus Martius.
119 *Cf.* Livy i. 60, 4.
120 *Cf.* Livy i. 60, 1-3.

haranguing them and summoning the citizens to liberty, which was all the information they could give him, he took with him his sons and the most trustworthy of his friends, and without communicating his design to any others, rode at full gallop in hopes of forestalling the revolt. But finding the gates shut and the battlements full of armed men, he returned to the camp as speedily as possible, bewailing and complaining of his misfortune. But his cause there also was now lost. For the consuls, foreseeing that he would quickly come to the city, had sent letters[121] by other roads to those in the camp, in which they exhorted them to revolt from the tyrant and acquainted them with the resolutions passed by those in the city. Titus Herminius and Marcus Horatius, who had been left by the king to command in his absence, having received these letters, read them in an assembly of the soldiers; and asking them by their centuries what they thought should be done, when it was their unanimous opinion the regard the decisions reached by those in the city as valid, they no longer would admit Tarquinius when he returned. After the king found himself disappointed of this hope also, he fled with a few companions to the city of Gabii, over which, as I said before, he had appointed Sextus, the eldest of his sons, to be king. He was now grown grey with age and had reigned twenty-five years. In the meantime Herminius and Horatius, having made a truce with the Ardeates for fifteen years, led their forces home.[122]

---

121 Livy (i. 59, 12; 60, 1) says that Brutus himself went to the camp before Ardea.
122 See the critical note.

Book V

1 The Roman monarchy,[1] therefore, after having continued for the space of two hundred and forty-four years from the founding of Rome and having under the last king become a tyranny, was overthrown for the reasons stated and by the men named, at the beginning of the sixty-eighth Olympiad[2] (the one in which Ischomachus of Croton won the foot-race), Isagoras being the annual archon at Athens. An aristocracy being now established, while there still remained about four months to complete that year, Lucius Junius Brutus and Lucius Tarquinius Collatinus were the first consuls invested with the royal power; the Romans, as I have said,[3] call them in their own language *consules* or "counsellors." These men, associating with themselves many others, now that the soldiers from the camp had come to the city after the truce they had made with the Ardeates, called an assembly of the people a few days after the expulsion of the tyrant, and having spoken at length upon the advantages of harmony, again caused them to pass another vote confirming everything which those in the city had previously voted when condemning the Tarquinii to perpetual banishment. After this they performed rites of purification for the city and entered into a solemn covenant; and they themselves, standing over the parts of the victims, first swore, and then prevailed upon the rest of the citizens likewise to swear, that they would never restore from exile King Tarquinius or his sons or their posterity, and that they would never again make anyone king of Rome or permit others who wished to do so; and this oath they took not only for themselves, but also for their children and their posterity However, since it appeared

---

1   *Cf.* Livy i. 60, 3 f.
2   507 B.C. For Dionysius' chronology see Intro. pp. xxvi ff.
3   iv. 76, 2.

that the kings had been the authors of many great advantages to the commonwealth, they desired to preserve the name of that office for as long a time as the city should endure, and accordingly they ordered the pontiffs and augurs to choose from among them the older men the most suitable one for the office, who should have the superintendence of religious observances and of naught else, being exempt from all military and civil duties, and should be called the king of sacred rites.[4] The first person appointed to this office was Manius Papirius, one of the patricians, who was a lover of peace and quiet.

2 After[5] the consuls had settled these matters, fearing, as I suspect, that the masses might gain a false impression of their new form of government and imagine that two kings had become masters of the state instead of one, since each of the consuls had the twelve axes, like the kings, they resolved to quiet the fears of the citizens and to lessen the hatred of their power by ordering that one of the consuls should be preceded by the twelve axes and the other by twelve lictors with rods only, or, as some relate, with clubs[6] also, and that they should receive the axes in rotation, each consul possessing them in turn one month. By this and not a few other measures of like nature they caused the plebeians and the lower class to be eager for a continuance of the existing order. For they restored the laws introduced by Tullus concerning contracts, which seemed to be humane and democratic, but had all been abrogated by Tarquinius; they also ordered that the sacrifices both in the city and in the country, which the members of the *pagi* and of the tribes, assembling together, used to offer up in common, should be performed once more as they had been performed in the reign of Tullius; and they restored to the people the right of holding

4   *rex sacrorum* or *rex sacrificulus*; *cf.* Livy ii. 2, 1 f.
5   *Cf.* Livy ii. 1, 8.
6   Thayer's Note: faces with clubs also: or very possibly, crowns.

assemblies concerning affairs of the greatest moment, of giving their votes, and of doing all the other things they had been wont to do according to former custom. These acts of the consuls pleased the masses, who had come out of long slavery into unexpected liberty; nevertheless, there were found among them some, and these no obscure persons, who from either simplicity or greed longed for the evils existing under a tyranny, and these formed a conspiracy to betray the city, agreeing together, not only to restore Tarquinius, but also to kill the consuls. Who the heads of this conspiracy were and by what unexpected good fortune they were detected, though they imagined they had escaped the notice of everybody, shall now be related, after I have first gone back and mentioned a few things that happened earlier.

3 Tarquinius, after being driven from the throne, remained a short time in the city of Gabii, both to receive such as came to him from Rome, to whom tyranny was a more desirable thing than liberty, and to await the event of the hopes he placed in the Latins of being restored to the sovereignty by their aid. But when their cities paid no heed to him and were unwilling to make war upon the Roman state on his account, he despaired of any assistance from them and took refuge in Tarquinii, a Tyrrhenian city, from whence his family on his mother's side had originally come.[7] And having bribed the magistrates of the Tarquinienses with gifts and been brought by them before the assembly of the people, he renewed the ties of kinship which existed between him and their city, recounted the favours his grandfather had conferred on all the Tyrrhenian cities, and reminded them of the treaties they had made with him. After all this, he lamented the calamities which had overtaken him, showing how, after having fallen in one day from the height of

---

7   The reference is obviously to Tanaquil, who was a native Etruscan (iii. 46, 5). But according to Dionysius (iv. 6 f.) she was the grandmother, not the mother, of Tarquinius Superbus.

felicity, he had been compelled, as a wanderer in want of the necessaries of life, to fly for refuge, together with his three sons, to those who had once been his subjects. Having thus recounted his misfortunes with many lamentations and tears, he prevailed upon the people, first of all to send ambassadors to Rome to possess terms of accommodation on his behalf, assuring them that the men in power there were working in his interest and would aid in his restoration. Ambassadors,[8] of his own selection, having then been appointed, he instructed them in everything they were to say and do; and giving them letters from the exiles who were with him, containing entreaties to their relations and friends, he gave them some gold also and sent them on their way.

4 When these men arrived in Rome, they said in the senate that Tarquinius desired leave to come there under a safe-conduct, together with a small retinue, and to address himself, first to the senate, as was right and proper, and after that, if he received permission from the senate, to the assembly of the people also, and there give an account of all his actions from the time of his accession to the sovereignty, and if anyone accused him, to submit himself to the judgment of all the Romans. And after he had made his defence and convinced them all that he had done nothing worthy of banishment, he would then, if they gave him the sovereignty again, reign upon such conditions as the citizens should determine; or, if they preferred no longer to live under a monarchy, as formerly, but to establish some other form of government, he would remain in Rome, which was his native city, and enjoying his private property, would live on an equality with all the others, and thus have done with exile and a life of wandering. Having stated their case, the ambassadors begged of the senate that they would preferably, on the principle of the right, recognized by all men, that

---

8   For chaps. 3, 3-6, 3 *Cf.* Livy ii. 3, 5 f.; 4, 3; 4, 7-5, 1.

no one should be deprived of the opportunity of defending himself and of being tried, grant him leave to make his defence, of which the Romans themselves would be the judges; but if they were unwilling to grant this favour to him, then they asked them to act with moderation out of regard for the city that interceded on his behalf, by granting her a favour from which they would suffer no harm themselves and yet would be looked upon as conferring great honour upon the city that received it. And they asked them, as being men, not to think thoughts too lofty for human nature or to harbour undying resentment in mortal bodies, but to consent to perform an act of clemency even contrary to their inclination, for the sake of those who entreated them, bearing in mind that it is the part of wise men to waive their enmities in the interest of their friendships and the part of stupid men and barbarians to destroy their friends together with their enemies.

5 After they had done speaking, Brutus rose up and said: "Concerning a return of the Tarquinii to this city, Tyrrhenians, say no more. For a vote has already been passed condemning them to perpetual banishment, and we have all sworn by the gods neither to restore the tyrants ourselves nor to permit others to restore them. But if you desire anything else of us that is reasonable which were not prevented from doing by the laws or by our oaths, declare it." Thereupon the ambassadors came forward and said: "Our first efforts have not turned out as we expected. For, though we have come as ambassadors on behalf of a suppliant who desires to give you an account of his actions, and though we ask as a private favour the right that is common to all men, we have not been able to obtain it. Since, then, this is your decision, we plead no longer for the return of the Tarquinii, but we do call upon you to perform an act of justice of another kind, concerning which our country has given us instructions — and there is neither law nor oath to hinder you from doing it — namely, to restore to the king the property formerly possessed by his grandfather, who never got anything of yours either by force or by fraud, but inherited his wealth from his father and brought it to you. For it is enough for him to recover what belongs to him and to live happily in some other place, without causing you any annoyance."

After the ambassadors had said this, they withdrew. Of the two consuls, Brutus advised retaining the fortunes of the tyrants, both as a penalty for the injuries they had done to the commonwealth, which were many and great, and for the advantage that would result from depriving them of these resources for war; for he showed that the Tarquinii would not be contented with the recovery of their possessions nor submit to leading a private life, but would bring a foreign war upon the Romans and attempt by force to get back into power. But Collatinus advised the contrary, saying that it was not the possessions of the tyrants, but the tyrants themselves, that had injured the commonwealth, and he asked them to guard against two things: first, not to incur the bad opinion of the world as having driven the Tarquinii from power for the sake of their riches, and, secondly, not to give the tyrants themselves a just cause for war as having been deprived of their private property For it was uncertain, he said, whether, if they got back their possessions, they would any longer attempt to make war upon them in order to secure their return from exile, but it was perfectly clear, on the other hand, that they would not consent to keep the peace if they were deprived of their property

6 As the consuls expressed these opinions and many spoke in favour of each, the senate was at a loss what to do and spent many days in considering the matter; for while the opinion of Brutus seemed more expedient, the course urged by Collatinus was more just. At last they determined to make the people the judges between expediency and justice. After much had been said by each of the consuls, the *curiae*, which were thirty in number, upon being called to give their votes, inclined to one side by so small a margin that the *curiae* in favour of restoring the possessions outnumbered by only one those that were for retaining them.[9] The Tyrrhenians, having received their answer from the consuls and given great praise to the commonwealth for having preferred justice to expediency, wrote to Tarquinius to send some persons to receive his possessions, while they themselves remained in the city, pretending to be employed in collecting his furniture and disposing of the effects that could not be driven or carried away, whereas in reality they were stirring up trouble in the city and carrying on intrigues, pursuant to the instructions the tyrant had sent them. For they employed themselves in delivering letters from the exiles to their friends in the city and in receiving others from these for the exiles; and engaging in conversation with many of the citizens and sounding their sentiments, if they found any easy to be ensnared through the feebleness of conviction, lack of means, or a longing for the advantages they had enjoyed under the tyranny, they endeavoured to corrupt them by holding out fair hopes and giving them money. And[10] in a large and populous city there were sure to be found, as we may suppose, some who would prefer a worse to a better form of government, and that not only among the obscure, but even among the men of distinction. Of this number were the two Junii, Titus and Tiberius, the sons of Brutus the consul, then just coming to manhood, and with them the two Vitellii, Marcus and Manius, brothers of the wife of Brutus, men capable of administering public affairs, and also the Aquilii, Lucius and Marcus, sons of the sister of

9   As there were thirty *curiae*, the vote could not have been carried by a majority of one. What Dionysius probably had in mind was that the change of a single vote would have reversed the result. For a similar inaccuracy of expression see vii. 64, 6.

10   For chap.6, 4-13, 1 *cf.* Livy ii. 3, 1-4, 7; 5, 5-10.

Collatinus, the other consul, of the same age with the sons of Brutus. It was at the house of the Aquilii,[11] whose father was no longer living, that the conspirators generally held their meetings and laid their plans for bringing back the tyrants.

7 Not only from many other circumstances has it seemed to me to be due to the providence of the gods that the affairs of the Romans have come to such a flourishing condition, but particularly by what happened upon this occasion. For so great a folly and infatuation possessed those unfortunate youths that they consented to write letters to the tyrant in their own hand, informing him not only of the number of their accomplices, but also of the time when they proposed to make the attack upon the consuls. They had been persuaded to do so by the letters that came to them from the tyrant, in which he desired to know beforehand the names of the Romans whom he ought to reward after he had regained the sovereignty. The consuls got possession of these letters by the following chance. The principal conspirators used to hold night sessions at the house of the Aquilii, the sons of the sister of Collatinus, being invited there ostensibly for some religious rites and a sacrifice. After the banquet they first ordered the servants to go out of the room and to withdraw from before the door of the men's apartment, and then proceeded to discuss together the means of restoring the tyrants and to set down in the letters in their own handwriting the decisions arrived at; these letters the Aquilii were to deliver to the Tyrrhenian ambassadors, and they in turn to Tarquinius. In the mean time one of the servants, who was their cup-bearer and a captive taken at Caenina, Vindicius by name, suspecting, from their ordering the servants to withdraw, that they were plotting some mischief, remained alone outside the door, and not only heard their conversation, but, by applying his eye to a crevice of the door that

---

11 Livy (ii. 4, 5) says they met at the house of the Vitellii.

afforded a glimpse inside, saw the letters they were all writing. And setting out from the house while it was still the dead of night, as if he had been sent by his masters upon some business, he hesitated to go to the consuls, lest, in their desire the keep the matter quiet out of goodwill for their kinsmen, they might do away with the one who gave information of the conspiracy, but went to Publius Valerius,[12] one of the four who had taken the lead in overthrowing the tyranny; and when this man had given him assurance of his safety by offering his hand and swearing oaths, he informed him of all that he had both heard and seen. Valerius, upon hearing this story, made no delay, but went to the house of the Aquilii about daybreak, attended by a large number of clients and friends; and getting inside the door without hindrance, as having come upon some other business, while the lads were still there, he got possession of the letters, and seizing the youths, took them before the consuls.

8 I am afraid that the subsequent noble and astonishing behaviour of Brutus, one of the consuls, which I am now to relate and in which the Romans take the greatest pride, may appear cruel and incredible to the Greeks, since it is natural for all men to judge by their own experience whatever is said of others, and to determine what is credible and incredible with reference to themselves. Nevertheless, I shall relate it. As soon, then, as it was day, Brutus seated himself upon the tribunal and examined the letters of the conspirators; and when he found those written by his sons, each of which he recognized by the seals, and, after he had broken the seals, by the handwriting, he first ordered both letters to be read by the secretary in the hearing of all who were present, and then commanded his sons to speak if they had anything to say. But when neither of them dared resort to shameless denial, but both

---

12 Livy (ii. 4, 6) says, *rem ad consules detulit*; but according to his account (ii. 2, 11) Valerius was already consul, as successor to Collatinus.

wept, having long since convicted themselves, Brutus, after a short pause, rose up and commanding silence, while everyone was waiting to learn what sentence he would pronounce, said he condemned his sons to death. Whereupon they all cried out, indignant that such a man should be punished by the death of his sons, and they wished to spare the lives of the youths as a favour to their father. But he, paying no heed to either their cries or their lamentations, ordered the lictors to lead the youths away, though they wept and begged and called upon him in the most tender terms. Even this seemed astonishing to everybody, that he did not yield at all to either the entreaties of the citizens or the laments of his sons; but much more astonishing still was his relentlessness with regard to their punishment. For he neither permitted his sons to be led away to any other place and put to death out of sight of the public, nor did he himself, in order to avoid the dreadful spectacle, withdraw from the Forum till after they had been punished; nor did he allow them to undergo the doom pronounced against them without ignominy, but he caused every detail of the punishment established by the laws and customs against malefactors to be observed, and only after they had been scourged in the Forum in the sight of all the citizens, he himself being present when all this was done, did he then allow their heads to be cut off with the axes. But the most extraordinary and the most astonishing part of his behaviour was that he did not once avert his gaze nor shed a tear, and while all the rest who were present at this sad spectacle wept, he was the only person who was observed not to lament the fate of his sons, nor to pity himself for the desolation that was coming upon his house, nor to betray any other signs of weakness, but without a tear, without a groan, without once shifting his gaze, he bore his calamity with a stout heart. So strong of will was he, so steadfast in carrying out the sentence, and so completely the master of all the passions that disturb the reason.

Book V

9 After he had caused his sons to be put to death, he at once summoned the nephews of his colleague, the Aquilii, at whose house the meetings of the conspirators against the state had been held; and ordering the secretary to read out their letters, that all present might hear them, he told them they might make their defence. When the youths were brought before the tribunal, either acting on the suggestion of one of their friends or having agreed upon it themselves, they threw themselves at the feet of their uncle in hopes of being saved by him.[13] And when Brutus ordered the lictors to drag them away and lead them off to death, unless they wished to make a defence, Collatinus, ordering the lictors to forbear a little while till he had talked with his colleague, took him aside and earnestly entreated him to spare the lads, now excusing them on the ground that through the ignorance of their youth and evil associations with friends they had fallen into this madness, and again begging him to grant him as a favour the lives of his kinsmen, the only favour he asked of him and the only trouble he should ever give him, and still again showing him that there was danger that the whole city would be thrown into an uproar if they attempted to punish with death all who were believed to have been working with the exiles for their return, since there were many such and some of them were of no obscure families. But being unable to persuade him, he at last asked him not to condemn them to death, but to impose a moderate punishment on them, declaring that it was absurd, after punishing the tyrants with banishment only, to punish the friends of the tyrants with death. And when Brutus opposed even the equitable punishment that he suggested and was unwilling even to put off the trials of the accused (for this was the last request his colleague made), but threatened and swore he would put them

---

13 Livy knows nothing of the episode here related. According to him (ii. 2, 3-10) Collatinus had already resigned his office at the request of Brutus and gone into exile.

439

all to death that very day, Collatinus, distressed at obtaining naught that he was asking, exclaimed: "Well then, since you are boorish and harsh, I, who possess the same authority as you, set the lads free." And Brutus, exasperated, replied: "Not while I am alive, Collatinus, shall you be able to free those who are traitors to their country. Nay, but you too shall pay the fitting penalty, and that right soon."

10 Having said this and stationed a guard over the lads, he called an assembly of the people, and when the Forum was filled with a crowd (for the fate of his sons had been noised abroad through the whole city), he came forward and placing the most distinguished members of the senate near him, spoke as follows: "I could wish, citizens, that Collatinus, my colleague here, held the same sentiments as I do in everything and that he showed his hatred and enmity towards the tyrants, not by his words only, but by his actions as well. But since it had become clear to me that his sentiments are the opposite of my own and since he is related to the Tarquinii, not alone by blood, but also by inclination, both working for a reconciliation with them and considering his private advantage instead of the public good, I have not only made my own preparations to prevent him from carrying out the mischievous designs he has in mind, but I have also summoned you for this same purpose.I shall inform you,first,of the dangers to which the commonwealth has been exposed and then in what manner each of us has dealt with those dangers. Some of the citizens, assembling at the house of the Aquilii, who are sons of the sister of Collatinus, among them my two sons and the brothers of my wife, and some others with them, no obscure men, entered into an agreement and conspiracy to kill me and restore Tarquinius to the sovereignty. And having written letters concerning these matters in their own handwriting and sealed them with their own seals, they were intending to send them to the exiles. These things, by the favour of some god, have become known to us through information given by this man — he is a slave belonging to the Aquilii, at whose house they held a session last night and wrote the letters — and the letters themselves have come into our possession. As for Titus and Tiberius, my own sons, I have punished them, and neither the law nor our oath has in any degree been violated through clemency on my part. But Collatinus is trying to take the Aquilii out of my hands and declares that, even though they have taken part in the same counsels as my sons, he will not allow them to meet with the same punishment. But if these are not to suffer any penalty, then it will be impossible for me to punish either the brothers of my wife or the other traitors to their country. For what just charge shall I be able to bring against them if I let these off? Of what, then, do you think these actions of his are indications? Of loyalty to the commonwealth, or of a reconciliation with the tyrants? Of a confirmation of the oaths which you, following us, all took, or of a violation of those oaths, yes, of perjury? And if he had escaped discovery by us, he would have been subject to the curses we then invoked and he would have paid the penalty to the gods by whom he had sworn falsely; but since he has been found out, it is fitting that he should be punished by us — this man who but a few days ago persuaded you to restore their possessions to the tyrants, to the end that the commonwealth might not make use of them in the war against our enemies, but that our enemies might use them against the commonwealth. And now he thinks that those who have conspired to restore the tyrants ought to be let off from punishment, with a view no doubt of sparing their lives as a favour to the tyrants, so that, if these should after all return as the result of either treachery or war, he may, by reminding them of these favours, obtain from them, as being a friend, everything that he chooses. After this, shall I, who have not spared my own sons, spare you, Collatinus, who are with us indeed in person, but with our enemies in spirit, and are trying to save those who have betrayed their country and to kill me who am fighting in its defence? Far from it! On the contrary, to prevent you from doing anything of the kind in future, I now deprive you of your magistracy and command you to retire to some other city. And as for you, citizens, I shall assemble you at once by your centuries and take your votes, in order that you may decide whether this action of mine should be ratified. Be assured, however, that you will have only one of us two for your consul, either Collatinus or Brutus."

11 While Brutus was thus speaking, Collatinus kept crying out and loudly protesting and at every word calling him a plotter and a betrayer of his friends, and now by endeavouring to clear himself of the accusations against him, and now by pleading for his nephews, and by refusing to allow the matter to be put to the vote of the citizens, he made the people still angrier and caused a terrible uproar at everything he said. The citizens being now exasperated against him and refusing either to hear his defence or to listen to his entreaties, but calling for their votes to be taken, Spurius Lucretius, his father-in-law, a man esteemed by the people, feeling concern about the situation, lest Collatinus should be ignominiously driven from office and from his country, asked and obtained from both consuls leave to speak. He was the first person who ever obtained this privilege, as the Roman historians relate, since it was not yet customary at that time for a private citizen to speak in an assembly of the people. And addressing his entreaties to both consuls jointly, he advised Collatinus not to persist so obstinately in his opposition nor to retain against the will of the citizens the magistracy which he had received by their consent, but if those who had given it thought fit to take back the magistracy, to lay it down voluntarily, and to attempt to clear himself of the accusations against him, not by his words, but by his actions, and to remove with all his goods to some other region till the commonwealth should be in a state of security, since the good of the people seemed to require this. For he should bear in mind that, whereas in the case of other crimes all men are wont to show their resentment after the deed has been committed, in the case of treason they do so even when it is only suspected, regarding it as more prudent, though their fears may be vain, to guard against the treason than, by giving way to contempt, to be undone. As for Brutus, he endeavoured to persuade him not to expel from his country with shame and vituperation his colleague with whom he had concerted the best measures for the commonwealth, but if Collatinus himself was willing to resign the magistracy and leave the country voluntarily, not only to give him leave to get together all his substance at his leisure, but also to add some gift from the public treasury, to the end that this favour conferred upon him by the people might be a comfort to him in his affliction.

12 When Lucretius thus advised both consuls and the citizens had voiced their approval, Collatinus, uttering many lamentations over his misfortune in being obliged, because of the compassion he had shown to his kinsmen, to leave his country, though he was guilty of no crime, resigned his magistracy. Brutus, praising him for having taken the best and the most advantageous resolution for both himself and the commonwealth, exhorted him not to entertain any resentment either against him or against his country, but after he had taken up his residence elsewhere, to regard as his country the home he was now leaving, and never to join with her enemies in any action or speech directed against her; in fine, to consider his change of residence as a sojourn abroad, not as an expulsion or a banishment, and while living in body with those who had received him, to dwell in spirit with those who now sent him on his way. After this exhortation to Collatinus he prevailed upon the people to make him a present of twenty talents, and he himself added five more from his own means. So Tarquinius Collatinus, having met with this fate, retired to Lavinium, the mother-city of the Latin nation, where he died at an advanced age. And Brutus, thinking that he ought not to continue alone in the magistracy or to give occasion to the citizens to suspect that it was because of a desire to rule alone that he had banished his colleague from the country, summoned the people to the field[14] where it was their custom to elect their kings and other magistrates, and chose for his colleague Publius Valerius,[15] a descendant, as I have stated earlier,[16] of the Sabine Valerius, a man worthy of both praise and admiration for many other qualities, but particularly for his frugal manner of life. For there was a kind of self-taught philosophy about him, which he displayed upon many occasions, of which I shall speak a little later.[17]

13 After this Brutus and his colleague, acting in everything with a single mind, immediately put to death all who had conspired to restore the exiles, and also honoured the slave who had given information of the conspiracy, not only with his freedom, but also by the bestowal of citizenship and a large sum of money. Then they introduced three measures, all most excellent and advantageous to the state, by which they brought about harmony among all the citizens and weakened the factions of their enemies. Their measures were as follows: In the first place, choosing the best men from among the plebeians, they made them patricians, and thus rounded out the membership of the senate to three hundred.[18] Next, they brought out and exposed in public the goods of the tyrants for the benefit of all the citizens, permitting everyone to have as large a

---

14 The Campus Martius.
15 *Cf.* Livy ii. 2, 11.
16 iv. 67, 3.
17 In chap. 48.
18 *Cf.* Livy ii. 1, 10 f.

portion of them as he could seize;[19] and the lands the tyrants had possessed they divided among those who had no allotments, reserving only one field, which lies between the city and the river.[20] This field their ancestors had by a public decree consecrated to Mars as a meadow for horses and the most suitable drill-field for the youth to perform their exercises in arms. The strongest proof, I think, that even before this the field had been consecrated to this god, but that Tarquinius had appropriated it to his own use and sown it, was the action then taken by the consuls in regard to the corn there. For though they had given leave to the people to drive and carry away everything that belonged to the tyrants, they would not permit anyone to carry away the grain which had grown in this field and was still lying upon the threshing-floors whether in the straw or threshed, but looking upon it as accursed and quite unfit to be carried into their houses, they caused a vote to be passed that it should be thrown into the river. And there is even now a conspicuous monument of what happened on that occasion, in the form of an island of goodly size consecrated to Aesculapius and washed on all sides by the river, an island which was formed, they say, out of the heap of rotten straw and was further enlarged by the silt which the river kept adding. The consuls also granted to all the Romans who had fled with the tyrant leave to return to the city with impunity and under a general amnesty, setting a time limit of twenty days; and if they did not return within this fixed time the penalties set in their case were perpetual banishment and the confiscation of their estates. These measures of the consuls caused those who had enjoyed any part whatever of the possessions belonging to the tyrants to submit to any danger rather than be deprived again of the advantages they had obtained; and, on the other hand, by freeing from their fear those who, through dread of

19 *Cf.* Livy ii. 5, 1 f.
20 *Cf.* Livy ii. 5, 2-4.

having to stand trial for the crimes they had committed under the tyranny, had condemned themselves to banishment, they caused them to favour the side of the commonwealth rather than that of the tyrants.

14 After[21] they had instituted these measures and made the necessary preparations for the war, they for some time kept their forces assembled in the plains under the walls of the city, disposed under their various standards and leaders and performing their warlike exercises. For they had learned that the exiles were raising an army against them in all the cities of Tyrrhenia and that two of these cities, Tarquinii and Veii, were openly assisting them toward their restoration, both of them with considerable armies, and that from the other cities volunteers were coming to their aid, some of them being sent by their friends and some being mercenaries. When the Romans heard that their enemies had already taken the field, they resolved to go out and meet them, and before the others could cross the river they led their own forces across and marching forward, encamped near the Tyrrhenians in the Naevian[22] Meadow, as it was called, near a grove consecrated to the hero Horatius. Both armies, as it chanced, were nearly equal in numbers and advanced to the conflict with the same eagerness. The first engagement was a brief cavalry skirmish, as soon as they came in sight of one another, before the foot were encamped, in which they tested each other's strength and then, without either winning or losing, retired to their respective camps. Afterwards the heavy-armed troops and the horse of both armies engaged, both sides having drawn up their lines in the same manner, placing the solid ranks of foot in the centre and stationing the horse on both wings. The right wing of the Romans was commanded by Valerius, the newly-elected consul, who stood

---

21 For chaps. 14-17 cf. Livy ii. 6, 1-7, 4.
22 This name is not attested elsewhere; Plutarch (*Popl.* 9) calls it Αἰσούελον, a form that may easily be a corruption of ΝΑΙΟΥΙΟΝ.

opposite to the Veientes, and the left by Brutus, in the sector where the forces of the Tarquinienses were, under the command of the sons of King Tarquinius.

15 When[23] the armies were ready to engage, one of the sons of Tarquinius, named Arruns, the most remarkable of the brothers both for the strength of his body and the brilliance of his mind, advanced before the ranks of the Tyrrhenians, and riding up so close to the Romans that all of them would recognize both his person and his voice, hurled abusive taunts at Brutus, their commander, calling him a wild beast, one stained with the blood of his sons, and reproaching him with cowardice and cravenness, and finally challenged him to decide the general quarrel by fighting with him in single combat. Then Brutus, unable to bear these reproaches and deaf also to the remonstrances of his friends, spurred forward from the ranks, rushing upon the death that was decreed for him by fate. For both men, urged on by a like fury and taking thought, not of what they might suffer, but only of what they desired to do, rode full tilt at each other, and clashing, delivered unerring blows against each other with their pikes, piercing through shield and corslet, so that the point was buried in the flank of one and in the loins of the other; and their horses, crashing together breast to breast, rose upon their hind legs through the violence of the charge, and throwing back their heads, shook off their riders. These champions, accordingly, having fallen, lay there in their death agony, while streams of blood gushed from their wounds. But the two armies, when they saw that their leaders had fallen, pressed forward with shouts and the clash of arms, and the most violent of all battles ensued on the part of both foot and horse, the fortune of which was alike to both sides. For those of the Romans who were on the right wing, which was commanded by Valerius, the other consul, were

---

23 *Cf.* Livy ii. 6, 7-9.

victorious over the Veientes, and pursuing them to their camp, covered the plain with dead bodies; while those of the Tyrrhenians who were posted on the enemy's right wing and commanded by Titus and Sextus, the sons of King Tarquinius, put the left wing of the Romans to flight, and advancing close to their camp, did not fail to attempt to take it by storm; but after receiving many wounds, since those inside stood their ground, they desisted. These guards were the *triarii*, as they are called; they are veteran troops, experienced in many wars, and are always the last employed in the most critical fighting, when every other hope is lost.

16 The sun being now near setting, both armies retired to their camps, not so much elated by their victory as grieved at the numbers they had lost, and believing that, if it should be necessary for them to have another battle, those of them now left would be insufficient to carry on the struggle, the major part of them being wounded. But there was greater dejection and despair of their cause on the side of the Romans because of the death of their leader; and the thought occurred to many of them that it would be better for them to quit their camp before break of day. While they were considering these things and discussing them among themselves, about the time of the first watch a voice was heard from the grove near which they were encamped, calling aloud to both armies in such a manner as to be heard by all of them; it may have been the voice of the hero to whom the precinct was consecrated, or it may have been that of Faunus,[24] as he is called. For the Romans attribute panics to this divinity; and whatever apparitions come to men's sight, now in one shape and now in another, inspiring terror, or whatever supernatural voices come to their ears to disturb them are the work, they say, of this god. The voice of the divinity exhorted the Romans to be of good courage, as having gained the victory,

---

24 Livy (ii. 7, 2) calls him Silvanus.

and declared that the enemy's dead exceeded theirs by one man. They say that Valerius, encouraged by this voice, pushed on to the Tyrrhenians' entrenchments while it was still the dead of night, and having slain many of them and driven the rest out of the camp, made himself master of it.

17 Such was the outcome of the battle. The next day the Romans, having stripped the enemy's dead and buried their own, returned home. The bravest of the knights took up the body of Brutus and with many praises and tears bore it back to Rome, adorned with crowns in token of his superior valour. They were met by the senate, which had decreed a triumph in honour of their leader, and also by all the people, who received the army with bowls of wine and tables spread with viands. When they came into the city, the consul triumphed according to the custom followed by the kings when they conducted the trophy-bearing processions and the sacrifices, and having consecrated the spoils to the gods, he observed that day as sacred and gave a banquet to the most distinguished of the citizens. But on the next day he arrayed himself in dark clothing, and placing the body of Brutus, suitably adorned, upon a magnificent bier in the Forum, he called the people together in assembly, and advancing to the tribunal, delivered the funeral oration in his honour. Whether Valerius was the first who introduced this custom among the Romans or whether he found it already established by the kings and adopted it, I cannot say for certain; but I do know from my acquaintance with universal history, as handed down by the most ancient poets and the most celebrated historians, that it was an ancient custom instituted by the Romans to celebrate the virtues of illustrious men at their funerals and that the Greeks were not the authors of it. For although these writers have given accounts of funeral games, both gymnastic and equestrian, held in honour of famous men by their friends, as by Achilles for

Patroclus and, before that, by Heracles for Pelops, yet none of them makes any mention of eulogies spoken over the deceased except the tragic poets at Athens, who, out of flattery to their city, invented this legend also in the case of those who were buried by Theseus.[25] For it was only at some late period that the Athenians added to their custom the funeral oration, having instituted it either in honour of those who died in defence of their country at Artemisium, Salamis and Plataea, or on account of the deeds performed at Marathon. But even the affair at Marathon — if, indeed, the eulogies delivered in honour of the deceased really began with that occasion — was later than the funeral of Brutus by sixteen years. However, if anyone, without stopping to investigate who were the first to introduce these funeral orations, desires to consider the custom in itself and to learn in which of the two nations it is seen at its best, he will find that it is observed more wisely among the Romans than among the Athenians. For, whereas the Athenians seem to have ordained that these orations should be pronounced at the funerals of those only who have died in war, believing that one should determine who are good men solely on the basis of the valour they show at their death, even though in other respects they are without merit, the Romans, on the other hand, appointed this honour to be paid to all their illustrious men, whether as commanders in war or as leaders in the civil administration they have given wise counsels and performed noble deeds, and this not alone to those who have died in war, but also to those who have met their end in any manner whatsoever, believing that good men deserve praise for every virtue they have shown during their lives and not solely for the single glory of their death.

---

25 The Seven who warred against Thebes. Their burial is the theme of Euripides' *Supplices*.

18 Such, then, was the death of Junius Brutus, who overthrew the monarchy and was appointed the first consul. Though he attained late to a place of distinction and flourished in it but a brief moment, yet he was looked upon as the greatest of all the Romans. He left no issue either sons or daughters, according to the writers who have investigate the history of the Romans most accurately; of this they offer many proofs, and this one in particular, which is not easily refuted, that he was of a patrician family, whereas those who have claimed to be descended from that family, as the Junii and Bruti, were all plebeian and were candidates for those magistracies only which were open by law to the plebeians, namely, the aedileship and tribuneship, but none of them stood for the consulship, to which the patricians only were eligible. Yet at a late period they obtained this magistracy also, when the plebeians too were allowed to hold it. But I leave the consideration of these matters to those whose business and interest it is to discover the precise facts.

19 After[26] the death of Brutus his colleague Valerius became suspected by the people of a design to make himself king. The first ground of their suspicion was his continuing alone in the magistracy, when he ought immediately to have chosen a colleague as Brutus had done after he had expelled Collatinus. Another reason was that he had built his house in an invidious place, having chosen for that purpose a fairly high and steep hill, called by the Romans Velia, which commands the Forum. But the consul, being informed by his friends that these things displeased the people, appointed a day for the election and chose for his colleague Spurius Lucretius, who died after holding the office for only a few days. In his place he then chose Marcus Horatius, and removed his house from the top to the bottom of the hill, in order that the Romans, as he himself said

---

26 *Cf.* Livy ii. 7, 5-8, 4.

in one of his speeches to the people, might stone him from the hill above if they found him guilty of any wrongdoing. And desiring to give the plebeians a definite pledge of their liberty, he took the axes from the rods and established it as a precedent for his successors in the consulship — a precedent which continued to be followed down to my day — that, when they were outside the city, they should use the axes, but inside the city they should be distinguished by the rods only. He also introduced most beneficent laws which gave relief to the plebeians. By one of these he expressly forbade that anyone should be a magistrate over the Romans who did not receive the office from the people; and he fixed death as the penalty for transgressing the law, and granted impunity to the one who should kill any such transgressor. In a second law it is provided: "If a magistrate shall desire to have any Roman put to death, scourged, or fined a sum of money, the private citizen may summon the magistrate before the people for judgment, and in the mean time shall be liable to no punishment at the hands of the magistrate till the people have given their vote concerning him." These measures gained him the esteem of the plebeians, who gave him the nickname of Publicola, which means in the Greek language *dēmokēdēs* or "the People's Friend." These were the achievements of the consuls that year.

20 The next year Valerius was appointed consul for the second time, and with him Lucretius.[27] In their consulship nothing worthy of note occurred except that a census was taken and war taxes were levied according to the plan introduced by King Tullius, which had

27 In subsequent chapters(22, 5; 40, 1) the praenomen of Lucretius is given as Titus, the same as in Livy (ii. 8, 9); and Naber wished to supply that name here. It may be, however, that after giving merely the family name of Valerius (who is already sufficiently familiar to the reader), Dionysius preferred to deal similarly with his colleague. Nevertheless, the omission of the praenomen is awkward, since the only Lucretius thus far mentioned has been Spurius Lucretius, whose death was recorded in the preceding chapter (19, 2).

been discontinued during all the reign of Tarquinius and was then renewed for the first time by these consuls. By this census it appeared that the number of Roman citizens who had reached manhood amounted to about 130,000. After this an army of Romans was sent to a place called Signurium[28] in order to garrison that stronghold, which stood as an outpost against the cities both of the Latins and of the Hernicans, from whence they expected war.

21 After[29] Publius Valerius, surnamed Publicola, had been appointed to the same magistracy for the third time, and with him Marcus Horatius Pulvillus for the second time, the king of the Clusians in Tyrrhenia, named Lars and surnamed Porsena, declared war on the Romans. He had promised the Tarquinii, who had fled to him, that he would either effect a reconciliation between them and the Romans upon the terms that they should return home and receive back the sovereignty, or that he would recover and restore to them the possessions of which they had been deprived; but upon sending ambassadors the year before to Rome with appeals mingled with threats, he had not only failed to obtain a reconciliation and return for the exiles, the senate basing its refusal on the curses and oaths by which they had bound themselves not to receive them, but he had also failed to recover their possessions, the persons to whom they had been distributed and allotted refusing to restore them. And declaring that he was insulted by the Romans and treated

---

28 The various spellings of this name given by the MSS. of Dionysius and Plutarch (see critical note) all seem to go back to a form Σιγνούριον, but no such place as Signurium is known. Nissen (*Ital. Landeskunde*, ii. 650, n. 4) holds that the reference must be to Signia, which was, in fact, the rendering adopted by Lapus, the earliest translator of Dionysius.

29 For chaps. 21, 1-23, 1 *cf.* Livy ii. 9. Livy (ii. 8, 5, 9) regarded Horatius Pulvillus as merely a *consul suffectus* of the first year, and hence ignores the third consulship mentioned by Dionysius. The events of this third consulship are assigned by him to the second consulship, those of the fourth to the third, and so on.

outrageously in that he could obtain neither one of his demands, this arrogant man, whose mind was corrupted by both his wealth and possessions and the greatness of his power, thought he now had excellent grounds for overthrowing the power of the Romans, a thing which he had long since been desiring to do, and he accordingly declared war against them. He was assisted in this war by Octavius Mamilius, the son-in-law of Tarquinius, who was eager to display all possible zeal and marched out of Tusculum at the head of all the Camerini and Antemnates, who were of the Latin nation and had already openly revolted from the Romans; and from among the other Latin peoples that were not willing to make open war upon an allied and powerful state, unless for compelling reasons, he attracted numerous volunteers by his personal influence.

22 The Roman consuls, being informed of these things, in the first place ordered all the husbandmen to remove their effects, cattle, and slaves from the fields to the neighbouring mountains, in the fastnesses of which they constructed forts sufficiently strong to protect those who fled thither. After that they strengthened with more effectual fortifications and guards the hill called Janiculum, which is a high mount near Rome lying on the other side of the river Tiber, taking care above all things that such an advantageous position should not serve the enemy as an outpost against the city; and they stored their supplies for the war there. Affairs inside the city they conducted in a more democratic manner, introducing many beneficent measures in behalf of the poor, lest these, induced by private advantage to betray the public interest, should go over to the tyrants. Thus they had a vote passed that they should be exempt from all the public taxes which they had paid while the city was under the kings, and also from all contributions for military purposes and wars, looking upon it as a great advantage to the state merely to make use of their persons in defending the country. And with their army long since disciplined and ready for action, they were encamped in the field that lies before the city.

But King Porsena, advancing with his forces, took the Janiculum by storm, having terrified those who were guarding it, and placed there a garrison of Tyrrhenians. After this he proceeded against the city in expectation of reducing that also without any trouble; but when he came near the bridge and saw the Romans drawn up before the river, he prepared for battle, thinking to overwhelm them with his numbers, and led on his army with great contempt of the enemy. His left wing was commanded by the sons of Tarquinius, Sextus and Titus, who had with them the Roman exiles together with the choicest troops from the city of Gabii and no small force of foreigners and mercenaries; the right was led by Mamilius, the son-in-law of Tarquinius, and here were arrayed the Latins who had revolted from the Romans; King Porsena had taken his place in the centre of the battle-line. On the side of the Romans the right wing was commanded by Spurius Larcius and Titus Herminius, who stood opposite to the Tarquinii; the left by Marcus Valerius, brother to Publicola, one of the consuls, and Titus Lucretius, the consul of the previous year, who were to engage Mamilius and the Latins; the centre of the line between the wings was commanded by the two consuls.

23 When the armies engaged, they both fought bravely and sustained the shock for a considerable time, the Romans having the advantage of their enemies in both experience and endurance, and the Tyrrhenians and Latins being much superior in numbers. But when many had fallen on both sides, fear fell upon the Romans, and first upon those who occupied the left wing, when they saw their two commanders, Valerius and Lucretius, carried off the field wounded; and then those also who were stationed on the right wing, though they were already victorious over the forces commanded by the

Tarquinii, were seized by the same terror upon seeing the flight of the others. While they were all fleeing to the city and endeavouring to force their way in a body over a single bridge,[30] the enemy made a strong attack upon them; and the city came very near being taken by storm, and would surely have fallen if the pursuers had entered it at the same time with those who fled. Those who checked the enemy's attack and saved the whole army were three in number, two of them older men, Spurius Larcius and Titus Herminius, who commanded the right wing, and one a younger man, Publius Horatius, who was called Cocles[31] from an injury to his sight, and one of his eyes having been struck out in a battle, and was the fairest of men in philosophical appearance and the bravest in spirit. This man was nephew to Marcus Horatius, one of the consuls, and traced his descent from Marcus Horatius, one of the triplets who conquered the Alban triplets when the two cities, having become involved in war over the leadership, agreed not to risk a decision with all their forces, but with three men on each side, as I have related in one of the earlier books.[32] These three men, then, all alone, with their backs to the bridge, barred the passage of the enemy for a considerable time and stood their ground, though pelted by many foes with all sorts of missiles and struck with swords in hand-to-hand conflict, till the whole army had crossed the river.

24 When they judged their own men to be safe, two of them, Herminius an Larcius, their defensive arms being now rendered useless by the continual blows they had received, began to retreat gradually But Horatius alone, though not only the consuls but the rest of the citizens as well, solicitous above all things that such a

---

30 For chaps. 23, 2-25, 3 *cf.* Livy ii. 10.
31 The word Cocles is perhaps related to κύκλωψ (literally "round-eyed," but used generally in the sense of "one-eyed").
32 In iii. 12 f.

man should be saved to his country and his parents,[33] called to him from the city to retire, could not be prevailed upon, but remained where he had first taken his stand, and directed Herminius and Larcius to tell the consuls, as from him, to cut away the bridge in all haste at the end next the city (there was but one bridge[34] in those days, which was built of wood and fastened together with the timbers alone, without iron, which the Romans preserve even to my day in the same condition), and to bid them, when the greater part of the bridge had been broken down and little of it remained, to give him notice of it by some signals or by shouting in a louder voice than usual; the rest, he said, would be his concern. Having given these instructions to the two men, he stood upon the bridge itself, and when the enemy advanced upon him, he struck some of them with his sword and beat down others with his shield, repulsing all who attempted to rush upon the bridge. For the pursuers, looking upon him as a madman who was courting death, dared no longer come to grips with him. At the same time it was not easy for them even to come near him, since he had the river as a defence on the right and left, and in front of him a heap of arms and dead bodies. But standing massed at a distance, they hurled spears, javelins, and large stones at him, and those who were not supplied with these threw the swords and bucklers of the slain. But he fought on, making use of their own weapons against them, and hurling these into the crowd, he was bound, as may well be supposed, to find some mark every time. Finally, when he was overwhelmed with missiles and had a great number of wounds in many parts of his body, and one in particular inflicted by a spear which, passing straight through one of his buttocks above the hip-joint, weakened

---

33 By a very slight change in the Greek (see critical note) Naber would make the sentence read, "to his country that gave him birth," a phrase frequently used by Dionysius.

34 The *pons sublicius*; see iii. 45.

him with the pain and impeded his steps, he heard those behind him shouting out that the greater part of the bridge was broken down. Thereupon he leaped with his arms into the river and swimming across the stream with great difficulty (for the current, being divided by the piles, ran swift and formed large eddies), he emerged upon the shore without having lost any of his arms in swimming.

25 This deed gained him immortal glory For the Romans immediately crowned him and conducted him into the city with songs, as one of the heroes; and all the inhabitants poured out of their houses, desiring to catch the last sight of him while he was yet alive, since they supposed he would soon succumb to his wounds. And when he escaped death, the people erected a bronze statue of him fully armed in the principal part of the Forum and gave him as much of the public land as he himself could plough round in one day with a yoke of oxen. Besides these things bestowed upon him by the public, every person, both man and woman, at a time when they were all most sorely oppressed by a dreadful scarcity of provisions, gave him a day's ration of food; and the number of people amounted to more than three hundred thousand in all. Thus Horatius, who had shown so great valour upon that occasion, occupied as enviable a position as any Roman who ever lived, but he was rendered useless by his lameness for further services to the state; and because of this misfortune he obtained neither the consulship nor any military command either. This was one man, therefore, who for the wonderful deed he performed for the Romans in that engagement deserves as great praise as any of those who have ever won renown for valour. And besides him there was also Gaius Mucius, surnamed Cordus, a man of distinguished ancestry, who also undertook to perform a great deed; but of him I shall speak a little later, after first relating in what dire circumstances the state found itself at that time.

26 After[35] the battle that has been described the king of the Tyrrhenians, encamping on the neighbouring hill, from whence he had driven the garrison of Rome, was master of all the country on that side of the river Tiber. The sons of Tarquinius and his son-in-law, Mamilius, having transported their forces in rafts and boats to the other, or Roman, side of the river, encamped in a strong position. And making excursions from there, they laid waste the territory of the Romans, demolished their farm houses, and attacked their herds of cattle when they went out of the strongholds to pasture. All the open country being in the power of the enemy and no food supplies being brought into the city by land and but small quantities even by the river, a scarcity of provisions was speedily felt as the many thousands of people consumed the stores previously laid in, which were inconsiderable. Thereupon the slaves, leaving their masters, deserted in large numbers daily, and the worst element among the common people went over to the tyrants. The consuls, seeing these things, resolved to ask those of the Latins who still respected the tie of kinship and seemed to be continuing in their friendship to send troops promptly to their assistance; and also resolved to send ambassadors both to Cumae in Campania and to the cities in the Pomptine plain to ask leave to import grain from there. The Latins, for their part, refused to send the desired assistance, on the ground that it was not right for them to make war against either the Tarquinii or the Romans, since they had made their treaty of friendship jointly with both of them. But Larcius and Herminius, the ambassadors who had been sent to convey the grain from the Pomptine plain, filled a great many boats with all sorts of provisions and brought them from the sea up the river on a moonless night, escaping the notice of the enemy. When these supplies also had soon been consumed and the people were oppressed by the same scarcity as before, the Tyrrhenian, learning

---

35 *Cf.* Livy ii. 11, 1-12, 1.

from the deserters that the inhabitants were suffering from famine, sent a herald to them commanding them to receive Tarquinius if they desired to be rid of both war and famine.

27 When[36] the Romans would not listen to this command, but chose rather to bear any calamities whatever, Mucius, foreseeing that one of two things would befall them, either that they would not adhere long to their resolution through want of the necessaries of life, or, if they held firmly to their decision, that they would perish by the most miserable of deaths, asked the consuls to assemble the senate for him, as he had something important and urgent to lay before them; and when they were met, he spoke as follows:

"Fathers, having it in my mind to venture upon an undertaking by which the city will be freed from the present evils, I feel great confidence in the success of the plan and believe I shall easily carry it out; but as for my own life, I have small hopes of surviving the accomplishment of the deed, or, to say the truth, none at all. As I am about to expose myself, then, to so great a danger, I do not think it right that the world should remain in ignorance of the high stakes for which I have played — in case it should be my fate to fail after all in the undertaking — but I desire in return for noble deeds to gain great praise, by which I shall exchange this mortal body for immortal glory. It is not safe, of course, to communicate my plan to the people, lest some one for his own advantage should inform the enemy of a thing which ought to be concealed with the same care as an inviolable mystery. But you, who, I am persuaded, will keep the secret inviolate, are the first and the only persons to whom I am disclosing it; and from you the rest of the citizens will learn of it at the proper season. My enterprise is this: I propose to go to the camp of the Tyrrhenians in the guise of a deserter. If I am disbelieved by them and put to death, the number of you citizens who remain will

36 For chaps. 27, 1-30, 1 *cf.* Livy ii. 12.

be only one less. But if I can enter the enemy's camp, I promise you to kill their king; and when Porsena is dead, the war will be at an end. As for myself, I shall be ready to suffer whatever Heaven may see fit. In the assurance that you are privy to my purpose and will bear witness of it to the people, I go my way, making the better fortune of my country the guide of my journey."

28 After he had received the praises of the senators and obtained favourable omen for his enterprise, he crossed the river. And arriving at the camp of the Tyrrhenians he entered it, having deceived the guard at the gates, who took him for one of their own countrymen since he carried no weapon openly and spoke the Tyrrhenian language, which he had been taught when a child by his nurse, who was a Tyrrhenian. When he came to the forum and to the general's tent, he perceived a man remarkable both for his stature and for his physical strength, clad in a purple robe and seated upon the general's tribunal with many armed men standing round him. And jumping to a false conclusion, as he had never seen the king of the Tyrrhenians, he took this man to be Porsena. But it seems he was the king's secretary, who sat upon the tribunal while numbering the soldiers and making a record of the pay due them. Making his way, therefore, to this man through the crowd that surrounded him and ascending the tribunal (for as he seemed unarmed nobody hindered him), he drew the dagger he had concealed under his garment and struck the man on the head. And the secretary being killed with one blow, Mucius was promptly seize by those who stood round the tribunal and brought before the king, who had already been informed by others of his secretary's death. Porsena, upon seeing him, said: "Most accursed of all men and destined to suffer the punishment you deserve, tell who you are and from whence you come and what assistance you counted on when you dared to commit such a deed? Did you propose to kill my secretary only, or me also? And who are your accomplices in this attempt, or privy to it? Conceal no part of the truth, lest you be forced to declare it under torture."

29 Mucius, without showing any sign of fear, either by a change of colour or by an anxious countenance, or experiencing any other weakness common to men who are about to die, said to him: "I am a Roman, and no ordinary man as regards birth; and having conceived a desire to free my country from the war, I came into your camp as a deserter with the purpose of killing you. I knew well that, whether I succeeded or failed in the attempt, death would be my portion; yet I resolved to give my life to my country from which I received it and in place of my mortal body to leave behind me immortal glory But being cheated of my hope, I slew, instead of you, your clerk, whom I had no cause to slay, misled by the purple, the chair of state, and the other insignia of power. As for death, therefore, to which I condemned myself when I was planning to set out on this undertaking, I do not ask to escape that; but if you would remit for me the tortures and the other indignities and give me assurances of this by the gods, I promise to reveal to you a matter of great moment which concerns your own safety." This he said with the purpose of tricking the other; and the king, being out of his wits and at the same time conjuring up imaginary perils as threatening him from many people, gave him upon oath the pledge he desired. Thereupon Mucius, having thought of a most novel kind of deceit that could not be put to an open test, said to him: "O king, three hundred of us Romans, all of the same age and all of patrician birth, met together and formed a plot to kill you; and we took pledges from one another under oath. And when we were considering what form our plot should take, we resolved not to set about the business all together, but one at a time, nor yet to communicate to one another when, how, where, or by what expedients each of us was to attack you, to the end that it might be easier for us to escape discovery. After we had settled these matters, we drew lots and it fell to my lot to make the first attempt. Since, therefore, you know in advance that many brave men will have the same purpose as I, induced by a thirst for glory, and that some one of them presumably will meet with better fortune than I, consider how you may sufficiently guard yourself against them all."

30 When the king heard this, he commanded his bodyguards to lead Mucius away and bind him, guarding him diligently. He himself assembled the most trustworthy of his friends, and causing his son Arruns to sit beside him, considered with them what he should do to escape the plots of these men. All the rest proposed such simple precautionary measures that they seemed to have no understanding of what was needed; but his son, who expressed his opinion last, showed a wisdom beyond his years. For he advised his father not to consider what precautions he should take in order to meet with no misfortune, but what he should do in order to have no need of precaution. When all had marvelled at his advice and desired to know how this might be accomplished, he said, "If you would make these men friends instead of enemies and would set a greater value of your own life than on the restoration of the exiles with Tarquinius." The king said his advice was most excellent, but that it was a matter calling for deliberation how an honourable peace could be made with them; for he said it would be a great disgrace if, after he had defeated them in battle and kept them shut up within their walls, he should then retire without having effected anything he had promised to the Tarquinii, just as if he had been conquered by those he had overcome and had fled from those who dared no longer even set foot outside their gates; and he declared that there would be one and only one honourable way of ending this war, namely, if some persons should come to him from the enemy to treat for friendship.

31 This is what the king then said to his son and to the others present. But a few days later he was obliged to take the initiative himself in proposing terms of accommodation, for the following reason: While his soldiers were dispersed about the country and plundering the provisions that were being conveyed to the city, and doing this continually, the Roman consuls lay in wait for them in a favourable place and destroying a goodly number, took even more of them prisoners than they slew. Upon this the Tyrrhenians were angered and talked matters over with one another as they gathered in knots, blaming both the king and the other commanders for the prolonging of the war, and desiring to be dismissed to their homes. The king, therefore, believing that an accommodation would be acceptable to them all, sent the closest of his personal friends as ambassadors.[37] Some, indeed, say that Mucius also was sent with them, having given the king his pledge upon oath that he would return; but others say that he was kept in the camp as a hostage till peace should be concluded, and this may perhaps be the truer account. The instructions given by the king to the ambassadors were these: Not to make the least mention of the restoration of the Tarquinii, but to demand the restitution of their property, preferably of all that the elder Tarquinius had left and they themselves had justly acquired and possessed, or, if that could not be, then to demand so far as possible the value of their lands, houses and cattle, and of the produce taken from the land, leaving it to the Romans to determine whether it was to their advantage that this should be paid by those who were in the possession and enjoyment of the land or defrayed by the public treasury. So far their instructions related to

37 Livy (ii. 13, 1-4) says the sending of this embassy was due to Porsena's concern for his own safety. He differs from Dionysius also in regard to the demands made by the king.

the Tarquinii. Then, for himself, they were to demand, upon his putting an end to the war, the so-called Seven Districts (this territory had formerly belonged to the Tyrrhenians, but the Romans had taken it from them in war and occupied it),[38] and, in order that the Romans should remain firm friends of the Tyrrhenians, they were to demand of them the sons of their most illustrious families to serve as hostages for the state.

32 When the embassy came to Rome, the senate, by the advice of Publicola, one of the consuls, voted to grant everything that the Tyrrhenian demanded, believing that the crowd of plebeians and poor people, oppressed by the scarcity of provisions, would cheerfully accept the termination of the war upon any terms whatever. But the people, though they ratified every other article of the senate's decree, would not hear of restoring the property. On the contrary, they voted that no resolution should be made to the tyrants either from private sources or from the public funds, and that ambassadors should be sent to King Porsena concerning these matters, to ask him to accept the hostages and the territory he demanded, but as regarded the property, that he himself, acting as judge between the Tarquinii and the Romans, should determine, after hearing both sides, what was just, being influenced by neither favour nor enmity. The Tyrrhenians returned to the king with this answer, and with them the ambassadors appointed by the people, taking with them twenty children of the leading families to serve as hostages for their country; the consuls had been the first to give their children for that purpose, Marcus Horatius delivering his son to them and Publius Valerius his daughter, who had reached the age for marriage. When these arrived at the camp, the king was pleased, and heartily commending the Romans, he made a truce with them for a specified number of days and undertook to act as judge of the

---

38 See ii. 55, 5.

controversy himself. But the Tarquinii were aggrieved at finding themselves disappointed of the greater hopes they had been placing in the king, having expected to be restored by him to the sovereignty; however, they were obliged to be content with the present state of things and to accept the terms that were offered. And when the men who were sent to defend the cause of the commonwealth, . . .[39] and the oldest of the senators had come from the city at the appointed time, the king seated himself upon the tribunal with his friends, and ordering his son to sit as judge with him, he gave them leave to speak.

32 While[40] the cause was still pleading, a messenger brought word of the flight of the maidens who were serving as hostages. It seems that they had asked leave of their guards to go to the river and bathe, and after obtaining it they had told the men to withdraw a little way from the river till they had bathed and dressed themselves again, so that they should not see them naked; and the men having done this also, the maidens, following the advice and example of Cloelia, swam across the river and returned to the city. Then indeed Tarquinius was vehement in accusing the Romans of a breach of their oaths and of perfidy, and in goading the king, now that he had been deceived by treacherous persons, to pay no heed to them. But when the consul defended the Romans, declaring that the maidens had done this thing of themselves without orders from their fathers and that he would soon offer convincing proof that the consuls had not been guilty of any treachery, the king was persuaded and gave him leave to go to Rome and bring back the maidens, as he kept promising to do. Valerius, accordingly, departed in order to bring them to the camp. But Tarquinius and his son-in-

---

39 Some words have probably been lost from the text at this point. Schnelle plausibly supplied "Valerius, one of the consuls," before "and." Kiessling, however, preferred to delete "and."

40 For chap. 33 f. *cf.* Livy ii. 13, 6-14, 4.

466

law, in contempt of all that was right, formed a wicked plot, sending out secretly a party of horse to lie in wait on the road, in order to seize not only the maidens as they were being brought back, but also the consul and the others who were coming to the camp. Their purpose was to hold these persons as pledges for the property the Romans had taken from Tarquinius, and not to wait any longer for the outcome of the hearing. But Heaven did not permit their plot to go according to their wish. For even as the horsemen who were intending to attack them upon their return were going out of the camp of the Latins, the consul was arriving with the maidens in time to forestall them, and he was already at the very gates of the Tyrrhenian camp when he was overtaken by the horsemen from the other camp who had pursued him. When the encounter between them occurred here, the Tyrrhenians quickly perceived it; and the king's son came in haste with a squadron of horse to their assistance and those of the foot who were posted before the camp also rushed up.

34 Porsena, resenting this attempt, assembled the Tyrrhenians and informed them that after the Romans had appointed him judge of the accusations brought against them by Tarquinius, but before the cause was determined, the exiles justly expelled by the Romans had during a truce been guilty of a lawless attempt upon the inviolable persons both of ambassadors and of hostages; for which reason, he said, the Tyrrhenians now acquitted the Romans of those charges and at the same time renounced all friendly relations with the Tarquinii and Mamilius; and he ordered them to depart that very day from the camp. Thus the Tarquinii, who at first had entertained excellent hopes either of exercising their tyranny again in the city with the assistance of the Tyrrhenians or of getting their property back, were disappointed in both respects in consequence of their lawless attempt against the ambassadors and hostages, and departed from the camp with shame and the detestation of all. Then the king of the Tyrrhenians, ordering the Roman hostages to be brought up to the tribunal, returned them to the consul, saying that he considered the good faith of the commonwealth as worth more than any hostages. And praising one maiden among them, by whom the others had been persuaded to swim across the river, as possessing a spirit superior both to her sex and age, and congratulating the commonwealth for producing not only brave men but also maidens the equals of men, he made her a present of a war-horse adorned with magnificent trappings. After the assembly he made a treaty of peace and friendship with the Roman ambassadors, and having entertained them, he returned to them without ransom all the prisoners, who were very numerous, as a present to take to the commonwealth. He also gave them the place where he was encamped, which was not laid out, like a camp, for a short stay in a foreign country, but, like a city, was adequately equipped with buildings both private and public, — though it is not the custom of the Tyrrhenians, when they break camp and quit the enemy's country, to leave these buildings standing, but to burn them. Thereby he made a present to the commonwealth of no small value in money, as appeared from the sale made by the quaestors after the king's departure. Such, then, was the outcome of the Romans' war with the Tarquinii and Lars Porsena, king of the Clusians, a war which brought the commonwealth into great dangers.

35 After the departure of the Tyrrhenians the Roman senate voted to send to Porsena a throne of ivory, a sceptre, a crown of gold, and a triumphal robe, which had been the insignia of the kings. And to Mucius, who had resolved to die for his country and was looked upon as the chief instrument in putting an end to the war, they voted that a portion of the public land beyond the Tiber should be given (just as previously in the case of Horatius, who had fought in front of the bridge), as much, namely, as he could plough round in one day; and this place even to my day is called the Mucian Meadows.[41] These were the rewards they gave to the men. In honour of Cloelia, the maiden, they ordered a bronze statue to be set up, which was erected accordingly by the fathers of the maidens on the Sacred Way, that leads to the Forum.[42] This statue I found no longer standing; it was said to have been destroyed when a fire broke out in the adjacent houses.

In this year[43] was completed the temple of Jupiter Capitolinus, of which I gave a detailed description in the preceding Book.[44] This temple was dedicated by Marcus Horatius, one of the consuls, and inscribed with his name before the arrival of his colleague; for at that time it chanced that Valerius had set out with an army to the aid of the country districts. For as soon as the people had left the fortresses and returned to the fields, Mamilius had sent bands of robbers and done great injury to the husbandmen. These were the achievements of the third consulship.

36 The consuls for the fourth year, Spurius Larcius and Titus Herminius, wen through their term of office without war. In their consulship Arruns, the son of Porsena, king of the Tyrrhenians, died while besieging the city of Aricia for the second year. For[45] as soon as peace was made with the Romans, he got from his father one half of the army and led an expedition against the Aricians, with a view of establishing a dominion of his own. When he had all but taken the city, aid came to the Aricians from Antium, Tusculum,and Cumae in Campania; nevertheless, arraying his small

41 *Cf.* Livy ii. 13, 5.
42 *Cf.* Livy ii. 13, 11.
43 Livy (ii. 8, 6-8) assigns this event to the first consulship.
44 iv. 61.
45 For §§ 2-4 *cf.* Livy ii. 14, 5-9.

army against a superior force, he put most of them to flight and drove them back to the city. But he was defeated by the Cumaeans under the command of Aristodemus, surnamed the Effeminate,[46] and lost his life, and the Tyrrhenian army, no longer making a stand after his death, turned to flight. Many of them were killed in the pursuit by the Cumaeans, but many more, dispersing themselves about the country, fled into the fields of the Romans, which were not far distant, having lost their arms and being unable by reason of their wounds to proceed farther. There, some of them half dead, the Romans brought from the fields into the city upon wagons and mule-carts and upon beasts of burden also, and carrying them to their own houses, restored them to health with food and nursing and every other sort of kindness that great compassion can show; so that many of them, induced by these kindly services, no longer felt any desire to return home but wished to remain with their benefactors. To these the senate gave, as a place in the city for build houses, the valley which extends between the Palatine and Capitoline hills for a distance of about four stades; in consequence of which even down to my time the Romans in their own language give the name of *Vicus Tuscus* or "the habitation of the Tyrrhenians," to the thoroughfare that leads from the Forum to the Circus Maximus. In consideration of these services the Romans received from the Tyrrhenian king a gift of no slight value, but one which gave them the greatest satisfaction. This was the territory beyond the river which they had ceded when they put an end to the war. And they now performed sacrifices to the gods at great expense which they had vowed to offer up whenever they should again be masters of the Seven Districts.

---

46 For explanations of this epithet see vii. 2, 4.

37 The[47] fifth year after the expulsion of the king occurred the sixty-ninth Olympiad,[48] at which Ischomachus of Croton won the foot-race for the second time, Acestorides being archon at Athens, and Marcus Valerius, brother of Valerius Publicola, and Publius Postumius, surnamed Tubertus, consuls at Rome. In their consulship another war awaited the Romans, this one stirred up by their nearest neighbours. It began with acts of brigandage and developed into many important engagements; however, it ended in an honourable peace in the third[49] consulship after this one, having been carried on during that whole interval without intermission. For some of the Sabines, deciding that the commonwealth was weakened by the defeat she had received from the Tyrrhenians and would never be able to recover her ancient prestige, attacked those who came down into the fields from the strongholds by organizing bands of robbers, and they caused many injuries to the husbandmen. For these acts the Romans, sending an embassy before resorting to arms, sought satisfaction and demanded that for the future they should commit no lawless acts against those who cultivated the land; and having received a haughty answer, they declared war against them. First an expedition was conducted by one of the consuls, who with the horse and the flower of the light-armed foot fell suddenly upon those who were laying waste the country; and there was great slaughter among the many men surprised most their plundering, as may well be imagined, since they were keeping no order and had no warning of the attack. Afterwards, when the Sabines sent a large army against them commanded by a general experienced in war, the Romans made another expedition against them with all their forces, led by both consuls. Postumius encamped on heights near Rome, fearing lest

---

47 For chaps. 37-39 *cf.* Livy ii. 16, 1 f.
48 503 B.C. *Cf.* Wilamowicz, *Aristoteles una Athen*, ii. 81, n. 14.
49 Literally "the fourth," reckoning inclusively. See chap. 49.

some sudden attempt might be made upon the city by the exiles; and Valerius posted himself not far from the enemy, on the bank of the river Anio, which after passing through the city of Tibur pours in a vast torrent from a high rock, and running through the plain belonging to both the Sabines and the Romans, serves as a boundary to both their territories, after which this river, which is fair to look upon and sweet to drink, mingles its stream with the Tiber.

38 On the other side of the river was placed the camp of the Sabines, this too at no great distance from the stream, upon a gently sloping hill that was not very strongly situated. At first both armies observed one another with caution and were unwilling to cross the river and begin an engagement. But after a time they were no longer guided by reason and a prudent regard for their advantage, but becoming inflamed with anger and rivalry, they joined battle. For, going to the river for water and leading their horses there to drink, they advanced a good way into the stream, which was then low, not yet being swollen with the winter's rains, so that they crossed it without having the water much above their knees. And first, when a skirmish occurred between small parties, some ran out of each camp to assist their comrades, then others again from one camp or the other to aid those who were being overpowered. And at times the Romans forced the Sabines back from the river, at times the Sabines kept the Romans from it. Then, after many had been killed and wounded and a spirit of rivalry had possessed them all, as is apt to happen when skirmishes occur on the spur of the moment, the generals of both armies felt the same eagerness to cross the river. But the Roman consul got the start of the enemy, and after getting his army across, was already close upon the Sabines while they were still arming themselves and taking their positions. However, they too were not backward in engaging, but, elated with a contempt of their foes, since they were not going to fight against both consuls nor the whole Roman army, they joined battle with all the boldness and eagerness imaginable.

39 A vigorous action ensuing and the right wing of the Romans, commanded by the consul, attacking the enemy and gaining ground, while their left was already in difficulties and being forced towards the river by the enemy, the consul, who commanded the other camp, being informed of what was passing, proceeded to lead out his army. And while he himself with the solid ranks of the foot followed at a normal pace, he sent ahead in all haste his legate, Spurius Larcius, who had been consul the year before, together with all the horse. Larcius, urging the horse forward at full speed, crossed the river with ease, as no one opposed him, and riding past the right wing of the enemy, charged the Sabine horse in flank; and there and then occurred a severe battle between the horse on both sides, who fought hand-to-hand for a long time. In the mean time Postumius also drew near the combatants with the foot, and attacking that of the enemy, killed many in the conflict and threw the rest into confusion. And if night had not intervened, the whole army of the Sabines, being surrounded by the Romans, who had now become superior in horse, would have been totally destroyed. But as it was, the darkness saved those who fled from the battle unarmed and few in number, and brought them home in safety. The consuls, without meeting any resistance, made themselves masters of their camp, which had been abandoned by the troops inside as soon as they saw the rout of their own army; and, capturing much booty there, which they permitted the soldiers to drive or carry away, they returned home with their forces. Then for the first time the commonwealth, recovering from the defeat received at the hands of the Tyrrhenians, recovered its former spirit and dared as before to aim at the supremacy over its neighbours. The Romans decreed a triumph jointly to both the consuls, and, as a special gratification to one of them, Valerius, ordered that a site should be given him for his habitation on the best part of the Palatine Hill and that the cost of the building should be defrayed from the public treasury. The folding doors of this house, near which stands the brazen bull, are the only doors in Rome either of public or private buildings that open outwards.[50]

40 These men[51] were succeeded in the consulship by Publius Valerius, surnamed Publicola, chosen to hold the office for the fourth time, and Titus Lucretius, now colleague to Valerius for the second time. In their consulship all the Sabines, holding a general assembly of their cities, resolved upon a war against the Romans, alleging that the treaty they had made with them was dissolved, since Tarquinius, to whom they had sworn their oaths, had been driven from power. They had been induced to take this step by Sextus, one of the sons of Tarquinius, who by privately courting them and importuning the influential men in each city had roused them all to united hostility against the Romans,[52] and had won over two cities, Fidenae and Cameria, detaching them from the Romans and persuading them to become allies of the Sabines. In return for these services they appointed him general with absolute power and gave him leave to raise forces in every city, looking upon the defeat they had received in the last engagement as due to the weakness of their army and the stupidity of their general. While they were employed in these preparations, some good fortune, designing to balance the losses of the Romans with corresponding advantages, gave them, in place of the allies who had deserted them, an

---

50 Plutarch (*Popl.* 20, 2) gives as the reason for this special distinction, "in order that by this concession he might be constantly partaking of public honour." — Perrin in *L.C.L.*; cf. also Pliny, *N.H.* xxxvi. 112.

51 For chaps. 40-43 *cf.* Livy ii. 16, 2-6.

52 Or, adopting Sylburg's second reading (see critical note), "had roused in all of them a common hostility."

unexpected accession of strength from among their enemies, of the following nature: A certain man of the Sabine nation who lived in a city called Regillum, a man of good family and influential for his wealth, Titus Claudius[53] by name, deserted to them, bringing with him many kinsmen and friends and a great number of clients, who removed with their whole households, not less than five hundred in all who were able to bear arms. The reason that compelled him to remove to Rome is said to have been this: The men in power in the principal cities, being hostile to him because of their political rivalry, were bringing him to trial on a charge of treason, because he was not eager to make war against the Romans, but both in the general assembly alone opposed those who maintained that the treaty was dissolved, and would not permit the citizens of his own town to regard as valid the decrees which had been passed by the rest of the nation. Dreading this trial, then, (for it was to be conducted by the other cities), he took his goods and his friends and came over to the Romans; and by adding no small weight to their cause he was looked upon as the principal instrument in the success of this war. In consideration of this, the senate and people enrolled him among the patricians and gave him leave to take as large a portion of the city as he wished for building houses; they also granted to him from the public land the region that lay between Fidenae and Picetia,[54] so that he could give allotments to all his followers. Out of these Sabines was formed in the course of time a tribe called the Claudian tribe, a name which it continued to preserve down to my time.

41 After all the necessary preparations had been made on both sides, the Sabines first led out their forces and formed two camps, one of which was in the open not far from Fidenae, and the other in

---

53 Livy (ii. 16, 4) calls him Attius Clausus and his native city Inregillum.
54 The site of this town is not known.

Fidenae itself, to serve both as a guard for the citizens and as a refuge for those who lay encamped without the city, in case any disaster should befall them. Then, when the Roman consuls learned of the Sabines' expedition against them, they too led out all their men of military age and encamped apart from each other, Valerius near the camp of the Sabines that lay in the open, and Lucretius not far distant, upon a hill from which the other camp was clearly in view. It was the opinion of the Romans that the fate of the war would quickly be decided by an open battle; but the general of the Sabines, dreading to engage openly against the boldness and constancy of men prepared to face every danger, resolved to attack them by night, and having prepared everything that would be of use for filling up the ditch and scaling the wall, he was intending, now that all was in readiness for the attack, to rouse up the flower of his army after the first watch and lead them against the entrenchments of the Romans. He also gave notice to the troops encamped in Fidenae that, as soon as they perceived that their comrades were come out of the camp, they also should march out of the city, with light equipment; and then, after setting ambuscades in suitable places, if any reinforcements should come to Valerius from the other army, they were to rise up and, getting behind them, attack them with shouts and a great din. This was the plan of Sextus, who communicated it to his centurions; and when they also approved of it, he waited for the proper moment. But a deserter came to the Roman camp and informed the consul of the plan, and a little later a party of horse came in bringing some Sabine prisoners who had been captured while they were out to get wood. These, upon being questioned separately as to what their general was preparing to do, said that he was ordering ladders and gang-boards to be constructed; but where and when he proposed to make use of them, they professed not to know. After learning this, Valerius sent his legate Larcius to the other camp to acquaint Lucretius, who had the

476

command of it, with weight intention of the enemy and to advise him in what way they ought to attack the enemy. He himself summoned the tribunes and the centurions, and informing them of what he had learned both from the deserter and from the prisoners, exhorted them to acquit themselves as brave men, confident that they had got the best opportunity they could wish for to take a glorious revenge upon their enemies; and after advising them what each of them should do and giving the watchword, he dismissed them to their commands.

42 It was not yet midnight when the Sabine general roused up the flower of his army and led them to the enemy's camp, after ordering them all to keep silence and to make no noise with their arms, that the enemy might not be apprised of their approach till they arrived at the entrenchments. When those in front drew near the camp and neither saw the lights of watch-fires nor heard the voices of sentinels, they thought the Romans guilty of great folly in leaving their sentry-posts unguarded and sleeping inside their camp; and they proceeded to fill up the ditches in many places with brushwood and to cross over without opposition. But the Romans were lying in wait by companies between the ditches and the palisades, being unperceived by reason of the darkness; and they kept killing those of the enemy who crossed over, as soon as they came within reach. For some time the destruction of those who led the way was not perceived by their companions in the rear; but when it became light, upon the rising of the moon, and those who approached the ditch saw not only heaps of their own men lying dead near it but also strong bodies of the enemy advancing to attack them, they threw down their arms and fled. Thereupon the Romans, giving a great shout, which was the signal to those in the other camp, rushed out upon them in a body. Lucretius, hearing the shout, sent the horse ahead to reconnoitre, lest there might be an ambuscade of the enemy, and he himself followed presently with the flower of the foot. And at one and the same time the horse, meeting with those from Fidenae who were lying in ambush, put them to flight, and the foot pursued and slew those who had come to their camp but were now keeping neither their arms nor their ranks. In these actions about 13,500 of the Sabines and their allies were slain and 4200 were made prisoners; and their camp was taken the same day.

43 Fidenae after a few days' siege was taken in that very part which was thought to be the most difficult of capture and was for that reason guarded by only a few men. Nevertheless, the inhabitants were not made slaves nor was the city demolished; nor were many people put to death after the city was taken. For the consuls thought that the seizing of their goods and their slaves and the loss of their men who had perished in the battle was a sufficient punishment for an erring city belonging to the same race,[55] and that to prevent the captured from lightly resorting to arms again, a moderate precaution and one customary with the Romans would be to punish the authors of the revolt. Having, therefore, assembled all the captured Fidenates in the forum and inveighed strongly against their folly, declaring that all of them, from youths to old men, deserved to be put to death, since they neither showed gratitude for the favours they received nor were chastened by their misfortunes, they ordered the most prominent of them to be scourged with rods and put to death in the sight of all; but the rest they permitted to live in the city as before, though they left a garrison, as large as the senate decided upon, to live in their midst; and taking away part of their land, they gave it to this garrison. After they had settled these matters, they returned home with the army from the enemy's

---

55 The Fidenates belonged to the Latin race.

country and celebrated the triumph which the senate had voted to them. These were the achievements of their consulship.

44 When[56] Publius Postumius, who was called Tubertus, had been chosen consul for the second time, and with him Agrippa Menenius, called Lanatus, the Sabines made a third incursion into the Roman territory with a larger army, before the Romans were aware of their setting out, and advanced up to the walls of Rome. In this incursion there was great loss of life on the side of the Romans, not only among the husbandmen, on whom the calamity fell suddenly and unexpectedly, before they could take refuge in the nearest fortresses, but also among those who were living in the city at the time. For Postumius, one of the consuls, looking upon this insolence of the enemy as intolerable, hastily took the first men he came upon and marched out to the rescue with greater eagerness than prudence. The Sabines, seeing the Romans advance against them very contemptuously, without order and separated from one another, and wishing to increase their contempt, fell back at a fast walk, as if fleeing, till they came into thick woods where the rest of their army lay in wait. Then, facing about, they engaged with their pursuers, and at the same time the others came out of the wood with a great shout and fell upon them. The Sabines, who were very numerous and were advancing in good order against men who were not keeping their ranks but were disordered and out of breath with running, killed such of them as came to close quarters, and when the rest turned to flight, they barred the roads leading to the city and hemmed them in on the unfortified ridge of a hill. Then, encamping near them (for night was now coming on), they kept guard throughout the whole night to prevent them from stealing away undiscovered. When the news of this misfortune was brought

---

56 For chaps. 44-47 *cf.* Livy ii. 16, 8 f. Livy reports no trouble with the Sabines during this year, but mentions a war with the Auruncans.

to Rome, there was a great tumult and a rush to the walls, and fear on the part of all lest the enemy, elated by their success, should enter the city in the night. There were lamentations for the slain and compassion for the survivors, who, it was believed, would be promptly captured for want of provisions unless some assistance should reach them quickly. That night, accordingly, they passed in a sorry state of mind and without sleep; but the next day the other consul, Menenius, having armed all the men of military age, marched out with them in good order and discipline to the assistance of those upon the hill. When the Sabines saw them approaching, they remained no longer, but roused up their army and withdrew from the hill, feeling that their present good fortune was enough; and without tarrying much longer, they returned home in great elation, taking with them a rich booty in cattle, slaves, and money.

45 The Romans, resenting this defeat, for which they blamed Postumius, one of the consuls, resolved to make an expedition against the territory of the Sabines speedily with all their forces; they were not only eager to retrieve the shameful and unexpected defeat they had received, but were also angered at the very insolent and haughty embassy that had recently come to them from the enemy. For, as if already victorious and having it in their power to take Rome without any trouble if the Romans refused to do as they commanded, they had ordered them to grant a return to the Tarquinii, to yield the leadership to the Sabines, and to establish such a form of government and such laws as the conquerors should prescribe. Replying to the ambassadors, they bade[57] them report to their general council that the Romans commanded the Sabines to lay down their arms, to deliver up their cities to them, and to be subject to them once more as they had been before, and after they

---

57 The verb of commanding is missing in the Greek text; see critical note.

had complied with these demands then to come and stand trial for the injuries and damage they had done them in their former incursions, if they desired to obtain peace and friendship: and in case they refused to carry out these orders, they might expect to see the war soon brought home to their cities. Such demands having been given and received, both sides equipped themselves with everything necessary for the war and led out their forces. The Sabines brought the flower of their youth out of every city armed with splendid weapons; and the Romans drew out all their forces not only from the city but also from the fortresses, looking upon those above the military age and the multitude of domestic servants as a sufficient guard for both the city and the fortresses in the country. And the two armies, approaching each other, pitched their camps a little distance apart near the city of Eretum, which belongs to the Sabine nation.

46 When each side observed the enemy's condition, of which they judged by the size of the camps and the information given by prisoners, the Sabines were inspired with confidence and felt contempt for the small numbers of the enemy, while the Romans were seized with fear by reason of the multitude of their opponents. But they took courage and entertained no small hopes of victory because of various omens sent to them by the gods, and particularly from a final portent which they saw when they were about to array themselves for battle. It was as follows: From the javelins[58] that were fixed in the ground beside their tents (these javelins are Roman weapons which they hurl and having pointed iron heads, not less than three feet in length, projecting straight forward from one end, and with the iron they are as long as spears of moderate length) — from these javelins flames issued forth round the tips of the heads

---

58 The word ὑσσός is used by Polybius and others for the Roman *pilum*. The usual Greek word for javelin is ἀκόντιον, and occurs at the end of the parenthesis just below.

and the glare extended through the whole camp like that of torches and lasted a great part of the night. From this portent they concluded, as the interpreters of prodigies informed them and as was not difficult for anyone to conjecture, that Heaven was portending to them a speedy and brilliant victory, because, as we know, everything yields to fire and there is nothing that is not consumed by it. And inasmuch as this fire issued from defensive weapons, they came out with great boldness from their camp, and engaging the Sabines, fought, few in number, with enemies many times superior, placing their reliance in their own good courage. Besides, their long experience joined to their willingness to undergo toil encouraged them to despise every danger. First, then, Postumius, who commanded the left wing, desiring to repair his former defeat, forced back the enemy's right, taking no thought for his own life in comparison with gaining the victory, but, like those who are mad and court death, hurling himself into the midst of his enemies. Then those also with Menenius on the other wing, though they were already in distress and being forced to give ground, when they found that the forces under Postumius were victorious over those who confronted them, took courage and advanced against the enemy. And now, as both their wings gave way, the Sabines were utterly routed. For not even those who were posted in the centre of the line, when once their flanks were left bare, stood their ground any longer, but being hard pressed by the Roman horse that charged them in separate troops, they were driven back. And when they all fled toward their entrenchments, the Romans pursued them,and entering with them, captured both camps. All that saved the army of the enemy from being totally destroyed was that night came on and their defeat happened in their own land. For those who fled got safely home more easily because of their familiarity with the country.

47 The next day the consuls, after burning their own dead, gathered up the spoils (there were even found some arms belonging to the living, which they had thrown away in their flight) and carried off the captives, whom they had taken in considerable numbers, and the booty, in addition to the plunder taken by the soldiers. This booty having been sold at public auction, all the citizens received back the amount of the contributions which they had severally paid for the equipment o the expedition. Thus the consuls, having gained a most glorious victory, returned home. They were both honoured with triumphs by the senate, Menenius with the greater and more honourable kind, entering the city in a royal chariot, and Postumius with the lesser and inferior triumph which they call *ouastês*[59] or "ovation," perverting the name, which is Greek, to an unintelligible form. For it was originally called *euastês*, from what actually took place, according to both my own conjecture and what I find stated in many native histories, the senate, as Licinius[60] relates, having then first introduced this sort of triumph. It differs from the other, first, in this, that the general who triumphs in the manner called the ovation enters the city on foot, followed by the army, and not in a chariot like the other; and, in the next place, because he does not don the embroidered robe decorated with gold, with which the other is adorned, nor does he have the golden crown, but is clad in a white toga bordered with purple, the native dress of the consuls and praetors, and wears a crown of laurel; he is also inferior to the other in not holding a sceptre, but everything else is the same. The reason why this inferior honour was decreed to Postumius, though he had distinguished himself more than any man in the last engagement, was the severe and shameful defeat he had

---

59 The verb *ovare* seems to have meant originally to shout *evoe* (εὐοῖ), thus being the equivalent of the Greek εὐάζειν, The form *ovatio* was awkward to transliterate into Greek, so Dionysius rendered it by the term οὐαστής (a slight change from εὐαστής), modifying θρίαμβος.

60 Licinius Macer.

suffered earlier, in the sortie he made against the enemy, in which he not only lost many of his men, but narrowly escaped being taken prisoner himself together with the troops that had survived that rout.

48 In[61] the consulship of these men Publius Valerius, surnamed Publicola, fell sick and died, a man esteemed superior to all the Romans of his time in every virtue. I need not relate all the achievements of this man for which he deserves to be both admired and remembered,because most of them have been already narrated in the beginning of this Book; but I think I should not omit one thing which most deserves admiration of all that can be said in his praise and has not yet been mentioned. For I look upon it as the greatest duty of the historian not only to relate the military achievements of illustrious generals and any excellent and salutary measures that they have devised and put into practice for the benefit of their states, but also to note their private lives, whether they have lived with moderation and self-control and in strict adherence to the traditions of their country This man, then, though he had been one of the first four patricians who expelled the kings and confiscated their fortunes, though he had been invested four times with the consular power, had been victorious in two wars to greatest consequence and celebrated triumphs for both — the first time for his victory over the Tyrrhenian nation and the second time for that over the Sabines — and though he had such opportunities for amassing riches, which none could have traduced as shameful and wrong, nevertheless was not overcome by avarice, the vice which enslaves all men and forces them to act unworthily; but he continued to live on the small estate he had inherited from his ancestors, leading a life of self-control and frugality superior to every desire, and with his small means he brought up his children in

---

61   *Cf.* Livy ii. 16, 7.

a manner worthy of their birth, making it plain to all men that he is rich, not who possesses many things, but who requires few. A sure and incontestable proof of the frugality he had shown during his whole lifetime was the poverty that was revealed after his death. For in his whole estate he did not leave enough even to provide for his funeral and burial in such a manner as became a man of his dignity, but his relations were intending to carry his body out of the city in a shabby manner, and as one would that of an ordinary man, to be burned and buried. The senate, however, learning how impoverished they were, decreed that the expenses of his burial should be defrayed from the public treasury, and appointed a place in the city near the Forum, at the foot of the Velia, where his body was burned and buried, an honour paid to him alone of all the illustrious men down to my time.[62] This place is, as it were, sacred and dedicated to his posterity as a place of burial, an advantage greater than any wealth or royalty, if one measures happiness, not by shameful pleasures, but by the standard of honour. Thus Valerius Publicola, who had aimed at the acquisition of nothing more than would supply his necessary wants, was honoured by his country with a splendid funeral, like one of the richest kings. And all the Roman matrons with one consent, mourned for him during a whole year, as they had done for Junius Brutus, by laying aside both their gold and purple; for thus it is the custom for them to mourn after the funeral rites of their nearest relations.

49 The[63] next year Spurius Cassius, surnamed Vecellinus, and Opiter Verginius Tricostus were appointed consuls. In their consulship the war with the Sabines was ended by one of them, Spurius, after a hard battle fought near the city of Cures; in this battle about 10,300 Sabines were killed and nearly 4000 taken

---

62 The burning and burial of bodies inside the city was later forbidden by one of the laws of the Twelve Tables.

63 *Cf.* Livy ii. 17.

prisoners. Overwhelmed by this final misfortune, the Sabines sent ambassadors to the consul to treat for peace. Then, upon being referred to the senate by Cassius, they came to Rome, and after many entreaties obtained with difficulty a reconciliation and termination of the war by giving, not only as much grain to the army as Cassius ordered, but also a certain sum of money per man and ten thousand acres[64] of land under cultivation. Spurius Cassius celebrated a triumph for his victory in this war; but the other consul, Verginius, led an expedition against the city of Cameria, which had withdrawn from its alliance with the Romans during this war. He took half the other army with him, telling no one whither he was marching, and covered the distance during the night, in order that he might fall upon the inhabitants while they were unprepared and un-apprised of his approach; and so it fell out. For he was already close to their walls, without having been discovered by anybody, just as day was breaking; and before encamping he brought up battering-rams and scaling ladders, and made use of every device used in sieges. The Camerini were astounded at his sudden arrival and some of them thought they ought to open the gates and receive the consul, while others insisted upon defending themselves with all their power and not permitting the enemy to enter the city; and while this confusion and dissension prevailed, the consul, having broken down the gates and scaled the lowest parts of the ramparts by means of ladders, took the city by storm. That day and the following night he permitted his men to pillage the town; but the next day he ordered the prisoners to be brought together in one place, and having put to death all the authors of the revolt, he sold the rest of the people and razed the city.

---

64 The word πλέθρον, here rendered "acre," was strictly an area 100 feet square, but it was often used for the Roman *iugerum* (28,800 sq. ft.), which in turn was only two-thirds the area of our acre.

50 In[65] the seventieth Olympiad (the one in which Niceas of Opus in Locris won the foot-race), Smyrus being archon at Athens, Postumus Cominius and Titus Larcius took over the consulship. In their year of office the cities of the Latins withdrew from the friendship of the Romans, Octavius Mamilius, the son-in-law of Tarquinius, having prevailed upon the most prominent men of every city, partly by promises of gifts and partly by entreaties, to assist in restoring the exiles. And a general assembly was held of all the cities that were wont to meet at Ferentinum[66] except Rome (for this was the only city they had not notified as usual to be present), at which the cities were to give their votes concerning war, to choose generals, and to consider the other preparations. Now it happened that at this time Marcus Valerius, a man of consular rank, had been sent as ambassador by the Romans to the neighbouring cities to ask them not to begin any revolt; for some of their people sent out by the men in power were plundering the neighbouring fields and doing great injury to the Roman husbandmen. This man, upon learning that the general assembly of the cities was being held so that all might give their votes concerning the war, came to the assembly; and requesting of the presidents leave to speak, he said that he had been sent as ambassador by the commonwealth to the cities that were sending out the bands of robbers, to ask of them that they would seek out the men who were guilty of these wrongs and deliver them up to be punished according to the provision which they had laid down in the treaty when they entered into their league of friendship, and also to demand that they take care for the future that no fresh offence should occur to disrupt their friendship and kinship. But, observing that all the cities had met together in order to declare war against the Romans — a purpose which he recognized, not only from many other evidences, but particularly

---

65 For chap. 50 f. *cf.* Livy ii. 18. This year was 499 B.C.
66 See note on iii. 34.

because the Romans were the only persons they had not notified to be present at the assembly, although it was stipulated in the treaty that all the cities of the Latin race should be represented at the general assemblies when summoned by the presidents — he said he wondered what provocation or what cause of complaint against the commonwealth had caused the deputies to omit Rome from the cities they had invited to the assembly, when she ought to have been the first of all to be represented and the first to be asked her opinion, inasmuch as she held the leadership of the nation, which she had received from them with their own consent in return for many great benefits she had conferred upon them.

51 Following him, the Aricians, having asked leave to speak, accused the Romans of having, though kinsmen, brought upon them the Tyrrhenian war and of having caused all the Latin cities, as far as lay in their power, to be deprived of their liberty by the Tyrrhenians. And King Tarquinius, renewing the treaty of friendship and alliance that he had made with the general council of their cities, asked those cities to fulfil their oaths and restore him to the sovereignty The exiles also from Fidenae and Cameria, the former lamenting the taking of their city and their own banishment from it, and the latter the enslaving of their countrymen and the razing of their city, exhorted them to declare war. Last of all, Tarquinius' son-in-law, Mamilius, a man most powerful at that time among the Latins, rose up and inveighed against the Romans in a long speech. And, Valerius answering all his accusations and seeming to have the advantage in the justice of his cause, the deputies spent that day in hearing the accusations and the defences without reaching any conclusion to their deliberations. But on the following day the presidents would no longer admit the Roman ambassadors to the assembly, but gave a hearing to Tarquinius, Mamilius, the Arician, and all the others who wished to make charges against the Romans, and after hearing them all through, they voted that the treaty had been dissolved by the Romans, and gave this answer to the embassy of Valerius: that inasmuch as the Romans had by their acts of injustice dissolved the ties of kinship between them, they would consider at leisure in what manner they ought to punish them.

While this was going on, a conspiracy was formed against the state, numerous slaves having agreed together to seize the heights and to set fire to the city in many places. But, information being given by their accomplices, the gates were immediately closed by the consuls and all the strong places in the city were occupied by the knights. And straightway all those whom the informers declared to have been concerned in the conspiracy were either seized in their houses or brought in from the country, and after being scourged and tortured they were all crucified.[67] These were the events of this consulship.

52 Servius Sulpicius Camerinus[68] and Manius Tullus Longus having taken over the consulship, some of the Fidenates, after sending for soldiers from the Tarquinii, took possession of the citadel at Fidenae, and putting to death some of those who were not of the same mind and banishing others, caused the city to revolt again from the Romans. And when a Roman embassy arrived, they were inclined to treat the men like enemies, but being hindered by the elders from doing so, they drove them out of the city, refusing either to listen to them or to say anything to them. The Roman senate, being informed of this, did not desire as yet to make war upon the whole nation of the Latins, because they understood that

---

67 Thayer note: Or maybe not. See W. Oldfather, TAPA 39:64.

68 Concerning this consulship (covered by chaps. 52-57) Livy says (ii. 19, 1) *nihil dignum memoria actum*. Both here and later (vi. 20 and x. l) the praenomen of Sulpicius is given by the MSS. as Servilius, an error which Dionysius could hardly have made.

they did not all approve of the resolutions taken by the deputies in the assembly, but that the common people in every city shrank from the war, and that those who demanded that the treaty should remain in force outnumbered those who declared it had been dissolved. But they voted to send one of the consuls, Manius Tullius, against the Fidenates with a large army; and he, having laid waste their country quite unmolested, as none offered to defend it, encamped near the walls and placed guards to prevent the inhabitants from receiving provisions, arms, or any other assistance. The Fidenates, being thus shut up within their walls, sent ambassadors to the cities of the Latins to ask for prompt assistance; whereupon the presidents of the Latins, holding an assembly of the cities and again giving leave to the Tarquinii and to the ambassadors from the besieged to speak, called upon the deputies, beginning with the oldest and the most distinguished, to give their opinion concerning the best way to make war against the Romans. And many speeches having been made, first, concerning the war itself, the most turbulent of the deputies were for restoring the king to power and advised assisting the Fidenates, being desirous of getting into positions of command in the armies and engaging in great undertakings; and this was the case particularly with those who yearned for domination and despotic power in their own cities, in gaining which they expected the assistance of the Tarquinii when these had recovered the sovereignty over the Romans. On the other hand, the men of the greatest means and of the greatest reasonableness maintained that the cities ought to adhere to the treaty and not hastily resort to arms; and these were the most influential with the common people. Those who pressed for war, being thus defeated by the advisers of peace, at last persuaded the assembly to do this much at least — to send ambassadors to Rome to invite and at the same time to advise the commonwealth to receive the Tarquinii and the other exiles upon the terms of impunity and a general amnesty, and after making a covenant concerning these matters, to restore their traditional form of government and to withdraw their army from Fidenae, since the Latins would not permit their kinsmen and friends to be despoiled of their country; and in case the Romans should consent to do neither of these things, they would then deliberate concerning war. They were not unaware that the Romans would consent to neither of these demands, but they desired to have a specious pretence for their hostility, and they expected to win over their opponents in the meantime by courting them and doing them favours. The deputies, having passed this vote and set a year's time for the Romans in which to deliberate and for themselves to make their preparations, and having appointed such ambassadors as Tarquinius wished, dismissed the assembly.

53 When the Latins had dispersed to their several cities, Mamilius and Tarquinius, observing that the enthusiasm of most of the people had flagged, began to abandon their hopes of foreign assistance as not very certain, and changing their minds, they formed plans to stir up in Rome itself a civil war, against which their enemies would not be on their guard, by fomenting a sedition of the poor against the rich. Already the greater part of the common people were uneasy and disaffected, especially the poor and those who were compelled by their debts no longer to have the best interests of the commonwealth at heart. For the creditors showed no moderation in the use of their power, but haling their debtors to prison, treated them like slaves they had purchased. Tarquinius, hearing of this, sent some persons who were free from suspicion to Rome with money, in company with the ambassadors of the Latins, and these men, engaging in conversation with the needy and with those who were boldest, and giving them some money and promising more if the Tarquinii returned, corrupted a great many of the citizens. And thus a conspiracy was formed against the aristocracy, not only by needy freemen, but also by unprincipled slaves who were beguiled by hopes of freedom. The latter, because of the punishment of their fellow-slaves the year before, were hostile toward their masters and in a mood to plot against them, since they were distrusted by them and suspected of being ready themselves also to attack them at some time if the opportunity should offer; and accordingly they hearkened willingly to those who invited them to make the attempt. The plan of their conspiracy was as follows: The leaders of the undertaking were to wait for a moonless night and then seize the heights and the other strong places in the city; and the slaves, when they perceived that the others were in possession of those places of advantage (which was to be made known to them by raising a shout), were to kill their masters while they slept, and having done this, to plunder the houses of the rich and open the gates to the tyrants.

54 But the divine Providence, which has on every occasion preserved this city and down to my own times continues to watch over it, brought their plans to light, information being given to Sulpicius, one of the consuls, by two brothers, Publius and Marcus Tarquinius of Laurentum, who were among the heads of the conspiracy and were forced by the compulsion of Heaven to reveal it. For frightful visions haunted them in their dreams whenever they slept, threatening them with dire punishments if they did not desist and abandon their attempt; and at last they thought that they were pursued and beaten by some demons, that their eyes were gouged out, and that they suffered many other cruel torments. In consequence of which they would wake with fear and trembling, and they could not even sleep because of these terrors. At first they endeavoured, by means of certain propitiatory and expiatory sacrifices, to avert the anger of the demons who haunted them; but accomplishing naught, they had recourse to divination, keeping secret the purpose of their enterprise and asking only to know whether it was yet the time to carry out their plan; and when the soothsayer answered that they were travelling an evil and fatal road, and that if they did not change their plans they would perish in the most shameful manner, fearing lest others should anticipate them in revealing the secret, they themselves gave information of the conspiracy to the consul who was then at Rome. He, having commended them and promised them great rewards if they made their actions conform to their words, kept them in his house without telling anyone; and introducing to the senate the ambassadors of the Latins, whom he had hitherto kept putting off, delaying his answer, he now gave them the answer that the senators had decided upon. "Friends and kinsmen," he said, "go back and report to the Latin nation that the Roman people did not either in the first instance grant the request of the Tarquinienses for the restoration of the tyrants or afterwards yield to all the Tyrrhenians, led by King Porsena, when they interceded in behalf of these same exiles and brought upon the commonwealth the most grievous of all wars, but submitted to seeing their land laid waste, their farm-houses set on fire, and themselves shut up within their walls for the sake of liberty and of not having to act otherwise than they wished at the command of another. And they wonder, Latins, that though you are aware of this, you have nevertheless come to them with orders to receive the tyrants and to raise the siege of Fidenae, and, if they refuse to obey you, threaten them with war. Cease, then, putting forward these stupid and improbable excuses for enmity; and if for these reasons you are determined to dissolve your ties of kinship and to declare war, defer it no longer."

55 Having given this answer to the ambassadors and ordered them to be conducted out of the city, he then told the senate everything relating to the secret conspiracy which he had learned from the informers. And receiving from the senate full authority to seek out the participants in the conspiracy and to punish those who should be discovered, he did not pursue the arbitrary and tyrannical course that anyone else might have followed under the like necessity, but resorted to the reasonable and safe course that was consistent with the form of government then established. Thus he was unwilling, in the first place, that citizens should be seized in their own houses and haled thence to death, torn from the embraces of their wives, children and parents, but considered the compassion which the relations of the various culprits would feel at the violent snatching away of those who were closest to them, and also feared that some of the guilty, if they were driven to despair, might rush to arms, and those who were forced to turn to illegal methods might engage in civil bloodshed. Nor, again, did he think he ought to appoint tribunals to try them, since he reasoned that they would all deny their guilt and that no certain and incontrovertible proof of it, besides the information he had just received, could be laid before the judges to which they would give credit and condemn the citizens to death. But he devised a new method of outwitting those who were stirring up sedition, a method by which, in the first place, the leaders of the conspiracy would of themselves, without any compulsion, meet in one place, and then would be convicted by incontrovertible proofs, so that they would be left without any defence whatever; furthermore, as they would not then be assembled in an unfrequented place nor convicted before a few witnesses only, but their guilt would be made manifest in the Forum before the eyes of all, they would suffer the punishment they deserved, and there would be no disturbance in the city nor uprisings on the part of others, as often happens when the seditious are punished, particularly in dangerous times.

Book V

56 Another historian, now, might have thought it sufficient to state merely the gist of this matter, namely, that the consul apprehended those who had taken part in the conspiracy and point them to death, as if the facts needed little explanation. But I, since I regarded the manner also of their apprehension as being worthy of history, decided not to omit it, considering that the readers of histories do not derive sufficient profit from learning the bare outcome of events, but that everyone demands that the causes of events also be related, as well as the ways in which things were done, the motives of those who did them, and the instances of divine intervention, and that they be left uninformed of none of the circumstances that naturally attend those events. And for statesmen I perceive that the knowledge of these things is absolutely necessary, to the end that they may have precedents for their use in the various situations that arise. Now the manner of apprehending the conspirators devised by the consul was this: From among the senators he selected those who were in the vigour of their age and ordered that, as soon as the signal should be given, they, together with their most trusted friends and relations, should seize the strong places of the city where each of them chanced to dwell; and the knights he commanded to wait, equipped with their swords, in the most convenient houses round the Forum and to do whatever he should command. And to the end that, while he was apprehending the citizens,[69] neither their relations nor any of the other citizens should create a disturbance and that there might be no civil bloodshed by reason of this commotion, he sent a letter to the consul who had been appointed to conduct the siege of Fidenae, bidding him come to the city at the beginning of night with the flower of his army and to encamp upon a height near the walls.

---

69 This word is suspicious here. Bücheler (see critical note) proposed to read "conspirators."

57 Having made these preparations, he ordered those who had given information of the plot to send word[70] to the heads of the conspiracy to come to the Forum about midnight bringing with them their most trusted friends, there to learn their appointed place and station and the watch-word and what each of them was to do. This was done. And when all the leaders among the conspirators had assembled in the Forum, signals, not perceived by them, were given, and immediately the heights were filling with men who had taken up arms in defence of the state and all the parts round the Forum were under guard by the knights, not a single outlet being left for any who might desire to leave. And at the same time Manius, the other consul, having broken camp at Fidenae, arrived in the Field[71] with his army. As soon as day appeared, the consuls, surrounded by armed men, advanced to the tribunal and ordered the heralds to go through all the streets and summon the people to an assembly; and when the entire populace of the city had flocked thither, they acquainted them with the conspiracy formed to restore the tyrant,and produced the informers. After that they gave the accused an opportunity of making their defence if any of them had any objections to offer to the information. When none attempted to resort to denial, they withdrew from the Forum to the senate-house to ask the opinion of the senators concerning them; and having caused their decision to be written out, they returned to the assembly and read the decree, which was as follows: To the Tarquinii who had given information of the attempt should be granted citizenship and ten thousand drachmae of silver to each and twenty acres[72] of the public land; and the conspirators should be seized and put to death, if the people concurred. The assembled

---

70 An infinitive with essentially this meaning seems to have fallen out of the text. See critical note.
71 The Campus Martius.
72 See note to chap. 49, 2.

crowd having confirmed the decree of the senate, the consuls ordered those who had come together for the assembly to withdraw from the Forum; then they summoned the lictors, who were equipped with their swords, and these, surrounding the guilty men in the place where they were hemmed in, put them all to death. After the consuls had caused these men to be executed, they received no more informations against any who had participated in the plot, but acquitted of the charges everyone who had escaped summary punishment, to the end that all cause of disturbance might be removed from the city. In such fashion were those who had formed the conspiracy put to death. The senate then ordered all the citizens to be purified because they had been under the necessity of giving their votes about shedding the blood of citizens, on the ground that it was not lawful for them to be present at the sacred rites and take part in the sacrifices before they had expiated the pollution and atoned for the calamity by the customary lustrations. After everything that was required by divine law had been performed by the interpreters[73] of religious matter according to the custom of the country, the senate voted to offer sacrifices of thanksgiving and to celebrate games, and set aside three days as sacred for this purpose. And when Manius Tullius, one of the consuls, fell from the sacred chariot in the Circus itself during the procession at the sacred games called after the name of the city[74] and died the third day after, Sulpicius continued alone in the magistracy during the rest of the time, which was not long.

58 Publius Veturius Geminus[75] and Publius Aebutius Elva were appointed consuls for the following year. Of these Aebutius was put in charge of the civil affairs, which seemed to require no small

---

73 The *pontifices*.
74 The *ludi Romani*.
75 *Cf.* Livy ii. 19 f. The Roman historian calls these consuls C. Vetusius and T Aebutius.

attention, lest some fresh uprising should be made by the poor. And Veturius, marching out with one half of the army, laid waste the lands of the Fidenates without opposition, and sitting down before the town, delivered attacks without ceasing; but not being able to take the wall by siege, he proceeded to surround the town with palisades and a ditch, intending to reduce the inhabitants by famine. The Fidenates were already in great distress when assistance from the Latins arrived, sent by Sextus Tarquinius, together with grain, arms and other supplies for the war. Encouraged by this, they made bold to come out of the town with an army of no small size and encamped in the open. The line of contravallation was now of no further use to the Romans, but a battle seemed necessary; and an engagement took place near the city, the outcome of which for some time remained indecisive. Then, forced back by the stubborn endurance of the Romans, in which they excelled because of their long training, the Fidenates, though more numerous, were put to flight by the smaller force. They did not suffer any great loss, however, since their retreat into the city was over a short distance and the men who manned the walls repulsed the pursuers. After this action the auxiliary troops dispersed and returned home, without having been of any service to the inhabitants; and the city found itself once more in the same distress and laboured under a scarcity of provisions. About the same time, Sextus Tarquinius marched with an army of Latins to Signia, then in the possession of the Romans, in expectation of taking the place by storm. When the garrison made a brave resistance, he was prepared to force them by famine to quit the place,and he remained there a considerable time without accomplishing anything worth mentioning; but finding himself disappointed of this hope also when provisions and assistance from the consuls reached the garrison, he raised the siege and departed with his army.

Book V

59 The following year[76] the Romans created Titus Larcius Flavus and Quintus Cloelius Siculus consuls. Of these, Cloelius was appointed by the senate to conduct the civil administration and with one half of the army to guard against any who might be inclined to sedition; for he was looked upon as fair-minded and democratic. Larcius, on his part, set out for the war against the Fidenates with a well-equipped army, after getting ready everything necessary for a siege. And to the Fidenates, who were in dire straits owing to the length of the war and in want of all the necessaries of life, he proved a sore affliction by undermining the foundations of the walls, raising mounds, bringing up his engines of war, and continuing the attacks night and day, in the expectation of taking the city in a short time by storm. Nor were the Latin cities, on which alone the Fidenates had relied in undertaking the war, able any longer to save them; for not one of their cities had sufficient strength by itself to raise the siege for them, and as yet no army had been raised jointly by the whole nation. But to the ambassadors who came frequently from Fidenae the leading men of the various cities kept giving the same answer, that aid would soon come to them; no action, however, followed corresponding to the promises, but the hopes of assistance they held out went no farther than words. Notwithstanding this, the Fidenates had not altogether despaired of help from the Latins, but supported themselves with constancy under all their dreadful experiences by their confidence in those hopes. Above all else, the famine was what they could not cope with and this caused the death of many inhabitants. When at last they gave way to their calamities, they sent ambassadors to the consul to ask for a truce for a definite number of days, in order to deliberate during that time concerning the conditions upon which they should enter into a league of friendship with the Romans. But this time was not sought by them for deliberating, but for securing reinforcements, as was revealed by

76 For chaps. 59-77 *Cf.* Livy ii. 21, 1, also 18, 4-8.

some of the deserters who had lately come over to the Romans. For the night before they had sent the most important of their citizens and such as had the greatest influence in the cities of the Latins to their general council bearing the tokens of suppliants.

60 Larcius, being aware of this beforehand, ordered those who asked for a truce to lay down their arms and open their gates first, and then to treat with him. Otherwise, he told them, they would get neither peace nor a truce nor any other humane or moderate treatment from Rome. He also, by stationing more diligent guards along all the roads leading to the city, took care that the ambassadors sent to the Latin nation should not get back inside the walls. Consequently the besieged, despairing of the hoped for assistance from their allies, were compelled to have recourse to supplicating their enemies. And meeting in assembly, they decided to submit to such conditions of peace as the conqueror prescribed. But the commanders at that time, it seems, were in their whole behaviour so obedient to the civil power and so far removed from tyrannical presumption (which only a few of the commanders in our days, elated by the greatness of their power, have been able to avoid), that the consul, after taking over the city, did nothing on his own responsibility, but ordering the inhabitants to lay down their arms and leaving a garrison in the citadel, went himself to Rome, and assembling the senate, left it to them to consider how those who had surrendered themselves ought to be treated. Thereupon the senators, admiring him for the honour he had shown them, decided that the most prominent of the Fidenates and those who had been the authors of the revolt — these to be named by the consul — should be scourged with rods and beheaded; but concerning the rest, they gave him authority to do everything he thought fit. Larcius, having thus been given full power in all matters, ordered some few of the Fidenates, who were accused by those of the opposite party, to be put to death before the eyes of all and confiscated their fortunes; but all the others he permitted to retain both their city and their goods. Nevertheless, he took from them one half of their territory, which was divided by lot among those Romans who were left in the city as a garrison for the citadel. Having settled these matters, he returned home with his army.

61 When the Latins heard of the capture of Fidenae, every city was in a state of the utmost excitement and fear, and all the citizens were angry with those who were at the head of federal affairs, accusing them of having betrayed their allies. And a general assembly being held at Ferentinum,[77] those who urged a recourse to arms, particularly Tarquinius and his son-in-law Mamilius, together with the heads of the Arician state, inveighed bitterly against those who opposed the war; and by their harangues all the deputies of the Latin nation were persuaded to undertake the war jointly against the Romans. And to the end that no city might either betray the common cause or be reconciled to the Romans without the consent of all, they swore oaths to one another and voted that those who violated this agreement should be excluded from their alliance, be accursed and regarded as the enemies of all. The deputies who subscribed to the treaty and swore to its observance were from the following cities:[78] Ardea, Aricia, Bovillae, Bubentum, Cora,

---

77 Thayer's Note: Neither the Etruscan Ferentinum nor the Hernican Ferentinum, but the Latin town by that name.

78 It will be observed that this list of cities is given in the order of the Roman alphabet, at least in so far as the initial letter is concerned. Only twenty-nine cities are named, in place of the thirty we should expect. The edition of Stephanus, to be sure, added the name Τρικρίνων after Τυσκλανῶν; but where he found it, no one knows. No Tricrium or Tricria is known to us, hence the name was emended to Trebia by Gelenius and to Tarracina by more recent scholars. As the Greek text gives, not the names of the cities themselves, but the names of their inhabitants, the exact form for the name of the city is uncertain in a few cases. Thus the forms may be either Cabum, Caba or Cabe; Fortinea or Fortinei; Querquetulum or Querquetula. Instead

Carventum, Circeii, Corioli, Corbio, Cabum,[79] Fortinea, Gabii, Laurentum, Lanuvium, Lavinium, Labici, Nomentum, Norba, Praeneste, Pedum, Querquetula, Satricum, Scaptia, Setia, Tibur, Tusculum, Tolerium, Tellenae, Velitrae. They voted that as many men of military age from all these cities should take part in the campaign as their commanders, Octavius Mamilius and Sextus Tarquinius, should require; for they had appointed these to be their generals with absolute power. And in order that the grounds they offered for the war might appear plausible, they sent the most prominent men from every city to Rome as ambassadors. These, upon being introduced to the senate, said that the Arician state preferred the following charges against the Roman state: When the Tyrrhenians had made war upon the Aricians, the Romans had not only granted them a safe passage through their territory, but had also assisted them with everything they required for the war, and having received such of the Tyrrhenians as fled from the defeat, they had saved them when they all were wounded and without arms, though they could not be ignorant that they were making war against the whole nation in common, and that if they had once made themselves masters of the city of Aricia nothing could have hindered them from enslaving all the other cities as well. If, therefore, the Romans would consent to appear before the general tribunal of the Latins and answer there the accusations brought against them by the Aricians, and would abide by the decision of all the members, they said the Romans would not need to have a war; but if they persisted in their usual arrogance and refused to make any just and reasonable concessions to their kinsmen, they threatened that all the Latins would make war upon them with all their might.

---

of Bovillae several scholars have preferred to read Bola.

79 For this form *cf.* De Sanctis, *Storia dei Romani*, i. 378, n. 5, and in Pauly-Wissowa *s.v.* Cabenses.

62 This was the proposal made by the ambassadors; but the senate was unwilling to plead its cause with the Aricians in a controversy in which their accusers would be the judges, and they did not imagine that their enemies would even confine their judgment to these charges alone, but would add other demands still more grievous than these; and accordingly they voted to accept war. So far, indeed, as bravery and experience in warfare were concerned, they did not suppose any misfortune would befall the commonwealth, but the multitude of their enemies alarmed them; and sending ambassadors in many directions, they invited the neighbouring cities to an alliance, while the Latins in their turn sent counter-embassies to the same cities and bitterly assailed Rome. The Hernicans, meeting together, gave suspicious and insincere answers to both embassies, saying that they would not for the present enter into an alliance with either, but would consider at leisure which of the two nations made the juster claims, and that they would give a year's time to that consideration. The Rutulians openly promised the Latins that they would send them assistance, and assured the Romans that, if they would consent to give up their enmity, they through their influence would cause the Latins to moderate their demands and would mediate a peace between them. The Volscians said they even wondered at the shamelessness of the Romans, who, though conscious of the many injuries they had done them, and particularly of the latest, in taking from them the best part of their territory and retaining it, had nevertheless had the effrontery to invite them, who were their enemies, to an alliance; and they advised them first to restore their lands and then to ask satisfaction from them as from friends. The Tyrrhenians put obstacles in the way of both sides by alleging that they had lately made a treaty with the Romans and that they had ties of kinship and friendship with the Tarquinii. Notwithstanding these answers, the Romans abated nothing of their spirit, which would have been a natural thing for those who were entering upon a dangerous war and had given up hope of any assistance from their allies; but trusting to their own forces alone, they grew much more eager for the contest, in the confidence that because of their necessity they would acquit themselves as brave men in the face of danger, and that if they succeeded according to their wish and won the war by their own valour, the glory of it would not have to be shared with anyone else. Such spirit and daring had they acquired from their many contests in the past.

63 While they were preparing everything that was necessary for the war and beginning to enrol their troops, they fell into great perplexity when they found that all the citizens did not show the same eagerness for the service. For the needy, and particularly those who were unable to discharge their debts to their creditors — and there were many such — when called to arms refused to obey and were unwilling to join with the patricians in any undertaking unless they passed a vote for the remission of their debts. On the contrary, some of them threatened even to leave the city and exhorted one another to give up their fondness for living in a city that allowed them no share in any thing that was good. At first the patricians endeavoured by entreaties to prevail upon them to change their purpose, but finding that in response to their entreaties they showed no greater moderation, they then assembled in the senate-house to consider what would be the most seemly method of putting an end to the disturbance that was troubling the state. Those senators, therefore, who were fair-minded and of moderate fortunes advised them to remit the debts of the poor and to purchase for a small price the goodwill of their fellow-citizens, from which they were sure to derive great advantages both private and public.

64 The author of this advice was Marcus Valerius, the son of Publius Valerius, one of those who had overthrown the tyranny and from his goodwill toward the common people had been called Publicola. He showed them that those who fight for equal rewards are apt to be inspired to action by an equal spirit of emulation, whereas it never occurs to those who are to reap no advantage to entertain any thought of bravery. He said that all the poor people were exasperated and were going about the Forum saying: "What advantage shall we gain by overcoming our foreign enemies if we are liable to be haled to prison for debt by the money-lenders, or by gaining the leadership for the commonwealth if we ourselves cannot maintain even the liberty of our own persons?" He then showed them that this was not the only danger which had been brought upon them in case the people should become hostile to the senate, namely, that they would abandon the city in the midst of its perils — a possibility at which all who desired the preservation of the commonwealth must shudder — but that there was the further danger, still more formidable than this, that, seduced by favours from the tyrants, they might take up arms against the patricians and aid in restoring Tarquinius to power. Accordingly, while it was still only a matter of words and threats, and no mischievous deed had been committed by the people as yet, he advised them to act in time and reconcile the people to the situation by affording them this relief; for they were neither the first to adopt such a measure nor would they incur any great disgrace on account of it, but could point to many others who had submitted, not only to this, but to other demands much more grievous, when they had no alternative. For necessity, he said, is stronger than human nature, and people insist on considering appearances only when they have already gained safety.

65 After he had enumerated many examples taken from many cities, he at last offered them that of the city of Athens, then in the greatest repute for wisdom, which not very long before, but in the time of their fathers, had under the guidance of Solon voted remission of debts to the poor; and no one, he said, censured the city for this measure or called its author a flatterer of the people or a knave, but all bore witness both to the great prudence of those who were persuaded to enact it and to the great wisdom of the man who persuaded them do so. As for the Romans, whose perilous situation was due to no trivial differences, but to the danger of being delivered up again to a cruel tyrant more savage than any wild beast, what man in his senses could blame them if by this instance of humanity they should cause the poor to become joint supporters, instead of enemies, of the commonwealth? After enumerating these foreign examples he ended with a reference to their own actions, reminding them of the straits to which they had been lately reduced when, their country being in the power of the Tyrrhenians and they themselves shut up within their walls and in great want of the necessaries of life, they had not taken the foolish resolutions of madmen courting death, but yielding to the emergency that was upon them and allowing necessity to teach them their interest, had consented to deliver up to King Porsena their most prominent children as hostages, a thing to which they had never submitted before, to be deprived of part of their territory by the cession of the Seven Districts to the Tyrrhenians, to accept the enemy as the judge of the accusations brought against them by the tyrant, and to furnish provisions, arms, and everything else the Tyrrhenians required as the condition of their putting an end to the war. Having made use of these examples, he went on to show that it was not the part of the same prudence first to refuse no terms insisted on by their enemies and then to make war over a trivial difference upon their own citizens who had fought many glorious battles for Rome's supremacy while the kings held sway, and had shown great eagerness in assisting the patricians to free the state from the tyrants, and would show still greater zeal in what remained to be done, if

506

invited to do so; for, though they lacked the means of existence, they would freely expose their persons and lives, which were all they had left, to any dangers for her sake. In conclusion he said that, even if these men from a sense of shame forbore to say or demand anything of this kind, the patricians ought to take proper account of them and to give them readily whatever they knew they needed, whether as a class or individually, bearing in mind that they, the patricians, were doing an arrogant thing in asking of them their persons while refusing them money, and in publishing to all the world that they were making war to preserve the common liberty even while they were depriving of liberty those who had assisted them in establishing it, though they could reproach them with no wrongdoing, but only with poverty, which deserved compassion rather than hatred.

66 After Valerius had spoken to this effect and many had approved of his advice, Appius Claudius Sabinus, being called upon at the proper time, advised the opposite course, declaring that the seditious spirit would not be removed from the state if they decreed an abolition of debts, but would become more dangerous by being transferred from the poor to the rich. For it was plain enough to everyone that those who were to be deprived of their money would resent it, as they were not only citizens in possession of all civil rights, but had also served their country in all the campaigns that fell to their lot, and would regard it as unjust that the money left them by their fathers, together with what they themselves had by their industry and frugality acquired, should be confiscated for the benefit of the most unprincipled and the laziest of the citizens. It would be the part of great folly for them, in their desire to gratify the worse part of the citizenry, to disregard the better element, and in confiscating the fortunes of others for the benefit of the most unjust of the citizens, to take them away from those who had justly acquired them. He asked them also to bear in mind that states are not overthrown by those who are poor and without power, when they are compelled to do justice, but by the rich and such as are capable of administering public affairs, when they are insulted by their inferiors and fail to keep justice. And even if those who were to be deprived of the benefit of their contracts were not going to harbour any resentment but would submit with some degree of meekness and indifference to their losses, yet even in that case, he said, it would be neither honourable nor safe for them to gratify the poor with such a gift, by which the life of the community would be devoid of all intercourse, full of mutual hatred, and lacking in the necessary employments without which cities cannot be inhabited, since neither the husbandmen would any longer sow and plant their lands, nor the merchants sail the sea and trade in foreign markets, nor the poor employ themselves in any other just occupation. For none of the rich would throw away their money to supply those who needed the means of carrying on any of these occupations; and in consequence wealth would be hated and industry destroyed, and the prodigal would be in a better condition than the frugal, the unjust than the just, and those who appropriated to themselves the fortunes of others would have the advantage over those who guarded their own. These were the things that created seditions in states, mutual slaughter without end,and every other sort of mischief, by which the most prosperous of them had lost their liberty and those whose lot was less fortunate had been totally destroyed.

67 But, above all, he advised them, in instituting a new form of government, to take care that no bad customs should gain admittance there. For he declared that of whatever nature the public principles of states were, such of necessity would be the lives of the individual citizens. And there was no worse practice, he said, either for states or for families, than for everyone to live always according to his own pleasure and for everything to be granted to inferiors by their superiors, whether out of favour or from necessity. For the desires of the unintelligent are not satisfied when they obtain what they demand, but they immediately covet other and greater things, and so on without end; and this is the case particularly with the masses. For the lawless deeds which each one by himself is either ashamed or afraid to commit, being restrained by the more powerful, they are more ready to engage in when they have got together and gained strength for their own inclinations from those who are like minded. And since the desires of the unintelligent mob are insatiable and boundless, it is necessary, he said, to check them at the very outset, while they are weak, instead of trying to destroy them after they have become great and powerful. For all men feel more violent anger when deprived of what has already been granted to them than when disappointed of what they merely hope for. He cited many examples to prove this, relating the experiences of various Greek cities which, having become weakened because of certain critical situations and having given admittance to the beginnings of evil practices, had no longer had the power to put an end to them and abolish them, in consequence of which they had been compelled to go on into shameful and irreparable calamities. He said the commonwealth resembled each particular man, the senate bearing some resemblance to the soul of a man and the people to his body. If, therefore, they permitted the unintelligent populace to govern the senate, they would fare the same as those who subject the soul to the body and live under the influence, not of their reason, but of their passions; whereas, if they accustomed the populace to be governed and led by the senate, they would be doing the same as those who subject the body to the soul and lead lives directed toward what is best, not most pleasant. He showed them that no great mischief would befall the state if the poor, dissatisfied with them for not granting an abolition of debts, should refuse to take up arms in its defence, declaring that there were few indeed who had nothing left but their persons, and these would neither offer any remarkable advantage to the state when present on its expeditions, nor, by their absence to do any great harm. For those who had the lowest rating in the census, he reminded them, were posted in the rear in battle and counted as a mere appendage to the forces that were arrayed in the battle-line, being present merely to strike the enemy with terror, since they had no other arms but slings, which are of the least use in action.

68 He said that those who thought it proper to pity the poverty of the citizens and who advised relieving such of them as were unable to pay their debts ought to inquire what it was that had made them poor, when they had inherited the lands their fathers had left them and had gained much booty from their campaigns, and, last of all, when each of them had received his share of the confiscated property of the tyrants; and after that they ought to look upon such of them as they found had lived for their bellies and the most shameful pleasures, and by such means had lost their fortunes, as a disgrace and injury to the city, and to regard it as a great benefit to the common weal if they would voluntarily get to the devil out of the city. But in the case of such as they found to have lost their fortunes through an unkind fate, he advised them to relieve these with their private means. Their creditors, he said, not only understood this best, but would attend to it best, and would themselves relieve their misfortunes, not under compulsion from others, but voluntarily, to the end that gratitude, instead of their money, might accrue to them as a noble debt. But to extend the relief to all alike, when the worthless would share it equally with the deserving, and to confer benefits on certain persons, not at their own expense, but at that of others, and not to leave to those whose money they took away even the gratitude owed for these services, was in no wise consistent with the virtue of Romans. But above all these and the other considerations, it was a grievous and intolerable thing for the Romans, who were laying claim to the leadership — a leadership which their ancestors had acquired through many hardships and left to their posterity — if they could not do what was best and most advantageous for the commonwealth also, by their own choice, or when convinced by argument, or at the proper time, but, just as if the city had been captured or were expecting to suffer that fate, must do things contrary to their own judgment from which they would receive very little benefit, if any, but would run the risk of suffering the very worst of ills. For it was far better for them to submit to the commands of the Latins, as being more moderate, and not even to try the fortune of war, than by yielding to the pleas of those who were of no use upon any occasion, to abolish from the state the public faith, which their ancestors had appointed to be honoured by the erection of a temple and by sacrifices performed throughout the year[80] — and this when they were merely going to add a body of slingers to their forces for the war. The sum and substance of his advice was this: to take for the business in hand such citizens as were willing to share the fortune of the war upon the same terms as every other Roman, and to let those who insisted upon any special terms whatever for taking up arms for their country go hang, since they would be of no use even if they did arm. For if they knew this, he said, they would yield and show themselves prompt to obey those who took the wisest counsel for the commonwealth; since all the unintelligent are generally wont, when flattered, to be arrogant, and when terrified, to show restraint.

69 These were the extreme opinions delivered upon that occasion, but there were many which took the middle ground between the two. For some of the senators favoured remitting the

---

80 *Cf.* ii. 75, 3.

debts of those only who had nothing, permitting the moneylenders to seize the goods of the debtors, but not their persons. Others advised that the public treasury should discharge the obligations of the insolvents, in order both that the credit of the poor might be preserved by this public favour and their creditors might suffer no injustice. Certain others thought that they ought to ransom the persons of those who were already being held for debt or were going to be deprived of their liberty, by substituting captives in their stead and assigning these to their creditors. After various views such as these had been expressed, the opinion that prevailed was that they should pass no decree for the time being concerning these matters, but that after the wars were ended in the most satisfactory manner, the consuls should then bring them up for discussion and take the votes of the senators; and that in the meantime there should be no money exacted by virtue of either any contract or any judgment, that all other suits should be dropped, and that neither the courts of justice should sit nor the magistrates take cognizance of anything but what related to the war. When this decree was brought to the people, it allayed in some measure the civil commotion, yet it did not entirely remove the spirit of sedition from the state. For some of the labouring class did not look upon the hope held out by the senate, which contained nothing express or certain, as a sufficient relief; but they demanded that the senate should do one of two things, either grant them the remission of debts immediately, if it wanted to have them as partners in the dangers of the war, or not delude them by deferring it to another occasion. For men's sentiments, they said, were very different when they were making requests and after their requests had been satisfied.

70 While[81] the public affairs were in this condition, the senate, considering by what means it could most effectually prevent the plebeians from creating any fresh disturbances, resolved to abolish the consular power for the time being and to create some other magistracy with full authority over war and peace and every other matter, possessed of absolute power and subject to no accounting for either its counsels or its actions. The term of this new magistracy was to be limited to six months, after the expiration of which time the consuls were again to govern. The reasons that compelled the senate to submit to a voluntary tyranny in order to put an end to the war brought upon them by their tyrant were many and various, but the chief one was the law introduced by the consul Publius Valerius, called Publicola (concerning which I stated in the beginning[82] that it rendered invalid the decisions of the consuls), providing that no Roman should be punished before he was tried, and granting to any who were haled to punishment by their orders the right to appeal from their decision to the people, and until the people had given their vote concerning them, the right to enjoy security for both their persons and their fortunes; and it ordained that if any person attempted to do anything contrary to these provisions he might be put to death with impunity. The senate reasoned that while this law remained in force the poor could not be compelled to obey the magistrates, because, as it was reasonable to suppose, they would scorn the punishments which they were to undergo, not immediately, but only after they had been condemned by the people, whereas, when this law had been repealed, all would be under the greatest necessity of obeying orders. And to the end that the poor might offer no opposition, in case an open attempt were made to

---

81 On the creation of the dictatorship (chaps. 70-77) *cf.* Livy ii. 18, 4-8. Livy follows the oldest authorities in making T. Larcius the first dictator, with Spurius Cassius his Master of the Horse, three years earlier than the date adopted by Dionysius.

82 Chap. 19, 4.

repeal the law itself, the senate resolved to introduce into the government a magistracy of equal power with a tyranny, which should be superior to all the laws. And they passed a decree by which they deceived the poor and, without being detected, repealed the law that secured their liberty. The decree was to this effect; that Larcius and Cloelius, who were the consuls at the time, should resign their power, and likewise any other person who held a magistracy or had the oversight of any public business; and that a single person, to be chosen by the senate and approved of by the people, should be invested with the whole authority of the commonwealth and exercise it for a period not longer than six months, having power superior to that of the consuls. The plebeians, being unaware of the real import of this proposal, ratified the resolutions of the senate, although, in fact, a magistracy that was superior to a legal magistracy was a tyranny; and they gave the senators permission to deliberate by themselves and choose the person who was to hold it.

71 After this the leading men of the senate devoted much earnest thought to searching for the man who should be entrusted with the command. For they felt that the situation required a man both vigorous in action and of wide experience in warfare, a man, moreover, possessed of prudence and self-control, who would not be led into folly by the greatness of his power; but, above all these qualities and the others essential in good generals, a man was required who knew how to govern with firmness and would show no leniency toward the disobedient, a quality of which they then stood particularly in need. And though they observed that all the qualities they demanded were to be found in Titus Larcius, one of the consuls (for Cloelius, who excelled in all administrative virtues, was not a man of action nor fond of war, nor had he the ability to command others and to inspire fear, but was a mild punisher of the

514

disobedient), they were nevertheless ashamed to deprive one of the consuls of the magistracy of which he was legally possessed and to confer upon the other the power of both, a power which was being created greater than the kingly authority. Besides, they were under some secret apprehensions lest Cloelius, taking to heart his removal from office and considering it a dishonour put upon him by the senate, might change his sentiments and, becoming a patron of the people, overthrow the whole government. And when all were ashamed to lay their thoughts before the senate, and this situation had continued for a considerable time, at last the oldest and most honoured of the men of consular rank delivered an opinion by which he preserved an equal share of honour to both the consuls and yet found out from those men themselves the one who was the more suitable to command. He said that, since the senate had decreed and the people in confirmation thereof had voted that the power of this magistracy should be entrusted to a single person, and since two matters remained that required no small deliberation and thought, namely, who should be the one to receive this magistracy that was of equal power with a tyranny, and by what legal authority he should be appointed, it was his opinion that one of the present consuls, either by consent of his colleague or by recourse to the lot, should choose among all the Romans the person he thought would govern the commonwealth in the best and most advantageous manner. They had no need on the present occasion, he said, of *interreges*, to whom it had been customary under the monarchy to give the sole power of appointing those who were to reign, since the commonwealth was already provided with the lawful[83] magistrate.

72 This opinion being applauded by all, another senator rose up and said: "I think, senators, this also ought to be added to the motion, namely, that as two persons of the greatest worth have at

---

83 Or, adopting Post's emendation, "the annual magistracy."

present the administration of the public affairs, men whose superiors you could not find, one of them should be empowered to make the nomination and the other should be appointed by his colleague, after they have considered together which of them is the more suitable person, to the end that, as the honour is equal between them, so the satisfaction may be equal also, to the one, in having declared his colleague to be the best man, and to the other, in having been declared the best by his colleague; for each of these things is pleasing and honourable. I know, to be sure, that even if this amendment were not made to the motion, they themselves would have thought proper to act in this manner; but it is better it should appear that you likewise approve of no other course." This proposal also seemed to meet with the approval of all, and the motion was then passed without further amendment. When the consuls had received the authority to decide which of them was the more suitable to command, they did a thing both admirable in itself and passing all human belief. For each of them declared, as worthy of the command, not himself, but the other; and they continued all that day enumerating one another's virtues and begging that they themselves might not receive the command, so that all who were present in the senate were in great perplexity. When the senate had been dismissed, the kinsmen of each and the most honoured among the senators at large came to Larcius and continued to entreat him till far into the night, informing him that the senate had placed all its hopes in him and declaring that his indifference toward the command was prejudicial to the commonwealth. But Larcius was unmoved, and in his turn continued to address many prayers and entreaties to each of them. The next day, when the senate had again assembled, and he still resisted and, in spite of the advice of all the senators, would not change his mind, Cloelius rose up and nominated him, according to the practice of the *interreges*, and then abdicated the consulship himself.

Book V

73 Larcius was the first man to be appointed sole ruler at Rome with absolute authority in war, in peace, and in all other matters They call this magistrate a dictator, either from his power of issuing whatever orders he wishes and of prescribing for the others rules of justice and right as he thinks proper (for the Romans call commands and ordinances respecting what is right and wrong *edicta* or "edicts")[84] so, as some write, from the form of nomination which was then introduced, since he was to receive the magistracy, not from the people, according to ancestral usage, but by the appointment of one man. For they did not think they ought to give an invidious and obnoxious title to any magistracy that had the oversight of a free people, as well as for the sake of the governed, lest they should be alarmed by the odious terms of address, as from a regard for the men who were assuming the magistracies, lest they should unconsciously either suffer some injury from others or themselves commit against others acts of injustice of the sort that positions of such authority bring in their train. For the extent of the power which the dictator possesses is by no means indicated by the title; for the dictatorship is in reality an elective tyranny. The Romans seem to me to have taken this institution also from the Greeks. For the magistrates anciently called among the Greeks *aisymnêtaí*[85] or "regulators," as Theophrastus writes in his treatise *On Kingship*,[86] were a kind of elective tyrants. They were chosen by the cities, not for a definite time nor continuously, but for emergencies, as often

---

84 The first explanation assumes that *dictator* comes from *dictare* and means "one who dictates, or prescribes;" the second derives the title from the circumstance that he was *dictus* ("named") by one individual rather than *creatus* ("elected"). Both explanations are found in Roman writers, though the second is patently absurd.

85 The word **aisymnêtês** is supposed to have meant "one mindful of what is just" or "one who awards the just portion"; in heroic days the name was applied to umpires at games.

86 The authenticity of this work was challenged by the ancients.

and for as long a time as seemed convenient; just as the Mitylenaeans, for example, once chose Pittacus to oppose the exiles headed by Alcaeus, the poet.

74 The first men who had recourse to this institution had learned the advantage of it by experience. For in the beginning all the Greek cities were governed by kings, though not despotically, like the barbarian nations, but according to certain laws and time-honoured customs, and he was the best king who was the most just, the most observant of the laws, and did not in any wise depart from the established customs. This appears from Homer, who calls kings *dikaspoloi* or "ministers of justice," and *themistopoloi* or "ministers of the laws." And kingships continued to be carried on for a long time subject to certain stated conditions, like that of the Lacedaemonians. But as some of the kings began to abuse their powers and made little use of the laws, but settled most matters according to their own judgment, people in general grew dissatisfied with the whole institution and abolished the kingly governments; and enacting laws and choosing magistrates, they used these as the safeguards of their cities. But when neither the laws they had made were sufficient to ensure justice nor the magistrates who had undertaken the oversight of them able to uphold the laws, and times of crisis, introducing many innovations, compelled them to choose, not the best institutions, but such as were best suited to the situations in which they found themselves, not only in unwelcome calamities, but also in immoderate prosperity, and when their forms of government were becoming corrupted by these conditions and required speedy and arbitrary correction, they were compelled to restore the kingly and tyrannical powers, though they concealed them under more attractive titles. Thus, the Thessalians called these officials *archoi*[87] or "commanders," and the Lacedaemonians *harmostai* or "harmonizers," fearing to call them tyrants or kings,[88] on the ground that it was not right for them to confirm those powers again which they had abolished with oaths and imprecations, under the approbation of the gods. My opinion, therefore, is, as I said, that the Romans took this example from the Greeks; but Licinius believes they took the dictatorship from the Albans, these being, as he says, the first who, when the royal family had become extinct upon the death of Amulius and Numitor, created annual magistrates with the same power the kings had enjoyed and called these magistrates dictators. For my part, I have not thought it worth while to inquire from whence the Romans took the name but from whence they took the example of the power comprehended under that name. But perhaps it is not worth while to discuss the matter further.

75 I shall now endeavour to relate in a summary manner how Larcius handled matters when he had been appointed the first dictator, and show with what dignity he invested the magistracy, for I look upon these matters as being most useful to my readers, since they will afford a great abundance of noble and profitable examples, not only to lawgivers and leaders of the people, but also to all others who aspire to take part in public life and to govern the state. For it is no mean and humble state of which I am going to relate the institutions and manners, nor were the men nameless outcasts whose counsels and actions I shall record, so that my zeal for small and trivial details might to some appear tedious and trifling; but I am writing the history of the state which prescribes rules of right

---

87 The word regularly used of these Thessalian commanders was ταγοί, and Bücheler proposed to restore that form here, ἀρχοί is probably a gloss that has replaced the word it was intended to explain.

88 But we hear of these harmosts only as governors sent out by the Lacedaemonians after the Peloponnesian War to rule the subject cities.

and justice for all mankind, and of the leaders who raised her to that dignity, matters concerning which any philosopher or statesman would earnestly strive not to be ignorant. As soon, therefore, as Larcius had assumed this power, he appointed as his Master of the Horse Spurius Cassius, who had been consul about the seventieth Olympiad.[89] This custom has been observed by the Romans down to my generation and no one appointed dictator has thus far gone through his magistracy without a Master of the Horse. After that, desiring to show how great was the extent of his power, he ordered the lictors, more to inspire terror than for any actual use, to carry the axes with the bundles of rods through the city, thereby reviving once more a custom that had been observed by the kings but abandoned by the consuls after Valerius Publicola in his first consulship had lessened the hatred felt for that magistracy. Having by this and the other symbols of royal power terrified the turbulent and the seditious, he first ordered all the Romans, pursuant to the best of all the practices established by Servius Tullius, the most democratic of the kings, to return valuations of their property, each in their respective tribes, adding the names of their wives and children as well as the ages of themselves and their children. And all of them having registered in a short time by reason of the severity of the penalty (for the disobedient were to lose both their property and their citizenship), the Romans who had arrived at the age of manhood were found to number 150,700. After that he separated those who were of military age from the older men, and distributing the former into centuries, he formed four bodies of foot and horse, of which he kept one, the best, about his person, while of the remaining three bodies, he ordered Cloelius, who had been his colleague in the consulship, to choose the one he wished, Spurius Cassius, the Master of the Horse, to take the third, and Spurius

---

89 He had been consul four years earlier (chap. 49), that is, in the last year of the 69th Olympiad.

Larcius, his brother, the remaining one; this last body together with the older men was ordered to guard the city, remaining inside the walls.

76 When he had got everything ready that was necessary for the war, he took the field with his forces and established three camps in the places where he suspected the Latins would be the most likely to make their invasion. He considered that it is the part of a prudent general, not only to strengthen his own position, but also to weaken that of the enemy, and, above all, to bring wars to an end without a battle or hardship, or, if that cannot be done, then with the least expenditure of men; and regarding as the worse of all wars and the most distressing those which men are forced to undertake against kinsmen and friends, he thought they ought to be settled by an accommodation in which clemency outweighed the demands of justice. Accordingly, he not only sent secretly to the most important men among the Latins some persons who were free from suspicion and attempted to persuade them to establish friendship between the two states, but he also sent ambassadors openly both to the several cities and to their league and by that means easily brought it about that they no longer entertained the same eagerness for the war. But in particular he won them over and set them against their leaders by the following service. The men who had received the supreme command over the Latins, namely, Mamilius and Sextus, keeping their forces all together in the city of Tusculum, were preparing to march on Rome, but were consuming much time in delay, either waiting for the cities which were slow in joining them or because the sacrificial victims were not favourable. During this time some of their men, scattering abroad from the camp, proceeded to plunder the territory of the Romans. Larcius, being informed of this, sent Cloelius against them with the most valiant, both of the horse and light-armed troops; and he, coming upon them unexpectedly, killed a few in the action and took the rest prisoners. These Larcius caused to be cured of their wounds, and having gained their affection by many other instances of kindness, he sent them to Tusculum safe and sound without ransom, and with them the most distinguished of the Romans as ambassadors. Through their efforts the army of the Latins was disbanded and a year's truce concluded between the two states.

77 After Larcius had effected these things, he brought the army home from the field, and having appointed consuls, laid down his magistracy before the whole term of his power had expired, without having put any of the Romans to death, banished any, or inflicted any other severity on any of them. This enviable example set by Larcius was continued by all who afterwards received this same power till the third generation before ours. Indeed, we find no instance of any one of them in history who did not use it with moderation and as became a citizen, though the commonwealth has often found it necessary to abolish the legal magistracies and to put the whole administration under one man. If, now, in foreign wars alone those who held the dictatorship had shown themselves brave champions of the fatherland, quite uncorrupted by the greatness of their power, it would not be so remarkable; but as it was, all who obtained this great power, whether in times of civil dissensions, which were many and serious, or in order to overthrow those who were suspected of aiming at monarchy or tyranny, or to prevent numberless other calamities, acquitted themselves in a manner free from reproach, like the first man who received it; so that all men gained the same opinion, that the only remedy for every incurable ill, and the last hope of safety when all others had been snatched away by some crisis, was the dictatorship. But in the time of our fathers, a full four hundred years after Titus Larcius, the institution became an object of reproach and hatred to all men under L. Cornelius Sulla, the first and only dictator who exercised his power with harshness and cruelty; so the Romans then perceived for the first time what they had along been ignorant of, that the dictatorship is a tyranny. For Sulla composed the senate of commonplace men, reduced the power of the tribunes to the minimum, depopulated whole cities, abolished some kingdoms and established others himself, and was guilty of many other arbitrary acts, which it would be a great task to enumerate. As for the citizens, besides those slain in battle, he put no fewer than forty thousand to death after they had surrendered to him, and some of these after he had first tortured them. Whether all these acts of his were necessary or advantageous to the commonwealth the present is not the time to inquire; all I have undertaken to show is that the name of dictator was rendered odious and terrible because of them. This is wont to be the case, not only with positions of power, but also with the other advantages which are eagerly contended for and admired in everyday life. For they all appear noble and profitable to those who hold them when they are used nobly, but base and unprofitable when they find unprincipled champions. For this result Nature is responsible, which to all good things has attached some congenital evils. But another occasion may be more suitable for discussing this subject.[90]

---

90 See critical note.

Book VI

1 Aulus Sempronius Atratinus[1] and Marcus Minucius, who
assumed the consulship the following year, in the seventy-first
Olympiad[2] (the one in which Tisicrates of Croton won the footrace),
Hipparchus being archon at Athens, performed no action either of
a military or administrative nature worthy of the notice of history
during their term of office, since the truce with the Latins gave them
ample respite from foreign wars, and the injunction decreed by the
senate against the exaction of debts till the war that was expected
should be safely terminated, quieted the disturbances raised in the
city by the poor, who desired to be discharged of their debts by a
public act; but they caused the senate to pass a most reasonable
decree which provided that any women of Roman birth who were
married to Romans should have full power to decide for themselves
whether they preferred to stay with their husbands or to return to
their own cities, and also provided that the male children should
remain with their fathers and the female and unmarried should
follow their mothers. For it happened that a great many women, by
reason of the kinship and friendship existing between the two
nations, had been given in marriage each into the other's state. The
women, having this liberty granted to them by the decree of the
senate, showed how great was their desire to live at Rome; for
almost all the Roman women who lived in the Latin cities left their
husbands and returned to their fathers, and all the Latin women
who were married to Romans, except two, scorned their native
countries and stayed with their husbands — a happy omen
foretelling which of the two nations was to be victorious in the war.

---

1   *Cf.* Livy ii. 21, 1.
2   For chaps. 2 f. *cf.* Livy ii. 21, 2-4.

Book VI

Under these consuls, they say, the temple was dedicated to Saturn upon the ascent leading from the Forum to the Capitol, and annual festivals and sacrifices were appointed to be celebrated in honour of the god at the public expense. Before this, they say, an altar built by Hercules was established there, upon which the persons who had received the holy rites from him offered the first-fruits as burnt-offerings according to the customs of the Greeks. Some historians state that the credit for beginning this temple was given to Titus Larcius, the consul of the previous year, others, that it was even given to King Tarquinius — the one who was driven from the throne — and that the dedication fell to Postumus Cominius pursuant to a decree of the senate. These consuls, then, had the opportunity, as I said, of enjoying a profound peace.

2 They[3] were succeeded in the consulship by Aulus Postumius and Titus Verginius, under whom the year's truce with the Latins expired; and great preparations for the war were made by both nations. On the Roman side the whole population entered upon the struggle voluntarily and with great enthusiasm; but the greater part of the Latins were lacking in enthusiasm and acted under compulsion, the powerful men in the cities having been almost all corrupted with bribes and promises by Tarquinius and Mamilius, while those among the common people who were not in favour of the war were excluded from a share in the public counsels; for permission to speak was no longer granted to all who desired it. Indeed, many, resenting this treatment, were constrained to leave their cities and desert to the Romans; for the men who had got the cities in their power did not choose to stop them, but thought themselves much obliged to their adversaries for submitting to a voluntary banishment. These the Romans received, and such of them as came with their wives and children they employed in

---

3   For chaps. 2 f. *cf.* Livy ii. 21, 2-4.

military services inside the walls,incorporating them in the centuries of citizens, and the rest they sent out to the fortresses near the city or distributed among their colonies, keeping them under guard, so that they should create no disturbance. And since all men had come to the same conclusion, that the situation once more called for a single magistrate free to deal with all matters according to his own judgment and subject to no accounting for his actions, Aulus Postumius, the younger of the consuls, was appointed dictator by his colleague Verginius, and following the example of the former dictator, chose his own Master of the Horse, naming Titus Aebutius Elva. And having in a short time enlisted all the Romans who were of military age, he divided his army into four parts, one of which he himself commanded, while he gave another to his colleague Verginius, the third to Aebutius, the Master of the Horse, and left the command of the fourth to Aulus Sempronius, whom he appointed to guard the city.

3 After the dictator had prepared everything that was necessary for the war, his scouts brought him word that the Latins had taken the field with all their forces; and others in turn informed him that they had captured by storm a strong place called Corbio, in which there was stationed a small garrison of the Romans. The garrison they wiped out completely, and the place itself, now that they had gained possession of it, they were making a base for the war. They were not capturing any slaves or cattle in the country districts, except those taken at Corbio, since the husbandmen had long before removed into the nearest fortresses everything that they could drive or carry away; but they were setting fire to the houses that had been abandoned and laying waste the country. After the Latins had already taken the field, an army of responsible size came to them from Antium, the most important city of the Volscian nation, with arms, grain, and everything else that was necessary for carrying on the war. Greatly heartened by this, they were in excellent hopes that the other Volscians would join them in the war, now that the city of Antium had set the example. Postumius, being informed of all this, set out hastily to the rescue before all the enemy's forces could assemble; and having led his army out by a forced march in the night, he arrived near the Latins, who lay encamped in a strong position near the lake called Regillus, and pitched his camp above them on a hill that was high and difficult of access, where, if he remained, he was sure to have many advantages over them.

4 The generals[4] of the Latins, Octavius of Tusculum, the son-in-law or, as some state, the son of the son-in-law of King Tarquinius, and Sextus Tarquinius — for they happened at that time to be encamped separately — joined their forces, and assembling the tribunes and centurions, they considered with them in what manner they should carry on the war; and many opinions were expressed. Some thought they ought to charge the troops under the dictator which had occupied the hill, while they could still inspire them with fear; for they regarded their occupation of the strong positions as a sign, not of assurance, but of cowardice. Others thought they ought to surround the camp of the Romans with a ditch, and keeping them hemmed in by means of a small guard, march with the rest of the army to Rome, which they believed might easily be captured now that the best of its youth had taken the field. Still others advised them to await the reinforcements from both the Volscians and their other allies, choosing safe measures in preference to bold; for the Romans, they say, would reap no benefit from the delay, whereas their own situation would be improved by it. While they were still debating, the other consul, Titus Verginius, suddenly arrived from Rome with his army, after making the march during the very next

---

4   For chaps. 4-13 (battle of Lake Regillus) see Livy ii. 19, 3-20, 13. Livy places the battle three years earlier than Dionysius.

night, and encamped apart from the dictator upon another ridge that was exceeding craggy and strongly situated. Thus the Latins were cut off on both sides from the roads leading into the enemy's country, the consul encamping on the left-hand side and the dictator on the right. This still further increased the confusion of their commanders, who had chosen safety in preference to every other consideration, and also their fear that by delaying they should be forced to use up their supplies of food, which were not plentiful. When Postumius observed the inexperience of these commanders, he sent the Master of the Horse, Titus Aebutius, with the flower both of the horse and light-armed troops with orders to occupy a hill which lay close beside the road by which provisions were brought to the Latins from home; and before the enemy was aware of it, the forces sent with the Master of the Horse passed by their camp in the night, and marching through a pathless wood, gained possession of the hill.

5 The generals of the enemy, finding that the strong places which lay in their rear were also being occupied, and no longer feeling any confident hopes that even their provisions from home would get through to them safely, resolved to drive the Romans from the hill before they could fortify it with a palisade and ditch. And Sextus, one of the two generals, taking the horse with him, rode up to them full speed in the expectation that the Roman horse would not await his attack. But when these bravely withstood their charge, he maintained the fight for some time, alternately retiring and renewing the attack; and then, since the nature of the ground offered great advantages to those who were already in possession of the heights, while bringing to those who attacked from below nothing but many blows and ineffectual hardships, and since, moreover, a fresh force of chosen legionaries, sent by Postumius to follow close upon the heels of the first detachment, came to the assistance of the Romans, he found himself unable to accomplish anything further and led the horse back to the camp; and the Romans, now secure in the possession of the place, openly strengthened the garrison there. After this action Mamilius and Sextus determined not to let much time intervene, but to decide the issue by an early battle. The Roman dictator, who at first had not been of this mind, but had hoped to end the war without a battle, founding his hopes of doing so chiefly on the inexperience of the opposing generals, now resolved to engage. For some couriers had been captured by the horse that patrolled the roads, bearing letters from the Volscians to the Latin generals to inform them that numerous forces would come to their assistance in about two days, and still other forces from the Hernicans. These were the considerations that reduced their[5] commanders to an immediate necessity of fighting, though until then they had not been of this mind. After the signals for battle had been raised on both sides, the two armies advanced into the space between their camps and drew up in the following manner: Sextus Tarquinius was posted on the left wing of the Latins and Octavius Mamilius on the right; Titus, the other son of Tarquinius, held the centre, where also the Roman deserters and exiles were posted. And, all their horse being divided into three bodies, two of these were placed on the wings and one in the centre of the battle-line. The left of the Roman army was commanded by Titus Aebutius, the Master of the Horse, who stood opposite to Octavius Mamilius; the right by Titus Verginius, the consul, facing Sextus Tarquinius; the centre of the line was commanded by the dictator Postumius in person, who proposed to encounter Titus Tarquinius and the exiles with him. The number of the forces of each army which drew up for battle was:on the side of

---

5   The pronoun αὐτῶν can hardly be correct. Hertlein wished to read "the commanders of both [armies]."

the Romans 23,700 foot and 1000 horse, and on that of the Latins and their allies about 40,000 foot and 3000 horse.

6 When they were on the point of engaging, the Latin generals called their men together and said many things calculated to incite them to valour, and addressed long appeals to the soldiers. And the Roman dictator, seeing his troops alarmed because they were going to encounter an army greatly superior in number to their own, and desiring to dispel that fear from their minds, called them to an assembly, and placing near him the oldest and most honoured members of the senate, addressed them as follows:

"The gods by omens, sacrifices, and other auguries promise to grant to our commonwealth liberty and a happy victory, both by way of rewarding us for the piety we have shown toward them and the justice we have practised during the whole course of our lives, and also from resentment, we may reasonably suppose, against our enemies. For these, after having received many great benefits from us, being both our kinsmen and friends, and after having sworn to look upon all our enemies and friends as their own, have scorned all these obligations and are bringing an unjust war upon us, not for the sake of supremacy and dominion, to determine which of us ought more rightly to possess it, — that, indeed, would not be so terrible, — but in support of the tyranny of the Tarquinii, in order to make our commonwealth enslaved once more instead of free. But it is necessary that you too, both officers and men, knowing that you have for allies the gods, who have always preserved our city, should acquit yourselves as brave men in this battle, remembering that the assistance of the gods is given to those who fight nobly and eagerly contribute everything in their power toward victory, not to those who fly from dangers, but to those who are willing to undergo hardships in their own behalf. We have many other advantages conducive to victory prepared for us by Fortune, but three in particular, which are the greatest and the most obvious of all.

7 "First, there is the confidence you have in one another, which is the thing most needed by men who are going to conquer their foes for you do not need to begin to-day to be firm friends and faithful allies to one another, but your country has long since prepared this boon for you all. For you have been brought up together and have received the same education; you were wont to sacrifice to the gods upon the same altars; and you have both enjoyed many advantages and experienced many evils in common, by the sharing of which strong and indissoluble friendships are wont to be formed among all men. Secondly, the struggle, in which your highest interests are at stake, is common to you all alike. For if you fall into the enemy's power it will not mean that some of you will meet with no severity while others suffer the worst of fates, but all of you alike will have lost your proud position, your sovereignty and your liberty, and will no longer have the enjoyment of your wives, your children, your property, or any other blessing you now have; and those who are at the head of the commonwealth and direct the public affairs will die the most miserable death accompanied by indignities and tortures. For if your enemies,[6] though they have received no injury, great or small, at your hands, have heaped many outrages of every sort upon all of you, what must you expect them to do if they now conquer you by arms, resentful as they are because you drove them from the city, deprived them of their property, and do not permit them even to set foot upon the land of their fathers? And finally, of the advantages I have mentioned you cannot, if you consider the matter aright, call this one inferior to any other — that the forces of the enemy have not proved to be so formidable as we conceived them to be, but are far short of the opinion we entertained of them. For,

---

6   The reference here is to the Tarquinii.

with the exception of the support furnished by the Antiates, you see no other allies present to take part with them in the war; whereas we were expecting that all the Volscians and many of the Sabines and Hernicans would come to them as allies, and were conjuring up in our minds a thousand other vain fears. But all these things, it appears, were only dreams of the Latins, holding out empty promises and futile hopes. For some of their allies have failed to send the promised aid,out of contempt for the inexperience of their generals; others, instead of assisting them, will keep delaying, wearing away the time by merely fostering their hopes; and those who are now engaged in making their preparations will arrive too late for the battle and will be of no further use to them.

8 "But if any of you, though convinced of the reasonableness of what I have said, nevertheless fear the numbers of the enemy, let them learn by a few words of instruction, or rather from their own memory, that what they dread is not formidable. Let them consider, in the first place, that the greater part of our enemies have been forced to take up arms against us, as they have often shown us by both actions and words, and that the number of those who willingly and eagerly fight for the tyrants is very small, in fact only an insignificant fraction of ours; and secondly, that all wars are won, not by the forces which are larger in numbers, but by those which are superior in valour. It would tedious to cite as examples all the armies of the Greeks as well as barbarians which, though superior in numbers, were overcome by forces so very small that the reports about the numbers engaged are not even credible to most people. But, to omit other instances, how many wars have you yourselves won, with a smaller force than you now have, when arrayed against enemies more numerous than all these the enemy have now got together? Well, then, can it be that, though you indeed continue to be formidable to those whom you have repeatedly overcome in battle, you are nevertheless contemptible in the eyes of these Latins and their allies, the Volscians, because they have never experienced your prowess in battle? But you all knew that our fathers conquered both of these nations in many battles. Is it reasonable, then, to suppose that the condition of the conquered has been improved after so many disasters and that of the conquerors impaired after so many successes? What man in his senses would say so? I should indeed be surprised if any of you feared the numbers of the enemy, in which there are few brave men, or scorned your own army, which is so numerous and so brave that none exceeding it either in courage or in numbers was ever assembled in any of our former wars.

9 "There is also this very great encouragement to you, citizens, neither to dread nor to shirk what is formidable, that the principal members of the senate are all present as you see, ready to share the fortunes of the war in common with you, though they are permitted by both their age and the law to be exempt from military service. Would it not, then, be shameful if you who are in the vigour of life should flee from what is formidable, while these who are past the military age, pursue it, and if the zeal of the old men, since it lacks the strength to slay any of the enemy, should at least be willing to die for the fatherland, while the vigour of you young men, who have it in your power, if successful, to save both yourselves and them and to be victorious, or, in case of failure, to suffer nobly while acting nobly, should neither make trial of Fortune nor leave behind you the renown that valour wins. Is it not an incentive to you, Romans, that just as you have before your eyes the record of the many wonderful deeds performed by your fathers,[7] whom no words can adequately praise, so your posterity while reap the fruits of many illustrious feats of your own, if you achieve success in this war also? To the

---

7   The text is uncertain here; "fathers" is Bücheler's emendation for "others" of the MSS. Furthermore, what is here translated as a single sentence has been thought by some scholars to be all that is left of two separate sentences.

end, therefore, that neither the bravery of those among you who have chosen the best course may go unrewarded, nor the fears of such as dread what is formidable more than is fitting go unpunished, learn from me, before we enter this engagement, what it will be the fate of each of them to receive. To anyone who performs any great or brave deed in this battle, as proved by the testimony of those acquainted with his actions, I will not only give at once all the usual honours which it is in the power of every man to win in accordance with our ancestral customs, but will also add a portion of the land owned by the state, sufficient to secure him from any lack of the necessities of life. But if a cowardly and infatuate mind shall suggest to anyone an inclination to shameful flight, to him I will bring home the very death he endeavoured to avoid; for such a citizen were better dead, both for his own sake and for that of others. And it will be the fate of those put to death in such a manner to be honoured neither with burial nor with any of the other customary rites, but unenvied and unlamented, to be torn to pieces by birds and beasts of prey. Knowing these things beforehand, then, do you all cheerfully enter the engagement, taking fair hopes as your guides to fair deeds, assured that by the hazard of this one battle, if it be attended by the best outcome and the one we all wish for, you will obtain the greatest of all advantages: you will free yourselves from the fear of tyrants, will repay to your country that gave you birth the gratitude she justly requires of you for your rearing, will save your children who are still infants and your wedded wives from suffering irreparable outrages at the hands of the enemy, and will render the short time your aged fathers have yet to live most agreeable to them. Oh, happy those among you to whom it shall be given to celebrate the triumph for this war, while your children, your wives and your parents welcome you back! But glorious and envied for their bravery will those be who shall sacrifice their lives for their country. Death, indeed, is decreed to all men, both the cowardly and the brave; but an honourable and a glorious death comes to the brave alone."

10 While he was still speaking these words to spur them to valour, a kind of confidence inspired by Heaven seized the army and they all, as if with a single soul, cried out together, "Be of good courage and lead us on." Postumius commended their alacrity and made a vow to the gods that if the battle were attended with a happy and glorious outcome, he would offer great and expensive sacrifices and institute costly games to be celebrated annually by the Roman people; after which he dismissed his men to their ranks. And when they had received the watchword from their commanders and the trumpets had sounded the charge, they gave a shout and fell to, first, the light-armed men and the horse on each side, then the solid ranks of foot, who were armed and drawn up alike; and all mingling, a severe battle ensued in which every man fought hand to hand. However, both sides were extremely deceived in the opinion they had entertained of each other, for neither of them thought a battle would be necessary, but expected to put the enemy to flight at the first onset. The Latins, trusting in the superiority of their horse, concluded that the Roman horse would not be able even to sustain their onset; and the Romans were confident that by rushing into the midst of danger in a daring and reckless manner they should terrify their enemies. Having formed these opinions of one another in the beginning, they now saw everything turning out just the opposite. Each side, therefore, no longer founding their hopes of safety and of victory on the fear of the enemy, but on their own courage, showed themselves brave soldiers even beyond their strength. And various and sudden shifting fortunes marked their struggle.

11 First, the Romans posted in the centre of the line, where the dictator stood with a chosen body of horse about him, he himself fighting among the foremost, forced back that part of the enemy that stood opposite to them, after Titus, one of the sons of Tarquinius, had been wounded in the right shoulder with a javelin and was no longer able to use his arm. Licinius and Gellius,[8] indeed, without inquiring into the probabilities or possibilities of the matter, introduce King Tarquinius himself, a man approaching ninety years of age, fighting on horseback and wounded. When Titus had fallen, those about him, after fighting a little while and taking him up while he was yet alive, showed no bravery after that, but retired by degrees as the Romans advanced. Afterwards they again stood their ground and advanced against the enemy when Sextus, the other son of Tarquinius, came to their relief with the Roman exiles and the flower of the horse. These, therefore, recovering themselves, fought again. In the meantime Titus Aebutius and Mamilius Octavius, the commanders of the foot on either side,[9] fought the most brilliantly of all, driving their opponents before them wherever they charged and rallying those of their own men who had become disordered; and, then, challenging each other, they came to blows and in the encounter gave one another grievous wounds, though not mortal, the Master of the Horse driving his spear through the corslet of Mamilius into his breast, and Mamilius running the other through the middle of his right arm; and both fell from their horses.

12 Both of these leaders having been carried off the field, Marcus Valerius, who had again been appointed legate,[10] took over the command of the Master of the Horse and with his followers attacked those of the enemy who confronted him; and after a brief resistance on their part he speedily drove them far out of the line. But to this body of the enemy also came reinforcements from the Roman exiles, both horse and light-armed men; and Mamilius,

8   To these two historians we may add Livy (ii. 19, 6).

9   These leaders commanded opposing wings of the two armies; see chap. 5, 5.

10 In v. 50, 3 he was mentioned as a πρεσβευτὴς (legatus), but there the word meant an ambassador.

having by this time recovered from his wound, appeared on the field again at the head of a strong body both of horse and foot. In this action not only Marcus Valerius, the legate, fell, wounded with a spear (he was the man who had first triumphed over the Sabines and raised the spirit of the commonwealth when dejected by the defeat it had received at the hands of the Tyrrhenians), but also many other brave Romans at his side. A sharp conflict took place over his body, as Publius and Marcus, the sons of Publicola, protected their uncle with their shields; but they delivered him to their shield-bearers un-despoiled and still breathing a little, and sent him back to the camp. For their own part, such was their courage and ardour, they thrust themselves into the midst of the enemy, and receiving many wounds, as the Roman exiles pressed closely round them, they perished together. After this misfortune the line of the Romans was forced to give way on the left for a long distance and was being broken even to the centre. When the dictator learned of the rout of his men, he hastened to their assistance with the horse he had about him. And ordering the other legate, Titus Herminius, to take a troop of horse, and passing behind their own lines, to force the men who fled to face about, and if they refused obedience to kill them, he himself with the best of his men pushed on towards the thick of the conflict; and when he came near the enemy, he spurred on ahead of the rest with a loose rein. And as they all charged in a body in this terrifying manner, the enemy, unable to sustain their frenzied and savage onset, fled and many of them fell. In the meantime the legate Herminius also, having rallied from their route those of his men who had been put to flight, brought them up and attacked the troops arrayed under Mamilius; and encountering this general, who both for stature and strength was the best man of his time, he not only killed him, but was slain himself while he was despoiling the body, someone having pierced his flank with a sword. Sextus Tarquinius, who commanded the left wing of the Latins, still held out against all the dangers that beset him, and was forcing the right wing of the Romans to give way But when he saw Postumius suddenly appear with the flower of the horse, he gave over all hope and rushed into the midst of the enemy's ranks, where, being surrounded by the Romans, both horse and foot, and assaulted on all sides with missiles, like a wild beast, he perished, but not before he had killed many of those who came to close quarters with him. Their leaders having fallen, the Latins at once fled *en masse*, and their camp, abandoned by the men who had been left to guard it, was captured; from this camp the Romans took much valuable booty. Not only was this a very great defeat for the Latins, from the disastrous effects of which they suffered a very long time, but their losses were greater than ever before. For out of 40,000 foot and 3000 horse, as I have said, less than 10,000 survivors returned to their homes in safety.

13 It is said that in this battle two men on horseback, far excelling in both beauty and stature those our human stock produces, and just growing their first beard, appeared to Postumius, the dictator, and to those arrayed about him, and charged at the head of the Roman horse, striking with their spears all the Latins they encountered and driving them headlong before them. And after the flight of the Latins and the capture of their camp, the battle having come to an end in the late afternoon, two youths are said to have appeared in the same manner in the Roman Forum attired in military garb, very tall and beautiful and of the same age, themselves retaining on their countenances as having come from a battle, the look of combatants, and the horses they led being all in a sweat. And when they had each of them watered their horses and washed them at the fountain which rises near the temple of Vesta and forms a small but deep pool, and many people stood about them and inquired if they brought any news from the camp, they related how the battle had gone and that the Romans were the victors. And it is said that after they left the Forum they were not seen again by anyone, though great search was made for them by the man who had been left in command of the city.[11] The next day, when those at the head of affairs received the letters from the dictator, and besides the other particulars of the battle, learned also of the appearance of the divinities, they concluded, as we may reasonably infer, that it was the same gods who had appeared in both places, and were convinced that the apparitions had been those of Castor and Pollux.

Of this extraordinary and wonderful appearance of these gods there are many monuments at Rome, not only the temple of Castor and Pollux which the city erected in the Forum at the place where their apparitions had been seen, and the adjacent fountain, which bears the names of these gods[12] and is to this day regarded as holy, but also the costly sacrifices which the people perform each year through their chief priests in the month called Quintilis,[13] on the day known as the Ides, the day on which they gained this victory. But above all these things there is the procession performed after the sacrifice by those who have a public horse and who, being arrayed by tribes and centuries, ride in regular ranks on horseback, as if they came from battle, crowned with olive branches and attired in the purple robes with stripes of scarlet which they call *trabeae*. They begin their procession from a certain temple of Mars built outside the walls, and going through several parts of the city and the Forum, they pass by the temple of Castor and Pollux, sometimes to the number even of five thousand, wearing whatever rewards for valour in battle they have received from their commanders, a fine sight and

---

11 The *praefectus urbi*; see chap. 2, end.

12 The only fountain known to us in this part of the Forum was regularly called the Fountain of Juturna.

13 Later called Julius, after Julius Caesar; in this month the Ides fell on the 15th.

worthy of the greatness of the Roman dominion. These are the things I have found both related and performed by the Romans in commemoration of the appearance of Castor and Pollux; and from these, as well as from many other important instances, one may judge how dear to the gods were the men of those times.

14 Postumius encamped that night on the field and the next day he crowned those who had distinguished themselves in the battle; and having appointed guards to take care of the prisoners, he proceeded to offer to the gods the sacrifices in honour of the victory. While he still wore the garland on his head and was laying the first burnt offerings on the altars, some scouts, running down from the heights, brought him word that a hostile army was marching against them.It consisted of chosen youth of the Volscian nation who had been sent out, before the battle was ended, to assist the Latins. Upon hearing of this he ordered all his men to arm and to stay in the camp, each under his own standards, maintaining silence and keeping their ranks till he himself should give the word what to do. On the other side, the generals of the Volscians, encamping out of sight of the Romans, when they saw the field covered with dead bodies and both camps intact, and no one, either enemy or friend, stirring out of the entrenchments, were for some time amazed and at a loss to guess what turn of fortune had produced this state of affairs. But when they had learned all about the battle from those who were making their escape from the rout, they consulted with the other leaders what was to be done. The boldest of them thought it best to attempt to take the camp of the Romans by assault, while many of the foe were still disabled from their wounds and all were exhausted by toil, and the arms of most of them were useless, some having their edges blunted and others being broken, and no fresh forces from home were yet at hand to relieve them, whereas their own army was large and valiant, splendidly armed and experienced in war, and by coming suddenly upon men who were not expecting it was sure to appear formidable even to the boldest.

15 But to the most prudent among them it did not seem a safe risk to attack without allies men who were valiant warriors and had just destroyed so great an army of the Latins, as they would be putting everything to the hazard in a foreign country where, if any misfortune happened, they would have no place of refuge. These advised, therefore, to provide rather for a safe retreat to their own country as soon as possible and to look upon it as a great gain if they sustained no loss from this expedition. But still others disapproved of both these courses, declaring that readiness to rush into battle was mere youthful bravado, while unreasoning flight back to their own country was shameful; for, whichever of these courses they took, the enemy would regard it as being just what they desired. The opinion of these, therefore, was that at present they ought to fortify their camp and get everything in readiness for a battle, and that, dispatching messengers to the rest of the Volscians, they should ask them to do one of two things, either to send another army that would be a match for that of the Romans or to recall the army they had already sent out. But the opinion that prevailed with the majority and received the sanction of those in authority was to send spies to the Roman camp, assured of safety under the title of ambassadors, who should greet the general and say that, as allies of the Romans sent by the Volscian nation, they were sorry they had come too late for the battle, since they would now receive little or no thanks for their zeal; but anyway they congratulated the Romans upon their good fortune in having won a great battle without the assistance of allies; then, after the ambassadors had tricked the Romans by the friendliness of their words and had got them to confide in the Volscians as their friends, they were to spy out everything and bring back word concerning the Romans' strength, their arms, their preparations, and anything they were planning to do. And when the Volscians should be thoroughly acquainted with these matters, they should then take counsel whether it was better to send for another army and attack the Romans or to return home with their present force.

16 After they had adopted this proposal, the ambassadors they had chosen came to the dictator, and being brought before the assembly, delivered their messages that were intended to deceive the Romans. And Postumius, after a short pause, said to them: "You have brought with you, Volscians, evil designs clothed in good words, and while you perform hostile acts, you want us to regard you as friends. For you were sent by your nation to assist the Latins against us, but arriving after the battle and seeing them overcome, you wish to deceive us by saying the very opposite of what you intended to do. And neither the friendliness of your words, simulated for the present occasion, nor the pretence under which you are come hither, is sincere, but is full of fraud and deceit. For you were sent, not to congratulate us upon our good fortune, but to spy out the weakness or the strength of our condition; and while you are ambassadors in name, you are spies in reality." When the men denied everything, he said he would soon offer them the proof; and straightway he produced their letters which he had intercepted before the battle as they were being carried to the commanders of the Latins, in which they promised to send them reinforcements, and produced the persons who carried the letters. After these were read out and the prisoners had given an account of the orders they had received, the soldiers were eager to stone the Volscians as spies caught in the act; but Postumius thought that good men ought not to imitate the wicked, saying it would be better and more magnanimous to reserve their anger against the senders rather than against the sent, and to let the men go in consideration of their ostensible title of ambassadors rather than to put them to death because of their disguised task of spying, lest they should give either a specious ground for war to the Volscians, who would allege that their ambassadors had been put to death contrary to the law of nations, or an excuse to their other enemies for bringing a charge which, though false, would appear neither ill-grounded nor incredible.

17 Having thus checked the rash impulse of the soldiers, he commanded the men to depart without looking back, and put them in charge of a guard of horse, who conducted them to the camp of the Volscians. After he had expelled the spies, he commanded the soldiers to get everything ready for battle, as if he were going to engage the next day. But he had no need of a battle, for the leaders of the Volscians broke camp before dawn and returned home. All things having now gone according to his wish, he buried his own dead, and having purified his army, returned to the city with the pomp of a magnificent triumph, together with huge quantities of military stores, followed by 5,500 prisoners taken in the battle. And having set apart the tithes of the spoils, he spent forty talents in performing games and sacrifices to the gods, and let contracts for the building of temples to Ceres, Liber and Libera,[14] in fulfilment of a vow he had made. It seems that provisions for the army had been scarce in the beginning, and had caused the Romans great fear that they would fail entirely, as the land had borne no crops and food from outside was no longer being imported because of the war. Because of this fear he had ordered the guardians of the Sibylline books to consult them, and finding that the oracles commanded that these gods should be propitiated, he made vows to them, when he

---

14 Liber and Libera were old Roman divinities presiding over the crops and particularly over the vine. They were later identified with the Greek Dionysus and Persephone (**Korê**). Though Dionysius speaks of temples, there was but a single building; see the note on iii. 69, 5.

was on the point of leading out his army, that if there should be the same abundance in the city during the time of his magistracy as before, he would build temples to them and also appoint sacrifices to be performed every year. These gods, hearing his prayer, caused the land to produce rich crops, not only of grain but also of fruits, and all imported provisions to be more plentiful than before; and when Postumius saw this, he himself[15] caused a vote to be passed for the building of these temples. The Romans, therefore, having through the favour of the gods repelled the war brought upon them by the tyrant, were engaged in feasts and sacrifices.

18 A few days later there came to them, as ambassadors from the Latin league, chosen out of all their cities. Those who had been opposed to the war, holding out the olive branches and the fillets of suppliants. These men, upon being introduced into the senate, declared that the powerful men in every city had been responsible for beginning the war, and said that the people had been guilty of this one fault only, that they had listened to corrupt demagogues who had schemed for private gain. And for this delusion, in which necessity had had the greatest share, they said every city had already paid a penalty not to be despised, in the loss of its young men, so that it was not easy to find a single household free from mourning. They asked the Romans to receive them now that they willingly submitted and neither disputed any longer about the supremacy nor strove for equality, but were ready to be for all future time subjects as well as allies and to add the good fortune of the Romans all the prestige which Fortune had taken from the Latins. At the end of their speech they made an appeal to kinship, reminded them of their unhesitating services as allies in the past, and bewailed the misfortunes that would fall on the innocent, who were far more

---

15 This is the reading of the MSS.; but the word for "himself" is probably a corruption, perhaps for "to them." See *L.C.L.* critical note.

numerous than the guilty, accompanying everything they said with lamentations, embracing the knees of all the senators, and laying the olive branches at the feet of Postumius, so that the whole senate was more or less moved by their tears and entreaties.

19 When the ambassadors had left the senate and permission to speak was given to the members who were wont to deliver their opinions first,[16] Titus Larcius, who had been appointed the first dictator the year before,[17] advised them to use their good fortune with moderation, saying that the greatest praise that could be given a whole state as well as to an individual was not to be corrupted by prosperity, but to bear good fortune with decorum and moderation; for all prosperity is envied, particularly that which is attended with arrogance and rigour toward those who had been humbled and subdued. And he advised them not to put any reliance on Fortune, since they had learned from their own experience in both adversity and prosperity how inconstant and quick to change she is. Nor ought they to reduce their adversaries to the necessity of running the supreme hazard, since such necessity renders some men daring beyond all expectation and warlike beyond their strength. He said they had reason to be afraid of drawing upon themselves the common hatred of all those they proposed to rule, if they should exact harsh and relentless penalties from such as had erred; for they would seem to have abandoned their traditional principles, forgetting to what they owed their present splendour, and to have made their dominion a tyranny rather than a leadership and protectorship, as it had been aforetime. He said that the error is a moderate and venial one when states that cling to liberty and have

---

16 Following Kiessling, who supplied "first." Entitled to speak first were the consuls-elect, if any, then the ex-magistrates, beginning with those who had held the consulship.

17 It had actually been the second year before; Kiessling proposed to delete "the year before."

once learned to rule are unwilling to give up their ancient prestige; and if men who aim at the noblest ends are to be punished beyond possibility of recovery when they fail of their hope, there will be nothing to prevent the whole race of mankind from being destroyed by one another, since all men have an innate craving for liberty. He declared that a government is far better and more firmly established which seeks to rule its subjects by its benefits rather than by punishments; for the former course leads to goodwill and the latter to terror, and it is a fixed law of Nature that everything that causes terror should be particularly detested. And finally he asked them to take as examples the best actions of their ancestors for which they had won praise, recounting the many instances in which, after capturing cities by storm, they had not razed them nor put all the male population to the sword or enslaved them, but by making them Roman colonies and by giving citizenship to such of the conquered as desired to live at Rome, they had made their city great from a small beginning. The sum and substance of his opinion was this: to renew the treaty they had previously made with the Latin league and to retain no resentment against any of the cities for the errors they had been guilty of.

20 Servius Sulpicius opposed nothing the other had said concerning peace and the renewal of the treaty; but, since the Latins had been the first to violate the treaty, and not now for the first time either — in which case they might deserve some forgiveness when they put forward necessity and their own deception as excuses — but often in the past too, so that they needed correction, he proposed that impunity and their liberty should be granted to all of them because of their kinship, but that they should be deprived of one half of their land and that Roman colonists should be sent thither to enjoy its produce and see to it that the Latins created no further disturbances. Spurius Cassius advised them to raze the Latin cities, saying he wondered at the simple-mindedness of those who urged letting their offences go unpunished, why they could not understand that, because of the inborn and ineradicable envy which the Latins felt towards the rising power of Rome, they were constantly fomenting one war after another against them and would never willingly give over their treacherous intent so long as this unfortunate passion dwelt in their hearts; indeed, they had finally endeavoured to bring a kindred people under the power of a tyrant more savage than any wild beast, thereby overturning all the covenants they had sworn by the gods to observe, induced by no other hopes than that, if the war did not succeed according to their expectation, they should incur either no punishment at all or a very slight one. He too asked them to take as examples the actions of their ancestors, who, when they knew that the city of Alba, of which both they themselves and all the other Latin cities were colonies, was envious of their prosperity and had made use of the impunity it had obtained for its first transgressions as an opportunity for greater treachery, resolved to destroy it in a single day, believing that to punish none of those who had committed the greatest and the most irremediable crimes was no better than to show compassion to none of those who were guilty of moderate errors. It would be an act of great folly and stupidity, surely not one of humanity and moderation, for those who would not endure the envy of their mother-city when it appeared beyond measure grievous and intolerable, to submit now to that of their mere kinsman, and for those who had punished enemies convicted in milder attempts of being such, by depriving them of their city, to exact no punishment now from such as had often shown their hatred of them to be irreconcilable. After he had spoken thus and had enumerated all the rebellions of the Latins and reminded the senators of the vast number of Romans who had lost their lives in the wars against them, he advised them to treat these also in the same manner as they had formerly treated the Albans, namely, to raze their cities and add their territory to that of the Romans; and as for the inhabitants, to make citizens of such as had shown any goodwill towards them, permitting them to retain their possessions, but to put to death as traitors the authors of the revolt by whom the treaty had been broken, and to make slaves of the poor, the lazy and the useless among the populace.

21 These were the opinions expressed by the leading men of the senate, but the dictator gave the preference to that of Larcius; and, no further opposition being made to it, the ambassadors were called in to the senate to receive their answer. Postumius, after reproaching them with an evil disposition never to be reformed, said: "It would be right that you should suffer the utmost severity, which is just the way you yourselves were intending to treat us, if you had succeeded in the many attempts you made against us." Nevertheless, he said, the Romans had not chosen mere rights in preference to clemency, bearing in mind that the Latins were their kinsmen and had had recourse to the mercy of those whom they had injured; but they were allowing these offences of theirs also to go unpunished, from a regard both to the gods of their race and to the uncertainty of Fortune, to whom they owed their victory "For the present, therefore, go your way," he said, "relieved of all fear; and after you have released to us the prisoners, delivered up the deserters, and expelled the exiles, then send ambassadors to us to treat of friendship and of an alliance, in the assurance that they shall fail of naught that is reasonable." The ambassadors, having received this answer, departed, and a few days later returned, having released the prisoners and expelled the exiles with Tarquinius from their cities, and bringing with them in chains all the deserters they had taken. In return for this they obtained of the senate their old treaty of friendship and alliance and renewed through the *fetiales* the oaths they had previously taken concerning it. Thus ended the war against the tyrants, after it had lasted fourteen years from their expulsion. King Tarquinius — for he still survived of his family — being now about ninety years of age and having lost his children and the household of his relations by marriage,[18] dragged out a miserable old age, and that too among his enemies. For when neither the Latins, the Tyrrhenians, the Sabines, nor any other free people near by would longer permit him to reside in their cities, he retired to Cumae in Campania and was received by Aristodemus, nicknamed the Effeminate,[19] who was at that time tyrant of the Cumaeans; and after living a few days there, he died and was buried by him.[20] Some of the exiles who had been with him remained at Cumae; and the rest, dispersing themselves to various other cities, ended their days on foreign soil.

22 After the Romans had put an end to the foreign wars, the civil strife sprang up again. For the senate ordered the courts of justice to sit and that all suits which they had postponed on account of the war should be decided according to the laws. The controversies arising over contracts resulted in great storms and terrible instances of outrageous and shameless behaviour, the plebeians, on the one hand, pretending they were unable to pay their debts, since their land had been laid waste during the long war, their cattle destroyed, the number of their slaves reduced by desertion and raids, and their fortunes in the city exhausted by their expenditures for the campaign, and the money-lenders, on the other hand, alleging that these misfortunes had been common to all and not confined to the debtors only, and regarding it as intolerable that they should lose, not only what they had been stripped of by the enemy in the war,

---

18 The only relation by marriage of whom we have been informed was Mamilius, his son-in-law; but *cf.* chap. 4, 1

19 Dionysius later (vii. 2, 4) gives two different explanations of this epithet.

20 Livy (ii. 21, 5) assigns his death to the following year.

but also what they had lent in time of peace to some of the citizens who asked for their assistance. And as neither the money-lenders were willing to accept anything that was reasonable nor the debtors to do anything that was just, but the former refused to abate even the interest, and the latter to pay even the principal itself, those who were in the same plight were already gathering in knots and opposing parties faced one another in the Forum and sometimes actually came to blows, and the whole established order of the state was thrown into confusion. Postumius, observing this, while he still retained the respect of all alike for having brought a severe war to an honourable conclusion, resolved to avoid the civil storms, and before he had completed the whole term of his sovereign magistracy he abdicated the dictatorship, and having fixed a day for the election, he, together with his fellow-consul, restored the traditional[21] magistrates.

23 The consuls[22] who next took over the annual and legal magistracy were Appius Claudius Sabinus and Publius Servilius Priscus. They saw, rightly, that to render the highest service to the state they must divert the uproar in the city to foreign wars; and they were arranging that one of them should lead an expedition against the Volscian nation, with the purpose both of taking revenge on them for the aid they had sent to the Latins against the Romans and of forestalling their preparations, which as yet were not far advanced. For they too were reported to be enrolling an army with the greatest diligence and sending ambassadors to the neighbouring nations to invite them to enter into alliance with them, since they had learned that the plebeians were standing aloof from the patricians and thought that it would not be difficult to capture a city suffering from civil war. The consuls, therefore, having resolved to

---

21 They are called traditional (literally, "ancestral") magistrates, though they had been functioning but fourteen years.
22 For chaps. 23-33 cf. Livy ii. 21, 5-27, 13.

lead an expedition against this people, and their resolution being approved of by the whole senate, they ordered all the men of military age to present themselves on the day they had appointed for making the levies of troops. But when the plebeians, though repeatedly summoned to take the military oath, would not obey the consuls, these were no longer both of the same mind, but beginning from this point, they were divided and continued to oppose one another during the whole time of their magistracy. For Servilius thought they ought to take the milder course, thereby adhering to the opinion of Manius Valerius, the most democratic of the senators, who advised them to cure the cause of the sedition, preferably by decreeing an abolition or diminution of the debts, or, failing that, by forbidding for the time being the haling to prison of the debtors whose obligations were overdue, and advised them to encourage rather than compel the poor to take the military oath, and not to make the penalties against the disobedient severe and inexorable, but moderate and mild. For there was danger, he said, that men in want of the daily necessities of life, if compelled to serve at their own expense, might get together and adopt some desperate course.

24 But the opinion of Appius, the chief man among the leaders of the aristocracy, was harsh and arrogant. He advised that they should show no leniency toward the people in anything, but should even allow the money-lenders to enforce payment of the obligations upon the terms agreed upon, and should cause the courts of justice to sit, and that the consul who remained in the city should, in accordance with ancestral custom and usage,[23] exact the punishments ordained by law against those who declined military service, and that they ought to yield to the people in nothing that

---

23 Some such word as "usage" seems to have been lost from the text after "and."
See critical note.

was not just nor aid them in establishing a pernicious power. "Why even now," he said, "they are pampered beyond all measure in consequence of having been relieved of the taxes they formerly paid to the kings and freed from the corporal punishments they received from them when they did not yield prompt obedience to any of their commands. But if they go further and attempt any disturbance or uprising, let us restrain them with the aid of the sober and sound element among the citizens, who will be found more numerous than the disaffected. We have on hand for the task no slight strength in the patrician youth who are ready to obey our commands; but the greatest weapon of all, and one difficult to be resisted, with which we shall subdue the plebeians, is the power of the senate; with this let us overawe them, taking our stand on the side of the laws. But if we yield to their demand, in the first place, we shall incur disgrace by entrusting the government to the people when we have it in our power to live under an aristocracy; and secondly, we shall run no little danger of being deprived of our liberty again, in case some man inclined toward tyranny should win them over and acquire a power superior to the laws." The consuls disputing in this manner, both by themselves alone and whenever the senate was assembled, and many siding with each, that body, after listening to their altercations and clamour and the unseemly speeches with which they abused one another, would adjourn without coming to any salutary decision.

25 Much time being consumed in this wrangling, one of the consuls, Servilius (for it had fallen to his lot to conduct the campaign), having, by much entreating and courting of the populace, prevailed upon them to assist in the war, took the field with an army not raised by a compulsory levy but consisting of volunteers, as the times required. Meanwhile the Volscians were still employed in their preparations and neither expected that the

Romans, divided into factions as they were and engaged in mutual animosities, would march against them with an army, nor thought they would come to close quarters with any who attacked them, but imagined that they themselves were at full liberty to begin the war whenever they thought fit. But when they found themselves attacked and perceived that they must attack in turn, then at last the oldest among them, alarmed by the speed of the Romans, came out of their cities with olive branches and surrendered themselves to Servilius, to be treated as he should think fit for their offences. And he, taking from them provisions and clothing for his army and choosing out of the most prominent families three hundred men to serve as hostages, departed, assuming that the war was ended. In reality, however, this was not an end of the war, but rather a postponement, as it were, and an opportunity for those who had been surprised by the unexpected invasion to make their preparations; and the Roman army was no sooner gone than the Volscians again turned their attention to war by fortifying their towns and reinforcing the garrisons of any other places that were suitable to afford them security. The Hernicans and the Sabines assisted them openly in their hazardous venture, and many others secretly; but the Latins, when ambassadors went to them to ask for their assistance, bound the men and carried them to Rome. The senate, in return for the Latins' steadfast adherence to their alliance and still more for the eagerness they showed to take part in the war (for they were ready to assist them of their own accord), granted to them a favour they thought they desired above all things but were ashamed to ask for, which was to release without ransom the prisoners they had taken from them during the wars, the number of whom amounted to almost six thousand, and that the gift might, so far as possible, take on a lustre becoming to their kinship, they clothed them all with the apparel proper to free men. As to the Latins' offer of assistance, the senate told them they had no need of it, since the national forces of Rome were sufficient to punish those who revolted. After they had given this answer to the Latins they voted for the war against the Volscians.

26 While[24] the senate was still sitting and considering what forces were to be taken into the field, an elderly man appeared in the Forum, dressed in rags, with his beard and hair grown long and crying out, he called upon the citizens for assistance. And when all who were near flocked to him, he placed himself where he could be clearly seen by many and said: "Having been born free, and having served in all the campaigns while I was of military age, and fought in twenty-eight battles and often been awarded prizes for valour in the wars; then, when the oppressive times came that were reducing the commonwealth to the last straits, having been forced to contract a debt to pay the contributions levied upon me; and finally, when my farm was raided by the enemy and my property in the city exhausted owing to the scarcity of provisions, having no means with which to discharge my debt, I was carried away as a slave by the money lender, together with my two sons; and when my master ordered me to perform some difficult task and I protested against it, I was given a great many lashes with the whip." With these words he threw off his rags and showed his breast covered with wounds and his back still bleeding from the stripes. This raising a general clamour and lamentation on the part of all present, the senate adjourned and throughout the entire city the poor were running about, each bewailing his own misfortunes and imploring the assistance of the neighbours. At the same time all who had been enslaved for their debts rushed out of the houses of the money lenders with their hair grown long and most of them in chains and fetters; and none dared to lay hold on them, and if anyone so much as touched them, he was forcibly torn in pieces, such was the

---

24 For chaps. 26, 1-29, 1 cf. Livy ii. 23 f.

madness possessing the people at that time, and presently the Forum was full of debtors who had broken loose from their chains. Appius, therefore, fearing to be attacked by the populace, since he had been the cause of the evils and all this trouble was believed to be due to him, fled from the Forum. But Servilius, throwing off his purple-bordered robe and casting himself in tears at the feet of each of the plebeians, with difficulty prevailed upon them to remain quiet that day, and to come back the next day, assuring them that the senate would take some care of their interests. Having said this, he ordered the herald to make proclamation that no money-lender should be permitted to hale any citizen to prison for a private debt till the senate should come to a decision concerning them, and that all present might go with impunity whithersoever they pleased. Thus he allayed the tumult.

27 Accordingly, they left the Forum for that time. But the next day there appeared, not only the inhabitants of the city, but also the plebeians from the neighbouring country districts and the Forum was crowded by break of day. The senate having been assembled to consider what was to be done about the situation, Appius proceeded to call his colleague a flatterer of the people and the leader of the poor in their madness, while Servilius called Appius harsh and arrogant and the cause of the present evils in the state; and there was no end to their wrangling. In the meantime some horsemen of the Latins came riding full speed into the Forum announcing that the enemy had taken the field with a great army and were already upon their own borders. Such were the tidings they brought. Thereupon the patricians and the whole body of the knights, together with all who were wealthy or of distinguished ancestry, since they had a great deal at stake, armed themselves in all haste. But the poor among them, and particularly such as were hard pressed by debt, neither took up arms nor offered any other assistance to the common cause, but were pleased and received the news of the foreign war as an answer to their prayers, believing that it would free them from their present evils. To those who besought them to lend their aid they showed their chains and fetters and asked them in derision whether it was worth their while to make war in order to preserve those blessings; and many even ventured to say that it was better for them to be slaves to the Volscians than to bear the abuses of the patricians. And the city was filled with wailing, tumult, and all sorts of womanish lamentations.

28 The senators, seeing these things, begged of the other consul Servilius, who seemed in the present juncture to have greater credit with the multitude, to come to the aid of the country. And he, calling the people together in the Forum, showed them that the urgency of the moment no longer admitted of quarrels among the citizens, and he asked them for the time being to march against the enemy with united purpose and not to view with indifference the overthrow of their country, in which were the gods of their fathers and the sepulchres of each man's ancestors, both of which are most precious in the eyes of all men; he begged them to show respect for their parents, who would be unable because of age to defend themselves, to have pity on their wives, who would soon be forced to submit to dreadful and intolerable outrages, and especially to show compassion for their infant children, who, after being reared for very different expectations, would be exposed to pitiless insults and abuses. And when by a common effort they had averted the present danger, then would be the time, he said, to consider in what manner they should make their government fair, impartial and salutary to all, one in which neither the poor would plot against the possessions of the rich nor the latter insult those in humbler circumstances — for such behaviour was anything but becoming to citizens — but in which not only the needy should receive some assistance from the state, but the money-lenders too, at least those who were suffering injustice, should receive moderate relief, and thus the greatest of human blessings and the preserver of harmony in all states, good faith in the observance of contracts, would not be destroyed totally and forever in Rome alone. After saying this and everything else that the occasion required, he spoke finally in his own behalf, about the goodwill which he had ever shown toward the people, and asked them to serve with him in this expedition in return for his zeal in their behalf; for the oversight of the city had been entrusted to his colleague and the command in war conferred upon himself, these duties having been determined for them by lot. He said also that the senate had promised him to confirm whatever agreements he should make with the people, and that he had promised the senate to persuade the people not to betray their country to the enemy.

29 Having said this, he ordered the herald to make proclamation that no person should be permitted to seize, sell, or retain as pledges the houses of those Romans who should march out with him against the enemy, or hale their family to prison for any debt, and that none should hinder any one who desired from taking part in the campaign; but as for those who should fail to serve, the money-lenders should have the right to compel them to pay their debts according to the terms which they had each advanced their money. When the poor heard this, they straightway consented, and all showed great ardour for the war, some induced by hopes of booty and others out of gratitude to the general, but the greater part to escape from Appius and the abusive treatment to which those who stayed in the city would be exposed.

Servilius,[25] having taken command of the army, lost no time, but marched with great expedition, that he might engage the enemy before they could invade the Romans' territory And finding them

---

25 For chap 29, 2-5 *cf.* Livy ii. 24, 8-25, 6.

encamped in the Pomptine district, pillaging the country of the Latins because these had refused their request to assist them in the war, he encamped in the late afternoon near a hill distant about twenty stades from the enemy's camp. And in the night his army was attacked by the Volscians, who thought they were few in number, tired out, as was to be expected after a long march, and lacking in zeal by reason of the disturbances raised by the poor over their debts, which seemed then to be at their height. Servilius defended himself in his camp as long as the night lasted, but as soon as it was day, and he learned that the enemy were employed in pillaging the country without observing any order, he ordered several small gates of the camp to be opened secretly, and at a single signal hurled his army against the foe. When this blow fell suddenly and unexpectedly upon the Volscians, some few of them stood their ground, and fighting close to their camp, were cut down; but the rest, fleeing precipitately and losing many of their companions, got back safely inside the camp, the greater part of them being wounded and having lost their arms. When the Romans, following close upon their heels, surrounded their camp, they made only a short defence and then delivered up the camp, which was full of slaves, cattle, arms and all sorts of military stores. There were also many free men taken in it, some of them being Volscians themselves and others belonging to the nations which had assisted them; and along with these a great quantity of valuables, such as gold and silver, and apparel, as if the richest city had been taken. All of this Servilius permitted the soldiers to divide among themselves, that every man might share in the booty, and he ordered them to bring no part of it into the treasury. Then, having set fire to the camp, he marched with his army to Suessa Pometia, which lay close by. For not only because of its size and the number of its inhabitants, but also because of its fame and riches, it far surpassed any city in that region and was the leader, so to speak, of the nation. Investing this place and calling off his army neither by day nor by night, in order that the enemy might not have a moment's rest either in taking sleep or in gaining a respite from fighting, he wore them down by famine, helplessness and lack of reinforcements, and captured them in a short time, putting to death all the inhabitants who had reached manhood. And having given permission to the soldiers to pillage the effects that were found there also, he marched against the rest of the enemy's cities, none of the Volscians being able any longer to oppose him.

30 When the Volscians had been thus humbled by the Romans the other consul, Appius Claudius, caused their hostages, three hundred men in all, to be brought into the Forum, and to the end that those who had once given the Romans hostages for their fidelity might beware of violating their treaties, he ordered them to be scourged in the sight of all and then beheaded. And when his colleague returned a few days afterwards from his expedition and demanded the triumph usually granted by the senate to generals who had fought a brilliant battle, he opposed it, calling him a stirrer up of sedition and a partisan of a vicious form of government, and he charged him particularly with having brought no part of the spoils of war back to the public treasury, but with having instead made a present of it all to whom he thought fit; and he prevailed upon the senate not to grant him the triumph. Servilius, however, looking upon himself as insulted by the senate, behaved with an arrogance unusual to the Romans. For having assembled the people in the field[26] before the city, he enumerated his achievements in the war, told them of the envy of his colleague and the contumelious treatment he had received from the senate, and declared that from his own deeds and from the army which had shared in the struggle he derived the authority to celebrate a triumph in honour of

---

26 The Campus Martius.

glorious and fortunate achievements. Having prescription thus, he ordered the rods to be crowned, and then, having crowned himself and wearing the triumphal garb, he led the procession into the city attended by all the people; and ascending the Capitol, he performed his vows and consecrated the spoils. By this action he incurred the hatred of the patricians still further, but won the plebeians to himself.

31 While[27] the commonwealth was in such an unsettled condition a kind of truce that intervened on account of the traditional sacrifices, and the ensuing festivals, which were celebrated at lavish expense, restrained the sedition of the populace for the moment. While they were engaged in these celebrations the Sabines invaded them with a large force, having long waited for this opportunity. They began their march as soon as night came on, in order that they might get close to the city before those inside should be aware of their coming; and they might easily have conquered them if some of their light-armed men had not straggled from their places in the line and by attacking farm-houses given the alarm. For an outcry arose at once and the husbandmen rushed inside the walls before the enemy approached the gates. Those in the city, learning of the invasion while they were witnessing the public entertainments and wearing the customary garlands, left the games and ran to arms. And, a sufficient army of volunteers rallying in good season about Servilius, he drew them up and with them fell upon the enemy, who were exhausted both by want of sleep and by weariness and were not expecting the attack of the Romans. When the armies closed, a battle ensued which lacked order and discipline because of the eagerness of both sides, but, as if guided by some chance, they clashed line against line, company against company, or man against man, and the horse and foot

---

27 *Cf.* Livy ii. 26, 1-3.

fought promiscuously. And reinforcements came to both sides, as their cities were not far apart; these, by encouraging such of their comrades as were hard pressed, caused them to sustain the hardships of the struggle for a long time. After that the Romans, when the horse came to their assistance, once more prevailed over the Sabines, and having killed many of them, returned to the city with a great number of prisoners. Then, seeking out the Sabines who had come to Rome under the pretence of seeing the entertainments, while actually intending to seize in advance the strong places of the city in order to help their countrymen in their attack, as had been concerted between them, they threw them into prison. And having voted that the sacrifices, which had been interrupted by the war, should be performed with double magnificence, they were again passing the time in merriment.

32 While[28] they were celebrating these festivals, ambassadors came to them from the Auruncans, who inhabited the fairest plains of Campania. These, being introduced into the senate, demanded that the Romans should restore to them the country of the Volscians called Ecetrans,[29] which they had taken from them and divided in allotments among the colonists they had sent thither to guard that people, and that they should withdraw their garrison from there; if they refused to do so, they might expect the Auruncans to invade the territory of the Romans promptly to take revenge for the injuries they had done to their neighbours. To these the Romans gave this answer: "Ambassadors, carry back the word to the Auruncans that we Romans think it right that whatever anyone possesses by having won it from the enemy through valour, he should leave to his posterity as being his own. And we are not afraid of war from the Auruncans, which will be neither the first nor the most formidable

---

28 For chaps. 32 f. *cf.* Livy ii. 26, 4-6.
29 The inhabitants of the city of Ecetra.

war we have been engaged in; indeed, it has always been our custom to fight with all men for the supremacy, and as we see that this will be a contest, as it were, of valour, we shall await it without trepidation." After this the Auruncans, who had set out from their own territory with a large army, and the Romans, with their own forces under the command of Servilius, met near the city of Aricia, which is distant one hundred and twenty stades from Rome; and each of them encamped on hills strongly situated, not far from one another. After they had fortified their camps they advanced to the plain for battle; and engaging early in the morning, they maintained the fight till noon, so that many were killed on both sides. For the Auruncans were a warlike nation and by their stature, their strength, and the fierceness of their looks, in which there was much of brute savagery, they were exceeding formidable.

33 In this battle the Roman horse and their commander Aulus Postumius Albus, who had held the office of dictator the year before, are said to have proved the bravest. It seems that the place where the battle was fought was most unsuitable for the use of cavalry, having both rocky hills and deep ravines, so that the horse could be of no advantage to either side. Postumius, ordering his followers to dismount, formed a compact body of six hundred men, and observing where the Roman battle-line suffered most, being forced down hill, he engaged the enemy at those points and promptly crowded their ranks together. The barbarians being once checked, courage came to the Romans and the foot emulated the horse; and both forming one compact column, they drove the right wing of the enemy back to the hill. Some pursued that part of them which fled towards their camp and killed many, while others attacked in the rear those who still maintained the fight. And when they had put these also to flight, they followed them in their difficult and slow retreat to the hilly ground, cutting asunder the sinews of both their feet and knees with side blows of their swords, till they came to their camp. And having overpowered the guards there also, who were not numerous, they made themselves masters of the camp and plundered it. However, they found no great booty in it, but only arms, horses and other equipment for war. These were the achievements of Servilius and Appius during their consulship.

34 After this[30] Aulus Verginius Caelimontanus and Titus Veturius Geminus assumed the office of consul, when Themistocles was archon at Athens, in the two hundred and sixtieth year after the foundation of Rome and the year before the seventy-second Olympiad[31] (the one in which Tisicrates of Croton won the prize[32] for the second time). In their consulship the Sabines prepared to lead out against the Romans a larger army than before, and the Medullini, revolting from the Romans, swore to a treaty of alliance with the Sabines. The patricians, learning of their intention, were preparing to take the field immediately with all their forces; but the plebeians refused to obey their orders, remembering with resentment their repeated breaking of the promises which they had made to them respecting the poor who required relief, . . . the votes that were being passed . . .[33] And assembling together a few at a

---

30   For chaps. 34-48 cf. Livy ii. 28, 1-33, 3.

31   492 B.C.

32   In the short distance foot-race.

33   The text is corrupt here, and no satisfactory emendation has been proposed. There is nothing to show definitely what votes Dionysius has in mind, but we naturally assume that they were votes of the senate, especially as he does not often use the verb ψηφίζεσθαι of the voting in the comitia. It is possible that the promises of the senate, mentioned in a few other chapters (28, 3; 43, 2; 44, 1; 56, 3) as well as this, are thought of as having been embodied in formal votes rather than as having been merely the individual statements of the leading senators. The reading proposed by Sylburg means: "since they (the senators) gave effect to none of the votes passed in the interest of such relief"; that of Kayser: "and they (the plebeians) opposed the votes passed by the others (the senators)"; that of Meutzner: the poor who required relief, "but met with treatment the very reverse of what was voted [for them] under stress

time, they bound one another by oaths that they would no longer assist the patricians in any war, and that to every one of the poor who was oppressed they would render aid jointly against all whom they met. The conspiracy was evident on many other occasions, both in verbal skirmishes and physical encounters, but it became especially clear to the consuls when those summoned to military service failed to present themselves. For whenever they[34] ordered anyone of the people to be seized, the poor assembled in a body and endeavoured to rescue the one who was being carried away, and when the consuls' lictors refused to release them, they beat them and drove them off; and if any either of the knights or patricians who were present attempted to put a stop to these proceedings, they did not refrain from beating them too. Thus, in a short time the city was full of disorder and tumult. And as the sedition increased in the city, the preparations of the enemy for overrunning their territory increased also. When the Volscians again formed a plan to revolt, and the Aequians, as they were called,[35] . . . ambassadors came from all the peoples who were subject to the Romans asking them to send aid, since their territories lay in the path of the war. For example, the Latins said that the Aequians had made an incursion into their country and were laying waste their lands and had already plundered some of their cities; the garrison in Crustumerium declared that the Sabines were near that fortress and full of eagerness to besiege it; and others came with word of still other mischief which either had happened or was going to happen, and to ask for prompt assistance. Ambassadors from the Volscians also appeared before the senate, demanding, before they began war, that

---

of a crisis."

34 The subject is missing, but the consuls are evidently meant.
35 Kiessling recognized a lacuna at this point, since mention ought to be made also of the Sabines (*cf.* chap. 42, 1).

the lands taken from them by the Romans should be restored to them.

35 The senate having been assembled to consider this business, Titus Larcius, esteemed a man of superior dignity and consummate prudence, was first called upon by the consuls to deliver his opinion. And coming forward, he said:

"To me, senators, the things which others regard as terrible and as requiring speedy relief appear neither terrible nor very urgent, I mean, how we are to assist our allies or in what manner repulse our enemies. Whereas the things which they look upon neither as the greatest of evils nor pressing at present, but continue to ignore as not likely to do us any injury, are the very things that appear most terrible to me; and if we do not soon put a stop to them, they will prove to be the causes of the utter overthrow and ruin of the commonwealth. I refer to the disobedience of the plebeians, who refuse to carry out the orders of the consuls, as well as to our own severity against this disobedient and independent spirit of theirs. It is my opinion, therefore, that we ought to consider nothing else at present than by what means these evils are to be removed from the state and how all of us Romans with one mind are to prefer public to private considerations in the measures we pursue. For the power of the commonwealth when harmonious will be sufficient both to give security to our allies and to inspire fear in our enemies, but when discordant, as at present, it can effect neither. And I should be surprised if it did not even destroy itself and yield the victory to the enemy without any trouble. Yes, by Jupiter and all the other gods, I believe this will soon happen if you continue to pursue such measures.

36 "For we are living apart from one another, as you see, and inhabit two cities, one of which is ruled by poverty and necessity, and the other by satiety and insolence; but modesty, order and justice, by which alone any civil community is preserved, remain in neither of these cities. For this reason we already exact justice from one another by force and make superior strength the measure of that justice, like wild beasts choosing rather to destroy our enemy though we perish with him, than, by consulting our own safety, to be preserved together with our adversary. I ask you to give much thought to this matter and to hold a session for this very purpose as soon as you have dismissed the embassies. As to the answers to be now given to them, this is the advice I have to offer. Since the Volscians demand restitution of what we are in possession of by right of arms, and threaten us with war if we refuse to restore it, let our answer be, that we Romans look upon those acquisitions to be the most honest and the most just which we have acquired in accordance with the law of war, and that we will not consent to destroy the fruits of our valour by an act of folly. Whereas, by restoring to those who lost them these possessions, which we ought to share with our children and which we shall strive to leave to their posterity, we shall be depriving ourselves of what is already ours and be treating ourselves as harshly as we would our enemies. As to the Latins, let us commend their goodwill and dispel their fears by assuring them that we will not abandon them in any danger they may incur on our account, so long as they keep faith with us, but will shortly send a force sufficient to defend them. These answers, I believe, will be the best and the most just. After the embassies have departed, I say we ought to devote the first meeting of the senate to the consideration of the tumults in the city and that this meeting ought not to be long deferred, but appointed for the very next day"

37 When Larcius had delivered this opinion and it had received the approval of all, the embassies then received the answers that I have reported, and departed. The next day the consuls assembled the senate and proposed that it consider how the civil disorders might be corrected. Thereupon Publius Verginius, a man devoted to the people, being asked his opinion first, took the middle course and said: "Since the plebeians last year showed the greatest zeal for the struggles in behalf of the commonwealth, arraying themselves with us against the Volscians and Auruncans when they attacked us with a large army, I think that all who then assisted us and took their share in those wars ought to be let off, and that neither their persons nor their property ought to be in the power of the money-lenders; and that the same principle of justice ought to extend to their parents as far as their grandfathers, and to their posterity as far as their grandchildren; but that all the rest ought to be liable to imprisonment at the suit of the money-lenders upon the terms of their respective obligations." After this Titus Larcius said: "My opinion, senators, is that to those who proved themselves good men in the wars, but all the rest of the people as well, should be released from their obligations; for only thus can we make the whole state harmonious." The third speaker was Appius Claudius, the consul of the preceding year, who came forward and said:

38 "Every time these matters have been up for debate, senators, I have always been of the same opinion, never to yield to the people any one of their demands that is not lawful and honourable, nor to lower the dignity of the commonwealth; nor do I even now change the opinion which I entertained from the beginning. For I should be the most foolish of all men, if last year, when I was consul and my colleague opposed me and stirred up the people against me, I resisted and adhered to my resolutions, undeterred by fear and yielding neither to entreaties nor to favour, only to demean myself now, when I am a private citizen, and to prove utterly false to the principle of free speech. You may call this independence of mind on my part nobility or arrogance, as each of you prefers; but, as long as

567

I live, I will never propose an abolition of debts as a favour to wicked men, but will go so far as to resist with all the earnestness of which I am capable those who do propose it, reasoning as I do that every evil and corruption and, in a word, the overthrow of the state, begins with the abolition of debts. And whether anyone shall think that what I say proceeds from prudence, or from a kind of madness (since I see fit to consider, not my own security, but that of the commonwealth), or from any other motive, I give him leave to think as he pleases; but to the very last I will oppose those who shall introduce measures that are not in accord with our ancestral traditions. And since the times require, not an abolition of debts, but relief on a large scale, I will state the only remedy for the sedition at the present time: choose speedily a dictator, who, subject to no accounting for the use he shall make of his authority, will force both the senate and the people to entertain such sentiments as are most advantageous to the commonwealth. For there will be no other deliverance from so great an evil."

39 This speech[36] of Appius was received by the young senators with tumultuous applause, as proposing just the measures that were needed; but Servilius and some others of the older senators rose up to oppose it. They were defeated, however, by the younger men, who arrived for that very purpose and used much violence; and at last the motion of Appius carried. After this, when most people expected that Appius would be appointed dictator as the only person who would be capable of quelling the sedition, the consuls, acting with one mind, excluded him and appointed Manius Valerius, a brother of Publius Valerius, the first man to be made consul, who, it was thought, would be most favourable to the people and moreover was an old man. For they thought the terror alone of the dictator's power was sufficient, and that the present situation

---

36 For chap. 39.1 *cf.* Livy ii. 30, 2-7.

required a person equitable in all respects, that he might occasion no fresh disturbances.

40 After[37] Valerius had assumed office and had appointed Quintus Servilius, a brother of the Servilius who had been the colleague of Appius in the consulship, to be his Master of the Horse, he summoned the people to an assembly. And a great crowd coming together then for the first time since Servilius had resigned his magistracy and the people who were being forced into the service had been driven to open despair, he came forward to the tribunal and said:

"Citizens, we are well aware that you are always pleased at being governed by any of the Valerian family, by whom you were freed from a harsh tyranny, and perhaps you would never expect[38] to fail of obtaining anything that was reasonable when once you had entrusted yourselves to those who are regarded as being, and are, the most democratic of men. So that you to whom my words will be addressed do not need to be informed that we shall confirm to the people the liberty which we bestowed upon them in the beginning, but you need only moderate encouragement to have confidence in us that we shall perform whatever we promise you. For I have attained to that maturity of age which is the least capable of trickiness, and have been sufficiently honoured with public office, which carries with it a minimum of shiftiness; and I am not intending to pass the remainder of my life anywhere else but among you, where I shall be ready to stand trial for any deception you may think I have practised against you. Of this, then, I shall speak no further, since, as I have said, no lengthy arguments are needed for those who are acquainted with the facts. But there is one thing

---

37 *Cf.* Livy ii. 30.
38 The words "you would never expect" are a conjecture of Jacoby. The MSS. are a hopeless jumble at this point.

which, having suffered from others, you seem with reason to suspect of all: you have ever observed that one or another of the consuls, when they want to engage you to march against the enemy, promises to obtain for you what you desire of the senate, but never carries out any of his promises. That you can have no just grounds for entertaining the same suspicions of me also, I can convince you chiefly by these two considerations: first, that the senate would never have made the mistake of employing me, who am regarded as the greatest friend of the people, for this service, when there are others better suited to it, and second, that they would not have honoured me with an absolute magistracy by which I shall be able to enact whatever I think best, even without their participation.

41 "For surely you do not imagine that I am joining in their deception knowingly and that I have concerted with them to do you some injury. For if it occurs to you to entertain these thoughts of me, do[39] to me what you will, treating me as the most depraved of all men. Believe, then, what I say and banish this suspicion from your minds. Turn your anger from your friends to your enemies, who have come with the purpose of taking your city and making you slaves instead of free men, and are striving to inflict on you every other severity which mankind holds in the greatest fear, and are now said to be not far from your confines. Withstand them, therefore, with alacrity and show them that the power of the Romans, though weakened by sedition, is superior to any other when harmonious; for either they will not sustain your united attack or they will suffer condign punishment for their boldness. Bear in mind that those who are making war against you are Volscians and Sabines, whom you have often overcome in battle, and that they have neither larger bodies nor braver hearts now than their ancestors had, but have conceived a contempt for you because they

---

39 The verb is missing from the text.

thought you were at odds with one another. When you have taken revenge on your enemies, I myself pledge that the senate will reward you, both by composing these controversies concerning the debts and by granting everything else you can reasonably ask of them, in a manner adequate to the valour you shall show in the war. In the mean time let every possession, every person, and every right of a Roman citizen be left secure from seizure for either debt or any other obligation. To those who shall fight zealously their most glorious crown will be that this city, which gave them birth, still stands intact, and glorious praise also from their fellow-soldiers will be theirs; and the rewards bestowed by us will be sufficient both to restore their fortunes by their value and to render their families illustrious by the honours bestowed. I desire also that my zeal in exposing myself to danger may be your example; for I will fight for my country as stoutly as the most robust among you."

42 While[40] he was speaking, all the people listened with great pleasure, and believing that they were no longer to be imposed upon, promised their assistance in the war; and ten legions were raised, each consisting of four thousand men. Of these each of the consuls took three, and as many of the horse as belonged to the several legions; the other four, together with the rest of the horse, were commanded by the dictator. And having straightway got everything ready, they set out in haste, Titus Veturius against the Aequians, Aulus Verginius against the Volscians, and the dictator Valerius himself against the Sabines, while the city was guarded by Titus Larcius together with the older men and a small body of troops of military age. The Volscian war was speedily decided. For these foes, looking upon themselves as much superior in number and recalling[41] the wrongs they had suffered, were driven to fight

40 For chaps. 42, 1-43, 1 *cf.* Livy ii. 30, 7-31, 6.
41 Gelenius supplied a negative, to give the meaning "unmindful of their former disasters."

with greater haste than prudence, and were the first to attack the Romans, which they did too impetuously, as soon as the latter had encamped within sight of them. There ensued a sharp battle, in which, though they performed many brave deeds, they nevertheless suffered greater losses and were put to flight; and their camp was taken, and a city of note, Velitrae by name, reduced by siege. In like manner the pride of the Sabines was also humbled in a very short time, both nations having wished to win the war by a single pitched battle. After this their country was plundered and some small towns were captured, from which the soldiers took many persons and great store of goods. The Aequians, distrusting their own weakness and learning that the war waged by their allies was at an end, not only encamped in strong positions and would not come out to give battle, but also effected their retreat secretly, wherever they could, through mountains and woods, and thus dragged out and prolonged the war for some time; but they were not able to preserve their army unscathed to the last, since the Romans boldly fell upon them in their rugged fastnesses and took their camp by storm. Then followed the flight of the Aequians from the territory of the Latins and the surrender of the cities they had seized in their first invasion, as well as the captured of some of the men who in a spirit of rivalry had refused to abandon the citadels.

43 Valerius, having succeeded in this war according to his desire and celebrated the customary triumph in honour of his victory, discharged the people from the service, though the senate did not regard it as the proper time yet, fearing the poor might demand the fulfilment of their promises. After this he sent out colonists to occupy the land they had taken from the Volscians, choosing them from among the poor; these would not only guard the conquered country but would also leave the seditious element in the city diminished in number. Having made these arrangements,[42] he asked the senate to fulfil for him the promises they had made, now that they had received the hearty co-operation of the plebeians in the later engagements. However, the senate paid no regard to him, but, just as before the young and violent men, who were superior to the other party in number, had joined together to oppose his motion, so on this occasion also they opposed it and raised a great outcry against him, calling his family flatterers of the people and the authors of vicious laws, and charging that by the very measure on which the Valerii prided themselves most, the one concerning the function of the assembly as a court of justice,[43] they had totally destroyed the power of the patricians. Valerius became very indignant at this, and after reproaching them with having exposed him to the unjust resentment of the people, he lamented the fate which would come upon them for taking such a course, as might be expected in such an unhappy situation, uttered some dire prophecies, inspired in part by the emotion he was then under and in part by his superior sagacity. Then he flung himself out of the senate chamber; and assembling the people, he said:

"Citizens, feeling myself under great obligations to you both for the zeal you showed in giving me your voluntary assistance in the war, and still more for the bravery you displayed in the various engagements, I was very desirous of making a return to you, not only in other ways, by particularly by not breaking the promises I kept giving you in the name of the senate, and, as an adviser and umpire between the senate and you, by changing at last the discord

42 For chap. 43, 2-48, 3 cf. Livy ii. 31, 7-32, 8.
43 This seems the best meaning to be obtained from the text offered by the MSS. (see critical note). The reference is obviously to the law granting the right of appeal (*provocatio*) from the sentence of a magistrate to the judgment of the people. But as Dionysius refers to this law in several places as permitting "an appeal to the people" or "to the judgment of the people," it is quite possible that we do not have his own words in the present passage.

that now exists between you into harmony. But I am prevented from accomplishing these things by those who prefer, not what is most advantageous to the commonwealth, but what is pleasing to themselves at the present moment, and who, being superior to all the rest both in number and in the power they derive from their youth rather than from the present situation, have prevailed. Whereas I, as you see, am an old man, and so are all my associates, whose strength consists in counsel which they are incapable of carrying out in action; and what was regarded as our concern for the commonwealth has turned out to have the appearance of a private grudge against both sides. For I am censured by the senate for courting your faction and misrepresented to you as showing greater goodwill to them.

44 "If, now, the people, after being treated well, had failed to keep the promises made by me to the senate in their name, my defence to that body must have been that you had violated your word, but that there was no deceit on my part. But since it is the promises made to you by the senate that have not been fulfilled, I am now under the necessity of stating to the people that the treatment you have met with does not have my approval, but that both of us alike have been cheated and misled, and I more than you, inasmuch as I am wronged, not alone in being deceived in common with you all, but am also hurt in my own reputation. For I am accused of having turned over to the poor among you, without the consent of the senate, the spoils taken from the enemy, in the desire to gain a private advantage for myself, and of demanding that the property of the citizens be confiscated, though the senate forbade me to act in violation of the laws, and of having disbanded the armies in spite of the opposition of the senators, when I ought to have kept you in the enemy's country occupied in sleeping in the open and in endless marching. I am also reproached in the matter

574

of sending the colonists into the territory of the Volscians, on the ground that I did not bestow a large and fertile country upon the patricians or even upon the knights, but allotted it to the poor among you. But the thing in particular which has occasioned the greatest indignation against me is that, in raising the army, more than four hundred well-to-do plebeians were added to the knights. If, now, I had been thus treated when I was in the vigour of my youth, I should have made it clear to my enemies by my deeds what kind of man they had abused; but as I am now above seventy years old and no longer capable of defending myself, and since I perceive that your discord can no longer be allayed by me, I am laying down my office and putting myself in the hands of any who may desire it in the belief that they have been deceived by me in any respect, to be treated in such manner as they shall think fit."

45 With these words Valerius aroused the sympathy of all the plebeians, who accompanied him when he left the Forum; but he increased the resentment of the senate against him. And immediately afterwards the following events happened: The poor, no longer meeting secretly and by night, as before, but openly now, were planning a secession from the patricians; and the senate, with the purpose of preventing this, ordered the consuls not to disband the armies as yet. For each consul still had command of his three legions, which were restrained by their military oaths, and none of the soldiers cared to desert their standards, so far did the fear of violating their oaths prevail with all of them. The pretext contrived for leading out the forces was that the Aequians and Sabines had joined together to make war upon the Romans. After the consuls had marched out of the city with their forces and pitched their camps near one another, the soldiers all assembled together, having in their possession both the arms and the standards, and at the instigation of one Sicinius Bellutus they seized the standards and revolted from the consuls (these standards are held in the greatest honour by the Romans on a campaign and like statues of the gods are accounted holy); and having appointed different centurions and made Sicinius their leader in all matters, they occupied a certain mount situated near the river Anio, not far from Rome, which from that circumstance is still called the Sacred Mount. And when the consuls and the centurions called upon them to return, mingling entreaties and lamentations, and making many promises, Sicinius replied: "With what purpose, patricians, do you now recall those whom you have driven from their country and transformed from free men into slaves? What assurances will you give us for the performance of those promises which you are convicted of having often broken already? But since you desire to have sole possession of the city, return thither undisturbed by the poor and humble. As for us, we shall be content to regard as our country any land, whatever it be, in which we may enjoy our liberty."

46 When these things were reported to those in the city, there was great tumult and lamentation and running through the streets, as the populace prepared to leave the city and the patricians endeavoured to dissuade them and offered violence to those who refused to obey. And there was great clamour and wailing at the gates, and hostile words were exchanged and hostile acts committed, as no one paid heed any longer to either age, comradeship, or the respect due to virtue. When those appointed by the senate to guard the exits, being few in number and unable any longer to resist them, were forced by the people to desert their post, then at last the populace rushed out in great multitudes and the commotion resembled the capture of a city; there were the lamentations of those who remained behind and their mutual recriminations as they saw the city being deserted. After this there were frequent meetings of the senate and accusations against those who were responsible for the secession. At the same time the enemy nations also attacked them, plundering their territory up to the very city. However, the seceders, taking the necessary provisions from the fields that lay near them, without doing any other mischief to the country, remained in the open and received such as resorted to them from city and the fortresses round about, who were already coming to them in great numbers. Not only those who were desirous of escaping their debts and the sentences and punishments they expected, flocked to them, but many others also who led lazy or dissolute lives, or whose fortunes were not sufficient to gratify their desires, or who were devoted to vicious practices, or were envious of the prosperity of others, or because of some other misfortune or reason were hostile to the established government.

47 At first great confusion and consternation fell upon the patricians, who feared that the seceders would at once come against the city together with the foreign enemies. Then, as if at a single signal, snatching up arms and attended each by his own clients, some went to defend the roads by which they expected the enemy would approach, others marched out to the fortresses in order to secure them, while still others encamped on the plains before the city; and those who by reason of age were unable to do anything of the kind took their places upon the walls. But when they heard that the seceders were neither joining the enemy, laying waste the country, nor doing any other mischief worth speaking of, they gave up their fear, and changing their minds, proceeded to consider upon what terms they might come to an agreement with them. And speeches of every kind, directly opposed to one another, were made by the leading men of the senate; but the most moderate speeches and those most suitable to the existing situation were delivered by the oldest senators, who showed that the people had not made this secession from them with any malicious intent, but partly compelled by irresistible calamities and partly deluded by their advises, and judging of their interest by passion rather than reason, as is wont to happen with an ignorant populace; and furthermore, that the greater part of them were conscious of having been ill advised and were seeking an opportunity of redeeming their offences if they could find plausible excuses for doing so. At any rate their actions were those of men who had already repented, and if they should be given good hope for the future by a vote of the senate granting them impunity and offering an honourable accommodation, they would cheerfully take back what was their own. In urging this course they demanded that men of superior worth should not be more implacable than their inferiors, nor defer an accommodation till the senseless crowd should be either brought to their senses by necessity or induced by it to cure a smaller evil by a greater, in depriving themselves of liberty as the result of delivering up their arms and surrendering their persons at discretion; for these things were next to impossible. But by treating the people with moderation they ought to set the example of salutary counsels, and to anticipate the others in proposing an accommodation, bearing in mind that while governing and administering the state was the duty of the patricians, the promoting of friendship and peace was the part of good men. They declared that the prestige of the senate would be most diminished, not by a policy of administering the government safely while bearing nobly the calamities that were unavoidable, but by a policy whereby, in showing resentment toward the vicissitudes of fortune, they would overthrow the commonwealth. It was the part of folly, while aiming at appearances, to neglect security; it was desirable of course, to obtain both, but if one must do without either, safety ought to be regarded as more necessary than appearances. The final proposal of those who gave this advice was that ambassadors should be sent to the seceders to treat of peace, since they had been guilty of no irreparable mischief.

48 This met with the approval of the senate. Thereupon they chose the most suitable persons and sent them to the people in the camp with orders to inquire of them what they desired and upon what terms they would consent to return to the city; for if any of their demands were moderate and possible to be complied with, the senate would not oppose them. If, therefore, they would now lay down their arms and return to the city they would be granted impunity for their past offences and amnesty for the future; and if they showed the best will for the commonwealth and cheerfully exposed themselves to danger in the service of their country, they would receive honourable and advantageous returns. The ambassadors, having received these instructions, communicated them to the people in the camp and spoke in conformity to them. But the seceders, rejecting these invitations, reproached the patricians with haughtiness, severity, and great dissimulation in pretending, on the one hand, to be ignorant of the demands of the people and of the reasons which had compelled them to secede from them, and, again, in granting them impunity from all prosecution for their secession, just as if they were still masters of the situation, though themselves standing in need of the assistance of their fellow-citizens against their foreign enemies, who would soon come with all their forces — enemies who could not be withstood by men who looked upon their preservation as not so much their own advantage as the good fortune of those who should assist them. They ended with the statement that when the patricians themselves understood better the difficulties that beset the commonwealth, they would know what kind of adversaries they had to deal with; and they added many violent threats. To all of which the ambassadors made no further answer, but departed and informed the patricians of the representations made by the seceders. When those in the city received this answer, they were in much more serious confusion and fear than before; and neither the senate was able to find a solution of the difficulties or any means of postponing them, but, after listening to the taunts and accusations which the leading men directed at one another, adjourned day after day; nor were the plebeians who still remained in the city, constrained by their goodwill toward the patricians or their affection for their country, of the same mind as before, but a large part even of these were trickling away both openly and secretly, and it seemed that no reliance could be placed upon those who were left. In this state of affairs the consuls — for the period that still remained of their magistracy was short — appointed a day for the election of magistrates.

49 When[44] the time came for them to assemble in the field[45] to elect their magistrates, and no one either sought the consulship or would consent to accept it if offered, the people themselves chose two consuls from among those who had already held this magistracy and who were acceptable to both the people and the aristocracy, namely Postumus Cominius and Spurius Cassius, Cassius being the one through whose efforts the Sabines had been conquered and had resigned their claims to the leadership. This was in the seventy-second Olympiad,[46] the year in which Tisicrates of Croton won the short-distance foot-race, Diognetus being then archon at Athens. Upon assuming office on the calends of September, earlier than had been customary with the former consuls, they convened the senate before attending to any other business and asked for an expression of its opinion concerning the return of the plebeians. The first senator they called upon to declare his views was a man, then in the maturity of his age, who was looked upon as a person of superior wisdom and was particularly commended for his political principles, since he pursued a middle course, being inclined neither to increase

---

44 For chaps. 49-60, 3 *cf.* Livy ii. 32, 5-7.
45 The Campus Martius.
46 491 B.C. For Dionysius' chronology see Intro. pp. xxvi ff.

the arrogance of the aristocratic party nor to permit the people to have their own way in everything — namely Agrippa Menenius. It was he who now urged the senate to an accommodation, speaking as follows:

"If all who are present, senators, chanced to be of the same opinion, and no one were going to oppose the accommodation with the people, but only the terms of it, be these just or unjust, on which we are to be reconciled with them were before you for consideration, I could have expressed my thoughts to you in few words. But since some consider that even this very point should be a matter for further consultation, whether it is better for us to come to an agreement with the seceders or go to war with them, I do not think it easy for me in a brief exposition of my views to advise you what ought to be done. On the contrary, a speech of some length is necessary, in order to show those among you who are opposed to the accommodation that they contradict themselves if, while intending to frighten you by playing on your fear of those difficulties that are the most trivial and easily corrected, they at the same time neglect to consider the evils that are greatest and incurable. And they have fallen into this predicament for no other reason than that in judging what is expedient they do not use reason but rather passion and frenzy. For how can these men be said to foresee in their minds any course that is profitable or possible, when they imagine that a state so powerful and mistress of so extensive a dominion, a state that is already becoming an object of hatred, and a cause of offence to her neighbours, will easily be able either without the plebeians to hold and preserve the subject nations or else to bring some other people into the commonwealth, a better people in place of one most knavish, who will fight to preserve their supremacy for them and will live with them under the same government in profound quiet, behaving themselves with self-restraint in both peace and war? For

581

there is no other possibility they could name that would justify their asking you not to accept the accommodation.

50 "How utterly silly either of those two expedients is, I would have you consider from the facts themselves, bearing in mind that since the humbler citizens grew disaffected toward you because of those who treated their misfortunes as neither fellow-citizens nor men of self-restraint should, and withdrew, indeed, from the city, yet neither are doing to you, nor have any thought of doing, any other mischief, but are considering only by what means they may be reconciled to you without dishonour, many of those who are not well disposed toward you, joyfully seizing upon this incident presented to them by Fortune, have become elated in their minds and look upon this as the long-desired opportunity for breaking up your empire. Thus, the Aequians and Volscians, the Sabines and Hernicans, who in any case have missed no opportunity to make war against us, being now exasperated also at their late defeats, are plundering our fields. As to the parts of Campania and Tyrrhenia which have continued to be doubtful in their allegiance to us, some of them are openly revolting and others are secretly preparing to do the same. Not even the kindred race of Latins, as it seems, longer remains steadfastly loyal to us, though it entered into relations of confidence with us, but a large part even of this people is reported to be disaffected, succumbing to the passion for change which all men crave. And we who used to besiege the cities of others now ourselves sit at home, pent within our walls, having left our lands unsown and seeing our farm-houses plundered, our cattle driven off as booty, and our slaves deserting, without knowing how to deal with these misfortunes. While we suffer all this, do we still hope that the plebeians will become reconciled to us, even though we know that it is in our own power to put an end to the sedition by a single decree?

51 "While our affairs in the open country are in this unhappy state, the situation within the walls is no less terrible. For we have neither provided ourselves with allies well in advance, as if we expected to be besieged, nor are we, unaided, sufficiently numerous to resist so many hostile nations; and even of this small and inadequate army the greater part consists of plebeians — labourers, clients, and artisans — not altogether trustworthy guardians for a tottering aristocracy. Moreover, the continual desertion of these now to the seceders has rendered all the rest liable to suspicion. But more than all these things, the impossibility of bringing in provisions while the country is in the power of the enemy already terrifies us, and when we are once in actual want, will terrify us still more; and, apart from this, the war allows not a moment's peace of mind. Yet surpassing all these calamities are the wretched wives, the infant children, and aged parents of the seceders wandering to and fro in the Forum and through every street, in pitiful garb and postures of mourning, weeping, supplicating, clinging to the hands and knees of everyone and bewailing the forlorn condition that afflicts them now and will afflict them even more — a dreadful and intolerable sight! No one, surely, is of so cruel a nature as not to have his heart touched at seeing these things, or to feel some sympathy for the misfortunes of his fellow-creatures. So that, if we are not going to trust the good faith of the plebeians, we shall have to get rid of these persons also, since some of them will be of no use while we are under siege and the others cannot be relied on to remain friendly. But when these too are driven away, what forces will be left to defend the city? And depending upon what assistance shall we dare to encounter these perils? Yet as for our natural refuge and our only trustworthy hope, the patrician youth, they are few, as you see, and it behooves us not to let our spirits rise because of them. Why, then, do those who propose that we submit to war indulge in nonsense and deceive us, instead of openly advising us to deliver up the city at once to our enemies without bloodshed and without trouble?

52 "But perhaps I myself am infatuated when I speak thus, and am asking you to fear things that are not formidable. The commonwealth is very likely threatened with no other danger as yet than a change of inhabitants, a matter of no serious consequence; and it would be very easy for us to receive into the body politic a multitude of labourers and clients from every nation and place. For this is the plan which many of the opponents of the plebeians keep prating of, and these by no means the most unimportant of them; to such a pitch of folly, indeed, have some already come, that instead of expressing salutary opinions they utter wishes impossible of realization. But I should like to ask these men: What superabundance of time will be afforded us to carry out these plans when the enemy is so near the city? What allowance will be made for the tarrying and delay of our auxiliaries who are to come, though we are in the midst of perils that do not tarry or delay? What man or what god will grant us security and will without molestation get together reinforcements from every quarter and conduct them hither? Besides, who are the people who will leave their own countries and remove to us? Are they such as have habitations, families, fortunes, and the respect of their fellow-citizens because of the distinction of their ancestors or a reputation for their own merit? And yet who would consent to leave behind his own blessings in order to share ignominiously the misfortunes of others? For they will come hither to share, not in peace and luxury, but in dangers and war, the successful issue of which cannot be foreseen. Or shall we bring in a multitude of homeless plebeians, like those driven from hence, who because of debts, judgments, and other like misfortunes will gladly remove to any place that may offer? But these, even though otherwise of a good and modest disposition — to concede them this much — yet just because of their being neither native born nor of like habits with us, and because they will not be acquainted with our customs, laws, and training, would no doubt be far, nay infinitely, worse than our own plebeians.

53 "The natives have here their wives, children, parents, and many others that are dear to them, to serve as pledges; yes, and there is their fondness for the soil that reared them, a passion that is implanted in all men and not to be eradicated; but as for this multitude which we propose to invite here, this people without roof or home, if they should take up their abode with us having none of these pledges here, in defence of what blessing would they care to face dangers, unless one were to promise to give them portions land and some part or other of the city, after first dispossessing the present owners — things we refuse to grant to our own citizens who have often fought in their defence? And possibly they might not be content with even these grants alone, but would also insist upon an equal share of honours, of magistracies, and of all the other advantages with the patricians. If, therefore, we do not grant them every one of their demands, shall we not have them as our enemies when they fail to obtain what they ask? And if we grant their demands, our country and our constitution will be lost, destroyed by our own hands. I do not add here that what we need at the present time is men trained to war, men of disciplined bodies; not husbandmen, labourers, merchants, or followers of menial trades, who will be obliged to learn military discipline and to give proof of their skill at one and the same time (and skill in any unwonted activity is difficult), such as a promiscuous collection of men resorting hither from every nation is bound to be. As for a military alliance, I neither see any formed to assist us, nor, if any allies unexpectedly appeared, should I advise you to admit them inconsiderately within your walls, since I know that many a city has been enslaved by troops introduced to garrison it.

54 "When you consider these things as well as those that I have mentioned earlier, and recall, further, the considerations which encourage you to make the accommodation, namely, that we are not the only people, nor the first, among whom poverty has raised sedition against wealth, and lowliness against eminence, but that in nearly all states, both great and small, the lower class is generally hostile to the upper (and in all these states the men in power, when they have shown moderation, have saved their countries, but when they have acted arrogantly, have lost not only their goods, but their lives as well); and when you remember that everything that is composed of many parts is generally affected with a disorder in some one of them, and, furthermore, that neither the ailing part of a human body ought always to be lopped off (for that would be to render the appearance of the rest ugly and its term of life brief) nor the disordered part of a civil community to be driven out (since that would be the quickest way of destroying the whole in time through the loss of its separate parts); and when you consider also how great is the power of necessity, the one thing to which even the gods yield, be not vexed at your misfortunes nor allow yourselves to be filled with arrogance and folly, as if everything were going to succeed according to our wishes, but relent and yield, deriving examples of prudence, not from the actions of others, but from our own.

SOPHRON EDITOR

CATALOGUE 2017

Caesar's Commentaries: The Complete Gallic War. Revised. 8vo., xxiv,507 pp.; Introduction, Latin text of all eight Books, Notes, Companion, Grammar, Exercises, Vocabularies, 17 Maps, illus., all based on Francis W. Kelsey.
ISBN 978-0-9850811 1 9 *$19.95*

Virgil's Aeneid Complete, Books I-XII. With Introduction, Latin text and Notes by W. D. Williams. 8vo., xxviii, 739 pp., 2 maps, Glossary, Index.
ISBN 978-0-9850811 6 4 *$27.95*

***Praxis Grammatica*. A New Edition.** John Harmer. 12 mo., xviii,116 pp.; Introduction by Mark Riley. ISBN 978-0-9850811 2 6 *$3.95*

The *Other* Trojan War. Dictys & Dares. 12 mo., xxii,397 pp.; Latin/English Parallel Texts; Frazer's Introduction & Notes, Index
ISBN 978-0-9850811 5 $14.95

The Stoic's Bible: *a Florilegium for the Good Life*. THIRD EDITION. Giles Laurén. 8vo., xxxii,720 pp., 3 illus., Introduction, Tables, Bibliography.
ISBN 978-0-9850811-0-2. $24.95

Why Don't We Learn from History? B. H. Liddell Hart. 12 mo., 126 pp.
ISBN 978-0-9850811 3 3 $4.95

Quintilian. Institutionis Oratoriae. Liber Decimus. Text, Notes & Introductory Essays by W. Peterson. Foreword by James J. Murphy. 8vo., cvi,291 pp., Harleian MS facsimile, Indexes. ISBN 978-0-9850811-8-8 *$19.95*

Schools of Hellas. Kenneth Freeman. 12 mo., xxi,279 pp., illus., Indexes.
ISBN 978-0-9850811-9-5 *$14.95*

Cornelius Nepos Vitae. 12 mo., xviii,424 pp., 3 maps, illus., notes, exercises, & vocabulary by John Rolfe. ISBN 978-0-9850811-7-1 *$14.95*

Greek Reader. Mark Riley. Based on the selection of Wilamowitz-Moellendorff, with additions, notes and a vocabulary. 12 mo., ix,368 pp., maps & illus.
ISBN 978-0-9897836-0-6 *$12.95*

Quintilian: *A Roman Educator and his Quest for the Perfect Orator*. REVISED EDITION. George A. Kennedy. 12 mo., xviii,184 pp. biblio., Index.
ISBN 978-0-9897836-1-3 *$9.95*

Diodorus Siculus. I. The Library of History in Forty Books. Vol. I. (books I-XIV). 8vo., xxxiii, 701 pp., illus. ISBN 978-0-9897836-2-0 *$25.00*

Diodorus Siculus. II. The Library of History in Forty Books. Vol. II. (books XV-XL). 8vo., xviii,610 pp., illus. ISBN 978-0-9897836-3-7 *$25.00*

La Dialectique. Paul Foulquié, in-8,. 160 pp.
ISBN 978-1-4954688-3-4 *$6.95*

Horace. The Complete Horace. 8vo., xli,620 pp, 2 illus., introduction & notes after Bennett & Rolfe. ISBN 978-0-9897836-4-4 *$19.95*

Grote's Legendary Greece. The Pre-history. Being Chapters 1-XXI of A History of Greece, Part I., 4th. Edit. Complete, ***without footnotes***, frontis. port., 5 maps, lvii,454 pp edited by G. Laurén. ISBN 978-0-9897836-6-8 *$17.50*

Grote's History of Greece I. Being Chapters I-XL of A History of Greece, Part II., 4th Ed. Complete ***without footnotes***, port., 9 illus., xii,705 pp. edited by G. Laurén.
ISBN 978-0-9897836-7-5 *$25.00*

Grote's History of Greece II. Being Chapters XLI-LXII of A History of Greece, Part II., 4th Ed. Complete *without footnotes*, 8 illus., vii,802 pp. edited by G. Laurén. ISBN 978-0-9897836-7-5 *$25.00*

Grote's History of Greece III. Being Chapters LXIII-LXXXI of A History of Greece, Part II., 4th Ed. Complete *without footnotes*, 8 illus., vii,794 pp. edited by G. Laurén. ISBN 978-0-9897836-7-5 *$25.00*

Grote's History of Greece IV. Being Chapters LXXXII-XCVIII of A History of Greece, Part II., 4th Ed. Complete *without footnotes*, 5 illus., vii,674 pp. edited by G. Laurén. ISBN 978-0-9897836-7-5 *$25.00*

Jebb's Isocrates. Edited with Intro. by Edward Schiappa, David Timmerman, G. Laurén; 12 mo., cxxv, 430 pp., 3 illus., notes, Greek Selections, biblio.
ISBN 978-0-9897836-5-1 *$17.50*

The Neo-Latin Reader. *Corrected*. *Selections from Petrarch to Rimbaud.* Mark Riley. illus., intro., notes, refs., 12 mo., xvii, 381 pp. ISBN 978-0-9897836-8-2 *$12.95*

The Mathematical Theory of Bridge. 134 Probability tables, their uses, simple formulas, applications & about 4000 probabilities.Émile Borel & André Chéron. Trans. by Alec Traub. Revised & corrected by G. Laurén. 8vo., xxviii,474 pp., illus., tables, notes.
ISBN 978-0-989783-9-9 *$25.00*

Emma the Porter. [Imma Portatrix] by Frederic Herman Flayder. Newly edited and translated by Mark Riley. 8vo., xxx,185 pp., intro., illus., notes.
ISBN 978-0-9991401-0-9 *$12.00*

Justin. Epitome of the Philippic Histories. Trans. J. S. Watson. Ed. G. Laurén. 12 mo., 500 pp., chron., illus., map, notes. ISBN 9780999116 $17.50

Dionysius of Halicarnassus. *The Roman Antiquites* **I.** Books 1-4.54. Trans. Earn. Cary. Ed. G. Laurén. 8vo., xliv+586 pp., frontis., Intro., biblio., notes.
ISBN 978-0-9991401-2-3
$25.00

Dionysius of Halicarnassus. *The Roman Antiquites* **II.** Books 5.55-13. Trans. Earn. Cary. Ed. G. Laurén. 8vo., 730 pp., frontis., Intro., notes. ISBN

Available from SOPHRON EDITOR (CreateSpace and Amazon worldwide)

In preparation:

Origins of Western Institutions: A Source Book.

Anglo-Latin Law: A Reader.

Giles Laurén, 4020 Grande Vista Blvd. #114, St. Augustine, FL 32084
enasophron@gmail.com